# THE BOOK OF IMMEDIATE MAGIC

Part 2

# THE BOOK OF IMMEDIATE MAGIC

## Part 2

Shadow Tree Series
Volume 4

Jacobus G. Swart

THE SANGREAL SODALITY PRESS
Johannesburg, Gauteng, South Africa

First edition, 2018
First printing, 2018


Published by The Sangreal Sodality Press
74 Twelfth Street
Parkmore 2196
Gauteng
South Africa
Email: jacobsang@gmail.com


Copyright © 2018 Jacobus G. Swart


All rights reserved. No part of this publication may be reproduced or transmitted in any form or by any means, electronic or mechanical, including photocopy, without permission in writing from the publisher. Reviewers who wish to quote brief passages in connection with a review written for inclusion in a magazine, newspaper or broadcast need not request permission.


ISBN 978-0-620-80794-4

Dedicated to Simon O'Regan

---

"Come from all Quarters whoso would be one with us, as we are willing to be one in search of spirit. .....Welcome indeed are they that enter with entitlement our closest circles of companionship."

—William G. Gray (*The Sangreal Sacrament*)

# Shadow Tree Series

Volume 1: The Book of Self Creation
Volume 2: The Book of Sacred Names
Volume 3: The Book of Seals & Amulets
Volume 4: The Book of Immediate Magic – Part 1 & 2
Volume 5: The Book of Fates & Oracles
Volume 6: The Book of Hebrew Incantations

# Contents

**Introduction** .......................................... I

**6. *Or Makif* — Magical Mediation** ..................... 1
   A. *Sefirotic* Sensibilities ............................. 1
      1. The Blessings of the *Sefirot* ................... 11
      2. A Kabbalistic Rule ............................ 11
      3. A Kabbalistic Creed ........................... 12
      4. A Kabbalistic Prayer .......................... 13
      5. A Kabbalistic Thanksgiving .................... 13
      6. Hebrew Sefirotic Prayer-Invocations ............ 14
   B. The Fifty Gates of Understanding: *Omer* ........... 28
      Week 1—Correcting the *Sefirah* of *Chesed* ...... 56
      Week 2—Correcting the *Sefirah* of *Gevurah* ..... 68
      Week 3—Correcting the *Sefirah* of *Tiferet* ..... 81
      Week 4—Correcting the *Sefirah* of *Netzach* ..... 97
      Week 5—Correcting the *Sefirah* of *Hod* ........ 111
      Week 6—Correcting the *Sefirah* of *Yesod* ...... 126
      Week 7—Correcting the *Sefirah* of *Malchut* .... 141

**7. *Or Yashar* — Magical Meditation** .................. 159
   A. The Need for Meditation ......................... 159
   B. Hebrew Magical Mantras ......................... 183

**8. *Or Sovev* — Astrological Considerations** .......... 203
   A. The Zodiac & Spiritual Transformation ............ 203
   B. The Power in Your Hands & Countenance ......... 231
   C. Sefirotic/Planetary Rituals ....................... 274
      1. Sticks & Stones ............................... 274
      2. *Netzach* (Victory/Venus): Love, Grace, Kindness
         & Joy ........................................ 316
      3. Venus Planetary Ritual for Love, Grace,
         Kindness & Joy ............................. 333

**9. *Or Ganuz* — Initiation: Mystical Rebirth** .......... 347
   A. Introduction ..................................... 347
   B. Preparation ..................................... 362
      1. Unification with the Higher Self ................ 366
      2. The Breath of Light ........................... 367
      3. The *Amen* Breath ............................ 368
   C. Personal Initiation: The Rite of Rebirth ............ 376
      1. Preparation & Opening ........................ 378
      2. Consecration of Consciousness ................ 379
      3. Balancing with the Four Elements ............. 380

4. The Ancient Charges .......................... 380
　　5. The Oath ................................... 382
　　6. Secret Identity ............................. 383
　　7. Uniting with the Hidden Ones ................ 383
　　8. Thanksgiving ............................... 386
　　9. Closing .................................... 387

**10. *Or Memale* — Oneness beyond All Being .......... 389**
　　A. The Art of Gifting .......................... 389
　　B. Self "Creation" vs "Uncreation" ................ 408
　　　1. The Desire for Results ..................... 409
　　　2. The Doubt Factor .......................... 410
　　　3. Reaffirming the *Status Quo* ................ 411
　　C. At the End of Everything! ..................... 416

**References & Bibliography ...................... 423**

**Illustrations**

Cover Illustration ......... 13th century Liturgical Calendar from Castile, Spain
Page 3 .................. Ten *Sefirot* in the Right Hand
Page 8 ........... Sefirotic array in the *Sha'arei Orah*
Page 22 ...................... Table of Sefirotic Gates
Page 33 .......... *Omer*—Seven *Sefirot*/Patriarchs/Weeks
Page 39 .... *Menorah Psalm* & the "Forty-two Letter Name"
Page 42 ... *Omer*—Seven Weeks/"Forty-two Letter Name"
Page 45 ...... *Omer*—Seven Weeks/Hexagram/"Forty-two Letter Name"/ Human Anatomy
Page 67 ....... *Omer*—Seventh Day/Hexagram/"Forty-two Letter Name"/Face
Page 79 ..... *Omer*—Fourteenth Day/Hexagram/"Forty-two Letter Name"/Right Shoulder
Page 95 ............ *Omer*—Twenty-first Day/Hexagram/ "Forty- two Letter Name"/Left Shoulder
Page 110 .......... *Omer*—Twenty-eighth Day/Hexagram/ "Forty-two Letter Name"/Right Hip
Page 125 ............ *Omer*—Thirty-fifth Day/Hexagram/ "Forty-two Letter Name"/Left Hip
Page 140 ........... *Omer*—Forty-second Day/Hexagram/ "Forty-two Letter Name"/Sexual Organ
Page 154 ... *Omer*—Forty-ninth Day/Hexagram/"Forty-two Letter Name"/Centre of Six Physical Locales
Page 166 ...... Twenty Hebrew Glyphs for Self Restoration
Page 172 ....... Mercy/Judgment Table of Hebrew Glyphs
Page 174 ........................ *Shem Vayisa Vayet*
Page 194 . Illustration of Enunciating a multipurpose *Hagah*
Page 205 ....... Table of the "Twelve Banners" & Twelve Permutations of "*Eh'yeh*"
Page 212 ...... Chart of Enunciating the "Twelve Banners"
Page 214 ... Chart of Zodiac/Banners: Hidden and Revealed
Page 215–226 ... Twelve Hexagrams—Hidden & Revealed affiliations to the twelve Zodiacal Signs/ Banners/*Shem Vayisa Vayet*
Page 229 ...................... Hexagram & the Body
Page 230 ......... Hexagram, Ineffable Name & the Body
Page 233 ................. Yetziratic Incantation Wheel
Page 234 .................. Planetary Order Key diagram
Page 237 ... Enunciation of Hebrew Seven "Double Letters"
Page 241 ......... Table of Hebew Glyphs/Planets/Days/ Facial Feature attributions
Page 242 ...... Planets & the Seven Appertures of the Face
Page 244 ..... Planets, Five Senses & the Hand illustration
Page 254 .. Table of Planets/*Sefirot*/Divine Name affiliations
Page 255 .......... *Chotamot* (Seals) of Seven Archangels

Page 255–256 .. *Chotamot* (Seals) of Seven Planetary Spirits
Page 257–263 ...... Tables of Planet/Archangel affiliations
with the Days/Hours & associated alignment
with the Twenty-four Permutations of *Adonai*/
"Twelve Banners"/Twelve Permutations
Permutations of "*Eh'yeh*"& Twenty-eight
"Lunar Camps."
Page 266 .... Table of Seven Sets of Attributes respectively
associated with the seven "Double Letters."
Page 267 ......... Table of Attributes and twenty-eight life
qualities listed in *Ecclestiastes 3:1-8* affiliated
with the seven "Double Letters."
Page 268 ............ Fourteen-Letter Name aligned with
the twenty-eight life qualities.
Page 270 ........... The 28 Camps of the Divine Presence
Page 271 .. Table of the Lunar Camps of the Divine Presence
Page 273 .................... *Chotam* (Seal) of *Tzadki'el*
Page 273 .................... *Chotam* (Seal) of *Hisma'el*
Page 320 .... Venus Love Ritual - *Sefirot*/Planet Alignments
Page 329 ......................... *Ayak Bachar* Square
Page 330 ............ *Ayak Bachar* Hebrew Letter Angles
Page 330 ............... *Petzgakotim Ayak Bachar* Seal
Page 331 ......................... *Petzgakotim Kamea*
Page 339 ................... *Chotam* (Seal) of *Kedem'el*
Page 400 ... Hands & *Mah* Extension of the Ineffable Name
Page 401 ................... Expansion of the letter *Alef*
Page 402 .. Expansion of the Ineffable Name *Mah* Extension

# Hebrew Transliteration

There are transliterations of Hebrew words and phrases throughout this work. In this regard I have employed the following method. The Hebrew vowels are pronounced:

> "a" — like "a" in "f**a**ther";
> "e" — like the "e" in "l**e**t" or the way the English pronounce the word "Air" without enunciating the "r";
> "I" — like the "ee" in "s**ee**k";
> "o" — like the "o" in "n**o**t" or the longer "au" in "n**au**ght"; or again like the sound of the word "**A**we";
> "u" — like the "oo" in "m**oo**d";
> "ai" — like the letter "y" in "m**y**" or "igh" in "h**igh**" or like the sound of the word "**eye**"; and
> "ei" — like the "ay" in "h**ay**."

The remaining consonants are as written, except for:

> "ch" which is pronounced like the guttural "ch" in the Scottish "Lo**ch**" or the equivalent in the German "I**ch**," and "tz" which sounds like the "tz" in "Ri**tz**" or like the "ts" in "hear**ts**."

In most cases an apostrophe (') indicates a glottal stop which sounds like the "I" in "bit" or the concluding "er" in "father," otherwise it is a small break to separate sections of a word or create a double syllable. For example, I often hear people speak of *Daat* (Knowledge), sounding one long "*ah*" between the "*D*" and the concluding "*T*." The correct pronunciation is however *Da'at*, the apostrophe indicating that the term comprises actually two syllables, "*dah*" and "*aht*." In this word a quick glottal stop separates the first syllable from the second. As a vowel it is the same sound made when one struggles to find the right word, and say something like "*er.....er.....er.....*"

One further rule is that the accent in Hebrew is, more often than not, placed on the last syllable of the word. Of course there are numerous instances which disprove this rule, but it applies almost throughout Hebrew incantations, e.g. those found in Merkavistic literature, etc.

"It is a great and mysterious magic which joins the clear spring and the heart of the world. The heart cannot live without the spring, but without the heart the spring itself would dry up... ... ... .

# INTRODUCTION

I commenced writing *"The Book of Self Creation,"*[1] the first volume of this series of texts on *"Practical Kabbalah"* (Jewish Magic), almost ten years ago, and I envisage several decades might still come to pass before I lay my head to rest having penned the concluding volume.....*Deo Volente!* Looking back at what has transpired over the last ten years, viz. the first four volumes of what I chose to term the "Shadow Tree Series" of magical texts having seen the light of day on the bookshelves of the world, I am impressed at how well these "mind children" of mine are faring out there in the greater domain of esoteric literature, and how they are holding up as beacons of light in a world where human predilections are more and more inclined towards ugliness, the bizarre, and the horrific.

As it is, the nastiest zombies, vampires, and anything gruesomely slimy, are not only swamping our cinema screens like veritable hurricanes of evil, but drowning out every sense of discernment between falsity and truth. It is plainly obvious that the whole of humanity is constantly being encouraged to be "aroused" by blood and gore, to indulge in emotional instability, and to enjoy the most invasive violence. In this regard, I have been informed categorically that if I want my "occult books" to sell, I had better satisfy the "needs" of readers of this material, which pertain mainly to sexuality and some sort of chaotic aggressive action from humans channelling the "domain of the darkly invisible." Really? I am an occultist who learned my "craft" from the best in the business, and not a single one of those who mentored me in this great Tradition ever tried to sell me such rubbish. In fact, I simply cannot get myself to be "turned on" by some dirty denizen of darkness, dredging up the dregs of doom from some or other demonic dimension of despair! In this regard, I am very happy to call it what it is—*sensationalist poppycock!*

I am well aware that "sensationalism" is very popular in the esoteric book market, and works which bear titles like "Work Wonders with Witchcraft" or "I was Flogged by Fiend," are virtually guaranteed to be best sellers by their titles alone. By all appearances titles may seem quite innocuous, but contents are another matter. In this regard, I am determined to avoid my writings being classified among a genre of esoteric books which can only be described as sheer *nastiness*, and which might include any revolting or stomach-turning activity one could think of which may or may not be humanly possible, or perhaps simply a figment of the author's imagination. Literature of that sort does *sell*, but in the end it defeats its own purpose by over-exposure, thus leading to a point where nothing other than boredom is left.

Be that as it may, I thought I might use the introduction to the second part of "*The Book of Immediate Magic*," to address some of the peculiar responses solicited by the publication of the previous volumes of the "Shadow Tree Series," in which the focus is as indicated mainly on Jewish Magic.[2] In fact, the very expression "Jewish Magic" led to a rather lively interaction on a "Jewish Magic" group internet site, between myself and an individual who was taking the line that the "universality" of the magical arts means one can do anything one wants with the practices comprising all magical traditions. In this regard, the issue revolved around a so-called "Full Moon Ritual" comprising an admixture of a variety of magical traditions. It certainly did not relate in any way whatsoever to "Jewish Magic," the soul topic of discussion on the said internet site. Since I queried the relationship of this ritual to "Jewish Magic," the initial response was that the practitioner of this lunar ritual was "partly Jewish." As I am sure common sense would indicate clearly enough, being Jewish or "partly Jewish" does not turn any odd magical ritual into "Jewish Magic," or verify the claim of the defendant that "it's what you make of it."

As I tried to clarify in the previous volumes of this series of tomes on "*Practical Kabbalah*," "Jewish Magic" is not a particularly eclectic system allowing for the inclusion of all manner of symbols of variant magical doctrines. Naturally the individual in question is perfectly entitled to conjoin magical systems as he pleases in terms of his own person, but it would not be acceptable to suggest that such a diverse conglomeration of magical traditions constitute "Jewish Magic" or, as is far too often the case, depict it to be authentic "*Practical Kabbalah*." It is for this reason that I usually suggest to my personal students, and everyone seriously interested in Jewish Magic, that they should avail themselves first with what this Tradition is and what it is not, before attempting a "marriage" of variant magical systems.

In other words, Jewish Magic is a fairly precise tradition, with its Divine Names, seals and symbols employed in an exact manner. I have witnessed far too often the employment of Jewish signs and symbols, not to mention Divine Names, for purposes for which they were plainly not designed. I concede that the said "universal minded" individual is entitled to do as he pleases with the "magical knowledge" at his disposal, and that such usage may include material derived from Jewish sources. However he cannot claim, nor convince me, that such a fusion of "cross cultural" resources amounts to authentic "Jewish Magic" (*Practical Kabbalah*).

As it is, the said individual was keen to remind me that "Kabbalah gets laughed at in occult circles," and was equally eager to emphasize that this tradition is dying. Of course, nothing is further from the truth, but that was not the actual issue. It would seem the individual in question was unaware of the affiliation of the expression "*Practical Kabbalah*" with "Jewish Magic." In fact, in primary Hebrew magical texts "Jewish Magic" is often referred to as "*Kabbalah Ma'asit*," which in translation means "*Practical Kabbalah*." In terms of it being a "dying tradition," it is worth noting that the value of "*Practical Kabbalah*" (Jewish Magic) is only just coming into its own with some of the hoards of primary Hebrew texts, dealing with the subject in question, only recently having been made available to a larger readership.

This contemporary "revelation" of Jewish magical texts is quite extraordinary. Relatively few of the extensive body of Jewish magical texts were available prior to the 21st century, at least in English translation, e.g. *Sefer Shimmush Tehillim*, translated into German in the 18$^{th}$ century by a certain Godfery Selig, and thence into a verbose and very poor English version incorporated in the so-called "*Sixth and Seventh Books of Moses*";[3] *Sefer Raziel ha-Malach* in a dismal translation;[4] *The Sword of Moses*, translated by Moses Gaster;[5] *Sepher ha-Razim* translated by Michael Morgan;[6] etc. In comparison to the enormous amount of primary material dealing with Jewish Magic ("*Practical Kabbalah*") in existence, the listed translations represented a mere fraction. Several of the most important Jewish magical texts were available only in manuscript prior to the advent of the world wide web, e.g. the mammoth *Shorshei ha-Shemot*;[7] an annotated facsimile of *A Fifteenth-Century Manuscript of Jewish Magic*;[8] etc.

The very important *Shoshan Yesod Olam* in *Collectanea of Kabbalistic and Magical Texts*, Bibliothèque de Genève: Comites Latentes 145,[9] was made available in electronic format again only in the 21st century because of the internet, as were several other magical manuscripts in the Jewish National Library, the Bar-Ilan University Library, the Library of the Jewish Theological Seminary, etc. On the other hand, most of the large collection of North African Jewish magical manuscripts is still held in private collections in manuscript form only, and the majority of the Jewish magical texts which were in print in the 18/19$^{th}$ and early 20$^{th}$ centuries, have been out of print and unavailable since the end of the second world war. Several were brought back into print by the late 20th century, because of the enthusiastic efforts of Meir Backal and others who were keen to inform a broader readership on the existence of this remarkable literature. Yet it was once again the creation of important online resources in the 21$^{st}$ century, which led to facsimiles of many of these great Jewish magical publications being now readily available in electronic format. There are far too many Jewish magical titles to list in any great detail in this introduction, but a fair inventory of both the primary and the secondary sources I have consulted in writing the published volumes comprising this "Shadow Tree Series" of texts on Jewish Magic,[10] can be found in the bibliography of the current text.

Considering the enormous amount of information shared in primary sources, it is to be expected that writing works on "*Practical Kabbalah*" is no easy matter, and it is naturally extremely difficult to maintain an objective stance when dealing with the topic at hand. In this regard, an anonymous critic of my works, noted that "*The Book of Sacred Names*"[11] is "an interesting reference for the obsessive." Being originally a classical concert pianist by profession, I know the importance of perusing all reviews of concert performances, since these will not only highlight the best of your ability, but will also indicate where there is room for improvement.....that is if "critics" are doing a proper job, and not messing around with personal antipathy towards the concert artist whose performance is supposed to be reviewed objectively. In this regard, I assumed that my insistence on ensuring that I substantiate every statement in a text dealing with Hebrew "Divine Names" in Jewish magical literature, with as many references as possible to primary Hebrew sources, to be what the said critic was talking about when he/she referred to my work appealing to the "obsessive."

On the other hand, the said individual claimed my work comprises "too many assumptions" which he/she maintained are "perhaps based on the influence" of my late mentor, William G. Gray, and it was further noted that "the books"—I suppose the plural is a reference to my entire literary output—"is a bit narrow minded." There is a gracious acknowledgement that "some of the material is worth reading." Again considering my "stubborn obsessiveness" with ensuring that I back as much of the subject matter addressed in my books with references to as many primary resources as I can in an extensive bibliography, I am not at all sure what this individual was really on about. I concede that I am particularly narrowly focussed on writing about "*Practical Kabbalah*/Jewish Magic" from more mainstream Jewish perspectives, that this is my particular "bag," and that it excludes most, though not all, of the interpretations of Christian Kabbalah and those of the Hermetic orders. However, the elucidations of the latter "traditions" have been dealt with, and shared over nearly a century and quarter, with virtually no references to the Jewish perspectives of doctrines and traditions which are primarily of Jewish origins!

Of course, it is important for me "to get it right" when it comes to the topics addressed in my publications on "*Practical Kabbalah*." In this regard, I take careful note of all opinions, suggestions, and especially "rectifications." However, what really pushes the upper limits of impudence, are individuals who are ultra-obsessed with their religious self importance, yet seek to investigate the "secrets" of this Tradition, but have to ascertain whether I am good enough for them to entrust their precious souls to my teachings. In this regard, I received a communiqué from an individual who quizzed me on my identity, i.e. whether I am a Jew, and, if not, as to my personal belief system. On confirming that I am a Jew, he launched into an intense interrogation as to exactly what kind of Jew I am, e.g. whether I follow the guidelines outlined in *Sefer Sha'arei Kedushah* ("Gates of Holiness"),[12] if I am fully "Torah observant," even whether I have "any knowledge of *Torah, Talmud*, and legal codes of the *Shulchan Aruch*"[13] [my italics], etc. Above all, whether I acquired my knowledge from a "Master Kabbalist," his reason for querying being that he saw that my work, in his own words, is "filled with many different sources such as *Shorshey Shemot*[14] [my italics] and other holy writs," and that he is interested in perusing my writings. In this regard, he noted that before he studies my work, he has to ascertain whether I am "the right vessel" to which he "can be a receptacle" of my knowledge.

    I carefully informed the individual in question that he would have noticed from the brief references to my own person in my publications, that I am not interested in extolling any personal virtues. In this regard my life stance, which has become more pronounced in my "retirement age," is to say as little as possible about myself, and to let this great Tradition speak for itself. After giving the individual a succinct overview of my training and background as a Kabbalist, as well as referencing my lifelong devotion to "*Practical Kabbalah*," the pressure was really on as to the "sacred" credentials of those who taught me.

    In reference to my mentioned stance about blowing my own trumpet, I had certainly no intention of going down the path of impressing this individual with the "sacred credentials" of those who shared the teachings of this great Tradition with me. In fact, I would like to make it clear to all interested in the material I am sharing in these tomes, that I will not be drawn into any such discussion with anyone for that matter. As far as I am concerned the success of my life and work speaks for itself, and I do not feel obligated to report to anyone as to the validity of my person, life, and the teachings which I have elected to share with everyone, whether Jewish or not, i.e. anyone keenly interested in the Tradition which has to date been most meaningful in terms of my personal wellbeing.

Now I am well aware that I am shooting myself in the foot as far as "good sales" of these books are concerned, but what needs to be said is that nobody is under any obligation to "buy" what I am sharing in these tomes, as I am equally under no obligation to yield to unnecessary confrontation with anyone, or indulge in what appears to be self righteous impertinence. To date I have informed those who seek teachers of only the "highest reputation," especially in terms of background and self aggrandisement, that they will surely find several authors out there who would be willing to spend a lot of time justifying their persons and the right to share what they know with them. As for myself, I am not interested in the least in whether they purchase these tomes, or whether or not they consider me worthy of their scrutiny. That is entirely their prerogative!

✸✸✸

As in the case of the previous volumes of this series, I again recommend to those who would be perusing, investigating and practicing the material shared in this volume, to consider commencing any study of Kabbalistic material by sitting in a restful, peaceful manner, and then, with eyes shut for a minute or so, to meditate on these words:

> "Open my eyes so that I may perceive the wonders of Your teaching."

Whisper the phrase repeatedly and allow yourself to sense, as it were, in a "feeling" manner, the meaning of the words you are uttering. Initially it is important not to attempt any mental deliberation on the meaning of the actual words being contemplated, but to simply reiterate them a number of times. In this regard, it is a good idea to read a section in its entirety, without trying to perceive any specific meaning, then to pause for a few seconds, and afterwards attempt to understand within yourself the general meaning of what was being said. In this manner you begin to fulfill an important teaching of *Kabbalah*, which tells you to unite two "worlds"—the inner and the outer within your own Being. By allowing yourself to "feel" the meaning of what you are reading, you learn to surrender to the words. You open yourself, again fulfilling one of the requirements of Kabbalistic study, which is to surrender the "me," the ego, and to remove arrogance and bias. You simply attempt to sense with your being what is being portrayed in the section you are perusing. This act is a serious step on the path of perfecting ones personality, because it stops the expansion of the ego, and increases chances of obtaining "True Knowledge."

✳✳✳

As I have noted before, none of the volumes comprising this "Shadow Tree Series" of texts on "Practical Kabbalah" (Jewish Magic) would have been written without the incomparable inspiration and support of my dear friends, my Companions in the Sangreal Sodality, as well as all my acquaintances whose incisive questioning inspired me to put pen to paper. In this regard, I offer my deepest gratitude to Simon O'Regan, to whom *"The Book of Immediate Magic"* is dedicated. He coined the title of this tome, and insisted that I share every detail of the "magical material" which came my way over the years of having been a dedicant to "Practical Kabbalah. That being said, I owe the wellbeing of my body, mind, soul and spirit to Gloria, the love of my life. I am profoundly grateful that she is the one who has held my heart in the palm of her hand for the past forty years. Her incredible ability to open her heart to every creature she encounters in her world, whether it be of the human, animal, plant or mineral kind, has made the expression "good living" infinitely meaningful. In this regard, acknowledgement is equally due to my late Mentor, William G. Gray, my Father-Brother, who liberally shared his heart and mind with me, and who not only awakened my eyes to the "Inner Ways of Truth and Goodness," but, above all, to that which is of the greatest value in living on this planet—"common sense."

    I need to reiterate that this text would not have been written without the love and support of my wonderful friends and associates in the "Great Work," with whom I have had the opportunity to share this great magical tradition over several decades. In this regard, I again offer my most profound thanks to my very dear friends and fellow Companions in South Africa, in Johannesburg Norma Cosani, Gidon Fainman, John Jones, Geraldine Talbot, Elizabeth Bennet, Francois le Roux, Ian Greenspan, Gerhardus Muller, Ryan Kay, and to Simon O'Regan who encouraged me to write this tome; in Pretoria to Carlien Steyn, Magriet Engelbrecht, Helene Vogel and Gerrit Viljoen; in sunny Durban to Marq and Penny Smith, and residing in the magnificent heart of the fairest of Capes, to Dirk Cloete and Sean Smith in beautiful Hout Bay.

I also wish to acknowledge my Sangreal Sodality Companions and friends residing beyond the South African borders, Marcus Claridge in Scotland, Hamish Gilbert in Poland, Bence Bodnar, Lukács Gábor, and Dániel Szeretõ in Hungary, Roberto Siqueira Rodrigues in Brazil, and all those "whose Identities are known unto Omniscience alone," not forgetting my "Fellow Questers" whose curiosity again contributed to the material shared in this volume. I also wish to pay tribute to my late friend Jonathan Helper, not only for his support in translating numerous and sometimes very obscure passages from the primary Hebrew sources employed in these tomes, but for having been my friend.

In conclusion I would like to offer my most profound gratitude to my Sangreal Companion and beloved friend Norma Cosani who carefully read and edited this text, and who worked the magic of "linguistic rectification" wherever necessary.

Happy Reading!

Jacobus Swart
Johannesburg
August 2018

**. ... ... ...Each day at dusk it receives a gift from the heart— one day, one single day for which it can continue to flow. When that day has passed, the spring begins to sing. Only the heart of the world hears that song, and it answers the spring with a song of its own... ... ... .**

# Chapter 6
# *Or Makif*— Light Embracing
# MAGICAL MEDIATION

## A. *Sefirotic* Sensibilities

The "Ten *Sefirot*" comprise the celebrated and much maligned central doctrine of *Kabbalah*. It has been used and abused in numerous ways, and mostly by those who are familiar with nothing more than the fanciful notions they have gleaned from the many misrepresentations of this doctrine in 20th century Hermetic magical literature perpetuated all over the world wide web. In terms of my thoughts on this matter, I believe I have expressed myself clearly in *"The Book of Self Creation,"* and certainly do not wish to belabour what I have said in the first volume of this *"The Shadow Tree Series"* of magical texts.[1]

Be that as it may, the *Sha'arei Orah* ("Gates of Light") by Rabbi Joseph Gikatilla,[2] a work in which the "Ten *Sefirot*" and their respectively associated Divine Names are extensively addressed, is *the* primary Hebrew text which profoundly impacted traditional *Kabbalah*, as well as the Christian and Hermetic varieties. It has been noted that "the first Christian Kabbalists recognized the importance of *Sha'arei Orah* and quoted it extensively,"[3] and the said impact of this text on Christian Hebraists in the Renaissance was entirely due to the very popular Latin translation of this text titled *"Portae Lucis"* by Paulus Riccius,[4] a Jewish convert, whose translations were included in Pistorius' *Ars Cabalistica*.[5] The popularity of the *Sha'arei Orah* during the Italian Renaissance, was equally due to the efforts of the famed Christian Kabbalist Johannes Reuchlin, who employed this translation to convince the Renaissance Pope Leo X of the value of Jewish writings, and to encourage him against the burning of Jewish writings as advised by Dominicans.[6]

Whilst there is hardly any indication in "Early *Kabbalah*" of the sefirotic array being employed for meditational purposes, Aryeh Kaplan was probably right in his assessment that the *Sha'arei Orah* "can be taken as a guide for those who wish to ascend spiritually through meditation on the ladder of the *Sefirot*," and that it "can be seen in its entirety as a guide to meditation."[7] There are indeed hints in this unique text to practical techniques based on the *Sefirot* and affiliated Divine Names, and in this regard Joseph Gikatilla wrote that "those who want their needs fulfilled by employing the Holy Names should try with all their strength to comprehend the meaning of each Name of God as they are recorded in the Torah, names such as *EHYE, YH, YHVH, AdoNaY, EL, ELOH, EloHIM, ShaDaY, TZVAOT*," and finally concluded his remarkable book with the words "we have given you ten keys for connecting (the Spheres). With these you will be able to enter many gates that are closed and many people will never merit entering them."[8] Again the late Aryeh Kaplan remarked that the ten *Sefirot* "may be looked upon as 'dials' in the mind that can be used to amplify the experiences associated with them."[9]

There are a few interesting and very effective magical/meditational activities based on the *Sefirot* delineated in traditional *Kabbalah*, and several in contemporary Hermetic Kabbalistic literature.[10] Amongst these is a practice based on an affiliation of the ten *Sefirot* to the nine phalanges of the central three fingers and the upper left portion of the palm of your right hand. When I explored the wonders of *Practical Kabbalah* in the early 1970's, a dear Israeli friend who was a veritable fountain of wisdom on Jewish Magic, alerted me to this curious practice, which he noted could be used in a special manner to meditatively trigger unique alignments with the sefirotic Tree within your own "Inner Being."

As mentioned, nine *sefirot* are assigned to the nine phalanges or digital bones of the three middle fingers in the regular order of appearance on the sefirotic Tree, with the tenth *sefirah* (*Malchut*—Kingdom) located at the base of the little finger,[11] as indicated in the following illustration:

*Magical Mediation* / 3

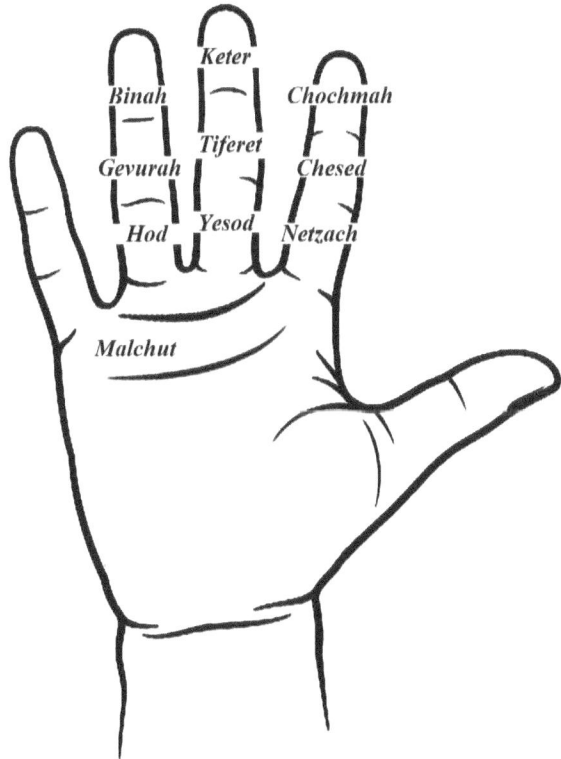

The "sefirotic powers" are "triggered" by means of the thumb for meditation/magical purposes. In this regard, it is important to familiarise yourself with the relative positions of the ten *sefirot* by touching the relevant locales on your fingers and hand with your thumb, and this action is be performed in the following manner:

1. Extend your right hand in front of you, palm facing upwards, and smile at your hand as you look at it for a couple of seconds, then say עץ החיים ביד שלי (*Etz ha-chayim b'yad sheli*—"The Tree of Life in my hand").
2. Close your eyes, continue smiling warmly inside yourself, and focus your attention on the central three fingers.
3. With closed eyes, and whilst still smiling, touch the upper phalanx of the middle finger with your thumb and say "*Keter.*" Continue touching the various phalanges of the three middle fingers in exactly the same manner, as you recite the names of their associated sefirotic appellatives, and doing so in their standard order of display on the

Kabbalistic Tree of Life. As indicated in the hand illustration, the order is:

a. Middle finger/upper phalanx—*Keter* (כתר–"Crown")
b. Index finger/upper phalanx—*Chochmah* (חכמה–"Wisdom")
c. Ring finger/upper phalanx—*Binah* (בינה–"Understanding")
d. Index finger/middle phalanx—*Chesed* (חסד–"Mercy")
e. Ring finger/middle phalanx—*Gevurah* (גבורה–"Severity")
f. Middle finger/middle phalanx—*Tiferet* (תפארת–"Beauty")
g. Index finger/lower phalanx—*Netzach* (נצח–"Victory")
h. Ring finger/lower phalanx—*Hod* (הוד–"Glory")
i. Middle finger/lower phalanx—*Yesod* (יסוד–"Foundation")

Complete tracing the Tree of Life in your hand by touching directly below the little finger with your thumb, and saying *Malchut* (מלכות–"Kingdom").

4. Conclude the procedure by opening your hand, and experiencing the entire layout of the sefirotic tree in your hand with closed eyes, and saying:

עץ החיים ביד שלי
ברוך שם כבוד מלכותו לעולם ועד

Transliteration:
*Etz ha-chayim b'yad sheli*
*Baruch shem k'vod malchuto l'olam va'ed*

Translation:
The Tree of Life in my hand.
Blessed be the Name of His glorious Kingdom throughout eternity.

I was informed that for this practice to be really effective, you need to do it with *Kavvanah*, i.e. to keep your attention firmly focussed in the palm of your hand. To fully achieve this, you have to ensure that you first touch a selected phalanx, and then, when you are fully conscious of the touch, and, as it were, mentally inhabiting that portion of your finger, to audibly utter the appellative of the associated *Sefirah*. This is to be done first thing on waking in the morning, and last thing prior to retiring to sleep at night. Also, as personal experience has taught me, this procedure should be practised on a daily basis for at least a month, in order to fully integrate it to, as it were, "programme" it into your "inner being" before attempting to expand the exercise in any way.

Unfortunately my earlier mentioned friend and informant on *Practical Kabbalah* never delineated any further procedures beyond the tracing of the ten *sefirot* in my hand in this manner, and he definitely said nothing in terms of "triggering sefirotic powers" for meditational or magical purposes. However, being always very enthusiastic about practices such as these, I added certain further "developments," so to speak. I also employed this very procedure to deliberately acknowledge daily, as it were, "events" in terms of their sefirotic associations, and especially in terms of their psycho/physical impact. In this regard, when I encountered joy, laughter, expansiveness of consciousness, gregariousness, good living, etc., I would consciously and deliberately touch the central phalanx of the index finger and say or think "*Chesed*." On the other hand, if I encountered aggression, anger, hatred, violence, etc., I would acknowledge it by touching the central phalanx of the ring finger and say or whisper "*Gevurah*." I have addressed sefirotic associations in terms of emotional qualities in the first volume of "*The Book of Immediate Magic*."[12] In the same manner I acknowledged whatever emotional responses I am manifesting, e.g. whatever mood I am at any moment.

I first practised the mentioned counting of the ten *sefirot* in the palm of my right hand for a couple of months, acknowledging them in the manner delineated whenever and wherever I encountered them in my daily life. Afterwards I elected to add to the procedure their commonly attributed array of ten Hebrew Divine Names, i.e. the set of Divine Name/*Sefirot* affiliations which is particularly popular amongst Hermetic Kabbalists, and which I have addressed in terms of "Opening" so-called sefirotic "Gates":[13]

| | | |
|---|---|---|
| *Keter* | אהיה | (*Eh'yeh*) |
| *Chochmah* | יהוה | (*YHVH*) |
| *Binah* | אלהים | (*Elohim*) |
| *Chesed* | אל | (*El*) |
| *Gevurah* | אלהים גבור | (*Elohim Gibor [Gibur]*) |
| *Tiferet* | יהוה אלוה ודעת | (*YHVH Eloha va-Da'at*) |
| *Netzach* | יהוה צבאות | (*YHVH Tzva'ot*) |
| *Hod* | אלהים צבאות | (*Elohim Tzva'ot*) |
| *Yesod* | שדי אל חי | (*Shadai El Chai*) |
| *Malchut* | אדני הארץ | (*Adonai ha-Aretz*) |

In terms of practicalities, you would again extend your hand to count the ten *sefirot* in the palm of your hand, and perform the entire procedure in the exact manner delineated earlier, but in the current instance you would include the Divine Name affiliated with each *sefirah*. For example, you would touch the tip of the upper phalanx of the middle finger, pronounce "*Keter*," and whisper the Divine Name אהיה (*Eh'yeh*). In each case, the best results can be achieved by maintaining an "inner smile" within yourself throughout the practice, and to cultivate a "feeling appreciation" of the practice.

It has been suggested that this set of Divine Names was assigned to the ten *Sefirot* by the late Israel Regardie of Golden Dawn fame. However, as I noted elsewhere,[14] I have examined a late 19th century French manuscript of what I believe to be a Hermetic *Kabbalah* text titled "*Ma'aseh ha-Tzafun [Tzafon]*" (*The Hidden Work [Work of the North?]*),[15] in which the Divine Names employed by Regardie and the Golden Dawn are listed in the exact manner in terms of their sefirotic affiliations. In this regard, the said text delineated a procedure of "opening" so-called "gates" in accordance with the vowels of the Divine Names respectively attributed to the ten *Sefirot*. As some readers would have noted, I have addressed the mentioned practice of "Opening Sefirotic Gates" in great detail in the first part of "*The Book of Immediate Magic*."[16]

It is quite possible for Israel Regardie to have derived those Divine Name/*Sefirot* attributions from the writings of Rabbi Moses Cordovero, as I am convinced did the anonymous French author of the mentioned "*Ma'aseh ha-Tzafun*" manuscript.[17] After all, Regardie was so impressed with Cordovero, that he titled his own introductory study of the ten *sefirot* "*Garden of Pomegranates*"[18] after Cordovero's *Pardes Rimmonim* (*Garden of Pomegranates*).[19] It is also worth considering that several mainstream Kabbalists wrote about the ten *sefirot* and their associated Divine Names, and that in this regard there are indeed variances to be found from one author to the next. However, assuming Regardie procured his set of sefirotic Divine Name attributions from the writings of Rabbi Moses Cordovero, it is worth noting that the great Rabbi listed all of those popular concepts and Divine Names attributed to the ten *sefirot* in the writings of Israel Regardie and the Hermetic Orders, e.g. שדי (*Shadai*) and אל חי (*El Chai*) are both attributed to *Yesod* (Foundation); אדני (*Adonai*) and ארץ (*Aretz*) are both attributed to *Malchut* (Kingdom); etc.[20]

A while back I have interacted with an individual who raised some concern about the דעת (*Da'at*) affiliation with the central *sefirah Tif'eret* (Beauty). However, it should be noted that whilst it is true that this appellative is employed in reference to the "non-*sefirah*" dividing the upper three *sefirot* from the lower seven, the word דעת (*Da'at*) is a common term referring to "knowledge" in general, and in Kabbalistic thinking true "knowledge" pertains to the "heart" rather than the "head." Consider also that in traditional *Kabbalah* a set of Biblical personalities are attributed to the ten *Sefirot*. In this regard, Moses is affiliated with *Tif'eret*, regarding which Moses Cordovero wrote in *Or Ne'erav* "Moses the man of *Da'at* which is subsumed within *Tiferet*."[21] Later in the same work Cordovero made the interesting statement "the third opposition is between *Chochmah* and *Binah*, and the balancing force is *Tif'eret* in the mystery of *Da'at*."[22]

It should be noted that Joseph Gikatilla, the great 13/14th century Kabbalist, equally addressed the term *Da'at* (Knowledge) in terms of the central sphere on the sefirotic Tree. In fact, he viewed the concept of *Da'at* to apply to the entire central line (Pillar) of the kabbalistic Tree of Life, and stated that "Israel, however, who is attached to the Middle Line, which is *TIFERET*, which is *DAT* (*Da'at*), can ascend."[23] Regarding the said *Tiferet* (Beauty)/*Da'at* (Knowledge) affiliation, he further noted that the "image of *TIFERET* is nothing less than the entire construction of the Constellation, all the Holy Names and Cognomens in which *YHVH*, may He be Blessed, dresses and adorns Himself. This sphere is known in the Torah as *DAT (Da'at)*....."[24] This is further clearly spelled out in the following English transcription of an illustration of the sefirotic array in Gikatilla's *"Sha'arei Orah"* ("Gates of Light").[25]

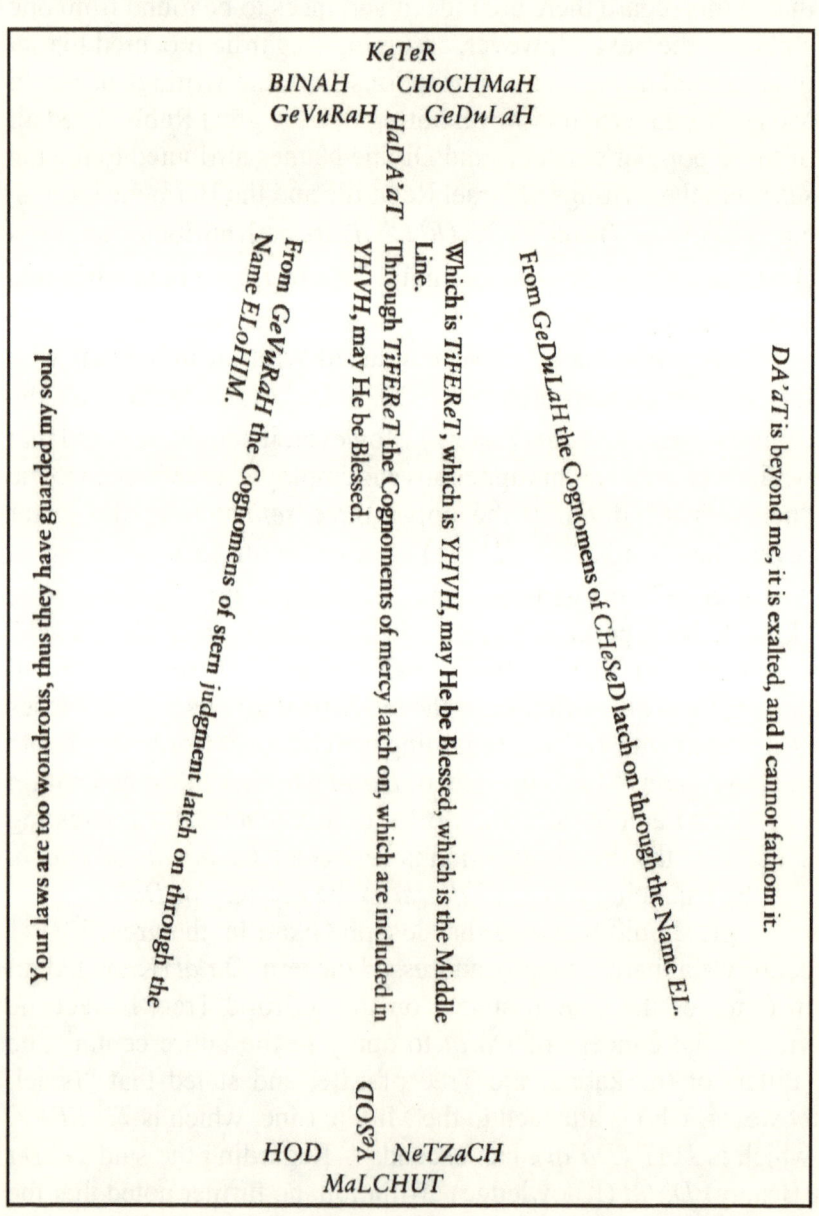

It should be clear that the Divine Name construct "*YHVH Elo'ah va-Daat*" is perfectly aligned with *Tif'eret* (Beauty), the *Sefirah* pertaining to the "chest" and perforce to the "Place" (מקום —*Makom*) of the "Heart." The said Divine Name combination translates correctly "*YHVH* God *and* the Knowledge,*"* which makes sense in terms of the mentioned association of the concept of "*Da'at*" (Knowledge) in a direct and specific manner with the central *sefirah* (*Tiferet*) on the Kabbalistic Tree of Life.[26] However, I personally find the standard translation "*YHVH* God of Knowledge" equally acceptable. It should be kept in mind that in mainstream *Kabbalah* the concept of "*Da'at*" (Knowledge) is attributed to both *Tif'eret* (Beauty) and *Yesod* (Foundation), "knowledge" in the case of the latter *sefirah* being more of the "carnal" kind, since *Yesod* (Foundation) is traditionally associated with the masculine reproductive organ.[27]

Whilst I am largely satisfied with the mentioned attribution of the said popular set of Divine Names to the ten *Sefirot*, I find the generally employed enunciations of some of the listed Divine Name constructs seriously problematic. Any vocalisation of the Ineffable Name, e.g. the manner in which it is enunciated by Hermetic and Christian Kabbalists ("*Jehovah*," "*Yahovah*," etc.), is unacceptable and strictly forbidden in Judaism, and perforce in Jewish *Kabbalah* as well. There are indeed a number of vocalisations of the Ineffable Name (יהוה) listed in Jewish Magic, each of which pertains directly to a specific magical intention. There is equally no vocalisation "*Sabaoth*" or "*Tsabaoth*" in reference to the צבאות association *Sefirot Netzach* (Victory) and *Hod* (Splendour), the correct pronunciation being "*Tzva'ot*."

I have also heard common Kabbalistic terms, e.g. the standard appellatives of the ten Sefirot, etc., being vocalised in the oddest fashion by individuals claiming to be "authorities" on the sefirotic tree. In this regard, the *sefirah* "*Malchut*" (Kingdom) is very often enunciated "*Mel-kooth*," "*Keter*" (Crown) vocalised "*Keether*"; "*Chochmah*" (Wisdom) rendered "*Choke-ma*"—as in "choking" your mother; "*Chesed*" vocally rendered "*Chess-set*" or even "*Cheese-set*"; etc. Whilst it would seem that the correct pronunciation of Hebrew terms is considered to be of little importance to many "non-Jewish" users of the Hebrew Divine Names and the Kabbalistic Tree of Life, it is certainly clear that with accurate 21st century enunciations of all manner of Hebrew terms readily available on the internet, there is really no excuse in ascertaining the correct vocalisation of the titles of the ten *sefirot* and Hebrew Divine Names, or Angelic Names for that matter.

Be that as it may, whilst I have attempted to greatly expand the current practice of counting the *sefirot*, it was clear to me that my earlier mentioned friend and remarkable informant on *Practical Kabbalah* did not know what this procedure might have further entailed. However, he encouraged me to employ the thumb of my right hand to trace the ten *sefirot* on my hand in the manner delineated.

A little more than a decade after learning this technique, I guessed what such possible associated meditational/magical purposes might be. In this regard, I should mention that following my all too brief sojourn into Lurianic *Kabbalah* in the early-1970's, I explored the works of my late mentor William G. Gray, the English Kabbalist and Ceremonial Magician. It was in his writings that I chanced upon the following highly original prayer-meditations, which I noticed combined beautifully with the tracing of the ten *Sefirot* in my hand. Such prayer-like meditations incorporating physical action, are effective in expanding consciousness in a most meaningful manner, especially in the current instance where one employs the *Sefirot* in a comprehensive manner as actualities for realising "Self," spiritual growth, and good living in this universe, i.e. what I referred to previously as "relating the 'centre' ('Self') to the 'circumference' (the 'All')."[28]

In working these invocations penned by my late mentor, I suggest you follow the exact procedure as delineated earlier in tracing the ten *Sefirot* on your hand, i.e. commencing with the open palm, then touching the phalanges of the three middle fingers in the exact order of their respective affiliations with the *Sefirot*, tracing either downwards from *Keter* (Crown) to *Malchut* (Kingdom), or *vice versa* upwards from *Malchut* to *Keter*. When necessary employ the open hand at appropriate moments, e.g. either at the beginning, in the middle, or at the end of the meditation, i.e. during the opening Hebrew phrase or prior to the concluding statement, as indicated in the shared set of prayer-invocations. I suggest you memorise each meditation, and perform them entirely with eyes shut, ensuring that you remain deeply surrendered as you mentally observe the action.

Keep in mind that this kind of magical/meditational activity requires a profound "feeling appreciation," and that with the utterance of each phrase you should allow the meaning of each phrase to invoke an inner response which floods your surrendered being.

## 1. THE BLESSINGS OF THE *SEFIROT*[29]

| | |
|---|---|
| ***Open hand*** | Blessed be the Light beyond all Being. |
| | Forever Blessed be the Living Spirit. *Amen.* |
| ***Keter*** | Blessed be the Breathing of Origination. |
| | Forever Blessed be the Living Spirit. *Amen.* |
| ***Chochmah*** | Blessed be Eternal Wisdom. |
| | Forever Blessed be the Living Spirit. *Amen.* |
| ***Binah*** | Blessed be Omniscient Understanding. |
| | Forever Blessed be the Living Spirit. *Amen.* |
| ***Chesed*** | Blessed be Perpetual Compassion. |
| | Forever Blessed be the Living Spirit. *Amen.* |
| ***Gevurah*** | Blessed be Almighty Justice. |
| | Forever Blessed be the Living Spirit. *Amen.* |
| ***Tiferet*** | Blessed be Transcendent Beauty. |
| | Forever Blessed be the Living Spirit. *Amen.* |
| ***Netzach*** | Blessed be Unceasing Victory. |
| | Forever Blessed be the Living Spirit. *Amen.* |
| ***Hod*** | Blessed be Surpassing Glory. |
| | Forever Blessed be the Living Spirit. *Amen.* |
| ***Yesod*** | Blessed be Infallible Foundation. |
| | Forever Blessed be the Living Spirit. *Amen.* |
| ***Malchut*** | Blessed be all Life throughout the Kingdom. |
| | Forever Blessed be the Living Spirit. *Amen.* |

## 2. A KABBALISTIC RULE[30]

| | |
|---|---|
| ***Malchut*** | Man of Earth, |
| ***Yesod*** | Faithfully Believe in Life. |
| ***Hod*** | Live Honourably; |
| ***Netzach*** | Conquer Yourself; |
| ***Tiferet*** | Be Equable of Energy; |
| ***Gevurah*** | Self Disciplined; |
| ***Chesed*** | Generously Merciful; |
| ***Binah*** | Understanding; |
| ***Chochmah*** | Wise; |
| ***Keter*** | Single of Spirit; |
| | and ultimately, |

| | |
|---|---|
| *Open hand* | You will live in Light Divine, Immortally beyond all limits, in Perfect Peace Profound. |

### 3. A KABBALISTIC CREED[31]
#### i. From Matter to Spirit

| | |
|---|---|
| *Malchut* | In Material Existence |
| *Yesod* | I Believe, |
| *Hod* | with Reason |
| *Netzach* | and Devotion, |
| *Tiferet* | in the Beauty |
| *Gevurah* | of Controlled |
| *Chesed* | abounding Love, |
| *Binah* | whose Understanding |
| *Chochmah* | Wisdom is the |
| *Keter* | Only Light, Illuminating |
| *Open hand* | Boundless Being in the Ultimate Unmanifest of Perfect Peace Profound. |

#### ii. From Spirit to Matter

| | |
|---|---|
| *Open hand* | Of Perfect Peace Profound out of the Ultimate Unmanifest, Boundless Being becomes Illumination as the |
| *Keter* | One True Light of |
| *Chochmah* | Wisdom, |
| *Binah* | Understanding all with |
| *Chesed* | Love outpoured |
| *Gevurah* | in full Control as |
| *Tiferet* | Beauty, whose |
| *Netzach* | Achievement is a |
| *Hod* | Brilliance finding its |
| *Yesod* | Foundation in |
| *Malchut* | Material existence. |

## 4. A KABBALISTIC PRAYER[32]

| | |
|---|---|
| *Open hand* | O Supreme Life Spirit, You alone are |
| *Keter* | Cause and Crown of Cosmos |
| *Chochmah* | With Your Wisdom |
| *Binah* | and Your Understanding. |
| *Open hand* | Grant us avoidance of the great Abyss in our Experience of Your Existence. |
| *Chesed* | Extend Your Mercy unto us |
| *Gevurah* | With all Your Might, |
| *Tiferet* | that we may realise the Blessed Beauty of Your Being. |
| *Netzach* | Let us lovingly Achieve |
| *Hod* | the Glory |
| *Yesod* | of Establishing ourselves immortally |
| *Malchut* | in Your most holy Kingdom Evermore. |
| | *Amen* |

## 5. A KABBALISTIC THANKSGIVING[33]

| | |
|---|---|
| *Open hand* | Gratitude to You, O Greatest |
| *Keter* | Sovereign Spirit |
| *Chochmah* | of Supernal Wisdom |
| *Binah* | and Omniscient Understanding, |
| *Open hand* | since we are enlightened by Experience of Your Existence. |
| *Chesed* | Thanks be for Mercifully |
| *Gevurah* | tempered Might, |
| *Tiferet* | and blessed be the Beauty |
| *Netzach* | of Achieving |
| *Hod* | Glory |
| *Yesod* | by Establishing our Living Entities |
| *Malchut* | within Your Everlasting Kingdom. |
| | *Amen* |

## 6. HEBREW SEFIROTIC PRAYER-INVOCATIONS

I am sure some readers might query whether such sefirotic prayer-meditations can be found in "traditional" *Kabbalah* which can be employed in the same manner, and, in this regard you might consider the following unique prayer-invocation by Rabbi Josef Tzayach.[34] This remarkable Kabbalist equally addressed the ten *Sefirot* in terms of the palm and nine phalanges of the central three fingers of the right hand, in conjunction with which you could employ his said personal prayer-blessing. It incorporates some of the Divine Names traditionally aligned with the ten *Sefirot*:

| | |
|---|---|
| **Keter** | *Eh'yeh Asher Eh'yeh*, Crown me. |
| **Chochmah** | *Yah*, grant me Wisdom. |
| **Binah** | *Elohim Chayim*, grant me Understanding. |
| **Chesed** | *El*, with the right hand of His Love, make me great. |
| **Gevurah** | *Elohim*, with the Terror of His Judgment, protect me. |
| **Tiferet** | *YHVH*, with His mercy, grant me Beauty. |
| **Netzach** | *Adonai Tzva'ot*, watch me Forever. |
| **Hod** | *Elohim Tzva'ot*, grant me beatitude from His Splendour. |
| **Yesod** | *El Chai*, make his covenant my Foundation. |
| **Malchut** | *Adonai*, open my lips and my mouth will speak of Your praise. |

Readers who prefer approaching the Kabbalistic Tree of Life from traditional Hebraic perspectives, will find the following great sefirotic invocation enormously beneficial. The material was shared in the mammoth *"Pardes Ha-Nisim"* text on *Practical Kabbalah*.[35] The incantation can be employed in the exact manner delineated, as indicated below:

1. Commence the procedure again by extending the palm of your right hand, and say:

עץ החיים ביד שלי

Transliteration:
*Etz ha-chayim b'yad sheli*
Translation:
The Tree of Life in my hand.

2. Continue by touching the relevant phalanges of your central three fingers in alignment with their sefirotic associations:

| | |
|---|---|
| **Keter** | חננו בקדושתיך ופניך<br>חננו בטובך ורצונך |
| **Chochmah & Binah** | *Binah  Chochmah*<br>חננו בחכמה ובינה |
| **Chochmah**<br>**Binah** | חיינו בחכמתיך וימלאו<br>חיינו בבינתך וימלאו |
| **Chesed &**<br>**Gevurah** | *Gevurah  Chesed*<br>חננו בקדושה וטהרה |
| **Chesed** | חננו בחסדיך וטובתיך<br>חיינו בחסדיך וימלאו |
| **Gevurah** | חננו בכוח וחיל<br>חננו בגבורח וימלאו |
| **Tiferet** | חננו בתפארתך וישועתך<br>חיינו בעזרתך וקדושתיך<br>חננו בתפארת וימלאו |
| **Netzach**<br>**& Hod** | *Hod  Netzach*<br>חיינו בנצח והוד |
| **Netzach** | חננו בחן וחסד<br>חננו בנצח וימלאו |
| **Hod** | חננו בהוד והדר<br>חננו בהוד וימלאו |
| **Yesod** | חננו באהבתיך וימלאו<br>חננו בשמחה וחדוה<br>חננו ביסוד וימלאו |

*16 / The Book of Immediate Magic — Part 2*

**Malchut**  חננו במלכות וימלא
חננו בחיים ופרנסה
חננו בברכה והצלחה
חננו בברכותיך וישועתיך

Transliteration:

**Keter**  chaneinu b'K'dushatecha u'Fanecha
chaneinu b'Tov'cha u'R'tzon'cha

**Chochmah & Binah**  *Chochmah*    *Binah*
chaneinu b'Chochmah u'Vinah

**Chochmah**  chayeinu b'Chochmatecha v'yimal'u
**Binah**  chayeinu b'Vinat'cha v'Yimal'u

**Chesed & Gevurah**  *Chesed*    *Gevurah*
chaneinu b'Kedushah v'Taharah

**Chesed**  chaneinu b'Chasadecha v'Tovatach
chayeinu b'Chasadecha v'Yimal'u

**Gevurah**  chaneinu b'Koach v'Chayil
chaneinu b'Gevurah v'Yimal'u

**Tiferet**  chaneinu b'Tif'artecha v'Y'shu'atecha
chayeinu b'Ezratech v'K'dushatecha
chaneinu b'Tiferet v'Yimal'u

**Netzach & Hod**  *Netzach*    *Hod*
chayeinu b'Netzach v'Hod

**Netzach**  chaneinu b'Chen v'Chesed
chaneinu b'Netzach v'Yimal'u

**Hod**  chaneinu b'Hod v'Hadar
chaneinu b'Hod v'Yimal'u

**Yesod**  chaneinu b'Ahav'tich v'Yimal'u
chaneinu b'Simchah v'Ched'va
chaneinu b'Yesod v'Yimal'u

| | |
|---|---|
| *Malchut* | *chaneinu b'Malchut v'Yimal'u*<br>*chaneinu b'Virkotecha v'Y'shu'atecha*<br>*chaneinu b'Chayim v'Parnasah*<br>*chaneinu biV'rachah v'Hatzlachah* |

Translation:

| | |
|---|---|
| *Keter* | Be gracious unto us in your Holiness and your Countenance.<br>Be gracious unto us in your Goodness and your Will. |
| *Chochmah & Binah* | Be gracious unto us in Wisdom and Understanding |
| *Chochmah* | We live in in your Wisdom, and we are fulfilled. |
| *Binah* | We live in your Understanding, and we are fulfilled. |
| *Chesed & Gevurah* | Be gracious unto us in Holiness and Purity. |
| *Chesed* | Be gracious unto us in your Mercy and your Goodness.<br>We live in your Mercy, and we are fulfilled. |
| *Gevurah* | Be gracious unto us in Power and Strength.<br>Be gracious unto us in Might, and we are fulfilled. |
| *Tiferet* | Be gracious unto us in your Beauty and Salvation.<br>We live in your Support and Holiness.<br>Be gracious unto us in Beauty, and we are fulfilled. |
| *Netzach & Hod* | We live in Victory and Splendour. |

| | |
|---|---|
| *Netzach* | Be gracious unto us in Grace and Kindness.<br>Be gracious unto us in Endurance, and we are fulfilled. |
| *Hod* | Be gracious unto us in Honour and Majesty.<br>Be gracious unto us in Glory, and we are fulfilled. |
| *Yesod* | Be gracious unto us in your Love, and we are fulfilled.<br>Be gracious unto us in Happiness and Delight.<br>Be gracious unto us in Foundation, and we are fulfilled. |
| *Malchut* | Be gracious unto us in the Kingdom, and we are fulfilled.<br>Be gracious unto us in your Blessedness and Salvation.<br>Be gracious unto us in Living and Livelihood.<br>Be gracious unto us in Blessings and Success. |

3. Continue by placing the three central fingers of your right hand flat on your forehead, and say:

חננו בכל ומכל כל

Transliteration:
>*chaneinu b'Chol u'm'Chol Chol*

Translation:
>Be gracious unto us in everything and everything.

4. Conclude the procedure by extending the palm of your right hand, and whilst experiencing the entire layout of the sefirotic tree in your hand with closed eyes, say:

עץ החיים ביד שלי
ברוך שם כבוד מלכותו לעולם ועד

Transliteration:
*Etz ha-chayim b'yad sheli*
*Baruch shem k'vod malchuto l'olam va'ed*

Translation:
The Tree of Life in my hand.
Blessed be the Name of His glorious Kingdom throughout eternity.

As you have probably noticed there are a number of statements pertaining to each *sefirah*, and the *Chochmah/Binah*; *Chesed/Gevurah*; and *Netzach/Hod* sefirotic pairs are addressed both conjointly and separately. In this regard, you would simply keep your thumb on a selected phalanx of a chosen finger, whilst reciting the entire set of associated statements. In the case of the mentioned sefirotic pairs being presented conjointly in the same phrase, you would simply move from one relevant phalanx to the next, e.g. *Chochmah* to *Binah*, etc., in the manner indicated in the phrase, and then repeat the same action with the phrases applicable to the associated *sefirot*.

Regarding the three central fingers being placed on the forehead prior to reciting the concluding incantationary phrase, the fingers positioned thus is meant to signal the letter ש (*Shin*), the latter representing in this instance the Divine Name שדי (*Shadai*) and שלום (*Shalom*—"Peace"). However, another manner in which this sign is employed to indicate the said Divine Name only, is to commence by placing the three central fingers on your forehead, followed by bending the thumb and little finger, representing the letters ד (*Dalet* [thumb]) and י (*Yod* [little finger]), and placing their tips on either side of the head. In this manner your hand position thus spells the Divine Name שדי (*Shadai*). According to an associate of mine, only the tips of your central fingers are placed on your forehead, and your two eyes respectively touched with the tips of the thumb and little finger. Having observed this practice performed by several associates and fellow practitioners of *Practical Kabbalah* over the years, I am fully satisfied that the manner in which I delineated the procedure is perfectly correct.

Having considered sefirotic meditation practices applied to the nine phalanges of the central three fingers and the upper palm of the right hand, I believe it is worth considering affiliated magical procedures. In this regard, we should revisit the earlier mentioned "Opening" of the ten sefirotic "Gates," which I have addressed in the first part of "*The Book of Immediate Magic*,"[36] and which were derived from a late 19th century manuscript which appears to have had its origins in "Hermetic *Kabbalah*."[37] Whatever their provenance may be, the said techniques pertaining to "*Opening the Ten Gates*" have proven to be very effective, similarly to the "divinising" practice titled "*Taking on the Name*," which is directly related to the ten *Sefirot,* and which I have shared elsewhere.[38] Briefly then, the "Opening" of the "Gates" procedure incorporates a magical/meditational alignment with each of the ten *Sefirot* from *Keter* (Crown) down to *Malchut* (Kingdom). As noted previously,[39] the practice affords you a method by means of which you can align mentally, emotionally, and physically with any of the ten sefirotic "Gates," and it is understood that interaction with your world will always be via the open "Gate." As noted before "it is your personal disposition, i.e. physically, emotionally, mentally and spiritually, which sets your relationship with your world," and "everything around you arranges itself, i.e. in terms of interacting with you, in accordance with your personal emotional/mental stance."[40] Hence it is understood that every person has, as it were, a "default Gate" open virtually all time. In this regard, it should be understood that whilst you might open any "Gate" at will, you will soon resort back to your standard "default Gate" in accordance with your basic nature as a person.

As I am sure readers who have perused the procedure in the first part of "*The Book of Immediate Magic*" have realised, you could very well work "Opening" all of the ten "Gates" in exact order from the first *sefirah* to the tenth, thus traversing the entire sefirotic Tree as an intense mental/emotional/physical meditation. As said previously "'*Opening the Ten Gates*' refers to unique procedures employed in the enhancement, within yourself and your environment, of 'Spirit Forces' affiliated with the ten *sefirot*. In this regard, a Divine Name directly affiliated with a *sefirah*, is vocalised in a specific manner, in order to allow the flow of the qualities of that *sefirah* to manifest within yourself, and which would be apparent to anyone you may encounter in your daily life."[41] Each sefirotic "Gate" is opened in accordance with the vowels comprising the associated Divine Name vocalised in their respectively related locales in the human body, these being "I" (*EE*)—Forehead; "E" (*EH*)—Throat; "A" (*AH*)—Heart; "O" (*OH*)—Liver [Solar Plexus]; and "U" (OO)—Genitals [Base of Spine].

As explained elsewhere "it would be necessary to establish the right vocal tension in the appropriate physical locale to start with, and then to commence the force flow of the Divine Name which will open the appropriate sefirotic 'Gate.' It is also worth noting that it is the first and last vowel tone of a Divine Name which is of particular importance. In other words, the point where you start, and the point you aim at in conclusion, the whole enunciation from beginning to end being a smooth, orderly flow of sound and mind."[42] Furthermore, during exhalation you need to slide your mental focus from one relevant locale to the next in your body as you chant or whisper the associated vowels of the Divine Name, in this regard consider again the following table:

| Sefirah | Divine Name | Associated Vowels | Physical Locales |
|---|---|---|---|
| 1. Keter | Eh'yeh | Eh–(Ee)–Eh | Throat–(Head)–Throat |
| 2. Chochmah | YHVH | Ee–Ah–Oh–Eh | Head–Heart–Solar Plexus–Throat |
| 3. Binah | Elohim | Eh–Oh–Ee | Throat–Solar Plexus–Head |
| 4. Chesed | El | Eh–(lllll) | Throat |
| 5. Gevurah | Elohim Gibor | Eh–Oh–Ee | Throat–Solar Plexus–Head |
| | | Ee–Oh | Head–Solar Plexus |
| 6. Tiferet | YHVH Eloah va-Da'at | Ee–Ah–Oh–Eh | Head–Heart–Solar Plexus–Throat |
| | | Eh–Oh–Ah | Throat–Solar Plexus–Heart |
| | | Ah–Ah–Ah | Heart–Heart–Heart |
| 7. Netzach | YHVH Tzva'ot | Ee–Ah–Oh–Eh | Head–Heart–Solar Plexus–Throat |
| | | Ah–Oh | Heart–Solar Plexus |
| 8. Hod | Elohim Tzva'ot | Eh–Oh–Ee | Throat–Solar Plexus–Head |
| | | Ah–Oh | Heart–Solar Plexus |
| 9. Yesod | Shadai El Chai | Ah–Ah–Ee | Heart–Heart–Head |
| | | Eh | Throat |
| | | Ah–Ee | Heart–Head |
| 10. Malchut | Adonai ha-Aretz | Ah–Oh–Ah–Ee | Heart–Solar Plexus–Heart–Head |
| | | Ah–Ah–Eh | Heart–Heart–Throat |

A vital factor in successfully opening any of the sefirotic "Gates" in the manner delineated here, pertains to the ten "qualities of action" which I delineated in the first part of *"The Book of Immediate Magic."* These are:

1. *Keter* — אהיה (*Eh'yeh*–"I am"): "Imagine and sense your physical body dissolving into 'Light,' and turning into an energy body. As you open the 'Gate of *Keter*' by means of the affiliated Divine Name, you sense your entire physical construct vibrating at a certain frequency. This is a kind of energy tension which you move into and maintain as you utter the Divine Name *Eh'yeh* in the manner delineated. This action is deliberate and intentional, and there is a condition of inner calm and outer tension being maintained."[43]

2. *Chochmah* — יהוה (*YHVH*): "In opening the 'Gate of *Chochmah*,' you have to shift your consciousness to the centre of your being, and be aware of past, present and future as one in the 'Eternal Now.' Whereas the first *sefirah* refers to *Eh'yeh*, the 'I am,' as it were, within an energetic 'Spirit Vehicle' or 'Energy Body,' the 'Gate of *Chochmah*' pertains to the eternality of that 'Energy Body.' In this regard you shift your consciousness to the centre, where, as said, you should sense past, present and future as one within your inner being. This is the 'awake aliveness,' the 'aliveness' and the 'awakeness' fully alert in the 'Now.' The Divine Name here is the ineffable יהוה (*YHVH*), the Divine Name which I noted elsewhere articulates the absolute totality of Divine Being.....All time and all manifestation 'exists' in the 'Now.' There is not really a past, present and a future."[44]

3. *Binah* — אלהים (*Elohim*): "First — 'Energy'; second — 'Time/Timelessness'; third — 'Space,' in which 'Forms' are affirmed and reaffirmed in the 'Eternal Now' of 'Self.' In this regard, opening the 'Gate of *Binah*' necessitates the 'Self Centre' freely expressing, as it were, radiating the power flow of its '*Is*-ness' outwards in all directions. It is a free flow of 'Spirit Force' between 'Centre' and 'Circumference.' Whilst in opening the 'Gate of

*Chochmah*' you realise the totality of 'beingness' in the 'Now,' in opening the 'Gate of *Binah*' you relate 'centre' and 'circumference,' and simply channel the free flow of 'Spirit Force' between your 'Self' and your environment."[45]

4. *Chesed* — אל (*El*): "Opening the 'Gate of *Chesed*' (Mercy or Lovingkindness) pertains to acceleration. In uttering the Name '*El*' in its appropriate locale in the throat.....you have to accelerate and expand the force flow between yourself and your environmental circumference..... You can easily facilitate and greatly enhance this process, by adopting within yourself a stance of kindness and loving empathy outpoured freely as the expansive acceleration of the mass of 'Spirit Force' spinning virtually out of control throughout the 'Whole'."[46]

5. *Gevurah* — אלהים גבור (*Elohim Gibor*–"Mighty *Elohim*"): "By opening the 'Gate of *Gevurah*' (Might or Severity), you apply the complete antithesis of *Chesed*. In this instance, you are applying strictest discipline and the maximum of your might by bringing the free expression of 'Spirit Force' under absolute control, as you bring it to a dramatic, sudden and immediate halt.....In this instance you imagine that you are holding the 'Whole' under a most tight control, so that there is no motion whatsoever. In other words, opening the 'Gate of *Gevurah*' blocks motion within yourself and your environment."[47]

6. *Tiferet* — יהוה אלוה ודעת (*YHVH Eloha va-Da'at*–"*YHVH Eloha* of [and the] Knowledge"): "Thus far you have taken the 'Energy' of *Keter* (Crown), realised it as a timeless condition of 'Self' in *Chochmah* (Wisdom), expressed it freely in *Binah* (Understanding), accelerated and increased it with joyous exuberance in *Chesed* (Lovingkindness), and brought it to a sudden halt in *Gevurah* (Might). In terms of practicalities, your physical body dissolves into an energy body in *Keter*, and in *Chochmah* you realise the centrality of the 'Self' within your energy body, experiencing timelessness and all time as one within the 'Now.' In *Binah* you enact the channelling of time and energy from your boundless being,

i.e. the focussing of force into forms, whilst in *Chesed* you accelerate the free flow of the channelled force, and in *Gevurah* you apply the blocking of the force flow, bringing it to an immediate halt..... In opening the 'Gate of *Tiferet*' (Beauty or Balance) you bring yourself to an absolute recognition of the balance of all forces in manifestation..... you allow all, i.e. *Keter* (Crown—Energy), *Chochmah* (Wisdom—Timeless Self), *Binah* (Understanding—Expressed Life Force), *Chesed* (Mercy—Abundant Increase), and *Gevurah* (Severity—Disciplined Decrease), to conjoin as one within the full realisation of *Ru'ach*, the awake 'One.' Since the *Ru'ach* is aligned with the 'heart,' it is on this portion of your anatomy that you have to focus your attention when you open the 'Gate of *Tiferet*'."[48]

7. *Netzach* — יהוה צבאות (YHVH Tzva'ot–"YHVH of Hosts"): "It is at *Netzach* and *Hod* where we enter the dynamics of three-dimensional existence, and where we start to respond to material life in terms of emotionality (*Netzach*) and analytical mental processes (*Hod*). The Hebrew term *Tzva'ot* has several meanings, i.e. armies, hosts, etc. In the current instance we might say it refers to the 'hosts' of feelings. Thus in opening the 'Gate of *Netzach*,' you firstly observe what is happening within your body and inner being in terms of emotional experiences, which could range from intense emotionality to simply feeling grateful..... following the opening of the 'Gate of *Netzach*,' simply invoke a deep sense of gratitude within your inner being, since that itself will conjoin the 'Centre' and the 'Circumference'.....Yet it should be understood that by opening the 'Gate of *Netzach*,' you allow yourself the full experience of emotionality. However, this is not the personal endurance of any specific emotion *per se*, but the totality of emotional experience. In this condition, you are meant to, as it were, read all your life experiences in terms of a 'feeling appreciation'."[49]

8. *Hod* — אלהים צבאות (*Elohim Tzva'ot*–"*Elohim* of Hosts"): "*Hod* refers to "thinking".....if one can get the destructive elements, i.e. the foolish arguments of the logical mind, under control, the 'Gate of *Hod*' can be

opened to encourage a 'thinking appreciation,' a greater perception on a mental level of all and sundry, without too much deconstruction. It should be clear that by opening any of the sefirotic 'Gates' by means of an affiliated Divine Name, you allow the specific, as it were, 'life quality' associated with that 'Gate' to express itself through you. In the case of opening the 'Gate of *Hod*,' it is not only better reasoning ability and mental perception to be stirred into action within you, but greater mindfulness is equally encouraged within yourself."⁵⁰

9. *Yesod* — שדי אל חי (*Shadai El Chai*–"*Shadai El* of Life*"*): "In opening the 'Gate of *Yesod*,' you allow yourself to neither see nor hear things external to yourself, but.... to encounter them literally inside you. In other words, the 'attachment' you are meant to trigger by opening the 'Gate of *Yesod*,' pertains to surrendering to life and love....love is the factor which breaks down the barriers of separateness, and allows us to, as it were, merge into a condition of becoming 'One'.....the best way to enact the opening of the 'Gate of *Yesod*' in your life, is to combine *Netzach* and *Hod*, feeling and thinking, into a single sense of perception, by means of which you can encounter the entirety of existence in the 'Oneness' of 'Self'."⁵¹

10. *Malchut* — אדני הארץ (*Adonai ha-Aretz*–"*Adonai* of the Earth"): "A thankful life (*Netzach*) is a thoughtful life (*Hod*).....and a thoughtful life is indeed a thankful life..... *Netzach*, *Hod* and *Yesod*, should unite in *Malchut*..... *Malchut* (Kingdom) is equally an acknowledgement of the 'Oneness-of-the-One.' This is what you are meant to realise, i.e. make real, by opening the 'Gate of *Malchut*'..... There is no separation between you and your world, and then there is no longer a need for attachment.....just as there is no separation between the 'Centre' (you) and the 'Circumference' (your world), there is likewise no fundamental difference between the Eternal One and your Self, except in what could be termed, conditions of consciousness. Hence the real consciousness behind opening the 'Gate of *Malchut*,' is the full realisation that the 'Centre' and the 'Circumference' are 'One.' Everything is God. Everything is אדני (*Adonai*)."⁵²

All of these details are combined into a coherent meditational procedure, which is worked in the following manner:

1. Smile warmly inside yourself and focus your attention firmly in the physical locale aligned with the opening vowel of the Divine Name associated with the selected *sefirah*.
2. Shape your mouth as if you are going to vocalise that vowel, then, during inhalation, "Inspeak" it in your mind as you virtually inhale the said vowel, and feel as if you are absorbing it into the relevant locale in your body.
3. With your attention still firmly focussed on the selected portion of your body in readiness to sound the opening vowel of the Divine Name aligned with the chosen sefirotic gate, commence exhaling without making any sound, and then let the sound "slip in," so to speak, and vocalise the opening vowel literally inside that part of your anatomy.
4. Continue the enunciation of the Divine Name by changing the shape of your mouth in accordance with the second vowel, and sense the sound sliding into the relevant locale in your body as you simultaneously slide your attention to this portion of your body.
5. Repeat this process by successively locating all the component vowels of a selected Divine Name construct. The entire action during exhalation is performed over a single exhalation.
6. Conclude by mentally and emotionally enacting within yourself the "quality of action" relevant to the selected sefirotic "Gate."

This meditation would be complete when you have worked the "*Opening the Ten Gates*" as a single procedure, incorporating the full compliment of *sefirot* from *Keter* (Crown) to *Malchut* (Kingdom). Of course, you can open any of the ten "Gates" anytime in accordance with personal requirements, e.g. the "Gate" of *Chesed* to interact with your "world" in terms of "loving-kindness," friendship, happiness, expansive wellbeing, prosperity, generosity, etc. It is in this regard that you could employ the earlier addressed "triggering" of the ten *sefirot* in your right hand in conjunction with "opening" the "gates," i.e. opening the necessary sefirotic "Gate" every time you touch a relevant phalanx of your fingers in response to, as it were, a "sefirotic stimulus" in your environment, or deliberately "trigger" an emotional/mental response within yourself in harmony with the selected *sefirah*.

Having considered meditations and magical practices pertaining to the ten *Sefirot* and their affiliation with the human hand, it is worth considering the application of the seven lower *Sefirot* in terms of psycho-spiritual self assessment. This most "magical" procedure in terms of personal transformation, is aligned with "The Fifty Gates of Understanding."

## B. The Fifty Gates of Understanding: *Omer*

There has been some mystical deliberation on the "Fifty Gates of Understanding,"[53] however more practical details regarding this interesting topic are somewhat sparse, except for one very important procedure which I wish to address here. Whilst there are variant interpretations of the "Fifty Gates," all are in agreement that they are traditionally associated with the seven weeks of "introspection and purification" between *Pesach* (Passover) and *Shavuot* (Feast of Weeks).[54] Called the *"Sefirat ha-Omer"* (Counting of the Sheaves [of wheat]), each week comprises a unique cycle of intensive psycho-spiritual self examination and adjustment of ones personal being towards a mindful fulfilment of the most ideal existence on this planet, i.e. relating Self (Centre) to כל (*Kol*—"All"), the "Whole of Creation" (Circumference).

Curiously enough the *gematria* of the word כל (*Kol*—"All") is fifty [כ = 20 + ל = 30 = 50]. In this regard Rabbi Joseph Gikatilla informed us that "the numerical sum of *Kol* is fifty, for all that is created came from the fifty gates of *Binah* (Understanding), and the sign of all Creation is *Kol*. The profound understanding of this is in the essence of the verse 'And God saw *Kol* (all) that He had done and behold it was very good' (*Genesis 1:31*)."[55] Of course, as I have noted elsewhere, "just as there is no separation between the 'Centre' (you) and the 'Circumference' (your world), there is likewise no fundamental difference between the Eternal One and your Self, except in what could be termed, conditions of consciousness.....the 'Centre' and the 'Circumference' are 'One.' Everything is God. Everything is אדני (*Adonai*)."[56] Likewise Joseph Gikatilla told us that at times the Divine Name *Adonai* "is referred to by the cognomen *Kol* ("All"), and the reason is that nothing is lacking from it; for all the emanations and a host of blessings and the source of existence are contained in it, and it is called *Kol* because all is within it."[57]

Be that as it may, whilst the "Counting of the *Omer*" is a standard practice worked annually amongst mainstream Jewish religionists,[58] I cannot see any reason why the same methodology cannot be applied by anyone, Jew and gentile alike, for the purpose of mindfully working "magical self rectification." It is in terms of this greater application, that I am sharing the *"Sefirat ha-Omer"* procedure which is, as noted, worked over a period of forty-nine days. Furthermore, whilst it is expected of every observant religious Jew to perform this procedure during a specific time period in accordance with the Jewish religious calendar, i.e. the seven weeks commencing on the second day of *Pesach* (Passover) and concluding fifty days later on *Shavuot* (Festival of Weeks), I equally cannot see any reason why anyone who wishes to do so, could not set up this cycle of serious self evaluation and unique adjustment of personal behaviour at any time, in accordance with personal requirements and the desire to do so.

Readers might ask why we should actually need to undertake such an extensive "self rectification." The reason pertains to freeing ourselves from what is termed in traditional Kabbalah the forty-nine "Gates of *Tum'ah*" (טמאה—"impurity") which causes *kilkul* (קלקול—"spiritual damage"), i.e. those factors within ourselves which corrupt, pollute, and defile us. This pertains to the calamitous, enslaving, impeding "psycho-physical" qualities we allow in our "Self-centres," and by means of which we rule ourselves (immediate circumference), and interact with the whole of existence (greater circumference). I call it the "do-you-know-who-I-am" existence of what my late mentor, William G. Gray, called the "Pseudo-Self."[59]

I am sure some would understand that this pertains to that which is called "sin," and, whilst they would not be far off the mark, I would again remind readers that this term pertains to "wrongful behaviour which damages us by the doing in such a way, that we fail to achieve anything like the 'Intention of God' in ourselves for our period of incarnation. Therefore, in 'falling short' of the mark by so far, we hinder our progression toward 'Perfection' by that much. In sinning against ourselves, we sin against the 'God-in-us'."[60]

In my estimation, the *Tum'ah* ("Spiritual Impurity") referred to here, indeed pertains to the "Pseudo-self," the "egoic self," which is built on qualities related exclusively to selfish behaviour, i.e. self aggrandisement, greed, jealousy, anger, hate, intolerance, intimidation, abuse, self justification, etc. In this regard, my late mentor noted "the typical picture of a so-called 'Selfish' person is actually that of someone who is pushing his Pseudo-Selfhood deliberately into a state of artificial and apparent autonomy apart from his Individuality."[61] Hence the practice of "Counting the *Omer*" pertains to an evaluation of your real status as a human being incarnated in the flesh, and your interactive relationship with your fellow humankind, and, for that matter, everything existing on this planet.

This period of serious and truthful introspection is also understood to purify the אור פנימי (*Or P'nimi*—"Inner Light"). In terms of the Centre/Circumference approach which I addressed in this and the first part of "*The Book of Immediate Magic*,"[62] it should be understood that everyone is functioning within the framework set by two aspects of "Divine Light"— one aspect is "within" (centre), i.e. the mentioned *Or P'nimi* ("Inner Light"), the other is "without" (circumference) and titled אור מקיף (*Or Makif*— "Encompassing Light"). In this regard, Rabbi Ariel bar Tzadok, quoting from "*Mesilot Chochmah*,"[63] wrote [my italics] "Light is the essence and the inner soul that is within the vessels. Now, these lights are divided into two aspects, these being the 'inner light' (*Ohr Penimi*) and the 'surrounding light' (*Ohr Makif*). Now, the light that gives life and radiates within the ten sefirot, which are the vessels, has an aspect that is cloaked within the vessels, in the same way as the soul is within the varying organs of the human body, giving them life and radiating within them from within.....Yet, there is a second (type of light) that is much stronger, which the vessels do not have the power to hold and contain within themselves. Thus this light remains outside [the vessels, surrounding them]. This then is the *Ohr Makif*. It surrounds the vessels and radiates upon them from the outside. This [division] of light is also true with regards to man below......For all light, in each and every universe has these two aspects of *Ohr Penimi*, the smaller light and *Ohr Makif*."[64]

In summary, as mentioned elsewhere, *Or P'nimi* is that portion of "Divine Light" (*Or Yashar*—"Direct Light") which is not only within you, but is the aspect of Divine Light which "unfolds itself in terms of your nature," i.e. assuming "the characteristics of its 'vessel,' i.e. of the one who bears it," and "unfolds itself as you evolve spiritually."[65] On the other hand the *Or Makif* cannot be absorbed into the physical body, but it is understood "to surround your body very closely," and we are told it is the "source of the 'Inner Light' (*Or P'nimi*)."[66] Furthermore, the closest aspect of the *Or Makif* "shapes or colours itself in accordance with your personality."[67]

I have addressed the concept of "Divine Light" as perceived from Kabbalistic perspectives, in some detail in the first part of "*The Book of Immediate Magic*."[68] However, in the current instance it is worth noting that working the forty-nine days of introspection, i.e. the "Counting of the *Omer*," pertains to more than just a process of personal psycho/spiritual "*tikkun*" (rectification). Since the *Or P'nimi* ("Inner Light") and the *Or Makif* ("Surrounding Light") interact, so to speak, and are impacted by your nature and behaviour, it is understood that "Counting the *Omer*" is equally working some restoration, virtually a cleansing, of the Divine Light within and around you.

Such purification of the Divine Light is important for you to have a truly meaningful life on all levels of being whilst incarnated in the flesh, especially since your perception of "Divine Being" within and around you, is fundamentally based on your "clarity of perception." In this regard it has been noted that the mind of the seeker "is filled with some particular content of understanding: he conceives God in some specific way. This conception is *penimi*. That which is 'within' the mind at that moment. This *penimi*, however, is inevitably attached to a *maqqif*, a conception beyond the mind's present grasp, one which at the same time both challenges the *penimi* and offers a conception on a higher level. Man's task is to seek out this *maqqif*, to bring it into his mind as a new *penimi*, and thus to seek a still-higher challenge and resolution."[69]

In terms of clearly comprehending the "Counting of the *Omer*," it is worth noting that each of the associated seven weeks of psycho-spiritual introspection is attributed to one of the seven lower *Middot* (qualities [*Sefirot*]), i.e. from *Chesed* (Loving-kindness) to *Malchut* (Kingdom) on the sefirotic tree,[70] on which it is said all physical manifestation is founded. We are informed that in "kabbalistic tradition, the ten sefirot are frequently divided into the top three and the bottom seven. These lower seven are distinguished from the upper three by their relative accessibility to our human awareness. We stand a chance at comprehending them, whereas the top three are unknowable. It is hardly surprising, therefore, that the seven weeks between the beginning of Pesach and *Shavuot* should find a sefirotic analogue."[71]

It should be further noted that each of the seven weeks comprising "*Sefirat ha-Omer*," is equally aligned with one of the seven "Holy Shepherds," also known as the seven אושפיזין (*Ushpizin*—"[Saintly] Guests"). They are seven supernatural visitors who, we are told in the *Sefer ha-Zohar*,[72] attend *Sukkot* (Festival of Booths). Each is said to attend one of the seven celebrations held every evening in the "tabernacles" constructed for this festival by every observant Jewish family. In fact, there are seven male and seven female sacred "spirit attendees" in the *Sukkah* (Tabernacle), whose presence is welcomed with songs including the wonderful incantation:[73]

תיבו תיבו אושפיזין עלאין
תיבו תיבו אושפיזין קדישין
תיבו תיבו אושפיזין דמהימנותא
תיבו בצלא דקודשא בריך הוא

Transliteration:
*tivu tivu ushpizin ela'in*
*tivu tivu ushpizin kedishin*
*tivu tivu ushpizin dimheimnutah*
*tivu b'tzila d'kudsha b'rich hu*

Translation:
Be seated (enter), be seated exalted guests;
Be seated, be seated holy guests;
Be seated, be seated guests of faithfulness;
Be seated in the shade of the Holy One, Blessed be He.

We are told that during their lives the seven *Ushpizin* perfected the seven sefirotic qualities respectively attributed to each of them, and to the seven weeks comprising *Omer*, these attributions being:

| Week 1 | Abraham | חסד (*Chesed*)<br>Compassion/Loving-Kindness |
| --- | --- | --- |
| Week 2 | Isaac | גבורה (*Gevurah*)<br>Strength/Judgment/Restraint |
| Week 3 | Jacob | תפארת (*Tiferet*)<br>Beauty/Harmony/Truth |
| Week 4 | Moses | נצח (*Netzach*)<br>Victory/Endurance |
| Week 5 | Aaron | הוד (*Hod*)<br>Splendour/Glory/Insight/Humility |
| Week 6 | Joseph | יסוד (*Yesod*)<br>Foundation/Bonding |
| Week 7 | David | מלכות (*Malchut*)<br>Kingdom/Leadership/Nobility |

*Kabbalah* approaches this period as a time of introspection on both the Divine and your own person. The "Seven Shepherds" are also respectively associated with the seven days comprising each of the seven weekly spiritual cycles, and the seven lower *sefirot* are equally allocated seven days each, the whole period then comprising, as indicated, the seven weeks of "Counting the *Omer*." In this regard, it is important to understand that each *sefirah* aligns with specific qualities, personality traits, and a specific part of the human anatomy.

In this instance the patriarchs/*sefirot* pertain to, as it were, a holographic understanding, i.e. *sefirot* within *sefirot*. For example, whilst the whole of the first week is affiliated with the Patriarch Abraham and the sphere of *Chesed* (Loving-Kindness) on the sefirotic Tree, the first day of each week is likewise assigned to the great Ancestor and the said sefirotic quality. In turn the second day pertains to Isaac and the quality of *Gevurah* (Strength), whilst the third relates to Jacob and *Tiferet* (Beauty), etc. In this manner, the said combination of *sefirot* respectively associated with the seven weeks and the seven days, is approached holistically, i.e. each *sefirah* comprises all of the others.

As can be seen, on the first day of each week we encounter a specific *sefirah* in all its "purity of self," so to speak, i.e. *Chesed* of *Chesed*; *Gevurah* of *Gevurah*; etc., whilst on the succeeding six days of each weeks, we encounter an admixture of two sefirotic qualities to contemplate and activate in our lives. Considering the statement that each *sefirah* pertains to a specific quality, character trait, and a part of the human anatomy, it is clear that on the first day of the week we deal with these in their direct alignment with a specific *sefirah*, and on the subsequent days, as it were, in pairs of spiritual qualities, human behaviour patterns, and bodily parts. The idea is not only to understand and reconcile opposing factors, e.g. חסד (*Chesed*) and גבורה (*Gevurah*)—expansiveness and restriction; joviality and seriousness; freedom of expression and self discipline; right hand and left hand; giving and taking, etc., but also to view, as it were, opposing qualities in direct relationship, literally within each other, e.g. *Gevurah* in *Chesed*—"Might" in "Mercy." In this regard, the following pattern is observed in "*Sefirat ha-Omer*":

Week 1—Abraham/*Chesed*
    Day 1—*Chesed* in *Chesed*
    Day 2—*Gevurah* in *Chesed*
    Day 3—*Tiferet* in *Chesed*, etc.
Week 2—Isaac/*Gevurah*
    Day 1—*Chesed* in *Gevurah*
    Day 2—*Gevurah* in *Gevurah*, etc.

These ancestral/sefirotic notions are not meant to be references to theoretical concepts, but to actual psycho-physical behaviour patterns pertaining to the primordial being of the seven, as it were, "Heroic Shepherds," collectively understood to embrace the most ideal way of meaningful living which humans can enact whilst incarnated in the flesh. As might be expected, the seven/sefirotic qualities pertaining to each of the "Seven Shepherds" in terms of their affiliation with the forty-nine days comprising the "Counting of the *Omer*," have been addressed and elaborated upon in numerous ways down the centuries. In this regard, an online commentator offered the following simple elucidation of the "Seven Shepherds" in terms of their affiliation with the seven weeks of "*Sefirat ha-Omer*."[74] For the sake of easy reference I have highlighted the names of the "Seven Shepherds," included the appellative of the *Sefirah* associated with each "Shepherd," as well as some bracketed delineations of Hebrew terms which a general readership might not understand:

1. **Abraham** (*Chesed*) learned all he could of God and lived a life of kindness sharing this knowledge.
2. **Isaac** (*Gevurah*) always listened attentively to his father.
3. **Jacob** (*Tiferet*) never spoke hastily but was a master of speech.
4. **Moses** (*Netzach*) gained the highest level of understanding possible and was able to speak to God face to face.
5. **Aaron** (*Hod*) had intuitive insight for making peace between people.
6. **Joseph**'s (*Yesod*) awe of his father Isaac, kept him from falling into sin with Potipher's wife.
7. **David's** (*Malchut*) reverence for God led him to compose the *T'hillim*, psalms of praise.
8. **Abraham** (*Chesed*) had humility before every guest (*Genesis 18:2-5*).
9. **Isaac** (*Gevurah*) took much joy in his life with his wife and children, overlooking their faults, and seeing only their good. (*Gen. 25:28*).
10. **Jacob** (*Tiferet*) achieved purity that which none before him could achieve, and was worthy that all his children would be part of Israel.
11. Though **Moses** (*Netzach*) led all of Israel, he attended to his father-in-law Jethro as a scholar listening to him and appointing judges throughout the nation.
12. **Aaron** (*Hod*) debated his colleagues and gave into their wishes leading to the golden calf.
13. **Joseph** (*Yesod*) was a teacher known for his discussions with students. He taught all of Egypt and his brethren and his children and their children to follow the laws and dream the will of God.
14. **David** (*Malchut*) was deliberate in action securing the boarders of Israel and Kingship and preparing the way for the construction of Solomon's Temple.
15. **Abraham**'s (*Chesed*) knowledge of the Torah was so great that he revealed the *Book of Creation* that which bestows kindness and truth.

16. **Isaac** (*Gevurah*) avoided excess business dealings, and at the end of his life was judged favorably, and blessed his sons in truth.
17. **Jacob** (*Tiferet*) abstained from worldly affairs and was rewarded with physical beauty and truth.
18. **Moses** (*Netzach*) abstained from pleasure with his wife in order to be ready to reveal Hashem's truth.
19. **Aaron** (*Hod*) had little time for sleep as he spent his nights dissolving arguments of couples with the truth.
20. **Joseph** (*Yesod*) circumcised his lips by only speaking after careful thought in truth.
21. **David** (*Malchut*) accomplished the writings of the *Psalms* and his victories all due to moderation in frivolity.
22. **Abraham** (*Chesed*) had tremendous patience trusting that God would fulfill his prophecy and grant Sarah and him a son. Without mentioning a word he held his patience to the very moment of the sacrifice of Isaac.
23. **Isaac** (*Gevurah*) was known for his good nature and was at peace with his neighbors in Israel.
24. **Jacob** (*Tiferet*) went to study in the *yeshivas* [Yeshivot - Jewish Religious Academies] of Shem and Eber, trusting in the sages, when he fled from Esau on his way to take a wife from the daughters of Laban. He also followed the will of his parents who were also his sages.
25. **Moses** (*Netzach*), belittled by his people for his choice of wife, or other mumbling defended the House of Israel and was uncomplaining and accepted the suffering.
26. **Aaron** (*Hod*) knew his place was to be high priest of Israel, which was a place to serve all Israel.
27. **Joseph** (*Yesod*) was content with his lot in life whether shepherd lad, dreamer, prisoner, servant, or viceroy of Egypt. He possessed an inner contentment from his visions on high.
28. **David** (*Malchut*) obtained kingship by limiting his words of slander and criticism. This was especially important while in the public eye.
29. **Abraham** (*Chesed*) claimed no credit for his achievements, but all was from God.
30. **Isaac** (*Gevurah*) was beloved by the people of the land of Caanan since he was friendly, displayed gratitude, and was

carefree with his neighbors. This also led him to love his son Esau and his wild spirit.

31. **Jacob**'s (*Tiferet*) love for God brought him to *Bet El*, the house of God, where he beheld the angels ascending and descending. His love for God taught him the importance of peace for to love God requires an environment without anger and hatred. He encouraged peace with his neighbors, his wives, between his children, and he pursued peace with his brother.

32. **Moses**' (*Netzach*) love for God brought him to a love for people.

33. **Aaron** (*Hod*) displayed acts of charity and kindness his whole life sometimes beyond measure by fashioning the Golden calf.

34. **Joseph** (*Yesod*) was straightforward in every action of his life. As a child his straightforwardness got him into trouble as he spoke his dreams. Even when he was testing his brethren, his straightforward side eventually burst forth as he told them his true identity.

35. When **David** (*Malchut*) was being cursed as he left Jerusalem with the impending attack from his son Absalom, the head of the *Beis Din* (*Beth Din*—supreme court) called him every dirty name. His general, Yoav wanted to kill him for the way he spoke, but David said let him speak for God told him to curse me. David saw admonition as always a means for correction. Similarly to when he received the admonition of God through the prophet Nathan for his actions with *Bat Sheva* [the mother of Solomon].

36. **Abraham** (*Chesed*) after his victory over the five kings, rescuing his nephew Lot, refuses any honor or reward that the Kings of Sodom and Gomorrah offer.

37. **Isaac** (*Gevurah*) shows no conceit in his learning, simply following the teachings of his father Abraham.

38. **Jacob** (*Tiferet*) as head of the seventy member house of Israel never showed delight in dictating decisions as he was aware that every decision that pleases one displeases another.

39. **Moses** (*Netzach*) carried the burden of the whole house of Israel by answering their disputes in righteousness. Sharing the burdens of your fellow man means placing oneself in

their position and not reacting spitefully to an inconvenience. For example, if a noisy truck privately owned by a couple begins unloading and loading cars in a nearby parking lot, one should look for a way to assist them instead of criticize them for the noise. If the president of the *shul* [Synagogue] hints at the need for more *tzedakah* [Deeds of Righteousness/Charitable Acts] even though you may already be a large contributor, prepare a contribution instead of a contrary word.

40. **Aaron** (*Hod*) always judged Israel favorably before God.
41. **Joseph** (*Yesod*) always directed his fellows with truth, never deceiving his path.
42. **David** (*Malchut*) established peace throughout the Land of Israel and with this in mind named his son Shlomo (His peace).
43. **Abraham** (*Chesed*) spent his years studying Torah in the fields, with others, and in his tents taking time composing his learning of the One God.
44. **Isaac** (*Gevurah*) asked his father only pertinent questions and gave answers to the point (*Genesis 22:7*).
45. **Jacob** (*Tiferet*) spent his life listening to his mother, to God, to his wives, and to his children. Jacob learned more than all the patriarchs before him and merited that all his children were complete following the Torah.
46. **Moses** (*Netzach*) learned all he could in order to teach the people.
47. **Aaron** (*Hod*) learned all he could in order to be an example of practising the commandments.
48. **Joseph** (*Yesod*) increased the wisdom of his father Jacob, his teacher.
49. **David** (*Malchut*) recorded his experiences in his *Psalms*.

There are further important biblical affiliations with the forty-nine days of *"Sefirat ha-Omer,"* e.g. *Psalm 67* which, as I noted elsewhere, is said to be based on the Priestly Blessing mentioned in *Numbers 6:24-26*,[75] and which is extensively employed in Hebrew protection amulets.[76] In this regard, the eight verses of this Psalm are so frequently depicted in the form of a *menorah* (seven-branched candelabrum), especially in *Shiviti* meditational plaques as indicated in the following illustration, that it acquired the appellative the *"menorah psalm."*[77]

*Magical Mediation* / 39

The numbered words and letters in the illustration pertain to the forty-nine days of the "Counting of the *Omer*." In this regard the seven verses of *Psalm 67* (verses 2[1] to 8[7]), without the twenty lettered introduction, comprise forty-nine words, and these words are respectively assigned to the forty-nine days, and individually focussed on during *"Sefirat ha-Omer."*[78] In kabbalistic tradition the forty-eight letters of *Psalm 67:5 [4]*, with an additional *Vav* (ו) to bring the total letters to the required forty-nine, are likewise affiliated with the forty-nine days of "Counting the *Omer*." This verse, which form the very central branch of the *"Menorah Psalm,"* reads:

ישמחו וירננו לאמים כי תשפ[נו]ט עמים מישור
ולאמים בארץ תנחם סלה

Transliteration:
> *yishm'chu viran'nu l'umim ki tishpot amim mishor ul'umim ba'aretz tanchem Selah*

Translation:
> O let the nations be glad and sing for joy; for Thou wilt judge the peoples with equity, and lead the nations upon earth. *Selah*

As in the case of the forty-nine words from *Psalm 67*, a single letter from this verse is equally focussed upon and vocalised one glyph per day during the *"Sefirat ha-Omer."* Hence it would take forty-nine days to spell the full verse, to, as it were, "invoke" the spiritual forces behind the letters and words of this verse, and to spiritually enact the joyous spirit of celebration on the fiftieth day, i.e. the day following the conclusion of the "Counting of the *Omer*."

There is yet more to consider in terms of unique affiliations applying to the forty-nine days, and which are of great importance in working the *"Sefirat ha-Omer"* procedure. This is the famous *"Forty-two letter Name of God"* and associated *"Ana Bechoach"* prayer, in which the capitals of the forty-two words comprising the said prayer combine to form the "Forty-two Letter Name of God."[79]

The prayer conjoined with the "Forty-two Letter Name of God" reads as follows:

אָנָא בְּכֹחַ גְּדוּלַת יְמִינְךָ תַּתִּיר צְרוּרָה
קַבֵּל רִנַּת עַמְּךָ שַׂגְּבֵנוּ טַהֲרֵנוּ נוֹרָא
נָא גִבּוֹר דּוֹרְשֵׁי יִחוּדְךָ כְּבָבַת שָׁמְרֵם
בָּרְכֵם טַהֲרֵם רַחֲמֵי צִדְקָתְךָ תָּמִיד גָּמְלֵם
חֲסִין קָדוֹשׁ בְּרוֹב טוּבְךָ נַהֵל עֲדָתֶךָ
יָחִיד גֵּאֶה לְעַמְּךָ פְּנֵה זוֹכְרֵי קְדֻשָּׁתֶךָ
שַׁוְעָתֵנוּ קַבֵּל וּשְׁמַע צַעֲקָתֵנוּ יוֹדֵעַ תַּעֲלוּמוֹת

Transliteration:
> Ana B'cho'ach G'dulat Yemincha Tatir Tz'rurah
> Kabel Rinat Am'chah Sagvenu Taharenu Nora
> Na Gibor Dorshei Yichudcha Kevavat Shomrem
> Bar'chem Taharem Rachamei Tzidkatcha Tamid Gomlem
> Chasin Kadosh B'rov Tuvcha Nahel Adatecha
> Yachid Ge'eh Le'am'cha Pneh Zochrei K'dushatecha
> Shav'atenu Kabel Ushma Tza'akatenu Yode'a Ta'alumot

Translation:
> Please now with might, with the strength of your right, untie the bound.
> Accept our song, strengthen us, purify in awe.
> Awesome in grace, we who see you as One, guard from harm.
> Cleanse us and bless, mix mercy with justice, and always redeem.
> Holy power, in your great goodness, guide your people.
> Exalted unique, turn to us, who recall your holiness.
> Receive our cry, hear our plea, you know what is hidden.[80]

The forty-two words comprising the "*Ana Bechoach*" prayer are respectively uttered over the first six days of each of the seven weeks, whilst the seven six-letter combinations forming the "Forty-two Letter Name of God" are in turn respectively focussed upon and enunciated on the seventh day of each of the seven weeks, as indicated in the full array of forty-nine proclamations comprising the "*Sefirat ha-Omer*." However, whilst the seven six-letter portions of the "Forty-two Letter Name of God" are held in the mind and enunciated in the manner delineated during the utterance of the full "*Ana Bechoach*" prayer, in the instance of their individual association with the seventh day of the seven weeks, each six-letter portion is divided into two three letter sections which are enunciated in the following manner:

| | | |
|---|---|---|
| Week 1— | אבג יתץ | *AViGe YaToTzi* |
| Week 2— | קרע שטנ | *KaRo' SaTaN'* |
| Week 3— | נגד יכש | *NaGiDa YeiCheiSha* |
| Week 4— | בטר צתג | *BiTaRo TzaTaG'* |
| Week 5— | חקב טנע | *CheKeVa Tin'I* |
| Week 6— | יגל פזק | *YaGaLi P'Z'Kei* |
| Week 7— | שקו צית | *ShuKoVa TzoYaT'* |

Whatever the Patriarchs, *Sefirot*, biblical verses, prayer and Divine Name associations may mean to individuals reading this tome, and whether you agree or not with the proponents of *Practical Kabbalah* that unique "Spiritual Forces" are invoked when practitioners focus on these special components of "*Sefirat ha-Omer*," it is important to understand that, in terms of applying this information meaningfully in a personal manner, the forty-nine days comprising the seven weeks of *Omer* are employed to "refine the soul." This is achieved by implementing certain directives which were referenced in a work titled the "*Pirkei Avot*" (Sayings of the Fathers).[81] Whilst this text is often carefully studied during the weeks comprising the "Counting of the *Omer*," I am well aware that I am writing my Jewish magical tomes for Jews and non-Jews alike, in fact, for anyone interested in working the techniques of *Practical Kabbalah*, to whom the expression "revelation at Mount Sinai" might be meaningless.

In terms of the application of Kabbalistic principles in "*Sefirat ha-Omer*," special attention should be paid to the following phrases from the "Opening Statement" employed daily during the forty-nine days:

לשם יחוד קודשא בריך הוא ושכינתיה (*l'shem yichud kud'sha b'rich hu u-sh'chinteih*—"For the sake of unifying the Holy One, blessed be He and the *Shechinah*").

This formula is often recited prior to performing a *Mitzvah*, i.e. a sacred commandment performed as a religious obligation, and also a "good deed."[82] It is equally employed by many orthodox religionists during the morning prayers with the additional phrase:

בדחילו ורחימו ליחד שם י"ה בו"ה ביחודא שלים
(*bid'chilu ur'chimu l'yacheid shem Y"H b'V"H b'yichuda sh'lim*—"in awe and reverence, to unify *YH* and *VH* in complete unity.")[83]

The complete statement is of particular importance in terms of the Kabbalistic perception of the "male" and "female" aspects of Divinity, and what it means in terms of Divine/human interrelationship. As elucidated elsewhere, the *Shechinah*, the "Countenance of God," is the universal "Mother Principle," "the Divine Presence as a Feminine Force" throughout the whole of creation.[84] I also noted that the *Neshamah*, the "Higher Self," is the "*Shechinah* inside us."[85]

The expression "to unify *YH* and *VH* in complete unity" pertains to what is called the "Mystery of Unification," which is delineated in highly sexual terms in Jewish Mysticism.[86] In this regard, we are informed in the *Zohar* that "the individual who is worthy of the World to Come must unify the name of the Blessed Holy One."[87] I noted elsewhere that we are informed that "the Blessed Holy One is the union of two pairs—the male and female aspects of God, and the male and female aspects of man in sexual union."[88] Hence the statement that "He must unify the upper and lower levels and limbs, uniting them all and bringing them all to the necessary place, where the knot is bound," and that "This unification is accomplished when one meditates and ascends, attaching himself to the Infinite Being (*Ain Sof*). It is here that all things, both on high and below, are bound together in a single desire."[89]

Understanding this in the light of the statement "to unify *YH* and *VH* in complete unity," we are told that *"Yod* is the mystery of the Holy Covenant. *Heh* is the Chamber, the place in which the Holy Covenant, which is *Yod* is concealed. And even though we have stated that this is the *Vav* here it is a *Yod*. The mystery is that the two are united as One."[90] As mentioned elsewhere, "the 'mystery of the Holy Covenant' is simply a euphemism for the circumcised penis, which is to be hidden inside the 'Chamber,' or Vagina of the Lesser *Heh*, or the *Shechinah* represented by all women on earth."[91]

Some attention should also be given to the three Divine Name constructs included in the "Opening Statement," i.e. יאהדונהי (*YAHDVNHY*); יאההויהה (*YAHHVYHH*); and איההיוהה (*AYHHYVHH*). The first, יאהדונהי, is the combination of the Ineffable Name (יהוה), associated with *Tiferet* (Beauty), and אדני (*Adonai*), affiliated with *Malchut* (Kingdom), which is believed to, as it were, enact the channel by means of which *Shefa*, Divine Abundance, flows into three dimensional existence. As stated elsewhere, the יאהדונהי (*YAHDVNHY*) Divine Name combination is also believed "to be the 'gate' through which prayers gain entry into the Divine Presence."[92] I have addressed this Divine Name combination fairly extensively in earlier volumes of this series of texts on *Practical Kabbalah*.[93]

The second and third Divine Name constructs, i.e. יאההויהה (*YAHHVYHH*) and איההיוהה (*AYHHYVHH*), are both combinations of the Ineffable Name (יהוה [*YHVH*]—*Tiferet*) and אהיה (*Eh'yeh*—*Keter*). In the first instance the Divine Name combination commences with *Yod* (י), the first letter of the four comprising the Ineffable Name, and in the second the Divine Name construct begins with *Alef* (א), the initial of the Divine Name *Eh'yeh*. These Divine Name combinations feature prominently in Kabbalistic *Siddurim* (Prayer Books)[94] and Lurianic *Kavvanot*.[95]

Whilst the daily "*Counting of the Omer*" incorporates the enunciation of an associated Hebrew letter from *Psalm 67* verse 5 [*4*], a single word from the forty-nine comprising the said Psalm, as well as an affiliated word from the "*Ana Bechoach*" prayer, it is worth considering an additional factor applicable to the seventh day of each week, during which, as noted, a six-letter portion of the "Forty-two Letter Name of God" is enunciated. In this regard, the earlier mentioned "magical vocalisation" of each tri-letter grouping, e.g. *AviGe YaToTzi* at the conclusion of Week 1; *KaRo' SaTaN'* at the end of Week 2; etc., is particularly effective, as is tracing the six letter portions of the said Divine Name on the surface of your body, as indicated in the following illustration:

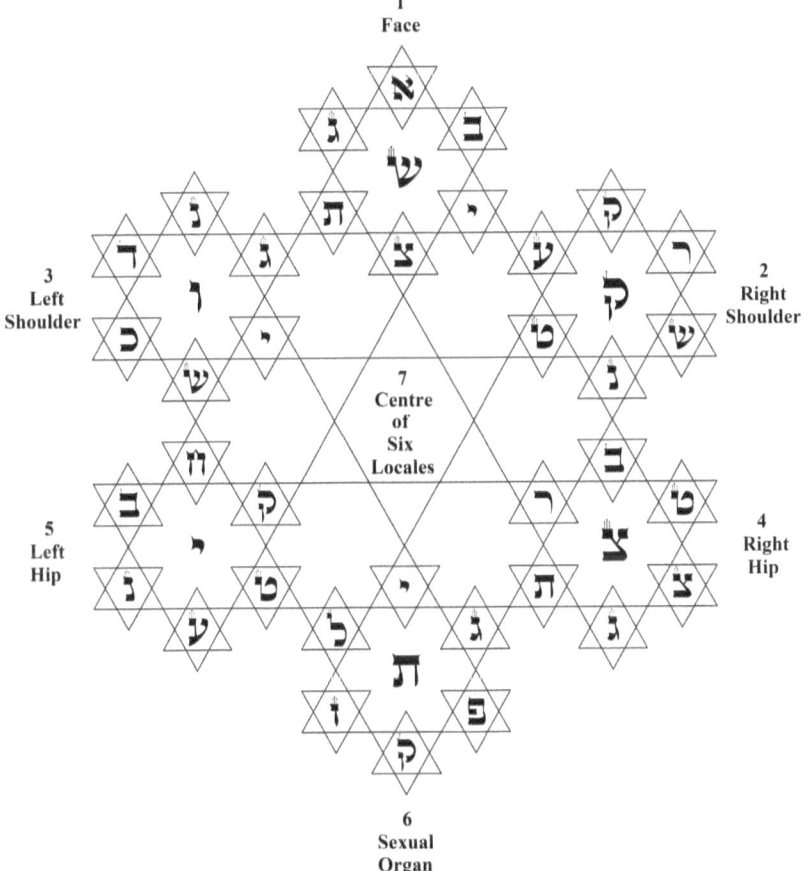

As indicated, you would scan and recite the six letters comprising each of the seven sectors of the "Forty-two Letter Name of God" to be respectively located within the six corners of a selected hexagram, and simultaneously, as it were, "encountering" or envisioning the said construct on the surface of the appropriate portion of your anatomy whilst enunciating the relevant six-letter portion of the said Divine Name seven times. I have addressed this unique arrangement of the "Forty-two Letter Name of God" in conjunction with the "Name of Seventy-two Names" in great detail elsewhere.[96]

However, before we peruse the full procedure of "Counting the *Omer*," it is necessary that we consider certain important directives pertaining to "*Sefirat ha-Omer*," of which I consider the following to be of great importance, whether or not you are a Jewish religionist:

1. No food should be consumed at least a half an hour prior to sunset on any of the days comprising the "Counting of the *Omer*." Of course, an evening meal can be consumed afterwards.
2. The procedure is performed every day from nightfall at any time till before dawn. It is generally practised immediately after sunset, this being the most comfortable time for most individuals who desire to devote the rest of the evening to other matters, e.g. family, friends, etc.
3. We are informed that practitioners should carefully avoid announcing the day after sunset to any querant, e.g. say "Today is the.....day," prior to having first pronounced the official daily "Counting of the *Omer*." In this regard, we are told that "it is best to reply with the number of days counted on the previous day."[97]
4. The procedure should be done whilst standing, however it is not considered a serious matter if done whilst being seated.
5. If one should forget to perform "*Sefirat ha-Omer*" during the night, the procedure could be executed during the following day. In this instance the rule is that it should be done without the accompanying blessing, following which one would continue with the counting in the normal manner over the remaining days. However, if practitioners forget to perform the "Counting of the *Omer*" for an entire day, they are obliged to perform the procedure without the blessing for the entire remaining period.

Again keep in mind that I am sharing the "Counting of the *Omer*" practice with anybody interested in working the procedure for its remarkable psycho-spiritual benefits, but who might not have any interest in the socio-religious expectations and regulations of mainstream Judaism. In this regard, the following arrangement of the practice aligns in some measure with a well-known kabbalistic *nusach* (order) of working the "Counting of the *Omer*,"[98] one which incorporates the Kabbalistic meditational practice of spelling words. It also includes religious sentiments which might be meaningless to anyone who is not practising the Jewish faith. However, the various elements comprising the full practice of "Counting the *Omer*," could be combined in the following manner for a truly magical process of "Self Rectification":

1. It is traditional to do the "Counting of the *Omer*" immediately after sunset, otherwise the procedure can be performed any time between sunset and dawn, and it is usually done whilst standing.
2. Enunciate the words and mentally scan the letters comprising the Divine Names of the "Opening Statement":

לשם יחוד קודשא בריך הוא ושכינתיה

[spell whisper]

יאהדונהי

ורחימו ודחילו      בדחילו ורחימו
[spell whisper]      [spell whisper]
איההיוהה      יאהדויהה

ליחד שם י"ה בו"ה

ביחודא שלים    יהוה    בשם כל ישראל

Transliteration:
[Top] *l'shem yichud kud'sha b'rich hu u-sh'chinteih*
[whisper] *Yod-Alef-Heh-Dalet-Vav-Nun-Heh-Yod*
[Right] *bid'chilu ur'chimu*

[whisper] *Yod-Alef-Heh-Heh-Vav-Yod-Heh-Heh*
[Left] *ur'chimu ud'chilu*
[whisper] *Alef-Yod-Heh-Heh-Yod-Vav-Heh-Heh*
[Centre] *l'yacheid shem Yod-Heh b'Vav-Heh*
[Bottom] *b'yichuda sh'lim Yod-Heh-Vav-Heh b'shem kol Yisra'el*

Translation:
[Top] For the sake of unifying the Holy One, blessed be He, and the *Shechinah*
[whisper] *Yod-Alef-Heh-Dalet-Vav-Nun-Heh-Yod*
[Right] in awe and reverence
[whisper] *Yod-Alef-Heh-Heh-Vav-Yod-Heh-Heh*
[Left] and reverence and awe
[whisper] *Alef-Yod-Heh-Heh-Yod-Vav-Heh-Heh*
[Bottom] to unify *Yod-Heh* and *Vav-Heh* in complete unity, *Yod-Heh-Vav-Heh*, in the name of all Israel.

3. Continue the "Opening Statement" saying:

הנני מוכן ומזומן לקיים מצות עשה של ספירת
העומר לעשות נחת רוח ליוצרנו ולעשות רצון
בוראנו

Transliteration:
*Hin'ni muchan um'zuman l'kayeim mitzvat aseh shel s'firat ha-omer la'asot nachat ruach l'yotz'reinu v'la'asot retzon bor'einu*

Translation:
I am hereby prepared and ready to fulfill the commandment (good deed) of working the Counting of the Omer, to give pleasure to our Creator and to do the will of our Maker.

4. Conclude the opening statement by reciting *Psalm 90:17*:

ויהי נעם אדני אלהינו עלינו ומעשה ידינו
כוננה עלינו ומעשה ידינו כוננהו

Transliteration:
*Vihi no'am Adonai Eloheinu aleinu uma'asei yadeinu konena aleinu uma'asei yadeinu kon'neihu*

Translation:

> And let the graciousness of *Adonai* our God be upon us; establish Thou also upon us the work of our hands; yea, the work of our hands establish Thou it.

5. Utter the following "Blessing" which is believed to, as it were, awaken the *Or Makif*, i.e. the mentioned "Light" which surrounds your personal Being. The four letters of the Ineffable Name are mentally traced and vocalised in accordance with the *Mah* (מה) extension, i.e. the *Milui d'Alfin* (*Alef* filling/spelling) of the four letters comprising the Explicit Name. This spelling applies to "*Olam ha-Yetzirah*" (World of Formation) which includes the human mind. It is for this reason that the *Mah* extension of the Ineffable Name has been employed in unique *Shiviti* amulets to purify the mind, and to open the heart to greater understanding.[99]

In the current instance of scanning and vocalising the said four letters, you might apply the simple technique of looking at the complete spelling of each letter, followed by enunciating it verbally. For example, look at the full spelling of יוד (*Yod*), mentally scan each letter consecutively as you think "*Yod-Vav-Dalet*," then say "*Yod*," etc.

ברוך אתה יהוה [יוד הא ואו הא] אלהינו
מלך העולם אשר קדשנו במצותיו וצונו על
ספירת העמר

Transliteration:

> *Baruch atah YHVH* [vocalised *Yod-Heh-Vav-Heh* while mentally scanning the glyphs comprising the *Mah* extension of the Ineffable Name] *Eloheinu Melech ha-olam asher kid'shanu b'mitzvotav v'tzivanu al s'firat ha-omer*

Translation:

> Blessed are You *YHVH* [vocalised *Yod Heh Vav Heh*] our God, King of the Universe, who sanctified us with his commandments and instructed us to count the *Omer*.

6. If you are familiar with the *"Opening the Ten Gates"* procedure, as well as with the ten affiliated spiritual "qualities of action," which I have addressed in the first part of *"The Book of Immediate Magic,"*[100] you could employ these in alignment with the respective sefirotic associations respectively applicable to the forty-nine days, doing so prior to the actual "Counting of the *Omer.*" In this regard, where you have one *Sefirah* applying to a day, you would open the related "Gate" once only. However, on most days there are two *Sefirot* applicable, and in these instances you would open first the "Gate" of the *Sefirah* applicable to the week, and immediately thereafter the one aligned with the day. For example, if you have to focus on "*Tiferet* (Beauty/Harmony referencing the day) in *Chesed* (Mercy/Lovingkindness referencing the week)," you would first open the "Gate" of *Chesed* (Week) and invoke within yourself the associated qualities, followed by the "Gate" of *Tiferet* (Day) and the invocation of the qualities affiliated with the latter *Sefirah*.

In terms of opening the "Gate of *Gevurah* (Might/Severity)," it should be noted that it has been stressed quite emphatically that it is *never* good to have this sefirotic "Gate" open for extended periods[101]—not even for a couple of hours. Whilst the aggressive condition, as it were, "channelled" via the "Gate of *Gevurah*" might be desirable in the case of soldiers, fighters, and assorted militants, as well as to restrict oneself momentarily in a condition of centred emotional, mental and physical discipline, it should be understood that anyone having this "Gate" open, will be encountered and approached by all in a stern, severe, and even an uncompromising manner for the period in which the "primal forces" of the *sefirah* of *Gevurah* are predominant within them. Thus it is imperative that on those days in which the concluding *Sefirah* "invoked" is *Gevurah* (Might), the practitioner concludes the counting procedure with the opening of the "Gate" which will assert greater harmony in his or her life, i.e. the "Gate of *Chesed*" or the "Gate of *Tiferet*."

7. Following the opening of the associated "Gate(s)," proclaim aloud (Count) the appropriate "*Omer.*" This is *the*

vital component of the procedure, which I share at the conclusion of these instructions, namely the full array of forty-nine proclamations and associated actions pertaining to the "*Sefirat ha-Omer*."

8. Scan and pronounce the earlier mentioned single Hebrew glyph from *Psalm 67* verse 5 [4], e.g. י (*Yod*) on Day 1; ש (*Shin*) on Day 2; etc., and spell the letters comprising the respectively associated words from *Psalm 67* and the "*Ana Bechoach*" prayer, doing so seven times. The latter prayer is applicable to the first six days of the week only, since the six letter portion of the "Forty-two Letter Name" is vocalised seven times on the seventh day of each week, i.e. Day 7–*AviGe YaToTzi*; etc.

9. Continue by enunciating the following statement:

הרחמן הוא יחזיר לנו עבודת בית המקדש
למקומה במהרה בימינו אמן סלה

Transliteration:
   ha-rachaman hu yachazir lanu avodat beit ha-mikdash lim'komah bim'heirah b'yameinu Omein Selah.

Translation:
   May the Merciful One restore unto us the service of the *Bet Hamikdash* (Holy Temple) to its place, speedily in our days *Amen Selah*.

This section of the "*Sefirat ha-Omer*" process pertains to the messianic expectations of Judaism. This statement can be interpreted both literally and mystically. Hence those practitioners who do not align with the sentiments expressed here in a literal sense, can approach this statement from the perspective of the "Holy Temple" being restored within the מקום (*Makom*), the sacred "Place" of *Tiferet* (Beauty) within their hearts.

10. Next recite the whole of *Psalm 67*, reading:

(Verse 1 [1-2]) למנצח בנגינת מזמור שיר אלהים
יחננו ויברכנו יאר פניו אתנו סלה
(Verse 2 [3]) לדעת בארץ דרכך בכל גוים ישועתך

(Verse 3 [4]) יודוך עמים אלהים יודוך עמים כלם
(Verse 4 [5]) ישמחו וירננו לאמים כי תשפוט עמים מישור ולאמים בארץ תנחם סלה
(Verse 5 [6]) יודוך עמים אלהים יודוך עמים כלם
(Verse 6 [7]) ארץ נתנה יבולה יברכנו אלהים אלהינו
(Verse 7 [8]) יברכנו אלהים וייראו אותו כל אפסי ארץ

Transliteration:
(Verse 1 [1-2]) *Lamnatze'ach bin'ginot mizmor shir Elohim yechoneinu vivar'cheinu ya'eir panav itanu selah*
(Verse 2 [3]) *lada'at ba'aretz darkecha b'chol goyim y'shu'atecha*
(Verse 3 [4]) *yoducha amim Elohim yoducha amim kulam*
(Verse 4 [5]) *yishm'chu viran'nu l'umim ki tishpot amim mishor ul'umim ba'aretz tanchem selah*
(Verse 5 [6]) *yoducha amim Elohim yoducha amim kulam*
(Verse 6 [7]) *eretz nat'nah y'vulah y'var'cheinu Elohim eloheinu*
(Verse 7 [8]) *y'var'cheinu Elohim v'yir'u oto kol afsei aretz*

Translation:
(Verse 1 [1-2]) For the Leader; with string-music. A Psalm, a Song. God be gracious unto us, and bless us; may He cause His face to shine toward us; *Selah*
(Verse 2 [3]) That Thy way may be known upon earth, Thy salvation among all nations.
(Verse 3 [4]) Let the peoples give thanks unto Thee, O God; let the peoples give thanks unto Thee, all of them.
(Verse 4 [5]) O let the nations be glad and sing for joy; for Thou wilt judge the peoples with equity, and lead the nations upon earth. *Selah*
(Verse 5 [6]) Let the peoples give thanks unto Thee, O God; let the peoples give thanks unto Thee, all of them.

(Verse 6 [7]) The earth hath yielded her increase; may God, our own God, bless us.
(Verse 7 [8]) May God bless us; and let all the ends of the earth fear Him.

11. Next enunciate the entire "*Ana Bechoach*" prayer, ensuring that during the enunciation your attention is fully focussed on the seven six-letter portions of the "Forty-two Letter Name of God," which are respectively aligned with the seven phrases of the said prayer. Conclude this portion with the standard expression:

ברוך שם כבוד מלכותו לעולם ועד

Transliteration:
*Baruch shem k'vod malchuto l'olam va'ed*
Translation:
Blessed be the Name of His glorious Kingdom throughout eternity.

12. In my estimation this is the appropriate moment when practitioners should contemplate the meaning of the sefirotic associations applicable to the day, i.e. how these are featuring in their lives, equally seeking an understanding of personal failure in terms of the successful expression of these principles in there lives, and how the affiliated "qualities" of *Chesed* (Loving-kindness), *Gevurah* (Discipline), *Tiferet* (Beauty), etc., may be realised in action in their daily lives.

13. Having gained some understanding as to the meaning of the sefirotic associations, and a clear realisation of personal failings in terms of meaningfully expressing those sefirotic qualities in their daily lives, practitioners can conclude the daily "*Sefirat ha-Omer*" procedure by uttering the following prayer-supplication:

רבונו של עולם אתה צויתנו על ידי משה
עבדך לספור ספירת העומר כדי לטהרנו
מקלפותינו ומטמאותינו כמו שכתבת בתורתך

[Leviticus 23:15-16] וספרתם לכם ממחרת השבת
מיום הביאכם את עמר התנופה שבע שבתות
תמימת תהיינה עד ממחרת השבת השביעית
תספרו חמשים יום
כדי שיטהרו נפשות עמך ישראל מזהמתם ובכן
יהי רצון מלפניך יהוה אלהינו ואלהי אבותינו
שבזכות ספירת העומר שספרתי היום יתקן מה
שפגמתי בספירה

(.....insert the appropriate sefirotic combination.....)

ואטהר ואתקדש בקדשה של מעלה ועל ידי זה
ישפע שפע רב בכל העולמות ולתקן את נפשותינו
ורוחותינו ונשמותינו מכל סיג ופגם ולטהרנו
ולקדשנו בקדשתך העליונה אמן סלה

Transliteration:

Ribono shel olam atah tzivitanu al y'dei Mosheh av'decha lispor s'firat ha-omer k'dei l'tahareinu miklipoteinu u-mitum'oteinu k'mo shekatavta b'toratecha

[Leviticus 23:15-16] u-s'fartem lachem mimacharat ha-shabat miyom ha-vi'achem et omer ha-t'nufah sheva shabatot t'mimot tih'yenah ad mimacharat ha-shabat ha-sh'vi'it tisp'ru chamashim yom

k'dei sheyitaharu nafshot am'cha Yisra'el mizuhamatam uv'chein y'hi ratzon milfanecha YHVH Eloheinu v'Elohei avoteinu shebiz'chut s'firat ha-omer shesafarti ha-yom y'tukan mah shepagamti bis'firah

(.....insert the appropriate sefirotic combination.....)

v'etaher v'etkadesh bik'dushah shel ma'lah v'al y'dei zeh yushpa shefa rav b'chol ha-olamot ul-takein et nafshoteinu v'ruchoteinu v'nish'moteinu mikol sig uf'gam ul-tahareinu ul-kad'sheinu bik'dushat'cha ha-elyonah Omein Selah

Translation:
> Master of the universe, you commanded us through Moses your servant to count *Sefirat Ha-Omer*, in order to purify us from our evil and uncleanness. As you have written in your *Torah*
> [*Leviticus 23:15–16*] "And ye shall count unto you from the morrow after the day of rest, from the day that ye brought the sheaf of the waving; seven weeks shall there be complete; even unto the morrow after the seventh week shall ye number fifty days,"
> so that the souls of your people Israel may be cleansed from their defilement. Therefore, may it be your will, *YHVH* our God and God of our fathers, that in the merit of the *Sefirat Ha-Omer* which I counted today, the blemish that I have caused in the *sefirah*
>
> (.....insert the appropriate sefirotic combination.....)
>
> be rectified and I may be purified and sanctified with holiness from above, and through this may abundant bounty flow upon all the worlds, and may it rectify our *Nefesh*, *Ruach* and *Neshamah* from every baseness and blemish, and may it purify and sanctify us with your exalted holiness *Amen Selah*.

It should be noted that whilst you might elect to perform the procedure during the standard forty-nine days between *Pesach* (Passover) and *Shavu'ot* (Festival of Weeks), you could easily set up your own "*Omer*" at any time, as Rabbi Simon Jacobson noted in an electronic version of his acclaimed work on the "Counting of the *Omer*."[102]

Herewith the full array of the forty-nine days comprising "*Sefirat ha-Omer*." In this regard, it should be noted that the exact meaning of each in terms of its sefirotic associations and affiliated psycho-spiritual "rectification," so to speak, have been deliberated and commented upon in many ways down the centuries. However, in constructing the comments on the various sefirotic combinations applicable to the forty-nine days, I have relied particularly on the writings of two remarkable authors whose works on the "Counting of the *Omer*" are, in my estimation, the very best of their genre.[103] These are the texts which I quoted, paraphrased, and commented upon in the annotations on the forty-nine sefirotic combinations respectively affiliated with the forty-nine days of personal introspection.

## WEEK 1—CORRECTING THE *SEFIRAH* OF *CHESED*

Rabbi Aryeh Kaplan informed us that "*Chesed*–Love connotes kindness and altruism," and that "*Chesed*–Love has to mean an unconditional giving."[104] He further maintained that "true altruism is to do something when you do not expect anything in return. Essentially then, *Chesed*–Love is the idea of giving oneself totally."[105]

My late mentor, William G. Gray, referred to the *sefirah Chesed* (Mercy/Loving-kindness) in terms of "Abounding Love" and "Perpetual Compassion," saying "Magnanimity and mercy are thine attributes; thou art concerned with care and consolation for thy creatures. Boundless are the blessings of thy bounty; and we are comforted by thy compassion."[106] Here we might consider the oft expressed phrase "God is Love" referencing the most vital principle in terms of meaningful existence. Yet, as I noted previously, whilst love "is such a *vital* thing, yet it can be deadly in the sense of losing oneself utterly into it."[107] David Cooper reminds us that *Chesed* is "kindness/compassion/ generosity/love of God/inspiring vision," but that it also has a "lack of limits or boundaries."[108]

Again Aryeh Kaplan equally noted that *Chesed* is "giving without bounds; being unrestrained, being unbounded, and perhaps undisciplined."[109] He also reminded us that if the Divine One "were to give freely of Himself, He would totally overwhelm creation with *Gedulah*–Greatness, the original name of *Chesed*–Love."[110] It is thus clear from the perspective of our human existence, that you might overindulge and even overwhelm those you love, literally kill them with kindness. These and other issues pertaining to your capacity to love and express kindness, need to be considered in the first week of "Counting the *Omer*."

## Day 1—*Chesed* in *Chesed*

היום יום אחד לעומר
חסד שבחסד

י

# אלהים אנא

Transliteration:
    *Ha-yom yom echad la-omer*
    *Chesed sheb'Chesed*
    *Yod*
    *Alef-Lamed-Mem-Yod-Mem Alef-Nun-Alef*

Translation:
    Today is the first day of *Omer*.
    Loving-kindness (Mercy) in Loving-kindness (Mercy)
    *Yod*
    *Alef-Lamed-Mem-Yod-Mem Alef-Nun-Alef*

**Comment:**

We are told that the first day of "Counting the *Omer*," pertains specifically to "the love aspect of love; the expression of love and its level of intensity."[111] We are equally informed that *Chesed* of *Chesed* pertains to "kindness and generosity vs. lack of limits or boundaries."[112]

Here the important factor is how one may actualise love inside oneself and in life. It should be noted that the sphere of *Chesed* (Lovingkindness) on the sefirotic tree pertains to the capacity to give, this being the quality specifically referenced by the expression יצר הטוב (*Yetzer ha-Tov*—"The Good Inclination"). Hence, on this, the first day of *Omer*, you need to not only assess your capacity to love and give, but equally how you give and express your love.

In this regard, it is very important to answer the following questions pertaining directly to this day and the sphere of *Chesed* (Loving-kindness) on the Kabbalistic Tree of Life, which Rabbi Simon Jacobson raised in his wonderful study on "Counting the *Omer*":[113]

Do you have and allow room for someone else in your life?
Are you afraid of personal vulnerability, of opening up and getting hurt?
How do you express your love?
Do you express love and give conditionally, i.e. only when it is comfortable to do so?
Are you able to communicate your love and true feelings—withholding perhaps because of fear of rejection, or expressing too much too early?
Whom do you love—only those with whom you have a good interrelationship?

Such questions and more need to be considered on this the first day of the "Counting of the *Omer*," representing the unimpeded flow of "Loving-kindness in Loving-kindness."

A recommended exercise for this day reads: "Find a new way to express your love to a dear one."[114]

### Day 2—*Gevurah* in *Chesed*

היום שני ימים לעומר
גבורה שבחסד

יחננו בכח

Transliteration:
    *Ha-yom sh'nei yamim la-omer*
    *Gevurah sheb'Chesed*
    *Shin*
    *Yod-Chet-Nun-Nun-Vav Bet-Kaf-Chet*

Translation:
    Today is the second day of *Omer*.
    Might (Severity) in Loving-kindness (Mercy)
    *Shin*
    *Yod-Chet-Nun-Nun-Vav Bet-Kaf-Chet*

**Comment:**

Whilst it has been said that the second day of "Counting of *Omer*," *Discipline* in *Loving-Kindness*, pertains to "the strength that enables one to be generous and kind,"[115] we are also reminded that "healthy love must always include an element of discipline. A degree of distance and respect for the other. An assessment of the person's capacity to contain your love. Love must be tempered and directed properly," and we are equally informed that "Love with discretion is necessary to avoid giving to those who would use loving to perpetuate negative behavior."[116]

This pertains to what I like to call the "kill-with-kindness-factor." I have observed this factor in families where parents overindulge their kids, and have seen the same in friendships where one party is so, as it were, "enamoured" with the other to the extent of allowing total leniency, and sometimes even accepting of serious mental and emotional abuse, in the relationship. Of course, this applies in two ways, i.e. being abused by the individual you love, or forcing an individual to do your bidding, and abide by your rules, in the name of "loving-kindness." The latter equally pertains to "*Gevurah* (Discipline) in *Chesed* (Loving-kindness)." I therefore fully align with Rabbi Jacobson who maintained that you should ask yourself on this second day of the "Counting of the *Omer*":

> Whether your love is disciplined enough?
> Whether you allow others to take advantage of your kind and altruistic nature?
> Whether you are injuring those you love by being their crutch?
> Whether you are hurting those you love "by forcing upon them" your personal values in the name of "love"?[117]
> Whether you are respecting the individual you love, or are being selfish?
> Whether your love is given appropriately?

I believe the following statement sums up the spirit of this day most magnificently: "Rain is a blessing only because it falls in drops that don't flood the fields."[118]

A recommended exercise for this day reads: "Help others on their terms.....not on yours."[119]

### Day 3—*Tiferet* in *Chesed*

היום שלשה ימים לעומר
תפארת שבחסד

מ

וִיבָרְכֵנוּ גְדוּלָת

Transliteration:
  Ha-yom sh'loshah yamim la-omer
  Tiferet sheb'Chesed
  Mem
  Vav-Yod-Bet-Resh-Kaf-Nun-Vav Gimel-Dalet-Vav-Lamed-Tav

Translation:
  Today is the third day of *Omer*.
  Harmony (Beauty) in Loving-kindness (Mercy)
  Mem
  Vav-Yod-Bet-Resh-Kaf-Nun-Vav Gimel-Dalet-Vav-Lamed-Tav

**Comment:**

This day pertains to the remarkable concept of *Harmony* in *Loving-Kindness*, which is plainly interpreted to mean "the beauty or compassion of kindness and generosity."[120] However, we are informed that "it is the power of *tiferet* which allows one to express a harmonious blend of the two spiritual poles of benevolence (*chesed*) and might (*gevurah*)."[121] It is said the "inner essence" of *Tiferet* (Beauty), the *sefirah* representing, as it were, the "heart" of the sefirotic Tree, pertains to רחמים (*Rachamim*—"Compassion"), and that the very concept of "Compassion" itself "synthesizes the contrasting elements of *ahavah* and *yirah*," respectively "love" and "fear/awe," combining these principles "into a force of discriminating compassion."¹²² Yet, it is understood that *Tiferet* (Beauty/Harmony) leans more in the direction of *Ahavah* (Love), hence kabbalistic tradition maintains "that *tiferet* always tends towards the right, the side of *chesed*."¹²³

Thus, in terms of the concept of *Tiferet* (Beauty/Harmony) in *Chesed* (Loving-kindness) being applicable to this third day of "Counting the *Omer*," we are correctly informed that "harmony in love is one that blends both the *chesed* and *gevurah* aspects of love,"¹²⁴ and that "harmonized love includes empathy and compassion."¹²⁵ However, we are reminded that *Tiferet* balances *Chesed* when "truth and harmony emerge from a place of loving-kindness."¹²⁶ In this regard, it is suggested you ask yourself, whether you are able:¹²⁷

> To recall past encounters which you thought were unfortunate at the time, yet which turned out for the best? To "establish a more balanced, truthful, and loving relationship" with everyone in your life, so as to "know when and how to give to the other in the most optimal way"?¹²⁸

A recommended exercise for the third day of "Counting the *Omer*" reads: "Offer a helping hand to a stranger."¹²⁹

### Day 4—*Netzach* in *Chesed*

היום ארבעה ימים לעומר
נצח שבחסד

ח

יאר ימינך

Transliteration:
> *Ha-yom arba'ah yamim la-omer*
> *Netzach sheb'Chesed*
> *Chet*
> *Yod-Alef-Resh Yod-Mem-Yod-Nun-Chaf*

Translation:
> Today is the fourth day of *Omer*.
> Endurance (Victory) in Loving-kindness (Mercy)
> *Chet*
> Yod-Alef-Resh Yod-Mem-Yod-Nun-Chaf

## Comment:

The fourth day of the "Counting of the *Omer*" references *Endurance* (*Netzach*) in *Loving-Kindness* (*Chesed*), which is said to be about "taking the initiative to be kind and generous and perseverance in same."[130] However, we are reminded that this day equally pertains to your "capacity to make and keep long-term loving commitments."[131] It should be understood that Endurance (*Netzach*) in Love (*Chesed*) is no easy matter, especially when you are constantly faced with challenges in personal relationships. In this regard, there will be times in any friendship or relationship when you feel closeness, and other times when you sense a distance between yourself and your partner or friend. Hence it is on this day that you are required to contemplate your commitment and endurance in intimate relationships. In this regard, Rabbi Jacobson encouraged you to ask yourself:[132]

> If your love is enduring?
> If it can withstand challenges and setbacks?
> If you give and withhold love according to your moods, and if it is constant regardless of the ups and downs of life?
> If you are willing to work at your relationships and fight for the love you have?
> If your love has spirit and valour?
> If you can be counted on in both the good times and the bad?

In this regard, the recommended exercise for this day reads: "Reassure a loved one of the constancy of your love."[133]

### Day 5—*Hod* in *Chesed*

היום חמשה ימים לעומר
הוד שבחסד

ו

## פניו תתיר

Transliteration:
> Ha-yom chamisha yamim la-omer
> Hod sheb'Chesed
> Vav
> Peh-Nun-Yod-Vav Tav-Tav-Yod-Resh

Translation:
> Today is the fifth day of *Omer*.
> Splendour (Glory) in Loving-kindness (Mercy)
> Vav
> Peh-Nun-Yod-Vav Tav-Tav-Yod-Resh

**Comment:**

This day pertains to *Hod* (Humility) in *Chesed* (*Loving-Kindness*), which is said to simply reference "sincerity of kindness and generosity."[134] The *sefirah* of *Hod* pertains to being "mindful" or "thoughtful," especially when viewed in terms of that special Hebrew concept termed הודאה (*Hoda'ah*— "acknowledgement" and "gratitude"). Considering the terms "mindful," "thoughtful," "acknowledgement" and "gratitude" conjointly, it is possible to sense the profound depth of the statement "arrogant love is not real love."[135]

I am reminded of the different stages of "soul unfoldment" which I referenced elsewhere.[136] In this regard, I noted that "a person whose consciousness is still firmly focussed in the *Nefesh* (Instinctual Self) is mainly concerned with personal needs, and sees those of others only in terms of his or her own needs." The "*Ru'ach* person, on the other hand, is the exact opposite of the previously mentioned individual. In this case the person is mainly concerned with the needs of others, and sees his or her personal requirements in terms of those of others. Such an individual is more altruistic, and seeks to make the world a better place for all."[137] Hence we are told that "Humility within loving-kindness means giving genuine consideration to the feelings, needs, rights, or perspective of others, and being willing to place their needs ahead of our own, whenever appropriate.....Searching for more numerous ways we can perform acts of *hod* within *chesed* in our relationships and in our communities would make the world we live in a much kinder place."[138] [my italics]

In terms of what has been said here, we are exhorted to consider the following questions:[139]

> Are you humbled by love?
> Are you arrogant sometimes, because you have the capacity to love?
> Knowing that love comes from the Eternal Living Spirit, do you enter into it with total humility, recognizing the great privilege of being able to love?
> Do you realise that through love you receive more than you give?

There are further questions to consider on this day, especially in terms of the qualities of thoughtfulness (*Hod*) aligned with loving-kindness (*Chesed*). In this regard you might ask yourself:[140]

> How likely you are "to take the first steps towards compromise or reconciliation" in an argument?
> Whether you consider yourself to be "superior to a person who looks dirty," and hence judge them for not being socially presentable?

Having contemplated those and perhaps related questions regarding *Hod* (Humility/Thoughtfullness) in *Chesed* (Loving-kindness), you might consider working the following recommended exercise: "Swallow your pride and reconcile with a loved one you have quarrelled with."[141]

## Day 6—*Yesod* in *Chesed*

היום ששה ימים לעומר
יסוד שבחסד

ו

אֻתָּנוּ צְרוּרָה

Transliteration:
>*Ha-yom shishah yamim la-omer*
>*Yesod sheb'Chesed*
>*Vav*
>*Alef-Tav-Nun-Vav Tzadi-Resh-Vav-Resh-Heh*

Translation:
>Today is the sixth day of *Omer*.
>Foundation (Bonding) in Loving-kindness (Mercy)
>*Vav*
>Alef-Tav-Nun-Vav Tzadi-Resh-Vav-Resh-Heh

**Comment:**

This day pertains to *Yesod* (*Bonding/Foundation*) in *Chesed* (*Loving-kindness*), which we are told pertains to "applying oneself to the task of being kind and generous."[142] Yet many people reading the word "bonding," would automatically assume that this pertains to "mating in a loving way," and they would certainly not be wrong in this assumption. All relationships are based on some kind of special "bonding," whether the latter be of the physical, mental, emotional or spiritual kind. In this regard, we are told categorically that "for love to be eternal it requires bonding; a sense of togetherness which actualizes the love with a joint effort,"[143] and that, similarly to the sexual bonding of lovers, this "bonding bears fruit; the fruit borne out of a healthy union."[144]

All of this is concisely summed up in the statement that "a relationship takes on emerging or permanent elements of bonding when we are able to rely on another person with unspoken trust."[145] We are informed that if you want to successfully achieve *Yesod* (Bonding) within *Chesed* (Loving-kindness), you need to ask yourself:[146]

How involved you are in the meaningful aspects of the other's life?
How much you are encouraging and supporting "the other's efforts, dreams and work, whatever that may be"?[147]
Do you treat those you care for "with deep and abiding respect at all times"[148] in body, mind, soul and spirit.

Hence we are encouraged on this day to "start building something constructive together with a loved one,"[149] i.e. anybody who holds a special place in your heart.

### Day 7—*Malchut* in *Chesed*

היום שבעה ימים
שהם שבוע אחד לעומר
מלכות שבחסד

סכֿלֿהֿ

אב"ג ית"ץ

Transliteration:
>Ha-yom shiv'ah yamim
>sheheim shavu'a echad la'omer
>Malchut sheb'Chesed
>Yod
>Samech-Lamed-Heh
>AViGe YaToTzi

Translation:
>Today is the seventh day
>which is one week of *Omer*.
>Kingdom (Leadership) in Loving-kindness (Mercy)
>Yod
>Samech-Lamed-Heh
>AViGe YaToTzi

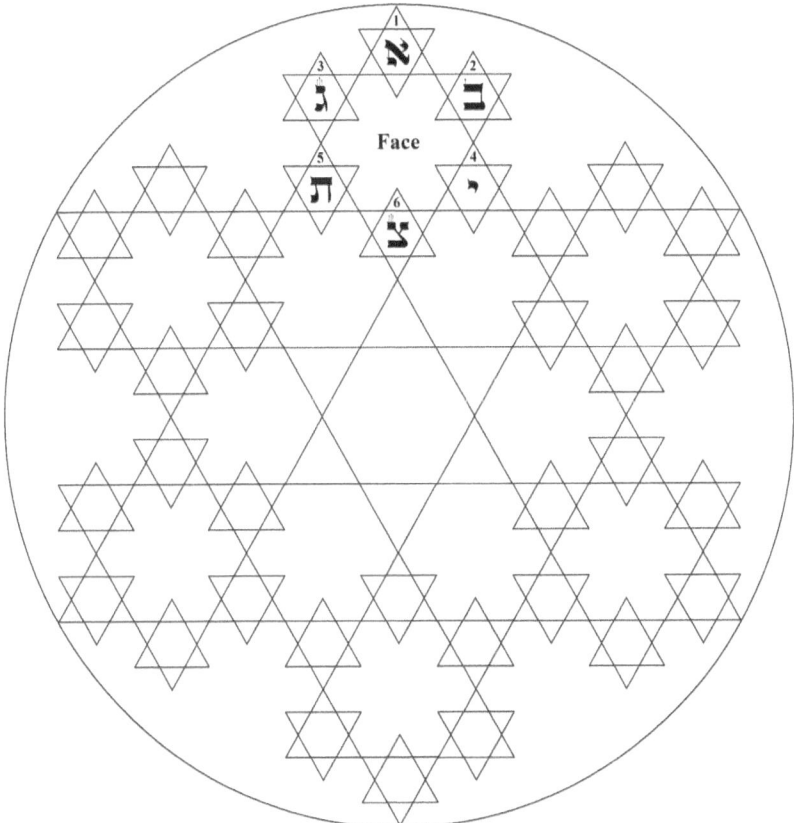

**Comment:**

*Malchut* (Leadership) in *Chesed* (Loving-kindness) is said to pertain to "receptivity or being accepting and inclusive as an expression of kindness and generosity."[150] Considering the, as it were, "noble bearing" of a "sovereign" within a "Kingdom," you are reminded of your own nobility, i.e. that "mature love" establishes "personal dignity, and intimate feeling of nobility and regalness."[151] In terms of the spirit of this day in which we consider *Malchut* (Sovereignty) in *Chesed* (Loving-kindness), it has been correctly stated that "for love to be complete it must have the dimension of personal sovereignty, a sense of freedom and dominion over the forces that detract from total living."[152]

William G. Gray, maintained that your body, mind, soul and spirit, including your personal space within this world, collectively comprise your personal "Kingdom" where you are meant to be the "Ruler." A sovereign is meant to govern with right and reason, and sometimes to make "self-sacrifice" for the good of his/her "people."[153] In this regard, William Gray noted that "surely you had to sacrifice *something* for the good of its people (who may be your family),"[154] to which I might add the query "What have you done to make this world a better place for someone or something?"

In terms of the "Kingship" and "Loving-kindness" we are considering here, you might ask yourself:[155]

> Are you a "King" in your "Inner Kingdom"?
> Do you make rules that you keep yourself?
> Can you control and govern your own emotional attributes?
> How far do you ever sacrifice yourself for the good of anything or anyone connected with you?
> What would you sacrifice for your own health and happiness? Your family or those who love you? Your beliefs?

On this completion of the first week of the "Counting of the *Omer*," it has been suggested that you "Highlight an aspect in your love that has bolstered your spirit and enriched your life.....and celebrate!"[156]

---

## WEEK 2—CORRECTING THE *SEFIRAH* OF *GEVURAH*

During the second week of the "Counting of the *Omer*" attention should be firmly focussed on the *sefirah Gevurah* (Might/Restraint/Discipline/Severity), which is said to be synonymous with דין (*Din*—"Judgement") and פחד (*Pachad*—"Fear"). Whereas *Chesed* (Loving-kindness/Mercy) is infinitely expansive, abundant and embracing, *Gevurah* (Discipline/Might) is absolute in its severity, contraction and restrictive discipline. In this regard, William G. Gray noted that "*Chesed* may be the accelerator of Life-energy, but it is *Geburah* that applies the most necessary brake. Extension of Infinity can only be controlled by contraction of the same degree."[157]

It is said that whilst *Gevurah* references "severity/strength/rigor/judgment/intention/withholding/awe of God," it also points to "excessive force, inflexibility, and inability to adapt."[158] However, in viewing the *Gevurah* (Restraint/Discipline) concept of the second week of "Counting the *Omer*" to be related to, or following on from, the *Chesed* (Loving-kindness/Mercy) of the first week, we are informed that "love (*chesed*) is the bedrock of human expression," whilst "discipline (*gevurah*) is the channel through which we express love."[159] In this regard, we are told that *Gevurah* (discipline) "gives our life and love direction and focus," and that the "discipline and measure" of this *sefirah* "concentrates and directs our efforts, our love in the proper directions."[160]

### Day 8—*Chesed* in *Gevurah*

היום שמונה ימים
שהם שבוע אחד ויום אחד לעומר
חסד שבגבורה

Transliteration:
> *Ha-yom sh'monah yamim*
> *sheheim shavu'a echad v'yom echad la'omer*
> *Chesed sheb'Gevurah*
> *Resh*
> *Lamed-Dalet-Ayin-Tav Kof-Bet-Lamed*

Translation:
> Today is the eighth day
> which is one week and one day of *Omer*.
> Loving-kindness (Mercy) in Might (Severity)
> *Resh*
> *Lamed-Dalet-Ayin-Tav Kof-Bet-Lamed*

**Comment:**

On the second day of "Counting the *Omer*" we encountered *Discipline* in *Loving-Kindness*. Whilst we are addressing the same principles in the current instance, this day pertains to *Loving-Kindness* in *Discipline*, i.e. "the *Chesed* of *Gevurah*," which is said to be a reference to "kindness as an expression of strength."[161] We are also informed that "the underlying intention and motive in discipline is love," and thus is *Chesed* of *Gevurah* "the love in discipline; awareness of the intrinsic love that feeds discipline and judgment."[162]

We are reminded that "your personal discipline and the discipline you expect of others is only an expression of love."[163] In this regard, one commentator noted that "it takes maturity to realize that the discipline we choose to apply in our own lives, as well as the discipline that we expect of others, is a strong expression of love."[164] However, there are certain times when discipline needs to be applied with a strong hand (*Gevurah*), especially when you care (*Chesed*) most profoundly for the individual so disciplined. My late mentor commented "have you ever made someone else afraid of you in order to curb bad or unsocial behaviour, like disciplining a child or training a pet because you really love them? In that case you should know why this concept (Gevurah) is on the Tree and understand the well-known text 'The Lord chastiseth whom he loveth' (*Proverbs 3:12*), and also 'The fear of the Lord is the beginning of Wisdom' (*Proverbs 9:10*)."[165]

Hence in considering "Loving-kindness in Discipline," you might ask yourself:

> Is your judgement and criticism of others tainted by contempt and irritation?[166]
> Are you secretly satisfied with the failure of the one you have been judging, or are your observations founded on love for the other?[167]
> Do you ever listen to yourself and think about how you may sound to others?[168]

In the "spirit" of this day, it was suggested that "before you criticize someone today think twice if it is out of care and love."[169]

### Day 9—*Gevurah* in *Gevurah*

היום תשעה ימים
שהם שבוע אחד ושני ימים לעומר
גבורה שבגבורה

נ

בּאֶרֶץ רנת

Transliteration:
> *Ha-yom tish'ah yamim*
> *sheheim shavu'a echad u'sh'nei yamim la'omer*
> *Gevurah sheb'Gevurah*
> *Nun*
> *Bet-Alef-Resh-Tzadi Resh-Nun-Tav*

Translation:
> Today is the ninth day
> which is one week and two days of *Omer*.
> Might (Severity) in Might (Severity)
> Nun
> Bet-Alef-Resh-Tzadi Resh-Nun-Tav

**Comment:**

It has been said that *Gevurah* (Discipline) of *Gevurah* (Discipline), is about "strength versus rigidity."[170] We are reminded that "*gevurah* within *gevurah* is a well of strength that we can harness physically, mentally, emotionally, and spiritually for constructive application in our behavior, relationships, and life. But, we must take caution, for unharnessed, pure *gevurah* within *gevurah* can be dangerous."[171] It is for this reason that we are advised that "pure *Gevurah*," so to speak, "should be applied only when complete and total concentration, discipline, and restraint—without any flexibility or compromise—are required."[172] Obviously external circumstances requiring the application of, as it were, "raw *gevurah*" to work "rectification" are fairly rare, however this day is about the "discipline factor of discipline"[173] applicable in your own personal life. In this regard, you may well query whether your discipline is "disciplined or is it excessive,"[174] and equally:[175]

> If you have enough discipline in your life and in your interactions?
> If you are organized, and employing your time efficiently?
> If you have problems with discipline and what you could do to enhance it?
> If you take time each day for personal accounting of your daily schedule and accomplishments?
> If your discipline incorporates the other six aspects pertaining to the "Counting of the *Omer*," i.e. Loving-kindness, Harmony, Endurance, Mindfulness (Humility), Bonding, and Leadership, since without these factors discipline cannot be effective and healthy?

You might further ask yourself:

> In what areas you might need *gevurah* within *gevurah* to improve yourself?[176]
> How you might apply *gevurah* within *gevurah* to restrain yourself "from offering constant criticism, verbalizing negative comments, or making wisecracks that put others down in a condescending manner"?[177]
> How you might employ *gevurah* within *gevurah* to overcome any manner of addiction?[178]

Rabbi Simon Jacobson, suggested that on this day you should work an exercise in which you are to "make a detailed plan for spending your day and at the end of the day see if you've lived up to it."[179]

### Day 10—*Tiferet* in *Gevurah*

היום עשרה ימים
שהם שבוע אחד ושלשה ימים לעומר
תפארת שבגבורה

בּ

דרכך עמך

Transliteration:
> Ha-yom asarah yamim
> sheheim shavu'a echad u'sh'loshah yamim la'omer
> Tiferet sheb'Gevurah
> Nun
> Dalet-Resh-Kaf-Chaff Ayin-Mem-Chaf

Translation:
> Today is the tenth day
> which is one week and three days of *Omer*.
> Harmony (Beauty) in Might (Severity)
> Nun
> Dalet-Resh-Kaf-Chaf Ayin-Mem-Chaf

### Comment:

The tenth day of "Counting the *Omer*" is referenced *Tiferet* (Beauty/Harmony) of *Gevurah* (Might), and in this regard we are informed that this is about "centeredness, balance and mercy as an expression of strength."[180] However, as noted earlier, the "inner essence" of *Tiferet* (Beauty) pertains to רחמים (*Rachamim*—"Compassion"), and thus on this day of *Tiferet* in *Gevurah*, we are encountering "Compassion" in "Discipline." We are told that "not just love but compassion has to drive discipline," and that compassion is unconditional love.[181] In this regard it is maintained that the reference here is to "love just for the sake of love, not considering the others position."[182]

Whilst I certainly align with the sentiments expressed here, I equally acknowledge that *Tiferet* in *Gevurah* "utilizes *gevurah* (first and foremost) with the appropriate amount of tiferet to take correct action in any given situation involving family and friends."[183] Above all, it is clear that this necessitates mindfulness, and, in the words of a great commentator, "it takes wisdom, patience, and humility to know how to achieve this, but it is essential. Tempering *gevurah* with *tiferet* creates harmony and balance within strength."[184]

Having considered the ideas shared, you should query yourself:

Whether your discipline has "an element of compassion"?[185]

Whether you are perhaps confronting a current situation with "either too much or too little *gevurah*"?[186]

Whether you could in situations requiring "rectification," so to speak, "apply the harmony and balance of tiferet to be more effective"?[187]

Whether there is an individual who constantly violates your personal space, and what you might do to inform this person that you "expect a certain level of *tiferet* within *gevurah*" in your relationship?[188]

In conclusion, it was recommended that you do the following exercise on this day: "Be compassionate to someone you have reproached."[189]

### Day 11—*Netzach* in *Gevurah*

היום אחד עשר יום
שהם שבוע אחד וארבעה ימים לעומר
נצח שבגבורה

ו

בכל שגבנו

Transliteration:
  *Ha-yom echad asar yom*
  *sheheim shavu'a echad v'arba'ah yamim la'omer*
  *Netzach sheb'Gevurah*
  *Vav*
  *Bet-Kaf-Lamed Shin-Gimel-Bet-Nun-Vav*

Translation:
  Today is the eleventh day
  which is one week and four days of *Omer*.
  Endurance (Victory) in Might (Severity)
  Vav
  Bet-Kaf-Lamed Shin-Gimel-Bet-Nun-Vav

**Comment:**

The sefirotic principles applying to the eleventh day of "Counting the *Omer*," pertains to *Netzach* (Endurance) in *Gevurah* (Discipline), which is said to pertain to "determination and persistence as expressions of strength."[190] This is clarified in the statement that "*netzach* within *gevurah* is the tenacious effort to persistently and consistently reinforce our commitments to reach our goals or objectives"[191] In this regard, it has been emphasised that "effective discipline must be enduring and tenacious."[192] It is certainly clear that "it takes discipline and strength and endurance to achieve any worthy objective or goal."[193]

Again, whilst keeping the point raised firmly in your mind, you might ask yourself the following questions:

> Is your discipline consistent or such only when forced?[194]
> Are you perceived as a weak disciplinarian?[195]
> Can you recall and relate when you discarded an undertaking, which you now wish you had completed?[196]
> Are there any hurdles imposed by yourself or others, which are preventing you from pursuing and reaching the goals you set out to achieve? If so, what are you intending to do about this?[197]

The exercise suggested for this day pertains to the one you enacted on the ninth day of the "Counting of the *Omer*," i.e. *Gevurah* in *Gevurah*, regarding which it is suggested that you "extend the plan you made" on that day "for a longer period of time, listing short-term and long-term goals and review and update it each day, and see how consistent you are; if you follow through."[198]

### Day 12—*Hod* in *Gevurah*

היום שנים עשר יום
שהם שבוע אחד וחמשה ימים לעומר
הוד שבגבורה

לֹ

גּוֹיִם טִהֲרֵנוּ

Transliteration:
> Ha-yom sh'neim asar yom
> sheheim shavu'a echad va-chamishah yamim la'omer
> Hod sheb'Gevurah
> Lamed
> Gimel-Vav-Yod-Mem Tet-Heh-Resh-Nun-Vav

Translation:
> Today is the twelfth day
> which is one week and five days of *Omer*.
> Splendour (Glory) in Might (Severity)
> Lamed
> Gimel-Vav-Yod-Mem Tet-Heh-Resh-Nun-Vav

### Comment:

*Hod* (Mindfulness/Humility) within *Gevurah* (Discipline) was said to pertain to "withdrawal or surrender as sincere expressions of strength."[199] This statement may appear somewhat ambiguous, but careful consideration will soon offer clarification. We are told that "whether *gevurah* is expressed in thought, speech or action, it can be severe and even destructive if it originates in arrogance. But when *gevurah* is filtered through *hod* (humility), it is tempered with gentleness and consideration for others."[200]

Besides, as Rabbi Simon Jacobson noted, "the results of discipline and might without humility are obvious. The greatest catastrophes have occurred as a result of people sitting in arrogant judgement of others."[201] Hence it is the cultivation of *Hod* (Humility) on all levels, which is so "critical in leading a meaningful, balanced, grounded, and happy life."[202]

You might ask yourself on this twelfth day of "Counting the *Omer*":

> If you are arrogant in the name of that which you consider just?[203]
> Whether you ever think that you "sit on a higher pedestal and bestow judgement" on those you relegate lower positions than yourself?[204]
> If you can describe a circumstance in which you "humbly accepted an outcome," despite the fact that it was not what you were hoping for?[205]

If in uncomfortable circumstances arising between yourself and loved ones, you are able to listen to your "inner voice" guiding you to do what is best for them instead of for yourself?[206]

Whether you have enough faith to accept those outcomes which you neither intended nor expected, and still retain your love for and service to the Eternal Living Spirit?[207]

In the light then of the sefirotic principles of *Hod* (mindfulness/humility) within *Gevurah* (discipline), it was suggested that on this day: "Don't judge anyone unless you are doing so selflessly with no personal bias."[208]

### Day 13—*Yesod* in *Gevurah*

היום שלשה עשר יום
שהם שבוע אחד וששה ימים לעומר
יסוד שבגבורה

א

יְשׁוּעָתְךָ נוֹרָא

Transliteration:
*Ha-yom sh'loshah asar yom
sheheim shavu'a echad v'shishah yamim la'omer
Yesod sheb'Gevurah
Alef
Yod-Shin-Vav-Ayin-Tav-Kaf Nun-Vav-Resh-Alef*

Translation:
Today is the thirteenth day
which is one week and six days of *Omer*.
Foundation (Bonding) in Might (Severity)

**Comment:**

The thirteenth day of the "Counting of the *Omer*" pertains to *Yesod* (Bonding/Foundation) within *Gevurah* (Strength/Discipline). These qualities have been depicted "focused attention and intention as applications of strength."[209] It has also been said that "for discipline to be effective it must be coupled with commitment and bonding."[210] It is clear that the factors listed in these statements are of vital importance in all manner of relationships, and they are succinctly summarised in the statement that the "bonding of *yesod* combined with the strength of *gevurah* makes it possible for people to stick together through thick and thin."[211] There is really not much more to be said, except to take careful note of the comment that "in disciplining yourself and others there has to be a sense that the discipline is important for developing a stronger bond,"[212] and "to strive to keep relationships strong and lasting, while restraining any tendencies to engage in behavior that whittles away the bond."[213]

Whilst again keeping the details shared firmly in your mind, you are exhorted to ask yourself the following questions:[214]

> Have you at any time worked hard at mending a rift with a friend or loved one?
> Is there currently a rift between yourself and loved ones resulting from some disagreement, and which needs resolution?
> How can you practice holding your tongue so as to not prevent the development of stronger relationships?

In terms of enacting the principles of *Yesod* (Bonding) in *Gevurah* (Discipline) in a practical manner on this day, you could work the following recommended exercise: "Demonstrate to your child or student," or, for that matter, anybody dear to you, "how your bonding with each other is an essential ingredient in discipline and growth."[215]

### Day 14—*Malchut* in *Gevurah*

היום ארבעה עשר יום
שהם שבוע שני שבועות לעומר
מלכות שבגבורה

מִ

יוֹדוֹךְ

קְרַ"ע שִׂטָ"ן

Transliteration:
> *Ha-yom arba'ah asar yom*
> *sheheim sh'nei shavu'ot la'omer*
> *Malchut sheb'Gevurah*
> *Mem*
> *Yod-Vav-Dalet-Vav-Chaf*
> *KaRo' SaTaN'*

Translation:
> Today is the fourteenth day
> which is two weeks of *Omer*.
> Kingdom (Leadership) in Might (Severity)
> *Mem*
> *Yod-Vav-Dalet-Vav-Chaf*
> *KaRo' SaTaN'*

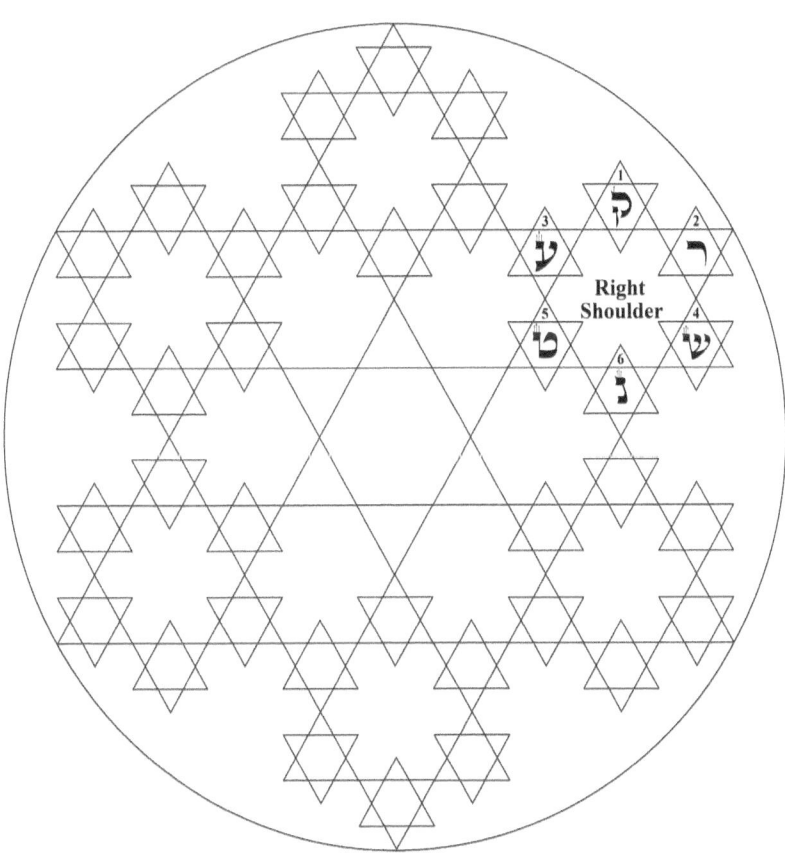

**Comment:**

*Malchut* (Sovereignty) in *Gevurah* (Discipline) has been delineated "receptivity and nurturance as expressions of strength."[216] However, in terms of the sefirotic qualities applicable to the fourteenth day of "Counting the *Omer*," we are told that "discipline, like love, must enhance personal dignity," and that "healthy discipline should bolster self-esteem and help elicit the best in a person; cultivating his sovereignty."[217]

We are informed that the *sefirah* of *Malchut* (Sovereignty/Rulership) is expressed in the harmonious synthesis of the *sefirot Chesed* (Loving-kindness/Mercy); *Gevurah* (Discipline/Might); *Tiferet* (Compassion/Beauty); *Netzach* (Endurance/Victory); *Hod* (Humility/Mindfulness); and *Yesod* (Bonding/Foundation), the result of which, we are told, "is leadership, nobility, dignity, and sovereignty.[218] In this regard, it is stated that *Malchut* (Sovereignty) in *Gevurah* (Discipline/Might), "introduces an element of maturity and self composure into relationships and, even more importantly, it consistently and constantly expresses itself with dignity and nobility no matter what is the issue, judgment, interaction, or reaction to a life situation."[219]

Keeping these details in mind, you are encouraged to ask yourself:

> If the discipline you apply on others is debilitating the human spirit, and whether it enfeebles or empowers you and those you interact with?[220]
> 
> If you consistently restrain yourself from judging others, "including those who are different" from you, and if not, whether you are judging others and in so doing separate yourself from them?[221]
> 
> If you can recount occasions when you do not display Malchut in Gevurah, and how you might rectify this?[222]

In the spirit of the sefirotic principles applying to this day, it was suggested that you work the following exercises: When disciplining anyone, foster his/her self-respect.[223]

# WEEK 3—CORRECTING THE *SEFIRAH* OF *TIFERET*

*Tiferet* (Beauty), the central *sefirah* on the sefirotic Tree which conjoins *Chesed* (Loving-kindness) and *Gevurah* (Discipline), has been delineated the "balance between *Chesed* and *Gevurah* in compassion," said to be "an abundance of heart."[224] As noted, the term רחמים (*Rachamim*—"Compassion") is a quality of *Tiferet*, the fundamental factor being "the dimension of truth, which is neither love or discipline and therefore can integrate the two."[225] In this regard, it was written "Abraham is *Chesed* (loving-kindness), which is on the right, Isaac is *Pachad* (fear), which is on the left, and Jacob, who is *Emet* (Truth), is in the middle."[226] Thus the attribute of "Truth" (אמת—*Emet*) is applied to *Tiferet* (Beauty/Compassion), regarding which it was said that "the attribute *EMET* (Truth) is the middle attribute which includes all, and that is why *YHVH*, may He be blessed, is called by this Name."[227]

In terms of the third week of our quest for "Self Rectification" and "Self Realisation" during the "Counting of the *Omer*," we are informed that "truth is accessed through selflessness: rising above your ego and your predispositions, enables you to realize truth."[228] Furthermore, it is maintained that "the imbalance of love and discipline (and for that matter, any distortion) is a result of a subjective, hence limited perspective; introducing truth, by suspending personal prejudices, allows you to express your feelings (including the synthesis of *chesed* and *gevurah*) in the healthiest manner."[229]

It is thus the harmonizing quality, i.e. the beautiful blending of opposites, which is perceived in the central *sefirah*, which is equated with the solar principle and the human heart, and is thus termed *Tiferet* (Beauty). However, we are reminded that *Tiferet* not only blends the opposing principles of "Mercy" (*Chesed*) and "Might" (*Gevurah*), since for it "to be complete it needs the inclusion of the following seven facets: love of compassion (*Chesed* in *Tiferet*), discipline of compassion (*Gevurah* in *Tiferet*), compassion of compassion (*Tiferet* in *Tiferet*), endurance of compassion (*Netzach* in *Tiferet*), humility of compassion (*Hod* in *Tiferet*), bonding of compassion (*Yesod* in *Tiferet*) and sovereignty of compassion (*Malchut* in *Tiferet*)."[230]

### Day 15—*Chesed* in *Tiferet*

היום חמשה עשר יום
שהם שני שבועות ויום אחד לעומר
חסד שבתפארת

יּ

## עָמִים נָֽא

Transliteration:
> Ha-yom chamishah asar yom
> sheheim sh'nei shavu'ot v'yom echad la'omer
> Chesed sheb'Tiferet
> Yod
> Ayin-Mem-Yod-Mem Nun-Alef

Translation:
> Today is the fifteenth day
> which is two weeks and one day of *Omer*.
> Loving-kindness (Mercy) in Harmony (Beauty)
> Yod
> Ayin-Mem-Yod-Mem Nun-Alef

**Comment:**

On this fifteenth day of "Counting the *Omer*," relating to *Chesed* (Loving-kindness/Mercy) in *Tiferet* (Beauty/Compassion), we are advised on this day to "examine the love aspect of compassion."[231] However, in terms of our earlier observations on *Tiferet*, it is clear that this *sefirah* "in its pure form is harmony/truth—the delicate balance between *chesed* (loving-kindness) and *gevurah* (strength-discipline)."[232]

As I am sure every reader knows well enough, truth can be both positive and negative.[233] In "clearing the air," being truthful with sincerity and honesty of heart, is certainly a good approach. However, it is well-known that "telling the truth" can equally be a weapon of vindictiveness. It is thus important to take heed of the message imparted by the sefirotic principles of *Chesed* (Loving-kindness) in *Tiferet* (Truth/Compassion). From the vantage point of these principles, we should endeavour "to preserve truth in a loving, kind, and caring manner that considers the individual and his or her relationship with others, promoting acceptance and understanding."[234]

Thus, keeping the principles of *Chesed* within *Tiferet* firmly in mind, you are encouraged to ask yourself in terms of "loving-kindness" and "compassion":

> Whether your compassion is "tender and loving or does it come across as pity"?[235]
> Whether your sympathy is "condescending and patronizing"?[236]
> Whether your compassion overflows "with love and warmth; is it expressed with enthusiasm, or is it static and lifeless"?[237]

You might also ask yourself in terms of "loving-kindness" and "truth":

> When you find it necessary to discipline anyone or express dissatisfaction, do you "come across too harshly" or do the recipients still feel your love?[238]
> When you present anyone with honest feedback, are you ready to employ words which are encouraging, rather than destructive and crushing rhetoric?[239]

On this day you are again counselled to work the following exercise: "When helping someone, extend yourself in the fullest way; offer a smile or a loving gesture."[240]

### Day 16—*Gevurah* in *Tiferet*

היום ששה עשר יום
שהם שני שבועות ושני ימים לעומר
גבורה שתפארת

מ

Transliteration:
> *Ha-yom shishah asar yom*
> *sheheim sh'nei shavu'ot u'sh'nei yamim la'omer*
> *Gevurah sheb'Tiferet*
> *Mem*
> *Alef-Lamed-Heh-Yod-Mem Gimel-Bet-Vav-Resh*

Translation:
> Today is the sixteenth day
> which is two weeks and two days of *Omer*.
> Might (Severity) in Harmony (Beauty)
> *Mem*
> *Alef-Lamed-Heh-Yod-Mem Gimel-Bet-Vav-Resh*

**Comment:**

This day is about *Gevurah* (Strength/Discipline) in *Tiferet* (Harmony/Truth/Compassion). In this regard, Rabbi Simon Jacobson informed us that "for compassion to be effective and healthy it needs to be disciplined and focused. It requires discretion both to whom you express compassion, and in the measure of the compassion itself. It is recognizing when compassion should be expressed and when it should be withheld or limited. Discipline in compassion is knowing that being truly compassionate sometimes requires withholding compassion. Because compassion is not an expression of the bestower's needs but a response to the recipient's needs."[241] This is so important! The term "Compassion" means "Common Passion," which is the "Fellow-Feeling" and "sympathy" which is invoked with the desire to help and to relieve. In my estimation true "Compassion" would dutifully respect "Divinity" within the one you are "feeling with," and then to give the service inspired within you by the sense of duty, honour, devotion, etc.. Most of us feel an inherent need to extend the "Mercy of our Maker" to our fellow humankind, and that is exactly how it should be.

However, the word "Mercy" comes from the Latin *"merces"* meaning to pay, reward and favour. In this regard, discretion is indeed vital in the expression and measure of your compassion. You need to know exactly how to pay and reward and extend your "favours," i.e. your "Compassion." Of course, you will aid and assist in the best possible manner in harmony with your

"Fellow-Feeling," and sometimes you assist more by allowing an individual his or her pain, in order that he/she may be relieved of it. I often hear the cries of people wanting to be free of their pains and desiring completeness, but do they realise that completeness means to be filled up, entire, perfect, with nothing lacking, accomplished, consummate, to be fulfilled and to be whole?

Regarding acts of "Loving-kindness," I noted elsewhere that "it is important that we should afford all the opportunity to get somewhere by their own efforts. We should bear *with* them, submit *with* them, carry *with* them, endure *with* them, share *with* them, live *with* them but never *for* them. The smooth, soft, calm warmth of true clemency, compassion and mercy, does not allow slothfulness, indolence, idleness or laziness. In one sense mercy and compassion are passive, but only in the true meaning of the word, which comes from roots meaning 'capable of suffering.' Mercy and compassion are also active, nimble and alert. When you are aware, you are passive enough to receive what comes, and active enough to live out what you have received."[242]

In terms of the principles of *Gevurah* in *Tiferet* pertaining to "Strength" in "Truth," we are told that this "involves applying the necessary strength, restraint, and discipline to ensure that truth is properly emphasized. The truth of *tiferet* must sometimes be reinforced with the strength of *gevurah* so that we do not inadvertently feed unacceptable behaviors, or reward poor choices and miscalculate, or fail to see the unvarnished truth."[243]

Once again keep what has been shared here firmly in your mind, as you ask yourself:[244]

> If you are "more compassionate with strangers than with close ones," and why this is so?
> If your compassion derives from a sense of guilt?
> If you are helping others at the expense of helping yourself?
> If your compassion for those who are close to you overshadow the needs of others?
> If your compassion is impulsive and careless?
> If you "assess the measure of compassion necessary for a given situation?
> If you are perhaps inflicting injury on an individual with your compassion?

If your compassion is overwhelming?
If your compassion is respectful, i.e. whether you give too much or too little?
If others are taking advantage of your compassionate nature?
If when you meet a person in need, you "impetuously express compassion out of guilt or pity without any discretion?
If you first determine the need, and then offer support in the best possible manner?

Further pertinent questions pertaining to *Gevurah* (Discipline) in *Tiferet* (Truth), which you might equally ask yourself:[245]

If you "held your tongue" and refrained from making a curt comment, because you realised that this would cause hurt feelings and worsen a situation?
How many times you corrected individuals in the last month with either a severe criticism or a positive comment?

The following exercise is recommended in the spirit of this day: "Express your compassion in a focused and constructive manner by addressing someone's specific needs."[246]

### Day 17—*Tiferet* in *Tiferet*

היום שבעה עשר יום
שהם שני שבועות ושלשה ימים לעומר
תפארת שבתפארת

כ

יודוך דורשי

Transliteration:
*Ha-yom shiv'ah asar yom
sheheim sh'nei shavu'ot u'sh'loshah yamim la'omer
Tiferet sheb'Tiferet
Kaf
Yod-Vav-Dalet-Vav-Chaf Dalet-Vav-Resh-Shin-Yod*

Translation:
> Today is the seventeenth day
> which is two weeks and three days of *Omer*.
> Harmony (Beauty) in Harmony (Beauty)
> *Kaf*
> Yod-Vav-Dalet-Vav-Chaf Dalet-Vav-Resh-Shin-Yod

## Comment:

This day pertains to *Tiferet* (Beauty/Harmony/Compassion/Truth) within itself. This remarkable sphere on the sefirotic Tree is the balance between *Chesed* (Loving-kindness/Mercy) and *Gevurah* (Might/Discipline), the three *sefirot* understood to be expressing "Greatness," "Power" and the "Glory" of the Divine One. In this regard, it is written לך יהוה הגדלה והגבורה והתפארת (*l'cha YHVH ha'g'dulah v'ha-g'vurah v'ha-tiferet*—"Thine *YHVH* is the greatness, and the power, and the glory") [*1 Chronicles 29:11*]. In my estimation the meaning of this verse is succinctly expressed in the statement that "*Tiferet* within *tiferet* accentuates the natural beauty of balance between compassion and truth so that the latter is expressed to another in a healthy manner which produces harmony," and that "achieving mastery of this *sefirah* combination is an important step towards lasting inner balance and self-esteem."[247]

We are reminded that *Tiferet* within *Tiferet* is "the expression of compassion and its intensity," and that "true compassion is limitless. It is not an extension of your needs and defined by your limited perspective. Compassion for another is achieved by having a selfless attitude, rising above yourself and placing yourself in the other person's situation and experience."[248] In this regard it was recommended that you ask yourself:[249]

> If you express and actualise the compassion and empathy in your heart, and what blocks you from expressing it?
> If your compassion is truly compassionate or self serving?
> If your compassion derives from a sense of guilt rather than genuine empathy, and how this impacts your compassion?
> If your compassion is expressed from a sense of duty offered as if it is frivolous?

If you are offering compassion habitually because you feel bad on encountering suffering, or are you applying yourself to scrutinise your compassion in terms of limitations and forms of expression?
If your compassion is well rounded, since your compassion is fully realised only when it comprises the qualities of the other six *sefirot* within *Tiferet*, i.e. loving-kindness (*Chesed*), Discipline (*Gevurah*), Endurance (*Netzach*), Humility (*Hod*), Bonding (*Yesod*), and Sovereignty (*Malchut*).

You are further exhorted on this day, to ask yourself:[250]

When faced with complex situations requiring a response, if you consider every option before thinking, saying or doing anything, or if you simply react thoughtlessly?
How you might deal with any situation from the *Kavvanah*, the focussed intention or stance of *Tiferet* within *Tiferet*?

Having considered and hopefully responded to these questions in a personally most meaningful manner, it is suggested that you work the following exercise: "Express your compassion in a new way that goes beyond your previous limitations: express it towards someone to whom you have been callous."[251]

### Day 18—*Netzach* in *Tiferet*

היום שמונה עשר יום
שהם שני שבועות וארבעה ימים לעומר
נצח שבתפארת

✶

שׁעְמִים יוֹזוּדךָ

Transliteration:
    *Ha-yom sh'monah asar yom*
    *sheheim sh'nei shavu'ot v'arba'ah yamim la'omer*
    *Netzach sheb'Tiferet*
    *Yod*
    Shin-Ayin-Mem-Yod-Mem Yod-Chet-Vav-Dalet-Chaf

Translation:
> Today is the eighteenth day
> which is two weeks and four days of *Omer*.
> Endurance (Victory) in Harmony (Beauty)
> *Yod*
> *Shin-Ayin-Mem-Yod-Mem Yod-Chet-Vav-Dalet-Chaf*

**Comment:**

The eighteenth day of "Counting the *Omer*" pertains to the principles of *Netzach* (Endurance/Victory) in *Tiferet* (Harmony/Compassion). In this regard we are told that *Netzach* in *Tiferet* "helps us to preserve the beautiful harmony of *Tiferet*."[252] This is said to pertain to "commitments, choices, pursuits, relationships, and chosen paths in life" which "can be a rollercoaster ride with their ups and downs, good times and bad."[253] Factually *Tiferet* (harmony) indeed needs the quality of *Netzach* (endurance), in order "to weather these difficult periods and reinforce and preserve relationship commitments."[254] In order to reach a more practical understanding of this, it is recommended to ask yourself:[255]

> If you have committed time and effort to a worthy goal or cause, and having done so on an enduring basis over a period of time, and if not, what stops you from making such a commitment?
> Are you aware of possible obstacles in your life which impede the achievement of important goals, and what can you do to establish reasonable boundaries to aid you to stay on course?
> Are you "too passive in setting goals and working in a dedicated manner to complete them,"[256] and what can you do to change this?

As noted earlier, *Tiferet* pertains to רחמים (*Rachamim*—Compassion). In this regard, you may also ask yourself:[257]

> If your compassion is enduring and consistent, reliable or whimsical?
> If you have the capacity to be compassionate even when you are engrossed in unrelated activities?
> If you are ready "to stand up and fight for another"?[258]

Keeping in mind the concepts pertaining to this day, you are encouraged to perform the following exercise: "In middle of a busy day take a moment and call someone that needs a compassionate word. Defend someone who is in need of sympathy even if it's not a popular position."[259]

### Day 19—*Hod* in *Tiferet*

היום תשעה עשר יום
שהם שני שבועות וחמשה ימים לעומר
הוד שבתפארת

תָּ

כּוּלָם כּבבת

Transliteration:
   Ha-yom tish'ah asar yom
   sheheim sh'nei shavu'ot v'chamishah yamim la'omer
   Hod sheb'Tiferet
   Tav
   Kaf-Vav-Lamed-Mem Kaf-Bet-Bet-Tav

Translation:
   Today is the nineteenth day
   which is two weeks and five days of *Omer*.
   Splendour (Glory) in Harmony (Beauty)
   Tav
   Kaf-Vav-Lamed-Mem Kaf-Bet-Bet-Tav

**Comment:**

We are told that "*hod* within *tiferet* is righteous truth."[260] Regarding the sefirotic principles of the nineteenth day of "Counting the *Omer*," it is said that "*Hod* adorns *Tiferet* with humility to make it even more beautiful and balanced," and that "when *hod* is coupled with *tiferet*, it manifests itself in quiet consideration and recognition of the other that comes from selflessness and not ego-based self-interest."[261] It should be realised that the current combination of sefirotic principles define good living, and thus require most careful consideration. It has been written that "*hod* within *tiferet* is a defining sefirah. With it, we can all live dignified lives. Without it, we are doomed."[262] It was further stated "achieving an ethical society requires *hod* within *tiferet*. First there must be an acceptance of that which is true, and also a balanced expression of *chesed* and *gevurah*. A society which lacks this balance will not be a healthy society. Too much *chesed* can lead to too much permissiveness.....and an attitude of 'anything goes.' Conversely, too much *gevurah* produces a totalitarian society where the strong.....and tolerance are suppressed."[263] It is thus maintained that *Hod* (Humility) "is essential in an ethical society and that comes from a foundation built on *hod* within *tiferet*."[264]

Naturally, in terms of the spirit of this day, what has been said about the principles of *Hod* in *Tiferet* within a healthy society, needs to be translated in terms applicable to your personal life and wellbeing. In this regard, we are reminded that *Tiferet* (compassion) must incorporate *Hod* (humility) "for it not to be condescending and pretentious,"[265] and thus is *Hod* , in the words of Rabbi Simon Jacobson, a recognition "that my ability to be compassionate and giving does not make me better than the recipient; it is the acknowledgement and appreciation that by creating one who needs compassion God gave me the gift of being able to bestow compassion. Thus there is no place for haughtiness in compassion."[266] Again, in terms of the vital principles applying not only to this day, but to the entirety of your life, you are encouraged to ask yourself:[267]

> If you feel superior because you are compassionate, and look down at those requiring your compassion?
> If you are grateful and humble before the Eternal One for having afforded you the ability to be compassionate?

You are further exhorted to equally query:[268]

> If you "try to give others the benefit of the doubt and to always look favourably upon them"?
> If your thoughts elevate you or leave you insecure, jealous, or haughty?

If you use your "gift of speech to express gratitude and appreciation and honor" to your fellow humankind, or to engage in slander, "complain, blame, criticize, and judge"?
If you behave in a dignified manner, displaying patience and courtesy, or if you rush around oblivious to the needs of others?
If in giving to those in need, you are doing so without seeking acknowledgement, or if you do so for self aggrandisement, believing yourself superior to the recipient?
If your personal needs, desires and expectations are "so tied into your ego needs that you neglect those that you love and regard"?
If arrogance and a lack of flexibility have in a given situation "prevented you from behaving in a way that required the nuance of truth and harmony"?

Having considered these questions with sincerity and truth, it is suggested that you perform the following exercise: "Express compassion in an anonymous fashion, not taking any personal credit."[269]

### Day 20—*Yesod* in *Tiferet*

היום עשרים יום
שהם שני שבועות וששה ימים לעומר
יסוד שבתפארת

ישמחו שמרם

Transliteration:
    *Ha-yom es'rim yom*
    *sheheim sh'nei shavu'ot v'shishah yamim la'omer*
    *Yesod sheb'Tiferet*
    Shin
    Yod-Shin-Mem-Chet-Vav
    Shin-Mem-Resh-Mem

Translation:
> Today is the twentieth day
> which is two weeks and six days of *Omer*.
> Foundation (Bonding) in Harmony (Beauty)
> Shin
> Yod-Shin-Mem-Chet-Vav
> Shin-Mem-Resh-Mem

**Comment:**

It is said that Bonding (*Yesod*) is required for Compassion (*Tiferet*) to be fully realised, and that this pertains to "creating a channel between giver and receiver. A mutuality that extends beyond the moment of need. A bond that continues to live on," which "is the most gratifying result of true compassion."[270]

In my estimation the concepts of *Yesod* (Bonding) in *Tiferet* (Compassion/Truth) pertaining to the twentieth day of the "Counting of the *Omer*," speak of reliability and commitment in the obligations underlying all manner of relationships in your life. These I believe are the underlying principles behind the statement that *Yesod* (Bonding/Foundation) "brings a quality of permanence and reliability to the *sefirah* of *tiferet*."[271] These principles and qualities are applicable in all relationships and commitments. In this regard, we are told that "the beautiful balance and truth of *tiferet*, when coupled with *yesod*, allows for a constancy in bonding that creates a fixed cornerstone to life's endeavours."[272]

In harmony with the spirit of this day, you are exhorted to ask yourself:

> If you bond with or stand apart from those for whom you have compassion?[273]
> If your interaction with those in need, derives entirely from a sense of pity, and whether "your interaction achieves anything beyond a single act of sympathy?"[274]
> "To whom are you bonded in complete harmony and truth such that you can be completely relied upon in both good and bad times to loyally give this other person your very best?"[275]

If your bond is "strong enough that you can convey messages the other may not wish to hear," and if this is mutual?[276]

To whom in your life do you feel completely connected," and how "you show that connection"?[277]

Once again, whilst keeping all principles perceived in mind, and having carefully evaluated yourself in terms of the listed queries, you are encouraged to work the following exercise: "Ensure that something eternal is built as a result of your compassion"[278]

### Day 21—*Malchut* in *Tiferet*

היום אחד ועשרים יום
שהם שלשה שבועות לעומר
מלכות שבתפארת

פ

וִירַנְנוּ

נָגִ"ד יְכַ"שׁ

Transliteration:
    Ha-yom echad v'esrim yom
    sheheim sh'loshah shavu'ot la'omer
    Malchut sheb'Tiferet
    Peh
    Vav-Yod-Resh-Nun-Nun-Vav
    NaGiDa YeiCheiSha

Translation:
    Today is the twenty-first day
    which is three weeks of *Omer*.
    Kingdom (Leadership) in Harmony (Beauty)
    Peh
    Vav-Yod-Resh-Nun-Nun-Vav
    NaGiDa YeiCheiSha

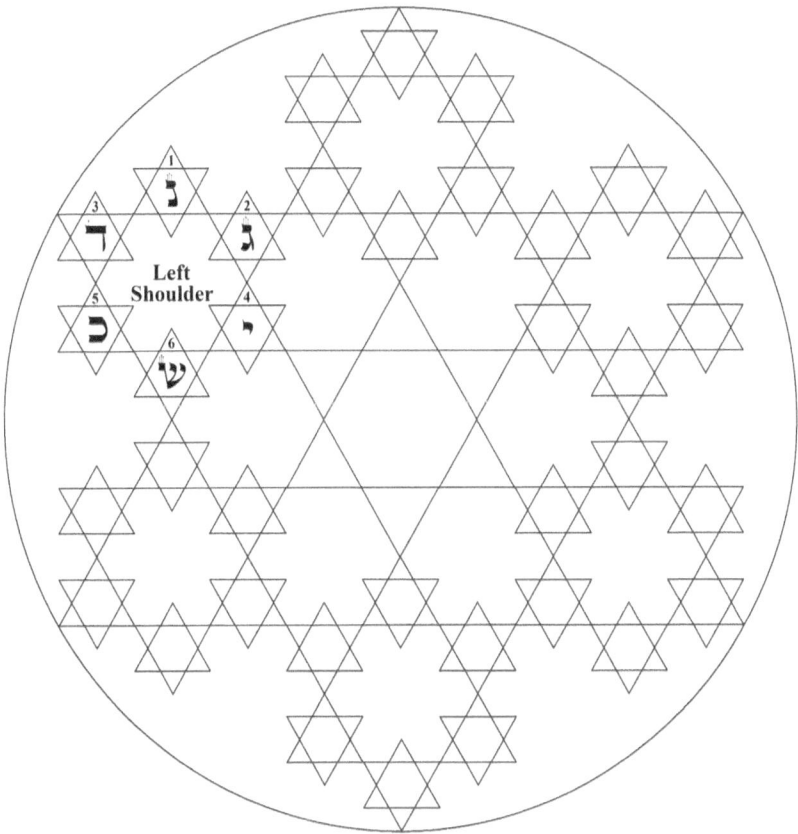

**Comment:**

At the conclusion of the third week of "Counting the *Omer*," we are examining the principles of *Malchut* (Dignity/Leadership/Nobility) in *Tiferet* (Compassion/Harmony/Truth) in our lives. In this regard, we are informed that "for compassion to be complete .....it must recognize and appreciate individual sovereignty. It should boost self-esteem and cultivate human dignity. Both your own dignity and the dignity of the one benefiting from your compassion."[279] It has been said that "*malchut* within *tiferet* is the epitome of the sefirah of *tiferet*."[280] Thus it is maintained that "when we independently choose to always act with kingship, dignity, leadership and nobility in our thoughts, speech, and actions, and in a way that reflects the truth and the beautiful balance that *tiferet* represents, we have mastered *malchut* within *tiferet*."[281]

However, *Malchut* is believed to be complete and fulfilled when it comprises the other six sefirotic qualities fully expressed within it, i.e. the qualities of *Chesed* (loving-kindness), *Gevurah* (restraint), *Tiferet* (balance), *Netzach* (endurance), *Hod* (humility), and *Yesod* (bonding) harmoniously interrelated and expressed whenever necessary in appropriate dosages. We are told that life continuously affords everyone "a chance to learn what truth is, and express it in harmonious ways throughout the day."[282] We are at times "presented with a life test where we are expected to actually implement this learned ability in a manner that serves as a model and inspiration for others."[283] To be able to deal with life in a wholesome manner, you need to be fully aware of your fallibilities. Owning up to your faults is in my estimation a sign of true spiritual growth. In this regard, you are advised to ask yourself:[284]

> If you can own up to some personal wrong doing, even when you know that the result might be painful?
> If you can perform a deed entirely out of character for the greater good, and recognise how this impacted your life?
> What is your greatest obstacle precluding you from "living a life of harmony and truth," and what you are willing to do to resolve this?

In terms of directing the Mercy of your Maker to your fellow humankind, i.e. expressing "complete compassion" (*Tiferet*) with "respectful dignity" (*Malchut*), you are encouraged to ask yourself:[285]

> If your compassion is "expressed in a dignified manner," and if you "manifest and emphasize majesty" in your compassion.
> If your compassion "elicit dignity in others"?
> If you are aware of the fact that in experiencing compassion as dignified, that "it will reflect reciprocally in the one who receives compassion"?

Having carefully considered the unique principles applying to this day, you are called upon to perform the following exercise: "Rather than just giving them charity help them help themselves in a fashion that strengthens their dignity."[286]

# WEEK 4—CORRECTING THE *SEFIRAH* OF *NETZACH*

The *sefirah* of *Netzach* (Victory/Endurance) is said to pertain to initiative, persistence, and determination to overcome.[287] In this regard, we informed that *Netzach* "stands for the active overcoming of obstacles, the conquest of anything that would interfere with the flow of divine energy."[288] The question arises as to exactly what one might consider to be interfering "with the flow of divine energy," and here opinions are going to vary so greatly, that it is highly likely that the variety of opinions regarding exactly what is and what is not "godly" is going to stir most "ungodly" religious arguments, accusations, and condemnations, i.e. a manifestation of not so sacred intolerance which will definitely "interfere with the flow of divine energy"!

In my estimation, what truly interrupts the flow of *Shefa* (Divine Abundance) in your life and world, is what my late mentor, William G. Gray, termed "the enemies within the gates." He noted that "these include all your faults, fallibilities and imperfections, to say nothing of any anti-human entities opposed to you making spiritual progress, and, on a broader scale, the obvious evils existing all over this earth,"[289] the latter being mainly of human making. William Gray noted that "life is a struggle, a fight, a constant conflict. Every one of us realises that. Against whom or what? Some would say "the Devil," others misfortune, others again fate or nature. All of these indicate external influences we are all up against. How many are enlightened enough to say: 'My own divided being?' The real battle of life begins and must end in one's self. That is the Victory we must gain here before we expect even the slightest sign of Perfect Peace Profound."[290]

As has been proven again and again, persistence and determination, qualities of *Netzach* (Victory/Endurance), are certainly necessary to overcome the worst in ourselves and in dealing with the vicissitudes of life. In this regard, we are informed that "endurance and ambition is a combination of determination and tenacity. It is a balance of patience, persistence and guts. Endurance is also being reliable and accountable, which establishes security and commitment.....It is an energy which comes from within and stops at nothing to achieve its goals."[291] We are further reminded that "effective endurance needs to encompass the following seven ingredients," i.e. all seven sefirotic qualities pertaining to the "Counting of the *Omer*," these being "love, discipline, compassion, endurance, humility, bonding and dignity,"[292] and regarding which it was written that "the problems people have with endurance and commitment are due to a lack of one or more of these seven components."[293]

### Day 22—*Chesed* in *Netzach*

היום שנים ועשרים יום
שהם שלשה שבועות ויום אחד לעומר
חסד שבנצה

ו

לאֻמִים בּרבּם

Transliteration:
>Ha-yom sh'nayim v'esrim yom
>sheheim sh'loshah shavu'ot v'yom echad la'omer
>Chesed sheb'Netzach
>Vav
>Lamed-Alef-Vav-Mem-Yod-Mem Bet-Resh-Bet- Mem

Translation:
>Today is the twenty-second day
>which is three weeks and one day of *Omer*.
>Loving-kindness (Mercy) in Endurance (Victory)
>Vav
>Lamed-Alef-Vav-Mem-Yod-Mem Bet-Resh-Bet- Mem

### Comment:

The sefirotic qualities applying to this day are *Chesed* (Loving-kindness) in *Netzach* (Endurance/Victory). It has been said the that *Netzach* is a "powerful raw force" which "can accomplish important objectives and goals,"[294] including establish "relationships that endure for a lifetime."[295] However, in terms of the guidance afforded by the principles of *Chesed* (Loving-kindness) in *Netzach* (Endurance), it is clear that "for anything to endure it needs to be loved,"[296] and that "a neutral or indifferent attitude will reflect in a marginal commitment."[297] It is for this reason that we are informed that endurance requires patience, that it can be counterproductive without love,[298] since "raw endurance can come across as harsh and aggressive, which undermines the cooperation of others."[299]

Thus we are told that employing *Netzach* (Endurance) without *Chesed* (Loving-kindness) is harsh, "which can result in isolation or distortion,"[300] and that "out of sheer determination one may often become controlling and demanding, driving others away."[301] We are therefore informed that "when the heart of *chesed* merges with the endurance of *netzach*, it helps to ensure that this attribute will be manifested in a loving, kind and considerate manner—a manner which makes a place for others and does not become severe or destructive to the human spirit."[302] In terms of this deliberation, you are encouraged to ask yourself:[303]

> If there are individuals within your circle of acquaintants who "insist on doing things only their way without seeking input from others," and what you could do to change this?
> If there are areas in which you appear harsh, demanding, stubborn and uncaring, and what you might do to work a change in this regard?
> If you are particularly impatient with certain individuals, and how you might alter this as a demonstration of Chesed (Loving-kindness) in Netzach (Endurance)?

In the light of the spirit of this day, Rabbi Simon Jacobson queried:[304]

> Whether your endurance is resulting in you appearing inflexible?
> Whether your "drive and determination" results in you being controlling and demanding?
> Whether all and sundry in your life are cooperating with you purely because of the enforcement of your will or out of love?
> Whether your endurance is unloving?

Whether you allow others to get hurt in order to get your own way?

Whether you believe "the end justifies the means," and whether you would stop at nothing to achieve your goals?

Whether you are still loving when your endurance prevails, and having overcome obstacles in your own way?

Whether you are driven by love or hate when you are defending yourself and others against unhealthy influences?

Having once again carefully considered the concepts and principles addressed here, you are encouraged to work the following exercise: "When fighting for something you believe in, pause a moment to ensure that it is accomplished in a loving manner."[305]

### Day 23—*Gevurah* in *Netzach*

היום שלשה ועשרים יום
שהם שלשה שבועות ושני ימים לעומר
גבורה שבנצח

ט

כי טהרם

Transliteration:
    *Ha-yom sh'loshah v'esrim yom*
    *sheheim sh'loshah shavu'ot u'sh'nei yamim la'omer*
    *Gevurah sheb'Netzach*
    *Tet*
    *Kaf-Yod Tet-Heh-Resh-Mem*

Translation:
    Today is the twenty-third day
    which is three weeks and two days of *Omer*.
    Might (Severity) in Endurance (Victory)
    *Tet*
    *Kaf-Yod Tet-Heh-Resh-Mem*

**Comment:**

The twenty-third day of "Counting the *Omer*" pertains to the sefirotic qualities of *Gevurah* (Strength/Discipline) in *Netzach* (Endurance). In this regard, you are advised to "examine the discipline of your endurance," since "endurance must be directed toward productive goals and expressed in a constructive manner."[306] We are reminded that *Netzach* (Endurance) is required in "achieving goals and objectives, establishing and building long-term relationships, serving God," and in "accomplishing one's mission in the world."[307]

Considered in terms of the principles applying this day in which *Gevurah* (Strength) is conjoined with *Netzach* (Endurance), we are told that "there is an added element of strength, discipline, and restraint that can have either a positive or negative effect. The effect is positive when *gevurah* expresses itself as self-control to modulate situations while, at the same time, energetically driving toward results. The effect is negative when the power of *gevurah* is used to achieve immoral, unethical and non-productive ends."[308] Keeping this in mind, you are encouraged to ask yourself:

> If you have "the enduring strength to break bad habits" and cultivate good ones in your life, and what you might do right away to facilitate the latter?[309]
> If your endurance come from strength or weakness, i.e. "does it come out of deep conviction or out of defensiveness?[310]
> If you are "tenacious out of stubbornness and an unwillingness to acknowledge errors"?[311]
> If your decisions are based on a personal agenda, which precludes you from reviewing them?[312]
> If you need to have a conversation with a loved one or a friend about your relationship, if you are mentally and emotionally prepared to have this interaction, and what you might do to ready yourself for it?[313]

If you have considered these questions in sincere honesty of heart, you are advised to work the following exercise: "Break one bad habit today."[314]

### Day 24—*Tiferet* in *Netzach*

היום ארבעה ועשרים יום
שהם שלשה שבועות ושלשה ימים לעומר
תפארת שבנצח

עׇ

תִשׁפוּט רוּחמִי

Transliteration:
    Ha-yom arba'ah v'esrim yom
    sheheim sh'loshah shavu'ot u'sh'loshah yamim la'omer
    Tiferet sheb'Netzach
    Ayin
    Tav-Shin-Peh-Vav-Tet Resh-Chet-Mem-Yod

Translation:
    Today is the twenty-fourth day
    which is three weeks and three days of *Omer*.
    Harmony (Beauty) in Endurance (Victory)
    Ayin
    Tav-Shin-Peh-Vav-Tet Resh-Chet-Mem-Yod

**Comment:**

The sefirotic qualities applying to the twenty-fourth day of the "Counting of the Omer" pertain to *Tiferet* (Harmony/Truth) in *Netzach* (Endurance). We are again reminded that endurance has both positive and negative aspects in its application, since "Netzach is a concentrated, dedicated momentum that achieves outcomes in every sphere of life."[315] In this regard, we are told that "that the "positive applications of *netzach* include tenacious and persistent efforts to achieve worthy goals," but that, on its own, *Netzach* (Endurance) "can easily become negative." Thus it is said that the inclusion of Tiferet (Harmony/Truth) results in "the drive and determination of *netzach*" being meaningfully "modulated by the balance and truth of *tiferet*, which respects boundaries and is considerate of multiple priorities, relationships, and responsibilities."[316] Thus, "the balance of *tiferet* influences *netzach* not to become so extreme that it consumes other life priorities and subtracts from the ability to maintain an integrated balance in all areas of life."[317]

This being said, we noted that compassion is equally a quality of *Tiferet*, and we are therefore informed that "healthy endurance, directed to develop good qualities and modifying bad ones, will always be compassionate."[318] In this regard, Rabbi Simon Jacobson noted "the compassion of endurance reflects a most beautiful quality of endurance: an enduring commitment to help another grow. Endurance without compassion is misguided and selfish. Endurance needs to be not just loving to those who deserve love, but also compassionate to the less fortunate."[319]

Having again carefully considered these points, you are advised to ask yourself:[320]

> If you are gracious in victory?
> If your determination compromises your compassion for others?
> If you are able to transcend your ego and empathize with competitors?

In terms of applying the principles of harmony and truth in your endurance, you might equally ask yourself:[321]

> Whether there is a lack of balance in your priorities, i.e. do you spend less time with loved ones than they require from you?
> Whether your health is suffering because of imbalances in your life, and what you might do to rectify this?
> How worthy your goals really are, and how persistent you are in achieving those goals, seeing them through without quitting?

Having considered all of the points raised, and attempted reasonable answers to the questions raised, you are advised to work the following exercise: "Be patient and listen to someone that usually makes you impatient."[322]

### Day 25—*Netzach* in *Netzach*

היום חמשה ועשרים יום
שהם שלשה שבועות וארבעה ימים לעומר
נצח שבנצח

מ

עַמִּים צִדְקָתֶךָ

Transliteration:

*Ha-yom chamishah v'esrim yom*
*sheheim sh'loshah shavu'ot v'arba'ah yamim la'omer*
*Netzach sheb'Netzach*
*Mem*
*Ayin-Mem-Yod-Mem Tzadi-Dalet-Kof-Tav-Chaf*

Translation:

Today is the twenty-fifth day
which is three weeks and four days of *Omer*.
Endurance (Victory) in Endurance (Victory)
Mem
Ayin-Mem-Yod-Mem Tzadi-Dalet-Kof-Tav-Chaf

### Comment:

The twenty-fifth day of "Counting the *Omer*" pertains to the concept of *Netzach* (Endurance) in *Netzach* (Endurance). This is said to pertain to "willpower and determination" which everyone has.[323] Thus we re told that all of us "have the capacity to endure much more than we can imagine, and to prevail under the most trying of circumstances."[324] In this regard, it has been correctly observed that *Netzach* (Endurance) "is the ability to steadfastly adhere to a path, whether positive or negative, to accomplish plans and goals, and to adhere to values and commitments. One that has *netzach* is able to stay focused on a course of action and be faithful to commitments whether in the physical, mental, emotional, or spiritual realm over extended periods of time."[325]

However, on this day we are facing, as it were, a double dose of *Netzach* (Endurance) for good or ill. Thus we are informed that "*netzach* within *netzach* is the extra power to reinforce pure *netzach* to produce an even more intensified drive and focused discipline to complete plans or goals. It is a booster that empowers endurance to stick to a path, objective or plan, whether good or bad, and to achieve its end."[326] It is therefore important that you ask yourself the following serious questions:[327]

> If you are stubbornly clinging to viewpoints that need to be reconsidered?
> What is the greatest challenge which is currently facing you, and if you are willing to commit yourself to this test, willingly enduring it in order to become a better person?
> If you display enduring commitment to those you love, and if they do the same towards you?

You should further ask yourself:[328]

> If your behaviour is erratic, i.e. inconsistent and unreliable, and, since you have will and determination, why this should be so?
> If you fear accessing your endurance and committing, if you are afraid that you might be trapped by commitment, and why this should be so?
> If "instead of cultivating endurance in healthy areas," you "developed a capacity for endurance of unhealthy experiences?"
> If you are enduring more pain than pleasure, and underestimate your capacity to endure?

The following exercise is recommended for this day: "Commit yourself to developing a new good habit."[329]

## Day 26—*Hod* in *Netzach*

היום ששה ועשרים יום
שהם שלשה שבועות וחמשה ימים לעומר
הוד שבנצח

׳

# מישור תמיד

Transliteration:
> Ha-yom shishah v'esrim yom
> sheheim sh'loshah shavu'ot v'chamishah yamim la'omer
> Hod sheb'Netzach
> Yod
> Mem-Yod-Shin-Vav-Resh Tav-Mem-Yod-Dalet

Translation:
> Today is the twenty-sixth day
> which is three weeks and five days of *Omer*.
> Splendour (Glory) in Endurance (Victory)
> Yod
> Mem-Yod-Shin-Vav-Resh Tav-Mem-Yod-Dalet

**Comment:**

This day pertains to the sefirotic principles of *Hod* (Humility) in *Netzach* (Endurance). We are informed that "*hod* within *netzach* introduces the ability to modify endurance with humility."[330] It is further stated that "*hod* influences *netzach* with the neutralizing factor of humility to keep it from becoming extreme in its intensity and thus harming our lives and others."[331] In this regard, we are told that "yielding—which is a result of humility—is an essential element of enduring."[332]

It is further maintained, that "true endurance sometimes requires the ability to yield or compromise appropriately rather than steadfastly clinging to a position once it becomes clear another course of actions is necessary."[333] This is applicable in all walks of life, and hence Rabbi Simon Jacobson wrote that "individuals have to learn this. Families have to learn this.

Business leaders have to learn this,"[334] because "standing fast can sometimes be a formula for destruction."[335]

We are also informed that "endurance is fueled by inner strength. *Hod* of *netzach* is the humble recognition and acknowledgement that the capacity to endure and prevail comes from the soul that God gave each person. This humility does not compromise the drive of endurance; on the contrary, it intensifies it, because human endurance can go only so far and endure only so much, whereas endurance that comes from the Divine soul is limitless."[336] Thus, if you clearly understood the vital messages shared here, you are advised to ask yourself:

> Whether you yield to the needs, requests, or demands of others too much or too little, and how can you rectify this?[337]
> Whether you know when to yield out of strength, or are you often afraid to yield?[338]
> Whether you attribute your success solely to your own strength and determination, and if this is due to you having convinced yourself that you are all powerful due to your level of endurance?[339]
> From whence you get the strength to endure in times when there appears to be no light at the end of the tunnel?[340]

Having again considered these questions most carefully, you are encouraged to work the following exercise: "When you awake, acknowledge God for giving you a soul with the extraordinary power and versatility to endure despite trying challenges. This will allow you to draw energy and strength for the entire day."[341]

### Day 27—*Yesod* in *Netzach*

היום שבעה ועשרים יום
שהם שלשה שבועות וששה ימים לעומר
יסוד שבנצח

Transliteration:
>Ha-yom shiv'ah v'esrim yom
>sheheim sh'loshah shavu'ot v'shishah yamim la'omer
>Yesod sheb'Netzach
>Mem
>Vav-Lamed-Alef-Vav-Mem-Yod-Mem Gimel-Mem-Lamed-Mem

Translation:
>Today is the twenty-seventh day
>which is three weeks and six days of *Omer*.
>Foundation (Bonding) in Endurance (Victory)
>Mem
>Vav-Lamed-Alef-Vav-Mem-Yod-Mem Gimel-Mem-Lamed-Mem

### Comment:

This twenty-seventh day of the "Counting of the *Omer*" relates to *Yesod* (Bonding) in *Netzach* (Endurance), or, as one commentator noted, "Bonding with Endurance."[342] In this regard, we are informed that "bonding is an essential quality of endurance," and that "endurance without bonding will not endure."[343] This is said to pertain to "unwavering commitment" to an individual, situation, experience, etc., which "you are bonding with, a commitment so powerful that you will endure all to preserve it. Endurance without bonding will not endure."[344]

It is maintained that whilst *Netzach* (Endurance) "can be a determined and steady force to accomplish goals," the union of *Netzach* (Endurance) with *Yesod* (Bonding) ensures the grounding of endurance, so that, while being resolute, we do not lose sight of the critical importance of maintaining strong relationships and worthy values."[346] In this regard, you might ask yourself:[347]

>Whether there are long standing disputes within your family or friendship circle requiring resolution, and what you might do about this situation?
>Whether there are individuals within your circle of acquaintances, whether they be relegated to be of the intimate or casual kind, of whom you are judgmental, and

how you might resolve these differences or perhaps adopt a neutral stance?

What are you doing to further greater unity, if not amongst the whole of humankind, at least amongst those who are closest to you?

Having considered the points addressed, and hopefully addressed the relevant queries, you are encouraged to work the following exercise: "To ensure that your new resolution should endure, bond with it immediately. This can be assured by promptly actualizing your resolution in some constructive deed."[348]

### Day 28—*Malchut* in *Netzach*

היום שמונה ועשרים יום
שהם ארבעה שבועות לעומר
מלכות שבנצח

Transliteration:
    *Ha-yom sh'monah v'esrim yom*
    *sheheim arba'ah shavu'ot la'omer*
    *Malchut sheb'Netzach*
    *Mem*
    *Bet-Alef-Resh-Tzadi*
    *BiTaRo TzaTaG'*

Translation:
    Today is the twenty-eighth day
    which is four weeks of *Omer*.
    Kingdom (Leadership) in Endurance (Victory)
    *Mem*
    *Bet-Alef-Resh-Tzadi*
    *BiTaRo TzaTaG'*

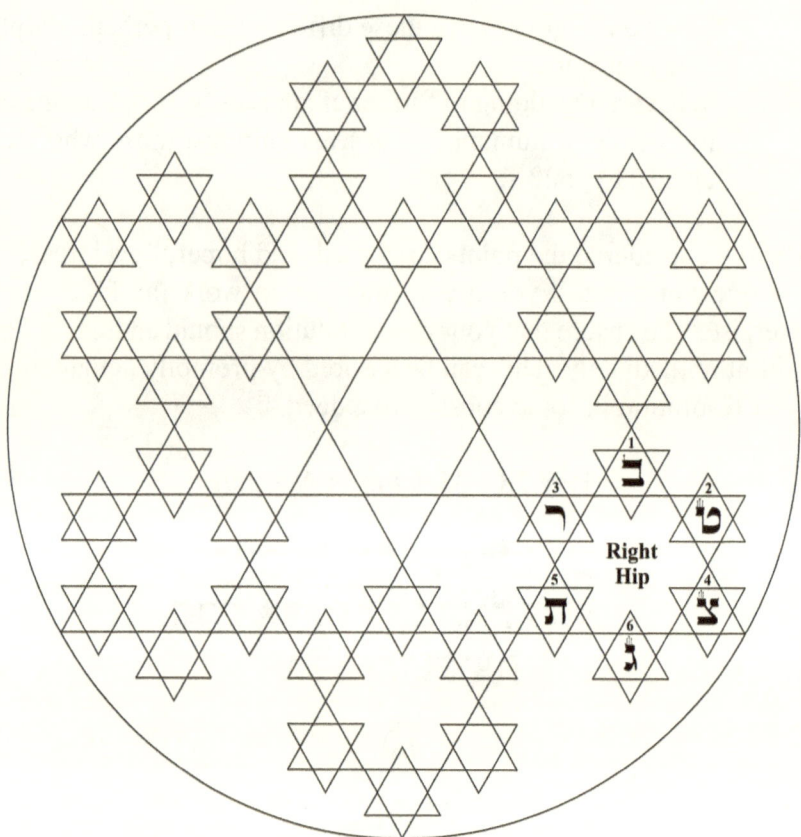

**Comment:**

The sefirotic qualities pertaining to the thirty-third day of "Counting the *Omer*" are *Malchut* (Sovereignty/Leadership/Nobility) in *Netzach* (Endurance). In this regard, it has been said that "sovereignty is the cornerstone of endurance."[349] We are told that the combination of *Malchut* (Leadership) in *Netzach* (Endurance) facilitates a holistic conjunction of all the *sefirot* in a "comprehensive way to ensure that our endurance is balanced and not distorted by extremes in our drive to actualize and achieve results."[350] *Malchut* in *Netzach* has been succinctly delineated "a steady course that incorporates a mature state of being that can overcome challenges and obstacles over time, while working towards a worthy outcome with dignity, sovereignty, leadership, and vision."[351]

Whilst keeping these details in mind, you are encouraged to ask yourself:

Whether your endurance is dignified, and bringing out the best in you?[352]

Amongst the many goals you have set yourself in your life, which have you achieved?[353]

What were the challenges you faced on your journey to the fulfilment of a goal, and what did you learn from the experience?[354]

Whether you are able to maintain a dignified, noble stance with your head held high when faced with hardships, rather than wallow in misery and cower in fear?[355]

Whether you are able to start again following a setback, or whether you submit and admit defeat?[356]

On this day you are encouraged to work the following exercise: "Fight for a dignified cause."[357]

## WEEK 5—CORRECTING THE *SEFIRAH* OF *HOD*

The *sefirah* of *Hod* is interpreted to be "Splendour," "Glory," "Majesty," "Acknowledgment," "Vigour," and, as I noted elsewhere, even "Beauty."[358] *Hod* is understood to be referencing "thinking," in contradistinction to *Netzach* which references "feeling." However, there is an affinity between what could be termed the "thinking-appreciation" as referenced by *Hod*, and the "feeling-appreciation" indicated by *Netzach*. I believe this to be expressed in the words "think" and "thank," both of which, as I mentioned previously, were derived from the same root.[359] This simply means a "thoughtful life" is a "thankful life," and that is in my estimation the reason why the *sefirah* of *Hod* is said to be referencing "humility." In this regard, Rabbi Simon Jacobson informs us that "if endurance is the engine of life humility is its fuel. As *gevurah* (discipline) gives *chesed* (love) focus, *hod* gives *netzach* direction."[360]

However, what should be understood right away is that the "humility" referenced here has absolutely nothing in common with the "false humility." In this regard, I previously observed how individuals, acting in the name of great "piety," employ "'humility' to intimidate and manipulate all and sundry in their vicinity into eating 'humble pie.' Sadly adopting a humble stance is in many instances itself a form of self-aggrandisement, e.g. 'there are none as humble [and as intolerant] as *we* are'."[361]

So how would one define the true humility referenced in the current instance in terms of the *sefirah* of *Hod*? We are told that "humility is modesty; it is recognizing how small you are which allows you to realize how large you can become."[362] Humility "is acknowledgement (from the root '*hoda'ah*'),"[363] and it indicates a condition of appreciation, i.e. thankfullness. In this regard, we are told that "it is saying 'thank you' to God,"[364] and that "it is clearly recognizing your qualities and strengths and acknowledging that they are not your own; they were given to you by God for a higher purpose than just satisfying your own needs."[365]

From a more personal angle, I once had an incredible, as it were, dream-vision in which I encountered the infinite vastness of "Divine Being," so to speak. Though all such experiences are inevitably modified in terms of the personal capacity of the experiencer, the impact of it left me with some understanding of the oft-quoted biblical phrase "the fear of the Lord is the beginning of Wisdom" (*Psalm 111:10*; *Proverbs 9:10*). The encounter left me with a profound sense of the meaning of true humility, which in my estimation is the most accurate assessment of comparison between "Cosmos" Itself and one single human being, regardless of how important that human may be in his or her own society. Yet, at the same time, I also realised that no matter how vast and superior "Cosmos" may be, it is still composed of its substructures which we call atoms, yet within which, we have recently proved, all the inherent "Power" resides. In relation to the "Cosmos," or "God" if you like (it's all the same), *WE* are such atoms.

Be that as it may, it is said that "*hod* (humility) is an umbrella under which its opposite on the *sefirot* tree—*netzach* (endurance)—is protected from harshness."[366] In fact, it has been noted that "humility is the silent partner of endurance. Its strength is in its silence. Its splendor in its repose. Humility leads to yielding, which is an essential element of Humility—and the resulting yielding—should not be confused with weakness and lack of self-esteem."[367] However, there is an important factor we need to keep in mind, and that is, as one commentator noted, that "when behaviors or actions are unworthy, *hod* is not a 'pushover'..... Rather, *hod* responds appropriately so as not to be mistakenly seen as endorsing negative opinions or actions through silence or inappropriate humbleness."[368]

In the previous week the focus was specifically on *Netzach* (Endurance), which we understood can be used for good or ill. It is for this reason that Rabbi Simon Jacobson maintains that "*Netzach* needs to be counterbalanced, and *hod* is a state of being that precludes, by its very definition, extreme acts of *netzach* that display exaggerated ego and self-centredness. Unbridled endurance must be tempered with humility in order to be healthy. Without *hod*, self-interests and unfettered desires can employ netzach to control every outcome and persist in pursuing distorted, selfish, unhealthy aims that adversely affect relationships and life in general."[369]

### Day 29—*Chesed* in *Hod*

היום תשעה ועשרים יום
שהם ארבעה שבועות ויום יאחד לעומר
חסד שבהוד

י

## תנהם וזסין

Transliteration:
> *Ha-yom tish'ah v'esrim yom*
> *sheheim arba'ah shavu'ot v'yom echad la'omer*
> *Chesed sheb'Hod*
> *Yod*
> *Tav-Nun-Heh-Mem Chet-Samech-Yod-Nun*

Translation:
> Today is the twenty-ninth day
> which is four weeks and one day of *Omer*.
> Loving-kindness (Mercy) in Splendour (Glory)
> *Yod*
> *Tav-Nun-Heh-Mem Chet-Samech-Yod-Nun*

**Comment:**

The sefirotic qualities pertaining to this day are *Chesed* (Lovingkindness) in *Hod* (Humility). In this regard, we are told that "healthy humility is not demoralizing," and that rather than fear, "it brings love and joy."[370] In the words of Rabbi Simon Jacobson, "humility that lacks love has to be re-examined for its authenticity."[371] He equally informs us that "humility can be confused with low self-esteem, which would cause it to be unloving."[372] It is said that *Hod*, "in its pure form, is free of any element of anger or arrogance," and that it "reflects an outward versus an inward, self-centered focus."[373]

In terms of the special qualities applying to the twenty-ninth day of "Counting the *Omer*," it has been correctly said that "when *chesed* combines with *hod*, humility is further accentuated with love and an even greater sensitivity and caring towards others."[374] It is further maintained that "humility brings love because it gives you the ability to rise above yourself and love another,"[375] and yet, we are equally reminded that *Hod* (humility) "does not manifest itself in weakness, but rather emanates from serene strength that seeks truth and understanding, and fosters harmony and peace."[376] Keeping these details in mind, you might ask yourself:[377]

> If you are "humble and happy or humble and miserable"?
> If your humility is resulting in you being "more loving and giving," or if it inhibits and constrains you?

You could further ask yourself:[378]

> Whether in you are offended "when people disagree with you," and end up in arguments rather than displaying humility?
> Whether, in dealing with others, you are able to "display patience, never becoming critical or judgmental," and how you might improve yourself to develop greater patience?

Having considered these questions, you are encouraged to work the following exercise: "Before praying with humility and acknowledgment of God, give some charity. It will enhance your prayers."[379]

### Day 30—*Gevurah* in *Hod*

היום שלשים יום
שהם ארבעה שבועות ושני ימים לעומר
גבורה שבהוד

שִׁ

סלֹה קדוּשׁ

Transliteration:
> *Ha-yom sh'loshim yom*
> *sheheim arba'ah shavu'ot u'sh'nei yamim la'omer*
> *Gevurah sheb'Hod*
> *Shin*
> *Samech-Lamed-Heh Kof-Dalet-Vav-Shin*

Translation:
> Today is the thirtieth day
> which is four weeks and two days of *Omer*.
> Might (Severity) in Splendour (Glory)
> *Shin*
> *Samech-Lamed-Heh Kof-Dalet-Vav-Shin*

**Comment:**

The thirtieth day of the "Counting of the *Omer*" incorporates the qualities of *Gevurah* (Discipline/Strength) in *Hod* (Humility/Splendour). In this regard, we are informed that "humility must be disciplined and focused."[380] Furthermore, since the qualities of respect and awe equally pertain to *Gevurah* (Strength), it is further maintained that "humility must include respect and awe for the person or experience you stand humble for."[381]

Whilst it is maintained that, from the perspective of the "Counting of the *Omer*, *Hod* (Humility) pertains to "looking outside of one's self and one's ego to understand another's perspective or position without becoming embroiled in unsettling conflict,"[382] it is also understood that there is a negative side to Hod, pertaining to the fact "that the people with whom we are interacting can interpret our silence or restraint as acceptance or recognition of their positions, opinions, or actions, even if these are immoral or unethical or even evil."[383]

We are also informed that *Gevurah* (Discipline/ Might) in *Hod* (Humility/Mindfulness) references "inner silence and the ability to intuit other people's viewpoints,"[384] in order to respond "in a disciplined, humble manner that makes a space for their convictions."[385] However, it is clearly understood that humility is not apathy, and that it "is devoid of jealousy, enmity, hatred, anger, arrogance, and other negative emotions,"[386] we are told that *Gevurah* (Discipline/Strength) in *Hod* (Humility) introduces "a balanced amount of discipline of strength, or restraint in *hod* when needed."[387] It "recognizes where we must assert ourselves in an appropriate, delicate manner, in order to clarify a position that could otherwise be taken as approval of an improper behavior."[388]

Keeping the ideas shared firmly in mind, you are encouraged to ask yourself:[389]

> When your humility is causing you to compromise, and when not, and equally when or when not your humility should cause you to compromise?
> Whether in the name of humility, you remain silent and fail to respond in the face of injustice and wickedness?
> Whether your humility is wanting, because you do not respect others?

And equally, whether you are employing humility to manipulate, control, and even insult others?

In terms of the spirit of this day, you are exhorted to perform the following exercise: "Focus in on your reluctance in any give area to see if it originates from a healthy, humble place."[390]

## Day 31—*Tiferet* in *Hod*

הַיּוֹם אֶחָד וּשְׁלֹשִׁים יוֹם
שֶׁהֵם אַרְבָּעָה שָׁבוּעוֹת וּשְׁלֹשָׁה יָמִים לָעוֹמֶר
תִּפְאֶרֶת שֶׁבְּהוֹד

ו

יוֹדוּךְ בָּרוֹב

Transliteration:
   Ha-yom echad v'sh'loshim yom
   sheheim arba'ah shavu'ot u'sh'loshah yamim la'omer
   Tiferet sheb'Hod
   Vav
   Yod-Vav-Dalet-Vav-Chaf Bet-Resh-Vav-Bet

Translation:
   Today is the thirty-first day
   which is four weeks and three days of *Omer*.
   Harmony (Beauty) in Splendour (Glory)
   Vav
   Yod-Vav-Dalet-Vav-Chaf Bet-Resh-Vav-Bet

**Comment:**

The thirty-third day of "Counting the *Omer*" incorporates the sefirotic qualities of *Tiferet* (Harmony/Compassion) in *Hod* (Splendour/ Humility). These principles are said to indicate that "just as humility brings compassion, compassion can lead one to humility,"[391] and that "if you lack humility, try acting compassionately, which can help bring you humility."[392] However, it is stated that "*Tiferet* within *hod* puts us on a path of aligning with the greater truth of our existence," which we are told pertains to "an 'inner essential I',"[393] which you share with every person in existence.

We are reminded that "that 'I' is God," and that "by ourselves we are nothing, but in and of God, we are a part of the

Essential Self.'"394 Hence, in my estimation, it is all a question of "separateness" and "oneness." In this regard, we are informed that your own "'inner essential I'.....only has relevance as part of the 'Great Essential I,' the One God."395 Thus, *Hod* pertaining to "humility," and "mindfulness" for that matter, is said "to be a way to begin the way back by helping us re-align our true self with the 'Essential Self'."396

However, it has been said that "*hod* can be motivated by either an appropirate level or an overabundance of *chesed* or *gevurah*. But when *hod* is influenced by *tiferet*, *hod* achieves the proper delicate balance necessary."397 In this regard, it is maintained that *Hod* (Humility) "does not provide undeserved approval, nor is it overly critical or silent, and that "when influenced by tiferet, emphasizes truth and balance and is not misguided, weak, or inappropriate, but rather a beautiful and balanced reaction to every relationship or situation."398

Once again, keeping this vital teaching in mind, you are encouraged to "examine if your humility is compassionate,"399 and to ask yourself:400

> If your humility is causing you "to be self-contained and anti-social, or does it express itself in empathy for others"?
> If your humility is "balanced and beautiful," or if it is awkward?

On the other hand you might ask yourself:401

> Whether you "socialize in a balanced way," and, if not, what you might do about it?
> Whether you are fully aware when to yield and be flexible, and when to set limits in your interaction with others?
> Whether you "display balanced empathy for others and an interest in their thoughts, words, and actions"?

In conclusion, you are encouraged to work the following exercise: "Express a humble feeling in an act of compassion."402

## Day 32—*Netzach* in *Hod*

היום שנים ושלשים יום
שהם ארבעה שבועות וארבעה ימים לעומר
נצח שבהוד

ר

עָמִים טוֹבֵךְ

Transliteration:
>Ha-yom sh'nayim v'sh'loshim yom
>sheheim arba'ah shavu'ot v'arba'ah yamim la'omer
>Netzach sheb'Hod
>Resh
>Ayin-Mem-Yod-Mem Tet-Vav-Bet-Chaf

Translation:
>Today is the thirty-second day
>which is four weeks and four days of *Omer*.
>Endurance (Victory) in Splendour (Glory)
>Resh
>Ayin-Mem-Yod-Mem Tet-Vav-Bet-Chaf

**Comment:**

The sefirotic qualities pertaining to the thirty-second day of the "Counting of the *Omer*" are *Netzach* (Endurance) in *Hod* (Humility). In this regard, we are told that "humility should not cause one to feel weak and insecure," and furthermore that "netzach of hod underscores the fact that true humility does not make you into a 'doormat' for others to step on; on the contrary, humility gives you enduring strength."[403] This is further emphasized in the observation that those who master the sefirotic qualities pertaining to this day, "are able to remain positively humble and modestly appropriate when asserting" their position "in a clear, grounded manner, even in the face of arrogant behavior. In such a case, netzach imbues hod with endurance so that it is able to stand its ground in a respectful manner."[404] We are therefore told that "when we steadfastly choose to think, speak, and act with humility in all situations, we have achieved netzach within hod. We accustom ourselves to listen carefully to all, thinking quietly about the person and the topic, and determining if and how we should react."[405]

Keeping once again these thoughts firmly in mind, you are urged to "examine the strength and endurance of your humility," and ask yourself:[406]

> If your humility can withstand challenges?
> If you are holding firm positions, or "waffle in the name of humility"?
> If your humility is perceived as weakness, as a result of which others are able to take advantage of you?

Additionally you might ask yourself:[407]

> Whether you have "established enduring, reasonable personal boundaries for the sake of" your "physical, emotional, and spiritual wellbeing," which no-one, yourself included, can violate?
> Whether in your relationships, you have remained silent in instances of improper behaviour, and what precluded you from speaking out?
> Whether you are able to encourage those "who may lack the confidence or ability to express" themselves, to bring out their "inner voice"?

You are encouraged to work the following exercise applicable to this day: "Demonstrate the strength of your humility by initiating or actively participating in a good cause."[408]

### Day 33—*Hod* in *Hod*

היום שלשה ושלשים יום
שהם ארבעה שבועות וחמשה ימים לעומר
הוד שבהוד

ו

אלהים נהל

Transliteration:
> Ha-yom sh'loshah u'sh'loshim yom
> sheheim arba'ah shavu'ot v'chamisha yamim la'omer
> Hod sheb'Hod
> Vav
> Alef-Lamed-Heh-Yod-Mem Nun-Heh-Lamed

Translation:
> Today is the thirty-third day
> which is four weeks and five days of *Omer*.
> Splendour (Glory) in Splendour (Glory)
> Vav
> Alef-Lamed-Heh-Yod-Mem Nun-Heh-Lamed

### Comment:

The thirty-third day of "Counting the *Omer*" incorporates the qualities of *Hod* (Humility/Mindfulness) in *Hod* (Humility), which we are reminded pertains to "humility in its purest form."[409] In this regard, we are informed that "when we demonstrate complete respect for ourselves, others, and God in our thought, speech, and action, and in all situations, no matter how stressful, we have mastered *hod* within *hod*."[410]

However, we are advised that "humility must also be examined for its genuineness."[411] In this regard, I am reminded of feigned humility which is a mask for arrogance and aggression, i.e. humility being employed as a tool towards selfish, or even self-aggrandising, ends. In this regard, I am reminded of the story of a highly esteemed Rabbi resting on a bench, and being overseen by two disciples who rapturously pondered the greatness of their astute leader. Looking at the peaceful countenance of the resting figure, the one disciple exclaimed "What a *Tzadik!* He is the kindest, most thoughtful person in the whole world!" "And so selfless," interjected the second, "he sacrifices himself every minute of every day for our wellbeing!" This went on for a while, until they eventually fell silent, having reached the stage where they could not find anything more to say. It is then that the Rabbi opened an eye to behold them, and retorted "And about my humility you say nothing!"

I believe it is for this reason that it is maintained that you "learn to cultivate your humility by interacting with people who are more refined than yourself, evoking in you modesty and humility that motivates you to grow."[412] In this regard, the principles of *Hod* (humility) in *Hod* (humility) are said to mean "that we not only refrain from judging or criticizing others, but we also do not view ourselves as superior to them, no matter how unlearned or how crude they appear to be."[413] This is beautifully summarised in the statement that "when we have mastered *hod* within *hod*, we are always empathetic and interested in the thoughts, wellbeing, and condition of others, seeking out ways to help, without ever seeking honor or public credit for acts of giving. We share our thoughts or make gentle suggestions without ever lording over any other human being."[414]

Keeping again the wonderful concepts shared in mind, you are urged to ask yourself:[415]

> Whether you are afraid to be too humble, and hence mask it with aggressive behaviour?
> Whether your humility is really humble, or just an expression of arrogance?
> Whether you are taking pride in your humility, flaunting it, and making it self-serving?
> Whether your humility is genuine or "part of a crusade," i.e. do you have expectations for being humble?

You should further ask yourself:[416]

> Whether you expect recognition and honour when you do something special?
> Whether you have enough inherent faith to make it through the challenges you have to face?
> In what manner you demonstrate an interest in the lives of others around you?

In conclusion you are exhorted to work the following exercise applicable to this day: "Be humble just for its own sake."[417]

## Day 34—*Yesod* in *Hod*

היום ארבעה ושלשים יום
שהם ארבעה שבועות וששה ימים לעומר
יסוד שבהוד

לֶ

יוֹדוֹךְ עֲדָתְךָ

Transliteration:
> *Ha-yom arba'ah u'sh'loshim yom*
> *sheheim arba'ah shavu'ot v'shishah yamim la'omer*
> *Yesod sheb'Hod*
> *Lamed*
> *Yod-Vav-Dalet-Vav-Chaf Ayin-Dalet-Tav-Chaf*

Translation:
> Today is the thirty-fourth day
> which is four weeks and six days of *Omer*.
> Foundation (Bonding) in Splendour (Glory)
> *Lamed*
> *Yod-Vav-Dalet-Vav-Chaf Ayin-Dalet-Tav-Chaf*

### Comment:

The thirty-fourth day of the "Counting of the *Omer*" pertains to *Yesod* (Bonding) in *Hod* (Humility). It is said "unity" is "the essence of *Yesod* within *Hod*," and that "*yesod* within *hod* is the ability to perceive the essence of another person or situation."[418] In this regard, we are told that "humility should not be a lonely experience. It ought to result in deep bonding and commitment. There is no stronger bond than one that comes out of humility."[419]

We are further informed that, whilst "*hod* in its purest form is the polar opposite of jealousy, enmity, anger, hatred, resentment, and arrogance, all of which are rooted in self-centeredness," it is understood that "when *yesod* within *hod* is added to the mix, relationships are balanced by a give-and-take dynamic which, in turn, leads to harmonious acceptance."[420] Therefore, it is emphasized that "when we have truly established a connection with something outside of ourselves, and when we display genuine humility, we are fully aware of our core that we could never abuse or otherwise harm another person, animal, or object. Humility includes bonding and having respect for other living creatures, as well as for the environment."[421]

Having considered the thoughts shared on this day, and keeping these in mind, you are encouraged to ask yourself:

If your humility is separating you from others, or bringing you closer?[422]
If your humility yields results, whether short term or long term?[423]
If your humility is establishing a firm, reliable foundation upon which you and others can build.[424]
Whether you have succeeded in bonding with humility to those who are dear to you?[425]

It is recommended that you conclude by working the following exercise: "Use your humility to build something lasting."[426]

### Day 35—*Malchut* in *Hod*

היום חמשה ושלשים יום
שהם חמשה שבועות לעומר
מלכות שבהוד

**Transliteration:**
*Ha-yom chamisha u'sh'loshim yom*
*sheheim chamisha shavu'ot la'omer*
*Malchut sheb'Hod*
*Alef*
*Ayin-Mem-Yod-Mem*
*CheKeVa TiN'I*

Translation:
> Today is the thirty-fifth day
> which is five weeks of *Omer*.
> Kingdom (Rulership) in Splendour (Glory)
> *Alef*
> Ayin-Mem-Yod-Mem
> CheKeVa TiN'I

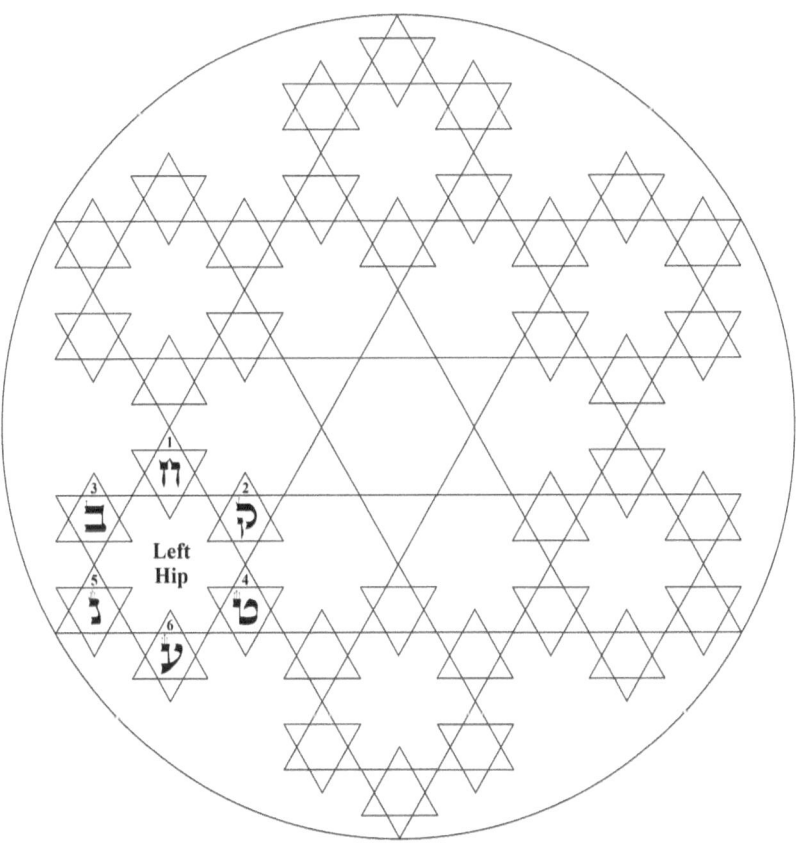

**Comment:**

The concluding day of the seven comprising the fifth week of the "Counting of the *Omer*" pertains to *Malchut* (Leadership/Rulership) in *Hod* (Humility). We are told "walking humbly is walking tall. Dignity is the essence of humility and modesty."[427] It is further stated "humility that suppresses the human spirit and denies individual sovereignty is not humility at all."[428] In this regard, it has been said that *Hod* "is a combination of patience and faith, which enables us to see the beauty and positive aspects of every person and situation despite life's interfering static."[429] Furthermore, we are told that "when *malchut* combines with *hod*, we are able to uplift relationships and situations to a higher level because malchut adds a noble presence - not through a display of ego, arrogance, or superiority, but rather through the very absence of these self-absorbed traits. This *sefirah* combination teaches us how to become vessels to receive the goodness of others, thus revealing God's majestic oneness in the world."[430]

Having reached the conclusion of the fifth week of "Counting the *Omer*," you are encouraged to ask yourself:

> Whether those around you consider you to be a humble person?[431]
> Whether your humility makes you feel dignified., and leaving you with a sense of being vibrant and alive?[432]
> Whether you show appropriate decorum and respect to everyone you encounter in your daily life, and if not, what you might do to rectify this situation?[433]

Having considered these questions, you are urged to work the following exercise: "Teach someone how humility and modesty enhance human dignity."[434]

---

## WEEK 6—CORRECTING THE *SEFIRAH* OF *YESOD*

The *sefirah* of *Yesod* (Foundation) is associated with sexuality, i.e. "Bonding." In this regard, Rabbi Simon Jacobson wrote that "Bonding is the ultimate emotional connection." He pointed out that "while the first five qualities (love, discipline, compassion, endurance and humility) are interactive, they manifest duality: the lover and the beloved. The emphasis is on an individual's feelings, not necessarily on mutuality. Bonding, on the other hand, is a complete fusion of the two."[435] Of course, the "bonding" reference here is not to sexuality *per se*, but rather to union on all levels of being. However, whilst here we are considering the principle of "bonding" from lofty perspectives, I believe it would be wrong to exclude the bonding of "sexuality." I trust that this what is meant by the statement that "the foundation of *Yesod* is different from an ordinary foundation. It does not just rest beneath the higher levels of the structure, but encompasses them all."[436]

Whilst some readers might suppose there is no spiritual element possible to sex, careful consideration will soon clarify that there are quite a number of spiritual elements present. For example, if the meaning of "God is Love [אהבה—*Ahavah*]") be taken literally, then thoughts connected with sexual stimulation should logically be classified with "God interests" also. Aroused sexual feelings should be synonymous with attraction to Divinity. In other words, sex and God should be simultaneous, and in one the other ought to be manifest. Only when we "want God" as passionately and urgently as we need sexual expression, will that expression of Infinity contact us.

The primary factor behind the principle of "bonding," the very foundation (*Yesod*) of existence on all levels, is the principle of "love." In this regard, I noted elsewhere that "'God is Love' used to be a favourite expression when so very few really understood what was meant by that phrase, except perhaps instinctively. Literally it is quite true, though we have used the word 'love' so casually, it has lost value. How shall we revalue it again? Interestingly, by rearrangement of the word we get *EVOL*(ve) out of it, and I firmly believe that our evolution godwards comes from our ability to really *love*."[437] The ever popular Kahlil Gibran noted that "The Power to love is God's greatest gift to man, for it never will be taken from the blessed who loves."[438]

Love is such a *VITAL* thing—yet it can be deadly, in the sense of losing oneself utterly into it. Indeed there is also the pain of love on all planes of existence, and most people know that "love hurts." That is why the ancients showed the bow of Eros as being fitted with an unlikely bowstring of bees. Love sang a soothing song like the humming of bees, yet it could sting painfully afterwards. I think it is with this in mind that Gibran maintained that "Man cannot reap love until after sad and revealing separation, and bitter patience, and desperate hardship."[439] However, I firmly believe that only genuine *Love* can release locked-up love, this being something beyond a matter of bodies and personalities. This is a unique "bonding" which is out of this world altogether, and absolutely separate from physical plane manifestations, a union so deep, true and absolute that it transcends incarnation and the events thereof altogether.

In this regard, Rabbi Jacobson noted that "without bonding no feeling can be truly realized. Bonding means connecting; not only feeling for another, but being attached to him. Not just a token commitment, but total devotion. It creates a channel between giver and receiver. Bonding is eternal. It develops an everlasting union that lives on forever through the perpetual fruit it bears. Bonding is the foundation of life. The emotional spine of the human psyche. Every person needs bonding to flourish and grow. The bonding between mother and child; between husband and wife; between brothers and sisters; between close friends. Bonding is affirmation; it gives one the sense of belonging; that 'I matter,' 'I am significant and important.' It establishes trust—trust in yourself and trust in others. It instills confidence. Without bonding and nurturing we cannot realize and be ourselves."[440]

We are told that whilst *Yesod* (Foundation) "is the healthy facility to bond with others.....It is also peace and grounding."[441] In this regard, it has been written that "bonding channels all five previous qualities into a constructive bond, giving it the meaning 'foundation'."[442] This is meaningfully highlighted in the statement that "the 'foundation' and grounding aspect of yesod occurs when one weaves all six of the *sefirot*," i.e. *Chesed* (loving-kindness); *Gevurah* (Discipline); *Tiferet* (Harmony); *Netzach* (Endurance); *Hod* (Humility); and *Yesod* (Foundation), "into a six-ply chord that creates the potential for honest, mutual, mature, and grounded bonding in all types of relationships."[443]

In summary Rabbi Simon Jacobson wrote that "whereas all other human feelings are individual emotions, separate storeys of a building, each a necessary component of human experience, bonding, channels and integrates them all into one bond which creates a foundation upon which the structure of human emotions firmly stands. Bonding is giving all of yourself not just part; it is not one emotion but all of them."[444]

## Day 36—*Chesed* in *Yesod*

היום ששה ושלשים יום
שהם חמשה שבועות ויום אחד לעומר
חסד שביסוד

מ

כולם יחיד

Transliteration:
*Ha-yom shishah u'sh'loshim yom*
*sheheim chamishah shavu'ot v'yom echad la'omer*
*Chesed sheb'Yesod*
*Mem*
*Kaf-Vav-Lamed-Mem Yod-Chet-Yod-Dalet*

Translation:
Today is the thirty-six day
which is five weeks and one day of *Omer*.
Loving-kindness (Mercy) in Foundation (Bonding)
*Mem*
*Kaf-Vav-Lamed-Mem Yod-Chet-Yod-Dalet*

**Comment:**

The thirty-sixth day of the "Counting of the *Omer*" pertains to *Chesed* (Mercy/Loving-kindness) in *Yesod* (Foundation/Bonding). In terms of *Yesod* being the *sefirah* referencing the "Foundation" of our existence, we are reminded that "love establishes a reliable base which allows bonding to build," that "love is the heart of bonding," that "you cannot bond without love."[445] In this regard it has been noted that "Bonding without love lacks the emotional glue and security that the *sefirah* of *chesed* brings to the building of foundational relationships, whether between self and God, self and other, or self and self."[446] Hence it is emphasized that the sefirotic principles applicable to this day pertain to *Chesed* being "a living force that sustains, nourishes, and grows as it deepens the bonding within enduring relationships."[447]

That being said, the survival of any loving relationship is not based on what you get out of it, but rather on what you put into it. This is why it is so important that *ha-Yetzer ha-Ra* ("the evil inclination"), referencing the "desire to receive," should be balanced with "*ha-Yetzer ha-Tov*" ("the good inclination"), i.e. the "desire to give." We are all familiar with what happens when two people "fall in love." There is an intense "desire to give" between the lovers, which is much stronger than the "desire to receive." This is a wonderful condition to be in, and should be maintained throughout the duration of the relationship. In fact, the "desire to give" should be continuously cultivated much more than the "desire to receive," if both parties desire their "bonding" to endure. Furthermore, at no stage in a relationship should there be a measuring of personal input, because the instant any party express the sentiment that the other could never compensate what he/she brought to the relationship, the alliance is factually over.

Since *Yetzer ha-Tov* ("desire to give") equates with *Chesed* (Loving-kindness) and *Yetzer ha-ra* ("desire to receive) aligns with *Gevurah* (Might), it is clear that cultivating the "good inclination" (*Yetzer ha-Tov*) in a relationship is equal to cultivating love. It is from this "giving" perspective that one can see the total sense of *Chesed* (Loving-kindness) being "a living force that sustains, nourishes, and grows as it deepens the bonding within enduring relationships."[448] Hence Rabbi Jacobson suggested that "if you have a problem bonding, examine how much you love the one (or the object) you wish to bond with."[449]

Having again considered the unique concepts applicable to this day, and keeping these in mind, you are encouraged to ask yourself:

> Whether you are trying to bond without first fostering a loving attitude?[450]
> Whether your bonding is expressed in a loving manner?[451]
> What actions you might take to restore a breach in a relationship?[452]
> Whether you have ever extended yourself and given to another person whom you did not know, why you did it, and how it made you feel?[453]

In conclusion, you are encouraged to work the following exercise applicable to this day: "Demonstrate the bond you have with your child or friend through an act of love."[454]

### Day 37—*Gevurah* in *Yesod*

היום שבעה ושלשים יום
שהם חמשה שבועות ושני ימים לעומר
גבורה שביסוד

ארץ גאה

Transliteration:
*Ha-yom shiv'ah u'sh'loshim yom*
*sheheim chamishah shavu'ot u'sh'nei yamim la'omer*
*Gevurah sheb'Yesod*
*Yod*
*Alef-Resh-Tzadi Gimel-Alef-Heh*

Translation:
Today is the thirty-seventh day
which is five weeks and two days of *Omer*.
Might (Severity) in Foundation (Bonding)
*Yod*
*Alef-Resh-Tzadi Gimel-Alef-Heh*

**Comment:**

The thirty-seventh day of the "Counting of the *Omer*" pertains to *Gevurah* (Discipline/Strength) in *Yesod* (Foundation/Bonding). On this day you are encouraged to "examine the discipline of your bonding."[455] After all, it has been correctly stated that "bonding must be done with discretion and careful consideration with whom and with what you bond," since "even the healthiest and closest bonding needs 'time out,' a respect for each individual's space."[456] However, we are also told that *Gevurah* in *Yesod* "is displayed when strength, restraint, and/or discipline assist bonding in difficult times that can put stress upon relationships."[457] In other words, relying on the discipline of inner strength (*Gevurah*), we can respond in a meaningful manner, "in order to facilitate the delicate balance required to preserve relationships."[458] In this regard, it is said that how "we sensitively respond to another is paramount in keeping relationships healthy and uplifted,"[459] and that *Gevurah* (Discipline/Strength) aids the maintenance of relationships, i.e. *Yesod* (Bonding/Foundation), "through restraint, thoughtfulness, wisdom, and understanding."[460]

Keeping again these vital concepts in mind, you are urged to ask yourself:[461]

> Whether you "overbond, i.e. whether you are too dependent on the one you bond with, or vice versa for that matter?
> Whether you have established a bond/relationship out of desperation?
> Whether the bond/relationship you share with others is healthy, and incorporating wholesome people?

Having responded to these questions in a manner most meaningful to yourself, you are encouraged to work the following exercise applicable to this day: "Review the discipline in your bonding experiences to see if it needs adjustment."[462]

### Day 38—*Tiferet* in *Yesod*

היום שמונה ושלשים יום
שהם חמשה שבועות ושלשה ימים לעומר
תפארת שביסוד

מ

נתנה לעמך

Transliteration:
   Ha-yom sh'monah u'sh'loshim yom
   sheheim chamishah shavu'ot u'sh'loshah yamim la'omer
   Tiferet sheb'Yesod
   Mem
   Nun-Tav-Nun-Heh Lamed-Ayin-Mem-Chaf

Translation:
> Today is the thirty-eighth day
> which is five weeks and three days of *Omer*.
> Harmony (Beauty) in Foundation (Bonding)
> *Mem*
> Nun-Tav-Nun-Heh Lamed-Ayin-Mem-Chaf

**Comment:**

The thirty-eighth day of "Counting the *Omer*" pertains to the concept of *Tiferet* (Harmony/Compassion) in *Yesod* (Foundation/Bonding). We are told that "*Yesod* is the bedrock of all relationships,"[463] and that when we achieve the mastery of *Tiferet* (Empathy) in *Yesod* (Bonding), we could ensure "that all our relationships are built on a foundation of trust, loyalty, and truth."[464] However, it has also been truthfully said that "bonding needs to be not only loving but also compassionate, feeling your friend's pain and empathizing with him."[465] Hence we are informed that with the support of *Tiferet* (Compassion) in *Yesod* (Bonding), "a proportionately balanced and mature equilibrium of bonding becomes harmonious and beautiful in its expression."[466] Keeping this information in mind, you might ask yourself:

> Whether your bonding or relationships are conditional, and whether you tend to withdraw in discomfort when faced with the difficulties of a friend, associate or companion.[467]
> Whether you can identify any of your relationships which you are aware of being unbalanced, and what you might do to improve it?[468]
> Whether you can identify a relationship in which you feel there is a good balance between giving and receiving?[469]
> What you consider to be a "dominant trait you have to balance better so that your relationships can improve"?[470]

Having considered the principles and queries addressed on this day, you are advised to work the following relevant exercise: "Offer help and support in dealing with an ordeal of someone you have bonded with."[471]

### Day 39—*Netzach* in *Yesod*

היום תשעה ושלשים יום
שהם חמשה שבועות וארבעה ימים לעומר
נצח שביסוד

**ב**

**יבולה פנה**

Transliteration:
*Ha-yom tish'ah u'sh'loshim yom
sheheim chamishah shavu'ot v'arba'ah yamim la'omer
Netzach sheb'Yesod
Bet
Yod-Bet-Vav-Lamed-Heh Peh-Nun-Heh*

Translation:
Today is the thirty-ninth day
which is five weeks and four days of *Omer*.
Endurance (Victory) in Foundation (Bonding)
Bet
Yod-Bet-Vav-Lamed-Heh Peh-Nun-Heh

**Comment:**

On this day we consider the qualities of *Netzach* (Victory/Endurance) in *Yesod* (Foundation/Bonding). In this regard, we are reminded that "an essential component of bonding is its endurance," this being "its ability to withstand challenges and setbacks," and that "without endurance there is no chance to develop true bonding."[472] Hence it is emphasized that "*netzach* within *yesod* translates into consistent and enduring effort to both establish and maintain the foundation of relationships and keep them healthy and everlasting."[473] That being said, we are warned that *Netzach* (Endurance) "is a driving quality that must always be applied carefully and in the right amounts to preserve bonding without smothering the independence of another,"[474] and in summary we are told that "Healthy bonding, reinforced by *netzach*, is essential because, without it, relationships are shallow, lack substance, permanence, and trust."[475]

In terms of these vital concepts, you are exhorted to ask yourself:[476]

> Whether you are totally committed to those you bond with?
> How much you will endure and how ready you are to fight to maintain this bond?
> Whether the individual(s) you bond with is/are aware of your devotion?

Following these deliberations, you are advised to work the following exercise applicable to this day: "Demonstrate the endurance level of your bonding by confronting a challenge that obstructs the bond."[477]

### Day 40—*Hod* in *Yesod*

היום ארבעים יום
שהם חמשה שבועות וחמשה ימים לעומר
הוד שביסוד

Transliteration:
*Ha-yom arba'im yom*
*sheheim chamishah shavu'ot v'chamishah yamim la'omer*
*Hod sheb'Yesod*
*Alef*
*Yod-Bet-Resh-Kaf-Nun-Vav Zayin-Vav-Kaf-Resh-Yod*

Translation:
Today is the fortieth day
which is five weeks and five days of *Omer*.
Splendour (Glory) in Foundation (Bonding)
*Alef*
*Yod-Bet-Resh-Kaf-Nun-Vav Zayin-Vav-Kaf-Resh-Yod*

## Comment:

On this day we focus on the qualities of *Hod* (Humility/Thoughtfulness) in *Yesod* (Bonding/Foundation). In this regard, Rabbi Simon Jacobson informs us that "humility is crucial in healthy bonding," because "arrogance divides people. Preoccupation with your own desires and needs separates you from others."[478] He noted that humility brings a greater appreciation and bonding with another individual, emphasizing that "bonding that is just an extension of your own needs is only bonding tighter with yourself," and that "healthy bonding is the union of two distinct people, with independent personalities, who join for a higher purpose than satisfying their own needs."[479] In this regard, we are reminded that bonding (*Yesod*) is enhanced by humility (*Hod*) "with sincere, appropriate and considerate expression of gratitude and appreciation of the give-and-take between self and God, self and other, and self and self."[480]

We are told that *Hod* (Humility/Mindfulness) in *Yesod* (Bonding/Foundation) "helps us to always express our thoughts, speech, and actions in a manner that does not take another person for granted but rather demonstrates our desire to keep every relationship alive and thriving."[481] However, it has been said that true humility derives from the recognition and acknowledgement of the Divine One in your life. In this regard, we are queried appropriately whether we are "aware of the third partner—God—in bonding?"[482] As Rabbi Jacobson noted succinctly, the Divine Partner affords us "the capacity to unite with another, despite our distinctions"?[483]

Keeping these concepts and life principles firmly in mind, you are encouraged to ask yourself:[484]

> Whether your bonding/relationship with anyone is unbalanced on the levels of giving and receiving, and what you might do to establish balance?
> Whether there is adequate expression of gratitude and appreciation, either verbally or in writing, to those who are generous to you, and what you might do to improve this?
> Whether you offer any gratitude to the Eternal Living Spirit, the Divine One, for the wonderful gifts of friendship with which you have been blessed?

Having answered these queries in a manner meaningful unto yourself, you are advised to work the following exercise pertinent to this day: "When praying acknowledge God specifically for helping you bond with others."[485]

### Day 41—*Yesod* in *Yesod*

היום אחד וארבעים יום
שהם חמשה שבועות ושלשה ימים לעומר
יסוד שביסוד

ר

אֱלֹהִים קְדוּשָׁתְךָ

Transliteration:

*Ha-yom echad v'arba'im yom*
*sheheim chamishah shavu'ot v'shishah yamim la'omer*
*Yesod sheb'Yesod*
*Resh*
*Alef-Lamed-Heh-Yod-Mem Kof-Dalet-Vav-Shin-Tav-Chaf*

Translation:

Today is the forty-first day
which is five weeks and six days of *Omer*.
Foundation (Bonding) in Foundation (Bonding)
Resh
Alef-Lamed-Heh-Yod-Mem Kof-Dalet-Vav-Shin-Tav-Chaf

**Comment:**

On this forty-first day of the "Counting of the *Omer*" we focus on the principles *Yesod* (Bonding) within *Yesod* (Bonding). On this day, said Rabbi Jacobson, "examine the bonding aspect of bonding. The forms it takes and its level of expression. Every person needs and has the capacity to bond with other people, with significant undertakings and with meaningful experiences."[486] In fact, it is maintained that "bonding breeds bonding. When you bond in one area of your life, it helps you bond in other areas."[487] In this regard, we are told that "*yesod* within *yesod* can be between brothers, siblings, husband and wife, parents and children, very close friends, and us and God."[488]

*Yesod* within *Yesod* references the total fullness of "Bonding," and thus this is "the apex of bonding and actualizing relationships and life experiences."[489] Thus it is said that this sefirotic combination is "absolutely essential to experience if we want to reach *malchut*.""[490] It is said this sefirotic combination "helps us to exercise the utmost sensitivity, personal wisdom, and understanding in approaching matters or relationships. The goal is to always connect to the common ground that will both preserve and strengthen bonding, while addressing life's demands and challenges to bring mutually beneficial, positive outcomes in all spheres."[491]

We are instructed that "for bonding to be possible it must embody the other six aspects of bonding," i.e. *Chesed* (Loving-kindness/Mercy), *Gevurah* (Discipline/Might), *Tiferet* (Empathy/Harmony), *Netzach* (Endurance/Victory), *Hod* (Humility/Mindfulness), and *Malchut* (Leadership/Kingship). Finally it is said that "succesful bonding must also include actualizing the bond in constructive deeds."[492]

With all of this in mind, you are encouraged to ask yourself the following questions:[493]

> Whether you have difficulty bonding, and if this is in all areas or only in certain ones?
> Whether you bond easily with your job, yet have difficulty bonding with people, or vice versa?
> Whether you have problems bonding with special events in your life?
> What the reason(s) is for not bonding, and whether it is due to you being too critical and finding fault in everything as an excuse for not bonding?
> Whether you are too locked in your own ways, and whether not bonding is a result of discomfort with vulnerability?
> Whether you have been hurt in your past bonding

experiences, or your trust has been abused?
Whether your fear of bonding is a result of deficient bonding you may have experienced in childhood?

If you have considered these questions in a manner meaningful to yourself, you are advised to work the following exercise for the day: "Begin bonding with a new person or experience you love by committing designated time each day or week to spend together constructively."[494]

### Day 42—*Malchut* in *Yesod*

היום שנים וארבעים יום
שהם ששה שבועות לעומר
מלכות שביסוד

צ

אלהינו

יג"ל פז"ק

Transliteration:
    *Ha-yom sh'nayim v'arba'im yom*
    *sheheim shishah shavu'ot la'omer*
    *Malchut sheb'Yesod*
    *Tzadi*
    *Alef-Lamed-Heh-Yod-Nun-Vav*
    *YaGaLi P'Z'Kei*

Translation:
    Today is the forty-second day
    which is six weeks of *Omer*.
    Kingdom (Rulership) in Foundation (Bonding)
    *Tzadi*
    *Alef-Lamed-Heh-Yod-Nun-Vav*
    *YaGaLi P'Z'Kei*

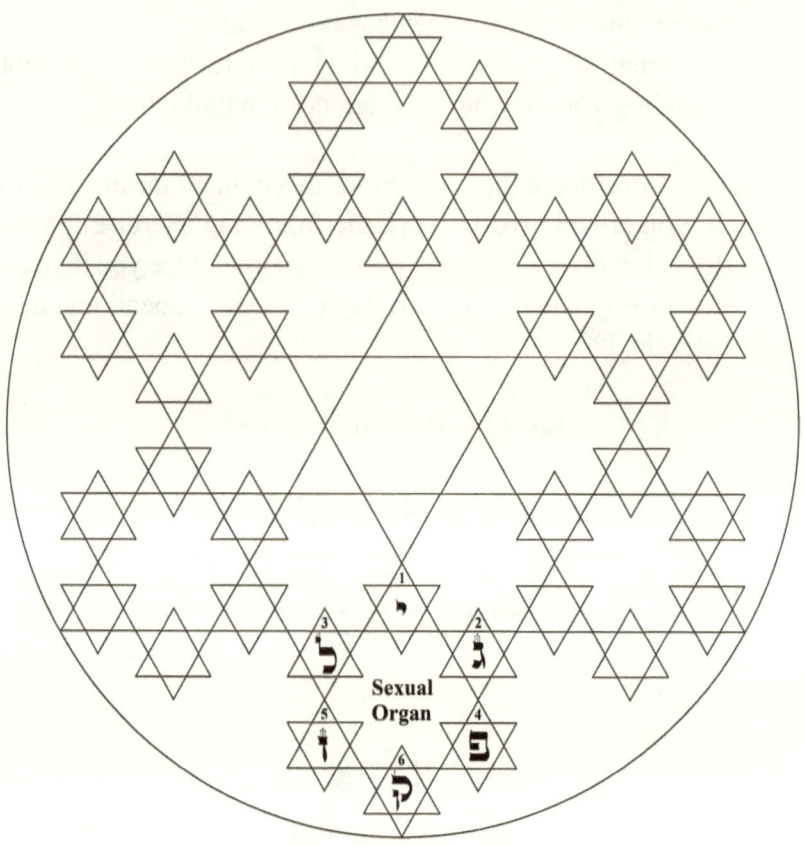

**Comment:**

The concluding day of the sixth week of the "Counting of the *Omer*" pertains to *Malchut* (Leadership/Kingship) in *Yesod* (Bonding/Foundation). We are told "bonding must enhance a person's sovereignty," and that "it should nurture and strengthen your own dignity and the dignity of the one you bond with."[495] In this regard, it has been appropriately stated that this sefirotic combination "can be characterized as a trait that is steady, mature, serene, deliberative, loving, kind, considerate, and restrained, and that has enduring energy focused on achieving goals and maintaining bonds in a balanced, truthful, and responsible manner," and that "relationships which are augmented by *malchut* within *yesod* don't end when faced with obstacles, rather they grow stronger and closer."[496]

It is for these reasons that the conjunction of *Malchut* (Leadership/Nobility) and *Yesod* (Bonding) is understood to bring to bear "a breadth and depth of personal development, experience, and actualization in building and maintaining highly effective relationships and fulfilling life goals."[497] It is thus understood that *Malchut* in *Yesod* "provides us with all the tools to organize, plan, execute, and accomplish challenging goals and missions, while helping us bond with people in all areas and walks of life."[498]

Keeping these ideas firmly in mind, you are exhorted to ask yourself:

> Whether your bonding inhibits the expression of your personality and qualities?[499]
> Whether it is overwhelming the one you bond with?[500]
> Whether you have cut yourself off from others who are different from you, using judgmental thoughts, speech, and actions?[501]
> When was the last time you offered any form of assistance to a complete stranger, and what might be keeping you from doing so?[502]

Having answered these questions, you are requested to work the following exercise applicable to this day: "Emphasize and highlight the strengths of the one you bond with."[503]

---

## WEEK 7—CORRECTING THE *SEFIRAH* OF *MALCHUT*

*Malchut* (Sovereignty), the last of the seven lower *Sefirot*, is recognised as very different from the preceding six, and has been delineated "a state of being rather than an activity."[504] Notwithstanding the relevancy of this observation, my oft mentioned mentor, William G. Gray, who liked to approach the sefirotic Tree from a "feeling appreciation" angle, "so that you will know something of how they feel to *you* from the inside," and maintained that "there is only one Tree of Life, *that which you grow for yourself*,"[505] commenced the journey up the sefirotic Tree by noting that Malchut is "your kingdom in this world."[506] In this regard he queried "What is it? Your home? Your job?" and responded "probably both and then some, but let us suppose it is your home. That is a kingdom of a very small kind even if it is a single room in somebody else's house. Whether you own it or just pay the rent, you are its 'king,' insofar as you are responsible for the place. Maybe you would prefer to call yourself 'co-ruler' if you share with a consort, but that still does not exempt you from liability. If you have the slightest say in making any rules for your home then as a ruler you have some rights in your 'kingdom.' A king is one who rules, governs, and if necessary, sacrifices himself on behalf of his people. Take a look round your home. Surely you had to sacrifice *something* for the good of its people (who may be your family). Even if only money for the landlord or owners, your home must have cost you something. So far as this world is concerned you can think of your home as your tenth Sphere on your Tree, the Kingdom where you are a sort of 'king'."[507]

Naturally questers in the "domain of spirit" would note that there must be a higher side to Malchut (Kingdom) then the reference to the "kingdom" of physical existence, and William Gray equally acknowledged this, by noting that "you know you will have your home only for a limited period. Some day you will move on in this world or into another one."[508] In this regard, he queried again appropriately "What happens to your kingdom then?" and noted that "you cannot take any of it with you, but you can have its equivalent *inside* you which goes wherever you do." With this in mind he queried his readers "Are you a king in your inner kingdom? Do you make rules that you keep yourself? Can you control and govern your own attributes, such as your temper, your impatience, your emotions and other impulses? How far do you ever sacrifice yourself for the good of anything or anyone connected with you? For instance, what would you sacrifice for the sake of your own health or happiness? Your family or those who love you? Your beliefs? Just how good, bad, or indifferent are you as a king in your tiny kingdom? Sit yourself down on your favorite throne and do a lot of thinking about this. How much are you kinglike in your life and living?"[509]

In terms of viewing the sefirah of *Malchut* (Sovereignty) from a practical, experiential perspective, William Gray noted that "some kinds of behavior are called 'regal' because they are typical of what a real king ought to do, like being generous, forgiving, or noble. Anybody can make a regal gesture, even a beggar. The Kingdom indicated on your Tree is not some faraway 'Kingdom of God' in distant heavens, it is *your* kingdom right here in your own home and in yourself."[510] In this regard, he suggested that "you can do one kingly thing right now. Make a small rule of conduct for yourself and determine to keep it. Don't attempt anything big, or anything you know is going to be difficult. Put a time limit on it for safety. Say to yourself something like: "Because I believe in my own kingship, I am making it a rule for myself to do so and so for the next week. Having heard, I will obey." Make it something very simple like saying a special prayer each day, but whatever it is *do it*. Real kings should abide by their own rulings. You may not think you have done anything especially regal, but you will have done so *if* you fulfil your own ruling."[511]

Approaching the sphere of *Malchut* (Kingdom/Sovereignty) from the position of the "Counting of the *Omer*," Rabbi Simon Jacobson informs us that "leadership is a passive expression of human dignity which has nothing of its own except that which it receives from the other six emotions."[512] However, I believe Rabbi Jacobson's views harmonize well with those of my late Mentor, since he also noted that *Malchut* (Sovereignty) "manifests and actualizes the character and majesty of the human spirit," since "it is the very fiber of what makes us human."[513] Thus he stated that "when love, discipline, compassion, endurance and humility are properly channelled into the psyche through bonding—the result is malchut. Bonding nurtures us and allows our sovereignty to surface and flourish."[514]

In the final analysis, the great Rabbi tells us that "Malchut is a sense of belonging. Knowing that you matter and that you make a difference. That you have the ability to be a proficient leader in your own right. It gives you independence and confidence. A feeling of certainty and authority. When a mother lovingly cradles her child in her hands and the child's eyes meet the mother's affectionate eyes, the child receives the message that I am wanted and needed in this world. I have a comfortable place where I will always be loved. I have nothing to fear. I feel like a king in my heart. This is *malchut*, kingship."[515] [my italics]

### Day 43—*Chesed* in *Malchut*

היום שלשה וארבעים יום
שהם ששה שבועות ויום אחד לעומר
חסד שבמלחות

ת

יְבָ֒רְכֵנוּ שׁוֹעָתֵנוּ

Transliteration:
Ha-yom sh'loshah v'arba'im yom
sheheim shishah shavu'ot v'yom echad la'omer
Chesed sheb'Malchut
Tav
Yod-Bet-Yod-Resh-Kav-Nun-Vav Shin-Vav-Ayin-Tav-Nun-Vav

Translation:
Today is the forty-third day
which is six weeks and one day of *Omer*.
Loving-kindness (Mercy) in Kingdom (Rulership)
Tav
Yod-Bet-Yod-Resh-Kav-Nun-Vav Shin-Vav-Ayin-Tav-Nun-Vav

Comment:

On this forty-third day of "Counting the *Omer*" we deal with Chesed (Loving-kindness) in Malchut (Sovereignty/Rulership). In this regard, we are told that "healthy sovereignty is always kind and loving,"[516] and that "an effective leader needs to be warm and considerate."[517] As noted earlier, *Malchut* (Kingdom) comprises all six preceding *Sefirot*, and thus a commentator said that this sphere on the sefirotic Tree "represents wholeness, completeness, sovereignty, leadership, kingship, dignity, and nobility." Hence it is maintained that "the emphasis on *chesed* within *malchut* floods *malchut* with beneficent kindness, goodness, and the nourishing light and love of God. *Chesed* within *malchut* influences and guides all relationships and interactions with acute sensitivity, care and love for ourselves, others, and God."[518]

Having considered the points raised most carefully, you are encouraged to ask yourself:

> Whether your rulership makes you more loving?[519]
> Whether you exercise your "authority and leadership in a caring manner, or whether you are imposing your authority on others?"[520]
> Whether you are satisfied with the level of *Chesed* (Loving-kindness) within *Malchut* (Rulership) which you display in your life, or whether you "waver in this attribute" when the pressures of life throw you off-track?[521]
> Whether you "display consideration and kindness to strangers?"[522]
> Whether you remember to manifest Chesed (Loving-kindness) in Malchut (Rulership) to your loved ones, and, if not, what you might do to facilitate a change?[523]

Having answered these questions in a manner meaningful to yourself, you are exhorted to work the following exercise applicable to this day: "Do something kind for your subordinates."[524]

### Day 44—*Gevurah* in *Malchut*

היום ארבעה וארבעים יום
שהם ששה שבועות ושני ימים לעומר
גבורה שבמלחות

נ

אלהים קבל

Transliteration:
*Ha-yom arba'ah v'arba'im yom*
*sheheim shishah shavu'ot u'sh'nei yamim la'omer*
*Gevurah sheb'Malchut*
*Nun*
*Alef-Lamed-Heh-Yod-Mem Kof-Bet-Lamed*

Translation:
> Today is the forty-fourth day
> which is six weeks and two days of *Omer*.
> Might (Severity) in Kingdom (Rulership)
> *Nun*
> Alef-Lamed-Heh-Yod-Mem Kof-Bet-Lamed

### Comment:

The forty-fourth day of the "Counting of the *Omer*," pertains to *Gevurah* (Discipline/Strength) in *Malchut* (Kingdom/Rulership), hence you are encouraged on this day to "examine the discipline of your sovereignty and leadership."[525] We are informed that "although sovereignty is loving, it needs to be balanced with discipline. Effective leadership is built on authority and discipline."[526] In this regard, it is said that the display of the sovereignty and dignity of *Malchut* "also projects an air of credibility and competency, supplying a sense of security and fairness to life situations and challenges. When augmented by *gevurah*, *malchut* is enhanced with added determination, assurance, and the will to make and execute difficult decisions in order to accomplish worthy ends."[527]

In terms of further factors in comprehending *Gevurah* (Discipline) in *Malchut* (Sovereignty), i.e. "determining the area in which you have jurisdiction and authority,"[528] that "dignity also needs discipline," and that "a dignified person needs to have a degree of reserve," Rabbi Simon Jacobson advises you to ask yourself:[529]

> Whether you recognize when you are not an authority?
> Whether you "exercise authority in unwarranted situations?"
> Whether you are aware of your limitations as well as your strengths?
> Whether you "respect the authority of others?"

There are several further questions pertaining to *Gevurah* (Discipline/Might) within *Malchut* (Kingdom/Nobility), which you equally should address on this day. Thus you are encouraged to ask yourself:[530]

Whether you have a predilection for speaking, or listening to *lashon hara* (evil tongue/gossip), and what you might do about that?

How you demonstrate respect for higher authority, i.e. the police, government, community leaders, etc.?

Whether you recall situations, i.e. amongst family or friends, where you "had the authority to act, but chose not to," why you made that choice, and how it turned out?

Whether you are inclined to impose your will and authority on your loved ones, friends, associates, etc., how they react, and what better approach you could take?

Having considered the listed deliberations applicable to this day, and having answered the relevant questions, you are urged to work the following relevant exercise: "Before taking an authoritative position on any given issue, pause and reflect if you have the right and the ability to exercise authority in this situation."[531]

### Day 45—*Tiferet* in *Malchut*

היום חמשה וארבעים יום
שהם ששה שבועות ושלשה ימים לעומר
תפארת שבמלחות

ח

וייראו  וישמע

Transliteration:
> *Ha-yom chamishah v'arba'im yom*
> *sheheim shishah shavu'ot u'sh'loshah yamim la'omer*
> *Tiferet sheb'Malchut*
> *Chet*
> *Vav-Yod-Yod-Resh-Alef-Vav Vav-Shin-Mem-Ayin*

Translation:
> Today is the forty-fifth day
> which is six weeks and three days of *Omer*.
> Harmony (Beauty) in Kingdom (Rulership)
> *Chet*
> *Vav-Yod-Yod-Resh-Alef-Vav Vav-Shin-Mem-Ayin*

## Comment:

This day pertains to the examination of *Tiferet* (Compassion/Harmony) in *Malchut* (Rulership/Nobility). We are advised that "a good leader is a compassionate one,"[532] and that *Tiferet* (Harmony) "is critical for successful leadership."[533] However, we are reminded that *Tiferet* is also "Truth," and that "when *malchut* is enhanced with *tiferet*, it becomes all the more beautiful, truthful, balanced, and harmonious in its overall stature and effectiveness."[534] This "state of being" is beautifully delineated in the statement that "wherever and whenever one is in a leadership role, whether at the head of a family, in a classroom, the workplace or the synagogue, or as the leader of a community, a government or a nation, *tiferet* within *malchut* facilitates calm, organized, clear, and open communications."[535] Such conditions of consciousness are said to aid "the achievement of common goals that all involved understand and accept, and where each is treated with dignity and respect."[536]

Having again considered the remarkable concepts applicable to this day, you are exhorted to ask yourself:[537]

> Whether your compassion is compromised because of your authority?
> Whether you "realize that an integral part of dignity is compassion?"
> Whether in your life and activities you "manage a smooth-running operation," and whether you are organized?
> Whether you issue clear instructions to those who are subordinate to you?
> Whether you have difficulty delegating power, and whether those sharing your organization, or your home, for that matter, are working as a team?
> Whether you have frequent meetings with staff, family, associates, etc., in order to coordinate collective goals and efforts?

Keeping the principles and questions applicable to this day firmly in mind, you are encouraged to work the following relevant exercise: "Review an area where you wield authority and see if you can polish it up and increase its effectiveness by curtailing excesses and consolidating forces."[538]

## Day 46—*Netzach* in *Malchut*

היום ששה וארבעים יום
שהם ששה שבועות וארבעה ימים לעומר
נצח שבמלחות

מ

אוֹתוֹ צִעֲקָתֵנוּ

Transliteration:
*Ha-yom shishah v'arba'im yom*
*sheheim shishah shavu'ot v'arba'ah yamim la'omer*
*Netzach sheb'Malchut*
*Mem*
*Alef-Vav-Tav-Vav Tzadi-Ayin-Kof-Tav-Nun-Vav*

Translation:
Today is the forty-sixth day
which is six weeks and four days of *Omer*.
Endurance (Victory) in Kingdom (Rulership)
*Mem*
*Alef-Vav-Tav-Vav Tzadi-Ayin-Kof-Tav-Nun-Vav*

### Comment:

The forty-sixth day of "Counting the Omer" pertains to *Netzach* (Endurance/Victory) in *Malchut* (Sovereignty/Kingdom). In this regard, we are told that "a person's dignity and a leader's success is tested by his endurance level. Will and determination reflect the power and majesty of the human spirit," and that this is "the strength of one's sovereignty."[539] It is said that "*Netzach* is needed in combination with *Malchut* when worthy situations, relationships, or goals require extra resolve, drive, and tenacity. This endurance is needed if we are to pursue goals and solutions in the face of all odds—even when others may be against us, even when a situation seems hopeless."[540] In this regard, you are encouraged to ask yourself:

Whether you are determined in reaching personal goals,[541] and whether you can recall times in recent years in which you "showed determination and endurance to reach a worthy goal" you have set for yourself, and if not, what prevented you from completing the task at hand?[542]

What is the longest amount of time you have devoted to a project or goal?[543]

What current goal you have set for yourself, whether it be in your personal life or career, and what timetables and goals you have set towards their accomplishment.[544]

What worthy causes you have ever fought for, and how that made you feel?[545]

How strong your conviction is "to fight for a dignified cause?"[546]

How confident you are in yourself, and whether your lack of endurance is a result of a low self-esteem?[547]

Whether you mask insecurities by finding excuses for a low endurance level?[548]

Having contemplated the points addressed, and carefully considered the relevant questions, you are urged to work the following exercise applicable to this day: "Act on something that you believe in but have until now been tentative about. Take the leap and just do it!"[549]

### Day 47—*Hod* in *Malchut*

היום שבעה וארבעים יום
שהם ששה שבועות וחמשה ימים לעומר
הוד שבמלחות

ס

Transliteration:
    *Ha-yom shiv'ah v'arba'im yom*
    *sheheim shishah shavu'ot v'chamishah yamim la'omer*
    *Hod sheb'Malchut*
    *Samech*
    *Kaf-Lamed Yod-Vav-Dalet-Ayin*

Translation:
> Today is the forty-seventh day
> which is six weeks and five days of *Omer*.
> Splendour (Glory) in Kingdom (Rulership)
> *Samech*
> Kaf-Lamed Yod-Vav-Dalet-Ayin

## Comment:

This forty-seventh day of the "Counting of the *Omer*" pertains to the sefirotic qualities of *Hod* (Humility/Mindfulness) in *Malchut* (Nobility/Rulership). In this regard, it is said that "sovereignty is God's gift to each individual," and that "*Hod* of *Malchut* is the humble appreciation of this exceptional gift."[550] In fact, *Hod* (Humility) in *Malchut* (Rulership) is an acknowledgement that all our achievements derive from the Divine One. In this regard, it is said that the current sefirotic combination is all about "knowing that everything that we accomplish or that happens to us in life comes from God."[551] This pertains to recognizing "that all the talents, blessings, and successes that rain down on us come from God and are not the sole result of our hard work and endeavors."[552] Thus we are informed that "armed with this *sefirah* combination, we approach all situations—and especially those where we are called upon to lead—with a humble self-awareness that helps us act with consideration of others."[553]

Having paid again close attention to the points raised, you are enjoined to ask yourself:

> Whether you appreciate the special qualities you were blessed with?[554]
> Whether your sovereignty and independence humble you, or are you an arrogant leader?[555]
> Whether, when playing a dominant role in a relationship, you believe that you are superior to those subordinate to yourself, and whether this attitude aids you in being more effective in your role?[556]
> Whether the dynamic in your family allows all "to play their role, be heard, participate, and feel that they are essential to the whole unit," and, if not, what you might do to improve this situation?[557]

How you feel when meeting those less formally educated and in a lower social status to yourself?⁵⁵⁸

Again keeping the principles and questions applicable to this day firmly in mind, you are advised to work the following relevant exercise: "Acknowledge God for creating you with personal dignity."⁵⁵⁹

### Day 48—*Yesod* in *Malchut*

היום שמונה וארבעים יום
שהם ששה שבועות וששה ימים לעומר
יסוד שבמלחות

אפסי תעלומות

Transliteration:
   Ha-yom sh'monah v'arba'im yom
   sheheim shishah shavu'ot v'shishah yamim la'omer
   Yesod sheb'Malchut
   Lamed
   Alef-Peh-Samech-Yod Tav-Ayin-Lamed-Vav-Mem-Vav-Tav

Translation:
   Today is the forty-eighth day
   which is six weeks and six days of *Omer*.
   Foundation (Bonding) in Kingdom (Rulership)
   Lamed
   Alef-Peh-Samech-Yod Tav-Ayin-Lamed-Vav-Mem-Vav-Tav

**Comment:**

On this penultimate day of "Counting the *Omer*," you are enjoined to address *Yesod* in *Malchut*, i.e. to "examine the bonding aspect of your sovereignty."⁵⁶⁰ It is said "the emphasis of *yesod* within *malchut* reinforces the ability of *malchut* to reach out to others in order to optimize relationships and create consensus."⁵⁶¹ You are advised that "*yesod* within *malchut* is a magnet that builds a solid, healthy foundation between self and self, self and other, and self and God."562 In this regard, you are reminded that you "are not meant to be an island," and that you "are expected to show respect for others and to bond with them while honoring their boundaries."563

Rabbi Simon Jacobson maintains "healthy independence should not prevent you from bonding with another person,"564 and that "self-confidence allows you to respect and trust another's sovereignty and ultimately bond with him,"565 or her for that matter. It is said this bond "will strengthen your own sovereignty, rather than sacrifice it."566

Having carefully contemplated these ideas, you are directed to ask yourself:567

> Whether your sovereignty prevents you from bonding, and whether this is due to inherent insecurities within yourself of which you are oblivious?
> If you "recognize the fact that a fear of bonding reflects on lack of self-confidence" in your personal sovereignty?
> Whether you are willing to converse with the individual with whom you are bonding, addressing any fears you may have that bonding will compromise your boundaries?

Having addressed these questions in a manner meaningful unto yourself, you are advised to work the following relevant exercise: "Actualize your sovereignty by intensifying your bond with a close one."568

### Day 49—*Malchut* in *Malchut*

היום תשעה וארבעים יום
שהם שבעה שבועות לעומר
מלכות שבמלכות

ה

ארץ

שק"ו צי"ת

Transliteration:
> *Ha-yom tish'ah v'arba'im yom*
> *sheheim shiv'ah shavu'ot la'omer*
> *Malchut sheb'Malchut*
> *Heh*
> *Alef-Resh-Tzadi*
> *ShuKoVa TzoYaT'*

Translation:
> Today is the forty-ninth day
> which is seven weeks of *Omer*.
> Kingdom (Rulership) in Kingdom (Rulership)
> Heh
> Alef-Resh-Tzadi
> ShuKoVa TzoYaT'

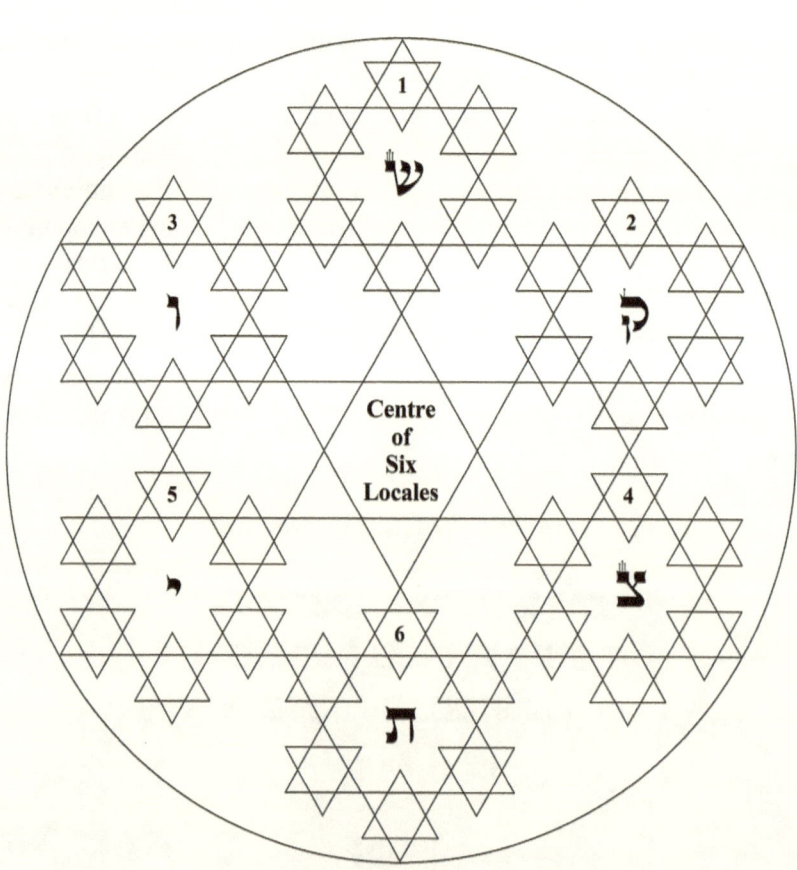

**Comment:**

The forty-ninth and final day of the "Counting of the *Omer*" pertains to *Malchut* (Nobility/Kingdom) in *Malchut*, hence we are advised on the forty-ninth day to "examine the sovereignty of your sovereignty."[569] In this regard, it is said "*Malchut* within *malchut* is the pinnacle toward which we have been striving. It is achieved when we genuinely respect others in all realms of life, whether physical, emotional, or spiritual."[570] It is maintained that *Malchut* (Sovereignty/Kingdom) in *Malchut* "is the scope of the combined wisdom and understanding that we have achieved through the cultivation and integration of the *sefirot* of *chesed, gevurah, tiferet, netzach, hod,* and *yesod*."[571]

We are advised that *Malchut* within *malchut* needs to be manifested in this world," and for this to happen we first need "to be aware of our own special individuality in order that we might understand and fulfill our own unique mission in this world. Second, we must demonstrate respect and regard for other people, each of whom has a unique mission too—and, just like us, the potential for *malchut*."[572] Thus, we are told that "whether it be in a very limited or wider area of responsibility, whether it would involve ourselves or other individuals, and whether it would or would not involve power, authority, and leadership, *Malchut* is a state of mind and self-composure that allows us to act with nobility and dignity both individually and in concert with others, in order to achieve outcomes that are worthy."[573] This is beautifully summarised in the statement that Malchut in Malchut, Sovereignty in Sovereignty, the Kingdom in the Kingdom, "is an integrated balance that acts with *emunah* (faith) to achieve unity, light, and holiness at all times."[574]

Here then at the conclusion of this amazing sefirotic journey of personal introspection, you are to consider the value of your own "Kingdom," i.e. the "Nobility" of your "Sovereignty," and ask:[575]

> Whether it comes from a profound inner confidence in yourself, or if it is merely a pretense to mask personal insecurities, and if this results in your sovereignty to be excessive?
> Whether you are aware of your uniqueness as a person, and of your personal contribution to the whole of existence?

Having for a last time considered the points raised and questions asked at the final stage of this journey, you are exhorted to conclude with the following exercise relevant to this day: "Take a moment and concentrate on yourself, on your true inner self, not on your performance and how you project to others; and be at peace with yourself knowing that God created a very special person which is you."[576]

---

Whilst some readers may well query the necessity of announcing each day the exact numerical position of the week and day in terms of the "Counting of the *Omer*," we are reminded "that this practice of verbally counting days and weeks makes us aware both of where we have been and where we are going, thus evoking a sense of movement from one state of being to another,"[577] and that "even as we look toward the future, counting each day forces us to acknowledge and appreciate the significance of the moment."[578] This, we are told, "evokes an essential lesson of *S'firat HaOmer*: that every moment of our lives is consequential, that every moment counts."[579]

The seven weeks of *Omer* culminate in the festival of *Shavuot* ("Festival of Weeks") in which Jewish religionists celebrate the revelation at Mount Sinai on the 50th day. This event and its specifically religious connotations, may have no special appeal for those who are not particularly religious, as well as for those whose religious sentiments lie elsewhere. However, *Shavuot* is about unity, and this is significant for those who followed the special path of personal introspection, to achieve that unique spiritual, mental, and emotional unity which they hope to integrate in their lives, and which is celebrated on *Shavuot*, the fiftieth day of the "Counting of the *Omer*." It is in recognition of this "unity" that Kabbalists introduced the practice of "Creating Perfection on the Night of *Shavuot*" (תקון ליל שבועות–*Tikkun leil Shavuot*),[580] which involves the studying of portions respectively of the "written" and "oral" *Torah*. In this regard, we are told that "in mystical symbolism, the Written Torah is associated with *Tiferet* and the Oral Torah is linked with *Malkhut*. The *tikkun* ritual is designed to hasten the divine marriage by joining *Tiferet* and *Malkhut*."[581] As noted, I acknowledge that this specific celebration may have no significance to those who do not follow the Jewish faith, but I would suggest that those who worked the "Counting of the *Omer*," conclude their journey by taking a break on the fiftieth day and performing a special meditational practice of their personal choice, during which they celebrate the wonderful "unity of spirit" they have achieved because of having undertaken this remarkable "Quest of Spirit." In this regard, you might well find a suitable meditation amongst the many shared in the following chapter.

. ... ... ...They sing strange, magic songs, songs without words, notes, or melody, joyous or sad. The songs of the clear spring and the heart of the world are woven of strands of light. These strands rise into the sky, reaching the seventh heaven, and high above the world they spread out like a net filled with glitter and sparkle... ... ... .

# Chapter 7
## *Or Yashar* — Light Unbending
## MAGICAL MEDITATION

### A. The Need for Meditation

Many who commence the path of "Spiritual Self Development" have the belief that the "higher" you develop yourself mentally and spiritually, the "thicker would become your skin" and the less you would be affected by the physical environment. I regret having to burst this fantasy bubble, but the opposite is in fact true. Your "skin" will actually become "thinner" as you develop spiritually, and as you become more sensitive to everything happening around you in the realm of material manifestation. Any person who has worked fully focussed with *Practical Kabbalah* for an extensive period of time, will testify that you become so sensitive, that you cannot walk into a space where people are socially active, and where there might be a conflict subjectively unfolding, without being impacted by the ambient atmosphere in a most direct manner.

In this regard, a very dear friend and Companion informed me of an experience he once had in a public place where an angry outburst was about to ensue between two individuals. He informed me that he became aware of the malignant energy in the locale when it was comparatively speaking only 1%. He further told me that by the time the said energy reached a level of around 5%, he was fully conscious of it, and this was long before anybody else realised there was something unpleasant afoot. My friend maintained that when the malevolent energy reached 20% of its eventual capacity, the ambient atmosphere had become most uncomfortable for him, and yet it appears everybody, except of course the perpetrators, were oblivious to the ensuing fracas.

Much of the violence we are encountering in the world today pertains to an overcrowded world in which one-up-man-ship has become a steadily more and more important, if deplorable, factor in human relationships. Of all the species on the planet, humans are the most likely to prey on their own kind on all levels of existence, and whilst most might not realise it all that fully, they have skills which destructively impact their fellow humankind on levels far exceeding average physical aggression. What is more, this kind of nastiness can be found even amongst the most highly sophisticated humans. Whilst it is fairly common for those who aspire to higher spiritual levels to think that no "evil" can exist on the loftiest "levels of spirit," they are bound to find "scoundrels" there as well. Each "level of being" has its own "Angels" and "Demons," these manifesting fairly often in the very body, mind, soul and spirit of the one claiming to have reached these lofty levels of spiritual being and existence.

As might be expected, much of human viciousness pertains again to what is termed the "evil eye." In fact this is a most serious problem in the world, and one which is very poorly understood despite the fact that it is extensively addressed in the literature of most magical traditions. Many have very grandiose ideas about what the "evil eye" is, e.g. someone deliberately directing rays of evil from their eyes to affect their victim in the most baleful manner, etc. As it is, the "evil eye" can range from something as simple as a petty jealousy about nothing of the slightest importance, to greed, intolerance, rivalry, resentment, dominance, out and out hatred, etc. Of course, any malevolence, whether perceived as petty or of the absolutely vindictive type, can impact a recipient in a most awful manner. The issue of the "evil eye" is large enough to manifest even on a national level, i.e. belligerence from one group to another, or one nation towards another, etc. In fact, it is rife amongst all sorts of human groupings, whether social, political, or spiritual, and so firmly ensconced in the "collective consciousness" of all nations, that it often results in civil unrest and even all out war.

Now, I am well aware that over-breeding is often the cause of serious conflict amongst herding animals, and, whether we like to hear this or not, humans are herding animals. However, it is clear that the inhumanity of humans to their own kind, as well as the constant scheming of these thinking monkeys, have no bounds. I have been told dismissively that more humans have died from mosquito bites than in a war, as if that would justify the ill treatment of even the most humble of our fellow humankind, or, for that matter, the death of even a single individual slain in cold blood for no greater reason than sheer jealousy, resentment, hatred, or anything related directly to the "evil eye." In the light of this state of affairs on our planet, it is no wonder that a large number of Jewish magical practices pertain to averting the "evil eye."

Of course, physical, mental, emotional and spiritual aggression of humans toward all and everything on this planet, can hardly be construed the only, as it were, "evil" we have to deal with. In this regard, I noted elsewhere that the "sum total of human suffering all round, i.e. feuds, wars, poverty, etc., must be incredible, and yet it seems to be considered quite a normal condition in this world, as long as it is happening to somebody else."[1] I conjectured that "I am sure all of us would like to see a world organised so that all humans were cared for and supplied according to needs, not necessarily wants; a world with a minimum of sickness, starvation and all the ills human creatures inflict on each other; a 'warless' world for certain."[2]

Naturally the fundamental factor is how to deal with these issues effectively. As said elsewhere, "what we need to know is how to keep ourselves together under the pressure of perdition itself, and how to survive in body, mind, soul and spirit whilst the 'forces of darkness and destruction' are hammering us into the ground, and proving by every means how helpless, futile and ineffective we are."[3] In this regard, I still maintain that "what is important is that we should *want* to do better in the first place,"[4] that "the only possible hope for this world is to alter the *SOUL* of humanity for the better,"[5] and that for this to happen "humans will have to alter *from within* to a drastic extent, and that can only be done by *spiritual* changes."[6]

In my estimation, such "spiritual changes" can be effectively worked within the "Inner Being" of every human on this planet, if he/she would commence a daily regime of meaningful meditation, in order to work the necessary alteration of him/herself "from within," i.e. the very "Self Centre," which will also impact the "without," i.e. the greater whole of physical existence. This is what "Immediate Magic" is all about, since "when we fully understand that consciousness is just one vast ocean, and thoughts are the waves we make in it,"[7] then all we need to do is "guide the 'currents of consciousness' which circulate through the 'Ocean of Awareness' we all share, so that everyone benefits because of the modulations we made. In one way it is like a flow of pure energy. Each separate mind that uses it, is processing it in some way which will affect other minds accepting it. We live in a 'sea' of each other's thoughts."[8]

It is therefore now my intention to address the manner in which we can keep ourselves together in the difficult situations we are met with in our daily lives, and in this regard we are obliged to "empower" ourselves, as said, "from within" by means of "magical meditation." To achieve this intention, it is in my estimation necessary to recognise three fundamental principles applicable to meditation, i.e. Rectification—Integration—Transformation. "Rectification" is in most instances the primary reason for individuals resorting to practising meditation. By this means they attempt to alter stressful life conditions which have an adverse impact on their general wellbeing, and thus work the necessary personal restoration. "Integration" is a reference to those qualities which you inculcate into yourself during the restoration process, i.e. coping mechanisms within yourself, in order to "pull yourself together," as the saying goes. "Transformation" happens when the meditation process facilitates the expansion of your consciousness, which allows you to achieve profound levels of understanding and achieve within yourself the sought after greater wellbeing.

Viewed from the angle of the five "Stages of Awareness," the concepts of which pertain to the so-called "Fivefold Path," and which I addressed under the title *"The Fivefold Path"* in the first volume of this series of texts on *Practical Kabbalah*,[9] the principle of "Rectification" would pertain to *Kavvanah* (Intention, Motivation and Dedication) and *Devekut* (Divine Union or Adhesion). "Integration" references *Devekut* and *Hishtavut* (Equanimity), this being the "awakening consciousness," which is, as it were, the result of a "Divine Union" which occurs between the *Nefesh* (Instinctual Self) and the *Ruach* (Conscious Self), and achieving equinimity, i.e. a level of consciousness in which you are no longer affected by insult or flattery. "Transformation" means that *Hitbodedut* (Meditation or Aloneness) leads to *Ru'ach ha-Kodesh* (Spirit which is Holy or Enlightenment), this being, as I noted, the achievement of a level of consciousness which embraces a greater whole to the one practitioners of meditation might have had prior to their forays into, as it were, their inner domains of spirit in search of self empowerment.

As it is, a large amount of the data shared in the earlier tomes of this series pertains exactly to personal empowerment, as is the sefirotic material shared in the previous chapter. Furthermore, Kabbalistic meditation is a vast topic, which has been addressed from a great variety of angles by several authors. In this regard, I have included a fairly extensive list of titles pertaining to "Jewish Meditation" in the bibliography of this tome.[10] The list includes both primary and secondary texts, including an array of Lurianic *Siddurim* (Prayer Books) incorporating Lurianic *Kavvanot* (Mystical Intentions). However, even a casual perusal of the books in question is likely to cause great consternation, since, beyond the meditational techniques of Abraham Abulafia, Yehudah Albotini and fellow "Ecstatic Kabbalists," whose meditational practices have been addressed in fair detail, and the relatively little elucidation of the *Kavvanot* and *Yichudim* (Unifications) of *Lurianic Kabbalah*, it would seem a great variety of very diverse practices are designated "Jewish meditation."

Be that as it may, it is not my intention to present a full analysis of what could be termed "Kabbalistic Meditation," and the limited space afforded me in this tome precludes me from sharing every single technique. Instead, I wish to focus on special meditational practices which will empower and enrich your life from "within," and, in my estimation, it is often the most simple which is the most effective. In this regard, there is the beautiful Jewish folktale of a villager who, whilst riding in the woods on the eve of *Yom Kippur* (Day of Atonement), decided to take a long lunch break. We are told that he "took his time eating and jumped on his horse, only to take a wrong turn on his way to town and lose his way in the woods. The sun set, and it was already time for the *Kol Nidre* prayer. When the villager saw that he would have to spend the holy night and day alone in the woods without even a prayer book, he burst into tears and said, 'Master of the Universe, what now? There's only one thing to do: I'll recite the letters of the Hebrew alphabet, and You, dear God, will make them into prayers as best you can'."[11]

The simple beauty and the pure "power of intention" of this story notwithstanding, a very important Jewish meditational/magical practice is referenced in this saga, i.e. the recitation of Hebrew letters. The twenty-two glyphs of the Hebrew Alphabet are said to be "vessels and chambers of God, and by means of the kavanah (focussed intention), man draws down within them the emanation of the supernal light"[12] I noted elsewhere that in "*Kabbalah* it is understood that when the letters of the Hebrew Alphabet, the *Otiot*, are spoken with a suitably associated godly stance or intention, the 'spiritual forces' inherent in those letters are invoked and manifested. Every sign of the *Otiot* is dominated by a *Maggid*, a Celestial Messenger. These Messengers or Angels, are rays of *Aur Ain Sof* (the Light of Eternal No-Thing), radiations of the boundless beneficence and qualities emanating from the Divine One."[13] In this regard, Moshe Idel referenced the stance of certain Kabbalists for whom "the highest domain of study, which transcends even the study of the *Zohar*, the most important text of Kabbalah, is knowledge of the 'spiritual force of the letters and their existence and their combination with each other,' for this knowledge enables the Kabbalist 'to create worlds'."[14]

I have already addressed the power and importance of the Hebrew alphabet in *Practical Kabbalah*,[15] and having paid special attention in the first part of "*The Book of Immediate Magic*" to the twenty-two Hebrew glyphs in aligning with the "Spirit Forces" inherent in the Hebrew alphabet,[16] we might now peruse the meditation practice of scanning Hebrew letters as a kind of "programming" of your "Inner Being," i.e. restoring and realigning your "Centre." Once again, as indicated earlier, the factors of primary importance in working kabbalistic meditation (*Hitbodedut*), are again restoration (*Kavvanah/Tikkun*), integration (*Devekut/Hishtavut*), and transformation (*Ruach ha-Kodesh*) on all levels of being, whether it be physical, mental, emotional or spiritual.[17]

In terms of achieving physical wellbeing by means of the Hebrew glyphs, there is the custom of scanning the text of the pages of the *Zohar* which is popularised by a modern-day kabbalistic sect.[18] I witnessed the remarkable impact of this practice in the instance of a female acquaintance who developed a very problematic psycho/physical condition. The body of the lady in question suddenly started to rock backwards and forwards by itself. At first it was a mild rocking, but over a period of a couple of months the rocking increased to such an extent, that she would literally fold her body in half as she moved backwards and forwards uncontrollably. This would happen even while she was sleeping. Doctors were stumped at trying to figure out what was going on, and it was the intervention of an individual who suggested she scans the pages of the *Zohar* which saved the day. As she let her eyes wander over the glyphs of the Aramaic text, without attempting to actually read or understand the words, she began to return to normal focal levels, and shortly thereafter the condition disappeared.

Regarding the scanning of the verses comprising the *Zohar* by the followers of the said contemporary kabbalistic cult, the practice is quite well-known elsewhere, especially amongst those Kabbalists who have a predilection for Kabbalistic *Tzerufim* (Hebrew Letter Combinations). This technique is still popular amongst Kabbalists of North African descent, i.e. Morocco, etc., for whom the meditation of tracing combinations of Hebrew letters for a variety of purposes is particularly important, and has been so for a very long time. It is this very valuable technique which I would like to share here especially in terms of the intention of spiritually empowering your "Self."

At the turn of the millennium I chanced upon the online writings of an individual who related his remarkable encounter with a Moroccan Kabbalist, to whom he confessed his psychological and personal health problems. In this regard, the author noted that the compassion of the said Kabbalist "was palpable and he proceeded to jot down some Hebrew letters for me on his business card. It was a meditation. I was to sit quietly and read it, and then close my eyes for a minute."[19] He further stated that this changed his life forever, that this gave him "what years of therapy could not," and that whilst "healing through psychotherapy was about releasing repressed emotions, acknowledging traumas and trying to re-examine those experiences," that "Kabbalah's healing approach.....is more of an energy channeling and a strengthening movement. One could say in one respect that therapy tries to get negative 'Stuff' out while Kabbalah tries to get positive 'Stuff' in."[20] I was naturally profoundly interested in what this was all about, and hence tried this very simple meditation of scanning and reciting the array of Hebrew letters. The results in terms of "self rectification" were simply astonishing, and I have been practising this technique for around fifteen years. I can vouch for its incredible power in affecting healing of body, mind and soul.

The set comprises altogether twenty Hebrew glyphs, as indicated below tracing from right to left:

| Vav | Vav | Heh | Nun | Bet | Nun | Kof | Tzadi | Bet | Alef |
|---|---|---|---|---|---|---|---|---|---|
| ו | ו | ה | נ | ב | נ | ק | צ | ב | א |
| Bet | Alef | Yod | Chet | Yod | Chet | Yod | Chet | Nun | Bet |
| ב | א | י | ח | י | ח | י | ח | נ | ב |

Whilst the collective meaning of the letters is perhaps not of particular importance, and whether intentional or not, it is clear that reading the letters in their exact order spell words like אב (*Av*—"father") spelled twice, three times if you include the fact that you can also read it when you read the letters in the rightmost column downwards; צקן (*Tzakan*—"beard"); בן (*Ben*—"son") also twice, הוו (*ha-Vav*—"the hook," "nail," "connection" or "link"); and חי (*Chai*—"live" or "alive"), the latter spelled three times.

As we know well enough, the concepts of "Father," "Beard," "Son," etc., are very important in *Kabbalah*, and a dissertation the size of this tome could be written on these very concepts alone. In this regard, we might note that אב (*Av*—"father") and בן (*Ben*—"son") are prominent in the concepts of the *Partzufim* ("Countenances" or "Configurations") attributed to the ten Sefirot, as addressed in the *Idra Rabba* ("Great Assembly") section of the *Sefer ha-Zohar*,[21] and expanded upon in particular in *Lurianic Kabbalah* of which there is an extensive literature available in English.[22]

If one presumes the twenty special Hebrew glyphs of the said unique meditation to be comprising a "hidden phrase" pertaining to some or other mystical/magical "kabbalistic mystery," you would do well to consider that the term אב (*Av*—"Father") might well be referencing *Arich Anpin* ("Long Faced") of *Keter* (Crown) on the sefirotic Tree, whilst בן (Ben—"Son") could be a reference to *Ze'ir Anpin* ("Short Faced" considered the "Impatient One"). In this regard, the צקן (*Tzaken*—"Beard") reference might then be pertaining to the symbolical *Dikna*, the "Beard" extending from *Arich Anpin*, and comprising thirteen strands said to reference thirteen *Tikunim* ("rectifications" or "restorations"), the latter said to reference "the 13 principles of Divine effluence that run from the *sefirah* of crown (super-consciousness) to the conscious *sefirot*."[23]

Now, the said "thirteen principles" pertain to what is called "thirteen qualities of compassion"[24] expressed in the thirteen portions in *Exodus 34:6-7* reading:

יהוה יהוה אל רחום וחנון ארך אפים ורב חסד ואמת נצר
חסד לאלפים נשא עון ופשע וחטאה ונקה

Transliteration:
*YHVH YHVH El rachum v'chanun erech apyim v'rav chesed v'emet, notzeir chesed la'alafim nosei avon vafesha v'chata'ah v'nakeh*

Translation:
(1)*YHVH* (2)*YHVH*, (3)*El* (4)compasionate [merciful] [5]and gracious, [6]slow to anger [long-suffering], (7)and abundant in kindness (goodness) (8)and truth, (9)preserver of kindness [keeping mercy] for thousands of generations [unto the thousandth generation], (10)forgiving iniquity (11)and willful transgression (12)and error (13) and who cleanses.

The "Thirteen Qualities of Compassion" are said to "originate in *Keter*, the highest *Sefirah*, the realm of total compassion, untainted by judgment,"[25] and they are primary to the *Selichot* (penitential) prayers recited prior to *Rosh Hashanah* (Jewish New Year Festival). In this regard, it has been noted that the said thirteen attributes "are traditionally the exact words that God taught Moses for the people to use whenever they needed to beg for Divine compassion," and that "the kabbalists introduced the current custom of reciting the Thirteen Attributes of Mercy before taking the Torah from the ark during the three pilgrimage festivals of Passover, Shavuot, and Sukkot, unless they occur on the Sabbath."[26]

The double usage of the Ineffable Name in these verses reminds me of the Zoharic double reference to *Matz'patz*, which is equally important in terms of the "Thirteen Aspects of Mercy." In this regard, we are informed regarding the biblical statement that "God made the two great lights" (*Genesis 1:16*), that the pair of "lights" were "at first in a single bond, mystery of the name complete as one: *YHVH Elohim*." Furthermore, it is said that the word "great" references these "lights" to have been "enhanced in name, both alike, to be called by the mystery of all: *Matz'patz Matz'patz*, supernal names of the thirteen qualities of compassion," and that "they are supernal, from the mystery on high, ascending for the benefit of the world, so that through them worlds endure." (*Zohar 1:20a*)[27]

The Divine Name מצפץ (*Matz'patz*), is a variant of the Ineffable Name (יהוה) constructed by means of the *Atbash* (את-בש) cipher, and is said to mean "*God protect.*" In this regard, the *Zohar* tells us that this Divine Name equally pertains to the quality of "compassion" (mercy).[28] Furthermore, as I noted elsewhere, "whilst מצפץ is a variant of the Ineffable Name, there is a close association between this Name and *Elohim*, the latter..... in the '*YHVH Elohim*' combination, titled 'the Complete Name' since it represents the union of the divine qualities of 'Compassion/Mercy' and 'Justice/Severity'."[29] Curiously enough, it was noted that the *gematria* of the Name *Matz'patz* [מ = 40 + צ = 90 + פ = 80 + צ = 90 = 300] is equal to that of the expression ברחמים (*b'rachamim*—"with mercy" [ב = 2 + ר = 200 + ח = 8 + מ = 40 + י = 10 + מ = 40 = 300), as well as to the *gematria* of the full spelling of the five letters comprising the Name *Elohim* [א = 1 + ל = 30 + פ = 80 + ל = 30 + מ = 40 + ד = 4 + ה = 5 + י = 10 + י = 10 + ו = 6 + ד = 4 + מ = 40 + מ = 40 = 300].[30] It was further noted that the thirteen letters in this expanded spelling of the Name *Elohim*, pertain directly to the "Thirteen Qualities of Compassion."[31]

Whilst I have shared a practice elsewhere incorporating the thirteen letters comprising the said full spelling of the Divine Name *Elohim*, which has to be performed regularly to align yourself with the thirteen qualities,[32] it is worth considering the following *Hagah* (Hebrew Mantra) which is equally employed to facilitate the same alignment with the "Thirteen Qualities of Compassion." This *Hagah* is so simple, even a child could perform it as if it were a nursery rhyme. In fact, some years back I shared it with an eight year old who was unhappy about a teacher who appeared to not like her, because she had difficulty remembering anything. It was not as if she had poor memory, she simply tended to get "stage fright" in the classroom, and this affected her recall.

I shared the said *Hagah* with her in a singsong manner, which she memorised instantly. I also told her that if she sang it all day, and opened her heart like a flower, and smiled from her chest while singing it, it would make everyone around her smile and everyone would be her friend.

As it is, the idea behind the *Hagah* is to "open the heart," encourage greater memory, to protect, to bring lovingkindness and compassion in the life of the user, and also to invoke affection for invocants in the hearts of all whom they may encounter. Here it is interesting to note that the *gematria* of the word אהבה ("Love") is 13, not at all a bad number in this tradition, since it references the "Thirteen Qualities of Compassion." Be that as it may, the said child smilingly performed the *Hagah* without question, and did so with great success, as you might if you perform it with the same stance throughout the day. This Kabbalistic rhyme reads:

מצפץ ברחמים
יהוה אלהים

(*Matz'patz* [*Matzapatz*] *b'rachamim*
*Yod Heh Vav Heh Elohim*)

That is all there is to it, and all you need to do is open your heart, smile from your chest, and sing it all day long in order to share in the infinite benefits of this wonderful *Hagah*.

Getting back to the earlier mentioned curious twenty-letter formula, whatever the origins and meaning of the formula may be, the individual sharing it maintained that the mentioned Kabbalist who shared it, was not willing to divulge whence it was derived, and the message was simply to just get on with the task of contemplating and reciting the letters comprising the meditation.[33]

Before addressing the actual technique of employing this meditation, I thought it expedient to reiterate some suggestions in order to ready yourself for meditations of this nature. Whilst these are not strictly necessary in the current instance, I observed elsewhere that for meditations involving *Kavvanah*, i.e. fully focussed attention and intention, to be truly successful, you should "prepare the subconscious mind" by cleaning your body beforehand, and donning fresh white, black or grey clothing, since bright colours can detract you from your "Focussed Attention" (*Kavvanah*)."³⁴ I noted that the same applies to the meditation room, which "should also comprise only objects and colours in keeping with the intention behind the specific meditation."³⁵ However, the most important factor in my estimation, is to refrain from discussing your meditations with anybody other than those who are "very close and sympathetic to your cause."³⁶

I further suggested that you cover your head with a טלית (*Talit*—prayer-shawl), if you have one readily available, or "the hood of a ritual garment or robe, or any cloth exclusively employed this purpose. As said, "this action causes a greater centering within oneself, a greater concentration of intention, as well as a sense of the closeness to the Divine Presence within and without." I affirmed that "all these activities have a strong influence in preparing the subconscious mind." I also mentioned that "you may sit either in a very brightly candle lit room, or else in a dimly lit or even dark room," the latter being entirely as suggested by your own "Inner Being."³⁷

In terms of the actual execution, the simplest way to work this practice of tracing and reciting the mentioned twenty Hebrew glyphs, is to sit in a comfortable and relaxed manner, to scan the letters from right to left, followed by shutting your eyes for a minute or two. However, in my estimation the full efficacy of a meditation depends on focus and intensity. Hence, in alignment with further suggestions from the individual who shared this technique,³⁸ I developed this scanning of the Hebrew letters into a "magical meditation" of the most impactive kind.

1. Commence by sitting and surrendering for a couple of minutes, and smile warmly inside yourself.
2. Focus your full attention on the first letter, and during inhalation imagine you are, as it were, drawing the letter and the inherent "spiritual force" of the glyph into your forehead.
3. Close your eyes and see the letter in your head, then chant or whisper the name of the letter intensely over the entire length of the exhalation.
4. Repeat the procedure with each letter comprising the array of twenty letters.

5. Conclude by taking another breath, and during exhalation allow the collective "spiritual forces" of the scanned glyphs to flow like a column of golden light downwards from the top of your head (*Keter*) to your feet (*Malchut*), as you flit your mind consecutively to the following physical locales:

| | |
|---|---|
| *Keter* (Crown) | Cranium |
| *Chochmah* (Wisdom) | Right Brain |
| *Binah* (Understanding) | Left Brain |
| [*Da'at* (Knowledge)] | [*Medulla Oblongata*/Brain Stem] |
| *Chesed* (Mercy) | Right Arm/Hand |
| *Gevurah* (Might) | Left Arm/Hand |
| *Tiferet* (Beauty) | Torso/Chest |
| *Netzach* (Endurance) | Right Leg/Kidney |
| *Hod* (Glory) | Left Leg/Kidney |
| *Yesod* (Foundation) | Sexual Organ |
| *Malchut* (Kingdom) | Feet |

6. Stay seated with eyes closed for a couple of minutes, and then focus your attention on the area in which you require healing or restoration, literally breathing the "Spiritual Force" into that specific situation, whether it be physical, emotional, mental, or spiritual.

7. Conclude by opening your eyes and uttering the standard Hebrew phrase ברוך שם כבוד מלכותו לעולם ועד (*Baruch shem k'vod malchuto l'olam va'ed*—"Blessed be the Name of His glorious Kingdom throughout eternity").

Regarding directing the "Spiritual Force" into the zone or situation needing restoration, we are informed that the individual who employed this technique for personal rectification, focussed the "Divine Force" in his "belly in order to get centered and nourish a basic sense of beingness."[39] Otherwise he suggested focussing on the heart "for healing and opening"; the sexual organ (genitals) "for healing and rectifying"; and the left brain "to become more detail-oriented."[40] To this list I personally added focussing on the right brain to increase creativity; and the nape of the neck, i.e. the bottom of the brainstem, to encourage greater reasoning ability and mental comprehension. I have personally found that I can sort out most psycho/physical problems by focussing the "Spiritual Force" into the solar plexus (liver), i.e. the physical zone understood to be the "brain" of the *Nefesh* (Instinctual Self).

Addressing the likely foundation of this meditation, and the manner in which it is functioning, the author who shared this amazing meditation referenced Moses Cordovero who wrote in his *Pardes Rimmonim* ("*Garden of Pomegranates*") that [my italics] "with the letters in general the commentators have said that there are a few (letters) that are of Judgment and a few that are of Mercy and a few in the middle. It is a principle in the divine Torah that *Aleph, Beth, Gimel, Dalet, Heh* and *Vav* are complete Mercy. *Zayin, Hhet, Tet* and *Yod* are Mercy. *Chaf, Lamed, Mem, Nun, Samech* and *Ayin* are a mixture of Judgment and Mercy. *Peh, Tzadi, Kof, Reish, Shin* and *Tav* are complete Judgment. When you want to write names, prayers and words, make the combination according to the action you want. If Mercy, the majority (of letters) should be Mercy; if Judgment, the majority should be Judgment."[41] Plainly then it is the first six of the twenty-two glyphs of the Hebrew alphabet which reflect "Complete Mercy," the succeeding four reflect "Mercy," the next six reflect a mixture of "Mercy" and "Judgment," and the concluding six which reflect "Complete Judgment," as indicated in the following table:

| Complete Mercy | Mercy | Mercy & Judgment | Complete Judgment |
|---|---|---|---|
| א Alef | ז Zayin | כ Kaf | פ Peh |
| ב Bet | ח Chet | ל Lamed | צ Tzadi |
| ג Gimel | ט Tet | מ Mem | ק Kof |
| ד Dalet | י Yod | נ Nun | ר Resh |
| ה Heh | | ס Samech | ש Shin |
| ו Vav | | ע Ayin | ת Tav |

In terms of the current meditation for "self rectification," it is clear "that the majority of its letters tilted towards Mercy."[42] I find perusing the balance of "Mercy glyphs" and "Judgment glyphs" in wellknown Hebrew incantations particularly interesting. Consider for example the famous prayer of Moses for the healing of his sister reading אל נא רפא נא לה (*El na r'fa na lah*—"Heal her now *El*, I beseech Thee") [*Numbers 12:13*]. This very brief prayer is popularly employed for healing in Hebrew amulets and incantations, and from the initials of its component words were derived אנרנל (*Enar'nal*), a most potent Hebrew Divine Name for healing purposes. We are reminded that the glyphs comprising this biblical phrase pertain mainly to "Mercy" or a balancing of "Mercy" and "Judgment," i.e. א (*Alef*)—"Complete Mercy"; ל (*Lamed*)—"Mercy/Judgment"; נ (*Nun*)—"Mercy/Judgment"; א (*Alef*)—"Complete Mercy"; ר (*Resh*)— "Complete Judgment"); פ (*Peh*)— "Complete Judgment"; א (*Alef*)—"Complete Mercy"; נ (*Nun*)—"Mercy/Judgment"; א (*Alef*)—"Complete Mercy"; ל (*Lamed*)—"Mercy/Judgment"; and ה (*Heh*) "Complete Mercy."[43]

As might be expected, any Divine/Angelic Name could be employed in the format delineated, and verbally expressed by spelling their component letters, e.g. the Divine Name אהיה (*Eh'yeh*) could be enunciated *Alef—Heh—Yod—Heh*, and the Angelic Name מיכאל vocalised *Mem—Yod—Ch[Kaf]—Alef—Lamed*. This particular practice is quite common, since there are many Divine Names in Jewish Magic which are not vocalised with vowels, but the component letters of which could be spelled out. This, considered a particularly powerful technique, can be applied to any Divine/Angelic Name the enunciation of which might be doubtful.

This is one of the techniques I have applied with the *Shem Vayisa Vayet* ("Name of Seventy-two Names") for meditional purposes. However, whilst it is good to work the technique of reciting the "Name of Seventy-two Names" letter by letter as you scan each of the seventy-two tri-letter combinations, i.e. והו—"*Vav–Heh–Vav*"; ילי—"*Yod–Lamed–Yod*"; סיט—"*Samech–Yod–Tet*"; etc., or even Abulafian style והו—"*VaHeVa*"; ילי—"*YoLaYo*"; etc.[44] I found reciting the various vocalisations, including the one I was taught some fifty years ago, to be equally effective for both meditational and magical purposes. In this regard, you would focus your full attention on each tri-letter portion whilst scanning the seventy-two tri-letter combinations, and reciting audibly or in a whisper the seventy-two "names":

| 1 Vehu וְהוּ | 2 Yeli יְלִי | 3 Sit סִיט | 4 Elem עָלָם | 5 Mahash מַהַשׁ | 6 Lelah לָלָה |
|---|---|---|---|---|---|
| 7 Acha אָכָא | 8 Kahet כַּהַת | 9 Hezi הָזִי | 10 Elad אָלָד | 11 Lav לָאוּ | 12 Haha הָהָע |
| 13 Yezel יָזֵל | 14 Mebah מָבָה | 15 Hari הָרִי | 16 Hakem הָקֶם | 17 Lav לָאוּ | 18 Keli כָּלִי |
| 19 Lov לָוּו | 20 Pahal פָּהָל | 21 Nelach נָלָךְ | 22 Yeyay יָיָי | 23 Melah מֶלָה | 24 Chaho חֲהוּ |
| 25 Netah נָתָה | 26 Ha'a הָאָא | 27 Yeret יָרָת | 28 Sha'ah שָׁאָה | 29 Riyi רִיִי | 30 Om אוֹם |
| 31 Lekav לָכָב | 32 Vesher וָשֶׁר | 33 Yichu יָחוּ | 34 L'hach לָהַח | 35 Kevek כּוֹק | 36 Menad מָנָד |
| 37 Ani אָנִי | 38 Cha'am חָעָם | 39 Reho רָהֹע | 40 Yeyiz יָיִז | 41 Hahah הָהַה | 42 Mich מִיךְ |
| 43 Veval וָול | 44 Yelah יָלָה | 45 Se'al סָאָל | 46 Ari עָרִי | 47 Eshal עָשָׁל | 48 Mih מִיה |
| 49 Vehu וְהוּ | 50 Dani דָּנִי | 51 Hachash הָחַשׁ | 52 Omem עָמֶם | 53 Nena נָנָא | 54 Nit נִית |
| 55 Mivah מָבָה | 56 Poi פּוּי | 57 Nemem נָמָם | 58 Yeyil יָיִל | 59 Harach הָרָח | 60 Metzer מָצָר |
| 61 Umab וּמָב | 62 Yahah יָהַה | 63 Anu עָנוּ | 64 Machi מָחִי | 65 Dameb דָּמָב | 66 Menak מָנָק |
| 67 Iya אִיע | 68 Chavu חָבוּ | 69 Ra'ah רָאָה | 70 Yabam יָבָם | 71 Hayi הָיִי | 72 Mum מוּם |

Readers may well wonder why it is necessary for me to focus yet again on the *"Name of Seventy-two Names,"* and, for that matter, on the subject of meditation, since I have already addressed this topic from a variety of angles in earlier volumes, which include the following meditation practices:

1. the *"Mother Breath,"* a unique meditational breathing technique the full practising of which is shared in the first part of *"The Book of Immediate Magic"*;[36]
2. *"Acknowledging and Invoking God Forces"* and *"Tuning in to God Forces,"* meditatively encountering and controling "God Forces," i.e. personal emotions;[37]
3. a set of meditation/magical techniques on the "Four Elements";[38]
4. a meditative technique to *"master the Spirit-Principle or Universal Element"*;[39]
5. a guided meditation to contacting *"Maggidim"* (Spirit Intelligences);[40]
6. a guided meditation to establishing an alignment with the Yohach Kalach *"Guardian Malachim: Spirit Messengers."*[41]
7. *"Word Meditation"* and *"Advanced Word Meditation"*;[42]
8. the twenty-two glyphs of *"The Hebrew Alphabet: Otiot"* as *"Gateways to Higher Awareness,"* which are also included in *"Aligning with 'Spirit Forces',"* the latter process equally including alignment with the *"The Potency of Achatri'el,"* and the *"Name of Seventy-two Names"*;[43]
9. meditation on the *Trisagion (Kedushah)*,[44] which "is said to align oneself with the actions of the 'Celestial Hosts',"[45] and which we are told has "the power to rid one of all negative influences."[46]
10. *"Taking on the Name"* to align with the "Eternal Living Spirit behind all existence and literally 'robe yourself in light'";[47]
11. *"Unification Meditations"* (*Yichudim*) with specific reference to a *"Universal Yichud"*;[48]
12. a unique *Yichud* on the three spellings of the letters comprising the Divine Name אהיה (*Eh'yeh*),[49] revisited later as *"Alignment with the Divine Self."*[50]

13. morning meditations on the twelve permutations of the Divine Names יהוה (*YHVH*) and אהיה (*Eh'yeh*),⁵¹ which I am revisiting in an advanced manner in the current tome;
14. the meditation on the six permutations of "*Shadai*" traced in a *Triquetra* pattern on the front of your body;⁵²
15. the meditation/magical use of the twenty-four permutations of the Divine Name אדני (*Adonai*);⁵³
16. reciting and meditating on the "*Menorah Psalm*"⁵⁴
17. prayer-meditations on the "*Ana Becho'ach*" prayer-meditation and associated "Forty-two Letter Name";⁵⁵
18. meditations on the "*Shem Vayisa Vayet*" ("Name of Seventy-two Names");⁵⁶
19. *Shiviti*" plaques, these being highly specialised and very beautiful visual constructs employed for both amuletic and meditational purposes;⁵⁷
20. a "*Machshavah Shiviti* amulet" to be meditated upon for "purity of thought";⁵⁸
21. a unique meditative technique of constructing and internalising Hebrew amulets;⁵⁹
22. the practice of "*Becoming a Living Kamea*" by means of employing meditative visualisation for a variety of purposes;⁶⁰
23. "*Tuning & Restructuring a Male Body*" with Divine Names employed meditatively;⁶¹
24. "*Clearing the Sacred Space*" and "*Contemplating Definitions: Gevulim*" (Boundaries),⁶² the practising of which I revisited in the first part of the current volume in terms of the full "*Clearing the Sacred Space*" procedure;⁶³
25. a "*Walking Meditation for Personal Aid*" and "*Hakafot*" ("Formulas for Circumambulation" such as "*Defining the Working Space*";⁶⁴
26. a variety of "*Sacred Chants*" for meditational purposes;⁶⁵
27. "*Merkavistic & Kabbalistic Mantric Meditation*";⁶⁶
28. Hebrew Keywords and Divine Names employed in *Hagah* meditation (Hebrew mantras);⁶⁷
29. "*Unification with the Higher Self,*" "*The Breath of Light,*" and "*The Amen Breath*";⁶⁸
30. "*Establishing a Body of Light*";⁶⁹
31. an "*Exercise in Absolute Reality*";⁷⁰ and

32. *"Opening the Gates,"* pertaining to channeling unique "Spirit Forces" by means of special actions within yourself;[71]

Thirty-two meditation techniques in all aligning, so to speak, with the "thirty-two wondrous paths of wisdom," and I have to date barely touched upon the vast depths of "Kabbalistic Meditation." Hence the necessity for revisiting this topic in the current text, and equally in future volumes to be included in the "Shadow Tree Series."

There are two special practices, i.e. the remarkable *Noten Kavod* ("Giving Respect") and superb *Lekaven Tiferet* ("Acknowledging Beauty") which I shared in the very first volume of this series of texts on *Practical Kabbalah*,[72] and which I have not included in this array of "magical meditations" addressed in my writings to date. Whilst the "Rite of Giving Honour" and the practice of "Acknowledging Beauty" might not be considered meditational practices in the strictest sense, some serious practitioners do consider them to be such, since these technique encourage focused mindfulness, a sorely needed quality to make the world a better place. To this end I noted regarding the incredibly effective *Noten Kavod* ("Giving Respect") practice, that "there will be no end to wars, abuse of the environment, etc., until respect for all manifestation returns to our world."[73] I also stated that the execution of this specific magico-meditational procedure directly impacts not only on that at which it is directed, but equally on the very being of the practitioner, since "it slowly infiltrates and alters the thought and desire of all life to emanate and give respect to the whole of manifestation, and all its constituent parts. With this activity, peace and serenity are automatically encouraged in yourself, your reality and everything else you may encounter."[74]

I previously elucidated different stages comprising the "Rite of Giving Honour," and noted that "when you are adept at doing this procedure as a matter of course throughout the day, it is a continual expression of יהוה (*YHVH*), the Ineffable Name of God."[75] I do not intend to address the separate stages of working "*Noten Kavod*" in any detail here, but I do believe we might review the complete practice which is as follows:

1.  Whatever and whoever you meet through your five senses, whether it be an object, subject or person, e.g. a stone, a book, food, drink, animal or person, be gracious enough to bow mentally to that which you are encountering, and, whilst doing so, to mentally express during an exhalation the sacred statement *Noten Kavod*. Smile warmly with your whole being, i.e. feel your whole body, heart and soul smile, and let the warmth of your being flow towards that which you are offering respect, whilst uttering the words *Noten Kavod*.

    It is suggested that you exhale through your mouth during the execution of this portion of the practice, the reason being that, as you mentally utter the words "*Noten Kavod*," you simultaneously imagine that "Divine Force," i.e. the warmth of your being flows out of your mouth and/or your entire being, in the form of a specific colour, element (fire, water, air or earth) towards that which you are honouring. This is normally done with a specific associated quality such as love, peace, health, etc., or even a combination of all of these. You should allow yourself to be guided by your own inner instincts as to what colour or elements you wish to emanate.

2.  Having performed the initial action during a single exhalation, during the succeeding inhalation imagine that you are receiving in return from that object, subject or person you are in contact with at that moment, the same respect, honour and warmth that you emanated. In this manner, by using imagination, you are inducing a beneficial return flow of "Divine Power" from the intended recipient to yourself, providing you allow yourself to receive such an acknowledgement by being open to the return flow.

Having worked this remarkable procedure for nearly five decades, and having witnessed the incredible impact it has on all, i.e. on practitioners and recipients alike, I have also encountered the enthusiastic feedbacks of those who have devoted themselves to performing the technique as a matter of course throughout their daily life. One practitioner queried whether it could be used in his business, i.e. applied on his customers, the intention being, in his own words, to "motivate them to do business in a more honest way." I personally believe the practice of *Noten Kavod* to be one of the most important techniques in "levelling the playing field," so to speak, i.e. in establishing the absolutely ideal arena for congenial interaction with your personal environment. In this regard, the earlier mentioned practitioner who wanted to employ it on all his clients in accordance with his stated intention, could and certainly should do so.

Another fellow practitioner noted that employing the *Noten Kavod* procedure on people who are antagonistic towards you, or perceived as personal enemies "is like forgiving them," which he noted is a difficult but healthy practice. As I am sure readers might have suspected from my eulogy, this is one of my all time favourite techniques, and one which has served me most beneficially for many decades. I use it all the time on everybody and everything. I use it on family, friends, animals, trees, the Sun and the Moon, in fact on everything I may encounter in my daily life. I employ it even on groups of people collectively in shopping centres, and once even in the most dangerous of circumstances. It was this incredibly simple and most effective procedure, which saved my wife and I when we were in great danger of being assaulted and killed by a belligerent mob. In fact, the leaders amongst those attackers took great care to get us out of harm's way as quickly as they possibly could, whilst protecting and treating us with great respect and kindness. I cannot sing the praises of the *Noten Kavod* procedure enough for anyone seriously interested in "Self Creation" and making the world a better place for all!

The wonderful thing about the "*Noten Kavod*" procedure is the remarkable, immediate, and beneficial impact it has on the intended recipient, whether the latter be of the humankind, a four legged friend, etc. Furthermore, it is one of those practices in which you are approaching life from a fully focussed personal stance incorporating acknowledgement and respect. Having worked this procedure for the major part of my life in this world, I have come to realise that whilst it is, as it were, "levelling the playing field" in terms of myself and the greater world around me, i.e. setting the the ideal condition for interaction between "Centre" (Self) and "Circumference" (the world), it does not mean that you necessarily have to like a recipient in order to give him/her/it respect. Hence this technique can be employed on anyone and anything, whether friend or foe.

I recall my late mentor, William Gray, telling me that we can still honour Divinity in anyone, whilst not particularly liking the way they may be behaving in life. It is purely a question of recognising that however revolting anyone may be, "God" is in them as well. The issue is that they might be presently part of the "unregenerate nature" of divine manifestation, which is being processed through a long and painful course of change involving maybe millions of years before they will be anything better. Of course, that does not help with the problem of how to deal with them, except at a distance as one would with say a rattlesnake. In fact, I can easily do the "*Noten Kavod*" procedure with a snake, or with anything or anyone, for that matter, whose behaviour might be personally inimical, whilst simultaneously maintaining a safe distance.

However, there are naturally situations in which one cannot avoid unpleasant circumstances deriving from those who would happily walk all over you without blinking an eye, and such unfortunate situations are sometimes very close to home, e.g. amongst those who are supposed to be ones nearest and dearest. Even in this instance it is important to recognise the Divine One in them as well, and to work the "*Noten Kavod*" procedure, whilst simultaneously accepting the fact that humans have this "bad" side to themselves, and realising that this is changeable with time and evolution. Therefore the best way to cope with it would be to place yourself in a position where you cannot be hurt, abused, etc., and to survive it with genuine love as distinct from "sentimental" love. I believe that is what is meant by "loving your enemy," and why it is so important. In my estimation the important thing is that we do not have to like or agree with each other, whilst still acknowledging that all of us, friends and enemies alike, are manifestations of the Divine One, and hence offering that individual respect in the magical manner expressed in the "*Noten Kavod*" procedure. This is certainly a difficult and uncompromising doctrine, but one worth realising.

It is worth revisiting the ancillary exercise to the "*Noten Kavod*" practice, i.e. the mentioned "*Lekaven Tiferet*" or "Finding Beauty" procedure, which, as in the case of "*Noten Kavod*" (Giving Respect), is a practice in which you (Centre) relate directly with the greater world (Circumference) in a most meaningful manner. It is likewise employed with everyone and everything. In this regard, the simplest way of working this process is to see and acknowledge the beauty in whatever you are observing.[76] Following this action, you would continue by aligning yourself with the Divine One in whatever way you choose to, and conclude the procedure, as I noted, "by uniting the beauty, which you have observed and acknowledged, with your Source by mentally saying *Baruch ha-Shem*, meaning 'Blessed be your Name',"[77] or offering the greater blessing expressed mentally, or aloud if possible:

ברוך אתה אדני אלהינו מלך העולם שככה לו בעולמו

Transliteration:
> *Baruch Atah Adonai Eloheinu Melech ha-Olam, Shekachah Lo ba-Olamo.*

Translation:
> Blessed are You *Adonai*, our God, King of the Universe, Who has created such as These in His world.

As some readers may know, it is often customary amongst Jews to say *"Baruch ha-Shem"* every time you hear something good. In this regard, my beloved friend Yoni Helper, may his memory be a blessing, who, as a religious Jew, practised one of the great Jewish "magical techniques" for bringing goodness and wellbeing into your life. Every time he heard something wonderful or saw anything beautiful, he would say *"Baruch ha-Shem"* (Blessed be the Name [God]). He used to quiz "so how are you doing Jacob?" I would respond "very well my dear Yoni," which elicited the inevitable exclamation *"Baruch ha-Shem!"* Then he would ask ".....and how is Gloria?" and I would say "she is doing so well Yoni," to which he would retort *"Baruch ha-Shem!"* This might be succeeded by "do you still make beautiful music?" and my rejoinder that "yes I still perform on occassion," inevitably induced another *"Baruch ha-Shem!"* He was a master of the art of *"Baruch ha-Shem,"* and in this manner he generated joy, goodness, and wellbeing not only in his own life, but in the lives of everybody who knew him. I am convinced the Divine One liked him so much that he decided to take my cheerful beloved Yoni into his personal care.

So by means of this wonderful exercise we deliberately turn our focus away from all ugliness, disorder and rage, so as not to unite ourselves with these "negativities," but instead to align ourselves with and focus on that which brings stability into our world. As I noted elsewhere, "it is through the act of finding beauty in anything that we are able to identify with that thing," and "the act of finding beauty in everything leads us to attain 'Seven Aspects of Bliss' from which will result 'Four Fulfilments of Joy'."[78] The "Seven Aspects of Bliss" are equated with the lower seven *Sefirot* on the Tree of Life, which we have addressed in some detail in the previous chapter, and which are as follows:

*Chesed* (Loving-kindness) — חדוה (*Chedva*—"Delight")
*Gevurah* (Severity, Strength) — דיצה (*Ditza* "Pleasure")
*Tiferet* (Beauty) — רינה (*Rina*—"Glad song")
*Netzach* (Endurance) — גילה (*Gila*—"Mirth")
*Hod* (Glory) — (*Simcha*—"Happiness")
*Yesod* (Foundation) — ששון (*Sasson*—"Joy")
*Malchut* (Kingdom) — צהלה (*Tzahalah*—"Jubilation")

We are taught that the "Jubilation" associated with Malchut (Kingdom), is a direct result of the first six aspects, and all of these conjoin to reveal the "Four Fulfilments of Joy":

אהבה (*Ahava*—"Love")
אחוה (*Achva*—"Brotherhood")
שלום (*Shalom*—"Peace")
רעות (*Rei'ut*—"Companionship")

The "Seven Aspects of Bliss" and the "Four Fulfilments of Joy" are sorely needed in our world, and can be so easily achieved by finding, contemplating, and acknowledging beauty in everything. As I noted in *"The Book of Self Creation,"* acknowledging beauty in everything is "a sure way to find the true meaning of Being," and is also "an attempt to achieve a full realisation of the 'Eternal Root of Splendour' beyond all being."[79] Personally speaking, the conjoined practice of *"Noten Kavod"* and *"Lekaven Tiferet"* pertains to the revelation of the Divine One and wellbeing in this world. By means of these simple practices we open ourselves to the flow of *Shefa* (Divine Abundance), as we deliberately turn our attention away from all ugliness, disorder and rage, and focus on that which brings stability into our world.

## B. Hebrew Magical Mantras

The main difference between *Practical Kabbalah* and other magical traditions is that Jewish Magic is primarily based on Divine Names. There are literally thousands of Hebrew Divine Name constructs created for a great variety of purposes, amongst which is the very one my querant is having to deal with. It is worth noting that the vast majority of Hebrew Divine Names, as elucidated amongst others by Rabbi Moses Zacutto in *"Shorshei ha-Shemot,"*[80] and as addressed in my own works on *Practical Kabbalah*, are not appellations of the Divine One *per se*. Each of these Divine Names constructs is, as it were, "programmed" to function in a specific manner within the vast "Sea of Collective Consciousness," the earlier mentioned "Ocean of Awareness" which is shared by us all.

A friend remarked that in *Practical Kabbalah* there are so many Divine Names for every purpose you might imagine, that it is difficult to select amongst them. As he noted, he certainly could not select all of them, if he wanted to employ them in a *Hagah* (mantra) to be uttered throughout the day. As might be expected, I encountered the same problem when I commenced my work with this amazing tradition nearly fifty years ago. However, there are a couple of "tricks," so to speak, in selecting the best possible combination of Names aligned with your basic purpose. In this regard, my first "trick" is to ascertain which, if any, of the Divine Names affiliated with my "purpose," is particularly popular. In my estimation the frequent use of certain Divine Names would cause them to be particularly empowered within the "Collective Consciousness" we all share, and hence I have found these to be particularly efficacious.

The second "trick" is to write down your intention, i.e. the purpose of the *Hagah*, and then to peruse each of the Divine Names associated with it. Most Sacred Names serve more than a single magical function, and by looking at all the "Powers" of each Name, you can ascertain those most suitable to the fundamental reason for the magical action. In this regard, a young man who was studying at a local tertiary institution, told me that he was looking to compile a set of Divine Names to be employed in a *Hagah* for the extensive purpose of "Improving memory and reasoning ability, health and general wellbeing, relationships, personal empowerment, and protection."

You might well ask how it is possible to have all those, seemingly diverse intentions, conjoined and dealt with in a single magical action? However, it is perfectly feasible to inspect the multi-functionality of several of the Hebrew Divine Names, of which I have listed a fair number in the first part of *"The Book of Immediate Magic."*[81] In terms of the requirements of the said individual, the first Divine Name which comes to mind is the well-known Divine Name construct אנקתם פסתם פספסים דיונסים vocalised *Anaktam Pastam Paspasim Dionsim* (sometimes *'naket'ma P'sotam P'sips'yema Dayev'n'soyam*). Known as the "Twenty-two Letter Name of God" which concludes the "Priestly Benediction" uttered during *Rosh Hashanah* (Jewish New Year), it is employed in a wide variety of Hebrew amulets and incantations.

This Divine Name combination does not have any specific meaning *per se*, however it is said to be a transposition of the twenty-two letters of the first five words of the priestly blessing in *Numbers 6:24–25*, reading:

יברכך יהוה וישמרך יאר יהוה

Transliteration:
*Y'varech'cha YHVH v'yishm'recha ya'er YHVH*
Translation:
*YHVH* bless thee and keep thee, shine *YHVH*

It is said that each letter of this Divine Name construct is the initial of a set of unique words, which pertains to an individual being freed from the prison of anxiety and fear.[82] The "power of protection" of this Divine Name complex is legendary, since, as I noted elsewhere, it relieves melancholy, depression, low self esteem, states of confusion, resentment, stress, banishes anxiety, terror, fear, nightmares (Night Demons), all feelings of trepidation, and protects one from the malicious actions of enemies, "the Evil Eye," spiritual and demonic assault, in fact, from all manner of evil.[83]

As I know well enough, so-called "psychic attack," and perforce "psychic defence," is of particular importance in a world beset by humans trying to destroy their fellow humankind for no better reasons than jealousy, resentment, one-up-man-ship, or simply because they delight in seeing others suffer because it gives them a sense of power. Whilst I am not an advocate of "Psychic Attack" at all, employing spiritual defence techniques against all manner of assault directed at oneself, or at the persons of those who are dear to us, or in support of those who are calling for help, might indeed incorporate counter assault. In this regard, I do not waste my time indulging in venom and hate against anyone seeking to harm me. Should I encounter any such situation, I would normally work to become centered to the point of feeling nothing whatsoever, then invoke the appropriate "God Force," i.e. emotional quality I have ascertained to be necessary in spiritually counteracting the onslaught, followed by taking appropriate "defensive action," whether the latter is perceived to be "counter attack" or not.

As noted earlier, the higher you evolve yourself spiritually, the more sensitive you become to the fluctuation of all manner of forces in your environment. With this kind of sensitivity, imagine being in the company of somebody who hates the very ground you walk on. That individual might sit there brooding, facing you with resentment and ill feelings of this, that, and the other, and might blast you with destructive energy just because of who you are. This is once again a matter of the "evil eye," and you will indeed be impacted in some or other way, depending on how you deal with the situation.

Readers familiar with the principles of "Self Creation," would observe that you are really only affected by the forces you "buy into," and this perception would indeed be correct. However, by having elected to be born into this realm of existence, including the associated emotional, mental, and spiritual domains, you have already "bought into" that which does not only affect all of us collectively, but equally impacts us individually whether we like it or not. Your day to day existence on this planet necessitates encountering all manner of forces, some benevolent and others malevolent. These will impact your life because you have elected to live here, i.e. you have "bought into" this level of existence in specific ways. In other words, you have on some primordial level of being set the "reality" you are now experiencing. Everybody living on this planet has done just that, and it is important to realise this when it comes to our human collective existence in three-dimensional manifestation, that we are all co-creators.

This might give the impression that individuals are trapped in the collective, and unable to do anything about it. Here is where

"Self Creation" comes in, and each individual can affect circumstances directly, depending on how much that individual is able to believe in him or herself. Unfortunately most people, who have literally submerged themselves into what could be termed the "fallen state of seperateness," have also lost the fundamental understanding that the answer to any problem they may encounter in life lies in how they deal with it.

To begin with, it is naturally vitally important to recognise that, whether we like it or not, "all is God" and there is nothing which is not "God." All aspects of manifestation are parts of the selfsameness of the great "I Am," hence viruses as well as all the assorted unpleasant manifestations we may encounter in life, are equally "entities" created by God, equally manifestations of the "Being" of the Infinite One, and have as much entitlement to a decent life existence as you believe you have. Of course, they threaten your essential wellbeing, and therein lies the problem on how to deal with them. There are also people who behave just like viruses, sapping the life force of all and sundry around them, and some of these individuals are believed to have themselves reached very lofty levels of spiritual development. All of us have at one time or another questioned the so-called "scum of the Earth," the villains, the sub-humans of so-called humanity, or what has been termed the "dregs of society," and asked with appropriate horror "What? Is God also in those? Are they equally manifestations of the Almighty, and can such revolting creatures be part of Its nature?" The answer has to be "yes they are," but they are part of the imperfect, unregenerate nature of Divine Being which is being processed through a long and painful course of change, involving maybe millions of years, before they will be anything better.

Having acknowledged the "power of protection" of the דיונסים פספסים פסתם אנקתם (*Anaktam Pastam Paspasim Dionsim*), it is worth noting that individuals who have a low self esteem, and who suffer melancholy and depression, can equally be relieved from such states of confusion and even resentment by means of the "Twenty-two Letter Name"[84] employed as a *Hagah*. In this specific regard, this Divine Name is often conjoined with other Hebrew "Names of Power" for the purposes of protection against all evil, whether the latter be of the spiritual or physical kind, as shown below:

אנקתם פסתם פספסים דיונסים
יוהך כלך צמרכד אזבוגה
*Anaktam Pastam Paspasim Dionsim*
*Yohach Kalach Tzamarchad Azbugah*

If this Divine Name combination is employed as a *Hagah*, you could simply utter it in a low voice continuously. However, there are different ways of using this Divine Name combination as a "mantra." For example, you might want to do this protection for somebody other than yourself. In this instance you would employ the entire Divine Name construct followed by the name of the individual, and then concluding by repeating again the entire Divine Name combination, e.g.:

אנקתם פסתם פספסים דיונסים יוהך כלך צמרכד
אזבוגה [.....insert name.....] אנקתם פסתם פספסים
דיונסים יוהך כלך צמרכד אזבוגה

Transliteration:
*Anaktam Pastam Paspasim Dionsim Yohach Kalach Tzamarchad Azbugah* [.....insert name.....] *Anaktam Pastam Paspasim Dionsim Yohach Kalach Tzamarchad Azbugah*

The "rule," so to speak, which applies here is to use only the first name of an individual you know personally, e.g. your wife, children, family, friends, associates, etc., and the name and surname of those whom you are not directly acquainted with. In other words, you may know someone personally and hence would use only his or her first name if you were performing this *"Hagah"* for the said individual. However, if you should receive a request to perform it for an individual with whom you are unacquainted, you would employ both the name and surname, and your *Nefesh* (Instinctual Self) would automatically link to that individual via the person of the one who requested you to perform this task in the first place. Some claim that the "name" of the individual should not only include the surname, but equally the name of his/her "mother." Whilst this is practically applicable where an individual has a Hebrew name, and is in fact aware of the identity of the "mother," which is not always the case, it is certainly not necessary or obligatory in terms of the success of the working, as I can attest in the personal capacity of having performed this practice numerous times over a period of fifty years with absolute success in every instance.

Of course, you could easily apply the same format of the *Hagah* for yourself, in this instance inserting your own name in the centre of the full phrase, and it is worth considering that there are again a few "tricks of the trade" when it comes to employing Divine Names in this mantric manner. It is very important to keep in mind that when you are uttering the *Hagah* for another individual, or yourself for that matter, that you perform the action as if you are addressing the recipient in a direct manner, like saying for example "How are you [.....so and so.....], how are you?" In the current instance you would speak to the recipient in one breath, saying in a low voice "*Anaktam Pastam Paspasim Dionsim Yohach Kalach Tzamarchad Azbugah*.....[personal name].....," then take a quick breath and conclude by affirming "*Anaktam Pastam Paspasim Dionsim Yohach Kalach Tzamarchad Azbugah*." This technique is one of the most powerful in terms of what a beloved companion of mine coined "Immediate Magic," and there are indeed further ways in which the "power" of this Divine Name construct can be most powerfully enhanced if needs be.

I should mention that it is an excellent idea to work the previously mentioned procedures in stages. What I mean is that you commence with working the *Hagah* comprising only the "Twenty-two Letter Name of God" for say a week, or at least until it has become fully "automated," i.e. pronouncing itself continuously in the back of your mind virtually unobserved by your conscious mind. This takes continuous effort on the part of the practitioner to ensure saying or whispering it at all times. When that is achieved, you would expand your "*Hagah*" with additional Divine Names which I have noted are pronounced twice with your personal name or the name of another recipient located in the centre. It becomes a lot easier to add Divine Names to your primary *Hagah*.

When you have achieved the "automated comfort," so to speak, of uttering the full Divine Name construct with your personal name or the name of another recipient, you can enhance the power of the Divine Name construct by including a most potent Divine Name. Vocalised *Achatri'el* (sometimes *Akatri'el* or *Aktri'el*), this Divine Name is understood to comprise enormous power, amongst which is the ability to vastly empower other Divine Names.[85] In the current instance in which you would be using a twofold enunciation of a Divine Name construct with a personal name included in the centre, the enhancement of the "Spiritual Forces" is achieved by adding the Divine/Angelic Name אכתריאל (*Achatri'el*) as a prefix and suffix to the entire construct. In other words, you would now pronounce the complete *Hagah* (Hebrew mantra) in the following manner:

אכתריאל אנקתם פסתם פספסים דיונסים
יוהך כלך צמרכד אזבוגה [.....insert name.....]
אנקתם פסתם פספסים דיונסים יוהך כלך
צמרכד אזבוגה אכתריאל

Transliteration:
> *Achatri'el Anaktam Pastam Paspasim Dionsim Yohach Kalach Tzamarchad Azbugah* [.....insert name.....] *Anaktam Pastam Paspasim Dionsim Yohach Kalach Tzamarchad Azbugah Achatri'el*

In the current instance you would commence the *Hagah* by uttering the Divine/Angelic Name אכתריאל (*Achatri'el*) prefix on its own, virtually announcing and calling this vast "Divine Power" into action. Following a momentary pause, you would continue by pronouncing the remainder of the opening phrase which includes the personal name. Then you take a breath before vocalising the concluding phrase in its entirety. Of course, the whole *Hagah* (Hebrew mantra) would be uttered in as rhythmic a manner as possible, and I should add that it helps a lot if one can encourage a good emotional disposition to accompany the work, e.g. one in which you are smiling from within yourself in a most friendly manner at yourself and your world.

In terms of the earlier mentioned request of my acquaintance for Divine Names which can be employed in a *Hagah* for the purpose of "improving memory and reasoning ability, health and general wellbeing, relationships, personal empowerment, and protection," and from the perspective of my mentioned "trick" to consider Divine Names which fulfil more than one function, you might wonder what the "Twenty-two Letter Name" has to offer beyond its "legendary" powers of protection. However, there is much more to this remarkable Divine Name than meets the eye, since it is also one of the Divine Names which encourages abundance, good living and blessings generally.[86] It is even used in incantations to find grace and loving-kindness in the eyes of a loved one, and equally for personal empowerment.[87] With a different vocalisation, i.e. *'naket'ma P'sotam P'sips'yema Dayev'nsoyam*, the same Divine Name construct is employed to improve memory, understanding and learning ability.[88] Considered from the perspective of the fundamental purpose of the magical action under consideration, this Divine Name would be vitally important since it satisfies several of the magical requirements:

1. It improves memory and reasoning ability;
2. It encourages general wellbeing from abundance, blessings and a good living perspective;
3. It works towards "personal empowerment" and encourages good relationships; and
4. It is certainly one of the greatest Divine Names in terms of its powers of protection.

In terms of satisfying the requirements of the mentioned query, both vocalisations of the "Twenty-two Letter Name of God" would be used. However, there are the other requirements in terms of the fundamental intention behind the current magical action to be considered, i.e. "health and general wellbeing," and whilst we investigate Divine Names pertaining to this purpose, it would be especially great if the chosen Divine Names equally align with the one already chosen. In this regard, I once again tend to seek the most popular first, and the "Forty-two letter Name of God" immediately comes to mind, which is equally famous in terms of finding protection against all sorts of dangers, since this Divine Name aligns with the sphere of *Gevurah* (Strength/Severity) on the sefirotic Tree.[89]

As you probably know already, the "Forty-two Letter Name of God" is divided into seven six-letter sections respectively related to the seven planets, and, as I noted previously, the entire "Forty-two Letter Name" is of great value in Jewish magic. However, only selected portions of this enigmatic Divine Name are employed for physical and spiritual protection, and as far as the current "magical intention" under discussion is concerned, it is the second tri-letter portions of the first and seventh sections of the "Forty-two letter Name" which are of particular importance, respectively יט'ץ (*YaToTzi*) and צי'ת (*TzoYaT'*). The *YatoTzi* tri-letter combination pertains to the sphere of *Chesed* (Lovingkindness or Mercy), and the *TzoYaT'* combination to the sphere of *Malchut* (Kingdom) on the sefirotic Tree.[90]

In terms of their employment in *Practical Kabbalah*, I noted that "if you focus your attention on any individual, and then utter the Name *YaToTzi* with *Kavvanah*, with the total meaning of the heartfelt intention of your soul, that individual will have received a very special blessing."[91] This tri-letter Divine Name combination is sometimes conjoined with the Name אדני (*Adonai*), vocalised *Adonaye* in the current instance, to form the Name אידתנצי (*Ayadotonatziye*), a Divine Name combination constructed for the purpose of magical protection, as well as the improvement of the health of a sickly individual.[92] We are further informed that the regular practice of uttering the Name *Ayadotonatziye* on waking in the morning and prior to falling asleep at night, will respectively "engender spiritual protection throughout the entire day" and "very clear answers in your dreams to any questions you might have."[93] In my estimation the use of אידתנצי (*Ayadotonatziye*) for the purposes of achieving the latter night-time aim, might render this Divine Name combination equally useful for the purposes of counteracting night time fears and bad dreams.

The יתץ (*YaToTzi*) Divine Name construct can be employed in conjunction with צית (*TzoYaT'*), the fourteenth and concluding portion of the "Forty-two Letter Name." Of course, the letters of these tri-letter Divine Name combinations are purely permutations of each other. As it is, *TzoYaT'* is a multi-functional portion of the "Forty-Two Letter Name," regarding which we are told this tri-letter combination has the ability to banish malevolent "Spirit Forces" and restore the wellbeing of an individual who suffers their affliction.[94] It should be noted that this Divine Name combination is sometimes conjoined with the Ineffable Name (vocalised יהוה (*YiHaV'Ha*) to form the Divine Name construct vocalised יצהיותה (*Yitzohayav't'ha*), again for the purposes of healing and protection.[95] In fact, the full combination *TzoYaT' Yitzohayav't'ha*, as well as its affiliated "Spirit Forces," are called upon for physical protection. The power of the concluding tri-letter portion of the "Forty-two Letter Name" employed in conjunction with the names of its associated Spirit Intelligences, i.e. גדיאל

(*Gadi'el*), צדקיאל (*Tzadki'el*), יהואל (*Yeho'el*), and תמאל (*Tama'el*), are said to increase the popularity of anyone invoking their support "in the Name of God."[96] In this regard, alignment with these "Spirit Forces" is understood to cause everyone you may encounter to like you, and, what is more, no special purification is required prior to invoking their support.

Now, we are informed the *TzoYaT'* Divine Name construct comprises the power to banish malevolent "Spirit Forces," and to "restore the wellbeing of an individual who suffers their affliction."[97] In this regard, we are also informed that *TzoYaT' Yitzohayav't'ha*, as well as their associated "Spirit Forces," could be called upon at any time anywhere for the purpose of protection against all manner of danger. Curiously enough, similarly to *YaToTzi*, which we noted can be employed to improve the health of a sickly individual, the combination *TzoYaT'* will encourage the speedy recovery of anyone suffering from a serious illness, especially when this Divine Name construct is uttered over the afflicted individual, in conjunction with the Names of the four listed Spirit Intelligences.[98]

So in terms of the listed magical intention of "Improving memory and reasoning ability, health and general wellbeing, relationships, personal empowerment, and protection," it is clear that the two enunciations of the "*Anaktam*" Divine Name combination, and the *YaToTzi/TzoYaT'*, as well as their respective combinations with the Divine Name *Adonai* and the Ineffable Name, are excellent in achieving every aspect of the primary magical intention. It is purely a question of combining the listed Divine Names in a meaningful way, which could be comfortably uttered in a rhythmical manner. In this regard, I would personally commence with יתץ אידתנצי (*Yatotzi Ayadotonatziye*) followed by אנקתם פסתם פספסים דיונסים (*Anaktam Pastam Paspasim Dionsim*). Next you would insert your first name, or the name and surname of an individual for whom you desire to perform this magical action, followed by the *'naket'ma P'sotam P'sipsiyema Dayev'nsoyam* enunciation of the "Twenty-two Letter Name," and concluding with the צית יצהיותה (*Tzoyat' Yitzohayav't'ha*) Divine Name construct.

You could again add the Divine Name אכתריאל (*Achatri'el*), the Name which focusses "Forces" into "Forms," so to speak, to the beginning and end of the *Hagah*, if you wish to further enhance and empower the collective "Divine Forces" of this Divine Name complex. In this instance the complete *Hagah* would read:

אכתריאל יתץ אידתנצי
אנקתם פסתם פספסים דיונסים
[.....fill in personal name.....]
אנקתם פסתם פספסים דיונסים [alternative vocalisation]
יצהיותה צית אכתריאל

Transliteration:
*Achatri'el Yatotzi Ayadotonatziye*
*Anaktam Pastam Paspasim Dionsim*
[.....fill in personal name.....]
*'naket'ma P'sotam P'sipsiyema Dayev'nsoyam*
*Yitzohayav't'ha Tzoyat' Achatri'el*

As far as uttering a *Hagah*, or any mantra for that matter, is concerned, it is purely a question of the symmetrical balance of the component parts requiring easy and rhythmical enunciation. In this regard, the rhythm and meter is dependent on the vocal accents in a Divine Name combination. In the instance of the *Hagah* (Hebrew mantra) under consideration, I was informed that the following accents apply:

A***CHA****tri'el*
***YA****totzi Ayadoto**NA**tziye*
*Anaktam **PAS**tam **PAS**pasim Di**ON**sim* [.....fill in name.....]
*'na**KE**t'ma P'so**TAM** P'sipsi**YE**ma Dayef'nso**YAM***
***YI****tzohaya**V'***t'ha **TZO***yat' A**CHA**tri'el*

Employing a rhythm, the speed of which is often indicated by nodding the head at a speed comfortable to the one employing the *Hagah* (magical mantra) , you would ensure that the beat always coincides with the accents in a Divine Name or Divine Name construct. In most instances the rhythm is a plain 1.....2.....1.....2.....1.....2..... Applying it in terms of the Divine Name combination comprising the *Hagah* currently under consideration, the rhythmic meter could be:

| | 1 | | 2 |
|---|---|---|---|
| 1 | Breathe......... | A-**CHA**tri'el | ......... |
| 2 | Breathe......... | **YA**totzi | Ayadoto– **NA**tziye ......... |
| 3 | Anaktam | **PAS**tam | **PAS**pasim Di-**ON**sim ......... |
| 4 | [Personal Name] | Breathe..... [E]na-**KE**t[e]'ma | P[e]so**TAM** ......... |
| 5 | ......P[e]sipsi– | **YE**ma | Da– **YEF**[e]nsoyam Breathe......... |
| 6 | **YI**tzohaya– | V[e]**It**[e]ha | **TZO**yat[e]...A-**CHA**tri'el ......... |

Keeping the accents of the words in mind, as well as the inclusion of inhalations at appropriate moments, I have arranged the *Hagah* over four lines. The rule here is that the opening "*Achatri'el*" is, as it were, an invocatory announcement, enunciated entirely separately from the remainder of the *Hagah*. The first portion from "*Yatotzi*" to the naming of the recipient, is uttered in a single breath, and the aim is to vocalise this phrase as if you were addressing the recipient directly in person. Following the utterance of the name of the recipient, a breath separates the first portion from the second which commences with the utterance of the variant enunciation of the "*Anaktam*" Divine Name construct, as well as the concluding statement from "*Yitzohayav't'ha*" to "*Achatri'el*." Here the second phrase, enunciated over a single exhalation, flows directly into the second "*Achatri'el*."

There are other ways of expressing the Divine Name combination comprising this *Hagah*, but the vocal accents of the component Divine Names need to be considered in every instance. Furthermore, easy vocalisation at a fair speed needs to be kept in mind at all times. As noted in the "Hebrew Transliteration" page at the very beginning of this tome, the bracketed "[e]" insert in the *Hagah* indicates the glottal stop vowel termed a "*sh'va*" in Hebrew, which is traditionally associated with *Gevurah* (Might) on the sefirotic Tree. It sounds like the "ea" in the English word "earn" or the "e" in "the." I usually indicate it with an apostrophe in my work.

It should be noted that in the current instance you do not need to actually read the Hebrew text of, or visualise, the Divine Names when they are employed as a *Hagah* (mantra). However, it is worth considering that the written text has a very strong talismanic impact, especially when internalised. Furthermore, whilst you could recite this Divine Name combination any day at any time, and it would be good to mentally "circulate" it all day long inside your heart or solar plexus, the important days, on which it should be uttered most mindfully, are Sunday (Sun), Monday (Moon), Wednesday (Mercury), Thursday (Jupiter), and Friday (Venus). Note that in this teaching a day starts at sunset (around 6 p.m.) of the previous day, e.g. Sunday begins at sundown on Saturday, Monday at dusk on Sunday, etc.

Be that as it may, on contemplating possible Divine Names which could be combined to serve the needs of my earlier mentioned acquaintance in improving memory, reasoning, general wellbeing, relationships, personal empowerment, etc., I understood that the fundamental factor in his query was "relationships." In this specific regard, one commentator on *Practical Kabbalah* referenced amongst the magical techniques to increase love, affection and friendship in the life of an individual, the following, as it were, "incantation." Whilst he did not specifically discuss this in any "incantationary" sense, it is truly a superb invocation which I have employed with great effect, though with some modification, to increase the unique factors listed in it, i.e. reverence, wisdom, intelligence (mindfulness), thankfulness, blessedness, success, humility, abundance, assistance (to support), love, and pleasure (to satisfy):[99]

יחולו היראה וירבו החכמה
יחולו החכמה וירבו השכל
יחולו השכל וירבו הודיה
יחולו הודיה וירבו הברכות
יחולו הברכות וירבו ההצלחות
יחולו ההצלחות וירבו הענוה
יחולו הענוה וירבו העושר
יחולו העושר וירבו העזרה
יחולו העזרה וירבו האהבה
יחולו האהבה וירבו הנחת
יחולו הנחת וירבו הקדושה

Transliteration:
*yachulu ha-yir'ah va-yirbo ha-chochmah*
*yachulu ha-chochmah va-yirbo has'kel*
*yachulu has'kel va-yirbo hodayah*
*yachulu hodayah va-yirbo ha-b'rachot*
*yachulu ha-b'rachot va-yirbo ha-hatzlachot*
*yachulu ha-hatzlachot va-yirbo ha-anavah*
*yachulu ha-anavah va-yirbo ha-osher*
*yachulu ha-osher va-yirbo ha-ezrah*
*yachulu ha-ezrah va-yirbo ha-ahavah*
*yachulu ha-ahavah va-yirbo ha-nachat*
*yachulu ha-nachat va-yirbo ha-k'dushah*

Translation:
Actualise Reverence and increase Wisdom
Actualise Wisdom and increase Intelligence
Actualise Intelligence and increase Thankfulness
Actualise Thankfulness and increase Blessedness
Actualise Blessedness and increase Success
Actualise Success and increase Humility
Actualise Humility and increase Abundance
Actualise Abundance and increase Assistance
Actualise Assistance and increase Love
Actualise Love and increase Pleasure
Actualise Pleasure and increase Holiness

As is the case with this kind of meditation, the best way to execute it is to vocalise the phrases slowly, i.e. enunciating them slowly enough in order to perceive the meaning of each word, but equally fast enough so as not to lose the overall meaning of each phrase.

It has been said that a Hebrew Divine Names mantra (*Hagah*) becomes effective when it has been uttered a hundred times or more. In this regard, readers might recall the "*Hagah* in Preparation for the Merkavistic Descent," which I referenced elsewhere, and which required utterance one hundred and twelve times in order to become effective.[100] In this regard, keeping count without being distracted by the very "counting" is somewhat problematic. The solution would be to have a string of beads of the required number, which will facilitate counting without being distracted. Of course, this is well-known to those familiar with the "*Rosary*" employed by Roman Catholics and Anglicans;[101] the "*Japamala*" or "*Mala*" beads popularly utilized by Hindus, Sikhs, Jains and Buddhists alike;[102] the "*Misbacha*" (*Subha*) beads of the Islamic faith,[103] etc. As it is, beads fulfill a most significant function in human society, in which the use of these items ranges from personal adornments to amulets constructed for a variety of magical purposes.[104]

This brings to mind the string of one hundred blue beads employed in Jewish Magic, albeit not specifically for the purpose of counting the number of times you are to utter a Hebrew mantra. However, this item is often employed for this very purpose, in addition to the magical intention behind its construction. In this regard, I noted elsewhere that Rabbi Shalom Mizrachi Sharabi, the great practitioner of *Practical Kabbalah* (Jewish Magic), "informed believers regarding the following 'Divine Secret' which was used to eradicate illness. In this instance you have to collect a hundred glass beads, which are to be threaded on a string. It is maintained that these beads should be blue, which I suspect has something to do with those traditionally associated with 'evil eye' amulets."[105]

In order to turn this item into a fully fledged magical item which could be employed to affect the intended purpose behind its construct, the practitioner was instructed to "utter the Name אגלא, here vocalised *Agila*, with each bead you thread on the strand,"[106] followed by the recitation of *Psalms 67, 23* and *16* three times in this exact order.[107] Having shared *Psalm 67* in the previous chapter, I include here *Psalms 23* and *16* only:

## Psalm 23

(Verse 1) מזמור לדוד יהוה רעי לא אחסר
(Verse 2) בנאות דשא ירביצני על מי מנחות ינהלני
(Verse 3) נפשי ישובב ינחני במעגלי צדק למען שמו
(Verse 4) גם כי אלך בגיא צלמות לא אירא רע כי אתה עמדי שבטך ומשענתך המה ינחמני
(Verse 5) תערך לפני שלחן נגד צררי דשנת בשמן ראשי כוסי רויה
(Verse 6) אך תוב וחסד ירדפוני כל ימי חיי ושבתי בבית יהוה לארך ימים

Transliteration:
   (Verse 1) *Mizmor l'david YHVH ro'i lo ech'sar*
   (Verse 2) *bin'ot deshe yarbitzeini al mei m'nuchot y'nahaleini*
   (Verse 3) *nafshi y'shoveiv yan'cheini b'ma'g'lei tzedek l'ma'an shemo*
   (Verse 4) *gam ki eleich b'gei tzalmavet lo ira ra ki atah imadi shivt'cha umish'antecha heimah y'nachamuni*
   (Verse 5) *ta'aroch l'fanai shulchan neged tzor'rai dishanta vashemen roshi kosi r'vaya*
   (Verse 6) *Ach tov vachesed yird'funi kol y'mei hayay v'shavti b'veit YHVH l'orech yamim*

Translation:
   (Verse 1) A Psalm of David. *YHVH* is my shepherd; I shall not want.
   (Verse 2) He maketh me to lie down in green pastures; He leadeth me beside the still waters.
   (Verse 3) He restoreth my soul; He guideth me in straight paths for His name's sake.
   (Verse 4) Yea, though I walk through the valley of the shadow of death, I will fear no evil, for Thou art with me; Thy rod and Thy staff, they comfort me.
   (Verse 5) Thou preparest a table before me in the presence of mine enemies; Thou hast anointed my head with oil; my cup runneth over.
   (Verse 6) Surely goodness and mercy shall follow me all the days of my life; and I shall dwell in the house of *YHVH* for ever.

### Psalm 16

(Verse 1) מכתם לדוד שמרני אל כי חסיתי בך

(Verse 2) אמרת ליהוה אדני אתה טובתי בל עליך

(Verse 3) לקדושים אשר בארץ המה ואדירי כל חפצי בם

(Verse 4) ירבו עצבותם אחר מהרו בל אסיך נסכיהם מדם ובל אשא את שמותם על שפתי

(Verse 5) יהוה מנת חלקי וכוסי אתה תומיך גורלי

(Verse 6) חבלים נפלו לי בנעמים אף נחלת שפרה עלי

(Verse 7) אברך את יהוה אשר יעצני אף לילות יסרוני כליותי

(Verse 8) שויתי יהוה לנגדי תמיד כי מימיני בל אמוט

(Verse 9) לכן שמח לבי ויגל כבודי אף בשרי ישכן לבטח

(Verse 10) כי לא תעזב נפשי לשאול לא תתן חסידך לראות שחת

(Verse 11) תודיעני ארח חיים שבע שמחות את פניך נעמות בימינך נצח

Transliteration:

(Verse 1) *Michtam l'david shomreni el ki chasiti vach*
(Verse 2) *amart la-YHVH adonai atah tovati bal alecha*
(Verse 3) *likdoshim asher ba'aretz heimah v'adirei kol cheftzi vam*
(Verse 4) *yirbu atz'votam acher maharu bal asich niskeihem midam uval esa et sh'motam al s'fatai*
(Verse 5) *YHVH m'nat chelki v'chosi atah tomich gorali*
(Verse 6) *Chavalim naflu li ban'imim af nachalat shafrah alai*
(Verse 7) *avarech et YHVH asher y'atzani af leilot yisruni chilyotai*
(Verse 8) *shiviti YHVH l'negdi tamid ki mimini bal emot*
(Verse 9) *lachein samach libi vayagel k'vodi af b'sari yishkon lavetach*
(Verse 10) *ki lo ta'azov nafshi lish'ol lo titein chasid'cha lir'ot shachat*
(Verse 11) *todi'eini orach chayim sova s'machot et panecha n'imot bimincha netzach*

Translation:

> (Verse 1) *Michtam* of David. Keep me, O God; for I have taken refuge in Thee.
> (Verse 2) I have said unto *YHVH*: 'Thou art my Lord; I have no good but in Thee';
> (Verse 3) As for the holy that are in the earth, they are the excellent in whom is all my delight.
> (Verse 4) Let the idols of them be multiplied that make suit unto another; their drink-offerings of blood will I not offer, nor take their names upon my lips.
> (Verse 5) *YHVH*, the portion of mine inheritance and of my cup, Thou maintainest my lot.
> (Verse 6) The lines are fallen unto me in pleasant places; yea, I have a goodly heritage.
> (Verse 7) I will bless *YHVH*, who hath given me counsel; yea, in the night seasons my reins instruct me.
> (Verse 8) I have set *YHVH* always before me; surely He is at my right hand, I shall not be moved.
> (Verse 9) Therefore my heart is glad, and my glory rejoiceth; my flesh also dwelleth in safety;
> (Verse 10) For Thou wilt not abandon my soul to the nether-world; neither wilt Thou suffer Thy godly one to see the pit.
> (Verse 11) Thou makest me to know the path of life; in Thy presence is fulness of joy, in Thy right hand bliss for evermore.

After having completed the recitation of these three Psalms (three times), the string of glass beads "empowered" in this manner is hung on the inside of the entrance to the home of the sick person, where it remains until the said individual is fully healed. As noted elsewhere, "it is understood that, with the help of *Hashem*, the 'Angel of Destruction' will not enter the premises."[108] As said, a further use of this item is to employ it in the manner of "prayer beads," in order to count the exact number of times, i.e. one hundred, this being necessary, as noted earlier, for a *Hagah* to work its "magic" effectively.

In conclusion, I believe we should consider a factor which is very important in performing a *Hagah* (mantra). Rather than "passive participation," i.e. one in which you repeat the mantra without paying much or special attention to it, those which I have addressed thus far initially require "active participation," i.e. being fully involved mentally, emotionally and physically, before allowing them to settle in the back of your mind. Taking this as a "given" in Jewish Magic, one often fails to make specific reference to this factor to those who are not familiar with this work. In this regard, it would be quite necessary to employ a *Hagah* in the manner of the "Sound Concentration" practice which I delineated in some detail elsewhere.[109] As it is, the effective use of Divine and Angelic Names, Hebrew incantations, etc., is dependent on having mastered this very skill.

For those who are unfamiliar with the "Sound Concentration" practice, and who might not have direct access to the text in which I addressed this technique, I noted previously that "The part of the mind in which verbal thoughts arise is brought under control by concentration on sounds imagined in your mind. Repeating a tune or a phrase from a song is relatively easy, hence it is better to select words of one or more syllables. Such words can be meaningless tonal constructs, or any simple term..... The chosen sound is repeated in the mind to block all other thoughts, and what is important here is to actually listen to yourself doing it, while being very careful not to attempt any explanation or analysis of the word or sound. You might even begin by uttering the sound aloud, and then saying it mentally, listening to yourself doing so. No matter how inappropriate the choice of sound may appear, persist with it. When the sound appears to repeat itself automatically, and even occur in sleep, you have mastered the skill." As mentioned in "*The Book of Self Creation*," "this information applies to Kabbalistic meditation, and is a key to the use of 'Words of Power'."[110] The vital factor in this instance is listening intently to yourself uttering a Divine Name, incantation, Hebrew mantra, or whatever.

During the years that I was coaching young pianists in unfolding their ability to be good concert artists, one of the most difficult tasks was to get them to not only perform a piano piece, i.e. getting the notes right, but to actually listen to the performance virtually as if they were members of an audience. Furthermore, to do this in, as it were, an "open" manner in the "Now," without ruminating on or judging the performance. Contrary to the idea that one should control every aspect of the performance, the best approach in my estimation is to surrender and go with the flow, virtually allowing the piece to perform itself. I believe the same approach applies in gaining good "Sound Concentration" skills. You utter the "*Hagah*" with the right "God Force," i.e. in a joyful, surrendered manner, and then listening to yourself virtually encompassing the utterance with your *Kavvanah* (Focussed Attention) without any hard concentration. It is allowing yourself to be aware of every sonic detail as you bathe in the physical or mental utterance of the "*Hagah*," i.e. allowing yourself to be enveloped by its full expression, virtually as if you are the resonating chamber—the perfect "musical instrument." In this regard, you do not have to do anything but listen, embrace and feel.

As an aside, as a musician I am so well acquainted with the skill of "Sound Concentration," that I can listen in my mind to the performance of a chosen orchestral work by a full symphony orchestra, encountering every detail and nuance of sound, i.e. hearing every instrument, without having to actually hear any sound recording via my physical ears. I only need to select the piece, surrender, and allow the "orchestra" of my "inner listening capacity" to perform it for me. Interestingly enough, in this instance the performance is always perfect in terms of my personal expectations, and naturally immensely satisfying. In other words, what I am trying to say is that the capacity of "encompassing listening" is enormously beneficial, not only in working "*Hagah*-magic" successfully in accordance with your personal intentions, but equally in truly mastering the art of meditation.

**. ... ... ...Day after day God's greatest angel comes to fashion the net into a new day. When it is ready he gives it to the heart of the world, and the heart gives it to the clear spring. Then the spring can gush until the next evening's twilight... ... ... .**

# Chapter 8
# *Or Sovev* — Light Surrounding
# ASTROLOGICAL CONSIDERATIONS

## A. The Zodiac & Spiritual Transformation

The "Science of Astrology" has been employed since very ancient times, in order to ascertain from cosmic perspectives the variety of ways in which physical existence unfolds on this planet. *Kabbalah*, teaching that all manifestation came into existence by means of the spoken word, addressed the twenty-two letters of the Hebrew alphabet as expressions of the "creative forces" of cosmos as viewed from our perspective as humans residing on this planet. It has always been of great importance to religionists, mystics, philosophers, and other thinkers to consider the manner in which everything "hangs together" in terms of the greater cosmos around them, especially as perceived from our perspectives as earth dwellers.[1]

Down the ages there were many who investigated the celestial "Science of Astrology," including several authors who penned a great array of texts dealing with this topic from Jewish perspectives.[2] Amongst this array of material, much of which still awaits publication, what to say translation into English, are a number of unique practical magical techniques designed to align the practitioner with the greater harmony of the "Heavenly Spheres" and its lofty "Spirit Forces" in such a manner, to allow the personal unfoldment and evolution of spirit, and to extend individual consciousness to embrace and unify with the greater "Whole."

It is on some of these magical practices employed for spiritual transformation, i.e. those techniques which are meant to work the "higher magic" of awakening the consciousness of the practitioner to higher spiritual awareness, which I am addressing in this chapter. Hence, in the current instance, the magical activity is psycho-spiritual alignment and attuning of your "Self" with "Universal Spiritual Forces," without any consideration of, or desire for, any specific material result.

In this regard, we will now reconsider the previously addressed twelve invocations comprising the twelve permutations of יהוה (*YHVH*) and אהיה (*Eh'yeh*), which are enunciated every morning during their respectively associated zodiacal periods,[3] doing so in conjunction with an associated set of unique vocalisations of the "Twelve Banners." The latter twelve enunciations are coordinated with the seventy-two tri-letter combinations of the *Shem Vayisa Vayet* ("Name of Seventy-two Names"), as affiliated with the twelvefold zodiacal cycle, and realised within the fourfold expression of the solar seasons upon our planet earth.

As it is, I have already addressed the "Twelve Banners" in terms of the so-called "*Tracing the Bet*," i.e. establishing a "*Body of Light*" and the four "*Gevulim*" (directional "Boundaries") in "*The Book of Self Creation*";[4] and shared the advanced employment of the mentioned "*Gevulim*" (directional "Boundaries") affiliated with the "Name of Seventy-two Names" in the first part of "*The Book of Immediate Magic*."[5]

Be that as it may, as mentioned above, there are twelve special invocations chanted every morning, usually after *Shacharit* (Jewish Morning Prayer),[6] each of which is comprised of a permutation of the Divine Names יהוה (*YHVH*) and אהיה (*Eh'yeh*), and each of which is equally affiliated with a single zodiacal sign. As said before, the cycle of invocations commences in *Aries*, i.e. "Spring in the Northern Hemisphere, and then continues in harmony with the flow of the four Seasons.

It has become customary amongst some Kabbalistic circles in the Southern Hemisphere to commence the cycle in the sign of *Libra*, September being the month of the Spring equinox in that part of the world."[7] The differences between the two hemispheres are indicated in the following table by the juxtaposed Zodiacal

*Astrological Considerations* / 205

signs, the one on the left referring to the Northern Hemisphere with the Southern Hemisphere to the right. I am employing a *Mapik* (an emphasis [dot]) in the second letter *Heh* of both the Ineffable Name (יהוה) and the Divine Name *Eh'yeh* (אהיה), in order to emphasise the exact location of this letter in each of the twelve permutations:

| ZODIACAL SIGN | DIVINE NAMES PERMUTATION |
|---|---|
| *Aries/Libra* | יהוה אהיה (YHVH AHYH) |
| *Taurus/Scorpio* | יההו אהיה (YHHV AHHY) |
| *Gemini/Sagittarius* | יוהה איהה (YVHH AYHH) |
| *Cancer/Capricorn* | הוהי היהא (HVHY HYHA) |
| *Leo/Aquarius* | הויה היאה (HVYH HYAH) |
| *Virgo/Pisces* | ההיו ההאי (HHYV HHAY) |
| *Libra/Aries* | והיה יהאה (VHYH YHAH) |
| *Scorpio/Taurus* | וההי יהחא (VHHY YHHA) |
| *Sagittarius/Gemini* | ויהה יאהה (VYHH YAHH) |
| *Capricorn/Cancer* | היהו האהי (HYHV HAHY) |
| *Aquarius/Leo* | היוה האיה (HYVH HAYH) |
| *Pisces/Virgo* | ההוי אההי (HHVY HHYA) |

Besides their associations with the Zodiac, each of the twelve permutations of the paired Divine Names is aligned with a biblical verse, in which either the initial letters or the concluding letters of the component words spell the related permutation. These verses are of great importance, since the vowels employed in the pronunciation of the various permutations were obtained from their respectively affiliated verses. Except in the instance of *Aries/Libra*, those enunciations which were derived from the concluding vowels of the associated biblical words are said to be "Hidden," and those procured from the initial vowels are indicated "Revealed."

Whilst I have earlier addressed the four letters comprising the Ineffable Name in terms of their linguistic usage to indicate specific vowels in Hebrew words, the said four letters are in the current instance enunciated in terms of their standard consonantal usage. It should be noted that the twelve permutations of the Divine Names יהוה (*YHVH*) and אהיה (*Eh'yeh*) are enunciated both separately and conjointly in these invocations. The differences of the respective Zodiacal alignment of each of the said Divine Name combinations in terms of the two hemispheres, are indicated by (N) Northern and (S) Southern hemispheres:

1. ***ARIES* (N)/*LIBRA* (S)—Hidden**
   **Biblical Verse:** *Psalm 96:11*
   יִשְׂמְחוּ הַשָּׁמַיִם וְתָגֵל הָאָרֶץ (*Yishm'chu Ha-shamayim V'tagel Ha-aretz*—"Let the heavens be glad, and let the earth rejoice")
   **Divine Names Permutation & Vocalisation:**

   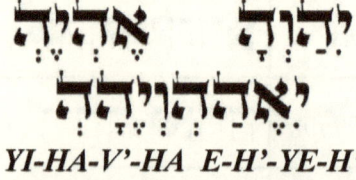

   YI-HA-V'-HA  E-H'-YE-H'
   YI-E-HA-H'-V'-YE-HA-H'

2. ***TAURUS* (N)/*SCORPIO* (S)—Revealed**
   **Biblical Verse:** *Jeremiah 9:23 [22]*
   יִתְהַלֵּל הַמִּתְהַלֵּל הַשְׂכֵּל וְיָדֹעַ (*Yit'halel Ha-mit'halel Has'kel V'yado'a*—"that glorieth glory in this, that he understandeth and knoweth")

*Astrological Considerations* / 207

**Divine Names Permutation & Vocalisation:**

YI-HA-HA-V' I-HA-HA-Y'
YI-I-HA-HA-HA-HA-V'-Y'

3. ***GEMINI* (N)/*SAGITTARIUS* (S)—Revealed**
   **Biblical Verse:** *Exodus 26:19/20*

   [19]יְדֹתָיו[20] וּלְצֶלַע הַמִּשְׁכָּן הַשֵּׁנִית (*Y'dotav [V]Ul'tzelah Ha-mishkan Ha-sheinit*—"[two] tenons and for the second side of the tabernacle")

   **Divine Names Permutation & Vocalisation:**

   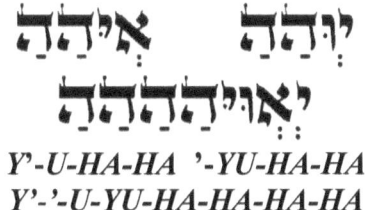

   Y'-U-HA-HA '-YU-HA-HA
   Y'-'-U-YU-HA-HA-HA-HA

4. ***CANCER* (N)/*CAPRICORN* (S)—Hidden**
   **Biblical Verse:** *Esther 5:13*

   זֶה אֵינֶנּוּ שֹׁוֶה לִי (*ZeH einenU[V] shoveH LI[Y]*—"This availeth me nothing")

   **Divine Names Permutation & Vocalisation:**

   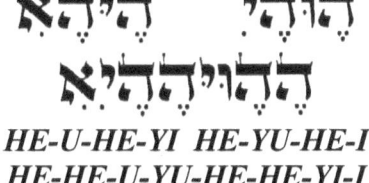

   HE-U-HE-YI HE-YU-HE-I
   HE-HE-U-YU-HE-HE-YI-I

5. ***LEO* (N)/*AQUARIUS* (S)—Revealed**
   **Biblical Verse:** *Deuteronomy 27:9*

   הַסְכֵּת וּשְׁמַע יִשְׂרָאֵל הַיּוֹם (*Hasket [V]Ushmah Yisra'el Ha-yom*—"Keep silence, and hear, O Israel, this day")

**Divine Names Permutation & Vocalisation:**

הָוִיהָ הָיאָהּ
הַהַוִייִאהָהּ

HA-U-YI-HA  HA-YU-I-HA
HA-HA-U-YU-YI-I-HA-HA

6. **VIRGO (N)/PISCES (S)—Hidden**
   **Biblical Verse:** *Genesis 49:11*

   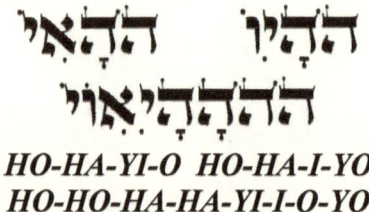 (*IroH v'lasoreikaH b'nI[Y] atonO[V]*—"Binding [his foal unto the vine], and his ass's colt")

   **Divine Names Permutation & Vocalisation:**

   הָהָיוּ הָהָאִי
   הֹהֹהָהָיִאוֹי

   HO-HA-YI-O  HO-HA-I-YO
   HO-HO-HA-HA-YI-I-O-YO

7. **LIBRA (N)/ARIES (S)—Hidden**
   **Biblical Verse:** *Genesis 12:15*

   וַיִּרְאוּ אֹתָהּ שָׂרֵי פַרְעֹה (*Va-yir'U[V] otaH sareI[Y] far'oH*—"And the princes of Pharaoh")

   **Divine Names Permutation & Vocalisation:**

   וּהָיֵה יָהָאֵה
   וִיֻהָהָיֵאֵהֹהֹ

   U-HA-YEI-HO  YU-HA-EI-HO
   U-YU-HA-HA-YEI-EI-HO-HO

8. **SCORPIO (N)/TAURUS (S)—Revealed**
   **Biblical Verse:** *Deuteronomy 26:15/16*

   וּדְבַשׁ [16] הַיּוֹם הַזֶּה יְהוָה [15] ([15] (*V)Ud'vash* [16] *Ha-yom Ha-zeh YHVH*—"[15] honey [16] *this day YHVH*")

*Astrological Considerations* / 209

**Divine Names Permutation & Vocalisation:**

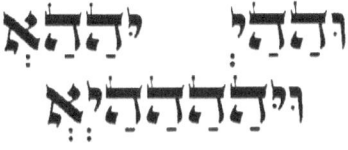

U-HA-HA-Y' YU-HA-HA-'
U-YU-HA-HA-HA-HA-Y-'

9. **SAGITTARIUS (N)/GEMINI (S)— Revealed**
**Biblical Verse:** *Genesis 50:11*

וַיַּרְא יוֹשֵׁב הָאָרֶץ הַכְּנַעֲנִי (*Va-yar Yoshev Ha-aretz Ha-k'na'ani*—"And when the inhabitants of the Land, the Canaanites")

**Divine Names Permutation & Vocalisation:**

VA-YO-HA-HA  YA-O-HA-HA
VA-YA-YO-O-HA-HA-HA-HA

10. **CAPRICORN (N)/CANCER (S)—Hidden**
**Biblical Verse:** *Psalm 34:3 (4)*

לַיהוָה אִתִּי וּנְרוֹמְמָה שְׁמוֹ (*Lu-YHVH itI[Y] un'rom'maH sh'mO[V]*—" to YHVH with me, and let us exalt His name")

**Divine Names Permutation & Vocalisation:**

HA-YI-HA-O  HA-I-HA-YO
HA-HA-YI-I-HA-HA-O-YO

11. **AQUARIUS (N)/LEO (S)—Revealed**
    **Biblical Verse:** *Leviticus 27:33*

    הָמֵר יְמִירֶנּוּ וְהָיָה הוּא (*Ha*-mer *Y'*mirenu *V'*hayah *Hu*—"[if] he change it at all, then both it and that [for which it is changed]")

    **Divine Names Permutation & Vocalisation:**

    HA-Y'-V'-HU  HA-'-Y'-HU
    HA-HA-Y'-'-V'-Y'-HU-HU

12. **PISCES (N)/VIRGO (S)—Hidden**
    **Biblical Verse:** *Deuteronomy 6:25*

    וּצְדָקָה תִּהְיֶה לָּנוּ כִּי (*U-tz'dakaH tih'yeH lanU(V) kI(Y)*—"And it shall be righteousness unto us, if [we observe]")

    **Divine Names Permutation & Vocalisation:**

    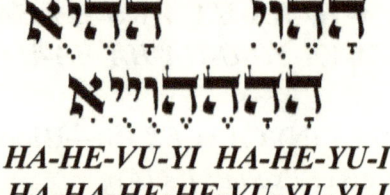

    HA-HE-VU-YI  HA-HE-YU-I
    HA-HA-HE-HE-VU-YU-YI-I

The twelve permutations and associated vocalisations are presented in the exact order as listed in the *"Sefer ha-Kanah."*[8] As noted earlier, these details are practiced in conjunction with an associated technique comprising once more the vocalisation of the "Twelve Banners," each enunciation having been again derived from a Biblical verse. These twelve utterances are in turn aligned with the "Name of Seventy-two Names" divided into twelve sectors respectively comprising six tri-letter portions, and each sector being arranged in the format of a hexagram.

Now, in the first part of *"The Book of Immediate Magic"* I shared a chapter titled *"Becoming a Living Kamea,"*[9] in which I addressed unique material derived from a privately owned anonymous Moroccan Hebrew manuscript incorporating a set of interesting Jewish magical techniques, which were clearly derived from a number of primary texts within the domain of *Practical Kabbalah*. At the time when I was examining this manuscript I was very keen to photocopy the text, but the owner would alas not grant me permission to do so, and I was allowed a mere two hours to copy portions of the said text by hand.

Suffice to say I managed to copy a fairly small portion of the work this way, but I ensured that I acquired at least some of those practices which were of personal interest to me, and which I have to date not seen anywhere else. These include two techniques which I respectively titled "*Becoming a Living Kamea*" and "*Keeping Human Evil in Check*," and which I shared in the previous part of "*The Book of Immediate Magic*."[10] Whilst the second technique was curious in itself, it was the first which greatly piqued my interest at the time. This procedure involved tracing a *Magen David* (Hexagram) in golden light directly on the front surface of the body, an action which is concluded with the Divine Name שדי (*Shadai*) equally visualised in the same golden light, and located in the centre of the hexagram, a locale which happens to be the centre of the chest.[11]

As noted previously, it is understood that this personal *Magen David* acts like a filter, "by means of which one can effectively communicate with the world, and through which the external environment may interact with oneself."[12] However, it is an additional portion in the said manuscript, which equally involved the tracing of *Magen David Chotamot* (Hexagram seals) in front of your anatomy, which relates to the daily recitation of the "Twelve Banners."

Whilst I was unable to note down all of the relevant details, I believe my familiarity with the related information regarding the twelve permutations of the Ineffable Name (יהוה) and their respective affiliation with the twelve signs of the Zodiac, which I delineated earlier and equally in some detail elsewhere,[13] and that I managed to copy a fair portion of the pertinent material from the manuscript, I am able to share the full application of this material in terms of the journey towards "Spiritual Awakening."

Having perused the enunciations of the twelve permutations of both the Ineffable Name (יהוה) and the Divine Name *Eh'yeh*

(אהיה), I am now listing the "Twelve Banners" in terms of their respective enunciation with unique sets of vowels which were again derived from twelve biblical verses, as enumerated in the following table.

In presenting the twelve permutations, I have resorted once more to the inclusion of the earlier mentioned *Mapik*, in order to draw a distinction between the two letters *Heh* in the Ineffable Name:

| 3<br>יְוֻהָהַ<br>Y'VuHaHa | 2<br>יִהָהַוְ<br>YiHaHaV' | 1<br>יִהַוֹהָ<br>YiHaVoHa |
|---|---|---|
| 6<br>הֹהַיִוֹ<br>HoHaYiVo | 5<br>הַוֻיִהָ<br>HaVuYiHa | 4<br>הָוֻהַיִ<br>HaVuHaYi |
| 9<br>וַיֹהָהַ<br>VaYoHaHa | 8<br>וֻהָהַיְ<br>VuHaHaY' | 7<br>וֻהַיֵהוֹ<br>VuHaYeiHo |
| 12<br>הַהֱוֻיִ<br>HaHeVuYi | 11<br>הַיְוְּהֻ<br>HaY'V'Hu | 10<br>הָיִהָוֹ<br>HaYiHaVo |

The collective format of the "Twelve Permutations" presented above, appears to indicate a magical "word square." I have discussed this very "word square" in both the second and third volumes of this series of texts on *Practical Kabbalah*.[14]

In order to understand the manner in which the "Twelve Banners," as well as the twelve permutations of the Divine Name אהיה (*Eh'yeh*), are vocalised in terms of their respective "Hidden" or "Revealed" designations, we need to consider the division of the twelve zodiacal signs into three quadruplicities respectively titled "Cardinal," "Fixed" and "Mutable." As readers probably know well enough, these apply to the three zodiacal periods comprising each of the "Four Seasons," i.e. Spring, Summer, Autumn and Winter, aligned with the four cardinal directions, i.e. East (Air), South (Fire), West (Water) and North (Earth) in the Northern

Hemisphere, and East (Air), North (Fire), West (Water) and South (Earth) in the Southern Hemisphere.

The four "Cardinal" signs, i.e. *Aries*, *Cancer*, *Libra* and *Capricorn*, respectively mark the rise, the very beginning of a solar season, whilst the four "Fixed" signs, i.e. *Taurus*, *Leo*, *Scorpio* and *Aquarius*, indicate the stable and absolute expression of the fullness of the central quality comprising their respectively associated season. The four "Mutable" signs, i.e. *Gemini*, *Virgo*, *Sagittarius* and *Pisces*, specify the waning or ending of their respectively affiliated season, which is the change prior to the rise of the succeeding season.[15]

Perusing the Divine Name/Zodiac affiliations respectively designated "Hidden" or "Revealed," we notice that all four "Cardinal" and two "Mutable" signs, i.e. *Virgo* and *Pisces*, are relegated the "Hidden" category. In this instance "Hidden" refers to the first of the three months comprising each of the "Four Seasons," as well as the periods marking the waning of Winter in preparation for the succeeding transformation into Spring, and the end of the Summer season being, as it were, readied for the transition into Autumn. Of course, the "Mutable" signs of *Virgo* and *Pisces* indicate the said seasonal changes in both the Northern and Southern Hemispheres, but in reverse since Winter in the North is Summer in the South, etc.

As indicated in the table overleaf, the vocalisations of the Ineffable Name derived from the capitals of their respectively associated biblical verses, and aligned with the four "Fixed" signs of the Zodiac, are listed "Revealed," i.e. *Taurus*, *Leo*, *Scorpio* and *Aquarius*. The same applies to two "mutable" signs of the Zodiac, i.e. *Gemini* and *Sagittarius*, the latter respectively marking the periods of transition from Spring into Summer and Autumn into Winter in the Northern Hemisphere, and vice versa in the Southern Hemisphere.

The "Twelve Banners" are automatically also aligned with the seven planets of traditional astrology, this being in agreement with the order of planets governing the twelve signs of the Zodiac. This is indicated in the following table in which the affiliations of the twelve permutations of the Ineffable Name (יהוה) with the twelve zodiacal signs and the seven planets, are listed in terms of their respective solar seasons from both Northern (N) and Southern hemisphere (S) perspectives:

| Revealed | | | | |
|---|---|---|---|---|
| | **Spring**<br>2. יהוה—Venus (*Taurus/Scorpio*)<br>3. יהוה—Mercury | **Summer**<br>5. יהוה—Sun (*Leo/Aquarius*) | **Autumn**<br>8. יהוה—Mars (*Scorpio/Taurus*)<br>9. יהוה—Jupiter (*Sagittarius/Gemini*) | **Winter**<br>11. יהוה—Saturn (*Aquarius/Leo*) |
| **Hidden** | **Spring**<br>1. יהוה—Mars (*Aries/Libra*) | **Summer**<br>4. יהוה—Moon (*Cancer/Capricorn*)<br>6. יהוה—Mercury (*Virgo/Pisces*) | **Autumn**<br>7. יהוה—Venus (*Libra/Aries*) | **Winter**<br>10. יהוה—Saturn (*Capricorn/Cancer*)<br>12. יהוה—Jupiter (*Pisces/Virgo*) |

The enunciations of the six permutations of the Ineffable Name designated "hidden," were respectively extracted from the concluding syllables of the four words of their respectively affiliated biblical verses, which in this instance appear to be unrelated to their respectively associated permutations. On the other hand, the six permutations designated "revealed" were respectively gleaned from the initial vowels of four words which collectively spell their respectively affiliated permutations. The twelve Ineffable Name/Zodiacal combinations are in turn aligned with the *Shem Vayisa Vayet* ("Name of Seventy-two Names"), as indicated below:

*Astrological Considerations* / 215

1. **Banner Permutation & Vocalisation:**

    יְהַוֹהַ (*Yihavoha*)—Hidden

    **Biblical Verse:** *Exodus 3:13*

    [וְאָמְרוּ] לִי מַה שְׁמוֹ מַה ([*v'amru*] *li mah sh'mo mah*—"[and they shall say] to me: What is His name? What.....")

    **Name of Seventy-two Names:**

    והו ילי סיט עלם מהש ללה (*Vehu Yeli Sit Elem Mahash Lelah*)

    **Astrological Associations:**

    (N) *Aries*    | Mars—Spring
    (S) *Libra*    |

2. **Banner Permutation & Vocalisation:**

יְהַֽהֲוּ (*Yihahav'*)—Revealed

**Biblical Verse:** *Jeremiah 9:23 [22]*

יִתְהַלֵּל הַמִתְהַלֵּל הַשְׂכֵּל וְיָדֹעַ (*yit'haleil ha-mit'haleil hash'keil v'yado'a*—"glorieth glory..... that he understandeth and knoweth")

**Name of Seventy-two Names:**

אכא כהת הזי אלד לאו ההע (*Acha Kahet Hezi Elad Lav Hahah*)

**Astrological Associations:**

(N) *Taurus* | Venus—Spring
(S) *Scorpio* |

3. **Banner Permutation & Vocalisation:**

יִוּהַדַה (*Y'vuhaha*)—Revealed

**Biblical Verse:** *Exodus 26:19/20*

יְדֹתָיו וּלְצֶלַע הַמִּשְׁכָּן הַשֵּׁנִית (*y'dotav ul'tzela ha-mishkan ha-sheinit*—"its tenons [sides] [19] and for the second side of the tabernacle" [20])

**Name of Seventy-two Names:**

יזל מבה הרי הקם לאו כלי (*Yezel Mebah Hari Hakem Lav Keli*)

**Astrological Associations:**

| (N) *Gemini* | Mercury—Spring |
| (S) *Sagittarius* | |

4. **Banner Permutation & Vocalisation:**

הָוּהָיִ (*Havuhayi*)—Hidden

**Biblical Verse:** *Exodus 4:3*

אַרְצָה וַיַּשְׁלִיכֵהוּ אַרְצָה וַיְהִי (*artza vayashlicheihu artza vay'hi*—"the ground, and he cast it on the ground, and it became")

**Name of Seventy-two Names:**

לוו פהל נלך ייי מלה חהו (*Lov Pahal Nelach Yeyay Melah Chaho*)

**Astrological Associations:**

| (N) *Cancer* (S) *Capricorn* | Moon—Summer |

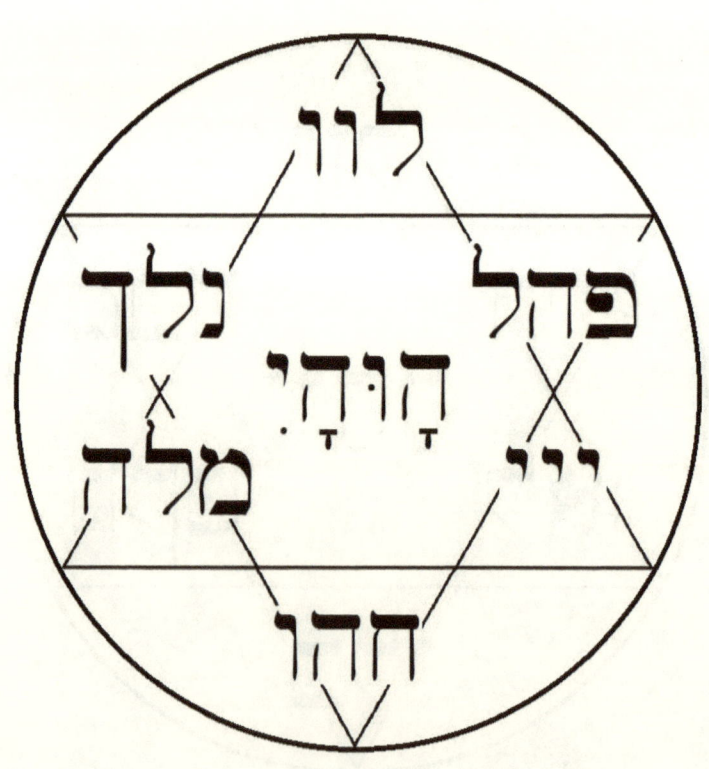

*Astrological Considerations* / 219

5. **Banner Permutation & Vocalisation:**

הַוִיָה (*Havuyiha*)—Revealed

**Biblical Verse:** *Deuteronomy 27:9*

הַסְכֵּת וּשְׁמַע יִשְׂרָאֵל הַיּוֹם (*ha-skeit ushma Yisra'eil ha-yom*—"Keep silence and hear O Israel this day")

**Name of Seventy-two Names:**

נתה האא ירת שאה ריי אום (*Netah Ha'ah Yeret Sha'ah Riyi Om*)

**Astrological Associations:**

| (N) *Leo* | Sun—Summer |
| (S) *Aquarius* | |

6. **Banner Permutation & Vocalisation:**
   הֹהָיִיוֹ (*Hohayivo*)—Hidden

**Biblical Verse:** *Genesis 49:11*
עִירֹה וְלַשֹּׂרֵקָה בְּנִי אֲתֹנוֹ (*iroh v'lasoreikah b'ni atono*—"his foal and his ass's colt unto the choice vine")

**Name of Seventy-two Names:**
לכב ושר יחו להח כוק מנד (*Lekav Vesher Yichu L'hach Kevek Menad*)

**Astrological Associations:**

| (N) *Virgo* | Mercury—Summer |
| (S) *Pisces* | |

7. **Banner Permutation & Vocalisation:**

וְהָיֵהֹ (*Vuhayeiho*)—Hidden

**Biblical Verse:** *Genesis 12:15*

וַיִּרְאוּ אֹתָהּ שָׂרֵי פַרְעֹה (*vayir'u otah sarei far'oh*—"and the princes of Pharaoh saw her")

**Name of Seventy-two Names:**

אני חעם רהע ייז ההה מיך (*Ani Cha'am Reho Yeyiz Hahah Mich*)

**Astrological Associations:**

(N) *Libra*  
(S) *Aries*  | Venus—Autumn

8. **Banner Permutation & Vocalisation:**

וְהַהַיְ (*Vuhahay'*)—Revealed

**Biblical Verse:** *Deuteronomy 26:15/16*

וּדְבַשׁ הַיּוֹם הַזֶּה יְהוָה ((*V*)***Ud*'vash *Ha*-yom *Ha*-zeh YHVH**—"[15] honey [16] *this day* YHVH'")

**Name of Seventy-two Names:**

וול ילה סאל ערי עשל מיה (*Veval Yelah Se'al Ari Eshal Mih*)

**Astrological Associations:**

(N) *Scorpio*  | Mars—Autumn
(S) *Taurus*

9. **Banner Permutation & Vocalisation:**

וַיִּהְדַ (*Vayohaha*)—Revealed

**Biblical Verse:** *Genesis 50:11*

וַיַּרְא יוֹשֵׁב הָאָרֶץ הַכְּנַעֲנִי (*vayar yoshev ha-aretz hak'na'ani*—"and when the inhabitants of the land, the Canaanites")

**Name of Seventy-two Names:**

והו דני החש עמם ננא נית (*Vehu Dani Hachash Omem Nena Nit*)

**Astrological Associations:**

(N) *Sagittarius*  | Jupiter—Autumn
(S) *Gemini*

10. **Banner Permutation Vocalisation:**

הָיִהְוֹ (*Hayihavo*)—Hidden

**Biblical Verse:** *Psalms 34:4 [5]*

לַיהוָה אִתִּי וּנְרוֹמְמָה שְׁמוֹ (*la-YHVH iti un'rom'mah sh'mo*—"to YHVH with me, and let us exalt His name")

**Name of Seventy-two Names:**

מבה פוי נמם ייל הרח מצר (*Mivah Poi Nemem Yeyil Harach Metzer*)

**Astrological Associations:**

(N) *Capricorn*  | Saturn—Winter
(S) *Cancer*

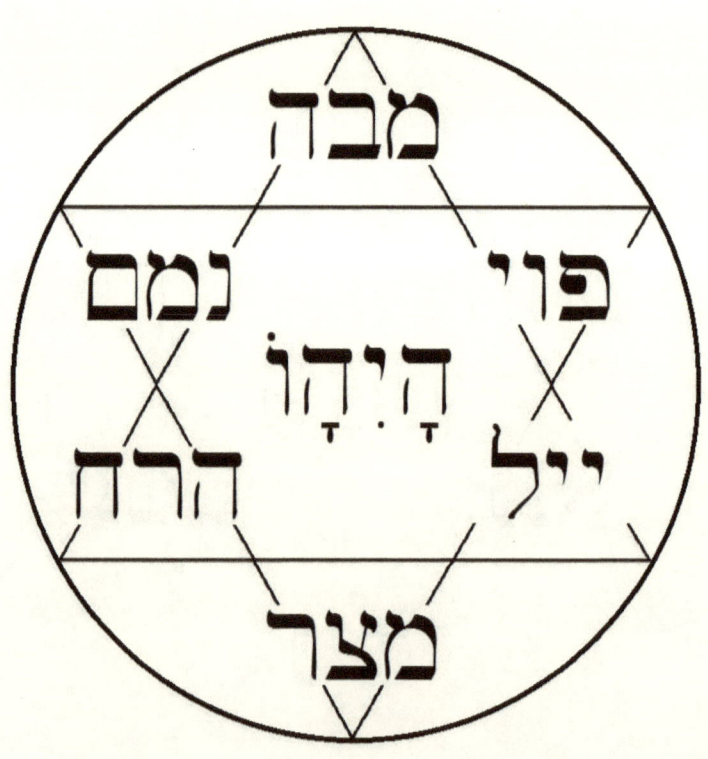

11. **Banner Permutation & Vocalisation:**

הַיְוְה (*Hay'v'hu*)—Revealed

**Biblical Verse:** *Leviticus 27:33*

הָמֵר יְמִירֶנּוּ וְהָיָה הוּא (*ha-meir y'mirenu v'hayah hu*—"to change he exchange it, he shall be.")

**Name of Seventy-two Names:**

ומב יהה ענו מחי דמב מנק (*Umab Yahah Anu Machi Dameb Menak*)

**Astrological Associations:**

(N) *Aquarius*  | Saturn—Winter
(S) *Leo*       |

12. **Banner Permutation & Vocalisation:**
דָּהֱוִי (*Hahevuyi*)—Hidden
**Biblical Verse:** *Deuteronomy 6:25*
וּצְדָקָה תִּהְיֶה לָּנוּ כִּי (*u'tz'dakah tih'yeh lanu ki*—"and it shall be righteousness unto us, if")
**Name of Seventy-two Names:**
איע חבו ראה יבם היי מום (*Iya Chavu Ra'ah Yabam Hayi Mum*)
**Astrological Associations:**

(N) *Pisces*
(S) *Virgo*

Jupiter—Winter

The full details shared are worked into a regimen of daily incantations which are, as said, recited after the *Shacharit* (Morning) prayers. Those readers who are not Jewish and/or not particularly interested in the standard religious practices of normative Judaism, may work these morning incantations after pronouncing the following very simple, beautiful and meaningful morning prayer which is traditionally uttered upon waking, prior to washing hands. It reads:[16]

מודה אני לפניך מלך חי וקים שהחזרת בי
נשמתי בחמלה רבה אמונתך

Transliteration:
> *modeh ani* [women say "*modah ani*"] *l'fanecha melech chai v'kayam shehechezar'ta bi nishmati b'chemlah rabah emunatecha*

Tranlation:
> I am thankful before you living and eternal King, for you have mercifully restored my soul within me. Great is Your faithfulness.

Again, those readers who are uncomfortable with uttering this prayer because of what they might consider the religious undertones, could simply continue with the actual procedure of mentally tracing and vocalising the permutation of the יהוה (*YHVH*)/אהיה (*Eh'yeh*) Divine Name combination appropriate to the specific Zodiacal period. Whilst I have addressed in some detail elsewhere,[17] it is in the current instance worked in conjunction with the additional portion of the "Twelve Banners" and six tri-letter section of the "Name of Seventy-two Names" relevant to the said selected zodiacal period.

One might consider this tracing of the Hebrew letters comprising each component of a Divine Name combination to be, as it were, a mental "engraving" of the Divine Name permutations whilst they are being vocalised in the following manner:

1. Commence the first portion of the procedure by reciting first the biblical verse relevant to the Zodiacal Period you are currently in. For example, every morning during the period of *Aries* (*Taleh*) in the Northern Hemisphere, or *Libra* (*Moznaim*) in Southern Hemisphere recite:

    [*Psalm 96:11*] יִשְׂמְחוּ הַשָּׁמַיִם וְתָגֵל הָאָרֶץ (*Yishm'chu Ha-shamayim V'tagel Ha-aretz*—"Let the heavens be glad, and let the earth rejoice")

2. Continue by intoning with great *Kavvanah*, that is with focussed intention and attention, the permutation of the associated two Divine Name permutations.

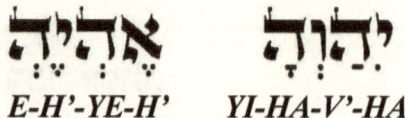

אֶהְיֶה      יְהֹוָה
E-H'-YE-H'      YI-HA-V'-HA

3. continue the phrase by following on with:

צבאות אלהי ישראל אלהים חיים ומלך עולם אל
שדי אל רחום וחנון רם ונשא שוכן עד מרום וקודש

Transliteration:
......*Tzva'ot Elohei Yis'rael Elohim Chayim uMelech Olam El Shadai, El Rachum v'Chanun, Ram v'Nisa, Shochen ad Marom, v'Kadosh*

Translation:
......of Hosts, God of the god-wrestler, living *Elohim* and King of the universe, *El Shadai*, *El* merciful and gracious, lofty and exalted, dwelling in eternity, and blessed.

4. Visualise and vocalise the composite "Name" comprising the letters of the two Divine Name permutations of the month conjoined in a special manner. For example, in the sign of *Aries/Libra* the Names יהוה and אהיה are intertwined like this:

יאההוהה

Considering the vowels employed in the pronunciation of these Divine Names, their conjoined enunciation during *Aries/Libra* would be:

יֶאֱהֹהוָיֶהֶ
YI-E-HA-H'-V'-YE-HA-H'

5. Continue with the second portion of the procedure by tracing a hexagram on the surface of your body. This is similar to the tracing of the "*Magen David*" on the surface of your body as addressed in the section dealing with

"*Becoming a Living Kamea*" in the first part of "*The Book of Immediate Magic,*"[18] the only difference being that, commencing at the uppermost point, the six points of the hexagram are mentally encircled anti-clockwise, as indicated below:

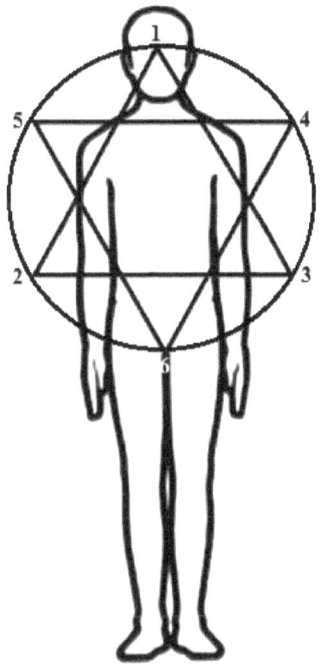

6. Recite the affiliated six tri-letter portions of the "Name of Seventy-Two Names," whilst simultaneously locating them in their respectively associated locales in the six corners of the hexagram as positioned on your body, these being in the current instance:

## והו ילי סיט עלם מהש ללה
***VEHU YELI SIT ELEM MAHASH LELAH***

7. Recite where applicable, i.e. in the instance of the "Banner-Permutations" listed "Hidden," the additional biblical verse affiliated to the relevant "Banner-Permutation," in the current instance [*Exodus 3:13*] לִי מַה שְׁמוֹ מַה (*li mah sh'mo mah*—"to me: What is His name? What.....")

8. Conclude by reciting the relevant "Banner-Permutation," i.e. either the standard one in the case of the "Revealed Banners" or the additional enunciation in the instance of the "Hidden Banners," simultaneously visualising it inside your heart centre. In this regard, it is worth noting that in all instances, the selected "Banner Permutation" is visualised without vowels. In the current instance it is the first "Banner Permutation" (Hidden):

יִהַוֹהַ

**YI-HA-VO-HA**

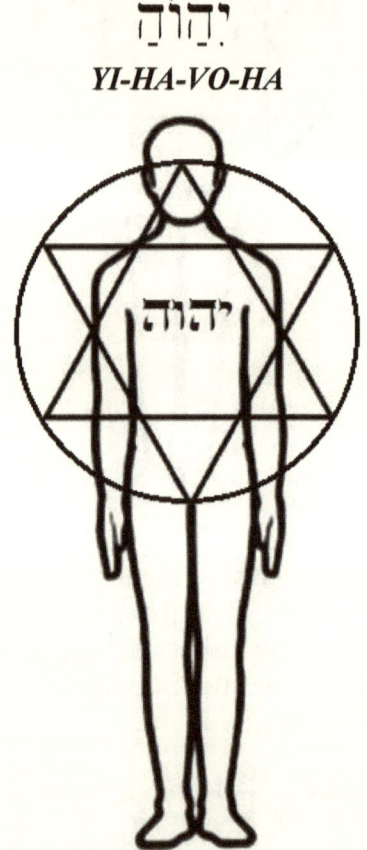

9. You may wish to conclude the procedure with the standard formula ברוך שם כבוד מלכותו לעולם ועד (*Baruch shem k'vod malchuto l'olam va'ed*—"Blessed be the Name of His glorious Kingdom throughout eternity").

As noted elsewhere, those who invoke these "Divine Names" at their proper times, are said to be able to interrupt and neutralise the negative impact of the "Spiritual Forces" of the twenty-eight Lunar Mansions, and also to completely neutralise whatever malevolence might be in store for the invocants.[19]

In conclusion, we need to consider the suitable times to perform these procedures. Generally speaking, and as I noted elsewhere, in Jewish thinking a day is measured from sunset to sunset rather than from sunrise to sunrise. In this regard, a day consists of two sub-cycles of which we might say the first commences at 6 p.m. (dusk) to 6 a.m. (dawn), and the second commences at 6 a.m. (dawn) and concludes at 6 p.m. (dusk).[20] Whilst one might follow this arrangement for convenience sake, it can hardly be considered ideal, or even correct. As everybody knows well enough, the hours of light and darkness change from one season to the next, in fact from month to month. Hence, if you wish to be really accurate in working the mentioned twelve invocations at the appropriate time, it would be necessary to ascertain the exact measure of daylight hours applicable throughout the year in the locale where you reside. Calculating sunrise to the exact minute has become a lot easier by the availability of a number of astrological/astronomical "apps" which can be downloaded into mobile phones.

## B. The Power in Your Hands & Countenance

Amongst the most important lessons I have learned on this lifelong journey as a dedicant to *Practical Kabbalah*, is that all "magical powers" are held within your very own being, and that all so-called "magical instruments" of mainstream "Ceremonial Magic," i.e. a *Sword*, *Rod*, *Cup*, *Shield*, *Cord*, colours, candles, herbs, incenses, etc., really serve to enhance your personal consciousness. Hence the most vital "instruments" in working "Real Magic" are in fact the various organs comprising your own body, i.e. your head, heart, throat, etc., supported by your mind, soul and spirit. If you fully comprehend this, you will realise that whilst it is wonderful to have a personal physical "Sacred Space" in which to work your "magical rituals," and employing all manner of "ritual gear" to enhance your magical activities, you could in fact do equally well without them. You might instead resort to the application of your "magical will," by relating the "centre" (Self) and the "circumference" (Environment) with the aid of your own tongue/respiratory system (*Sword*/Air); spine/skeletal-nervous system (*Rod*/Fire); heart/ cardiovascular system (*Cup*/Water); and skin/flesh (*Shield*/Earth).

As it is, the great instruments of "magical communication" between the "Self-centre" and the "All-circumference," are your own hands and face controlled with clear consciousness in a magical manner. These organs of your physical anatomy could be considered "magical circuit boards," since they are etched with unique "tracts," so to speak, by means of which the seven subtle "planetary forces" of our solar system are conducted into our lives and world. Magically speaking, the quantity and quality of these "planetary powers" can be controlled by *Kavvanah*, the powerfully focussed intention and attitude, of the one who consciously directs these subtle forces via his/her face and hands into the surrounding greater circumference.

However, it is important to consider how "everything hangs together" in terms of the greater cosmos, as understood from our perspectives as earth dwellers. In this regard, we understand from the *Sefer Yetzirah* that the twenty-two glyphs of the Hebrew alphabet comprise the fundamental building blocks of all creation.[21] We are further instructed that the said glyphs are divided into three "Mother Letters" pertaining to the three "active Elements"— א (*Alef*–Air), מ (*Mem*–Water), ש (*Shin*–Fire); seven "Double Letters" affiliated with the "Seven Planets," i.e. ב (*Bet/Vet*–Saturn), ג (*Gimel/Djimel*–Jupiter), ד (*Dalet/Thalet*–Mars), כ (*Kaf/Chaf*–Sun), פ (*Peh/Feh*–Venus), ר (*Resh/Resh*–Mercury), ת (*Tav/Thav*– Moon); and twelve "Single Letters" aligned with the twelve signs of the Zodiac i.e. ה (*Heh*–Aries), ו (*Vav*–Taurus), ז (*Zayin*– Gemini), ח (*Chet*–Cancer), ט (*Tet*–Leo), י (*Yod*–Virgo), ל (*Lamed* –Libra), נ (*Nun*–Scorpio), ס (*Samech*–Sagittarius), ע (*Ayin*–Capricorn), צ (*Tzadi*–Aquarius), ק (*Kof*–Pisces). The affiliation of the Hebrew alphabet with the said Elements and Celestial Bodies are schematically presented in the following illustration termed the *"Yetziratic Incantation Wheel"*[22] for want of a better title:

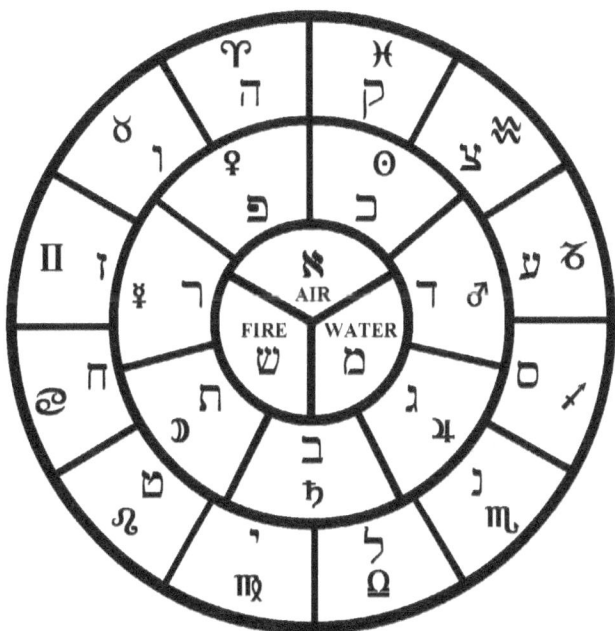

As indicated, in this chapter we are addressing certain magical practices pertaining to sevenfold "powers" aligned with the "Seven Planets." I am fully aware that, astronomically speaking, the Sun and the Moon are not "planets" *per se*, but for the sake of convenience, and in alignment with the primary teachings of *Practical Kabbalah*, I will continue to refer to the listed seven celestial bodies as "planets." They are the basis of an extensive "Doctrine of Sevens," i.e. seven *sefirot* (spheres) on the Kabbalistic "Tenfold Tree of Faith," of which more anon.

In examining the mentioned order of attribution of the seven planets to the seven "Double Letters," it is clear the planets are listed in terms of their relative distance from our own planet. However, there are several "planetary orders" indicating the motion or "flow" of the planetary forces calculated in terms of specific cyclical circumstances, i.e. the hours of the day, the days themselves; the Zodiac; etc., all measured in terms of the planetary placement along the parameter of the following glyph:

As noted earlier, the "natural" order of the planets in terms of our locale on earth, is: 1. Moon, 2. Mercury, 3. Venus, 4. Sun, 5. Mars, 6. Jupiter, 7. Saturn. In this instance commencing at the glyph of Saturn located bottom-right on the illustration, we can follow the entire layout by tracing anti-clockwise along its parameter. However, if we look at the planetary order of the days of the week, we note that Day 1–Sunday is governed by the Sun; Day 2–Monday by the Moon; Day 3–Tuesday by Mars; Day 4–Wednesday by Mercury; Day 5–Thursday by Jupiter; Day 6–Friday by Venus; and Day 7–Saturday by Saturn. In this instance, if we commence with the Sun (Sunday), and move from thence to the locale of the Moon (Monday) in the illustration, continuing thence with the pattern suggested by the planetary order of the days and concluding with Saturn (Saturday), the pattern outlines a sevenfold star. There are several such patterns pertaining to the twelve zodiacal signs, cycles of years, etc.

It should be noted that in Jewish mysticism the concept of the "seven days" does not only refer to the seven daily cycles comprising what is termed the "week," but also applies to cosmic cycles, i.e. a "cosmic day" or "cosmic week." The seven days are divided into six "active" working days and one "passive" day of rest. Considered from an "As Above, So Below" perspective, there is amongst others the doctrine of the *Shemitot*. Whilst the latter concept refers to "Cosmic Cycles," it is a specific term indicating seven cosmic eras, each of which lasts around 7000 years.[23] In this regard, we are informed that each of these cosmic periods are under the dominance of a specific *Sefirah*, and it has been said that we are currently in the *Shemitah* of *Gevurah* (Strength/Severity), a period marked by strict judgment (*Din*).[24] Each *Shemitah* is viewed as a "Cosmic Week," in which the first six millennia pertain to the six days, and the seventh to the Sabbath day of assimilation. In my estimation what is of particular importance, is the understanding that such sevenfold cycles apply throughout the whole of existence from the smallest aspect of the microcosm to the largest consideration of the macrocosm, all of which are believed to be interrelated.

Be that as it may, readers who are well acquainted with the doctrines of the Hermetic Orders, might object to the rigid focus in mainstream Kabbalah on "Seven Planets." They could well insist that the "ten planets" of 20th century astrology are correctly attributed to the ten [eleven] *Sefirot*.[25] However, herein lie certain difficulties, 1. the entire "astrological system" in traditional Kabbalah is based on the division of the twenty-two Hebrew glyphs into the earlier mentioned three "Mother Letters" affiliated with the three active Elements; seven "Double Letters" aligned with seven "Planets" only; and twelve "Single Letters" attributed to the twelve Zodiacal signs; 2. the contentious attributions of the, as it were, "modern" Planets" attributed to *Keter* (Crown), the first *Sefirah*, and to the second, *Chochmah* (Wisdom). Whilst the Latin literature penned by the Renaissance esotericists regarding planetary attributions to the sefirotic tree, i.e. Giordano Bruno, Athanasius Kircher, *et al.*, had a direct impact on the thinking of the late 20th century Hermetic occultists, it is clear that the discovery of three further planets in our solar system had the "moderns" attempting to rearrange the *sefirot*/planet doctrines of traditional Kabbalah. In this regard, one commentator observed laconically that "In recent times Kabbalists have overlaid *Hokhmah*, traditionally the Zodiac, with Uranus, and *Keter*, traditionally *Reshit hagilgulim*, the Prime Swirlings or fiery mist of the Galaxy, with Neptune. These last placings, like the further superimposition of the recently discovered Pluto on *Daat*, are only speculative."[26] [my italics]

From what I have observed regarding this issue over the five decades that I have been involved with this tradition, the term "speculative" is actually not applicable in the case of those esotericists who will accept nothing less than full confirmation of the correctness of the attribution of "ten planets" to the kabbalistic "Tree of Life." However, the general tendency today is to return to the "seven planets" doctrine of ancient astrology, which readily aligns with the teachings of traditional Kabbalah. In this regard, there has been some conjecture that the attribution of the planets to the *sefirot* is exclusively "Hermetic." There are a number of primary Hebrew texts in which the planets are aligned with sefirot, and such attributions were already made in the 13th century by Joseph ben Shalom Ashkenazi, a contemporary of Abraham Abulafia.[27]

It should be noted that the affiliation of the seven planets to seven *sefirot* were by no means uniform. Some Jewish thinkers and certain Christian thinkers, i.e. the French author Guy Lefèvre de La Boderie [1541–1598],[28] student of the celebrated Christian Kabbalist Guillaume Postel [1510–1585], Athanasius Kircher [1602–1680], and Gerard Encausse (Papus) [1865–1916] following Kircher, attributed the seven planets to the lower seven *sefirot*, i.e. *Chesed*—Saturn, *Gevurah*—Jupiter; *Tif'eret*—Mars; *Netzach*—Sun; *Hod*—Venus; *Yesod*—Mercury; and *Malchut*—Moon.[29] Elsewhere Kircher offered the same set of attributions with the two planets associated with *Tif'eret* and *Netzach* interchanged, i.e. *Tif'eret*—Sun and *Netzach*—Mars.[30] It is worth noting that Elijah ben Solomon Zalman, the famous Gaon of Vilna known as the "Gra" [1720–1797], insisted on the following array of sefirotic/planetary attributions: *Chesed*—Moon; *Gevurah*—Mars; *Tif'eret*—Sun; *Netzach*—Venus; *Hod*—Mercury; *Yesod*—Saturn; and *Malchut*—Jupiter.[31] In this regard, we are informed that this set of attributions "fits most closely to the teachings of the Zohar," and "is based on the ordering of the planets as found in the Zohar [*Tikuney Zohar* 70 (*128b*)]."[32]

Be that as it may, whilst there is no connection whatsoever between Kircher's attributions and the standard set acknowledged by modernday "Hermeticists," there are correspondences to be found in the array shared by the "Gra." As it is, the popular set of sefirotic/planetary attributions, *senza* the inclusion of the later discovered planets, was introduced to the Renaissance Hebraists and Christian Kabbalists by Yohanan Alemanno [1435–1510],[33] an Italian Kabbalist who was the friend and teacher of Pico dela Mirandola [1463–1494], the "Father" of "Christian Kabbalah." It has been said that Alemanno derived his attribution of the planet Saturn to the sphere of *Binah* (Understanding) on the sefirotic Tree from the writings of the earlier mentioned Joseph ben Shalom Ashkenazi.[34] Be that as it may, Yohanan Alemanno's sefirotic/

planetary array comprises Saturn–*Binah* (שבתאי–*Shabetai*); *Chesed*—Jupiter (צדק–*Tzedek*); *Gevurah*—Mars (מאדים–*Madim*); *Tif'eret*—Sun (חמה–*Chamah* [also *Shemesh*]); *Netzach*—Venus (נוגה–*Nogah*); *Hod*—Mercury (כוכב–*Kochav*); and concluding with the Moon–*Yesod* (לבנה–*Levanah*).[35]

This array was adopted by most of the, if you will, "Renaissance Hermeticists," i.e. Francesco Giorgi [1466–1540],[36] Heinrich Cornelius Agrippa von Nettesheim [1486–1535],[37] Giordano Bruno [1548–1600],[38] the great Robert Fludd [1574–1637],[39] and Angelo Berardi [1636–1694].[40] A slight variant of Alemanno's set of sefirotic/planetary attributions was offered by Giulio Camillo [1480–1544], i.e. *Binah*–Saturn; *Chesed*—Jupiter; *Gevurah*— Mars; *Ti'feret*—Sun; *Netzach* & *Hod*—Venus; *Yesod*—Mercury; and *Malchut*—Moon.[41]

Of course, in dealing with the seven Planets and their sefirotic associations, it is important to keep in mind the mentioned seven "Double Letters," i.e. the seven Hebrew glyphs, each of which is vocalised in a dual manner, as indicated in the following table:

| Plosive—Malevolent | Fricative—Benevolent |
|---|---|
| בּ—*Bet* | ב—*Vet* |
| גּ—*Gimel* ("g" as in "go") | ג—*Djimel* ("g" as in "George") |
| דּ—*Dalet* | ד—*Thalet* (hard "*th*" as in "that") |
| כּ—*Kaf* | כ—*Chaf* ("ch" as in the German "ich" or the Scottish "loch") |
| פּ—*Peh* | פ—*Feh* |
| ר—*Resh* (Guttural "*r*") | ר—*Resh* (Palatal "*r*") |
| תּ—*Tav* | ת—*Thav* (soft "*th*" as in "think") |

In order to distinguish between the "hard" (plosive) and "soft" (fricative) enunciations, a *Dagesh* (dot) is inserted in the centre of the letter to be enunciated in the "plosive" manner. Here the basic premise is that the "fricative" enunciation is "benevolent," and the "plosive" is "malevolent." In this regard, I noted in *"The Book of Sacred Names,"* that each of the said double letters has "two meanings, as well as two applications: one positive, the other negative."[42] I further commented that "only three of the seven have been retained in modern Hebrew. Three of the rest are apparently used by very few individuals, and the double of the remaining one, *Resh*, is said by some to have been lost, whilst some maintain it to be a well-guarded secret."[43] I should mention that the, as it were, "discarded" double enunciation of the letter ג (Gimel) is employed in the Hebrew versions of certain common appellatives, i.e. ג׳ירפה (*Djirafah*—"Giraffe"), ג׳ין (*Djin*— "Gin"), etc.

As I noted elsewhere, "it is understood that the two-fold usage of the seven 'double letters' comprises the invocation of sets of polarised potencies, each portrayed and 'invoked' respectively by means of one of the 'double letters' and their respective positions on the Kabbalistic 'Tree of Life.' It has been said that the 'hard' sound pertains to *Gevurah* (Severity) and the 'soft' to *Chesed* (Mercy). The 'negative quality' is associated with the plosive sound and the 'positive' with the fricative, e.g *Bet* with a *Dagesh* is '*B*'—a plosive sound considered to pertain to *Gevurah* (Severity); without the *Dagesh* the pronunciation is '*V*'—a fricative sound linked to *Chesed* (Mercy).'"[44] As one might expect, the "double letters" found in Hebrew Divine and angelic Names in terms of their plosive/fricative enunciations can be most confusing. In this regard, an acquaintance, who is a fellow quester in the domain of *Practical Kabbalah*, was met with this very confusion when attempting to ascertain the *Gevurah/Chesed* enunciations within the earlier mentioned *Hagah* (Hebrew Mantra) comprising, amongst others, the *Anaktam Pastam Paspasim Dionsim Yohach Kalach Tzamarchad Azbugah* Divine Name combination. He observed correctly that, in his own words, "in *Anaktam* and *Pastam* the letter *T* sounds like *Tav* instead of *Thav*. In *Pastam* and *Paspasim* the letter *P* sounds like *Peh* instead of *Feh*," and equally "in *Kalach* the first *K* sounds like *Kaf* instead of *Chaf*." He further noted that "in *Azbugah* the *G* sounds like *Gimel* instead of *Djimel*."

The said acquaintance made the interesting observation that, from his personal investigations into this topic, he "learned that the fricative sound of a consonant allows a continuous flow of air in the oral cavity while the plosive one interrupts the flow of air because of the contact between two parts of the oral cavity. My first conclusion about why the fricative is benevolent is because the flow of air into or from our lungs is a symbol of the Life Force like when God breathed into Adam's nostrils the breath of life, therefore, the fricative sound does not interrupt that life force flow, so to speak."

I am not really informed regarding any specific reasons facilitated by Jewish thinkers as to why certain Divine Names have a preponderance of "plosive" letters rather than "fricative" ones from the seven "Double Letters." In my estimation, this is likely more due to Hebrew linguistic conventions, rather than to mystico/magical propensities. What I do know is that many uses and enunciation formats of the twenty-two letters of the Hebrew Alphabet employed in a number of "Divine Names" constructed for magical reasons, were intentional, since such Divine Name constructs were carefully "programmed," so to speak, within our "collective consciousness" in order to affect definite outcomes. In this regard, the pronunciation is extremely important, since at times the enunciation of a Divine Name varies in accordance with specific intentions.

As a case in point, the Divine Name *Agala'a* is at times enunciated *Agila*, and the Divine Name combination *Anaktam Pastam Paspasim Dionsim* is, as I noted earlier, sometimes vocalised *'naket'ma p'sotam p'sips'yema dayev'nsoyam*, all depending on the purpose of its employment. As mentioned, the second vocalisation of the "*Anaktam*" Divine Name construct is employed for the purposes of improving memory, understanding and learning ability. Whilst the vowels employed in this instance are apparently directly affiliated to the vowels appearing in the relevant portion of the Biblical "Priestly Blessing" from whence the Divine Name in question was derived, we are either afforded very vague information, or have no indication as to why this Divine Name is vocalised in a certain manner in one instance and differently in another. Personally speaking, my only criteria when it comes to Hebrew Divine Names and incantations, is to take primary sources and the ancient practitioners of this art at their word, ensuring that I follow instructions "to a t." This stance has to date stood me in good stead with excellent results all round.

As might be expected, there is a lot more to consider in terms of the "benevolent/malevolent" concepts applying to the dual enunciations of the seven "Double Letters," i.e. the respective affiliations of these Hebrew glyphs not only with the seven "Planets," but equally with the seven days of the week, and with a range of unique qualities which are, as it were, "invoked" by the variant vocalisations of each of the "Double Letters." In this regard, we are told that there are seven benevolent versus seven malevolent qualities aligned with the dual enunciation of the seven "Double Letters" of the Hebrew alphabet, i.e. Wisdom/Folly, Wealth/Poverty, Mastery/Slavery, Life/Death, Beauty/Ugliness, Prosperity/Desolation, and Peace/Evil [War].

As noted earlier, the original details regarding the seven "Double Letters," were derived from the *Sefer Yetzirah* ("The Book of Creation").[45] However, the subject matter addressed in this enigmatic work, has been elaborated upon by many commentators in numerous ways over the ages since the appearance in the 9th century.[46] In terms of the planetary attributions of the seven "Double Letters," the issue is how to ascertain the correct planetary/quality alignment with the seven "Double Letters" from the conglomeration of conflicting opinions of versions of versions of versions of the *Sefer Yetzirah*, and the contradictory perspectives expressed in the commentaries on this enigmatic text.

As far as the personal "microcosmos" of each individual is concerned, we are informed in the *Sefer Yetzirah* that the seven "Double Letters" are, as noted, affiliated with the seven "Planets"; the mentioned seven unique Qualities; the seven Days of the week; and equally with the seven openings of the face. Thus, in order to ascertain the most accurate attributions, I consulted the earliest manuscripts of the *Sefer Yetzirah* I could find,[47] and solved all the anomalies and contradictions I chanced upon with the use of plain common sense. I believe the affiliation of the seven planets with the "Double Letters" as delineated in these early manuscripts to be correct, and hence maintain those correspondences in my own dealings with *Practical Kabbalah*.

That being said, it is worth noting that whilst the following table of correspondences agrees with the magical system shared in this tome, there are variances of opinion as to the exact assignment of the seven "double" letters to the planets, days, and the seven apertures of the face. As indicated, the seven "double" letters are aligned with the seven planets in terms of the attributions found in the said manuscripts of the "*Sefer Yetzirah*." However, since I prefer to align with the neat, coherent systems based on common sense, I adhere to the planetary/day/facial attributions presented in, amongst others, the *Kuzari* by Yehudah Halevi,[48] and *Sheirit Josef* by Josef Tzayach:[49]

| Letter | Quality | Planet | Day | Facial Feature |
|---|---|---|---|---|
| ב | Wisdom | Saturn | Saturday | Mouth |
| ג | Wealth | Jupiter | Thursday | Right Ear |
| ד | Mastery | Mars | Tuesday | Right Nostril |
| כ | Life | Sun | Sunday | Right Eye |
| פ | Beauty | Venus | Friday | Left Ear |
| ר | Prosperity | Mercury | Wednesday | Left Nostril |
| ת | Peace | Moon | Monday | Left Eye |

Viewed in terms of the human face, the set of attributions could be portrayed in the following manner:

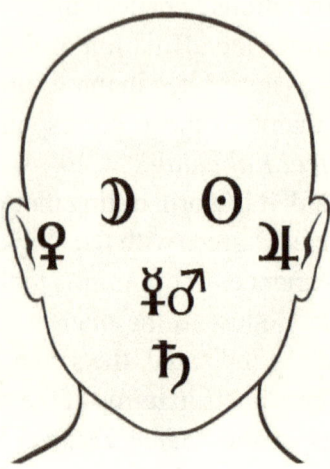

I understand this alignment of the seven planets with the seven apertures of the face, is based on the way humans approach various life situations. For example, statements like "smelling danger," "smelling fear" or "smelling prey" are quite common, hence the Mars and Mercury affiliation with the sense of smell. On the other hand, sight is aligned with light, and for us this has to do with solar and lunar qualities. We see by the light of the Sun and the Moon. As far as hearing is concerned, it is good to keep in mind that we experience joy, humour, and even affection via our ears, since we listen to jokes and the enchanting voices of those who charm us, hence the Jupiter and Venus association with hearing. However, it is also well to remember that humans often find themselves in disastrous circumstances because of their ears. In this regard, we might recall the ancient Greek saga of the beautiful sirens whose magnificent voices ensnared sailors and led them to their doom.[50]

Be that as it may, an important "magical instrument" remains to be considered, before we peruse the practical applications of the listed items in what could be termed the "Magic of the Seven Planets." Earlier we noted that the quantity and quality of the "planetary forces," can be consciously directed via the face and hands of the one who controls these powers with *Kavvanah*, the powerfully focussed intention. We have addressed the seven apertures of the face aligned with the "seven planets," hence we need to turn our attention next to the human hand as a "magical instrument." I wrote elsewhere on the symbolical meaning of the image of hands in Hebrew amulets,[51] but in the current instance I wish to focus specifically on the "subtle forces" understood to be inherent in the fingers and palm of the human hand. In this regard, it should be noted that the face and the hands employed conjointly, comprise two of the most powerful "instruments" in the "magical arsenal" of the serious practitioner.

As noted, your countenance is aligned with "planetary forces," which can be internalised into the Self-centre or externalised into the Environment-circumference, in accordance with the will of the one employing the listed alignments with specific intentions. Likewise, your hands are aligned with "spirit forces," the latter being expressed through the respectively associated portions of your hands, in order to affect either the Self or the greater environment in harmonic symbiosis with the will of the kabbalist/magician. In this regard, Gershon ben Shlomo d'Arles, amongst other mediaeval authors, informed us that the five fingers of the hand align with the five senses,[52] these alignments being determined by the common usage of the fingers in terms of the seven apertures of the face. The little finger is employed to clean the ears, hence it is aligned with the sense of hearing. The ring finger is employed to clean the eyes, thus it is affiliated with the sense of sight. The middle finger is often used to stroke and feel, therefore it is associated with the sense of touch. The index finger is employed to clean the nose, and is therefore allied with the sense of smell. In conclusion, it is well-known that infants suck their thumbs, hence the thumb corresponds with the sense of taste.[53]

The human hand is also aligned with the "seven planets," as any good chiromancer knows well enough.[54] As indicated in the following illustration, the planetary alignments of the fingers are the little finger—Mercury; the ring finger—Sun; the middle finger—Saturn; the index finger—Jupiter; and the thumb—Venus. It is interesting that it is the "Mercury" finger which is employed to impact the "Jupiter/Venus" ears, and the "Jupiter" finger which is working the same on the "Mars/Mercury" nostrils.

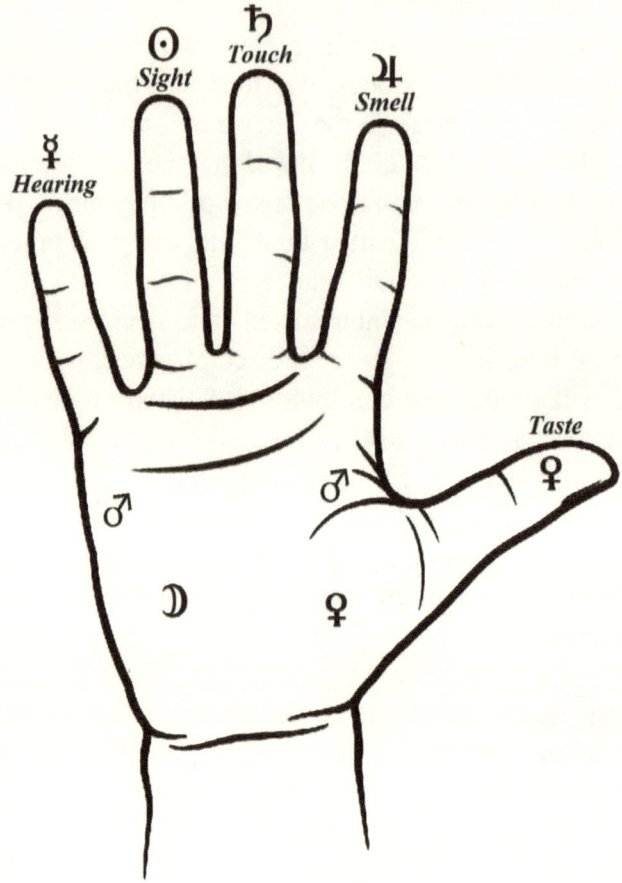

The planets/senses indicated by the fingers are also affiliated with the four Elements. Mercury (hearing) pertains to the Element of Air, and so does Jupiter (smell). Sun (sight) is associated with the Element of Fire, and Saturn (touch) as well as Venus (taste) are both aligned with a combination of the Water and Earth Elements. As in the instance of the affiliated sefirotic meditations addressed in the first chapter of this tome, the thumb is again employed to "trigger" the "spirit forces" inherent in the other fingers and the palm of the hand. In this regard, you need to turn your attention to training yourself to fully acknowledge and activate the "planetary forces," which we noted are located in your hands and face. The procedure involved is one of, as it were, "entrainment" and surrendering to the "frequencies" of the "spirit forces" to be harnessed in, and channeled via, the face and the hands of the practitioner. The process involved is somewhat similar to what is termed "anchoring" in "*Neuro Linguistic Programming.*"[55] In this regard, commence by working the following procedure with your hands:

1. Extend any one of your hands in front of you, palm facing towards your face.
2. Close your eyes, smile inside yourself, and focus your attention on your five fingers.
3. Commencing with the little finger, gently bend the finger as you focus on it, then smile and name it "*Kochav*" (כוכב—Mercury). Repeat this procedure with the ring finger naming it "*Shemesh*" (שמש—Sun). Next work the procedure with the middle finger, smiling at it and calling it "*Shabetai*" (שבתאי—Saturn). Continue with the index finger, working the same procedure, and with your warmest smile name it "*Tzedek*" (צדק—Jupiter). Conclude by focussing on your thumb, sensing it extending downwards and expanding into the palm of the hand, then smile and name it "*Nogah*" (נוגה—Venus).

In this instance it is important to bring your full attention to bear on each finger, simultaneously allowing yourself to have a great "feeling appreciation" of it. It is when you feel your consciousness virtually occupying the selected finger, that you smile not only *at* but also *with* that finger, and then assign it a planetary appellative. You might also want to exercise this portion of the procedure regularly over a number of days, before proceeding with the next portion of the procedure.

Having worked the entire procedure with both hands, you next need to invoke five emotional qualities relevant to the five planets, which will "empower" the respectively associated fingers. If you have mastered the various practices pertaining to the previously addressed "*Tuning in on God Forces*,"[56] you will be able to "invoke" within yourself any emotional condition at will, without having to resort to imagery. The aim here is to have the energy of an emotional quality as pure as possible, i.e. untainted by imagery based on specific life circumstances or human conditions.

If you need to intensify an emotional quality, i.e. make it stronger within yourself, you could employ any of the Sefirotic/Planetary attributes, which I addressed in the first part of "*The Book of Immediate Magic*,"[57] to boost relevant emotional qualities.

What is important is that you acquire the ability to simply switch from one "God Force" (emotion) into another at will, i.e. turn depression (Saturn) into say joy (Jupiter), or anger (Mars) into a sense of harmonious balance and perfect peace (Sun), etc. As noted elsewhere,[58] the, as it were, "gateway" to all emotions is your upper chest, i.e. the portion of your anatomy which you would strike as you exclaim "oh woe is me!" in the drama of total emotional abandonment. All emotions are held in your upper chest, whether it be anger, rage, profound sadness or exuberant joviality. All you need to do is place your attention directly below your throat in your upper chest, and think sadness whilst feeling it arise in your chest, and you will immediately trigger the said emotional quality without having to resort to any associated mental image.

Again the greatest skill would be to trigger a "God Force" in this manner, without having to resort to thinking of some image or incident associated with the desired emotional quality. In this regard, whilst being fully aware of your upper chest, you might for example bring to mind the sphere of *Gevurah* (Might) and its association with the planet *Madim* (Mars), as well as the emotional quality of anger. Ask yourself what anger feels like in your chest. Do not attempt to explain it mentally, but simply to allow yourself a "feeling appreciation" of the "God Force." Repeat the word "anger" over and over slowly in your mind, and allow the word to trigger the relevant emotional response inside your upper chest. Allow this emotion to manifest as intensely as you can bear it. If you think you can take it to maximum level, you could change the keyword to "rage." When you feel that you have reached the peak of your anger experience, acknowledge the "Spirit" behind this "God Force" by saying "*Shalom Ru'ach* (or *Maggid*) *m'Madim*" (Salutations Spirit from Mars). That is the fundamental procedure pertaining to "invoking" any emotional quality ("God Force") in your upper chest, and perforce within your entire being.

So then to continue the, as it were, "entrainment" of your hands with the earlier mentioned "Planetary Forces," you have to, as indicated, invoke the relevant emotional qualities to be

## Astrological Considerations / 247

conjoined with the relevant fingers. This is done in the following manner:

1. Once again extend any one of your hands in front of you, palm facing towards your face.
2. Close your eyes, smile inside yourself, and focus your attention on your five fingers.
3. Commencing with the middle finger (Saturn), focus on it and smile *with* it, then invoke the appropriate "God Force" (emotional quality) employing any of the earlier mentioned methods. The "God Force" of Saturn, could be anything from the very negative, e.g. sadness, disappointment, distrust, disillusionment, etc., to the more positive, e.g. sternness, seriousness, caution, etc. You do not require the emotional quality to be absolutely overwhelming. In fact, a soft yet insistent sense of the "God Force" is good enough.
4. Employing a "feeling appreciation," take a deep breath and on exhalation say *"Shabetai"* (Saturn), then fill your middle finger with, as it were, the fullness of the Saturn emotional quality you have invoked inside yourself.
5. Next, turn your attention to your index finger. Again focus on it and smile *with* it, then continue by invoking within yourself the "God Force" of Jupiter, e.g. happiness, exuberance, enthusiasm, humour, laughter, the desire to embrace all, etc. As in the case of the middle finger, take a deep breath and on exhalation say *"Tzedek"* (Jupiter), and fill your forefinger to capacity with the "God Force" of Jupiter which you have invoked inside yourself.
6. Repeat this practice with your ring finger in exactly the manner delineated. After having invoked the "God Force" of the Sun, i.e. a sense of great vibrancy in a condition of harmonious balance with the "whole" in the "Now," inhale and on exhalation say *"Shemesh"* as you virtually inflate your ring finger with the said "God Force."
7. Next, perform the same procedure with your thumb. In this instance you need to invoke within yourself the sensuality and love pertaining to Venus. The emotional quality pertaining to this planet is not only sensuality, but also the

sense of encompassing love. Take an inbreath and on exhalation say "*Nogah*" as you fill your thumb, as well as the portion which extends from it into your hand, with the "God Force" of Venus.

8. In conclusion, work this technique with the little finger, the latter being aligned with Mercury. It is somewhat difficult to attribute an emotion to this planet, since it represents more a sense of bright awakeness and sharpness of mind. In this regard, bring yourself into a condition in which you perceive yourself as being awake, alert, and mentally agile. Perceive yourself as being filled with the "power" of intelligence, and being filled with the realisation of yourself being an awake "Self." Then, after inhalation, say "*Kochav*" as you feel the awakeness of your being penetrate and fill your little finger.

9. If time allows, perform the said practice with the fingers of the other hand. This can be postponed for a later, more convenient time, but it is important to understand that the technique should be executed with both hands.

In the next exercise you are required to touch the tips of the four fingers with your thumb, and with each touch to "trigger" the relevant emotion in your upper chest, focussing especially on the centre of your chest, and then aligning this, as it were, "planetary thread" with related locales on your face. The procedure is as follows:

1. Once again extend any one of your hands in front of you, palm facing towards your face.
2. Close your eyes, smile inside yourself, and focus your attention on your five fingers.
3. Commencing with the middle finger (Saturn), touch the tip of this finger with your thumb and trigger the emotional quality associated with *Shabetai* (Saturn) in your chest, i.e. sadness, sternness, etc. Be fully aware of the presence of the "God Force" in your chest, which you acknowledge with a quick "*Shalom Ruach m'Shabetai*" ("Greetings Spirit from Saturn").

4. Next raise your hand to your chest, and tap the centre of the chest, the locale where you feel the maximum intensity of the "God Force," three times with the Saturn finger. If you were employing this technique as a fully fledged magical practice, rather than the preparatory "Self programming" you are working currently, you would focus on the quality of Saturn you wish to emphasize as you tap, e.g. הצבת גבולות (*Hatzavat g'vulot*—"Setting Boundaries"), or any of the Saturn qualities listed in the earlier mentioned tables of Sefirotic/Planetary attributes.[59]

5. Conclude by stroking along your mouth (Saturn) with the same finger (Saturn).

6. Bring your hand back in front of your body, and smile again warmly inside yourself, whilst this time focussing your attention on your index finger. You now commence the aligned "God Force" of Jupiter by touching the tip of your index finger with your thumb, and triggering the emotional quality associated with *Tzedek* (Jupiter) in your chest, i.e. joy, exuberance, expansiveness, etc. Be again fully aware of the powerful presence of this "God Force" in the centre of your chest, which you acknowledge by saying, whispering or thinking "*Shalom Ruach m'Tzedek*" ("Greetings Spirit from Jupiter").

7. Next, raise your hand and, with your fingers spread, place the palm flat on the centre of your upper chest, i.e. the locale where you feel the maximum intensity of the "God Force." This time press the forefinger three times against the chest, and, if you are employing this technique for magical purposes, focus on the quality of Jupiter you want to emphasize as you press the finger three times on your chest, e.g. מרגיש משגשג (*Margish M'sagseg*—"Feeling Prosperous"), or any of the Jupiter qualities listed in the tables comprising the mentioned tables of Sefirotic/Planetary attributes.[60]

8. Conclude by touching the opening of your right ear (Jupiter) with your index finger (Jupiter).

9. Bring your hand back in front of your body, and, as before, smile warmly as you bring your attention to your ring finger (Sun). This time you align the "God Force" of the

Sun by touching the tip of your ring finger with your thumb, and triggering the emotional quality associated with *Shemesh* (Sun) in your chest, i.e. a vibrant/energetic sense of balance and "nowness" or vitality, etc. Be again fully aware of the presence of this "God Force" in the centre of your chest, which you acknowledge by saying, whispering or thinking "*Shalom Ruach m'Shemesh*" ("Greetings Spirit from the Sun").

10. As before, raise your hand and place your palm flat on the centre of your chest, then press the ring finger three times against the chest, again, if you are employing this technique for magical purposes, focusing on the quality of the Sun you wish to emphasize as you press the finger three times against your chest, e.g. בטוח (*Batuach*—"Confident/Trusting"), or any of the Sun qualities listed in the mentioned tables of Sefirotic/Planetary attributes.[61]

11. Conclude by touching the lid of your right eye (Sun) with your ring finger (Sun).

12. Bring your hand again back in front of your body, and smile warmly as you bring your attention to your thumb (Venus). Employing either your index (Jupiter) or ring finger (Sun), align the "God Force" of Venus by touching the tip of your thumb with either of the said fingers, and triggering the emotional quality associated with *Nogah* (Venus) in your chest, i.e. sensuality, graceful, loving, etc. Be once again fully aware of the presence of this "God Force" in the centre of your chest, which you acknowledge by saying, whispering or thinking "*Shalom Ruach m'Nogah*" ("Greetings Spirit from Venus").

13. Again raise your hand, placing the palm flat on the centre of your chest, this time pressing the thumb three times against the chest, and, if you are employing this technique for magical purposes, focusing on the quality of Venus you wish to emphasize as you press the thumb against your chest, e.g. חושני (*Chushani*—"Sensual"), or any of the Venus qualities noted in the tables of Sefirotic/Planetary attributes, which as noted was addressed in the first part of "*The Book of Immediate Magic*."[62]

14. Conclude by touching the opening of your left ear (Venus) with the back of your thumb (Venus).
15. As before, return your hand to the front of your body, with the palm facing towards your face. Smile warmly as you bring your attention to your little finger (Mercury). Align the "God Force" of Mercury by touching the tip of your little finger with the thumb, and triggering the quality associated with *Kochav* (Mercury) in your chest, i.e. alertness, mental agility, communicative ability, etc. Be fully aware of the presence of this "God Force" in the centre of your chest, which you acknowledge by saying, whispering or thinking "*Shalom Ruach m'Kochav*" ("Greetings Spirit from Mercury").
16. Raise your hand, placing the palm flat on the centre of your chest, this time pressing the little finger three times against the chest. If you are employing this technique for magical purposes, focus on the quality of Mercury you wish to emphasize as you press your little finger against your chest, e.g. המחשי (*Hemcheishi*—"Perceptive"), or any of the Mercury qualities listed in the mentioned tables of Sefirotic/Planetary attributes.[63]
17. Conclude by lightly closing the left side of your nose (Mercury) with your little finger (Mercury).
18. Lastly we come to the "God Forces" of Mars, which are aligned with your chest and face in quite a different manner. Whilst the central portion of your hands is affiliated with Mars, it is not preferable to "entrain" the palm of your hands with the "God Forces" of Mars, especially when you wish to employ the hands to function magically in, as it were, a "giving" manner. Besides, the "God Forces" of anger, rage, might, etc., are extremely easily invoked inside humans, virtually as if these emotional qualities are the most natural to humankind. Hence, the procedure of aligning the "God Forces" of *Madim* (Mars) requires you to simply invoke a sense of disciplined might, fierceness, or even anger, in your upper chest. Then, simply place your palm with a measure of force on your chest, i.e. strike your upper chest, and, whilst feeling your hand thus in contact with this portion of your

upper torso, acknowledge the "God Force" by saying, whispering or thinking "*Shalom Ruach m'Madim*" ("Greetings Spirit from Mars").

19. Afterwards, raise your hand and place it over your face in such a manner that the three middle fingers, symbolising the letter ש (*Shin*), are resting on your forehead with your nose (Mars) pressing against the centre of your palm (Mars). Some readers might recognise this gesture to be somewhat similar to the action of placing your hand over your face to indicate exasperation. Be that as it may, whilst having your hand positioned over your face thus, be fully aware of the "God Force" you are aligning with. If you should be employing this technique for magical purposes, focus on the quality of Mars you desire to emphasize whilst you are aware of your nose against your palm, e.g. החלטי (*Hechaleiti*—"Tenacious" or "Decisive"), or any of the Mars qualities listed in the previously addressed tables of Sefirotic/Planetary attributes.[64]

20. Again note that this technique is worked with both hands, which could be enacted during the same session, or worked separately. Whatever the case may be, conclude the procedure by bringing your hand to a normal restful position prior to closing with the standard formula:

ברוך שם כבוד מלכותו לעולם ועד

Transliteration:
*Baruch shem k'vod malchuto l'olam va'ed*
Translation:
Blessed be the Name of His glorious Kingdom throughout eternity.

As you have probably noticed, the Moon is not included amongst these planetary alignment procedures. The Moon is associated with sexuality and especially the *Nefesh* (Instinctual Self). It is understood that the "God Forces" of *Levanah* (Moon) are powerfully present in all living creatures, and these are enhanced or "empowered" by means of a variety of "Lunar" procedures, which I will be addressing separately in a future volume.

The important factor in dealing with any of these "God Forces," is that you should never be, as it were, overwhelmed by any emotional quality, however strong it may be. In this regard, it is important to have the full experience of the "God Force," but always remain the observer or "witness." There is also the possibility of interacting with the qualities of different "God Forces" in a single working. In this regard, you might invoke the quality of *Shabetai*, by touching your middle finger with your thumb whilst feeling perhaps "disillusionment," but instead of tapping with your middle finger (Saturn) three times on your chest, you simply place your hand flat on your chest, and press your ring (Sun) or forefinger (Jupiter) three times against your chest as you "transmute" the Saturn "God Force" into that of the Sun or Jupiter, whilst simultaneously invoking the relevant emotional quality directly inside your upper chest. This is afterwards confirmed by touching the appropriate portion of your face as you say either "*Shalom Ruach m'Shemesh*" in the case of the solar "God Force," or "*Shalom Ruach m'Tzedek*" in the instance of having invoked the "God Force" of Jupiter.

Such "emotional transmutations" can be worked with any "God Force," and this action might not always be from a so-called "negative" emotion to a "positive" one. There might be times when you feel it necessary to convert "disappointment" (Saturn) to "anger" (Mars). In this instance, you would commence with Saturn by acknowledging the associated "God Force," i.e. touching the middle finger (Saturn) with your thumb and saying "*Shalom Ruach m'Shabetai*," then slap your chest with your flat hand, an action meant to trigger *Madim* (Mars). This is followed by focussing on an appropriate emotional quality, e.g. anger, or any of the Mars qualities listed in the earlier mentioned tables of Sefirotic/Planetary attributes.[65] This is then affirmed in your face prior to interacting with a recipient in your environment whom you deem should be impacted by the "God Force" of *Madim* (Mars).

It is clear that the delineated procedures of aligning "God Forces" in your hands, chest and face, pertain specifically to controlling the "centre," i.e. the personal stance and emotional qualities by means of which the practitioner wishes to impact his/her environment. This is the foundation of "Planetary Magic" addressed in this tome. However, having "set" the "centre" (Self), you will next require a number of magical tools by means of which you could impact the "circumference" (environment) in accordance with a specific intention to achieve a specific outcome. These could include the "Four Elements," sefirotic considerations, Divine Names, "Spirit Intelligences" and their respectively affiliated "Magical Seals," "Incantations," etc. In fact, in terms of practical requirements for the successful implementation of the "planetary magical techniques" shared here, any or all of the following affiliated sevenfold correspondences, amongst others, could be employed:

1. the earlier mentioned seven Divine Names affiliated with seven *Sefirot*, all of which are aligned with the Seven Planets:

| Planet | Sefirah | Divine Name |
|---|---|---|
| *Shabetai* (Saturn) | *Binah* | Elohim |
| *Tzedek* (Jupiter) | *Chesed* | El |
| *Madim* (Mars) | *Gevurah* | Elohim Gibor |
| *Shemesh* (Sun) | *Tiferet* | YHVH Eloha va-Da-at |
| *Nogah* (Venus) | *Netzach* | YHVH Tzva'ot |
| *Kochav* (Mercury) | *Hod* | Elohim Tzva'ot |
| *Levanah* (Moon) | *Yesod* | Shadai El Chai |

2. seven Archangels aligned with the seven Planets, these being, according to Eleazar of Worms (Garmiza), קפציאל (*Kaftzi'el*)—Saturn; צדקיאל (*Tzadki'el*)—Jupiter; סמאל (*Sama'el*)—Mars; מיכאל (*Micha'el*)—Sun; ענאל (*Ana'el*)—Venus; רפאל (*Rafa'el*)—Mercury and גבריאל (*Gavri'el*)—Moon.[66]

3. seven special *Chotamot* (seals) assigned to the seven Archangels, which I have redrawn below in harmony with the originals listed in *Shoshan Yesod Olam*:[67]

*Astrological Considerations* / 255

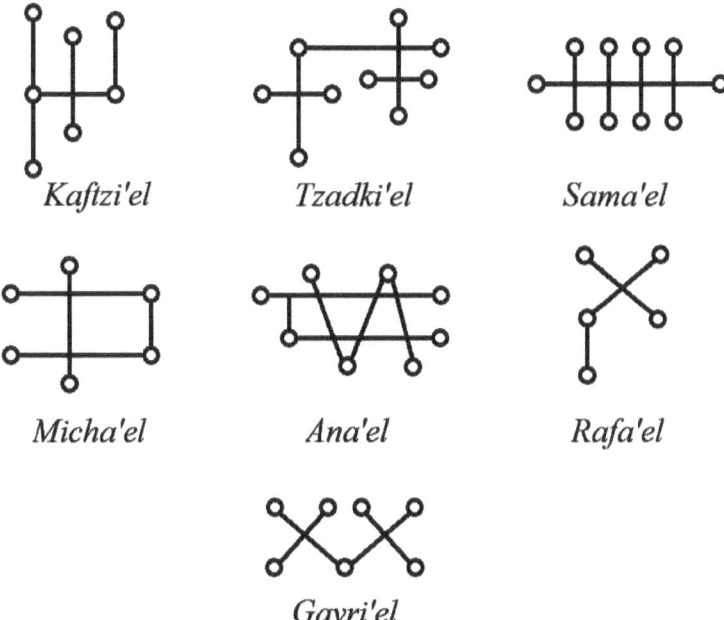

4. seven *chotamot* (magical seals/sigils) associated with seven "Planetary Intelligences" and seven subservient "planetary spirits."[68] However, in terms of the requirements of the practices addressed here, I am focussing specifically on the seven magical seals of the seven "subservient spirits." From what I have been taught, and in my personal experience, these serving "Spirit Intelligences" are particularly effective in achieving speedy results in terms of delivering their respective, as it were, planetary obligations:

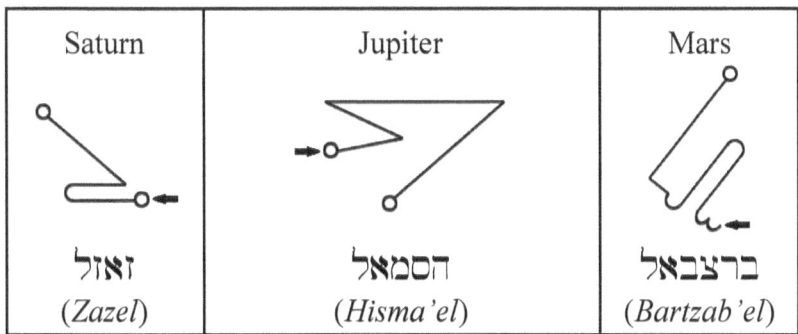

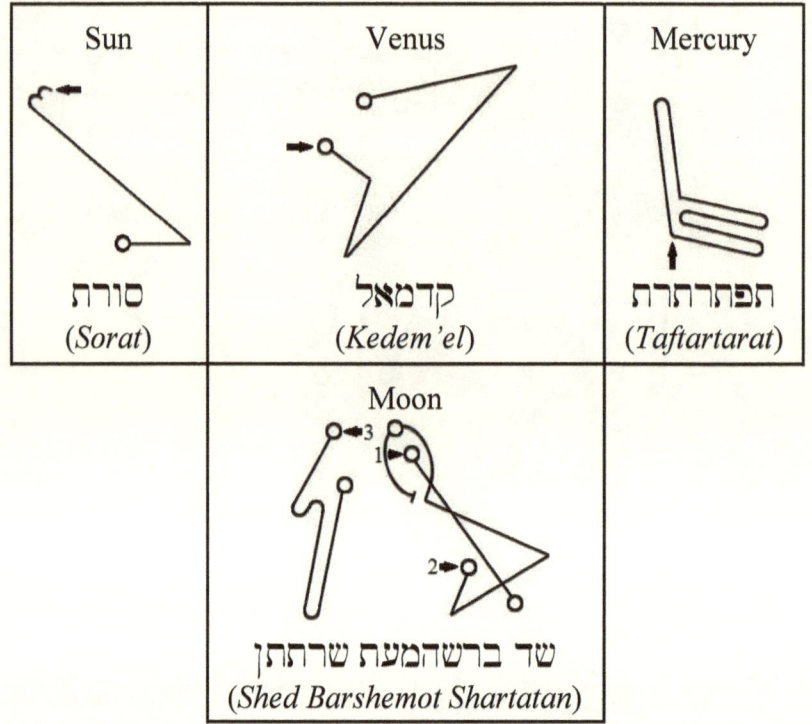

The little arrow(s) included with each *Chotam* (Seal) indicate the commencement of each *Sigil*, if you should wish to draw it mentally or trace it with your hand in the air.

5. the Archangel/Planetary associations with the seven days, and their respective affiliations with the twenty-four hours of the day; the twenty-four permutations of the Divine Name אדנ"י (*Adonai*) corresponding to the twelve night-time hours, as well as the twelve permutations respectively of the Ineffable Name (יהו"ה) and the Divine Name אה"יה (*Eh'yeh*) related to the twelve day-time hours; and the twenty-eight "Lunar Camps" aligned with the 168 hours of the week.

All of these correspondences are arranged in accordance with the order employed in the system shared in this series of texts on *Practical Kabbalah*. The emboldened Angelic Name at the hour of daybreak, references the Archangel in charge of the entire day:

Astrological Considerations / 257

## Day 1 – Sunday – Sun – *Micha'el*

| Saturday 18h00 to Sunday 06h00 ||||
|---|---|---|---|
| 18h00<br>Mercury<br>*Rafa'el*<br>יאהויב<br>אדני [ADNY]<br>אדין [ADYN] | 19h00<br>Moon<br>*Gavri'el*<br>יאהויב<br>אנדי [ANDY]<br>אניד [ANYD] | 20h00<br>Saturn<br>*Kaftzi'el*<br>יאהויב<br>איננד [AYND]<br>אידנ [AYDN] | 21h00<br>Jupiter<br>*Tzadki'el*<br>יאהויב<br>דניא [DNYA]<br>דנאי [DNAY] |
| 22h00<br>Mars<br>*Sama'el*<br>יאהויב<br>דינא [DYNA]<br>דיאנ [DYAN] | 23h00<br>Sun<br>*Micha'el*<br>יאהויב<br>דאינ [DAYN]<br>דאני [DANY] | 00h00<br>Venus<br>*Ani'el*<br>הויגהו<br>ניאד [NYAD]<br>נידא [NYDA] | 01h00<br>Mercury<br>*Rafa'el*<br>הויגהו<br>נאיד [NAYD]<br>נאדי [NADY] |
| 02h00<br>Moon<br>*Gavri'el*<br>הויגהו<br>נדאי [NDAY]<br>נדיא [NDYA] | 03h00<br>Saturn<br>*Kaftzi'el*<br>הויגהו<br>יאדנ [YADN]<br>יאנד [YAND] | 04h00<br>Jupiter<br>*Tzadki'el*<br>הויגהו<br>ידאנ [YDAN]<br>ידנא [YDNA] | 05h00<br>Mars<br>*Sama'el*<br>הויגהו<br>ינדא [YNDA]<br>ינאד [YNAD] |
| Sunday 06h00 to 18h00 ||||
| 06h00<br>**Sun**<br>***Micha'el***<br>יהוית<br>יהוה [YHVH]<br>אהיה [AHYH] | 07h00<br>Venus<br>*Ani'el*<br>יהוית<br>יההו [YHHV]<br>אההי [AHHY] | 08h00<br>Mercury<br>*Rafa'el*<br>יהוית<br>יוהה [YVHH]<br>איהה [AYHH] | 09h00<br>Moon<br>*Gavri'el*<br>יהוית<br>הוהי [HVHY]<br>היהא [IIYIIA] |
| 10h00<br>Saturn<br>*Kaftzi'el*<br>יהוית<br>הויה [HVYH]<br>היאה [HYAH] | 11h00<br>Jupiter<br>*Tzadki'el*<br>יהוית<br>ההיו [HHYV]<br>ההאי [HHAY] | 12h00<br>Mars<br>*Sama'el*<br>הויצהו<br>והיה [VHYH]<br>יהאה [YHAH] | 13h00<br>Sun<br>*Micha'el*<br>הויצהו<br>וההי [VHHY]<br>יההא [YHHA] |
| 14h00<br>Venus<br>*Ani'el*<br>הויצהו<br>ויהה [VYHH]<br>יאהה [YAHH] | 15h00<br>Mercury<br>*Rafa'el*<br>הויצהו<br>היהו [HYHV]<br>האהי [HAHY] | 16h00<br>Moon<br>*Gavri'el*<br>הויצהו<br>היוה [HYVH]<br>האיה [HAYH] | 17h00<br>Saturn<br>*Kaftzi'el*<br>הויצהו<br>ההוי [HHVY]<br>ההיא [HHYA] |

### Day 2 – Monday – Moon – *Gavri'el*

| Sunday 18h00 to Monday 06h00 | | | |
|---|---|---|---|
| 18h00<br>Jupiter<br>*Tzadki'el*<br>יקהויר<br>אדני [ADNY]<br>אדין [ADYN] | 19h00<br>Mars<br>*Sama'el*<br>יקהויר<br>אנדי [ANDY]<br>אניד [ANYD] | 20h00<br>Sun<br>*Micha'el*<br>יקהויר<br>אינד [AYND]<br>אידן [AYDN] | 21h00<br>Venus<br>*Ani'el*<br>יקהויר<br>דניא [DNYA]<br>דנאי [DNAY] |
| 22h00<br>Mercury<br>*Rafa'el*<br>יקהויר<br>דינא [DYNA]<br>דיאנ [DYAN] | 23h00<br>Moon<br>*Gavri'el*<br>יקהויר<br>דאינ [DAYN]<br>דאני [DANY] | 00h00<br>Saturn<br>*Kaftzi'el*<br>הויעהו<br>ניאד [NYAD]<br>נידא [NYDA] | 01h00<br>Jupiter<br>*Tzadki'el*<br>הויעהו<br>נאיד [NAYD]<br>נאדי [NADY] |
| 02h00<br>Mars<br>*Sama'el*<br>הויעהו<br>נדאי [NDAY]<br>נדיא [NDYA] | 03h00<br>Sun<br>*Micha'el*<br>הויעהו<br>יאדנ [YADN]<br>יאנד [YAND] | 04h00<br>Venus<br>*Ani'el*<br>הויעהו<br>ידאנ [YDAN]<br>ידנא [YDNA] | 05h00<br>Mercury<br>*Rafa'el*<br>הויעהו<br>ינדא [YNDA]<br>ינאד [YNAD] |
| Monday 06h00 to 18h00 | | | |
| 06h00<br>**Moon**<br>**Gavri'el**<br>ישהויט<br>יהוה [YHVH]<br>אהיה [AHYH] | 07h00<br>Saturn<br>*Kaftzi'el*<br>ישהויט<br>יההו [YHHV]<br>אההי [AHHY] | 08h00<br>Jupiter<br>*Tzadki'el*<br>ישהויט<br>יוהה [YVHH]<br>איהה [AYHH] | 09h00<br>Mars<br>*Sama'el*<br>ישהויט<br>הוהי [HVHY]<br>היהא [HYHA] |
| 10h00<br>Sun<br>*Micha'el*<br>ישהויט<br>הויה [HVYH]<br>היאה [HYAH] | 11h00<br>Venus<br>*Ani'el*<br>ישהויט<br>ההיו [HHYV]<br>ההאי [HHAY] | 12h00<br>Mercury<br>*Rafa'el*<br>הוינהו<br>והיה [VHYH]<br>יהאה [YHAH] | 13h00<br>Moon<br>*Gavri'el*<br>הוינהו<br>וההי [VHHY]<br>יההא [YHHA] |
| 14h00<br>Saturn<br>*Kaftzi'el*<br>הוינהו<br>ויהה [VYHH]<br>יאהה [YAHH] | 15h00<br>Jupiter<br>*Tzadki'el*<br>הוינהו<br>היהו [HYHV]<br>האהי [HAHY] | 16h00<br>Mars<br>*Sama'el*<br>הוינהו<br>היוה [HYVH]<br>האיה [HAYH] | 17h00<br>Sun<br>*Micha'el*<br>הוינהו<br>ההוי [HHVY]<br>ההיא [HHYA] |

## Day 3 – Tuesday – Mars – *Sama'el*

| Monday 18h00 to Tuesday 06h00 | | | |
|---|---|---|---|
| 18h00<br>Venus<br>*Ani'el*<br>ינהויג<br>אדני [ADNY]<br>אדין [ADYN] | 19h00<br>Mercury<br>*Rafa'el*<br>ינהויג<br>אנדי [ANDY]<br>אניד [ANYD] | 20h00<br>Moon<br>*Gavri'el*<br>ינהויג<br>אינד [AYND]<br>אידן [AYDN] | 21h00<br>Saturn<br>*Kaftzi'el*<br>ינהויג<br>דניא [DNYA]<br>דנאי [DNAY] |
| 22h00<br>Jupiter<br>*Tzadki'el*<br>ינהויג<br>דינא [DYNA]<br>דיאן [DYAN] | 23h00<br>Mars<br>*Sama'el*<br>ינהויג<br>דאין [DAYN]<br>דאני [DANY] | 00h00<br>Sun<br>*Micha'el*<br>הוידהו<br>ניאד [NYAD]<br>נידא [NYDA] | 01h00<br>Venus<br>*Ani'el*<br>הוידהו<br>נאיד [NAYD]<br>נאדי [NADY] |
| 02h00<br>Mercury<br>*Rafa'el*<br>הוידהו<br>נדאי [NDAY]<br>נדיא [NDYA] | 03h00<br>Moon<br>*Gavri'el*<br>הוידהו<br>יאדן [YADN]<br>יאנד [YAND] | 04h00<br>Saturn<br>*Kaftzi'el*<br>הוידהו<br>ידאן [YDAN]<br>ידנא [YDNA] | 05h00<br>Jupiter<br>*Tzadki'el*<br>הוידהו<br>ינדא [YNDA]<br>ינאד [YNAD] |
| Tuesday 06h00 to 18h00 | | | |
| 06h00<br>**Mars**<br>***Sama'el***<br>ייהויכ<br>יהוה [YHVH]<br>אהיה [AHYH] | 07h00<br>Sun<br>*Micha'el*<br>ייהויכ<br>יההו [YHHV]<br>אההי [AHHY] | 08h00<br>Venus<br>*Ani'el*<br>ייהויכ<br>יוהה [YVHH]<br>איהה [AYHH] | 09h00<br>Mercury<br>*Rafa'el*<br>ייהויכ<br>הוהי [HVHY]<br>היהא [HYHA] |
| 10h00<br>Moon<br>*Gavri'el*<br>ייהויכ<br>הויה [HVYH]<br>היאה [HYAH] | 11h00<br>Saturn<br>*Kaftzi'el*<br>ייהויכ<br>ההיו [HHYV]<br>ההאי [HHAY] | 12h00<br>Jupiter<br>*Tzadki'el*<br>הוישהו<br>והיה [VHYH]<br>יהאה [YHAH] | 13h00<br>Mars<br>*Sama'el*<br>הוישהו<br>וההי [VHHY]<br>יההא [YHHA] |
| 14h00<br>Sun<br>*Micha'el*<br>הוישהו<br>ויהה [VYHH]<br>יאהה [YAHH] | 15h00<br>Venus<br>*Ani'el*<br>הוישהו<br>היהו [HYHV]<br>האהי [HAHY] | 16h00<br>Mercury<br>*Rafa'el*<br>הוישהו<br>היוה [HYVH]<br>האיה [HAYH] | 17h00<br>Moon<br>*Gavri'el*<br>הוישהו<br>ההוי [HHVY]<br>ההיא [HHYA] |

## Day 4 – Wednesday – Mercury – *Rafa'el*

| Tuesday 18h00 to Wednesday 06h00 | | | |
|---|---|---|---|
| 18h00<br>Saturn<br>*Kaftzi'el*<br>יבהויט<br>אדני [ADNY]<br>אדין [ADYN] | 19h00<br>Jupiter<br>*Tzadki'el*<br>יבהויט<br>אנדי [ANDY]<br>אניד [ANYD] | 20h00<br>Mars<br>*Sama'el*<br>יבהויט<br>אינד [AYND]<br>אידנ [AYDN] | 21h00<br>Sun<br>*Micha'el*<br>יבהויט<br>דניא [DNYA]<br>דנאי [DNAY] |
| 22h00<br>Venus<br>*Ani'el*<br>יבהויט<br>דינא [DYNA]<br>דיאנ [DYAN] | 23h00<br>Mercury<br>*Rafa'el*<br>יבהויט<br>דאינ [DAYN]<br>דאני [DANY] | 00h00<br>Moon<br>*Gavri'el*<br>הוירהו<br>ניאד [NYAD]<br>נידא [NYDA] | 01h00<br>Saturn<br>*Kaftzi'el*<br>הוירהו<br>נאיד [NAYD]<br>נאדי [NADY] |
| 02h00<br>Jupiter<br>*Tzadki'el*<br>הוירהו<br>נדאי [NDAY]<br>נדיא [NDYA] | 03h00<br>Mars<br>*Sama'el*<br>הוירהו<br>יאדנ [YADN]<br>יאנד [YAND] | 04h00<br>Sun<br>*Micha'el*<br>הוירהו<br>ידאנ [YDAN]<br>ידנא [YDNA] | 05h00<br>Venus<br>*Ani'el*<br>הוירהו<br>ינדא [YNDA]<br>ינאד [YNAD] |
| Wednesday 06h00 to 18h00 | | | |
| 06h00<br>**Mercury**<br>***Rafa'el***<br>יצהוית<br>יהוה [YHVH]<br>אהיה [AHYH] | 07h00<br>Moon<br>*Gavri'el*<br>יצהוית<br>יההו [YHHV]<br>אההי [AHHY] | 08h00<br>Saturn<br>*Kaftzi'el*<br>יצהוית<br>יוהה [YVHH]<br>איהה [AYHH] | 09h00<br>Jupiter<br>*Tzadki'el*<br>יצהוית<br>הוהי [HVHY]<br>היהא [HYHA] |
| 10h00<br>Mars<br>*Sama'el*<br>יצהוית<br>הויה [HVYH]<br>היאה [HYAH] | 11h00<br>Sun<br>*Micha'el*<br>יצהוית<br>ההיו [HHYV]<br>ההאי [HHAY] | 12h00<br>Venus<br>*Ani'el*<br>הויגהו<br>והיה [VHYH]<br>יהאה [YHAH] | 13h00<br>Mercury<br>*Rafa'el*<br>הויגהו<br>וההי [VHHY]<br>יההא [YHHA] |
| 14h00<br>Moon<br>*Gavri'el*<br>הויגהו<br>ויהה [VYHH]<br>יאהה [YAHH] | 15h00<br>Saturn<br>*Kaftzi'el*<br>הויגהו<br>היהו [HYHV]<br>האהי [HAHY] | 16h00<br>Jupiter<br>*Tzadki'el*<br>הויגהו<br>היוה [HYVH]<br>האיה [HAYH] | 17h00<br>Mars<br>*Sama'el*<br>הויגהו<br>ההוי [HHVY]<br>ההיא [HHYA] |

## Day 5 – Thursday – Jupiter – *Tzadki'el*

| Wednesday 18h00 to Thursday 06h00 | | | |
|---|---|---|---|
| 18h00<br>Sun<br>*Micha'el*<br>יחהויק<br>אדני [ADNY]<br>אדין [ADYN] | 19h00<br>Venus<br>*Ani'el*<br>יחהויק<br>אנדי [ANDY]<br>אניד [ANYD] | 20h00<br>Mercury<br>*Rafa'el*<br>יחהויק<br>איגד [AYND]<br>אידן [AYDN] | 21h00<br>Moon<br>*Gavri'el*<br>יחהויק<br>דניא [DNYA]<br>דנאי [DNAY] |
| 22h00<br>Saturn<br>*Kaftzi'el*<br>יחהויק<br>דינא [DYNA]<br>דיאן [DYAN] | 23h00<br>Jupiter<br>*Tzadki'el*<br>יחהויק<br>דאין [DAYN]<br>דאני [DANY] | 00h00<br>Mars<br>*Sama'el*<br>הויבהו<br>ניאד [NYAD]<br>נידא [NYDA] | 01h00<br>Sun<br>*Micha'el*<br>הויבהו<br>נאיד [NAYD]<br>נאדי [NADY] |
| 02h00<br>Venus<br>*Ani'el*<br>הויבהו<br>נדאי [NDAY]<br>נדיא [NDYA] | 03h00<br>Mercury<br>*Rafa'el*<br>הויבהו<br>יאדן [YADN]<br>יאנד [YAND] | 04h00<br>Moon<br>*Gavri'el*<br>הויבהו<br>ידאן [YDAN]<br>ידנא [YDNA] | 05h00<br>Saturn<br>*Kaftzi'el*<br>הויבהו<br>ינדא [YNDA]<br>ינאד [YNAD] |
| Thursday 06h00 to 18h00 | | | |
| 06h00<br>**Jupiter**<br>*Tzadki'el*<br>יטהוין<br>יהוה [YHVH]<br>אהיה [AHYH] | 07h00<br>Mars<br>*Sama'el*<br>יטהוין<br>יההו [YHHV]<br>אההי [AHHY] | 08h00<br>Sun<br>*Micha'el*<br>יטהוין<br>יוהה [YVHH]<br>איהה [AYHH] | 09h00<br>Venus<br>*Ani'el*<br>יטהוין<br>הוהי [HVHY]<br>היהא [HYHA] |
| 10h00<br>Mercury<br>*Rafa'el*<br>יטהוין<br>הויה [HVYH]<br>היאה [HYAH] | 11h00<br>Moon<br>*Gavri'el*<br>יטהוין<br>ההיו [HHYV]<br>ההאי [HHAY] | 12h00<br>Saturn<br>*Kaftzi'el*<br>הויעהו<br>והיה [VHYH]<br>יהאה [YHAH] | 13h00<br>Jupiter<br>*Tzadki'el*<br>הויעהו<br>וההי [VHHY]<br>יההא [YHHA] |
| 14h00<br>Mars<br>*Sama'el*<br>הויעהו<br>ויהה [VYHH]<br>יאהה [YAHH] | 15h00<br>Sun<br>*Micha'el*<br>הויעהו<br>היהו [HYHV]<br>האהי [HAHY] | 16h00<br>Venus<br>*Ani'el*<br>הויעהו<br>היוה [HYVH]<br>האיה [HAYH] | 17h00<br>Mercury<br>*Rafa'el*<br>הויעהו<br>ההוי [HHVY]<br>ההיא [HHYA] |

### Day 6 – Friday – Venus – *Ani'el*

| Thursday 18h00 to Friday 06h00 | | | |
|---|---|---|---|
| 18h00<br>Moon<br>*Gavri'el*<br>ייהויג<br>אדני [ADNY]<br>אדינ [ADYN] | 19h00<br>Saturn<br>*Kaftzi'el*<br>ייהויג<br>אנדי [ANDY]<br>אניד [ANYD] | 20h00<br>Jupiter<br>*Tzadki'el*<br>ייהויג<br>אינד [AYND]<br>אידנ [AYDN] | 21h00<br>Mars<br>*Sama'el*<br>ייהויג<br>דניא [DNYA]<br>דנאי [DNAY] |
| 22h00<br>Sun<br>*Micha'el*<br>ייהויג<br>דינא [DYNA]<br>דיאנ [DYAN] | 23h00<br>Venus<br>*Ani'el*<br>ייהויג<br>דאינ [DAYN]<br>דאני [DANY] | 00h00<br>Mercury<br>*Rafa'el*<br>הוילהו<br>ניאד [NYAD]<br>נידא [NYDA] | 01h00<br>Moon<br>*Gavri'el*<br>הוילהו<br>נאיד [NAYD]<br>נאדי [NADY] |
| 02h00<br>Saturn<br>*Kaftzi'el*<br>הוילהו<br>נדאי [NDAY]<br>נדיא [NDYA] | 03h00<br>Jupiter<br>*Tzadki'el*<br>הוילהו<br>יאדנ [YADN]<br>יאנד [YAND] | 04h00<br>Mars<br>*Sama'el*<br>הוילהו<br>ידאנ [YDAN]<br>ידנא [YDNA] | 05h00<br>Sun<br>*Micha'el*<br>הוילהו<br>ינדא [YNDA]<br>ינאד [YNAD] |
| **Friday 06h00 to 18h00** | | | |
| 06h00<br>**Venus**<br>**Ani'el**<br>יפהויז<br>יהוה [YHVH]<br>אהיה [AHYH] | 07h00<br>Mercury<br>*Rafa'el*<br>יפהויז<br>יההו [YHHV]<br>אההי [AHHY] | 08h00<br>Moon<br>*Gavri'el*<br>יפהויז<br>יוהה [YVHH]<br>איהה [AYHH] | 09h00<br>Saturn<br>*Kaftzi'el*<br>יפהויז<br>הוהי [HVHY]<br>היהא [HYHA] |
| 10h00<br>Jupiter<br>*Tzadki'el*<br>יפהויז<br>הויה [HVYH]<br>היאה [HYAH] | 11h00<br>Mars<br>*Sama'el*<br>יפהויז<br>ההיו [HHYV]<br>ההאי [HHAY] | 12h00<br>Sun<br>*Micha'el*<br>הויקיו<br>והיה [VHYH]<br>יהאה [YHAH] | 13h00<br>Venus<br>*Ani'el*<br>הויקיו<br>וההי [VHHY]<br>יההא [YHHA] |
| 14h00<br>Mercury<br>*Rafa'el*<br>הויקיו<br>ויהה [VYHH]<br>יאהה [YAHH] | 15h00<br>Moon<br>*Gavri'el*<br>הויקיו<br>היהו [HYHV]<br>האהי [HAHY] | 16h00<br>Saturn<br>*Kaftzi'el*<br>הויקיו<br>היוה [HYVH]<br>האיה [HAYH] | 17h00<br>Jupiter<br>*Tzadki'el*<br>הויקיו<br>ההוי [HHVY]<br>ההיא [HHYA] |

Astrological Considerations / 263

## Day 7 – Saturday – Saturn – *Kaftzi'el*

| Friday 18h00 to Saturday 06h00 ||||
|---|---|---|---|
| 18h00<br>Mars<br>*Sama'el*<br>ישהויק<br>אדני [ADNY]<br>אדין [ADYN] | 19h00<br>Sun<br>*Micha'el*<br>ישהויק<br>אנדי [ANDY]<br>אניד [ANYD] | 20h00<br>Venus<br>*Ani'el*<br>ישהויק<br>אינד [AYND]<br>אידן [AYDN] | 21h00<br>Mercury<br>*Rafa'el*<br>ישהויק<br>דניא [DNYA]<br>דנאי [DNAY] |
| 22h00<br>Moon<br>*Gavri'el*<br>ישהויק<br>דינא [DYNA]<br>דיאן [DYAN] | 23h00<br>Saturn<br>*Kaftzi'el*<br>ישהויק<br>דאין [DAYN]<br>דאני [DANY] | 00h00<br>Jupiter<br>*Tzadki'el*<br>הויוהו<br>ניאד [NYAD]<br>נידא [NYDA] | 01h00<br>Mars<br>*Sama'el*<br>הויוהו<br>נאיד [NAYD]<br>נאדי [NADY] |
| 02h00<br>Sun<br>*Micha'el*<br>הויוהו<br>נדאי [NDAY]<br>נדיא [NDYA] | 03h00<br>Venus<br>*Ani'el*<br>הויוהו<br>יאדן [YADN]<br>יאנד [YAND] | 04h00<br>Mercury<br>*Rafa'el*<br>הויוהו<br>ידאן [YDAN]<br>ידנא [YDNA] | 05h00<br>Moon<br>*Gavri'el*<br>הויוהו<br>ינדא [YNDA]<br>ינאד [YNAD] |
| Saturday 06h00 to 18h00 ||||
| 06h00<br>**Saturn**<br>**Kaftzi'el**<br>יצהויי<br>יהוה [YHVH]<br>אהיה [AHYH] | 07h00<br>Jupiter<br>*Tzadki'el*<br>יצהויי<br>יההו [YHHV]<br>אההי [AHHY] | 08h00<br>Mars<br>*Sama'el*<br>יצהויי<br>יוהה [YVHH]<br>איהה [AYHH] | 09h00<br>Sun<br>*Micha'el*<br>יצהויי<br>הוהי [HVHY]<br>היהא [HYHA] |
| 10h00<br>Venus<br>*Ani'el*<br>יצהויי<br>הויה [HVYH]<br>היאה [HYAH] | 11h00<br>Mercury<br>*Rafa'el*<br>יצהויי<br>ההיו [HHYV]<br>ההאי [HHAY] | 12h00<br>Moon<br>*Gavri'el*<br>הויתהו<br>והיה [VHYH]<br>יהאה [YHAH] | 13h00<br>Saturn<br>*Kaftzi'el*<br>הויתהו<br>וההי [VHHY]<br>יההא [YHHA] |
| 14h00<br>Jupiter<br>*Tzadki'el*<br>הויתהו<br>ויהה [VYHH]<br>יאהה [YAHH] | 15h00<br>Mars<br>*Sama'el*<br>הויתהו<br>היהו [HYHV]<br>האהי [HAHY] | 16h00<br>Sun<br>*Micha'el*<br>הויתהו<br>היוה [HYVH]<br>האיה [HAYH] | 17h00<br>Venus<br>*Ani'el*<br>הויתהו<br>ההוי [HHVY]<br>ההיא [HHYA] |

Whilst most of the mentioned correspondences are readily comprehensible in terms of the material shared, I believe it important to revisit some of the details shared in these tables. I have earlier referenced the seven Archangels in terms of their planetary associations, as listed by Eleazer of Worms;[69] the twenty-four permutation of אדני (*Adonai*); and the two sets of twelve permutations of יהוה (*YHVH*) and אהיה (*Eh'yeh*), hence these need no further discussion. It is worth bearing in mind that the said twenty-four permutations and twelve sets of permutations of the Ineffable Name and the Divine Name *Eh'yeh*, are equally aligned with the twelve Zodiacal signs,[70]

As mentioned earlier, the invocation of the sets of twelve permutations at their proper times, i.e. their respectively associated months and hours, are understood to neutralise the negative impact of the powers of the "Twenty-eight Mansions" of the Moon, and equally "to completely neutralise whatever malevolence might be in store for the invocants."[71] In this regard, I was taught that these daily invocations neutralise and rectify astrological dispositions, which afford practitioners the opportunity to perform planetary ritual procedures without having to be concerned about whether a relevant planet is "retrograde," etc. This topic is quite extensive, and the current tome does not afford enough space to address the subject matter in greater detail. Hence I will offer an introduction only, and leave further elaborations to be addressed in future volumes.

Readers who are familiar with Hebrew will find a lot of details regarding the twenty-eight Lunar mansions in the famous "*Commentary on the Sefer Yetzirah*" attributed to the *Raavad*.[72] Briefly, the twenty-eight "Mansions of the Moon" pertain to the twenty-eight days of the lunar month, or more precisely of the "sidereal month." This topic was of particular importance in Chinese, Japanese and Hindu astrology, and the "Lunar Mansions" is of equal significance in Islamic Astrology. In this regard, we should acknowledge the contribution medieval moslem astrologers like Abu'l-Rayhan Muhammad ibn Ahmad Al-Biruni made to the study of the twenty-eight "mansions" of the moon,[73] and how greatly "Lunar Astrology" impacted the thoughts of Jewish mystics who resided in Moslem lands in the Middle Ages.[74]

Whilst this aspect of Lunar Astrology was derived from ancient oriental sources, it was given a unique treatment in Kabbalistic traditions, involving special verses from the Hebrew

Bible, the seven "double letters" in the Hebrew alphabet aligned with "seven *Sefirot*," as well as the "seven planets" of traditional astrology. These were in turn associated with a set of Divine Names, and the entire combination worked into a harmonious whole with the twelve signs of the Zodiac, as well as with the hours of the day. Most importantly, the Kabbalistic approach to this topic pertains to the *Shechinah*, the "Female" aspect of Divinity, or the "Divine Presence" in manifestation, specifically to "Her" being associated with "time." In this regard, the *Zohar* (*1:198a*) informs us that עת (*Et* - "time") is "a supernal rung."[75] It continues by asking "And who is this *Et?*" to which we are told that it is the letter ה (*Heh*), and then, by adding the letter *Heh* as a suffix to *Et*, further elucidates that "it is called עתה (*Atah*)," a term meaning "Now." Daniel Matt explained that the reason for "time" being "a supernal rung" is that the *Shechinah* "is known as 'time' since She conducts the world according to a cosmic schedule, enabling phenomenon to unfold in its proper time," and further that "She is also symbolized by the letter ה (*Heh*), the final letter of the divine name יהוה (*YHVH*)."[76]

Since the *Shechinah* is traditionally associated with both "Time" and the "Moon," we can understand why the twenty-eight "Lunar Mansions" are collectively considered to be, as it were, an expression of the "Divine Presence" in manifestation. Furthermore, these twenty-eight Lunar *Ittot* (times) are associated with the twenty-eight "qualities of time" listed in *Ecclestiastes 3:1-8* reading:

> "To every thing there is a season, and a time to every purpose under the heaven:
> A time to be born, and a time to die;
> A time to plant, and a time to pluck up that which is planted;
> A time to kill, and a time to heal;
> A time to break down, and a time to build up;
> A time to weep, and a time to laugh;
> A time to mourn, and a time to dance;
> A time to cast away stones, and a time to gather stones together;
> A time to embrace, and a time to refrain from embracing;
> A time to seek, and a time to lose;
> A time to keep, and a time to cast away;

A time to rend, and a time to sew;
A time to keep silence, and a time to speak;
A time to love, and a time to hate;
A time for war, and a time for peace."

There are fourteen benevolent "times" and fourteen malevolent ones. Kabbalistically speaking these are considered to pertain to the "good" and "bad" time cycles of the twenty-eight "Lunar Mansions," fourteen from the aspect of *Chesed* (Mercy or Benevolence) and fourteen from the aspect of *Din* or *Pachad* (respectively "judgment" and "fear," also *Gevurah*).[77] As an aside, it is worth perusing the exposition of *Et Tovah* ("good time," also called "*Et Ratzon*" "time of favour") and *Et Ra* ("bad" or "evil" time) in "*Gates of Light*" (*Sha'arei Orah*) by Joseph Gikatilla.[78]

The fourteen positive and fourteen negative aspects listed in these verses were arranged in a particular manner in Kabbalah to coincide with the seven "double letters" of the Hebrew alphabet, as well as with the seven attributes or qualities associated with these letters. According to all the manuscripts of the "Saadia"[79] and "Long"[80] versions of the *Sefer Yetzirah* which I have consulted, and which are quite different from the much later and currently popular "*Gra* version,"[81] the seven "attributes" are associated with the "double letters" in the following manner:

| ב | Bet/Vet | Life/Death |
|---|---|---|
| ג | Gimel/Djimel | Peace/War |
| ד | Dalet/Thalet | Wisdom/Folly |
| כ | Kaf/Chaf | Wealth/Poverty |
| פ | Peh/Feh | Prosperity/Desolation |
| ר | Resh/Resh | Beauty/Ugliness |
| ת | Tav/Thav | Mastery/Slavery |

Aryeh Kaplan listed the order in which Kabbalists associated these attributes with the mentioned twenty-eight "times" in *Ecclesiastes*

3, to be "somewhat different than that of the Scripture."[82] He also mentioned that it does not correspond to the order found in the *Sefer Yetzirah*. Accordingly the correct order is said to be:

| ר | ן | ט | ט | ל | ו | ו |
|---|---|---|---|---|---|---|
| Mastery | Beauty | Prosperity | Wealth | Wisdom | Peace | Life |
| A time to laugh / A time to dance | A time to embrace / A time to keep | A time to be born / A time to plant | A time to gather stones / A time to seek | A time to sew / A time to keep silence | A time to love / A time for peace | A time to heal / A time to build up |
| A time to weep / A time to mourn | A time to refrain from embracing | A time to die / A time to pluck up | A time to cast away stones / A time to lose | A time to rend / A time to speak | A time to hate / A time for war | A time to kill / A time to break down |
| Slavery | Ugliness | Desolation | Poverty | Folly | War | Death |

It is worth noting that the listed twenty-eight qualities, is that the fourteen "good" aspects related to *Chesed* (Mercy), have been said to have originated from the fourteen glyphs comprising the biblical phrase יהוה אלהינו יהוה (*YHVH Eloheinu YHVH*), whilst the fourteen "evil" aspects affiliated with *Gevurah* (Might), are to have been derived from the fourteen glyphs comprising the transposition of the said biblical expression, i.e. בוזו במוכסז כוזו (*Kuzu B'mochsaz Kuzu*), the so-called "Fourteen Letter Name of God." Aryeh Kaplan therefore noted that "these 28 letters can therefore be used to transmit the appropriate concepts."[83] He delineated the said affiliations in the following manner:

| Seed | י *Y* to be born<br>ה *H* to plant | כ *K* to die<br>ו *U* to uproot |
|---|---|---|
| Life | ו *V* to heal<br>ה *H* to build | ז *Z* to kill<br>ו *U* to wreck |
| Wealth | א *E* to hoard stones<br>ל *L* to seek | ב *B* to throw stones<br>ם *M* to lose |
| Grace | ה *H* to embrace<br>י *Y* to safeguard | ו *U* to shun<br>כ *K* to discard |
| Wisdom | נ *N* to be still<br>ו *U* to sew | ס *S* to speak<br>ז *Z* to tear |
| Peace | י *Y* of peace<br>ה *H* to love | כ *K* of war<br>ו *U* to hate |
| Dominance | ו *V* of dancing<br>ה *H* to laugh | ז *Z* of mourning<br>ו *U* to weep |

We are informed that the fourteen qualities comprising the "times of evil" of the twenty-eight Lunar Mansions, can be neutralised by means of the daily enunciations of the twelve permutations of יהוה (*YHVH*) and אהיה (*Eh'yeh*). In this regard, I shared the affiliations of these permutations with the Zodiac as well as with the twelve daylight hours. As indicated elsewhere, and reiterated here, the glyphs comprising the "Forty-two Letter Name" are equally associated with the twelve zodiacal signs, and the seven days of the week.[84] We are informed that by means of the Forty-two Letter Name are the twenty-eight Lunar Mansions associated with the twelve signs of the zodiac.[85] In this regard, the forty-two letters comprising this Divine Name, are conjoined in a unique

*Astrological Considerations* / 269

manner with the three letters comprising the Divine Name יהוה
(*YHVH*), i.e י (*Yod*), ה (*Heh*) and ו (*Vav*). The combination יהו
(*YHV*) is repeated forty-two times, and the individual letters
comprising the "Forty-two Letter Name" respectively located after
each *Yod*, as indicated below:[86]

יאהו יבהו יגהו ייהו יתהו יצהו יקהו ירהו יעהו ישהו
יטהו ינהו ינהו יגהו ידהו ייהו יכהו ישהו יבהו יטהו
ירהו יצהו יתהו יגהו יחהו יקהו יבהו יטהו ינהו יעהו
ייהו יגהו ילהו יפהו יזהו יקהו ישהו יקהו יוהו יצהו
ייהו יתהו

Transliteration:
> *YAHV YBHV YGHV YYHV YTHV YTzHV YKHV YRHV*
> *YAHV YShHV YTHV YNHV YNHV YGHV YDHV YYHV*
> *YKHV YShHV YBHV YTHV YRHV YTzHV YTHV YGHV*
> *YChHV YKHV YBHV YTHV YNHV YAHV YYHV YGHV*
> *YLHV YPHV YZHV YKHV YShHV YKHV YVHV YTzHV*
> *YYHV YTHV*

In order to align this Divine Name construct with the twelve signs
of the Zodiac, the 168 letters are divided into into twelve fourteen-
letter combinations, as shown below:[87]

| | |
|---|---|
| *Teleh* (Aries) | יאהויבהויגהויי |
| *Shor* (Taurus) | הויתהויצהויקהו |
| *Te'omim* (Gemini) | ירהויעהוישהויט |
| *Sartan* (Cancer) | הוינהוינהויגהו |
| *Aryeh* (Leo) | ידהויהויכהויש |
| *Betulah* (Virgo) | הויבהויטהוירהו |
| *Moznaim* (Libra) | יצהויתהויגהויח |
| *Akrav* (Scorpio) | הויקהויבהויטהו |
| *Keshet* (Sagittarius) | ינהויעהוייהויג |
| *Gedi* (Capricorn) | הוילהויפהויזהו |
| *Deli* (Aquarius) | יקהוישהויקהויו |
| *Dagim* (Pisces) | הויצהויתהויתהו |

Each of the fourteen-letter Divine Name combinations is often divided into three or four parts, each of which varies in the number of component glyphs from one zodiacal sign to the next, e.g. *Aries*—הוית הויצ הויקהו; *Taurus*—יאהוי בהוי גהויי; *Gemini*— הוין הוינ הויגהו; *Cancer*—ירהויע הויש הויט; *Leo*—הויב הויט הויוהו; *Virgo*—ידהוי יהויכ הויש; *Libra*—הויק הויב הויטהו; *Scorpio*—יצהוית הויג הויח; *Sagittarius*—הויל הויפ הויזהו; *Capricorn*—ינהויע הויי הויג; *Aquarius*—הויצ הויי הוית הו; and *Pisces*—יק הויש הויק הויו.⁸⁸

We need to also consider the said Divine Name combinations applied to the Lunar Mansions. In this instance, the 168 Hebrew letters are arranged into twenty-eight six-letter combinations, as indicated in the following illustration from a famous commentary on the *Sefer Yetzirah*,⁸⁹ which a contemporary interpreter delineated a "magic circle"⁹⁰ whilst it is in fact nothing of the kind. Aryeh Kaplan delineated it "the 28 camps of the Divine Presence":⁹¹

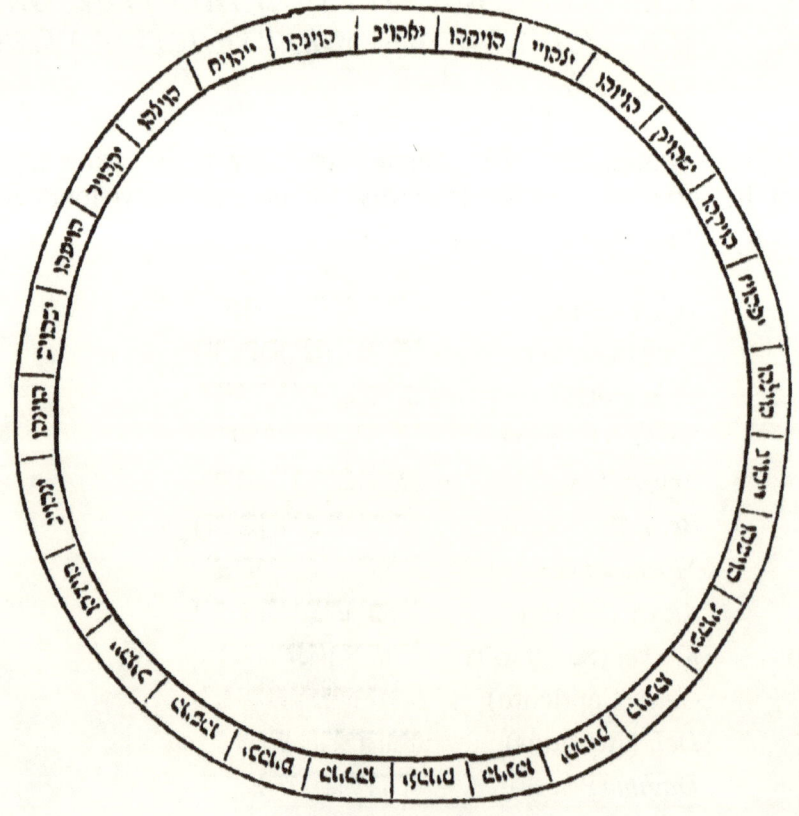

Herewith the full array of these Divine Name combinations aligned with the twenty-eight Lunar Mansions:

| 4 | 3 | 2 | 1 |
|---|---|---|---|
| הויצהו | ייהוית | הויגהו | יאהויב |
| 8 | 7 | 6 | 5 |
| הוינהו | ישהויט | הויעהו | יקהויר |
| 12 | 11 | 10 | 9 |
| הוישהו | ייהויכ | הוידהו | ינהויג |
| 16 | 15 | 14 | 13 |
| הויגהו | יצהוית | הוירהו | יבהויט |
| 20 | 19 | 18 | 17 |
| הויעהו | יטהוין | הויבהו | יחהויק |
| 24 | 23 | 22 | 21 |
| הויקהו | יפהויז | הוילהו | ייהויג |
| 28 | 27 | 26 | 25 |
| הויתהו | יצהויי | הויוהו | ישהויק |

As you have probably noticed from the contents of the earlier listed tables comprising correspondences of planets, angels, and Divine Names, these twenty-eight Divine Name combinations are arranged over the seven days of the week, i.e. four Divine Name constructs ruling 6 hours each. Thus on the first day of the week, Sunday, commencing at sunset on Saturday, the Divine Name combination יאהויב will be applicable for the first six hours from dusk to midnight, which is succeeded by the Divine Name combination הויגהו which is "active," so to speak, from midnight to dawn on Sunday, etc.

As might be expected, there are many practical deliberations as far as the magical application of the items listed are concerned. In this regard, let us consider for example the scenario of simply finding greater joy in living. The process of acquiring expansive happiness in your life is supported by numerous activities especially designed to facilitate the ideal circumstances in which "greater happiness" may flourish. These range from carrying special amulets, uttering magical mantras, enunciating unique Divine Names, etc., and these practices are indeed very effective. Yet, many who have employed these procedures, will testify that whilst there is ample evidence to prove the success of these magical activities, there are many instances in which "magical practices" have failed. These individuals would rightly query the fundamental factor in assuring success.

In this regard, the important factor is the very being of the practitioner/invocant, i.e. the one employing these techniques. I have noted elsewhere "every moment requires us to be alert to fresh possibilities in the *Now*. In the 'all-possible-possibilities' of the Eternal Now' we certainly cannot afford to be concerned about the past or the future, i.e. with the '*has been*' (memories) or the '*would be*' (expectations). These factors rob us of our 'Now-ness,' and tie us to the wheel of cause and effect where we instantly find ourselves in a rut, totally unable to see the miraculous 'all-possible-possibilities'."[92]

This brings us right back to a point I made in the very first volume of this "Shadow Tree Series" of magical texts, that magic is defined "the science and art of causing change to occur in conformity with will,"[93] and whilst "will" refers to the *Ru'ach*, i.e. the Reasoning Self, this conscious "Self" will only "initiate a magical action." It is "the *Nefesh*, the Instinctual Self, that has to work the 'change'," which can be achieved only if "there is no interference from the 'cage of logic,' the reasoning mind."[94] As noted, "the greatest pitfall in *Kabbalah* and Magic, leading to the worst frustrations and inability, is in fact the *desire to have results*. This lust for results annihilates all our efforts. Desire destroys the deed, because there is egotistical identification, fear of failure, and even a reciprocal desire not to achieve the original desire, and all this, arising as it does from our dualistic natures, will wreck any hoped for outcome."[95] It is for this very reason that I recommended to practitioners of the magical arts to surrender "studying and working with a desire for results," and that they should work for the joy of it, "practising for the sake of the 'art,' i.e. 'for the heck of it'."[96]

Hence, before considering the scenario of engendering happiness by magical means, I again suggest that you work any magical procedure "because you want to....., without caring whether it will work or not, or whether it will produce any effects or not. Do not seek any outcome, even if the working is done for a specific purpose, simply work 'uninvolved,' which does not mean 'do not care' or not to put in effort. Just do not let spiritual

*Astrological Considerations / 273*

intellectual, egotistical, or emotional expectations cloud and destroy your efforts. Thus it is that at the end of the working, you should immediately wipe it from your mind."[97]

In terms of the suggested scenario of establishing greater happiness, and perforce a greater sense of wellbeing in life, by means of any or all the shared sets of "sevenfold correspondences," you could elect to work with the sphere of *Chesed* (Loving-kindness), this *sefirah* being aligned with צדק (*Tzedek*—"Jupiter"), and associated with the expansiveness of joy termed חדוה (*Chedvah*—"Delight"). In this regard, you recognise your index finger and right ear to be affiliated to the said planet, and equally acknowledge the following correspondences to the said *Sefirah*:

1. the Divine Name אל (*El*), with which you will affirm the "God Force" alignment, or personal stance, which you will establish deliberately by "opening" the appropriate "Gate";
2. the Archangel צדקיאל (*Tzadki'el*) and "his" *Chotam* (Seal/Sigil), which you will internalize, the latter being:

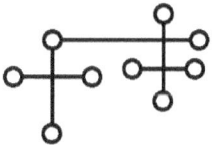

3. the subservient "Planetary Spirit" הסמאל (*Hisma'el*) and the following associated *Chotam* (Seal/Sigil), which you will trace with your eyes and right hand as you enunciate the name of the said "Spirit Intelligence":

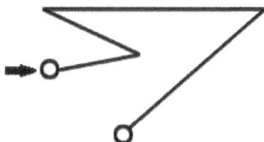

Having aligned the "centre" (Self) with a selected "God Force," impacting the "circumference" is basically a matter of triggering the appropriate "God Force," i.e. emotional quality, by means of the relevant hand/face locales; if necessary having added further intensification by "opening" the associated sefirotic "Gate"; invoking the support of allied "Spirit Forces" by enunciating their appellatives, and "internalising" their respective magical seals; or, if so intended, communicating the magical intention behind the activity directly with an intended recipient in your environment. Such procedures could naturally be expanded upon, e.g. with *Lachashim* (incantations) incorporating appropriately aligned Divine Names, the earlier listed Archangelic associations, and the "internalising" of their respectively affiliated *Chotamot* (magical seals/sigils).

## C. Sefirotic/Planetary Rituals

### 1. STICKS & STONES

Before we address larger planetary rituals in conjunction with specific intentions, it is worth considering component physical materials which, by means of their planetary associations or "signatures" might enhance and empower relevant ritual procedures.

Several readers of this series of texts on *Practical Kabbalah* have noted the distinct "lack of ritual gear" in Jewish Magic (*Practical Kabbalah*), the only ritual objects employed being an engraved *kiddush* cup occasionally, metal and paper amulets, roots, herbs, oils, stones, etc.[98] Interestingly enough, there is quite an inventory of herbs and their uses to be found in traditional Jewish folk medicine, which includes an array of *Segulot*, i.e. magical uses.[99] In this regard, there has been much cross-cultural influence between Jews and their Christian neighbours, e.g. in Eastern Europe regarding which one commentator noted to be "an essentially binary framing of mutual influence: either Slavic culture is understood to reflect a Jewish impact, or Jewish culture to reflect a Slavic one."[100] Here one cannot fail to recognize the vital role of the popular *Ba'alei Shem*, the "Masters of the Name," who "performed a shamanic function: to restore social order or provide personal security, they mediated between empiric reality and divine realms this world and the netherworld, spirits and living beings. They employed magical remedies and mystical devices, Lurianic and popular Kabbalah, local fold herbal remedies and traditional Hebrew acronyms, encrypted biblical verses (*gematriah*) and amulets (*kameya'*)."[101] We are told that "Jews and gentiles from all walks of life (the wealthiest Polish magnates included) turned to *ba'alei shem* to cure infertility, sexual disorders, and seminal emissions, to ensure safe childbirth, control epidemics, protect a person or personal habitat from a disaster like murder, fire, robbery, or the evil eye, predict fate, reveal suppressed desires or "read" dreams, banish Lilith or other demons (*mazikim*), treat depression, and exorcise evil spirits (*dybbuks*)."[102]

Whilst the East European *Ba'alei Shem* ("Masters of the Name") disappeared from the world scene, despite the claims of some moderns who style themselves under this appellative, it is clear that the thoughts they shared on plants and herbs, still impact those who seek natural cures for all manner of illness, and, as hinted, some of these involve practices which are distinctly "magical." For example, in terms of herbs being employed in amulets, it is quite common today in the State of Israel, to find a small portion of rue or garlic and plain rock salt folded in small squares of ordinary paper, which would then be taped together with the two endings of a plain red ribbon, and worn around the neck for magical protection, etc.

Regarding the most important herbs popular amongst practitioners of *Practical Kabbalah*, which were employed for medical/magical purposes, we should pay some attention to רוטא (*Ruta*—"Rue").[103] This herb was considered to be so powerful, that the Hebrew name of this herb, i.e. רוטא (*Ruta*), written on an amulet or included in an incantation, is to this day considered to be a powerful divine name imparting the very magical/healing powers of the herb it identifies. However, it should be noted, that there is also a Divine Name רוטא pertaining to *Gevurah* (Might) on the sefirotic Tree, which is quite distinct from the said herb of that name, and which is equally employed in amulets for healing and protection against epidemics. The distinction between the two items is in their differing vocalisations, i.e. *Ruta* in reference to the herb, and *Ri'ut'o* in the instance of the Divine Name construct, the latter said to have been derived from the four emboldened letters in *Genesis 43:11* reading צרי ומעט דבש נכאת (*tzori u-m'at d'vash n'chot*—"balm, and a little honey, spicery").[104]

Considering the similarity of the spelling of the appellatives of the said two items and their applications in Jewish Magic, it is no wonder that they should come to be viewed as one and the same in the popular mind. Here we have a "Holy Name" and a "Holy Plant." Special conditions were required when harvesting this pungent herb for magical purposes. In this regard, I previously shared an amulet comprising a letter square of the first nine letters of the Hebrew alphabet, as well as the names of the four main Archangels, i.e. *Gavri'el*, *Ori'el*, *Micha'el* and *Rafa'el*. We are told this amulet should be placed together with the *Rue* inside a red silk pouch to be carried on the person of the one requiring the magical benefits afforded by this, as it were, "herb amulet."

However, as mentioned, there are certain rules as to when and how to cut the said herb to be employed in this magical fashion. In this regard, we are told that the *Ruta* (Rue) "should be cut with a golden coin or disc on a Wednesday prior to sunrise while the moon is still shining, and during a period when the moon is in the ascent, i.e. from New Moon to Full Moon."[105] Furthermore, *Deuteronomy 6:4–9* and the *Vihi No'am* prayer, the latter prayer comprising the concluding verse of *Psalm 90* and the whole of *Psalm 91*, should be recited prior to cutting the herb. This is followed by the cutting of the *Ruta* (Rue) whilst uttering the words:

אני לוקט אותך בשם יאי לשמירת [פלוני בן פלוני]
מן הדבר ומן המגפה

Transliteration:
> *Ani loket otcha b'shem YAY l'shmirat [.....Ploni ben Ploni.....] min ha-dever v'min ha-magefah*

Translation:
> "I am collecting you in the Name *YAY* for the protection of [.....fill in the name of the recipient.....] from the pestilence and from the plague."

As mentioned elsewhere, "afterwards the amulet and the rue are placed in the mentioned silk pouch, and suspended around the neck of the individual for whom it was constructed."[106]

Besides protection against "pestilence" and "plague," rue was employed in Jewish folk medicine and magic for a great variety of purposes. In this regard, it was noted that "Rue is mentioned in medical books in recipes for management of diarrhoea and treatment of wind, warts, dysuria, dysmenorrhoea, and hard swellings, aphasia, muscle spasms, tension, shaking, and facial palsy; bladder complaints, alopecia (topically applied), and dysuria (rue cooked in oil). It also appears as a simple in a lexicon of *materia medica*. Rue leaves were used against fever, black bile, and phlegm, rue oil against convulsion and tetany, fevers, and colic, and rue seeds against entropion and roughness of the eyelids; wild rue is in a quasi-medical formula for incense, and in a recipe for weak and dim vision and drooping eyelids."[107]

We are further informed that "al-Kindi notes a variety of uses for the plant and its products. The resin serves as a component in expectorants and is also used for treating the gall bladder, joint infections, and nervous diseases, and to prepare poultices to dress the spleen, liver, kidneys, and stomach. Shabbetai Donolo mentions the plant and its medical uses. Maimonides states that the plant is a hot and dry medication. The leaves served as a component in 'theriac,' a food for those who were bitten, and a component in an enema to treat constipation accompanied by heartburn. The resin of the plant was a component in a medication that caused 'sexual excitation and stiffened the male sexual organ so that it does not droop.' Ibn al-Baytar reports that the resin of the plant is hot and dry, and is effective in treating eye diseases and sores in the throat and armpits. The oil of rue and its medical properties are described as well. According to al-Qazwini, this is a famous plant with extensive uses, including improving virility, aborting foetuses, and treating epilepsy, headaches and toothache, blindness, and skin diseases."[108]

Raphael Patai mentioned a one time practice in which "barren women are wont to pluck grass from the slits of the Western Wall, growing there between the rows of the stones of the wall. This they boil and drink the infusion as a charm."[109] In this regard, he noted that rue was employed for the same purpose, and, quoting from one primary source on Jewish medicine, wrote "For pregnancy. If the woman should put some rue into her womb after the intercourse, and sleep lying on her back, she will conceive at once."[110] This magical plant still features prominently in the *"Ritual Medical Lore of Sephardic Women."*[111] In this regard, it was reported that to the question "'Did you use any herbs, like *majorana* [marjoram] or *ruda* [rue]?' one of the women replied, 'Ah! Ruda yes. When the eye hurt, this I remember from my grandmother, they washed the ruda, they mashed it well, they put it with a little sugar in a thin rag, and it was placed on the eye. And it was good. It is good even today.' The other woman immediately added, 'It is also used for *ayin arah* [evil eye].' Both of the women continued discussing the beneficial aspects of the herb, rue."[112]

It should therefore come as no surprise that even the very Hebrew name of this plant, רוטא (*Ruta*), is considered to be enormously powerful in terms of, as it were, "spiritually channeling" its medicinal and magical benefits. Hence, it is equally clear why sprigs and branches of this and other plants, whose "magical benefits" have been studied in terms of the "*Doctrine of Signatures*," are considered to be equally beneficial in enhancing magical rituals the fundamental intentions of which align with affiliated planetary forces, and which might perforce be enhanced by their associated herbs, flowers, shrubs, trees, etc.

### a. PLANTS

In terms of sharing a list of plants which may be employed to enhance "planetary rituals," I have consulted a variety of sources, both primary and secondary.[113] Hence, if you feel the need to enhance your planetary rituals with plants or their essences, I would recommend the following list of plants and their respective planetary alignments, which will be of good service. As you will notice, whilst there are many plants directly affiliated with a single planet, the majority conjoin two or more planetary powers. Thus it is worthwhile to consider the planetary force fundamental to the purpose of your intended ritual activity, and equally the additional planetary powers which might be incorporated in harmonious alignment with the selected primary planetary power. Herewith the said list of planetary/plant substances:

### i. Saturn

| | |
|---|---|
| Saturn | Alder Buckthorn [*Rhamnus frangula*]. |
| | Amaranth [*Amaranthus*]. |
| | Ashweed [Wild Masterwort, Goatweed, Bishop's Weed, Herb Gerard/*Aegopodium podagraria*]. |
| | Barley [*Hordeum vulgare*]. |
| | Beech Tree [*Fagus silvatica*]. |
| | Beet [Mangel-wurzel, Stock Beet, Silver Beet/*Beta Rubra*]. |
| | Beetroot [*Beta vulgaris*]. |
| | Beets (Red) [(*Beta*) *Hertensis*]. |
| | Birdsfoot [*Lotus corniculatus*]. |

Bistort [*Bistorta polygonaceae*].
Bittersweet Nightshade [*Solanum dulcamara*].
Cockle Weed [Bearded Darnel/*Lolium temulentum*].
Cornflower [Bluebottle, Bullweed/Centaurea cyanus].
Cowbane [Water Hemlock/*Cicuta virosa*].
Elm [*Ulmus campestris*].
Eryngium [Sea Holly/*Eryngium maritimum*].
Eryngo (Common) [*Eryngium campestre*].
Fenugreek [*Foenum graecum*].
Flatleaf Eryngo [*Eryngium planum*].
Fleawort [*Plantago psyllium*].
Hellebore [Christmas Rose/*Helloborus niger*].
Hellebore (White) [*Veratrum album*].
Hemlock [*Conium maculatum*].
Hemp [*Cannabis sativa*].
Holly [*Olex aquifolium*].
Buckshorn Plantain [*Plantago coronopus*].
Horsetail [*Equisetum arvense*].
Ivy [*Hedera helix*].
Jew's Ear [*Auricularia judae*].
Knapweed [*Centaurea nigra*].
Maize [Indian Corn/*Zea mays*].
Male Fern [*Aspedium filix mas*].
Medlar [*Mespilus germanica*].
Monkshood [*Aconitum*].
Pansy [*Viola tricolor*].
Polypody Root [*Polygonum vulgare*].
Quince [*Cydonia vulgaris*].
Rye [*Secale cereale*].
Scotch Pine [*Pinus sylvestris*].
Senna [*Cassia angustifolia*].
Shepherd's Purse [*Capsella bursa pastoris*].
Solomon's Seal [*Polygonatum officinale*].
Sorb Tree [*Sorbus domestica*].

|  |  |
|---|---|
|  | Spleenwort [*Asplenium*].<br>Tamarind [*Tamarindus indica*].<br>Twayblade [*Listera ovata*].<br>White Plum [Blackthorn, Sloe/*Prunus spinosa*].<br>Willow Herb [*Epilobium angustifolium*].<br>Winter Green [*Gaultheria procumbens*].<br>Yew [*Taxus baccata*]. |
| Saturn & Jupiter | Comfrey [*Symphytum officinalis*].<br>Fumitory [*Fumaria officinalis*].<br>Henbane [*Hyoscyamus niger*].<br>Mullein [Aaron's Rod/*Verbascum thapsiforme*]. |
| Saturn, Jupiter & Mars | Flax [*Linum usatissimum*]. |
| Saturn, Jupiter & Sun | Poplar [*Populus*] (all varieties). |
| Saturn & Mars | Aconite [Monkshood/*Aconitum napellus*].<br>Aloe (all varieties).<br>Belladonna [Deadly Nightshade/*Atropa belladonna*].<br>Hawthorn [*Crataegus oxyacantha*].<br>Sea Onion [Squill/*Scilla maritima*]. |
| Saturn, Mars & Moon | Onion [*Allium cepa*]. |
| Saturn & Sun | Rue [*Ruta graveolens*]. |
| Saturn & Venus | Burdock [Burr Fruit/*Arctium lappa*]. |
| Saturn, Venus & Mercury | Black Elder [Elderberries/*Sambucus nigra*]. *(Dwarf Elder [*Sambucus ebulus*] is under the influence of Mars).<br>Red Foxglove [Digitalis/*Digitalis purpurea*]. |
| Saturn & Mercury | Caraway [*Carvum carvi*]. |

*Astrological Considerations* / 281

| | |
|---|---|
| Saturn, Mercury & Moon | Mandrake [*Mandragora officinarum*]. |
| Saturn & Moon | Chickweed [*Stellaria media*].<br>Corn Poppy [*Papaver rhoeas*].<br>Florentine Iris [*Iris florentina*].<br>German Iris [*Iris germanica*].<br>Hawkweed [Mouse-ear/*Hieracium pilosella*].<br>Opium Poppy [*Papaver somniferum*].<br>Pale Iris [*Iris pallida*].<br>Periwinkle [*Vinca minor*].<br>Royal Fern [*Osmunda regalis*]. |

### ii. Jupiter

| | |
|---|---|
| Jupiter | Agrimony [*Agrimonia eupatoria*].<br>Alexander [Alisander].<br>Alexandrian Parsley [*Smyrnium olusatrum*].<br>Apricot [*Prunus armeniaca*].<br>Arnica [*Arnica montana*].<br>Asparagus [*Asparagus officinalis*].<br>Beets (White).<br>Bilberries [Whortleberries/*Vaccinium myrtillus*].<br>Borage [*Borago officinalis*].<br>Bugloss [*Echium vulgare*].<br>Carnation [*Dianthus cariophyllus*].<br>Carrageen [Irish Moss/*Cetraria islandica*].<br>Chervil [*Anthriscus cerefolium*].<br>Chicory [*Cichorium intybus*].<br>Couch Grass [Dog Grass/*Agroyron cannium*].<br>Dandelion [*Taraxacum officinalis*].<br>Elecampane [*Inula campana*].<br>*(Elecampane [*Inula helenium*] is under the influence of Jupiter)<br>Ginseng [*Panax ginseng*].<br>Hedge-Nettle [Stachys, Woundwort/*Betonica officinalis*]. |

Horse Chestnut [*Aesculus hippocastanum*].
Houseleek [Sempervivum/*Sempervivum tectorum*].
Jasmine [*Jasminum*].
Manna [Flowering Ash/*Fraxinus ornus*].
Maple [Sycamore/*Acer pseudoplatanus*].
Masterwort [*Imperatoria*].
Meadowsweet [*Spiraea ulmaria*].
Melilot [Sweet Clover/*Melilotus officinalis*].
Polypody [*Polypodium vulgare*].
Raspberry [*Rubus idaeus*].
Rose Hip [*Rosa Canina*].
Sage [*Salvia officinalis*].
Samphire [*Crithmum maritimum*].
Sugarcane [*Saccharum officinalis*].
Tomato [*Solanum lycopersicum*].
Water Betony [Brown Wort, Bishopswort/ *Stachys macrantha*].
Wood Betony [*Stachys officinalis*].

| | |
|---|---|
| Jupiter & Saturn | Comfrey [*Symphytum officinalis*]. Fumitory [*Fumaria officinalis*]. Henbane [*Hyoscyamus niger*]. Mullein [Aaron's Rod/*Verbascum thapsus*]. |
| Jupiter, Saturn & Mars | Flax [*Linum usatissimum*]. |
| Jupiter, Saturn & Sun | Poplar [*Populus*] (all varieties). |
| Jupiter & Mars | Basil [*Ocimum Basilicum*]. Chinese Rhubarb [*Rheum palmatum*]. Dogrose [*Rosa canina*]. Madder [*Rubia tinctorum*]. Oak [*Quercus robur*]. |
| Jupiter, Mars & Moon | Hyssop [*Hyssopus officinalis*]. *(Hedge Hyssop [*Gratiola officinalis*] is under the influence of Mars) |

| | |
|---|---|
| Jupiter & Sun | Almond [*Amygdalum*].<br>Ash [*Fraxinus excelsior*].<br>Celandine [*Chelidonium majus*].<br>Centaury [*Centaurium umbellatum*].<br>Centaury (Lesser) [*Erythria centaurium*].<br>Cinquefoil [Five-leaf, Finger-grass/*Potentilla reptans*].<br>Gentian (Yellow) [*Gentiana lutea*].<br>*(Gentian [*Gentiana*] is under the influence of Mars)<br>Grapewine [*Vitis vinifera*].<br>Lemon Balm [*Melissa officinalis*].<br>Laurel [Bay/*Laurus nobilis*].<br>Liverwort [*Hepaticae*] (all varieties).<br>Myrrh [*Myrrha*].<br>Olive [*Oleo europea*].<br>Palm [*Arecaceae*].<br>Scarlet Pimpernel [*Anagallis arvensis*]. |
| Jupiter, Sun & Venus | Apple [*Pirus malus*].<br>Marshmallow [*Althaea officinalis*].<br>Wild Strawberry [Wood Strawberry/*Fragaria vesca*]. |
| Jupiter, Sun & Mercury | Juniper [*Juniperus communis*].<br>Lavender [*Lavandula vera*]. |
| Jupiter, Sun & Moon | Mistletoe [*Viscum album*]. |
| Jupiter & Venus | Chestnut [*Castanea sativa*].<br>Fig [*Ficus carica*].<br>Peppermint [*Mentha piperita*]. *(all other varieties of Mint are under the influence of Venus)<br>Rose [*Rosa damascena*].<br>Sandalwood (White & Red) [*Santalum*].<br>Sorrel [*Rumex acetosa*].<br>Tansy [*Tanacetum vulgaris*]. |

| | |
|---|---|
| Jupiter, Venus & Mercury | Coltsfoot [*Tussilago farfara*]. |
| Jupiter, Venus & Moon | Lime [*Tilia Europaea*]. |
| Jupiter & Mercury | Anise [*Pimpinella anisum*].<br>Endive [*Chichorium endivia*].<br>Fennel [*Foeniculum vulgare*].<br>Houndstongue [*Cynoglossum officinale*].<br>Licorice [*Liquiritia officinalis (Glycyrhiza glabra)*].<br>Lungwort [*Pulmonaria officinalis*].<br>Oats [*Avena Sativa*]. |
| Jupiter & Moon | Nutmeg [*Myristica fragrans*]. |

### iii. Mars

| | |
|---|---|
| Mars | All-Heal [*Prunellinae*].<br>Anemone [*Anemone*].<br>Asarabacca [Hazelwort, Wild Spikenard/*Asarum europaeum*].<br>Avens [Holy or Blessed Thistle/*Carduus benedictus*].<br>Barberry [*Berberis vulgaris*].<br>Black Radish [*Raphanus sativus*].<br>Box [*Buxus sempervirens*].<br>Brooklime [Speedwell/*Veronica beccabunga*].<br>Broom [*Genisteae*].<br>Broomrape [*Orobanche*].<br>Bruscus [Butcher's Broom/*Nameruscus aculeatus*].<br>Bryony [*Bryonia dioica*]. *(*Bryonia alba* is under the influence of Mercury)<br>Cuckoopint [Wake-robin/*Arum maculatum*].<br>Dead Nettle [Blind Nettle, Lamium/*Lamium album*]. |

*Astrological Considerations* / 285

|   |   |
|---|---|
|   | Dwarf Elder [*Sambucus ebulus*]. *(Elder [*Sambucus nigra*] is under the influence of Venus, Saturn & Mercury). Dyer's Broom [*Genista tinctoria*]. Everlasting Flower [Immortelle, Goldflower/*Helichrysum arenarium*]. Figwort [Knotty Brownwort/*Scrophularia nodosa*]. Garlic [*Allium sativum*]. Gentian [*Gentiana*]. *(Gentian [*Gentiana lutea*] is under the influence of Sun & Jupiter) Hedge Hyssop [*Gratiola officinalis*]. *(Hyssop [*Hyssopus officinalis*] is under the influence of Jupiter, Mars & Moon) Hop [*Humulus lupulus*]. Horseradish [*Amoracia rusticana*]. Mustard [*Sinapis*] (all varieties). *(White and Black Mustard are under the influence of Mars & Sun) Nettle [Stinging Nettle]/*Urtica dioica*]. Nettle [Small Stinging Nettle]/*Urtica urens*]. Paprika [Red Pepper/*Capsicum*] (all varieties). Pine [*Pinus*] (all varieties). Pineapple [*Ananas sativus*]. Red Cedar [Savin/*Sabina*]. Restharrow [Thorny Harrow/*Ononis spinosa*]. Sarsaparilla [*Smilax utilis*]. Henna [*Cassia obovata*]. Spurge-laurel [Mezereon/*Mezereum*]. Tarragon [*Artemesia dracunculus*]. Tobacco [*Nicotiana tabacum*]. |
| Mars & Saturn | Aloe [*Aloe*] (all varieties). Belladonna [Deadly Nightshade/*Atropa belladonna*]. Hawthorn [*Crataegus oxyacantha*]. Sea Onion [Squill/*Scilla maritima*]. |

| | |
|---|---|
| Mars, Saturn & Jupiter | Flax [*Linum usatissimum*]. |
| Mars, Saturn & Moon | Onion [*Allium cepa*]. |
| Mars & Jupiter | Basil [*Ocimum basilicum*].<br>Chinese Rhubarb [*Rheum palmatum*].<br>Dogrose [*Rosa canina*].<br>Madder [*Rubia tinctorum*].<br>Oak [*Quercus robur*]. |
| Mars, Jupiter & Moon | Hyssop [*Hyssopus officinalis*]. *(Hedge Hyssop [*Gratiola officinalis*] is under the influence of Mars) |
| Mars & Sun | Plantain (Common) [*Plantago major*].<br>Ribwort [*Plantago lanceolata*].<br>Mustard (White & Black) [*Sinapis alba/negra*]. *(all varieties of Mustard are under the influence of Mars)<br>Tormentil [Bloodwort, Rootwort/ *Tormentilla*]. |
| Mars & Venus | Catnip [*Nepeta cataria*].<br>Coriander [*Coriandrum sativum*].<br>Cursed Crowfoot [Marsh Crowfoot/ *Ranunculus sceleratus*].<br>Geranium [Herb Robert/*Geranium robertianum*]. |
| Mars, Venus & Mercury | Wormwood [*Artemisia absinthium*]. |
| Mars & Mercury | Honeysuckle [Woodbine/*Lonicera caprifolium*].<br>[Poison Nut, Emetic Nut/*Strychnos nux vomica*]. |
| Mars, Venus & Moon | Daisy [*Bellis perennis*]. |

### iv. Sun

| | |
|---|---|
| Sun | Bergamot [*Citrus bergamium*].<br>Burnet [*Sanguisorba minor*].<br>Butterbur [*Petasites*].<br>Calamus [*Calamus aramaticus*/*Acorus calamus*].<br>Cinnamon [*Cinnamonum ceylanicum*].<br>Cloves [*Caryophyllus*/*Syzygium aromaticum*].<br>Dittany [*Dictamnus albus*].<br>German Chamomile [*Matricharia chamomile*].<br>Ginger [*Zingiber officinale*].<br>Lemons [*Citrus limonum*].<br>Lovage [*Ligusticum levisticum*].<br>Marigold [*Calendula officinalis*].<br>Oranges [*Citrus aurantium*]<br>Passionflower [*Passiflora incarnata*].<br>Peony [*Paeonia officinalis*].<br>Pepper (white & black) [*Piper*].<br>Rice [*Oryza sativa*].<br>Roman Chamomile [*Anthemis nobilis*].<br>Rosemary [*Rosmarinus officinalis*].<br>Saffron [*Crocus sativus*]<br>St. John's Wort [*Hypericum perforatum*].<br>Sundew [*Drosera rontundifolia*].<br>Sunflower [*Helianthus anuus*].<br>Viper's Buglass [Blueweed/*Echium vulgare*].<br>Zedoary [*Curcuma zedoaria*]. |
| Sun & Saturn | Rue [*Ruta graveolens*]. |
| Sun, Saturn & Jupiter | Poplar [*Populus*] (all varieties). |
| Sun & Jupiter | Almond [*Amygdalum*].<br>Ash Tree [*Fraxinus excelsior*].<br>Celandine [*Chelidonium majus*]. |

Centaury [*Centaurium umbellatum*].
Centaury (Lesser) [*Erythria centaurium*].
Cinquefoil [Five-leaf, Finger-grass/*Potentilla reptans*].
Gentian (Yellow) [*Gentiana lutea*].
*(Gentian [*Gentiana*] is under the influence of Mars)
Grapewine [*Vitis vinifera*].
Lemon Balm [*Melissa officinalis*].
Laurel [Bay/*Laurus nobilis*].
Liverwort [*Hepaticae*] (all varieties).
Myrrh [*Myrrha*].
Olives [*Oleo europea*].
Palm [*Arecaceae*].
Scarlet Pimpernel [*Anagallis arvensis*].

| | |
|---|---|
| Sun, Jupiter & Venus | Apple [*Pirus malus*].<br>Marshmallow [*Althaea officinalis*].<br>Wild Strawberry [Wood Strawberry/*Fragaria vesca*]. |
| Sun, Jupiter & Mercury | Juniper [*Juniperus communis*].<br>Lavender [*Lavandula vera*]. |
| Sun, Jupiter & Moon | Mistletoe [*Viscum album*]. |
| Sun & Mars | Plantain (Common) [*Plantago major*].<br>Ribwort [*Plantago lanceolata*].<br>Mustard (White & Black) [*Sinapis alba/negra*]. *(all varieties of Mustard are under the influence of Mars)<br>Tormentil [Bloodwort, Rootwort/*Tormentilla*]. |
| Sun & Venus | Angelica [*Angelica archangelica*].<br>Ground Ivy [Alehoof, Creeping Charlie/*Glechoma hederacea*].<br>Thyme [*Thymus vulgaris*].<br>Wild Angelica [*Angelica sylvestris*].<br>Wild Thyme [*Thymus serpyllum*]. |

| | |
|---|---|
| Sun, Venus & Mercury | Eyebright [*Euphrasia officinalis*]. |
| | |
| Sun & Mercury | Elecampane [*Inula helenium*]. |
| | *(Elecampane [*Inula campana*] is under the influence of Jupiter) |
| | Marjoram [*Marjorana hortensis*]. *(Sweet Marjoram [*Origanum marjorana*] is under the influence of Mercury) |
| | Walnut [*Juglans regia*]. |

### v. Venus

| | |
|---|---|
| Venus | Alder (Black & Common) [*Alnus glutinosa*]. |
| | Alkanet [Dyer's Alkanet/*Alkanna tinctoria*]. |
| | Archangel (Red, White & Yellow). |
| | Artichoke [*Cynara scolymus*]. |
| | Beans (all varieties). |
| | Birch Tree (Silver) [*Betula pubescens* (*Alba*) & *Betula pendula* (*Verrucosa*)]. |
| | Bramble [Blackberry/*Rubus fructicosus*]. |
| | Bugle [*Ajuga reptans*]. |
| | Bulwort [Bishop's Weed/*Ammi majus*]. |
| | Chick-pea [*Cicer arietinum*]. |
| | Columbine [*Aquilegia vulgaris*]. |
| | Cowslip [*Primula veris*]. |
| | Dahlia [*Dahlia pinnata*]. |
| | Goldenrod [*Solidago virga aurea*]. |
| | Gromwell [*Lithospermum minus*]. |
| | Groundsel [*Senecio vulgaris*]. |
| | Ladies Bedstraw [*Galium verum*]. |
| | Lady's Mantle [*Alchemilla vulgaris*]. |
| | Magnolia [*Magnoliaceae*]. |
| | Mint [*Menthae*] (all varieties). |
| | *(Peppermint is under the influence of both Venus & Jupiter) |
| | Morello Cherry [Sour Cherry/*Prunus cerasus*]. |
| | Motherwort [*Leonurus cardiaca*]. |
| | Mugwort [*Artemisia vulgaris*]. |

Navelwort [Cotyledon/*Cotyledon umbilicus*].
Orchids [*Orchis*] (all varieties).
Peach [*Persica vulgaris*].
Pear [*Pyrus communis*].
Penny Royal [*Mentha pulegium*].
Primrose [*Primula officinalis*].
Sanicle [*Sanicula europaea*].
Soapwort [Soap Plant, Soapweed/*Saponaria officinalis*].
Spicknel [*Meum athamanthicum*].
Teasel [Fuller's Thistle/*Dipsacus sativus*].
Vervain [*Verbena officinalis*].
Wood Sorrel [Clover Sorrel/*Oxalis acetosella*].
Yarrow [*Achillea millefolium*].

| | |
|---|---|
| Venus & Saturn | Burdock [Burr Fruit/*Arctium lappa*]. |
| Venus, Saturn & Mercury | Black Elder [Elderberries/*Sambucus nigra*]. *(Dwarf Elder [*Sambucus ebulus*] is under the influence of Mars).<br>Red Foxglove [Digitalis/*Digitalis purpurea*]. |
| Venus & Jupiter | Chestnut [*Castanea sativa*].<br>Fig [*Ficus carica*].<br>Peppermint [*Mentha piperita*]. *(all other varieties of Mint [*Menthae*] are under the influence of Venus)<br>Rose [*Rosa damascena*].<br>Sandalwood (White & Red) [*Santalum*].<br>Sorrel [*Rumex acetosa*].<br>Tansy [*Tanacetum vulgaris*].<br>Wheat [*Triticum sativum*]. |
| Venus, Jupiter & Sun | Apple [*Pirus malus*].<br>Marshmallow [*Althaea officinalis*].<br>Wild Strawberry [Wood Strawberry/*Fragaria vesca*]. |

*Astrological Considerations* / 291

| | |
|---|---|
| Venus, Jupiter & Mercury | Coltsfoot [*Tussilago farfara*]. |
| Venus, Jupiter & Moon | Lime [*Tilia europaea*]. |
| Venus & Mars | Catnip [*Nepeta cataria*].<br>Coriander [*Coriandrum sativum*].<br>Cursed Crowfoot [Marsh Crowfoot/*Ranunculus sceleratus*].<br>Geranium [Herb Robert/*Geranium robertianum*]. |
| Venus, Mars & Mercury | Wormwood [*Artemisia absinthium*]. |
| Venus, Mars & Moon | Daisy [*Bellis perennis*]. |
| Venus & Sun | Angelica [*Angelica archangelica*].<br>Ground Ivy [Alehoof, Creeping Charlie/*Glechoma hederacea*].<br>Thyme [*Thymus vulgaris*].<br>Wild Angelica [*Angelica sylvestris*].<br>Wild Thyme [*Thymus serpyllum*]. |
| Venus, Sun & Mercury | Eyebright [*Euphrasia officinalis*]. |
| Venus & Moon | Arrach [Goosefoot plant/*Atriplex hortensis*].<br>Running Bean [Dwarf Bean/*Phaseolus vulgaris*].<br>Violet [*Viola odorata*]. |

### vi. Mercury

| | |
|---|---|
| Mercury | Acacia (all varieties).<br>Azalea [*Rhododendron*].<br>Bittersweet [Amara Dulcis/*Solanum dulcamara*]. |

Bryony [*Bryonia alba*]. *(*Bryonia dioica* is under the influence of Mars)
Buttercup [*Ranunculus acris*].
Calamint [Mountain Balm, Wild Basil/*Calamintha montana*].
Calamint [*Calamintha arvensis*].
Carrot [*Daucus carota*].
Celery [*Apium graveolens*].
Cubeb Pepper [*Piper cubeba*].
Dill [*Anethum graveolens*].
Germander [*Teucrium scordium*].
Harefoot [Hop Trefoil, Hopclover/*Trifolium arvense*].
Hazel [*Corylus avella*].
Hedge-mustard [*Alliaria officinalis*].
Lavender [*Lavandula officinalis*].
Licorice [*Glycyrrhiza glabra*].
Maidenhair [*Adiantum capillus veneris*].
Marsh Trefoil [Buckbean/*Trifolium fibrinum*].
Mercury (Annual) [*Mercurialis annua*].
Mercury (Perennial) [*Mercurialis perennis*].
Mulberry [White & Black/*Morus*].
Myrtle [*Myrtus communis*].
Origanum [Oregano/*Origanum vulgare*].
Parsley [*Apium petroselinum hortense*].
Parsnip [*Pastinaca sativa*].
Southernwood [*Artemisia abrotanum*].
Summer Savory [*Satureia hortensis*].
Sweet Marjoram [*Origanum marjorana*].
*(Marjoram [*Marjorana hortensis*] is under the influence of the Sun & Mercury)
Valerian [*Valeriana officinalis*].
Wall Pellitory [*Parietaria officinalis*].
White Horehound [*Marrubium vulgare*].
Winter Savory [*Satureia montana*].

Mercury & Saturn     Caraway [*Carvum carvi*].

*Astrological Considerations* / 293

| | |
|---|---|
| Mercury, Saturn & Venus | Black Elder [Elderberries/*Sambucus nigra*]. *(Dwarf Elder [*Sambucus ebulus*] is under the influence of Mars). Red Foxglove [Digitalis/*Digitalis purpurea*]. |
| Mercury, Saturn & Moon | Mandrake [*Mandragora*]. |
| Mercury & Mars | Honeysuckle [Woodbine/*Lonicera caprifolium*]. Vomic [Poison Nut, Emetic Nut/*Strychnos nux vomica*]. |
| Mercury & Jupiter | Anise [*Pimpinella anisum*]. Endive [*Chichorium endivia*]. Fennel [*Foeniculum vulgare*]. Houndstongue [*Cynoglossum officinale*]. Licorice [*Liquiritia officinalis (Glycyrrhiza glabra)*]. Lungwort [*Pulmonaria officinalis*]. Oats [*Avena Sativa*]. |
| Mercury, Jupiter & Sun | Juniper [*Juniperus communis*]. Lavender [*Lavandula vera*]. |
| Mercury, Jupiter & Venus | Coltsfoot [*Tussilago farfara*]. |
| Mercury & Mars | Honeysuckle [Woodbine/*Lonicera caprifolium*]. Vomic [Poison Nut, Emetic Nut/*Strychnos Nux vomica*]. |
| Mercury & Sun | Elecampane [*Inula helenium*]. *(Elecampane [*Inula campana*] is under the influence of Jupiter) Marjoram [*Marjorana hortensis*]. *(Sweet Marjoram [*Origanum marjorana*] is under the influence of Mercury) Walnut [*Juglans regia*]. |

| | |
|---|---|
| Mercury, Mars & Venus | Wormwood [*Artemisia absinthium*] |
| Mercury & Moon | Lily-of-the-Valley [*Convallaria majalis*]. |

### vii. Moon

| | |
|---|---|
| Moon | Accanthus [*Accanthus mollis*].<br>Adder's Tongue [*Ophioglossum*].<br>Atriplex [Orache, All-seed, Notchweed/*Atriplex silvestris*].<br>Bearsbreech [*Acanthus spinosus*].<br>Brank Ursine [*Acanthus mollis*].<br>Cabbage [*Braccicae*] (all varieties).<br>Cucumber [*Cucumis sativus*].<br>Duckweed [*Lenticula palustris*].<br>Goose Grass [Galium/Cleavers/*Galium aparine*].<br>Lady's Smock [Cuckoo Flower/*Cardamine pratense*].<br>Lettuce [*Lactuca sativa*].<br>Monk's Pepper [*Agnus castus*].<br>Moneywort [*Lysimachia nummularia*].<br>Moonwort [*Ruta lunaria*].<br>Orpine [*Sedum telephium*].<br>Papaya [*Carica papaya*].<br>Privet [*Ligustrum vulgare*].<br>Pumpkin [Gourd/*Cucurbita Pepo*].<br>Saxifrage [*Saxifraga*].<br>Sedum [*Telephium vulgare*].<br>Speedwell [*Veronica officinalis*].<br>Turmuric [*Curcuma longa*].<br>Wall Pepper [Sharp stone-crop/*Sedum acre*].<br>Wallflower [*Cheiranthus cheiri*].<br>Water Chestnut [*Trapa natans*].<br>Watercress [*Nasturtium officinale*].<br>Water Lily [*Nymphaea alba*].<br>White Lily [*Lilium album*].<br>Willows [*Salices*] (all varieties). |

## Astrological Considerations / 295

| | |
|---|---|
| Moon & Saturn | Chickweed [*Stellaria media*].<br>Corn Poppy [*Papaver rhoeas*].<br>Florentine Iris [*Iris florentina*].<br>German Iris [*Iris germanica*].<br>Hawkweed [Mouse-ear/*Hieracium pilosella*].<br>Opium Poppy [*Papaver somniferum*].<br>Pale Iris [*Iris pallida*].<br>Periwinkle [*Vinca minor*].<br>Royal Fern [*Osmunda regalis*]. |
| Moon, Saturn & Mars | Onion [*Allium cepa*]. |
| Moon, Saturn & Mercury | Mandrake [*Mandragora*]. |
| Moon & Jupiter | Nutmeg [*Myristica fragrans*]. |
| Moon, Jupiter & Mars | Hyssop [*Hyssopus officinalis*]. *(Hedge Hyssop [*Gratiola officinalis*] is under the influence of Mars) |
| Moon, Mars & Venus | Daisy [*Bellis perennis*]. |
| Moon, Jupiter & Sun | Mistletoe [*Viscum album*]. |
| Moon, Jupiter & Venus | Lime [*Tilia Europaea*]. |
| Moon & Venus | Arrach [Goosefoot plant/*Atriplex hortensis*].<br>Running Bean [Dwarf Bean/*Phaseolus vulgaris*].<br>Violet [*Viola odorata*]. |
| Moon & Mercury | Lily-of-the-Valley [*Convallaria majalis*]. |

It is worth noting that incenses comprising a mix of aromatic herbs and resins, have always been very popular items amongst esotericists of all sorts. Whilst there is a great variety of incenses to satisfy the demands of the most discerning olfactory sense amongst esotericists, when it comes to choosing a single one which will not only satisfy your nose, but equally create the right ambient atmosphere in which to meditate and work all manner of spiritual/magical procedure, and without discrediting the carefully formulated "Planetary Suffumigations," you would do very well to settle for a good quality frankincense in all your ritual work.

If this is not satisfactory in terms of specific personal requirements, you could equally employ good essential oils, of which there are infinite varieties to align with planets known and unknown. These can be employed to impregnate the atmosphere of your "Sacred Space" by means of an "Essential Oil Burner," and the latter can equally be appropriately constructed for magical purposes.

### b. MINERALS

Minerals can equally be employed to enhance planetary ritual work, and in this regard I have again consulted a number of primary and secondary sources.[114] In this regard, it should be noted that the following index of "Planetary Gems" and stones is not meant to be a complete lapidary like the one compiled in the court of the great Spanish King, Alfonso X.[115] The intention here is purely to share a set of "gemstones" which can be employed for magical purposes, i.e. to be focussed upon in harmony with specific magical intentions, or, in the instance of those who, like myself, have found the mediaeval "Doctrine of Signatures," as well as the concept of "Magical Contagion," to be profoundly meaningful, to align oneself and one's actions with specifically selected "cosmic forces" benefitting harmoniously affiliated physical "outcomes."

Whilst Joshua Trachtenberg informed us that "precious and semiprecious stones, in particular, have been credited with superior occult powers by many peoples,"[116] readers may well wonder what any of this has to do with Jewish Magic (*Practical Kabbalah*), considering the distinct rarity of "Magical Instruments" in this tradition. It should be noted that "one of the most widely attested magical activities in late antiquity is the production of magical gems,"[117] and we are reminded that "Jews were the leading importers of and dealers in gems during the early Middle Ages, and Christian Europe attributed to them a certain specialization in the magic properties of precious stones: *Christianos fidem in verbis, Judaeos in lapidibus pretiosis, et Paganos in herbis ponere* ('Christians put their trust in words, Jews in precious stones, and pagans in herbs'), ran the adage."[118] As we know well enough, this statement is not quite accurate, especially considering the fact that the *Ba'alei Shem* ("Masters of the Name") employed Divine Names (words), herbs and stones in their magical activities.

However, we know that gemstones were employed as amulets, especially when engraved with a Divine Name, and one might conjecture that the Jewish so-called special interest in "magical gems" commenced with the חושן משפט (*Choshen Mishpat*), the mysterious "breastplate" of the High Priest referenced in *Exodus 28:15—21* reading:

> (15) And thou shalt make a חושן משפט (*Choshen Mishpat*—'Breastplate of Judgment'), the work of the skilful workman; like the work of the *efod* thou shalt make it: of gold, of blue, and purple, and scarlet, and fine twined linen, shalt thou make it.
> (16) Four-square it shall be and double: a span shall be the length thereof, and a span the breadth thereof.
> (17) And thou shalt set in it settings of stones, four rows of stones: a row of אדם (*Odem*—'carnelian'), פטדם (*Pit'dam*—'topaz'), and ברקת (*Bareket*—'smaragd') shall be the first row;
> (18) and the second row נפך (*Nofech*—'carbuncle'), ספיר (*Sapir*— 'sapphire'), and יהלם (*Yahalom*—'emerald');
> (19) and the third row לשם (*Leshem*—'jacinth'), שבו (*Shevo*— 'agate'), and אחלמה (*Ach'lamah*—'amethyst');
> (20) and the fourth row תרשיש (*Tarshish*—'beryl'), and שהם (*Shoham*—'onyx'), and ישפה (*Yash'feh*—'jasper'); they shall be inclosed in gold in their settings.
> (21) And the stones shall be according to the names of the children of Israel, twelve, according to their names; like the engravings of a signet, every one according to his name, they shall be for the twelve tribes.

As indicated, the twelve stones are translated "carnelian," "topaz," "smaragd," "carbuncle," "sapphire," "emerald," "jacinth," "agate," "amethyst," "beryl," "onyx," and "jasper" in the English Bible. However, the terms "smaragd" and "emerald" refer to the same mineral, and there has been some conjecture on exactly which twelve stones are referenced by their Hebrew appellatives. In this regard, the Hebrew text of the relevant section on gemstones in the *Sefer Gematriot*, a 14th century text dealing with the magical properties of the twelve gemstones in the "Breastplate of Judgment," which was shared by Joshua Trachtenberg and portions translated in his groundbreaking "*Jewish Magic & Superstition*,"[119] is here presented with some modification in complete English translation, with interspersed bracketed elucidations:

אדם (*Odem*—variously interpreted carnelian/ruby/sard/red haematite/red stone)[120] pertains to ראובן (*R'uvein*—"Reuben") because of the red appearance of his face [blushing] following the mounting of his father's bed [with *Bilhah*, his father's handmaid], and his confession that he did so shamelessly (*Genesis 49:3–4*). This is the stone called *rubino*, and its use is to protect a woman who wears it from suffering a miscarriage. It is also good for women who suffers excessively in childbirth, and when mixed [powdered] with food and drink, it is good for fertility like the דודאים (*duda'im*—"mandrakes") which Reuben found. This is why the word אדם (*Odem*) [normally spelled אודם] is written without a ו (*Vav*) [in the Bible], because mandrakes have the shape of אדם (*Adam*—man). Sometimes the stone *rubino* is conjoined with another stone and is called *rubin felsht* (רובין פלשט—mixed[?] ruby). Likewise did Reuben save Josef, and they joined together, as it is said, "And Reuben heard it, and delivered him out of their hand" (*Genesis 37:21*), and as it is written "and Reuben answered them, saying: 'Spoke I not unto you, saying: Do not sin against the child; [and ye would not hear? therefore also, behold, his blood is required'."] (*Genesis 42:22*); "and Pharaoh took off his signet ring [from his hand, and put it upon Joseph's hand]" (*Genesis 41:42*). That ring was *felsht* including a mix within it, and that was found to be a mixed ruby.

פטדה (*Pitdah*—variously rendered topaz/diamond/chrysolite/jade/emerald/Yellowish-green Serpentine/green stone),[121] the stone of שמעון (*Shim'on*—"Simeon") is a פרזמא (*Prezma*—"prase") suggested to be ירקן (*Yarkan*—Jade)[122] but it appears to me to be an emerald, and green pertains to Zimri, the son of Salu ["a prince of a father's house among the Simeonites.....who was slain with the Midianitish woman"] (*Numbers 25:14*), who left them [the Simeonites] green in the face [ashamed], and again with no king and no judge, and them marked for the offence with דרקון (*darkon*—"dropsy" [the "green disease"]). This is the darkness which fell upon their faces. Its [*Pitdah*] benefit and consequence is to cool the body, as it is written "The topaz of Ethiopia shall not equal it" (*Job 28:19*). Ethiopia and Egypt were rife with lewdness, and that is why it [*Pitdah*] is found there to cool the body, and also [employed] in [matters of] love, as it is said, 'Because YHVH hath heard that I am hated [He hath therefore given me this son also.' And she called his name Simeon]" (*Genesis 29:33*).

ברקת (*Bareket*—variously rendered emerald/smaragd/carbuncle/ruby/amethyst/rock crystal/green olivine/green feldspar/marble).[123] This is the carbuncle flashing like ברק (*barak*—"lightning") and glows like a flame, and it is the good stone which Noah placed in the ark, as is said, "A light (צהר—*tzohar*) shalt thou make to the ark") (*Genesis 6:16*), of which the *Gematria* (numerical value) equals לאור האבן (*l'or ha-even*—"in light of the stone") [צ = 90 + ה = 5 + ר = 200 = 295; ל = 30 + א = 1 + ו = 6 + ר = 200 + ה = 5 + א = 1 + ב = 2 + ן = 50 = 295]. This is the stone אקדח (*Ek'dach*— carbuncle [precious]) stone of the prophets [see *Isaiah 54:12*], and flaming like burning coals, it is the stone of לוי (*Leivi*—"Levi"), as it is said, the Levites should enlighten all on the *Torah*, as is written "They shall teach Jacob [Thine ordinances, and Israel Thy law]" (*Deuteronomy 33:10*), and as written "A man's wisdom maketh his face to shine, [and the boldness of his face is changed]" (*Ecclesiastes 8:1*). At the birth of Moses [a Levite], the whole house was filled with light.[124] This was the radiation of the skin of Moses' countenance. And this stone is of good benefit to its bearer, makes man wise, and illuminates the eyes, and opens the heart. Eating and drinking it pulverized with other medictions, restores the aged to youth, as it is said, "his eye was not dim, nor his natural force abated" (*Deuteronomy 34:7*).

נפך (*Nofech*—variously rendered emerald/smaragd/turquoise/carbuncle/jasper, red garnet/ruby/almandine garnet/green stone).[125] It is the smaragd which is interpreted איזמרגדין [said to be a "carbuncle"; the Hebrew term translates "emeraldine"]. It is green in reference to the hue [shame] of the face of יהודה (*Y'hudah*—"Judah") when he overcame his lust and confessed his [illicit] relations with Tamar [his daughter in law] (*Genesis 38:13–26*). Also, when his father [Jacob] was suspicious of Joseph's death, as it is written "An evil beast hath devoured him" (*Genesis 37:20*), and [Judah] was cleared, as it is written "from the prey, my son, thou art gone up" (*Genesis 49:9*), his face lit up with joy, and thus is his stone clear and not dark like Simeon's. The benefit of this stone pertains to increase גבורה [*Gevurah*—"might"/"strength"], bringing victory to the one who wears it in a battle [war]. Therefore the tribe of Judah were heroes [mighty]. It is called נפך (*nofech*) because the enemy turns (הופך—*hofech*) away from those who carry it, as it is written "Thy hand shall be on the neck of thine enemies." (*Genesis 49:8*).

ספיר (*Sapir*—variously rendered sapphire/lapis lazuli/blue stone), the stone of יששכר (*Yissachar*—"Issachar"),[126] who "had understanding of the times" (*I Chronicles 12:32*) and in the giving of the *Torah*. It is azure-blue, good for healing, and good to pass across the eyes, as it is said, "It shall be health to thy navel, and marrow to thy bones." (*Proverbs 3:8*)

יהלם (*Yahalom*—variously rendered diamond/crystal/emerald/amethyst).[127] This is the stone of זבלון (*Z'vulun*—"Zebulun"), and it is the gem called *pirleh* (פירלה misprinted פירכה)[128] [said to be בדלח (*b'dolach*—"bdellium")].[129] It brings success in trade, and is good to carry on the road [during travels], because it promotes peace and increases love [affection], and brings sleep, as it is said, יזבלני אישי (*yiz'b'leini ishi*—"Now will my husband dwell [sleep] with me") (*Genesis 30:20*).

לשם (*Leshem*—variously rendered jacinth/opal/agate/ligure/jacinth/hyacinth/amber/sapphire/turquoise).[130] This is the stone of דן (*Dan*—"Dan"), which is the *topatziah*[?]. The face of a man is reflected in it upside down, which is a symbol of Micah's graven image which was overturned [by the Danites] (*Judges 18:14–31*).

שבו (*Shebo*—variously rendered agate/banded agate/turquoise/quartz crystal).[131] This is the stone of נפתלי (*Naftali*—"Naftali"), which is the *turkiska* (טורקישקא). It establishes an individual firmly in strength, and prevents him from stumbling and falling. Its power is coveted by knights and horsemen, since it makes a man to be secure on his mount, as it is said נפתולי אלהים נפתלתי (*naftulei Elohim niftalti*—"With mighty wrestlings [tribulations of Elohim] have I wrestled") (*Genesis 30:8*).

אחלמה (*Ach'lamah*—variously rendered amethyst/crystal).[132] In the *Targum* it is interpreted עין עגלא (*ein ig'la*—"eye of the calf" [a precious stone]).[133] This is the stone called *cristalo* [crystal], which is very common and well-known. It is the stone of גד (*Gad*—"Gad"), because the tribe of Gad are very numerous and renowned, as it is said "and teareth the arm, yea, the crown of the head" (*Deuteronomy 33:20*). There is another gem called *diamanti* which is like the *cristalo*, except that it has a faintly reddish hue; the tribe of Gad used to carry this with them. It is useful in מלחמה (*milchamah*—"war"), for it strengthens the heart so that it does not grow faint, for Gad used to move into battle ahead of his brothers, and it is called אחלמה (*ach'lamah*—amethyst). In this regard, it is said יחלמו בניהם (*yach'l'mu v'neihem*—"Their young ones wax strong") (*Job 39:4*), and also ותחלימני והחייני (*v'tachalimeini v'hachayeini*—"wherefore recover Thou me, and make me to live"; alternatively "You have restored me to health and have revived me") (*Isaiah 38:16*) with strength [An affinity is drawn between the words *ach'lamah* (amethyst), *milchamah* (war), *yach'l'mu* (wax strong/break away), and *tachalimeini* (you recovered me/you have restored me)]. This stone [*ach'lamah*—amethyst] is good against *Mazikin* [injurious demons] and *Ruchot* [demonic spirits], so that one who wears it is not seized by that faintness of heart which they call *glolir*[?].

תרשיש (*Tarshish*—variously rendered beryl/jacinth/topaz/aquamarine/serpentine).[134] This is the *yakint* [jacinth]. The *Targum* calls it the "sea-green" which is its color. It is the stone of אשר (*Asher*—"Asher"). Its utility is to burn up food. No bad food will remain in the bowels of one who consumes it [powdered], but will be transferred into a thick oil. For it is written, "As for Asher, his bread shall be fat" (*Genesis 49:20*), and his daughters shall be married to kings and high priests, as it is written in the chronicles (*1 Chronicles 7:31*) "[Malchiel (Asher's grandson)] who was the father of Birzayit [literally 'olive-infant']," to sons of priests (*Kohanim*) who were annointed with olive oil. His land will overflow with oil like a spring. Sometimes the sapphire is found in combination with the jacinth (*yakint*), because the daughters of the tribe of Asher intermarried with the tribe of Issachar. Isacchar relates to the sapphire, and the Torah is likened to water. And this is the good jacinth (*yakint*), and the sapphire aligns well with Asher, because the bread of Asher is fat for all creatures, and the faces of stout people are ruddy. The jacinth (*yakint*) is sometimes of a reddish hue.

שהם (*Shoham*—variously rendered onyx/lapis-lazuli/agate/sardonyx/sard).[135] This is the stone called *nikli* [*nichilus*, an agate]. It is the stone of יוסף (*Yosef*—"Joseph") and it bestows grace. It is called שהם (*shoham*—"onyx") since the letters [of the word can be rearranged to] read השם, as it is said "And *YHVH* was with Joseph, [and he was a prosperous man] (*Genesis 39:2*). It is good to wear in a place where people gather, in order to cause them to hear his words, and to achieve success, so that he will be a successful man.

ישפה (*Yashfeh*—jasper).[136] This is [the stone] for בנימין (*Benyamin*—"Benjamin"). It is called דיאשפי (*diaspi*[?]), and is found in a variety of colors: green, black, red, because Benjamin knew that Joseph had been sold, and often considered revealing this to Jacob, and his face would turn all colors as he debated whether to disclose his secret or to keep it hidden. But he restrained himself and kept the matter concealed. This stone jasper [*yashfeh*], because it was a bridle on his tongue, has also the power to restrain the blood.

In terms of the earlier mentioned biblical statement "like the engravings of a signet" (*Exodus 28:21*), and the comment that "Aaron shall bear the names of the children of Israel in the breastplate of judgment upon his heart, when he goeth in unto the holy place, for a memorial before *YHVH* continually," [*Exodus 28:29*] it is understood that the stones were engraved with the appellatives of the twelve tribes. As it is, many semiprecious stones were, and still are, engraved with Hebrew Divine Names, very often the Name שדי (*Shadai*), or באל שדי (*b'El Shadai*), יהוה שדי (*YHVH Shadai*), even שדי צבאות (*Shadai Tzva'ot*), etc.,[137] and these were either set in rings or worn as pendants for amuletic purposes. However, in terms of the following set of minerals respectively aligned with planetary associations, the fundamental purpose is not the production of amulets *per se*, but rather the focussing of so-called "planetary forces" for specific magical intentions in terms of certain practices shared in the current tome, of which more anon.

In compiling the list of "planetary gems" shared in this tome, I did not rely on specifically Jewish sources. The aim is to offer the broadest array of planetary/gemstone associations, as shared in both western and oriental traditions. In this regard, you will notice that, similar to the earlier listing of plants, in most instances a single gemstone is affiliated with a range of planets, as acknowledged, amongst others, in the "Lapidary" of Alfonso X.[138] Keeping this in mind, I have personally selected minerals to be included in ritual work, e.g. to enhance a fundamental planetary force, etc., always in terms of the specific intentions. This might pertain to a singular planetary power or combined planetary influences. In the case of a singular planetary force, I am always careful to ensure that I do not include stones which have been linked to a planetary force inimical to the task at hand. On the other hand, where the said task might benefit from a planetary force harmonious to the one affiliated with the specific intention of the selected ritual work, I gladly combine a variety of stones.

No doubt there are many who would disagree with this list of planetary/gemstone attributions, but in my estimation the actions of esoteric traditions, whether Eastern or Western, affiliating a specific gemstone with a variety of planets, have "empowered" that object, i.e. turned it into a "power object" to be employed in terms of results determined by the specific forces, which are understood to be inherent in that object.

The following array of minerals and their planetary affiliations comprise those which are fairly readily available, but the list is by no means complete:

### i. Saturn

| | |
|---|---|
| Saturn | Alum. |
| | Apache Tear. |
| | Dionesia. |
| | Coal. |
| | Jet. |
| | Obsidian. |

*Astrological Considerations* / 305

|  |  |
|---|---|
|  | Odontolite (Bone Turquoise).<br>Petrified Wood.<br>Sapphire [Blue]. *(Yellow Sapphire is under the influence of Jupiter, Venus, Mercury & Moon)<br>Serpentine. |
| Saturn, Jupiter, Mars, Sun & Venus | Diamond. |
| Saturn, Jupiter, Mars, Venus & Mercury | Amethyst. |
| Saturn, Jupiter, Venus, Mercury & Moon | Chalcedony. |
| Saturn, Jupiter, Mars, Sun & Mercury | Topaz. |
| Saturn & Mars | Asbestos.<br>Onyx. |
| Saturn, Mars & Sun | Sardonyx. |
| Saturn, Mars & Mercury | Hematite. |
| Saturn & Venus | Lapis-Lazuli. |
| Saturn & Moon | Pyrites [Tin-coloured]. *(Pyrites Ash-coloured are under the influence of Jupiter; Gold-coloured are under the influence of the Sun; Copper-coloured are under the influence of the Sun & Venus; and Silver-coloured are under the influence of the Moon) |

## ii. Jupiter

| | |
|---|---|
| Jupiter | Aegirine.<br>Bezoar.<br>Chelidon.<br>Iris.<br>Lepidolite.<br>Pyrites [Ash-coloured]. *(Pyrites Tin-coloured are under the influence of Saturn & the Moon; Gold-coloured are under the influence of the Sun; Copper-coloured are under the influence of the Sun & Venus; and Silver-coloured are under the influence of the Moon)<br>Sugilite.<br>Yellow Jargoon. *(Red Jargoon is under the influence of Mars, and and White Jargoon is under the influence of Venus) |
| Jupiter, Saturn, Mars, Sun & Venus | Diamond. |
| Jupiter, Saturn Mars, Venus & Mercury | Amethyst. |
| Jupiter, Saturn, Mars, Sun & Mercury | Topaz. |
| Jupiter, Saturn, Venus, Mercury & Moon | Chalcedony. |
| Jupiter, Mars, Sun & Mercury | Jacinth. |
| Jupiter, Mars, Sun & Venus | Carnelian. |

| | |
|---|---|
| Jupiter, Mars & Venus | Carbuncle |
| Jupiter, Mars, Venus & Mercury | Emerald. |
| Jupiter & Sun | Citrine. |
| Jupiter, Sun & Venus | Amber [Lapis Lyncurius]. |
| Jupiter, Venus, & Mercury | Turquoise. |
| Jupiter, Venus, Mercury & Moon | Sapphire [Yellow]. *(Blue Sapphire is under the influence of Saturn) |
| Jupiter & Mercury | Tourmaline. |

### iii. Mars

| | |
|---|---|
| Mars | Acanthite.<br>Actinolite.<br>Aragonite.<br>Bloodstone.<br>Coral [Red]. *(Corals are under the influence of Venus)<br>Flint [Thunderstone/Elf-shot].<br>Haematite.<br>Jargoon [Red]. *(Yellow Jargoon is under the influence of Jupiter, and White Jargoon is under the influence of Venus)<br>Jasper [Red]. *(Jasper is under the influence of Venus & Mercury)<br>Lava.<br>Rhodocrosite<br>Rhodonite. |
| Mars & Saturn | Asbestos.<br>Onyx. |

| | |
|---|---|
| Mars, Saturn, Jupiter, Sun & Venus | Diamond. |
| Mars, Saturn Jupiter, Venus & Mercury | Amethyst. |
| Mars, Jupiter, Sun & Mercury | Jacinth. |
| Mars, Jupiter, Sun & Venus | Carnelian. |
| Mars, Jupiter, Venus & Mercury | Emerald |
| Mars, Saturn, Jupiter & Mercury | Topaz. |
| Mars, Saturn & Sun | Sardonyx. |
| Mars, Saturn & Mercury | Hematite. |
| Mars, Jupiter & Venus | Carbuncle. |
| Mars & Sun | Garnet. Sard. |
| Mars, Sun & Venus | Ruby. |
| Mars, Venus & Mercury | Agate. |

| | |
|---|---|
| Mars, Venus & Moon | Beryl. |
| Mars & Mercury | Bloodstone [Heliotrope].<br>Magnetite [Loadstone]. |
| Mars & Moon | Rock Crystal. |

### iv. Sun

| | |
|---|---|
| Sun | Aetites.<br>Alectoria.<br>Brazilian Chrysoberyl.<br>Pyrites [Gold-coloured]. *(Pyrites Tin-coloured are under the influence of Saturn & the Moon; Ash-coloured are under the influence of Jupiter; Copper-coloured are under the influence of the Sun & Venus; and Silver-coloured are under the influence of the Moon)<br>Sunstone.<br>Tiger's Eye.<br>Zircon. |
| Sun, Saturn, Jupiter, Mars & Venus | Diamond. |
| Sun, Saturn, Jupiter, Mars, & Mercury | Topaz. |
| Sun, Saturn & Mars | Sardonyx. |
| Sun & Jupiter | Citrine. |
| Sun, Jupiter & Venus | Amber [Lapis Lyncurius]. |

| | |
|---|---|
| Sun, Jupiter, Mars & Mercury | Jacinth. |
| Sun, Jupiter, Mars & Venus | Carnelian. |
| Sun & Mars | Garnet.<br>Sard. |
| Sun, Mars & Venus | Ruby. |
| Sun & Venus | Pyrites [Copper-coloured]. *(Pyrites Tin-coloured are under the influence of Saturn & the Moon; Ash-coloured are under the influence of Jupiter; Gold-coloured are under the influence of the Sun; and Silver-coloured are under the influence of the Moon) |
| Sun, Venus & Mercury | Opal. |
| Sun, Venus & Moon | Quartz Crystal. |

### v. Venus

| | |
|---|---|
| Venus | Azurite [Lapis Linguis/Lapis Lingua].<br>Cat's-Eye.<br>Celestite.<br>Chrysocolla.<br>Kunzite.<br>Lapis Armenus [Armenian Stone].<br>Moss Agate [Mocha Stone].<br>Olivine.<br>Sodalite.<br>Stalactite.<br>White Jargoon. *(Red Jargoon is under the influence of Mars, and Yellow Jargoon is under the influence of Jupiter) |

| | |
|---|---|
| Venus & Saturn | Lapis-Lazuli. |
| Venus, Saturn Jupiter, Mars & Mercury | Amethyst. |
| Venus, Saturn, Jupiter, Mars & Sun | Diamond. |
| Venus, Saturn, Jupiter, Mercury & Moon | Chalcedony. |
| Venus, Jupiter, Mars & Sun | Carnelian. |
| Venus, Jupiter & Sun | Amber [Lapis Lyncurius]. |
| Venus, Jupiter & Mars | Carbuncle |
| Venus, Jupiter, Mars & Mercury | Emerald. |
| Venus, Jupiter & Mercury | Turquoise. |
| Venus, Jupiter, Mercury & Moon | Sapphire [Yellow]. *(Blue Sapphire is under the influence of Saturn) |
| Venus, Mars & Sun | Ruby. |
| Venus, Mars & Mercury | Agate. |
| Venus, Mars & Moon | Beryl. |

| | |
|---|---|
| Venus & Sun | Pyrites [Copper-coloured]. *(Pyrites Tin-coloured are under the influence of Saturn & the Moon; Ash-coloured are under the influence of Jupiter; Gold-coloured are under the influence of the Sun; and Silver-coloured are under the influence of the Moon) |
| Venus, Sun & Mercury | Opal. |
| Venus, Sun & Moon | Quartz Crystal. |
| Venus & Mercury | Armena.<br>Chrysolite [Peridot].<br>Chrysoprase.<br>Jade.<br>Jasper. *(Red Jasper is under the influence of Mars)<br>Malachite. |
| Venus, Mercury & Moon | Pearl. |
| Venus & Moon | Coral. *(Red Coral is under the influence of Mars) |

### vi. Mercury

| | |
|---|---|
| Mercury | Aventurine.<br>Mica.<br>Pumice stone.<br>Sphene [Titanite]<br>Touchstone [Lapis Lydius]. |
| Mercury, Saturn, Jupiter, Mars & Venus | Amethyst. |

| | |
|---|---|
| Mercury, Saturn, Jupiter, Venus & Moon | Chalcedony. |
| Mercury, Saturn, Jupiter, Mars, & Sun | Topaz. |
| Mercury & Jupiter | Tourmaline. |
| Mercury, Jupiter, Mars & Sun | Jacinth. |
| Mercury, Jupiter & Venus | Turquoise. |
| Mercury, Jupiter, Venus & Moon | Sapphire [Yellow]. *(Blue Sapphire is under the influence of Saturn) |
| Mercury, Mars, Jupiter & Venus | Emerald. |
| Mercury & Mars | Bloodstone [Heliotrope]. Magnetite [Loadstone]. |
| Mercury, Mars & Venus | Agate. |
| Mercury, Sun & Venus | Opal. |
| Mercury & Venus | Armena. Chrysolite [Peridot]. Chrysoprase. Jade. Jasper. *(Red Jasper is under the influence of Mars) Malachite. |

314 / *The Book of Immediate Magic — Part 2*

| | |
|---|---|
| Mercury, Venus & Moon | Pearl. |
| Mercury & Moon | Aquamarine. |

### vii. Moon

| | |
|---|---|
| Moon | Adamite.<br>Adularia.<br>**Androdamas.**<br>Pyrites [Silver-coloured]. *(Pyrites Tin-coloured are under the influence of Saturn & the Moon; Ash-coloured are under the influence of the Jupiter; Gold-coloured are under the influence of the Sun; and Copper-coloured are under the influence of the Sun & Venus)<br>Marble.<br>Selenite [Moonstone]. |
| Moon & Saturn | Pyrites [Tin-coloured]. *(Pyrites Ash-coloured are under the influence of the Jupiter; Gold-coloured are under the influence of the Sun; Copper-coloured are under the influence of the Sun & Venus; and Silver-coloured are under the influence of the Moon) |
| Moon, Saturn, Jupiter, Venus, & Mercury | Chalcedony. |
| Moon, Jupiter, Venus & Mercury | Sapphire [Yellow]. *(Blue Sapphire is under the influence of Saturn) |
| Moon & Mars | Rock Crystal. |
| Moon, Sun & Venus | Quartz Crystal. |

| | |
|---|---|
| Moon, Mars & Venus | Beryl. |
| Moon & Venus | Coral. *(Red Coral is under the influence of Mars) |
| Moon, Venus & Mercury | Pearl. |
| Moon & Mercury | Aquamarine. |

Having addressed some of the material which you may employ to "enhance" or "empower" any planetary magical practice you wish to undertake, the question may well arise as to what such enhancement or empowerment is actually all about. In terms of *Practical Kabbalah*, it is all about focussing and "drawing down" *Ruchaniyut* which I have addressed in some detail elsewhere, and which pertains to "Spiritual Force" which is "localized inside all material existence."[139] In this regard, I noted that "all of us have this 'Spiritual Power' within our beings, and so have trees, stones, the sun, moon and the stars."[140] From practical perspectives, this means that those who are aware of the, as it were, "qualities of *Ruchaniyut*" within everything, whether it be a plant, a stone, a tree or a mountain, the sun, moon and the stars, etc., can attract, so to speak, the "spiritual forces" (*Ruchaniyut*) inside these objects, thus focussing them in terms of harmoniously associated intentions, i.e. relevant purposes.

It is with this in mind that I wrote "Having discovered *Ruchaniyut* inside matter, Kabbalists can for example attract the Spiritual Forces (*Ruchaniyut*) of the celestial bodies, etc. It is understood that the very existence of our world hinges on this hidden force, which can be consciously drawn down through certain actions into the body of the Kabbalist, who is thereby able to achieve modifications in the terrestrial realm and even exert some control in *Tzeva Marom* (the celestial domain)."[141] Let us now consider a planetary ritual which was constructed and worked to beneficially affect the outcome of certain intentions, and which did so most effectively. Unfortunately the limited space in this tome allows only one planetary ritual to be shared, however the one elected certainly offers an excellent example on how such rituals can be constructed from the material addressed both in this and the first part of *"The Book of Immediate Magic."*[142] In this regard, I have selected the following "Venus Planetary Ritual" employed for the purpose of increasing love, grace and loving-kindness.

## 2. *NETZACH* (VICTORY/VENUS): LOVE, GRACE, KINDNESS & JOY

Love and happiness rank amongst the most vital factors necessary to ensure that our existence on this planet is meaningful. With love in our lives we thrive, expand and grow, without it we dwindle into very sad, grey figures. It is the latter situation which drives humans who are lonely and longing for intimate relationships, to seek out magical ways of encouraging love in their lives. However, if you want to raise the ire of so-called "authorities" and self-styled "adepts" in the "magical arts," simply post a query regarding "love spells," or volunteer information pertaining to "engendering love" by "magical means" on a internet social sites. The backlash can be thoroughly ugly, and full of assumptions regarding the person who posted the query. In this regard, the denigratory responses to a simple query reveal a lot more about the nature of those who are berating the querant, than they do about the being of the person who raises the question in the first place.

In one instance, an individual posted the simple request "need love spell," which resulted in a torrent of unpleasantness and assumptions regarding this person relying on magic to save him/herself from having "to develop the sort of personality that someone likes." The presumptions got worse as the conversation continued, until I offered the querant what I considered a meaningful response, which equally elicited condemnation and a barrage of condescending rhetoric. In this regard, I responded with the example of a fellow practitioner who successfully employed the forthcoming planetary ritual for "love, grace, kindness and joy." This engendered further haughty, disdainful responses regarding the magical efforts of the said individual. To add insult to injury, the main culprit in dishing out verbal castigation is an individual who is styled an "adept" in the magical arts. Furthermore, the said "adept" is to date fully unacquainted with my associate who successfully employed, as it were, "Kabbalistic love magic."

The fact of the matter is that the individual, who was being maligned and verbally assaulted, was not a kid asking for a "love spell," but a forty year old adult and a very astute practitioner of the magical arts. His intention was to simply set the right circumstances or environment to generate "love, grace, kindness and joy" in his life. The "planetary ritual" he employed worked exceptionally well, and a very shy, introverted individual found love and affection, not of the fleeting kind but rather of the equal kind between true lovers. As I noted elsewhere, "if anyone can employ magical incantations to create the right environment to generate business and a good living, I cannot for the life of me see why they cannot attempt to generate the appropriate environment in which they might find love. I am well aware of the general suggestion that individuals who are incapable of finding stable relationships, should engage in serious introspection to ascertain the 'flaws' within themselves which preclude them from forming stable relationships. Whilst such reasoning may apply in some cases, this approach is based on a serious generalization which precludes any recognition of individuals who might be nothing more than very shy by nature. This is certainly not a mental disease nor a character flaw."[143]

As might be expected, there are numerous techniques employed in *Practical Kabbalah* to encourage love and happiness, ranging from the use of unique Hebrew amulets to special incantations. In this regard, in harmony with the topic addressed in this chapter, dealing also with "Planetary Magic," we will consider a ritual which was employed by my mentioned associate, friend and fellow practitioner of this great Tradition, in order to successfully engender love and happiness in his life.

The first factor which has to be considered in seeking out magical ways to facilitate intimate relationships in your life, is the fundamental intention behind the action. Reasons might vary from seeking a close union or marriage with a loving partner, to interaction with a variety of partners, the latter being the preferred choice by those who do not have any desire to be "tied down," so to speak. This being said, over the years of working with individuals who supposedly wanted "open relationships," I have noticed just how those very individuals eventually committed themselves to a single partner.

Of course, the single word which applies here is "love," and this is what needs to be kept in mind when you next write the necessary, as it were, "statement of intent." In Kabbalisic tradition the word "love" is often viewed in harmony with other special qualities, which individuals require in order to realise, i.e. make real, "love" in their lives. Thus we find the Hebrew expression חן וחסד ואהבה (*chen v'chesed v'ahavah*—"grace and kindness and love") being generally employed in amulets and incantations pertaining to matters of the heart. It is worth considering that you do not need to employ Hebrew in writing down the "statement of intent," since this could be done in your mother tongue, and preferably in a single, simple phrase like "to increase and strengthen love, grace and loving-kindness in my life." Do not try to be too elaborate in this statement, because your own *Nefesh* (Instinctual Self) is not really concerned with elaborations, but rather with the most basic, clearly stated fundamental intentions.

It should be understood that any major "magical practice" for a specific purpose, most of the time necessitates a number of successive smaller magical activities. In this regard, the magical process is not just about "creating circumstances," and, as one of my associates noted, "setting the scene when interacting with others," but more about maintaining your own "inner poise," so to speak. In other words, the outcome of having worked a major magical ritual for an intended purpose, necessitates a number of smaller "magical activities" being executed along the way whilst out and about in your world. The initial ritualistic procedure is just the beginning of a much larger magical activity, which will not be completed, as it were, today, tomorrow or the day after.

I am reminded of a daunting magical task which was set for me in the early 1970's, albeit not one pertaining specifically to "love," but to the increase of personal knowledge and the capacity to understand. I recall how I cowered under the enormity of the task at hand, because I had to learn the fullness of magical skill through a single magical procedure. That is in fact my primary intention in sharing with you a unique "planetary ritual" for gaining "love, grace and loving-kindness." In terms of aiming to enhance these qualities in your life, it is understood that if you increase these special ideals within yourself, they are likely to conjoin into a single quality, which is likely to expand in all kinds of directions. It is equally likely to impact relationships on several

*Astrological Considerations* / 319

levels, whether it be of the romantic kind or the social kind, e.g. in your work environment, etc. I have addressed this topic to some extent elsewhere,[144] and will likely deal with it in much greater detail in future volumes of this series of texts on *Practical Kabbalah*.

Learning by example should, in my estimation, be reckoned amongst the best ways of acquiring skill in the construction of successful planetary ritual practices. Hence, in terms of working a Venus planetary "*Ritual for Love, Grace, Kindness and Joy*," it is worth considering the manner in which one such ritual was efficiently compiled and executed by a skilled practitioner of the magical arts, whom, as I noted, is a close associate of mine. Again, the primary factor for the said individual was a recognition that any planetary ritual necessitates certain requirements. Thus the initial task pertained to the compilation of a list of items which might be employed to enhance and empower the ritual activity, and, as it were, "draw down" the necessary *Ruchaniyut* (Spiritual Forces) to facilitate the desired result. In this regard, he commenced with a clear recognition of the primary purpose of the ritual activity, including the main qualities involved, which in the current instance were noted to be:

1. Purpose: To increase love, grace and lovingkindness in his life.
2. Main Qualities: Grace, Joy, and Pleasure.

The said individual noted that his intention was not only to, in his own words, "set the scene when interacting with others," but equally to develop and maintain his own inner poise and harmony. With a clear purpose in mind, and equally with the clarity of his conscience, he next needed to list the items which he intended to include in the ritual itself. In this regard, he commenced with the necessary planetary influences, so to speak. In the current instance he acknowledged נוגה (*Nogah*—Venus) to be the primary planetary force relevant to the said purpose. He then considered the alignment of the לבנה (*Levanah*—Moon), שמש (*Shemesh*—Sun) and צדק (*Tzedek*—Jupiter) with Venus. To this end he understood that the Venus/Moon affiliation pertains in a large measure to that which is "instinctual" and to "sexuality," whilst the Venus/Sun combination speaks more of "lovers," and since Jupiter is jovial and expansive, the Venus/Jupiter alignment references grace (Venus), joy (Jupiter), and obviously a lot of pleasure. Considered from sefirotic perspectives, these planetary associations would indicate interactions between *Netzach* (Victory/Endurance—Venus), *Yesod* (Foundation—Moon), *Tiferet* (Beauty/Harmony—Sun), and *Chesed* (Mercy/Loving-kindness—Jupiter), as shown in the following illustration:

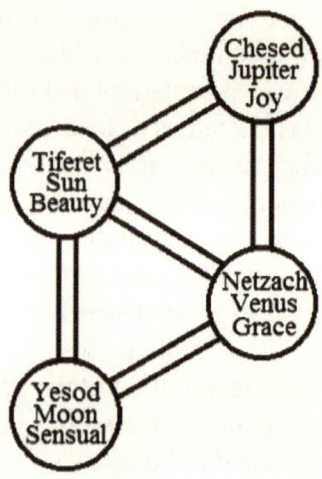

These planetary combinations are certainly most benevolent, especially so in terms of the fundamental purpose of expanding grace, loving-kindness and love in joyful living.

Having elected the planetary forces, he next decided the period in which it would be best to work the said "Venus ritual." In this regard, it was felt that the most harmonious seasonal association would be anytime from mid-Spring through Summer, but no later than mid-Autumn. As can be expected, this presented a "zodiacal problem," so to speak, since the ritual was to be worked in the Southern Hemisphere in Johannesburg, South Africa, where the said period comprises עקרב (*Akrav*—Scorpio), קשת (*Keshet*—Sagittarius), גדי (*G'di*—Capricorn), דלי (*D'li*—Aquarius), and דגים (*Dagim*—Pisces), in contrast to the Northern Hemisphere where the same seasons comprise שור (*Shor*—Taurus), תאומים (*Te'omim*—Gemini), סרטן (*Sartan*—Cancer), אריה (*Aryeh*—Leo), and בתולה (*B'tulah*—Virgo). After careful consideration, it was decided to perform this said Venus ritual on a relevant day and time closest to the Full Moon in *Aquarius*. In terms of the seasons, this is the seasonal period in the Southern Hemisphere which aligns with *Leo* in the Northern Hemisphere, the latter zodiacal period being under the rulership of the Sun. Furthermore, the Hebrew glyph associated with *Aquarius* is צ (*Tzadi*), the letter representing a צדיק (*Tzadik*), a righteous individual, and equally the initial of the word צדק (*Tzedek*—Jupiter). Hence *Aquarius* was felt to be most harmonious in terms of the primary purpose of the said ritual, as perceived from the angle of the associated solar period in the Southern Hemisphere.

It is customary to work any, as it were, "ritual of increase," i.e. increasing love, money, etc., during an upcycle, e.g. during the said Summer months; the waxing lunar cycle commencing with the New Moon up to Full Moon; etc. In terms of working the current ritual, the appropriate days would be those aligning with any of the relevant planetary forces, i.e. Sunday (Sun), Monday (Moon), Thursday (Jupiter), or Friday (Venus). In terms of the said "upcycle" considerations applicable at the time, it was decided to execute the current ritual during the "Hour of the Moon," on the Sunday which was then the day of the Full Moon in *Aquarius* in the Southern Hemisphere. Hence there was a strong Sun/Moon affiliation during the time when the said individual enacted this "Venus Ritual." In this regard, the appropriate hours during which the said ritual could be performed, would be those aligned with the moon between sunset on Saturday to sunrise on Sunday. Consulting the earlier shared tables of planetary hours, it is clear that if sunset is at 18h00 hours on Saturday, the first night-time "Hour of the Moon" would be between 19h00 and 20h00, and the second between 02h00 to 03h00. It was further agreed that all necessary preparations would be done in the "Hour of Mercury" preceding the Lunar hour.

The next consideration regarding requirements which would contribute to the success of the ritual in question, was the creation of a meaningful adjuration. In terms of the actual "Venus Ritual," it was decided to commence the procedure with the opening of the "Gate of *Netzach*," Venus being the planetary affiliation of this *sefirah*, and this "opening" being executed by means of the earlier addressed יהוה צבאות (*YHVH Tzva'ot*) and its associated qualities. Whilst the "Opening" of the said "Gate" necessitates uttering the vowels of the relevant Divine Name in their associated bodily locales, all further Divine Names are intoned in a standard manner without any physical considerations.

Be that as it may, it was further decided to include the Divine Name combination appropriate to the day on which the said ritual was to be enacted, i.e. Sunday/Sun/*Tiferet*. In this regard, the relevant Divine Name combination is יהוה אלוה ודאת (*YHVH Eloha va-Da'at*).

Following these Divine Name combinations respectively applicable to the main planetary influence (Venus), and the planet of day (Sunday/Sun), some attention was paid to a relevant set of Divine Names which might be employed in the mentioned adjuration. In terms of the extensive list of Divine and Angelic Names, as well as incantationary formulas shared in the first part of *"The Book of Immediate Magic,"*[145] it was determined that the following planetary/sefirotic/Divine Name disposition applicable to the said *"Ritual for Love, Grace, Kindness and Joy,"* should include:

1. נוגה (*Nogah*–Venus)—נצח (*Netzach*–Grace)—צמרכד (vocalised *Tzemiroch'da*);
2. צדק/נוגה (*Tzedek*–Jupiter/*Nogah*–Venus)—חסד/נצח (*Chesed*–Loving-Kindness/*Netzach*–Grace)—אדירירון (*Adiriron* or *Adiryaron*);
3. לבנה (*Levanah*–Moon)—יסוד (*Yesod*–Foundation/Bonding)—אל שדי (*El Shadai*); and
4. Moon/Jupiter—*Yesod*/*Chesed*—יגלפזק (*Y'galp'zak*).

It was recognised that since the Ineffable Name features prominently in the "Opening the Gate of *Netzach*" procedure, as well as in the Divine Name construct applicable to the day (Sunday) on which this ritual was to be worked, it did not require any incorporation in the set of Divine Names to be included in the adjuration. Naturally one could incorporate any Divine Name aligning with the primary purpose of the adjuration, and in this regard the various options include:

a. יהוה (*YHVH*) and יאהדונהי (*Yahadonahi*), respectively associated with *Tiferet* (Beauty, and the union of *Tiferet* (Beauty) and *Malchut* (Kingdom);

b. the Twelve Banners, i.e. יהוה יההו יוהה הויה ההיו והיה וההי ויהה היהו היוה ההוי (*YHVH YHHV YVHH HVHY HVYH HHYV VHYH VHHY VYHH HYHV HYVH HHVY*), which pertain to Venus/Moon/Jupiter in the sense that they are employed, amongst other purposes, to encourage "sexual unity" and to facilitate joy and pleasure;[146]

c. אהיה אשר אהיה (*Eh'yeh asher Eh'yeh*) is likewise employed for the purpose of encouraging sexual union, as well as for grace, love, kindness;[147]

d. אכתריאל (*Achatri'el*), which, I noted previously "will stir great love amongst a married couple, and will equally make a woman greatly beloved by all who meet her."[148] This remarkable Divine/Angelic Name is not only employed for the purpose of encouraging grace, love and kindness, but is understood to greatly increase the power of all Sacred Names to which it may be conjoined;

e. אנהליכה (*Eneh'layechah*), which I noted elsewhere is a Divine Name which was "constructed from the combination of נלך (*Nelach*), the twenty-first portion of the *Shem Vayisa Vayet*, and the Divine Name אהיה (*Ehyeh*)."[149] I further mentioned that this Divine Name combination is claimed to have "the power to do many things in the world";[150]

f. הלז (*Heilaze*), which is a Divine Name derived from the three words in *Genesis 47:23* reading הא לכם זרע (*hei lachem zera*— "here is seed for you"), and is hence equally employed for the purposes of encouraging joy and pleasure, and, as can be expected, sexual union.[151]

It was further decided to include the names of Spirit Intelligences, and in this regard the relevant Planetary/Sefirotic/Angelic Name associations are:

1. Primary Planetary Influence: נוגה (*Nogah*–Venus)—נצח (*Netzach*–Victory)—חניאל (*Chani'el*);
2. שמש (*Shemesh*–Sun)—תפארת (*Tiferet*–Beauty)—מיכאל (*Micha'el*);
3. צדק (*Tzedek*–Jupiter)—חסד (*Chesed*–Mercy)—צדקיאל (*Tzadki'el*); and
4. לבנה (*Levanah*–Moon)—יסוד (*Yesod*–Foundation)—גבריאל (*Gavri'el*)

There are once again many alternative options when it comes to Angelic Names which can be incorporated in the adjuration under consideration,[152] and these are far more numerous than the relevant Divine Names:

אביאל (*Avi'el*); אהביאל (*Ahavi'el*); אוריאל (*Ori'el*); בואל (*Bo'el*); ברכיאל (*Barchi'el*); גזריאל (*Gazri'el*); זקפיאל (*Zakfi'el*); חסדיאל (*Chasdi'el*); טריאל (*Tari'el*); יופיאל (*Yofi'el*); נגדיאל (*Nagdi'el*); נוריאל (*Nuri'el*); נזריאל (*Nazri'el*); סנדלפון (*Sandalfon*); עוזיאל (*Ozi'el*); עזריאל (*Azri'el*); פחדיאל (*Pachdi'el*); פקדיאל (*Pakdi'el*); רחמיאל (*Rachmi'el*); שבריאל (*Shavri'el*); שמריאל (*Shamri'el*); שמשיאל (*Shamshi'el*); תמוניאל (*T'muni'el*); and סריגורא (*Sarigora*).

Whilst some readers might think that it would be necessary to include all of the listed Divine and Angelic Names, it was decided to settle for a fairly brief, impactive incantation, in which the set of Divine/Angelic Names were those determined to be directly associated with the planetary/sefirotic qualities underpinning the primary intention of the ritual in question, and should thus be included in the adjuration. Additionally, it was decided to include from amongst the remainder of the associated Divine/Angelic Names, only those employed fairly regularly in Hebrew amulets and adjurations for grace, love and kindness.

In this regard, one might think that it would be absolutely imperative to include the Ineffable Name, since it is employed for a great variety of purposes, and it is indeed very effective in amulets and incantations for the very purposes sought after in the current instance. The same can be said for the well-known יאהדונהי (*Yahadonahi*) Divine Name combination, which we noted earlier is "the 'gate' through which prayers gain entry into the Divine Presence." However, since the Ineffable Name is already included in the Divine Name construct employed in "Opening the Gate of *Netzach*," and equally in the Divine Name combination pertaining to the *sefirah* associated with the Sun, i.e. *Tiferet*, it was decided not to include it in the incantation as well.

Following a traditional format in the construction of the said adjuration, the final construction reads:

יהי רצון מלפניך יאהדונהי אלהי הצבאות בכח שמות
הקדושים והגדולים האלה יגלפזק אל שדי צמרכד
אדירירון ועל ידי המלאכים מיכאל גבריאל צדקיאל
חניאל חסדיאל רחמיאל אהביאל שמשיאל שתתנני
לאהבה לחן ולחסד שתצליחוני בזה מה שארצה זמן
פרעון אוריאל מעתה ועד עולם אמן וחן יהי רצון

Transliteration:
> *Y'hi ratzon milfanecha Yahadonahi Elohei ha-tzva'ot b'koach shemot ha-k'doshim v'ha-g'dolim ha-eleh Y'galp'zak El Shadai Tzemiroch'da Adiriron, v'al y'dei ha-malachim Micha'el Gavri'el Tzadki'el Chani'el Chasdi'el Rachmi'el Ahavi'el Shamshi'el, shetit'neni l'ahavah l'chen v'l'chesed sh'tatz'lichuni b'zeh mah she'ertzeh, z'man peira'on Ori'el me'atah v'ad olam omein v'chen y'hi ratzon*

Translation:
> May it be your will *Yahadonahi Elohei ha-tzvaot* in the power of these holy and great Names *Y'galp'zak El Shadai Tzemirochda Adiriron*, and through the angels *Micha'el Gavri'el Tzadki'el Chani'el Chasdi'el Rachmi'el Ahavi'el Shamshi'el*, that I will find grace, love and loving-kindness for me to have success in this that I desire, payback time *Oriel* from now unto eternity *amen* and thus be it so willed.

Additionally you may include all or any of the listed Divine and Angelic Names in this incantation. However, in vocalising this Hebrew incantation in a low voice, the important trick is to keep the words and phrases flowing along as rhythmically as possible.

Bearing in mind that in the majority of instances the accent is on the last syllable of Hebrew words, and speaking as if you were reciting a rhyme, this incantation should flow as smoothly as oil. Furthermore, you will truly experience the power of this incantation, if you can get a pulse going in uttering the Hebrew phrases. In this regard, you should always keep to the rhythm, as this renders the hypnotic impact, and what is enhancing the psycho-spiritual effectiveness of the incantation. Hebrew offers you everything necessary for the successful vocalisation of incantations, i.e. rhythm, rhyming, alliteration, etc. William G. Gray, my late mentor, loved alliteration, and whilst some may feel that he overdid it, so to speak, alliteration is not only a good "memory device," but equally a great "incantationary device."

Be that as it may, in the current instance, the ritual for love, grace, kindness and joy included an amulet comprised of an unique formula, which was meant to encourage and facilitate the said qualities. In exactly the same manner delineated in "*The Book of Seals & Amulets*," it was decided "to fashion a kind of 'spirit force-form' which could be perceived to be an 'artificial elemental' or a 'spirit *golem*'."[153] As noted in the said text, "Method being very important, a way had to be found to conjoin 'subtle forces' in a unique manner."[154] Furthermore, as mentioned, the "'spirit powers' first had to be identified, and then amalgamated to form, as it were, a single 'entity'."[155] This process was enacted in the same manner as in the previously listed instance by conjoining selected Hebrew glyphs into a "Magic Square," which "would function as a kind of spirit 'circuit-board'," and by means of which, the necessary "spirit forces" would be triggered and enhanced to affect the fundamental purpose of the construct.

In the current instance, the earlier mentioned "*Yetziratic Incantation Wheel*" was again employed to determine the correct elemental/planetary/zodiacal/letter associations. Having earlier established the Hebrew letter associated with the zodiacal sign (Aquarius), i.e. צ (*Tzadi*), the next step would be to ascertain the "Double Letters" respectively affiliated with the chosen planets, as well as the "Mother Letter" aligned with the "Element of Water," the latter being harmoniously associated with the flowing quality of "Love," and this being the fundamental intention of working the Venus ritual. In this instance the full compliment of associated Hebrew glyphs were combined in the following manner:

פ *(Peh)*—Venus—Earth
צ *(Tzadi)*—Aquarius—Air/Fire
ג *(Gimel)*— Jupiter—Air
כ *(Kaf)*—Sun—Fire
ת *(Tav)*—Moon—Water
מ *(Mem)*—Water.

Employing these letters in the exact listed order we arrive at the letter combination פצגכתם *(PtzGKTM)*. It was decided to construct a "Sacred Name" and magical seal (sigil) from these glyphs, employing the same methodology as addressed in terms of the *Tagiom* formula which was constructed to encourage and facilitate good living, and which I addressed in "*The Book of Seals & Amulets*."[156] As indicated, the "Element" associations indicated one quality of "Earth," one of "Air," one of "Fire," two of "Water," and one of an "Air/Fire" combination, i.e. the quality of "Fire" being applicable to *Aquarius* in terms of its relevant season in the Southern Hemisphere.

Naturally, to be able to pronounce this word, we need to insert some vowels, and, as I noted elsewhere,[157] the vowels employed in Hebrew words are equally affiliated with the "Elements," i.e. "I" (*ee*) with the Element of Air, "A" (*ah*) with the Element of Fire, "O" (*oh*) with the Element of Water, "E" (*eh*) with the Element of Earth, and "U" (*oo*) the "Universal Element." Hence, to further intensify the powers of the "Elements" associated with the Hebrew glyphs comprising the Sacred Name construct, it was decided to incorporate four vowels in the following order:

E [*Eh*] — *Afar* — Earth
A [*Ah*] — *Esh* — Fire
O [*Oh*] — *Mayim* — Water
I [*Ee*] — *Ruach* — Air

You may well wonder how to locate the vowels in the said Sacred Name construct. In this regard, it was agreed that the letter פ [*Peh*—Venus—Earth] should be vocalised with its natural vowel, i.e. "E" [*Eh*], which is equally affiliated with the "Element of Earth." This was thought to be particularly appropriate in terms of balancing the Air/Fire qualities affiliated with the succeeding letter

צ *(Tzadi—Aquarius)*. As it is, no vowel was assigned the letter צ *(Tzadi)*, because it was understood that, despite the association of this letter with *Aquarius* as well as the planet Saturn in the Northern Hemisphere, and equally with the Sun and Fire in terms of its seasonal association in the Southern Hemisphere, the Hebrew glyph itself is, as indicated, closely aligned with צדק *(Tzedek—Jupiter)*. Hence it was determined to conjoin the enunciation of the צ *(Tzadi)* with the succeeding ג *(Gimel)*. Furthermore, since the latter is the "Double Letter" associated with צדק *(Tzedek—Jupiter)* as well as the "Element of Air," and the succeeding letter כ *(Kaf)* is aligned with the *Sun* and the "Element of Fire," it was agreed to intersperse the said Hebrew glyphs with the vowel "A" [*Ah*] representing the "Element of Fire." It was further decided that the balancing of the "Airy" ג *(Gimel)* with the vowel aligned with "Fire," the most harmonious arrangement would be to in turn balance the "Fiery" כ *(Kaf)* with the vowel "O" [*Oh*] aligned with the "Element of Water."

Two glyphs remain, ת *(Tav–Moon)* related to the "Element of Water," and מ *(Mem)* the letter directly aligned with Water. In this regard, it was considered ideal to intersperse these letters with the vowel associated with the "Element of Air," i.e. "I" [*ee*], between the two concluding Hebrew glyphs. Reading from right to left the full Hebrew letter/vowel combination reads:

מ–i–ת–o–כ–a–ג–צ–e–פ

Thus *PeTzGaKoTiM* (פצגכותמ) became the "Name of Power" referencing the fundamental intention and purpose of the current "Venus ritual." However, the intention here is not primarily the construction of a "Name of Power" which can be employed to as it were, "invoke" associated planetary/elemental forces, but ultimately, as I noted elsewhere, "to fashion a kind of 'spirit force-form' which could be perceived to be an 'artificial elemental' or a 'spirit *golem*,' so to speak, to achieve the hoped-for objective."[158] Hence the necessity of identifying and conjoining the relevant "subtle forces" selected from the range of planetary/elemental/ Hebrew glyph qualities. As I mentioned previously, "these 'spirit powers' first had to be identified, and then amalgamated to form, as it were, a single 'entity'."[159] In this regard, I referenced the notion that "every letter of the Hebrew alphabet was, and still is, considered to be the 'embodiment' of a Spirit Intelligence, each being an 'Angel'," and thus it is that Divine Names "actually are the respective qualities or aspects of Divinity hidden within their inner meanings."[160]

Therefore, in order to facilitate an even greater empowerment of the *Petzgakotim* construct, as well as the creation of a relevant "spirit force-form" in harmony with the current primary magical intention, it was decided to convert and conjoin the Hebrew glyphs comprising the said "Magical Name" into a single *Chotam* (Seal/Sigil). This was achieved by means of the previously addressed *AYaK BaChaR* or *AIK BeKaR* system[161] which is popularly called "*Qabalah of the Nine Chambers*."[162] As noted before, "this system is comprised of a square of nine boxes ('chambers'), each of which contains three letters and the numerical value of each being reducible to the same single digit, e.g. א [1] – י [10] – ק [100] = 1; ב [2] – כ [20] – ר [200] = 2; etc.,"[163] as shown below:

The fundamental components of the mentioned magical sigil are acquired by tracing, in exact order, the angles of the boxes containing the component letters of the four primary Hebrew letters selected, i.e. פ (Venus), צ (*Aquarius*) ג (Jupiter), ב (Sun), ת (Moon), and מ (Water). However, in terms of the *gematria* (numerical value) of each Hebrew glyph, i.e. פ = 80 (8), צ = 90 (9), ג = 3, ב = 20 (2), ת = 400 (4), and מ = 40 (4), it is clear that the *gematria* of the two concluding glyphs can be reduced to the same simple value. In fact, both of these letters located are in the same *Ayak Bachar* angle, which, in terms of the rules of application, is employed only once . The resultant angles are:

# 330 / The Book of Immediate Magic — Part 2

פצגכתה

Conjoining all of these angles in their exact order will yield a number of potential forms, of which the following construct was selected to be the seal/sigil of *Petzgakotim*:

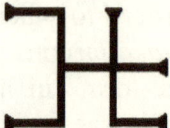

This special *Chotam* (Seal/Sigil) was located in the centre of the following unique "Magic Square" constructed from seven glyphs, i.e. the six comprising the Name פצגכתם (*Petzgakotim*) plus the letter א (*Alef*). The latter glyph was selected because it is understood to represent the Divine One, and equally to link the "infinity" of אהיה (*Eh'yeh*), the "I am/will be" of the "Divine Originator" in *Keter* (Crown) on the sefirotic Tree, with אדני (*Adonai*), the manifestation of the Eternal Living Spirit in *Malchut* (Kingdom) of material existence. As noted elsewhere, "the letter *Alef* being representative of the 'Holy One,' it is worth noting that the spelling of several important Divine Names commence with this glyph, e.g. אדן (*Adon*) and אדני (*Adonai*); אל (*El*), אלוה (*Eloah*) and אלהים (*Elohim*), אדיר (*Adir*—'Mighty One'); etc., and likewise the names of a number of important 'Divine Qualities' equally start with the letter *Alef*, e.g. אין (*Ain*—'Nothing'); אור (*Or* [*Aur*]—'Light'); אחד (*Echad*—'One'); אני (*Ani*—'I am' or 'Self'); אמת (*Emet*—'Truth'); אולם (*Olam*—'Eternity'); and many more."[164]

In terms of the entire talismanic construct, it is generally understood that it "would function as a kind of spirit 'circuit-board,' so to speak, through which, the required spirit forces could be, as it were, 'triggered' and 'enhanced' for the proposed purpose."[165]

*Astrological Considerations* / 331

| מ | ת | כ | א | ג | צ | פ |
|---|---|---|---|---|---|---|
| ת | כ | מ | א | פ | ג | צ |
| כ | מ | ת | א | צ | פ | ג |
| א | א | א | ⌷⌵ | א | א | א |
| ג | פ | צ | א | ת | מ | כ |
| צ | ג | פ | א | מ | כ | ת |
| פ | צ | ג | א | כ | ת | מ |

     The important task would be to align yourself with each of the component glyphs of the פצגכתם (*PeTzGaKoTiM*) construct. In this regard, I noted previously "that perhaps the most important practice, as far as *Practical Kabbalah* and everything it entails is concerned, is alignment with the 'Spirit Forces' inherent in the twenty-two glyphs comprising the Hebrew alphabet."[166] If this alignment was enacted as delineated in the first part of "*The Book of Immediate Magic*,"[167] then there is no need to repeat the said action here. However, if the said alignment procedures were not performed previously, it would be necessary in the current instance to perform the required alignment with at least the six letters comprising the *Petzgakotim* construct.

     The primary practice is quite simple, and good enough in terms of current requirements. All that needs to be done is to look intently for a minute or so at a large image of a selected Hebrew glyph, then close the eyes and see it reflected on the blank screen of your inner vision whilst simultaneously enunciating the name of the said glyph. Of course, in terms of visualising the Hebrew glyphs whilst uttering their respective appellatives, greater skill can be developed with regular practice, to the point where you can clearly see the selected glyph hanging in space in front of your eyes. This practice is an important precursor to the procedure of establishing *Gevulim* ("Boundaries"),[168] and equally to visualising and reciting the letters of a Divine Name construct.

Having completed the construction of this, as it were, "Spirit Force-form," and worked the required alignment with the component letters, attention had to be given to the preparation of the "sacred space" in which this "*Ritual for Love, Grace, Kindness and Joy*" were to be performed. Since readers may want to work this ritual personally, I will address the preparation and the ritual procedure in terms of the items which could be incorporated, in order to enhance and empower the various "celestial forces" at play. In this regard, it should be noted that the colour of Venus/*Netzach* is green, and hence this colour should be a major component of the decor, i.e. a green altar cloth, green candles, green leaves, shrubs, etc. However, keep in mind that in terms of plants, you need to ensure that you include those that have an affinity with "Venus" and/or the planetary combination applicable to the primary purpose for working the ritual in question. For example, you may consider including readily available green ferns, however all ferns are affiliated with Saturn, though some are also aligned with the Moon, but they are not at all suitable for the current ritual procedure.

As indicated in the earlier list of plants and their planetary associations, there is a fair variety of easily accessible herbs, flowers, trees, fruits, and vegetables which are either directly affiliated with Venus, or aligned with a combination of the planetary forces applicable to the current ritual. In this regard, some of the most readily available in the wild in some parts of the world, or in any good nursery elsewhere, are:

1. **Herbs:** Alkanet, Angelica [including the wild variety], Archangel (Red, White & Yellow), Artemisia (Mugwort), Creeping Charlie (Ground Ivy), Galium (Ladies Bedstraw), Lady's Mantle, Mint [all varieties], Penny Royal, Soapwort, Sorrel, Thyme [including the wild variety], Vervain (*Verbena*]), Oxalis (Wood Sorrel/Shamrock), and Yarrow.
2. **Flowers:** Bugle, Columbine, Cowslip, Dahlia, Goldenrod, Magnolia, Orchids, Primrose, Roses, Tansy, Teasel (Fuller's Thistle), and Violets.
3. **Fruits:** Apples, Brambles (Blackberries), Chestnuts, Figs Morello Cherries (Sour Cherries), Peaches, Pears, and Limes.

4. **Vegetables:** Beans, Artichokes, Chick-peas, and Running Bean (Green Beans).

Any of these items, even if only a vase of roses, a basket of apples, and/or a bowl filled with beans, will enhance the current ritual. It should also be kept in mind that wheat is aligned with Venus, and hence a sheath, a few ears of wheat, or a couple of "corn dollies," will equally intensify the link with the said planet. You could also burn a little incense to add to the ambience of your work space, perhaps a little sandalwood. Both the white and red varieties are aligned with both Venus and Jupiter. Otherwise you could easily acquire an essential oil of any of the listed herbs/flowers, the fragrance of which could be spread throughout the room by means of an essential oil burner.

In conclusion, ensure that you place a small table or your altar in the Western quarter of your Temple, the sector aligned with the "Element of Water," the Archangel גבריאל (*Gavri'el*), and the concept of "Love." Ready the altar surface for the ritual work by locating on it the green candles (with matches), and whatever else you think necessary to work the rite, not forgetting your ritual script and/or written incantation, as well as the unique "*Petzgakotim* Letter Square" which must be located within easy reach and be clearly visible.

### 3. VENUS PLANETARY RITUAL
### FOR LOVE, GRACE, KINDNESS & JOY

#### a. Ritual Purification
#### performed during the
#### "Hour of the Sun"

It is important to ensure that you are appropriately prepared in body, mind, soul and spirit, prior to working any planetary ritual practice. In this regard, the actual act of concentrating with focussed intention (*Kavvanah*) and clarity of conscience on the task at hand, is enough to prepare yourself mentally and emotionally for such practices. However, the physical preparedness is another matter altogether. In this regard, it would be necessary to get yourself, as it were, "cleansed" of all unwanted "spiritual forces" (*Ruchaniyut*) which are attached to you, and which may detract from the task at hand. It is for this reason that it is suggested that you perform a physical "ritual purification," i.e. take a ritual bath, prior to working planetary rituals. Jewish practitioners may simply perform a ritual submersion in their local *Mikvah*, whilst others who prefer to perform such sacred ablutions in the comfort of their own homes, can follow the following procedure which I have already addressed in the first part of the current volume,[169] and reiterate here for the sake of convenience:

1. Clean yourself fully prior to the sacred immersion, and then enter the ritual bath.
2. Prepare your ritual bath, to which has been added some salt, and whatever herbal substances might be deemed suitable. The famous "*Key of Solomon*" includes a so-called "Exorcism of the Water" to be uttered over the water.[170] Should you be interested in Hebrew versions of the incantations and prayers in the grimoire, there is an easily accessible text titled *Mafteach Shlomo*, comprising a Hebrew translation of the *"Key of Solomon."*[171] I personally prefer reciting the first four verses of *Psalm 29* over the water during the preparation of a ritual bath. These verses read:

(verse 1) הבו ליהוה בני אלים הבו ליהוה כבוד ועז

(verse 2) הבו ליהוה כבוד שמו השתחוו ליהוה בהדרת קדש

(verse 3) קול יהוה על המים אל הכבוד הרעים יהוה על מים רבים

(verse 4) קול יהוה בכח קול יהוה בהדר

Transliteration:
(verse 1) *havu l'YHVH bnei eilim havu la-YHVH kavod va'oz*
(verse 2) *havu la-YHVH k'vod sh'mo hishtachavu la-YHVH b'hadrat kodesh*
(verse 3) *kol YHVH al ha-mayim El ha-kavod hirim YHVH al mayim rabim*
(verse 4) *kol YHVH ba-koach kol YHVH be-hadar*

Translation:
> (verse 1) Give unto *YHVH*, O sons of the mighty, Give unto *YHVH* glory and strength.
> (verse 2) Give unto *YHVH* the glory due unto His name; worship *YHVH* in the beauty of holiness.
> (verse 3) The voice of *YHVH* is upon the waters; *El* of glory thundereth, *YHVH* is upon many waters.
> (verse 4) The voice of *YHVH* is full of power; the voice of *YHVH* is full of majesty.

3. Utter whatever incantation/prayer you deem appropriate prior to immersion. The "*Key of Solomon*" suggests the recitation of portions of *Psalm 27:1*; *Psalm 14:1*; *Psalm 69:1*; *Exodus 15:1*; and *Psalm 106:1*.[172] In this regard, I prefer reciting a single verse, i.e. *Psalm 18:16* [17] reading:

ישלח ממרום יקחני ימשני ממים רבים

Transliteration:
> *Yishlach mimarom yikacheini yamsheini mimayim rabim*

Translation:
> He sent from on high, He took me; He drew me out of many waters.

4. Immerse yourself slowly and submerge fully in the water of the ritual bath, and utter the following blessing after resurfacing:

ברוך אתה יהוה אלהינו מלך העולם אשר
קדשנו במצותיו וצונו על הטבילה

Transliteration:
> *Baruch atah YHVH Eloheinu melech ha-olam asher kidshanu b'mitzvotav v'tzivanu al ha-t'vilah*

Translation:
> Blessed are you, *YHVH* our God, King of the Universe, who has consecrated us to do good deeds, and commanded us regarding ritual immersion.

5. Immerse yourself fully a second time, followed by uttering the following blessing:

ברוך אתה יהוה אלהינו מלך העולם אשר קדשנו בטבילה במים חיים

Transliteration:
> Baruch atah YHVH Eloheinu melech ha-olam asher kidshanu bit'vilah b'mayim chayim

Translation:
> Blessed are you, *YHVH* our God, King of the Universe, who has consecrated us by submersion in living waters.

6. Immerse yourself a third time, and after surfacing conclude by uttering a concluding blessing, e.g.

ברוך שם כבוד מלכותו לעולם ועד אמן

Transliteration:
> Baruch Shem K'vod Malchuto l'Olam Va'ed Omein

Translation:
> Blessed be the Name of His glorious Kingdom throughout eternity *Amen*.

### b. Preparatory Practices performed during the "Hour of the Sun"

It is of great importance to understand that all magical procedures are, as it were, "Centre/Circumference affairs," i.e. the "Centre" (Self) must be fully aligned with the "Circumference" in order to affect the desired outcome. It is not simply a matter of arranging your personal workspace or temple to align with "Cosmic Forces," or, as I noted elsewhere, "dressing up in important-looking costumes,"[173] and uttering certain words which you believe the "Spirits" or the Divine One would like to hear, as you wave a stick around in a demanding manner. Whilst I certainly believe in the validity of preparing the "Circumference," i.e. setting up your workspace, to become, as it were, a "portal" for interacting with "Celestial Forces," it is of equal importance to adjust yourself, the

"Centre," to be fully aligned with the "spirit" of the magical task you are about to undertake.

My late mentor, William G. Gray, once noted that you have to "adjust yourself to fulfill the need Divinity in you has for Itself decreed." Of course, the context of this statement was quite different to the current topic, but the principle applies nevertheless. You have to adjust your body, mind, soul and spirit, for the ritual practice to have a successful outcome. In this regard, you need to do certain procedures which will trigger the relevant "God Forces," i.e. emotional qualities, and turn you into the living expression of נוגה (*Nogah*–Venus). In terms of the current ritual, all preparatory practices should be performed during the "Hour of the Sun," prior to the hour (Venus) during which you would be working this "*Ritual for Love, Grace, Kindness and Joy*." These practices could include:

1. "*Surrendering*"; "*Body Awareness*"; and "*Toning and Tuning the Body*," techniques which I have addressed in great detail in "*The Book of Self Creation*."[174]
2. The complete "*Mother Breath*" and "*Shadai Triquetra*" procedures addressed in the first part of "*The Book of Immediate Magic*."[175]
3. The "*Taking on the Name*" procedure, which was equally discussed in the first volume of this series of texts on *Practical Kabbalah*.[176]

Conclude by kindling all candles, and/or light your selected incense prior to continuing with the enactment of the Venus ritual procedure.

### c. Ritual Procedure performed during the "Hour of Venus."

Having prepared yourself physically, mentally, emotionally and spiritually, commence the ritual by standing in the centre of the room and facing East:

1. Establish the *Gevulim* (Boundaries) on the four walls of your working space, and enact the "*Clearing the Sacred*

Space" in the manner delineated in the first part of the current volume,[177] or perform the much simpler "*Clearing the Sacred Space*" and "*Defining the Working Space*" delineated in "*The Book of Self Creation*."[178] If you are unfamiliar with these procedures, you could work any "clearing"/"banishing" practice with which you are *au fait*.

2. Turning to face West, you could start the actual Venus ritual procedure by uttering the following relevant biblical verses in a low voice:

לריח שמניך טובים שמן תורק שמך (*l'rei'ach shmaneicha tovim shemen torak shmeicha*—"Thine ointments have a goodly fragrance; thy name is as ointment poured forth") [Song of Songs 1:3]

אמרתי אעלה בתמר אחזה בסנסניו (*Amarti e'eleh b'tamar ochazah b'sansinav*—"I said: 'I will climb up into the palm-tree'.") [Song of Songs 7:9]

3. Continue with an acknowledgment of the earlier mentioned Divine Name associated with the day on which you are working the ritual procedure, i.e. Sunday—Sun— *Tiferet* (Beauty). In this regard, enunciate or chant in a low voice:

יהוה אלוה דאת (*YHVH Eloha va-Da'at*)

In this instance you are not opening the "*Gate of Tiferet*," but simply vocalise the Divine Name of the day in a standard manner. It would be equally pertinent to enunciate the Divine Name combination pertaining to the Zodiacal Period, i.e. the relevant portions from the "*Name of Seventy-two Names*" pertaining to the current Zodiacal decanate. However, the entire "*Shem Vayisa Vayet*" is recited twice in the "*Gevulim*" and "*Clearing the Sacred Space*" practices, and this action would automatically include the combination appropriate to the decan in which the current ritual is being enacted.

*Astrological Considerations* / 339

4. If you have worked the earlier addressed procedure of triggering "God Forces" in your hand, body and face, invoke the required Venus "Planetary Force" in the following manner:

   a. Extend your active hand in front of you, palm facing towards your face.
   b. Close your eyes, smile inside yourself, and focus your attention on your five fingers.
   c. Smile warmly as you bring your attention to your thumb. Employing either your index or ring finger, align the "God Force" of Venus by touching the tip of your thumb with either of the said fingers, and triggering the emotional quality associated with *Nogah* (Venus) in your chest, i.e. sensuality, graceful, loving, etc. Be fully aware of the presence of this "God Force" in the centre of your chest, which you acknowledge by saying, whispering or thinking "*Shalom Ruach m'Nogah*" ("Greetings Spirit from Venus").
   d. Raise your hand, placing the palm flat on the centre of your chest. Press the thumb three times against the chest, as you focus on the quality of Venus you wish to emphasize, i.e. חושני (*Chushani*—"Sensual").
   e. Conclude by touching the opening of your left ear with the back of your thumb.

5. Trace the *chotam* (seal/sigil) of קדמאל (*Kedem'el*) towards the West with your dominant hand and eyes, whilst simultaneously enunciating the name of the subservient "Planetary Spirit" of Venus:

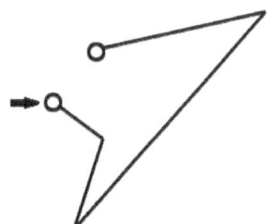

6. Intensify your alignment with the Venus "God Force" by performing the *"Opening the Gate of Netzach"* procedure in the manner delineated earlier. It is via this sefirotic "gate" that you will link with the set of Divine/Angelic Names employed in the Venus incantation. As mentioned earlier, the said sefirotic "Gate" is opened by vocalising the component vowels of the associated Divine Name, i.e. יהוה צבאות (*YHVH Tzva'ot*), in their associated locales in your body, whilst simultaneously allowing yourself the full experience of intense "feeling appreciation."

   The "God Force" could be greatly enhanced by sensing the exhilaration of "Divine Force" spinning joyously around you (*Chesed*—Jupiter), and literally dancing on your skin, creating a sense of acute sensuality (*Yesod*—Moon), as you smile warmly within, allowing yourself to be filled with love, grace and kindness (*Netzach*—Venus). You might encourage within yourself the emotional qualities of affection, passion, devotion, tenderness, and admiration for life and the living, all qualities pertaining to Venus.

7. This is followed by opening the "Nil Centre" within yourself, a practice which I addressed in the first part of *"The Book of Immediate Magic."*[179] Whilst keeping your attention firmly focussed inside the emptiness of the "Nil Centre," enunciate the incantation comprising the Divine/Angelic Names pertinent to the purpose of the current ritual.

8. If you have used an alternative procedure to "Clearing the Sacred Space," you would next need to recite the complete *Shem Vayisa Vayet* ("Name of Seventy-two Names"):

והו ילי סיט עלם מהש ללה אכא כהת הזי אלד לאו
ההע יזל מבה הרי הקם לאו כלי לוו פהל נלך ייי
מלה חהו נתה האא ירת שאה ריי אום לכב ושר יחו
להח בוק מנד אני חעם רהע ייז ההה מיך וול ילה
סאל ערי עשל מיה והו דני החש עמם ננא נית מבה
פוי נמם ייל הרח מצר ומב יהה ענו מחי דמב מנק
איע חבו ראה יבם היי מום

Transliteration:
> *Vehu Yeli Sit Elem Mahash Lelah Acha Kahet Hezi*
> *Elad Lav Hahah Yezel Mebah Hari Hakem Lav*
> *Keli Lov Pahal Nelach Yeyay Melah Chaho Netah*
> *Ha'ah Yeret Sha'ah Riyi Om Lekav Vesher Yichu*
> *L'hach Kevek Menad Ani Cha'am Reho Yeyiz*
> *Hahah Mich Veval Yelah Se'al Ari Eshal Mih Vehu*
> *Dani Hachash Omem Nena Nit Mivah Poi Nemem*
> *Yeyil Harach Metzer Umab Yahah Anu Machi*
> *Dameb Menak Iya Chavu Ra'ah Yabam Hayi Mum*

9. Approach the table/altar on which your "*Petzgakotim* Letter Square" is located. You will need to connect with this item by establishing "lines of force" between yourself and the "*Petzgakotim* Square." As delineated elsewhere,[180] the practice is as follows. Select the following bodily zones individually in the exact listed order:

   a. Forehead
   b. Throat
   c. Heart
   d. Navel
   e. Sexual organ

   Having selected the specific physical locale, turn your attention to your "Nil Centre." On inhalation imagine you are drawing "Divine Spiritual Force" in the form of golden light into the chosen locale inside your body, e.g. the forehead. Focus your attention on the *Petzgakotim Kamea*, and, whilst whispering "*OO*" during exhalation, sense the golden light flow from the selected physical locale (forehead), linking like a laser beam with the centre of the *Petzgakotim* amulet. As noted elsewhere, it is not particularly important to visualise this force thread, "since it happens automatically anyway when you look at something. You are only doing it consciously and strengthening the bond."[181] Repeat this procedure with all five physical zones, thus establishing five lines of "Spiritual Force" with the central seal (sigil) of the "*Petzgakotim Letter Square*."

10. Having established the said five lines of "Spiritual Force" between yourself and the *Kamea*, raise your hands and point your fingers at the object. Ensure that you point your hands and fingers towards the object in a relax manner, and in the manner employed with the listed five bodily zones, direct "lines of force" from your fingers or hands, linking them again to the centre of the amulet. You might have to repeat this action several times to get the full sense of being connected to the item in question.

11. Turning your attention back to your "Nil Centre," identify intensely with the "Element of Water." This is achieved in the manner delineated elsewhere, in which you envision the said Element as a deep cool blue pond or blue mist inside the "Nil Centre." As noted elsewhere, smile warmly at the Element, "feeling your *Ruchaniyut*, Spiritual Force, linking with the Element. Keep focussing on the image of the Element of Water, and sense the specific qualities associated with it,"[182] i.e. the flowing qualities of coolness and Love. As noted elsewhere, "what you should allow to happen, is the sense of being absorbed into, or turning into, the image and quality of that Element."[183]

12. Whilst still smiling warmly inside yourself, focus on the *Petzgakotim* seal (sigil) in the centre of the *Kamea*. Then, during successive inhalations, draw the image and qualities of the Watery Element into your body, and during exhalation, whilst whispering intensely the name "*Petzgakotim*," forcefully push the "elemental force" along all the "lines of force" established between yourself and the amulet, sensing it flowing into the centre of the *Kamea*. Repeat this action as many times as you feel necessary, until you sense the object is fully "charged" with the Element.

13. With the "*Petzgakotim* Letter Square" turned into a fully charged "power object," the next step would be to "internalise" it. Keep smiling warmly, and look unblinkingly for around a minute or two at the *chotam* (seal/sigil) in the centre of the amulet, doing so in a relaxed manner. As noted elsewhere, this is sometimes called the "soft look," in which you employ "a sort of soft stare in which you perceive the full image in absolute detail with

your eyes focussed on the centre."[184] When ready, inhale and imagine you are absorbing the complete image of the *Kamea* into your head, close your eyes and perceive the afterimage of the object inside your head for a couple of seconds, before letting the image fall or sink into the blackness of your "Nil Centre" as you whisper *Petzgakotim* during exhalation. In this manner you "internalise" the amulet, and connect it with the "Infinite Oneness." Perform this action three or seven times.

14. Conclude the procedure by keeping your eyes closed and invoking in your own inner being the presence of the "Spirit Force" acting through the *Kamea*, as you utter the following Hebrew adjuration:

a. Pronounce with a deep, strong and resonant voice:

פצגכתם אני משביעך בגוף

Transliteration/Translation:
> *Petzgakotim, ani mashbi'acha ba-guf*
> ("*Petzgakotim*, I invoke you in the Body").

Feeling the whole body resonate with the sound, chant:

*PETZ–GAH–KOH–TEEMMMMM*

Pause and feel the "Presence" inside your body. This is a "feeling appreciation" in which no visualisation is necessary.

b. As before, say aloud:

פצגכתם אני משביעך בנפש

Transliteration/Translation:
> *Petzgakotim, ani mashbi'acha ba-Nefesh*
> ("*Petzgakotim*, I invoke you in the *Nefesh*").

With attention focussed on your solar plexus (liver), which in old Kabbalistic teaching is the locale of the Instinctual Self [*Nefesh*], whisper intensely:

*PETZ–GAH–KOH–TEEMMMMM*

Pause and feel the "Presence" inside your very gut.

c. As before, say aloud:

פצגכותם אני משביעך ברוח

Transliteration/Translation:
> *Petzgakotim, ani mashbi'acha ba-Ruach—*
> ("*Petzgakotim*, I invoke you in the *Ruach*).

With attention focussed on the heart, the locale of the "Awake Self" [*Ruach*], exhale from your mouth without verbalising anything, as you think in your heart:

PETZ–GAH–KOH–TEEMMMMM

Pause and feel the "Presence" inside your heart.
d. As before, say aloud:

פצגכותם אני משביעך בנשמה

Transliteration/Translation:
> *Petzgakotim, ani mashbi'acha ba-Neshamah*
> ("*Petzgakotim*, I invoke you in the *Neshamah*").

In total silence and in perfect peace, think above the eyes inside the forehead:

PETZ–GAH–KOH–TEEMMMMM

Pause and feel yourself being "*Petzgakotim*." Do absolutely nothing, but simply *be* "*Petzgakotim*."
e. Conclude the adjuration with the standard formula:

ברוך שם כבוד מלכותו לעולם ועד אמן

Transliteration:
> *Baruch Shem K'vod Malchuto l'Olam Va'ed Omein*

Translation:
> Blessed be the Name of His glorious Kingdom throughout eternity *Amen*.

The pause between the fourth adjuration and the concluding statement is extremely important. You are "*Petzgakotim*." You *are* the magic that you are working. This is the point where the "magician" and the "magic" are

"One." If the practitioner can achieve the realisation that this specialised "form of force," which was created from the Fire, Air and Water elements, is in fact him or herself, the magic is done and the end result a *fait accompli!* Do not forget to remove the "*Petzgakotim Kamea*" from the table top at the conclusion of the ritual, and to carry it on your person, e.g. inside your pocket, wallet, handbag, etc. You only need to quickly think or whisper the concluding adjuration every now and again, in order to re-invoke and re-empower the "spirit force" acting through this unique *Kamea*.

In conclusion, as you have probably noticed, a variety of planetary "God Forces" were brought into play in the current ritual, i.e. emotional qualities associated with Venus, the Moon, Jupiter and the Sun. However, it is generally understood that, since the so-called "Seven Planets" are respectively affiliated with fairly definite emotional qualities, i.e. "God Forces," one can really only invoke the inherent forces of a single "planet" at a time. The idea is that your emotional stance should be in alignment with the "spirit forces" you are employing or invoking in a magical action. In this regard, we are instructed to work with the "Spirit Intelligences," *chotamot* (magical seals), and "planetary square" of one planet at a time, doing so in harmony with an associated "God Force" or emotional quality within yourself.

However, kabbalistic teaching maintains that your manifested existence comprises different "Levels of Being." As noted, you are an "Awake Self" (*Ru'ach*), which acts in life in conjunction with an "Instinctual Self" (*Nefesh*), as well as the physical body (*Guf*), these being the major components of human existence. Due to the positioning of the planets, astrologically speaking, the physical body may be under a specific planetary influence at a specific time, which would impact your physical anatomy in some or other perceived fixed manner. In this regard, one could consciously elect to align the "Lower Self" (*Nefesh*) with a planetary "God Force" (emotional quality), which is quite different from the "Spirit Force" of the "Planet" which may be impacting the physical body at any specific time. Furthermore, the "planetary position," so to speak, of the "Middle Self" (*Ru'ach*) could equally be personally established by opening one of the Sefirotic "Gates," or even by affirming, as it were, a default "Spirit Force" for the "Awake Self."

In this manner, each of the different aspects of "manifested Being," i.e. the body (*Guf*), the "Instinctual/Feeling Self" (*Nefesh*), and the "Awake/Thinking Self" (*Ru'ach*), could be aligned with different "Planetary" aspects. For example, it is perfectly possible to maintain the centralised and harmonious "Solar" position of *Tiferet* (Beauty) in the "Awake Self," whilst invoking within the *Nefesh* (Lower Self) the "God Force" of "thankfulness" or a "feeling appreciation," i.e. a quality of *Nogah* (Venus) aligned with *Netzach* (Victory), and then focussing mentally on the "planetary seal" of *Kochav* (Mercury) which is affiliated with *Hod* (Splendour). After all, there are the so-called *Tzinorot* ("Channels" or "Paths") on the sefirotic Tree, these being the interactive possibilities between the mentioned *sefirot*, which can be readily employed on a number of levels in terms of their respective planetary "God Force" affiliations.

**. ... ... ...But the angel of God who shapes the new day from the shining net has to be created anew each time. His head, body, arms and legs come only from the good deeds of men; but evil deeds destroy him... ... ... .**

# Chapter 9
## *Or Ganuz* — Light Concealed
## INITIATION: MYSTICAL REBIRTH

### A. Introduction

In the previous chapter I addressed the five senses in terms of their affinity with the five fingers of the human hand, and it is worth noting that in many magical traditions the five senses are brought into play in magical activity. However, the sense of touch appears to be somewhat neglected in magical studies. Being psychodramas, most magical rituals depend upon sensual representation for their efficacy. All of their sense-elements are "magical" because they are unfamiliar and therefore "alerting." In this regard consider for example a magical Temple or "Sacred Space." You have a sense of "impact" immediately on entering the premises, i.e. the *sight* of all the symbols, colours and patterns; the *sound* of the music and chanting, or possibly more impressive, the silence and sense of "Presence"; the *smell*, which couples with *taste*, of the incense. Now then, where does *touch* come in? For those who follows the magical procedures of the Western Inner Tradition, there is of course the experience of wearing a gown-robe with a girdle and possibly a hood, and officiants will handle solid symbols at intervals, but it occurs to me that touch is the most neglected sense of all, and yet it is the most basic and primal of all our senses.[1]

It is certainly the first sense we develop while still in the womb, followed by hearing during gestation. After "quickening" babies will respond to external sounds, and the unborn's reaction to music has been documented.[2] Taste and smell are probably developed during the pre-birth period to some extent, and sight is actually the last sense to appear, which most babies take some time to focus and learn how to use. Touch is undoubtedly the first sense to arrive and the last to go. So, how does it fit in with magical rituals, and why is this not studied more and coordinated with greater care? My late mentor, William G. Gray, addressed the sense of touch to some extent in his writings, but there has not really been any detailed study on this subject.[3] In Judaism we might consider the touch sense being dealt with ritualistically in terms of the *Tallit* (Prayer Shawl) and *Tefillin* (Phylacteries),[4] even though this is not the primary intention in terms of the use of these items. As it is, the sense of touch features especially prominently in the "hand/face-magic" which I addressed in the previous chapter. These examples notwithstanding, my feeling is that the "touch sense" in ritual has been mostly overlooked, and insufficiently covered by most of the ritualistic writers. To leave out the touch-sense altogether would be absurd, but it needs coordinating and a good deal of careful study.

I suppose it has been dealt with to some extent in past times, but definitely not very well. Ceremonial scourging and cutting of the flesh feature prominently in the "Rites of Passage"[5] of some tribal societies around the globe, and ritual scourging, as introduced by Gerald Gardner,[6] also appears to have become popular in the ranks of certain modern "Witch" and pagan movements, but the action has become in some cases symbolical rather than actual.[7] Such activities are said to be carefully calculated to sharpen attention, like the ceremonial whack on the back by a Zen Roshi during Zazen sitting.[8] At the other end of the scale there is ceremonial sex,[9] the most intimate practice of all, which is about the closest an ordinary human comes to "ecstasy" by a touch-practice, but abuse and reprehensible practices by those who join sex cults and pagan groups mainly for any spare sex they can get, has led to social ignominy.[10]

Whilst a state of "sexual ecstasy" for most humans would be the highest peak experience they can ever achieve whilst embodied, there are "in-between" touch-needs as well. This is where the study of ritual "encasement," clothing and artifacts worn as a ritualistic stimulus comes in. For example, there is the theory of Wilhelm Reich, that Life, or "God" under another name, is constantly in a state of orgasm. This was said to create a "fluid" in space which, as the source of life, could heal all diseases and virtually do anything provided you could harness it.[11] This idea is in fact quite old. Paracelcus termed it *Azoth*,[12] combining the first and last letters of the alphabet, Mesmer named it "*Animal Magnetism*,"[13] his pupil, Baron von Reichenbach, called it "*Od*,"[14]

Wilhelm Reich titled it "*Orgone*," connecting it with "Orgasm," and Kabbalists call it "*Avir*" or "*Ruchaniyyut*." It is curious that all the listed men were German. Reich was a Freudian[15] who launched out on his own with his "bionics," which he claimed had cured cancer and caused rain. He was an Austrian Jew who settled in New York in 1939, where he founded the Orgone Institute and did well out of his "Orgonomy."[16] He started a little farm-commune which he called "Organon," and also practised as a psychiatrist which was his main source of income.

Israel Regardie, the well-known occultist, was a Reichian therapist and thought the world of Wilhelm Reich.[17] Reich was a non-practising Jew who could not have cared a curse about any "Inner Tradition," what to say the Jewish Kabbalah, and he apparently disliked mysticism of any kind. Having been one of Sigmund Freud's pupils, it was said of him that he carried on where Freud left off. He had an interest which was somewhat uncommon at that period, and that was an entirely open attitude to sex. He claimed it should be freely "discussable," taken as natural and normal, and that sexual repressions and prurience were responsible for about half the evils on earth. He saw this from a psychiatrist's viewpoint. He then became absorbed in his "orgonics," his boxes which he called "accumulators," and his "bions" which he claimed were the "Life-force" in action. He believed he could harness the "Life-fluid," and his chief invention was the "orgone accumulator," which was nothing more than a largish cabinet, just big enough for an average adult to sit in upright. The inside was lined with metal (inorganic), while the outside was wood (organic), and between the two was a packing of sawdust, paper, asbestos, wool, or some such material. All you had to do was simply sit inside the cabinet naked for about two periods of half an hour a day.

Strictly speaking Reich, who was technically an atheist, worked on the "God is Love" principle. He was taking this quite literally and trying to convert it into physical, mechanical terms. The theory is interesting, though I do wonder if the practice was of the slightest use, except for the faith-factor it evoked from people. I am also not sure whether there was anything in the "Orgone Box" idea in principle, but believe it would bear investigating or experimenting with in an up-to-date way. Reich started making and marketing his boxes in the USA shortly after the war, and fell foul of the Federal Food, Drugs and Cosmetics Act. The whole thing turned into a very expensive lawsuit, and he got a two year sentence, plus his unsold boxes confiscated and destroyed.[18] After a few months in prison he had a massive heart-attack and died.

Now I believe Reich was sincere, but barking hopelessly up the wrong tree while pointing to the right one without realising what he was doing. To my mind his "boxes" do smack a bit of "pyramidology," which consists amongst other things of sitting or squatting and meditating under a plain pyramidal frame about six feet high. All sorts of claims are made for this practice, and it just seems to be the shape itself which is important. The frame is often of wooden rods fitted together with metal or plastic joints.[19] Extraordinary what people will think of, but what interests me is the motivation behind it. In every case, it is a human being looking outside the area of their bodies for some reflecting agent, to bring out from inside themselves whatever is likely to help them with their life-problems, and I believe this to be a very important factor which needs recognition and examination. On the surface it works something like this.

Humans are conscious of some inadequacy, necessity, insufficiency, or a specific quality they do not have within themselves but which they desire most ardently. Let us call this the *"N"-Factor* for *"Need."* This sets them searching or *"Questing"* (*"Q"-Factor*) for whatever. The *"O"-Factor* is for the *"Objective"* which, if they can bring it within the range of their experience, or is offered from other sources, will then become the *"A"* for *"Attainment"-Factor*. Thus we have the formula:

$$\frac{N}{Q} + O = A$$

Of course, this does not mean that *"Need"* and the *"Quest"* by themselves will produce the *"Objective,"* but only an effort to reach it. The *"Objective"* has to be *added*. From where? That is the *"X"-Factor*. Call it "God" if you like. So:

$$\frac{N+X}{Q} = OA$$

Boiled down to basics this means that in our need to *be ourselves* we search for specific objectives, which only "God" can supply via whatever channels are open or may be available.

Most people will admit that they cannot be conscious of God in the sense we are aware of say a table or any material thing, but that they can be conscious of God's effects, or phenomena pointing to Its Existence, with which they themselves may react. In other words "Indicators of Infinite Identity." Reflectors of "the Light." Everything depends on how suitable these may be for such a purpose, because that is such a variant factor that it can scarcely be classified. For example we use Temples on this Earth for "encountering God," purely because they have been laid out and arranged with special symbolism intended for that purpose alone: to "meet God reflectively." Theoretically we should be able to do this in any environment, some admittedly better than others, or should we say more suitable.

Thus one wonders if the "Orgone Boxes" were in reality a kind of "mini Temple," which, by compressing the electro-magnetic and natural "force-fields" around a person, brought them in closer and more direct contact with the "Source" of their life-energy. I have been told that this is equally the result of wearing a chain-mail suit of armour, i.e. there is an actual effect on the one wearing it. After all, the medieaval Knights factually wore leather, or woollen suits (organic material), with flexible metal (inorganic) over them. They were literally wearing "Orgone Boxes" for hours on end, except of course that Reich reversed the order with the metal on the inside, but in my estimation the principle is there all the same. A live body radiates electronic energy which is subject to natural laws, e.g. metal conducts while dielectrics such as silk, leather, etc., are non-conductive, or at best highly resistant. The metal lining to the box would have the effect of distributing the electronic energy equally over its entire surface, while the wooden cover would act as a non-conductor, providing it was dry.

To some extent, it is vaguely reminiscent of the biblical "Ark of the Covenant," which was, after all, a plain box which was a primitive electrical condenser on account of the pitch lining and the metallic exterior, as well as the metallic "*Cherubim* Angels" on the cover. In theory Reich's box was little more than that, or perhaps more of a "Faraday Cage" for isolating someone from ambient electro-magnetic effects. In Rosicrucian/Masonic systems initiates employed what is called a "*Pastos*" (literally "bridal bed"), a sort of closeable coffin in which the "Master" lay for indefinite periods.[20] To my mind the "*Pastos*" was an early form of the Orgone Box. Referring to the "death-rebirth" form of Initiation, my late Mentor, William G. Gray, wrote:

"For any human being to achieve a spiritual state of existence, enabling it to appreciate and deal with Inner energies as the actualities of Life they really are, it needs to undergo some soul-changing experience, completely altering its essential nature into compatible characteristics. In other words we have to experience hell in order to handle heaven. Humans have to be subjected to traumatic experiences, which are sufficiently strong enough to alter their essential selves into entirely different types of being, before they become able to deal with what might be called Divine conditions of consciousness on a direct relationship.

This was well-known in olden days, when mystics would be put through an arranged series of experiences, calculated to cause such changes in normal souls, and culminate in what was known as 'enlightenment,' because the soul would live in a condition wherein everything seemed to consist of sheer light-energy. Such a process was known as 'initiation' and could be drastic in the extreme, sometimes resulting in death due to the severity of the ordeal undergone. One of the most stringent was literal burial for at least three days, during which the human concerned would be plunged into the hell of himself, afterwards emerging either the victor over, or the vanquished by such an experience."[21]

The Tomb/Womb in the Earth Mother is one of the oldest known initiatory practices. Technique varies here and there, but the same fundamentals apply. Nowadays it is worked in laboratories by suspension in a tank of water at body heat to minimise weight, and is known as "sensory deprivation."[22] It is interesting that nearly all the old methods are being translated into modern psychological terms of investigating human consciousness. Even the old "witches cradle" is used now in the form of a steel body-harness, rotatable in any plane at different speeds.[23] Originally it was something like a net into which the body was gathered, and the whole lot suspended by a rope, sometimes over a smoking fire burning hallucinogenic herbs. Now they just administer these orally by means of pills or injections.[24]

Of course, as you probably know well enough, the spiritual "death-rebirth" idea is not the exclusive property of esotericists at all. We all know the Christian "reborn" claims, especially as proclaimed by the charismatic "Evangelical Christian" movement,[25] though I dare say their modern day "baptism" hardly equates with the same as practiced in ancient days. There is also still a faint trace of the "death-revival" theme in the full consecration of a Roman Catholic Priest. Clad in a simple alb (a white robe), the candidate lies prostrate on the steps of the altar and is covered completely by a black pall or coffin cover. The consecrating bishop then recites the formula that so and so had died to the ordinary world, and looks for resurrection in Christ. Then he calls the priest by his new religious name, and bids him like Lazarus to come forth. The pall is removed by its four corners, and the priest arises and gives thanks and praise to God. On the other hand, the Christian Initiation known as the "Confirmation Service" is now absolutely dull, uninspiring and, according to my Christian friends, easily forgotten.

This Initiation theme is a "back to the womb" impulse.[26] In this regard, the "Mystical Rebirth" theme applied with the "Mystical Marriage," which has to occur before and after a "rebirth" or "waking up," is a very real and recurring idea both in Jewish Mysticism and the Western Mystery Tradition.[27] This is where the "soul-mate" theory of one's "other half," or matching soul of opposite sex, and all the rest of it also come in. One's real "other half" is factually ones own opposite polarity, or the female side of males and the male side of females. In other words the Jungian *Anima* and *Animus*.[28] The "Mystical Marriage" is in fact a perfect mating match between the male and female side of the same soul, if one could imagine such a thing. After all, it is only doing in miniature what *Life* itself is supposed to do at the end of Time, and was supposed to have done at the very beginning.

To understand this is not very difficult when one looks at our lives in general. We commence physical life as a fertilised egg which is eventually expelled from a maternal body, and has to live on its own, adapting to external environments, which are not nearly so convenient or comfortable. As someone said a long way back, a man spends the first few moments of his life crawling out of a hole, and the rest of his life trying to get back into it. I do not know how that translates for a woman, but the crudity is apt as crudities often are, since that is exactly what we do. Spiritually we do the same thing. Having "emerged" from "God" into this world, we are trying to get back into "*IT*." It is just the return half of the ticket so to speak. Just a natural instinct out of which every religion, and religious custom known to man, developed through the ages. All our philosophies, all our science, and all our culture stem from that one single source.

Be that as it may, "Initiation" is such a misunderstood practice. If we look at the history of the practice, we notice that in ancient times it required candidates to be tested to the very limits of their capacities for bearing stresses of mind and body.[29] The reason was to fetch their very deepest "Inner" abilities, raising them to the focal points of their awareness, thus revealing their potentials not only to their Initiator, but also themselves. They had to face tempests (water and air), as well as deserts and forest fires (fire and earth). They also had to cope with and survive the spiritual equivalents of such conditions. Today we do something of this nature on "survival courses," though with some help from modern equipment.[30] It is all part of a process to condition human consciousness along lines leading to a higher than normal human state of existence. Now, the "Mystical Rebirth" is similar to the "double birth" of some people, including my own some years back, which, though rarely recognised, is not unique at all. It is a very intense form of "Initiation into Life," so to speak, which usually happens after "near-death" conditions, or a very serious illness from which a "miraculous" recovery is made.[31] Sometimes a very severe shock will trigger it. That is why old-time initiations employed such drastic shock treatments in trying to awaken latent spirituality in candidates, all of which were useless unless the subject was first very carefully primed and prepared through a long course of conditioning. In other words, everything had to be exactly right for that one moment, and sometimes this took years.

As might be expected, some of these "initiation ideas" did survive into modern times like the "Water Initiation," or earlier mentioned "Baptism,"[32] to which I do not attach much importance, unless carried out in the original way, all conditions having been met. Even so, this is only valuable in a percentage of cases as an initiatory exercise. In old times, baptism was the culmination of a probationary period marked by fasting, prayer, meditation, and other psycho-physical stress exercises which might go on for weeks. The candidate was ducked under water forcibly and held till almost at last gasp. Then pulled upright by his Initiator who "breathed" his "New Name" into one ear from behind. A second ducking followed, with Name breathed into other ear. Then a third and last time with Name given into both ears. It was an unforgettable experience. The only groups I know of who still practice baptism in a similar manner, are some of the African Christian movements who nearly drown their members to ensure that their sins are "properly washed away."

I once witnessed such a baptism ceremony which was executed in a river in South Africa by a priest who was very thorough at his job. He held the candidate under water until bubbles started surfacing. The poor man frenziedly tried to escape, and was swimming as fast he could towards the riverbank, with a very grim and determined priest fast at his heels. The priest eventually captured the man and, for good measure, held him under water somewhat longer than I presume was customary, meaning the candidate almost drowned. Generally however, initiations are not what they used to be, though what we live through today as normal life, would terrify some of the ancients out of their wits. They would certainly think themselves in Hell.

The Water Initiation method through ducking adults is of course standard Pentecostal Christian practice, and is also standard in Greek and Russian Orthodox Churches, except that in these movements it is usually done when a person is still a baby. The priests are expert in cupping the nose and mouth of the child for a few seconds while they dip them naked into a large basin of tepid water. In early days baptism was done in rivers, much as some do now, and as described with John the Baptist in the Christian Bible, the idea was to free the soul from past sins, which would be washed away by the river. Very religious Jews still have the ceremony of *Tashlich*, i.e. "casting their sins on the waters" once a year by shaking the ends of their garments over running water,[33] just as Hindus believe the Ganges washes away the sins of the bathers and carries them out to sea.[34]

Another initiatory process which in earlier times had to be survived, was the alternative way of absorbing "Inner Tradition" directly from nature itself by solitary contemplative reaction with direct environment, as the old hermits used to do. The danger here is mental imbalance interfering with the process. If balance can be maintained, remarkable results can be gained in this way, though only by exceptionally strong and capable souls operating for limited periods. My late mentor, William G. Gray, once shared with me his recollections of what it felt like in the Egyptian desert far away from all human contact. He noted that the "Presence" felt so close and alive, but stated that he did not find Bedouins, who live almost permanently in the desert, to be particularly spiritual people. In his estimation, they simply take God for granted and hope He has something good to offer them in another life of Heavenly luxury. In this regard, he noted that their only "luxury" on Earth is dreaming, and that they were particularly good at that.

An initiation practice called "Fire Initiation," "Practising the Presence," *Latihan*, etc., has gained some attention amongst some followers of the Western Inner Tradition. This is all good and well, provided it is realised that this is only a step to something higher. This kind of "opening" and practice of submission to a pure flow of Energy/Power perceived to be of Divine origin, features particularly prominently in "*Subud*," where it is termed *Latihan*.[35] The idea got some popularity a while back, but following studies of some time later, showed up poor results in terms of mental instability and psychic unbalance among a marked percentage of followers, and so the movement in general developed a doubtful reputation.[36] It is one of those things which work quite well when handled carefully, and given to a few when they are absolutely ready, but it is not recommended for indiscriminate practice. I did undergo the "opening" of *Subud* around thirty years ago, and encountered *Latihan* in a most direct manner, which was certainly a most amazing and unforgettable experience. Yet I later found that the continuing practice of *Latihan* in the *Subud* sense became a kind of, as it were, spiritual masturbation. People were getting their "emotional rocks off" so to speak, and thereby ridding themselves of a lot of psychic stress. The procedure termed "*Practicing the Presence*," which I addressed in "*The Book of Self Creation*,"[37] is equally a way of allowing the automatic flow of pure "Conscious Energy" from "Inner Sources" by itself, through a similar process of total surrender. The difference between the two practices is that "*Practicing the Presence*" is not an end in itself, whereas *Latihan* is considered such.

This reminds me of an initiation practice called the "*Initiation of the Rod*." It is one of five initiations respectively offered to the "*Officers of the Quarters*" in Sangreal Sodality Temples, i.e. the "*Officer of the Sword*" located in the East, associated with the "Element of Air," and aligned with the Archangel רפאל (*Rafa'el*); the "*Officer of the Rod*" located in the South [North in the Southern Hemisphere], associated with the "Element of Fire," and affiliated with the Archangel מיכאל (*Micha'el*); the "*Officer of the Cup*" located in the West, associated with the "Element of Water," and aligned with the Archangel גבריאל (*Gavri'el*); the "Officer of the Shield" located in the North [South in the Southern Hemisphere], associated with the "Element of Earth," and conjoined with the Archangel אוריאל *Ori'el*); and lastly the "*Officer of the Cord*," who has no fixed position in the Temple, is associated with *Avir*, the Universal Element, and affiliated with the Archangel סובביאל (*Sov'vi'el* [*Sababiel*, *Savaviel* or *Suvuviel* according to William G. Gray]).[38]

Considering the fact that much of these "initiatory systems" incorporate Hebrew terms, i.e. Hebrew Divine and Angelic Names, and kabbalistic concepts, it might be presumed that initiatory practices are fundamental to Jewish esotericism. However, in Jewish Magic there are currently no special initiations, or anything pertaining to the grade initiations aligned with the ten *sefirot*, as employed in the modern Hermetic Orders, in order to become a competent practitioner of *Practical Kabbalah*. In my estimation, the only requirement is personal capacity to work any of the techniques shared in a capable manner, e.g. *Kavannah* (Focused Intention/attitude), capability, acting with the strength of a firm faith in yourself, etc.

That being said, an acquaintance reminded me that the Kabbalistic ritual of a master passing on the Ineffable Name to his disciple whilst facing a body of running water, as delineated by Eleazar of Worms,[39] is in fact an "initiation" practice. After all, this procedure has been noted to be "one of the most important rituals preserved in our sources concerning the way to pass on a secret tradition,"[40] and Gershom Scholem called it a "rite of initation in the strictest sense."[41] Elements of it align with the baptism practices addressed earlier. In this regard, Elliot R. Wolfson's translation of the relevant section from the writings of Eleazar of Worms reads:

"YHWH—His unique, glorious, and awesome name. We will explain its meaning according to the capacity to speak and to know about the glory of the supernal name of the Lord and His fear.....The [name] is transmitted only to the meek ('the reserved' according to Scholem, who maintained the Hebrew term might also be translated 'the initiate'), who do not get angry, and to the God-fearing, who perform the commandments of their Creator. It is transmitted only over water, as it is written, 'The voice of the Lord is over the waters' (Ps. 29:3). Before the master teaches his disciples they should bathe in water and immerse themselves in [the ritual bath that measures] forty *se'ah* (the traditional measure of a *Mikveh*). They should don white clothes and fast on the day he will teach them [the name], and they should stand in the water up to their ankles. Then the master opens his mouth in fear and says: 'Blessed are You, O Lord, our God, king of the universe, Lord, God of Israel, You are one and Your name is one, and You have commanded us to conceal Your great name, for Your name is awesome, Blessed are You, Lord, who reveals His secret to those who fear Him, the One who knows all secrets. The master and his disciples should look at the water and say, 'The ocean sounds, O Lord, the ocean sounds its thunder, the ocean sounds its pounding, more majestic than the breakers of the sea is the Lord, majestic on high' (Ps. 93:3–4). 'The voice of the Lord is over the waters, the God of glory thunders, the Lord, over the mighty waters (Ps. 29:3). 'The waters saw You, O God, the waters saw You and were convulsed; the very deep quaked as well' (Ps. 77:17). 'Your way was through the sea, Your path, through the mighty waters; Your tracks could not be seen' (Ibid., 20). Afterwards they should go near the water or to a synagogue or study-house where there is water in a pure vessel, and the master should say: Blessed are you, Lord, our God, king of the universe, who has sanctified us with his commandments and commanded us and separated us from the nations, and revealed to us His secrets and instructed us in the knowledge of His great and awesome name."[42]

It would seem that there was quite a tradition regarding certain Divine Names being enunciated over water.[43] In this regard I referenced in "*The Book of Self Creation*"[44] a practice in which the practitioner has to prepare a "mantle of righteousness," which is a special garment (*Malbush*).[45] Then, after a period of physical and spiritual preparation, the practitioner has to enter a body of water and utter a Divine Name over the water. The effectiveness of this "initiation" procedure, was to determine the readiness of the practitioner for higher work, which was indicated by the resultant colours appearing above the waters following the uttering of the Divine Name. This procedure has been correctly delineated by my mentioned acquaintance, who also translated the primary Hebrew text into English,[46] to be "more of a self initiation."

Whilst these techniques of uttering Divine Names over a body of water are correctly interpreted "initiations," they do not quite fit the current understanding of "initiation" as interpreted, for example, by contemporary Hermetic Orders. I believe the fundamental problem pertains to the actual meaning of the term "initiation," since it is made to mean a variety of things, some of it quite fantastic, whereas it basically means "introduction." For example, William G. Gray, my late mentor, passed on to me what he knew of the tradition we share. However, that did not involve a formal "Initiation" *per se*, but when he tried to awaken within me, or fetch out of me, certain qualities of character, or certain spiritual abilities, so to speak, he worked a number of "initiations" to stir, start, initiate, or "awaken" that which was potentially within me. In this regard, "initiation" was the beginning with further unfolding or development being entirely in my own hands. That is the problem with teaching anything actually. We think we bring advancement to individuals by putting something, i.e. knowledge, *into* them, whereas true "initiation," so to speak, would really be when we fetch something meaningful, i.e. knowledge, *out* of them.

As can be expected, there is an enormous tradition globally surrounding the concept of "Initiation," e.g. the earlier mentioned "baptism" or "water initiation," etc., or a variety of "Rites of Passage" amongst different communities around the world, like the Jewish *Brit Milah* (Covenant of Circumcision),[47] etc. Whilst this practice often generates some truly heated debates all round, it should be noted that it is a very serious initiatory practice which still survives as a "Rite of Passage" practised not only by Jews, but by many other nations and communities around the globe.[48] Those who consider the practice barbaric, might be further shocked to learn that, as symbol of regeneration or freeing the glans from its grave, some societies performs subincision along a portion of the urethra tract, this being viewed as a rebirth in the same way as the snake sloughing its skin.[49] Be that as it may, amongst the majority of races practising circumcision, it is customarily performed as part of a "Rite of Passage" during which the boy is initiated into manhood. In this instance circumcision, in which the penis is released from the protective foreskin, is symbolic of the cutting away of the boy from the mother and the subsequent release into the secret traditions and realms of the male.

Now, most "occult initiations" in Western esoteric groups are pretty similar, but the "degree" initiations vary greatly. I personally do not believe in them much except for recognition. They were previously celebrations that some soul had reached specific stages of realisation, which marked him or her out from the rest of the crowd. The trouble was that such degrees could only be celebrated by those who had reached these levels themselves, which left very few indeed capable of administering them. Besides, I am not sure if the whole of the so-called "initiatory structure" of the Mysteries is not hopelessly out of date altogether, and totally meaningless in the light of modern history. William Gray told me that the older he got, the more dissatisfied he became with all that had gone before. Ceremonies were kept up for lack of something better, but the thing is that if we really demand something better, we shall have to supply it ourselves or do without. It is for that reason that he was constantly reviewing some of the Rites, and started to demand more and more intensity during initiations. For example, we currently work the Inner Court Initiations of our Sangreal Sodality Temple in Johannesburg with the Candidates in "open states," which means that prior to the start of the initiation rite, their consciousness is expanded beyond the limits of the body. This ensures that they would encounter every aspect of the initiation with maximum intensity. As the degree of being in an "open" state varies from one individual to the next, it is virtually impossible to guarantee that a Candidate will have the fullest experience on all levels, i.e. body, mind, soul and spirit, during the initiation.

It is however most important that Initiators should explain to candidates all the responsibilities and obligations Initiation entails, and how it does *not* immediately give them all sorts of supernatural powers they are not entitled to. Nobody should ever accept initiation blindly or mistakenly, thinking it is some wonderful thing which will suddenly be able to solve all problems, or have all personal troubles taken care of by powerful Angels or subservient spirits. Never suppose there will be a "live happily ever after" once an initiation ceremony is over. An initiation is a *beginning*. No more. The ending lies entirely in the hands of the newly initiated, and will not even be achieved in one lifetime. Most initiations are really reiterations of something that happened a long time ago in former births. They are "join-ups" of consciousness that broke off a long time back.

Never expect that initiation will suddenly create "Cosmic Consciousness" or any such thing, and yet I meet with that kind of thinking quite frequently. Especially in Western esotericism, in which many in their attempt to break into "Inner Areas," come up against their own "self barriers" with a bump as it were, and get shocked and surprised by the encounter. In point of fact, an experience of Inner realities is the last thing many might be able to handle. They hurt and man prefers to live in his phoney, Disney-like version of an occult never-never land, where all is just love and beautiful bliss. Man frequently, but often very late, discovers he is living on the surface of life. Sadly there is many a time the thought that if enough money is spent, he must get anything he wants, and God is thought to be "purchasable." Many modern religions do think this way, and strangely seem to have the same fundamental beliefs as the ancient Egyptians who had similar ideas. Heaven is for the rich, and simply a copy of luxurious Earth-Life. Gods could be purchased, and were bribable if enough priests were paid to "fix things." In the same way, many people appear to believe the dollar is an answer to everything in this world....and the next! Buy an expensive enough funeral, and a good place in Heaven is assured.

The final word in this introduction is that "initiation" is a practice designed to push candidates towards the point where they will wake up to whom and what they really are. "Waking Up" or "Becoming Aware" was Gurdjieff's constant cry,[50] but suppose too many people "woke up" all at once? The sudden shock would blow their minds away from any hope of stability. "No man may look upon God and live." Very true. God help Western, or any kind of man, who suddenly awakes unprepared to face the shock of him or herself in the "Mirror of Truth"! We dare only wake up at a safe rate in this "Mystical Marriage."

## B. Preparation

I am hoping to share certain techniques which, though not necessarily obligatory, I recommend as preparations for the successful working of this self initiation procedure. However, since initiation is part of a personal quest for "illumination," and that this is not a purely spiritual objective, but involves our very existence in this place in time and space, it is important to realise, as I have noted elsewhere, that as individuals "we are not an isolated islands, we are living in this world, and that the great work is the process of trying to make this world a better place for all life on this planet."[51] The Biblical allegory of Adam and Eve in the Garden of Eden explains it quite simply. God placed Adam in the Garden to *tend* it, and as each one of us is a cell in the body of the "Great Adam," so to speak, each one of us must contribute to the "tending" of this Outer Kingdom. In this regard, I noted that "to do this, one has to establish oneself as a partner of Divinity,"[52] and commence with the realisation that the world *can* be made a better place, even if the possible personal contribution appears to be minimal, and that it would take considerable effort over a long period of time to bring about a modicum of "rectification."

Each individual should understand that, in a way, every single one of us is the *Messiah*, so to speak, since all of us have the responsibility to act as the "saviours" of our "Selves" and our world. All of us have to work towards *Tikkun*, the restoration of ourselves and this manifested realm, to our original conjoined state of "wholeness." This is more important than the concept of the *Messiah* as a literal, political figure, who will come to instantly alter everything for the better for a specific group of people. There is a passage in the *Talmud* (*Avot D'Rabbi Natan*) which reads: "If you are holding a sapling in your hand, and someone tells you the Messiah has come, plant the sapling first, then go look for the Messiah."[53]

Again, as I noted previously, "Each person, not religious groups and teachers, has the responsibility to improve and better this world for all existing in it, and one should constantly remind oneself of this important task. That is in fact the real secret. We need to remind ourselves that we cannot be completely happy while the world around us is suffering, since however beautiful our 'worldly home' is, we are not '*at* home' because this home is unsatisfactory."[54] In this regard, I am reminded of the retort I received back in the 1970's, when I raised this issue with an individual who queried "but is everything not as it should be, is it not right and perfect in itself?" The said individual faced me with a very sweet, pious, sentimental countenance, insisting that every moment is exactly as it should be, and this at a time when forests were being destroyed by napalm—the "ultimate deodorant" one observer commented acerbically, and everything else was being consumed by conflagrations engendered by the scourge earth policies of politicians; buildings were collapsing, as they still do, on thousands of people because of man's inhumanity to man, for no more than "they are wrong and we are right," or "we are better than they" motivations; infants merely months old were being raped by individuals who were supposed to care for them, and the perpetrators felt absolutely nothing.....the list is endless!

I recall asking "What is the difference between a single individual suffering or thousands?" "What is the difference between a human being tortured or an animal having to endure the same?" "What is the difference between animals and trees being thoughtlessly attacked by those who claim to think for themselves?" In fact, as far as practitioners of ritual magic are concerned, I queried "What kind of magic requires you to knock rusty nails into the trunk of a tree?" In other words, I do not align with the thinking that "*this* is the lowest and *that* is the highest," "*this* is expendable and *that* must be preserved." Not a single one of the seemingly random situations I referred to is isolated from the other, since all existence is part of the "Selfsameness" of one "Great Consciousness" called "I AM." We have work to do, meaning that we do not necessarily have to only "rectify" what is wrong, but also to strengthen what is right. We have to counter balance evil by empowering that which makes our planet beautiful. In the Sangreal Sodality we might call it "The Quest for Best in the West," without specific reference to any particular group of people in a single locale on this planet.

The burden of responsibility towards the "restoration" of ourselves and our world, i.e. the restoration of "Divine Balance, belongs to all. Yet, this task cannot be enforced on all and sundry, since the betterment of this "Outer Kingdom" must be achieved in non-violent ways. I noted previously, that "we have to recognise 'spiritual democracy'," and that "what is important is *Kavvanah*, which we noted refers to focussed intention, attitude, motivation, and goals. Naturally, when we have to make decisions, it is difficult to predict the final outcome. Only after things have happened, can we know whether results were produced satisfactorily. Who can really know in advance the outcome of a violent act? We need to know how to deal with our conflicts, both individually and globally, in an imaginative and non-aggressive manner."[55]

In my estimation, "there can be no justification for violence, whether such be physical, mental, emotional or spiritual,"[56] and therefore I believe that the best we can do is "to make the Divine Presence so strong in our lives, that it goes beyond our human natures altogether. Hence, by bringing 'God Forces' into our lives, we intentionally and mindfully direct these into the world at large."[57] In this regard, we might follow the advice of my late Mentor, who suggested that we "Shun dangers by intuition."[58] It is in fact important that we learn to work more fully in the realm of intuition, which is thinking through identification. First identify with something, then think, i.e. allow yourself to be taught by what you are identifying with. *That* is what *IN*-tuition is all about.

Many readers would say that "intuition" also pertains to "inner guidance," i.e. a kind of instinctive understanding based on what I term a "feeling appreciation," and, from a spiritual perspective, a kind of automatic knowing free from the conscious mind. A variety of practices can be used to develop this, as it were, "inner sensitivity," and I have already shared several in these volumes on *Practical Kabbalah*. Amongst these I would especially reference the practices titled "*Invocation of Subtle Energy,*" *Practising the Presence: "Spontaneous Dance,"* and "*Exercising the Spirit Body,*"[59] which, when worked regularly, will unfold awareness and sensitivity to the flow of all manner of forces around you, especially those which impact your *Or Makif* (Surrounding Light). In this manner you, the "Awake One," employ your "inner circumference," i.e. "Energy Body," to interact with your "outer circumference." By further aligning with the latter, i.e. the ability is further empowered by consciously aligning yourself with the greater world around you on a direct energy level. Thus you can consciously direct the manner in which the "outer circumference" unfolds itself around you, and equally how it interacts with you. In this regard, the "*Rite of Noten Kavod (Giving Respect): A Doorway to Higher Consciousness,*" "*The Rite of Lekavven Tiferet: Acknowledging Beauty,*"[60] and, for want of a better title, the "*Yahadonahi Shadai*" procedure which I shared in the first part of "*The Book of Immediate Magic,*"[61] will facilitate this endeavour.

All these procedures necessitate that you approach your environment with a warm, friendly "inner smile." In all instances you would focus on a single or a collection of objects, whether they be mineral, vegetable, animal or human, in order to execute any of the three procedures. Whilst it is more common to work the first procedure with attention focussed on a specific object, the "*Yahadonahi Shadai*" procedure is commonly worked with the greater expanse of the world around you. After all, אדני (*Adonai*) is the Divine Name referencing *Malchut*, the greater "Kingdom" of manifestation, in which everything *is* in fact *Adonai*. You are *Adonai*, and I am *Adonai*. A tree is *Adonai*, and so is every stone. There is nothing which is not *Adonai*. In this regard, as noted previously, one way of working the "*Yahadonai Shadai*" procedure is to smile warmly, extend "your personal consciousness outwards as far as possible towards the furthest horizon. The 'Whole' is then embraced with the warmth of your smile, and the entirety of your surrounding circumference is imagined to be turning around you during inhalation, after which the Divine Name יאהדונהי (*Yahadonahi*) [or simply אדני (*Adonai*)] is uttered. This is followed by absorbing or drawing the 'Whole' into your heart during the succeeding inhalation, followed by the mental utterance of the Divine Name שדי (*Shadai*) in the heart during the pause prior to, or whispered during, the concluding exhalation."[62]

It is also important to consciously establish an affinity between yourself and your "Divine Self," which is in fact a conscious recognition of an alignment which is already there, i.e. the affiliation between that higher aspect of your "Self" within the אור ישר (*Or Yashar*—"Direct Light") and אור פנימי (*Or P'nimi* —"Inner Light"), the latter being the portion of "Divine Light" within yourself. In this regard, the practices titled "*Exercise in Absolute Reality*" and "*Mastering the Universal Element*," as well as "*Unification with the Higher Self*," "*The Breath of Light*," and "*The Amen Breath*."[63] are of great value. The first two routines pertain to merging with the potencies of the "Infinite Nothingness," and the latter three to establishing a relationship with your "Higher Self." In my estimation, these practices are important in reaching the required condition physically, mentally, emotionally and spiritually, which is necessary for the successful working of the self-initiation "*Rite of Rebirth*" I am sharing in this tome. I have addressed all of these practices in great detail elsewhere.[64] However, the first two procedures I discussed at the conclusion of the previous chapter in terms of applications in which a magical practice is enacted in a condition outside time and space, so to speak. Hence I will now revisit the latter three practices in terms of their value as preparatory practices to the forthcoming "Rite of Self Initiation."

The said procedures are adaptations of techniques originally shared in the so-called "*Armour of Light*" writings of Olive Charlotte Blythe Pixley.[65] In terms of the material shared here, these practices are:

### 1. UNIFICATION WITH THE HIGHER SELF

1. Work the following procedure on going to sleep at night and first thing on waking in the morning. Remain relaxed and surrendered inside your body, and turn the palms of

your hands to face upwards. Identify with Peace by surrendering to the feeling of what Peace represents. Utter the following "Words of Power" several times, sensing their meaning and how they impact on you:

### *Shefa shel Shalom v' Emet*
### Abundance of Peace and Truth

2. Repeat the word *Shalom*, "Peace," over and over, each time allowing yourself to "feel" the meaning of the word, and simultaneously surrendering deeply in order to allow it to permeate your entire being.
3. Next, think of a "Shining Being of Light" at your feet, with the soles of Its feet placed against your own.
4. Having established this special connection with the "Shining Being of Light, turn your attention to your forehead or the top of your head, and sense a "Channel of Light" linking you with your "Source," an "Infinite Point of 'Is'–ness," diagonally above you.
5. Having recognised your link with "Divine Power" via the two extremes of your body, i.e. feet and head, take a deep breath, and during inhalation draw the "Divine Force" as golden Light, from your "Infinite Source" down into your head. Continue by mentally directing the flow of this "Light" during the exhalation, by letting it flash like a blazing circle of golden light flowing from your right temple around and through the head of the Being of Light, and back into your head via your left temple, thus establishing a complete circle of "Divine Force" linking you with the shining figure of your *Neshamah*, your "Divine Self." In this manner your feet are dedicated to Divine Service, and open your head to Divine Inspiration.
6. Work this procedure rapidly three times.

## 2. THE BREATH OF LIGHT

Having completed the *"Unification with the Higher Self,"* established contact with the Being of Light, the Infinite Point of Radiance, and having enacted the "Circle of Light" linking your own head to that of the "Radiant Being of Light," you may proceed with the next practice:

1. Continue by remaining entirely relaxed, the palms of the hands still facing upwards, the soles of your feet resting against those of the Being of Light, and sensing your "Infinite Point of Radiance" diagonally above you.
2. Next, focus your attention on your solar plexus, which I noted earlier is the "brain" of your "Instinctual Self." This time, sense your "Infinite Source of Radiance" to be directly above this point of your anatomy. Then, during inhalation, visualise and sense the golden "Divine Light" being drawn down into your body via the solar plexus, from whence it divides and flows in two directions, upwards to the top of your head and downwards to the soles of your feet. Reverse this action during exhalation, i.e. sensing the "Divine Force" flowing back into the Solar Plexus, from whence it returns into the infinity of the One Eternal Spirit, the "Infinite Source" above you.
3. Repeat the procedure for as long as you desire, ensuring that you stay mentally focussed.

### 3. THE *AMEN* BREATH

"Divine Energy" is drawn from your "Radiant Being of Light" via your feet, from whence it is directed directly into your hands, almost as if there are two laser beams respectively connecting your hands directly with the insteps of your feet. Your connection with your "Infinite Source" and your "Radiant Being of Light" being already well established, you may commence the current procedure:

1. Turn your palms downward, then, whilst taking a deep breath and softly sounding "*AH*" during the inhalation, imagine intense golden light, or "Divine Energy," being drawn from the feet of the "Being of Light," through the souls and insteps of your feet upwards towards your hands. Retain the Divine Force in your hands as you exhale and whisper "*MEN*." Repeat this action three times.
2. Next, again during inhalation, draw the "Divine Force" upwards from your hands to your elbows while whispering "*EE*," then from your elbows to your throat while changing the whisper to "*AH*." During the brief pause between the

inhalation and exhalation, feel the "Divine Energy" gathered in your throat, and then direct the golden light back into your "Infinite Source," either directly from your throat or via the top of the head, as you whisper "*OH*" or "*OO*." Experience and sense the Divine Force uniting with the "All of Nothing," the universal *OMNIL*. Repeat this portion of the procedure also three times.

In the latter procedure, as noted elsewhere, "you are quietly declaring '*Amen IAO*.' As noted before, the Divine Name '*IAO*' represents the totality of your 'Being,' of which this exercise is the full expression. Hence, these deliberate acts of alignment are meant to facilitate a cleaving to *Atzilut* (the World of Emanation), so to speak. It is ultimately via the *Neshamah*, the Divine Higher Self, that one is able to govern the world, and the downward flow of *shefa* (spiritual influx) is reliant on *Kavvanah*, literally your conduct, demeanour and stance. This factor is vital in drawing down the 'Light of the World of Emanation,' and radiating it via your own being into all spheres of manifestation."[66]

However, as I noted elsewhere regarding practices of this nature, "the power of these techniques does not originate entirely inside the Self, but, like the material body, the success of these practices is reliant on factors in its surroundings. So the power of these techniques originates in the repeated inhalation of the Life-Force of the Eternal Living Spirit."[67] I further maintained that the "Power" should "be drawn from the Divine,"[68] and thus your primary perception should be of an abundant fountain of pure Divine Power which you are being prepared to integrate into yourself and your world. This abundant "Source" is represented in the listed procedures as the "Infinite Point of 'Is'-ness" or the "Infinite Point of Radiance," which is, as it were, a "focus" by means of which you align with the Eternal No-Thing, *Ayn Sof Aur*, or "God" if you like.

As is the case with so many psycho-spiritual practices, all of the listed techniques pertain to actions in which the *Neshamah* (Higher Self) converts "Light" (Divine Energy) into "forces" which can be easily absorbed and channelled by humans. I stated previously that *you* are the medium through which the sovereign and splendid "Divine Force" is relayed and established in the world, and that "you are the receptive conclusion of the operation."[69] Your primary task is to acquire "the bright Being of the Divine," and relay it into your circumference every moment of your life. As said, "in this manner you may construct within yourself a fresh and hallowed essence, and in conveying this to your world, you contribute towards the *Tikkun*, the raising and restoration of both the human race and this planet."[70] This comprises in fact a three-fold process involving the Divine (*Ayn Sof*), the Higher Self (*Neshamah*) and you as Lower/Middle Self (*Nefesh* and *Ruach*). The more fully this threefold awareness is understood by the practitioner of the listed techniques, the faster will be the results. Each of the three points is decisively installed in the initial "*Unification with the Higher Self*" procedure, which is presented antecedent to any of the other operations. In other words, there is the factual self and the communication with the "Higher Self brilliance" at the feet, as well as with the Eternal Living Spirit as the "Infinite Point of Radiance" overhead, all of which are primary to the listed procedures.

That being said, it should be clearly understood that breathing is the primary practice underlying not only the listed procedures, but all the techniques shared in these tomes on Jewish Magic. Breathing is not a power in itself, but the conveyer of both the physical and spiritual qualities of light and sound, in fact, the very life-force we share in this world. The success of this "Rite of Rebirth" is dependent on a good memory, fair visualisation skills, and "Conscious Breathing" which I addressed in some detail elsewhere.[71] As you know well enough, within the scope of your perceptions, sound is conveyed upon the air and the life-force, including the flow of "subtle forces," follow the same principles in their operations on this level of existence, where all is communicated on the air or with breath.

As I noted in the first part of "*The Book of Immediate Magic*," conscious breathing practices "afford you control over your emotions and over life in general; facilitate a better condition of balance, greater concentration, and centring of the mind; are often employed to strengthen health and physical wellbeing; are well known for the many empowering effects they had on the body, mind, soul and spirit, such as relieving stress, relaxation, restoring vitality, and even the improvement of libido," and "can be harnessed in the enhancement and focussing of the 'subtle energy' surrounding your body for a variety of purposes, just as that can be employed to focus the 'life force' coursing through your body in a manner resulting in greater consciousness."[72]

In summary, the listed recommended practices thus commence with envisioned "Conscious Breathing" establishing a route from your "Infinite Point of Radiance," via the "Higher Self" as mediator, to the human self who establishes this divine life. Each practice is executed on the pulse of an inhalation and exhalation, in order to establish a vehicle for light and sound. In this regard, it is worth noting that whilst all the workings incorporate the envisioning of "Light," it is not important to *see* it in absolute clarity, but rather to *feel* or *sense* it as intensely as possible. It is further important to understand that this *Light* is a real power. Just as there are numerous types of matter with distinct applications in the physical realm, so there are manifold characteristics and varieties of, as it were, "light essence" in the "Realm of Light," rendering diverse services in accordance with distinctive frequencies.

It will appear that there is an immense amount of preparation for this Rite of Personal Initiation, and there certainly is. These preparations do not however pertain only to the "*Rite of Rebirth*" as a once-off occurrence, but will be found to have a whole range of effects benefiting your life in numerous ways. I will share some of these with you shortly, but I want to stress that the intensity and value of the Initiation Rite which I am sharing here, is dependent on how well the practitioner is prepared to have the full experience and benefit of the working. So I want to urge you to give a lot of attention to techniques already shared in the previous volumes of this series of texts on *Practical Kabbalah*,[73] as well as to those I am addressing in the current tome. Do not hurry or attempt to work this initiation procedure when you are not absolutely ready to enact all aspects of the Rite. Take as much time as you need to practice the various exercises, since you will in any case be afforded a lot of time in having to memorise this entire "Rite of Initiation," which will be worked in a "landscape" within your "Inner Being" without any access to the ritual script.

To continue with the preparations for the "*Rite of Rebirth*," special attention must be given to two practices which will improve your, as it were, "extrasensory" skills, i.e. "*Sound Concentration*," and "*Image Concentration*."[74] The first practice necessitates one gaining control over the portion of the mind in which verbal thoughts arise. In this regard, you would simply repeat selected words comprised of one or more syllables. Similar to uttering mantras, the chosen sound is repeated mentally, and in this regard it is important to listen to yourself uttering the sound. As noted elsewhere, "when the sound appears to repeat itself automatically, and even occur in sleep, you have mastered the skill."[75] With the second practice, i.e. "*Image Concentration*," you are learning to control that portion of your brain in which pictorial images arise. In this instance you would select any simple shape, perhaps a triangle, circle, square, etc., and observe it mentally without distortion for around 15 minutes. Whilst you would practice this visualisation with closed eyes, you should later attempt to do so with eyes open. In this regard you would gain the skill of projecting the mental image onto any blank surface in your environment. Again, as mentioned elsewhere, "this skill is fundamental to the internalizing and projection of 'sigils' in talismanic work, and in the creation of thought-forms."[76]

Further procedures which will afford the necessary skills in the successful execution of this "self initiation," are "*Establishing the Body of Light*,"[77] and two practices pertaining to working with the four "Magical Elements," i.e. the procedure of invoking and accumulating the "Four Elements,"[78] as well as the practice titled "*Balancing with the Elements*."[79] I have addressed the construction of the "*Body of Light*," and shared an excellent procedure for invoking the "Four Elements" in the first part of the current tome,[80] hence these need no further elucidation here. However, "*Balancing with the Elements*" is an integral procedure in the current self-initiation "*Rite of Rebirth*," and hence it needs to be readdressed here. In this regard, I stated elsewhere that "the human body is divided into four principal regions, corresponding to the elements. The feet up to the buttocks, correspond to the Earth Element. The genitals, the abdominal region with all the internal organs such as the bladder, bowels, gall, liver, stomach, etc. up to the diaphragm relate to the Water Element. The chest, lungs, heart, arms and the neck correspond to the Air Element, and finally the head and its organs pertain to the Fire Element."[81] The practice of "Balancing with the Elements" necessitates the, as it were, "loading" of the four regions of your physical anatomy, with their respectively associated "Elements" in the following manner:

1. The different elements are invoked in the manner delineated in the first part of *"The Book of Immediate Magic."*[82] It is customary to commence by loading the Element of Earth in the lower regions of the body, followed by Water in the abdominal area, Air in the upper torso, and finally Fire in the head. In this regard, select the Element you wish to work with, then focus on your "Nil Centre" and visualise the qualities of that Element within it. Then commence drawing the said "Elemental force" upwards into your chest during inhalation as you "inspeak" the related vowel tone, and during the exhalation allow it to flow and settle into the associated locale in your body. Do this seven times.
2. Repeat the procedure with all four Elements and their respective regions in the human anatomy.
3. Conclude by smiling with your entire body, and feeling the warmth of the smile, the *Ruchaniyut*, permeating your entire physical structure.

Bear in mind that, as I mentioned elsewhere, that the "Inner Forces" you are attempting to contact by means of this "Rite of Self initiation," will not necessarily hear the physical words you are uttering. They perceive "the nuances of intention" as expressed in the imagined pictures you emanate and create not only in your mind, or expressed via your mouth, but also in your own "ambient atmosphere," so to speak. In this regard, I noted that "in a small way you are doing what God, or your *Neshamah*, is doing all the time, and that is 'to make the word flesh'."[83] You will be doing the same through your own being during this special *"Rite of Rebirth,"* in order "to get your intentions expressed and heard on 'Inner Levels'."[84]

During this time of preparation you might also acquire such items which you feel may be conducive to the successful working of this Rite, e.g. special clothing, which could be a simple black robe with a hood, or any other item of clothing you like, such items being entirely optional. You may equally want to light the room with candles, etc., though the entire rite could be worked in total physical darkness. All such items are entirely optional. What is however important is that you need to select a "Magical Name" for yourself, which will represent your "Identity" within the "Inner

Realms." In other words, your "magical identity" is reflected in your "magical name." Of course, you can get yourself a "magical identity" any way you want, since the fundamental rule applicable here is personal appeal. In this regard, I am aware of an instance in which an individual created his "magical identity" by conjoining his personal name with the Ineffable Name. The idea originally appealed to him, and he went with it. The "Magical Identity" might be something which you wish to realise or achieve in your life. In my case my first "magical name" was *Yahdam*, which I interpreted to mean that I reflect Divinity (*Yah*) inside myself, i.e. in my "blood" metaphorically speaking. Having, as it were, fully realised this "magical identity," I took the opportunity to elect another Divine Name in which concepts which I found personally appealing were conjoined. What is important is that this "magical name" is known to yourself and "Spirit" only, and perhaps to your most trusted Companions within your family of faith.

Now, in order to prepare yourself to undertake the "inner journey" into the deepest recesses of your *Nefesh* (Instinctual Self), where you will be working this ritual of self initiation, you need to employ a procedure which will help you enter into, as it were, a trance state. There are of course several ways in which a trance state can be achieved, and in this regard the earlier mentioned "*Sound Concentration*" and "*Image Concentration*" practices are excellent ways to induce a state of trance. These practices, which require intense focus and concentration, will however not suffice in inducing the required surrendered trance condition to commence the said journey into your "Inner World."

As readers know probably well enough, there are other trance inducing techniques, such as hypnosis. In fact, getting into a trance state is relatively easy. It can be achieved through meditation, mantras, breathing exercises employed over extended periods, fasting, *Yichudim* (Unification Exercises combining meditation, mantras and breathing) such as those I addressed in "*The Book of Self Creation*."[85] Related here are Yogic postures, dancing, chanting, or simply sitting quietly while alternately and rapidly relaxing and contracting the anal muscles for long periods until a trance state ensues. Some practitioners prefer the use of faster but psychologically very risky routes, such as sexual practices or the ingestion of mind expanding plant substances. It has been said that the "longer" methods achieve a more permanent state, whereas the "faster" ones are of a temporary nature. However, it is difficult to assess which method is better without knowing the mental, emotional and physical factors, i.e. the psychological makeup, of the one employing any of these trance inducing methods. As far as I am concerned, all of these methods are risky and should therefore be approached with caution. It is simply impossible to know which are dangerous for a specific person, without being well acquainted with the personality of the said individual.

Be that as it may, for our purposes here we do not actually need to enter into a deep trance at all. The requirement is to be fully alert whilst being in a state of profound surrender, and to achieve this I recommend the following simple technique of autosuggestion:

1. Without resorting to hard concentration, close your eyes, and whilst looking slightly upwards, focus your gaze gently on the dark screen in front of your eyes.
2. Slowly repeat the following instructions. Say each phrase aloud, and then repeat them mentally while simultaneously attempting to enact or experience the meaning of the words in your body and being. An easy way of doing this is to allow yourself to *feel* the meaning of the words rather than *think* them. Your instruction to your "subconscious self" should also be done with a warm inner smile, like this:

"I surrender myself.....(pause/repeat/experience).....My right arm is heavy.....(pause/repeat/ experience).....My right hand is heavy.....(pause/repeat/experience).....My right arm is sinking.....(pause/repeat/experience).....My right arm is heavy.....(pause/repeat/experience)....."

Repeat this portion of the procedure with the left arm, then continue with:

"My right leg is heavy.....(pause/repeat/experience).....My right foot is heavy.....(pause/repeat/ experience).....My right leg is sinking.....(pause/repeat/experience).....My right leg is heavy.....(pause/repeat/experience)....."

Again repeat the latter portion of the procedure with the left leg, afterwards continuing with:

"My arms are heavy.....(pause/repeat/experience).....My legs are heavy.....(pause/ repeat/ experience).....My arms and legs are heavy.....(pause/repeat/experience).....My body is heavy.....(pause/repeat/experience).....I surrender myself .....(pause/repeat/experience).....My body is heavy..... (pause/repeat/experience)..."

This activity will facilitate just the right "expanded state of consciousness," to enable you to successfully work the *"Rite of Rebirth."* What is more, you can easily return to normal focal levels by bringing your attention to focus back on your body as a whole, then to open your eyes, make fists, open fists, take a deep breath and stretch.

## C. PERSONAL INITIATION: THE RITE OF REBIRTH

It should be stressed that this Rite is worked in the Name of an acknowledged "God Force," or "Universal Divine Identity" which is of great significance to the one working the rite. Readers who prefer to acknowledge such, as it were, "Universal Consciousness" by means of Divine Names aligned with mainstream Kabbalistic teachings, could employ the Ineffable Name (יהוה); *Eh'yeh* (אהיה); *Adonai* (אדני) or *Yahadonahi* (יאהדונהי); שדי (*Shadai*); or, in terms of special and unique preferences, any of the Divine Names associated with the ten *Sefirot*, or even a set of Divine Names. What is important is that you decide in whose Name the *"Rite of Rebirth"* will be performed, since you will bind yourself to that "Identity" through every aspect of your behaviour, as well as the service you will provide to life. All of this will be in the Name of that "Spiritual Identity" you are seeking to serve.

As indicated, this personal initiation is done in the imagination as a form of creative visualisation or guided meditation. It can be physically enacted if required, but it is vitally important to experience the actions within your own "Inner Being" where all true initiation is worked. It is thus imperative that the

*Initiation: Mystical Rebirth* / 377

entire procedure is memorised, which means you have to slowly learn the words over the period that you are doing the preparatory practices. Again keep in mind that all actions from the *"Consecration of Consciousness"* onwards, are done in the imagination.

For about one to two hours prior to the performance of the actual *"Rite of Rebirth,"* you need to do the various exercises to help you enter into the said appropriate expanded state of consciousness in which you will work the initiation. So you also need to familiarise yourself with these, and recollect their exact order. Of course, you will need to lie down, and find a comfortable position in which you will remain for the duration of the procedure. So here are the various exercises to be done prior to the Rite, which will bring you into the correct "open" state as said:

1. "Surrendering"; "Body Awareness"; and "Toning and Tuning the Body," techniques which, I noted earlier, I have addressed in the first volume of this series of texts on Jewish magic.[86]
2. The advanced manner of working the "Mother Breath," which I addressed in the first part of the current tome,[87] and which will bring you into a state of focussed balance, and commence the expansion of your consciousness.
3. Continue by using the simple method discussed earlier, in order to aid you in entering into an "open" or trance state, or use any such method which you find comfortable and within your clarity of conscience.
4. When you feel the sought-after expanded state of consciousness is being reached, continue by entering with full conviction into the "Inner Adytum of Spirit" as a magical landscape where the Initiation will take place. This is done in the following manner:

   a. While you are deeply surrendered and relaxed, imagine your bioflux emanation, your aura, surrounding your body as a warm, brilliant, golden light, in which all stress simply melts away.
   b. Next, use the practice of *"Picture Speech"*[88] in which, as you exhale, you imagine the "Element of Air" flowing out

of your mouth in the shape of billowing blue clouds, which begin to fill the room. Continue performing this action until you are surrounded by a thick blue mist.

c. Continue by letting the mist form itself into a swirling, spherical "spirit-energy" vehicle, similar to the one delineated elsewhere in terms of the procedure pertaining to the creation of a *"Body of Light."*[89] During the *"Rite of Rebirth,"* you will use this vehicle of swirling blue mist to raise and carry you into the Inner Realm, the mythical landscape where the initiation is to take place. While you are still acquiring the skill to create this vehicle, you should get used to forming and dissipating it.

It should be noted that this *"Rite of Rebirth"* is presented here in the format worked in the Northern Hemisphere. Readers living in the Southern Hemisphere need to reverse the positions of North and South, that is the positions of the Elements of Fire and Earth.

### 1. PREPARATION & OPENING

Ensure that you will work this procedure at a time and place where you can proceed without the possibility of being disturbed or interrupted. You might want to do the working on the day of the Full Moon, or as close to it as possible. A good suggestion is to fast for twenty-four hours prior to the rite (some prefer to fast up to a week), and to consciously and deliberately remove all "toxic thoughts and feelings" which might arise during that day. Allow yourself about three hours for the rite, and start by taking a nice, relaxed bath. You could also prepare the room you will be working in by lighting a pleasant incense, but do not create so much smoke as to cause you to choke, and thus distract you from the "Inner Work" you are about to undertake. You should also keep the illumination of the room fairly low, perhaps lighting only one or two candles. Your preparations could also be accompanied by soft, peaceful music or chanting, which should be set to fade or end prior to the commencement of the actual initiation. This is however optional and many individuals who have worked this *"Rite of Rebirth"* have preferred total silence.

## Initiation: Mystical Rebirth / 379

When you are clean, robed, and ready to start the procedure, enter your sacred space or room where you will work, close the door, and lie down in a comfortable position, which is the position you will remain in for the duration of the Rite. For about one to two hours prior to the actual Initiation, you need to do the various exercises to help you enter into the appropriate expanded state of consciousness. Again, you need to familiarise yourself with these preparatory exercises beforehand, and memorise their exact order. Having found the position in which you will remain for the duration of the Initiation, proceed with the listed exercises which will facilitate the expansion of your consciousness, as well as entrance into the "Inner" landscape.

Finally, form the billowing blue mist into a spherical vehicle, as it were a *Merkavah*, which surrounds your body as explained previously. Then experience yourself being raised higher and higher by this vehicle of swirling blue mist, and carried into the Inner realm, the mythical landscape where the initiation will take place.

When you feel yourself gently come to rest, imagine the mist clearing and see yourself standing in a clear, moonlit landscape. In front of you, above the horizon, is shining a brilliant star, which is your earlier mentioned "*Infinite Point of Radiance*." When you are thus located in this "Inner" world, you can continue with the next part of the "Rite of Rebirth," which is the consecration of your consciousness.

### 2. CONSECRATION OF CONSCIOUSNESS

[*Imagine you are facing towards the East, which is where you can see a bright star, this being your Infinite Source of Light and Truth. Stretch out your arms sideways as if to embrace the star, and address it with the following invocation*]

> I ASK IN THE NAME OF THE ETERNAL PRESENCE, WHO IS WITHOUT END, WHOSE BEGINNING SPRINGS FORTH ETERNALLY WITHIN ALL LIVING INTELLIGENCE, WITHIN US ALL, THAT THE AWAKENING OF MY CONSCIOUSNESS BE CONSECRATED, AS IT EXPANDS TO EMBRACE THE WHOLE IN THE PROCESS OF MY ILLUMINATION, *EH'YEH* - I AM.

[*Lower the arms and form the Cosmic Cross or the Kabbalistic Cross in the manner delineated in the first part of the current tome.*][90]

> *Touch forehead say:* IN THE NAME OF THE WISDOM
> *Touch solar plexus, say:* AND OF THE LOVE
> *Touch right shoulder, say:* AND OF THE JUSTICE
> *Touch left shoulder, say:* AND OF THE INFINITE MERCY
> *Moving hand over the head, encircle all points, say:* OF THE ONE ETERNAL SPIRIT.
> *Raise both hands in prayer position over the heart, say:* AMEN (*OMEIN*)

### 3. BALANCING WITH THE FOUR ELEMENTS[91]

LET THE ELEMENTS OF MY EXISTENCE BE SACRED TO ME. THE AIR OF ASPIRATION, THE FIRE OF FERVENCY, THE WATER OF WILLINGNESS, THE EARTH OF OUR ENDEAVOURS, AND THE TRUTH THAT TIES THE LAWS OF LIFE TOGETHER SO THAT SPIRIT MAY BE MANIFEST BY MATTER.

[*The four regions of the body linked to the four elements are balanced respectively with Earth, Water, Air and Fire.*]

### 4. THE ANCIENT CHARGES[92]

I HERE AND NOW AFFIRM THE ANCIENT CHARGES OF MY EXISTENCE UPON THE HOLY TREE OF LIFE.

FIRST, IN THE NAME OF *EH'YEH*, I AFFIRM THAT I WILL ALWAYS SEEK THE SINGLE SPIRITUAL LIGHT WITHIN MYSELF, WHICH SHOWS MY ETERNAL ENTITY AND GRANTS ME *KETER*, THE COSMIC CROWN OF EVERLASTING LIFE.

SECOND, IN THE NAME OF *YHVH*, I AFFIRM THAT I RECOGNIZE *CHOCHMAH*, WISDOM, AS AN ATTRIBUTE OF DIVINITY WE MAY SHARE IN SOME DEGREE, AND THUS DEDICATE MYSELF TO ITS REALISATION.

THIRD, IN THE NAME OF *ELOHIM*, I AFFIRM THAT I WILL APPROACH ALL ASPECTS OF THE SACRED MYSTERIES WITH MODESTY AND HOPE OF REACHING REVELATION IN *BINAH*, A DIVINELY UNIVERSAL UNDERSTANDING.

FOURTH, IN THE NAME OF *EL*, I AFFIRM THAT I WILL DIRECT *CHESED*, THE MERCY OF MY MAKER TO ALL, AND CARE FOR MY FELLOW CREATURES WITH COMPASSION.

FIFTH, IN THE NAME OF *ELOHIM GIBUR*, I AFFIRM THAT I WILL APPLY *GEVURAH*, DISCIPLINE, ON MYSELF, IN ORDER TO LEARN TO LIVE AS A RESPONSIBLY WELL-REGULATED MEMBER OF THESE MYSTERIES.

SIXTH, IN THE NAME OF *YHVH ELOHA VA-DA'AT*, I AFFIRM THAT I WILL ATTEMPT AN ARRANGEMENT OF MYSELF TO BE IN *TIFERET*, HARMONY, WITH ALL THE SACRED SPHERES IN THE PLAN OF PERFECTION.

SEVENTH, IN THE NAME OF *YHVH TZ'VA'OT*, I AFFIRM THAT I WILL APPLY *NETZACH*, THAT IS TO PERSEVERE WITH PROBLEMS ON MY PATH, SO THAT THESE WILL SOLVE THEMSELVES AND SUBLIMATE INTO A SPIRITUAL SUCCESS.

EIGHTH, IN THE NAME OF *ELOHIM TZV'A'OT*, I AFFIRM THAT I WILL APPLY *HOD*, THAT IS TO STUDY THE MYSTERIES WITH RESPECTFUL REASON IN ORDER TO MAKE UP MY MIND.

NINTH, IN THE NAME OF *SHADAI EL CHAI*, I AFFIRM THAT I WILL FIRMLY LIVE OUT THE PRACTICE OF THIS LIVING FAITH AS I PURSUE THE PRINCIPLES OF *YESOD*, ITS FOUNDATION, AND THE SECRET OF ITS SPIRITUAL STRENGTH.

TENTH, IN THE NAME OF *ADONAI HA-ARETZ*, I AFFIRM THAT IN *MALCHUT*, THIS WORLD, I WILL KEEP THE LAWS INTENDED FOR THE GOVERNMENT OF MUNDANE AFFAIRS, BUT LIVE WITHIN THE LIGHT OF THE INNER REALM AS AN ACTIVE AND INITIATED MEMBER OF THESE MYSTERIES.

## 5. THE OATH[93]

I CALL ON THE MIGHTY ONES OF THE HEAVENS AND OF THE EARTH, TO WITNESS THAT THIS WILL BE MY CODE OF CONDUCT AND A GENERAL GUIDE FOR ALL MY THOUGHTS AND ACTIONS IN OUR WORLD.

FIRSTLY, THAT FROM THE PAST, I WILLINGLY ACCEPT A PROPER PORTION OF MY FORBEARS' FAULTS WHICH CAUSED THE WORST OF EVERYTHING ENCOUNTERED ON THIS EARTH AND IN MY PRESENT PERSON.

SECONDLY, THAT FROM THIS PRESENT I WILL WORK AND PRAY WITH MY WHOLE HEART AND SOUL FOR THE PERFECTION OF MYSELF AND SPECIES AS I DO BELIEVE THE WILL DIVINE IN ME DIRECTS BY OUR MOST BLESSED BLOOD.

THIRDLY, THAT FOR THE FUTURE I WILL STRIVE TO SERVE THE.....[*here fill in the name of the spiritual identity* in whose Name you are working this "Self Initiation"].....FAITHFULLY SO THAT WE WILL BECOME THE BEST OF BEINGS POSSIBLE TO PEOPLE ON THIS PLANET, AND EVENTUALLY PASS BEYOND EMBODIMENT OF EARTH TO PERFECT PEACE PROFOUND.

I AFFIRM THIS [*form the Cosmic Cross or the Kabbalistic Cross in the accustomed manner*]

IN THE NAME OF THE WISDOM
AND OF THE LOVE
AND OF THE JUSTICE
AND OF THE INFINITE MERCY
OF THE ONE ETERNAL SPIRIT
*AMEN (OMEIN)*

## 6. SECRET IDENTITY[94]

I CALL ON THE MIGHTY ONES OF THE HEAVENS AND OF THE EARTH TO WITNESS MY INTENTIONS AS EXPRESSED IN MY SECRET NAME, WHICH I HAVE CHOSEN AS MY COGNOMEN AMONGST THE COMPANY OF MY COSMIC FAMILY OF FAITH.

MY NAME WILL BE.....[*here fill in the chosen name*], which means.....[*here fill in the meaning*]. I WILL BEAR THIS NAME WITH HONOUR AS AN OBLIGATION TO MY LIFE IN SPIRIT. IT WILL BE TO ME A SPECIAL SYMBOL OF THE.....[*here fill in the name of the spiritual identity*].....I SEEK TO SERVE. MAY IT BRING ME EVERY BLESSING WHILE I WORK AND WAIT WITHIN THIS WORLD.

THIS REFLECTS MY INTENTIONS TO THE HIGHEST ONES, WHICH I NOW CONFIRM [*here form the Cosmic Cross or the Kabbalistic Cross in the accustomed manner*]

IN THE NAME OF THE WISDOM
AND OF THE LOVE
AND OF THE JUSTICE
AND OF THE INFINITE MERCY
OF THE ONE ETERNAL SPIRIT
*AMEN (OMEIN)*

## 7. UNITING WITH THE HIDDEN ONES[95]

[*Invoke the Forces of Air, by giving a hailing sign with your arm(s) outstretched towards the East*]

COME FORTH HOLY HIDDEN ONES OF THE EASTERN LIGHT OF DAWN, WHOSE LIFE ELEMENT IS AIR AND SYMBOL IS THE SWORD. CONSECRATE AND ENTER INTO MY BEING WHILE I, AN ASPIRANT OF LIGHT, START MY QUEST FOR ENLIGHTENMENT.

*Imagine a powerful wind starting up in the East, swirling around, and forming itself into a small tornado. Stretch out your arms sideways as if to embrace the swirling Element of Air. Imagine It rushing towards you and completely encircling your being. Feel yourself in the centre of this swirling mass. Sense the power and qualities of the Element. Then absorb the Element with its qualities into your being with three inhalations, and as you do so, it dwindles as it is completely assimilated into your being.*

*[Conclude by forming the Cosmic Cross or the Kabbalistic Cross in the accustomed manner]*

> IN THE NAME OF THE WISDOM
> AND OF THE LOVE
> AND OF THE JUSTICE
> AND OF THE INFINITE MERCY
> OF THE ONE ETERNAL SPIRIT
> *AMEN (OMEIN)*

*Turn to face the South [North in the Southern Hemisphere]. Invoke the Forces of Fire, by giving the hailing sign with your arm(s) outstretched towards the South [North in the Southern Hemisphere].*

> COME FORTH HOLY HIDDEN ONES OF THE SOUTHERN [NORTHERN] LIGHT OF DAY, WHOSE LIFE ELEMENT IS FIRE AND SYMBOL IS THE ROD. CONSECRATE AND ENTER INTO MY BEING WHILE I, AND ASPIRANT OF LIGHT, START MY QUEST FOR ENLIGHTENMENT.

*Imagine a flame in the distance, which grows quickly into a powerful conflagration, swirling around, and forming itself into a dancing inferno of fire. Stretch out your arms sideways as if to embrace the swirling Element of Fire. Imagine It rushing towards you and completely encircling your being. Feel yourself in the centre of this swirling mass. Sense the power and qualities of the Element. Then absorb the Element with its qualities into your being with three inhalations, and as you do so, it dwindles as it is completely assimilated into your being.*

*[Conclude by forming the Cosmic Cross or the Kabbalistic Cross in the accustomed manner]*

IN THE NAME OF THE WISDOM
AND OF THE LOVE
AND OF THE JUSTICE
AND OF THE INFINITE MERCY
OF THE ONE ETERNAL SPIRIT
*AMEN (OMEIN)*

*Turn to face the West. Invoke the Forces of Water, by giving the hailing sign with arm(s) outstretched towards the West.*

COME FORTH HOLY HIDDEN ONES OF THE WESTERN LIGHT OF DUSK, WHOSE LIFE ELEMENT IS WATER AND SYMBOL IS THE CUP. CONSECRATE AND ENTER INTO MY BEING WHILE I, AN ASPIRANT OF LIGHT, START MY QUEST FOR ENLIGHTENMENT.

*Imagine a pool of water in the distance, which begins to swirl around as if it is stirred by a magical hand. It rises, swirling around and forming quickly into a powerful vortex. Stretch out your arms sideways as if to embrace the swirling Element of Water. Imagine It rushing towards you and completely encircling your being. Feel yourself in the centre of this swirling mass. Sense the power and qualities of the Element. Then absorb the Element with its qualities into your being with three inhalations, and as you do so, it dwindles as it is completely assimilated into your being.*

*[Conclude by forming the Cosmic Cross or the Kabbalistic Cross in the accustomed manner]*

IN THE NAME OF THE WISDOM
AND OF THE LOVE
AND OF THE JUSTICE
AND OF THE INFINITE MERCY
OF THE ONE ETERNAL SPIRIT
*AMEN (OMEIN)*

*Turn to face the North [South in the Southern Hemisphere]. A little away, in front of you there is a stone cavern. It is the womb/tomb of the Earth Mother. Imagine you are entering the cavern. Feel the heaviness and powerful presence of the enormous, moss covered stoneface walls. See the faces of your ancestors carved in the stones, and feel yourself linked to them by, as it were, your "soul root." Then, invoke the Forces of Earth, by giving the hailing sign with arm outstretched towards the depths of the cavern, which is the North [South in the Southern Hemisphere].*

> COME FORTH HOLY HIDDEN ONES OF THE NORTHERN [SOUTHERN] LIGHT OF NIGHT, WHOSE LIFE ELEMENT IS EARTH AND SYMBOL IS THE SHIELD. ENTER INTO MY BEING WHILE I, AN ASPIRANT OF LIGHT, START MY QUEST FOR ENLIGHTENMENT.

*Feel the presence of your ancestors, as well as the power of the Element of Earth, rumbling around you, and forming itself into a very intense pressure as it were. Stretch out your arms sideways as if to open yourself to and embrace the Element of Earth. Imagine it pressing down on you, completely surrounding your being. Feel yourself in the centre of this mass. Sense the power and qualities of the Element. Then absorb the Element with its qualities into your being with three inhalations, and as you do so, it fades as it is completely assimilated into your being.*

*[Conclude by forming the Cosmic Cross or the Kabbalistic Cross in the accustomed manner]*

> IN THE NAME OF THE WISDOM
> AND OF THE LOVE
> AND OF THE JUSTICE
> AND OF THE INFINITE MERCY
> OF THE ONE ETERNAL SPIRIT
> *AMEN (OMEIN)*

## 8. THANKSGIVING[96]

*Sense the cavern dissolving around you, until the stones completely fade away, and you find yourself standing again in a cleared area, surrounded by the moonlit sky. The bright Star of Light and Truth is now directly overhead. Turn again to face the East, and continue with this Thanksgiving:*

THANK YOU, OH HOLY HIDDEN ONES, THAT I HAVE WORKED THIS WAY OF LIGHT; THAT I COULD LAY MY LIFE BEFORE THE ALTAR OF MY ASPIRATIONS AND BELIEFS. CONSECRATE MY LIFE WHICH COMES INTO YOUR COMPANY WITH LOYALTY AND LOVE.

I ALSO THANK YOU, OH LORD OF GREATER LIFE, FOR THIS INVALUABLE GIFT. THANK YOU FOR WHAT I HAVE RECEIVED FROM YOUR LOVING HANDS. I PRAY THAT I MAY PROVE WORTHY OF THE FAITH AND FELLOWSHIP WITHIN THESE MYSTERIES.

IN PEACE I CAME.
WITH POWER I WORKED.
IN PEACE I NOW LEAVE WITH PROFUNDITY OF PURPOSE.

[*Conclude by forming the Cosmic Cross or the Kabbalistic Cross in the accustomed manner*]

IN THE NAME OF THE WISDOM
AND OF THE LOVE
AND OF THE JUSTICE
AND OF THE INFINITE MERCY
OF THE ONE ETERNAL SPIRIT
AMEN (OMEIN)

## 9. CLOSING

*Finally, imagine you are lying down. Then perform again the earlier addressed "The Breath of Light," which is to be aware of the Being of Light with its feet resting against the soles of your feet, as well as to sense your "Infinite Point of Radiance" which is the star directly above you. Then inhale normally, simultaneously visualizing and experiencing Divine Energy being drawn from the "Infinite Point of Radiance" into your body through the solar plexus, from whence it spreads simultaneously upwards to the head and downwards to the feet. When you breathe out, imagine and feel the breath and Divine Energy flowing back to the Solar Plexus from whence it flows back to the "Infinite Point of Radiance." Do it three times.*

*Thereafter conclude by becoming again deeply surrendered and relaxed, and imagining your aura, surrounding your body as a warm, brilliant, golden light. Again use the practice of "Picture Speech" in which, as you exhale, you imagine the Element of Air flowing out of your mouth in the shape of billowing blue clouds. It fills the Inner World, until you are again surrounded by a thick blue mist. The mist is again formed into the spherical vehicle surrounding your body, raising it higher and higher, and carrying it back to the realm of ordinary living. When you feel yourself gently coming to rest, imagine the mist clearing, and feel yourself back in the room in which you have been working. Open your eyes, make fists, open fists, take a deep breath and stretch. With this action you have concluded this "Rite of Rebirth"!*

**. ... ... ...If people help each other, and live in peace and the fear of God, they give the angel life. But if there are always on earth more of those who kill, or steal, or deceive, the angel will not appear... ... ... .**

# Chapter 10
## *Or Memale* — Light Abounding
## THE ONENESS BEYOND ALL BEING!

### A. The Art of Gifting

In working magical techniques to generate income or improve finances, etc., an important point to consider is the power of "giving" in the process of "receiving." In fact, it is vitally important to balance the "*ha-Yetzer ha-Ra*" ("the evil inclination"), referencing the "desire to receive," with "*ha-Yetzer ha-Tov*" ("the good inclination"), the latter being the focus of the "desire to give." As noted elsewhere, "if one should predominate or overpower the other, disastrous results will inevitably ensue."[1] In balancing the said two "inclinations," you have to deal with the בלבול (*bilbul*—"confusion") which more often than not "exists in human hearts between good and evil inclinations."[2] In this regard, I align with the quote purportedly uttered by Winston Churchill "we make a living by what we get. We make a life by what we give." However, from the perspective of the "magical" empowerment of good living on this planet, serious practitioners of Jewish Magical traditions know well enough that it is of the utmost importance that they should "give" in order to "receive," this being part of the process, as I noted elsewhere, "of balancing acts of 'giving' and 'receiving,' so as to magically encourage the free flow of 'abundance' in their lives."[3]

This being said, in Kabbalistic terms, balancing the "desire to receive" with the "desire to give" is not quite as simple as one might expect. In comprehending the whole of manifestation to be the embodiment of the *Shechinah*, the feminine counterpart of the Divine One, we are told that "the Sh'chinah is not merely a two way clearing house through which all divine qualities and human deeds pass."[4] In fact, it is understood that the whole of existence is a continuous balancing act of sefirotic forces, in order to maintain the harmony of *Din* (Judgment) and *Chesed* (Loving-kindness), between that which is delineated in kabbalistic literature to be respectively "bitter" and "sweet." The concepts of "sweetness" and "bitterness" in terms of human behaviour were understood to have been referenced in the famous biblical tale of Samson and the lion. This intriguing saga triggered the imagination of both Jewish and Christian thinkers. We are informed that "Samson had killed a lion in whose carcass a swarm of bees subsequently nested and produced honey; he invented the following riddle based on this incident: 'Out of the eater came what is eaten, and out of the strong came what is sweet.'....In die *Lehrtafel* this riddle is combined with the cabalistic sephirot: sweetness and bitterness correspond to Gedulah (or Hesed) and Gebura (Din), respectively (*Lehrtafel* 1:92)."[5]

Now, we are told that "the s'firot when in proper loving flow are harmonious and the Sh'chinah receiving the divine abundance via her partner Tiferet, distributes it to the world below. Sometimes the harmony is broken, and then there is an imbalance, a preponderance comes from the left side, Din (Judgment), also known as G'vurah (Power Strength). When Din is not in flow with her partner Hesed (Love, Loving-kindness) – which is to say, when judgment and power overrule loving kindness – there is an imbalance, both in the upper and in the lower realms. Too much of the Din power flowing into the Sh'chinah causes her to be bitter. We can see.....how it is that the Sh'chinah is referred to as the 'Great sea into which all rivers flow.' As sea she collects the fullness of all the rivers and nourishes the world with her water, which water changes from *sweet to bitter and bitter to sweet*, according to whether there is more Din or more Hesed."[6]

As noted elsewhere, Kabbalistic teaching has it that a great shattering happened within the unity of "Divine Being," so to speak, which resulted in the forces of *Din* (Judgment) and *Chesed* (Mercy) becoming wholly imbalanced and, as it were, jumbled. Thus we are informed that "at present, the Shekhinah and humanity are in exile. This exile takes place in this world—a world where everything is 'mixed up,' as when a hurricane and storm wind come and turn the whole world upside down. This world is therefore known as the *Heichalei HaTemurot* ('The Chambers of Exchanges'), where evil is called good and good is called evil; [for them] light is darkness and darkness is light, [they make] bitter sweet and sweet bitter."[7] This is where *Tikkun Olam* ("Restoration of the Universe") enters the fray, as well as the belief that humankind has the capacity to aid the restoration of the universe, to release the obstructions by intentionally focussing the energy flow of consciousness so that *Shefa* (Divine Abundance) may flow unimpeded into manifestation. In this regard, it is understood that proper intention (*Kavvanah*) in your meditations, prayers, and sacred activities re-stabilizes the, as it were, "Divine Being," and facilitates the refocusing of "Divine Energy" along its proper lines.

A major part of the process of releasing the free flow of *Shefa* (Divine Abundance) in your life, pertains to what I delineated the *"Art of Gifting."* Never mind how poor you may regard yourself to be, there is always something you have which could contribute to the well-being of your fellow creatures who share this planet with you, whether they be of the human or animal kind. In giving freely and unconditionally to life, you serve not only the world around you, but importantly so you equally encourage your own personal well-being in this world. In this regard, I am reminded of how many decades ago in my remote youth, I attempted to establish a contact with, as it were, the archetype of Death personified as a kind of "Divine Mother." My late Mentor, William G. Gray, was not impressed at all, and after castigating me in the strongest possible terms, informed me that since I had "invoked" the "spirit of Death," and sort of dedicated myself to "Her," that I had better listen to what "She" had to say, because "She" would interact with me in all manner of unexpected ways.

It was not long after this interaction with my late Mentor, when I was powerfully confronted with the dual aspects of the "nature" of "Mother Death" in two incidents. The first occurred while I was sitting at a bus-stop in front of a hospital I visited earlier. A fairly elderly man was walking towards the bus shelter. He looked awful, and appeared to be suffering from a peculiar skin condition resulting in the flaking of his epidermis, which exposed dark-red patches of raw flesh. All in all he was not in good shape as he struggled to walk under the intense stoop of his torso, in clothes that had also seen better days. His gaze was fixed to the ground, and I never saw him look up even once. He was constantly wringing his hands whilst sighing intermittently. All in all he was a most desperate apparition.

The said individual approached the bus-stop, and sat down to my right fairly close to me. With the constant sighing and wringing of his hands, I became increasingly more aware of his presence, as if it was sort of being emphasised in my mind. I was just about to move away, when my attention was drawn to my left where I saw an elderly woman who was also approaching the bus-stop. She was in a worse condition than the man on my right, dragging herself along on crutches, and emanating sheer despair and depression. She sat down on my left, again fairly close. I was literally stuck between two people who seemed to have lived too long, and I became painfully aware of this fact. The intensity of the experience was such, that I felt my blood pulsating in my temples and a hissing inside my head.

As is so often the case with humans seeking a meaningful answer to the difficulties they encounter in life, I found what I thought was the answer to these tragedies playing out on either side of me, i.e. what I call the "cop out," and being very young and having learned the word "*Karma*," I thought this must be it. Hence I decided to get up and stand in the sun, but before I could do so, a little fox terrier appeared out of nowhere, and was struggling towards me. It was the ugliest little thing I ever saw. It was so old that its face was drawn and eyes slanted, giving the impression of being the plague incarnated. It walked dreadfully slowly with its hind legs wide apart. The one leg was considerably thinner than the other, and this sorely distressed little creature walked up to me. I was wearing a pair of open "clogs," and it placed its cold nose directly on my right foot.

At that instant I was literally surrounded by "Mother Death" in what could be termed her most gruesome aspects, and there was simply no escape. I was fascinated and shocked at my own fascination with the situation, whilst simultaneously thinking that it would surely be kinder to put them all to sleep, as one tends to do with a suffering animal, and wondering why Death was not dealing with them expediently, rather than leaving them crippled, crawling and senile wrecks, this being the penalty of having lived too long in one body. Animals have more sense than we do. When they feel their bodies failing, they can just curl up, dehydrate as fast as they can and wish themselves to death. I believe humans could do that once, but now they try to hang on to useless bodies beyond belief. I recall thinking that it was really the helplessness of the condition which was so awful, and at that moment getting old appeared to me a most horrible prospect, with the worst part of it being the consciousness of the process. The awareness of it. The feeling that everything you might really still want to do having to be put off until another lifetime, i.e. all the various awarenesses that accompany the end of life in one body, as well as the impatience of waiting for Death.

At the time I was thinking what a relief Death must be, and then I remembered the odd message my Mentor received from his mother when she died. "Death doesn't solve any problems, it just makes new ones," and I was wondering what she meant. Dying I do not mind, but the dreary drag to death seemed horrible. I remember asking "do we have to go through all of that first?" At that moment it was as if "Mother Death" was glaring at me saying "Look.....look.....look you little worm! You think you can call on me! You want to look at my countenance.....my face is crawling with maggots!" I must have sat for only about a minute or two in this situation, with thoughts racing through my mind at an incredible speed, when the spell was suddenly broken, or, perhaps better, the experience was both transformed and intensified by somebody else, another lady, who crossed the road in front of me. She appeared to be much older than the two people on either side of me. She was absolutely beautiful, and her bearing was sheer grace. Her hair was snow white and she carried herself with sparkle and poise, and in that instant I suddenly saw, as it were, "the other side of Death." My "Deadly Mother" had a dual face —one side indeed maggot ridden, whilst the other was exquisitely beautiful, and I suppose it all depends on which side you are aligned with, and are experiencing in your life.

It was a special experience for me in particular, and my firm belief is that "Fate" stages such things for the express purpose of producing results in terms of our spiritual awakening. In this case a change of consciousness in me which to date has had far-reaching results, one which at the time I could neither understand nor realise until much later. That incident may have altered my life only fractionally, and I might still find out *why* for many years to come. On relating the incident to William Gray, he recounted a somewhat similar experience he had a long while back. He was visiting a friend in hospital, when he passed by one of the wards where he witnessed a peculiar scene. A woman was sitting up in bed and crying her eyes out. Another woman, with a blanket wrapped round her shoulders, had dragged herself out of bed, and crawled along the floor to the side of the weeping woman. Slouching on the floor, she was cuddling one of the weeper's hands between hers, and held it to her shrivelled cheek. My dear Mentor told me he could just hear her murmuring words of comfort like "Don't worry dear, I'm sure it'll be all right. I'm sorry dear." He related how he witnessed a nurse scolding the woman on the floor for dragging herself out of bed when she was seriously ill with cancer, whilst the weeping woman had a hysterectomy and would get over it in no time. William Gray said he was touched, and went on his way to fulfil the purpose of his visit.

When he got back on the bus, he noticed a church nearby with one of those "Wayside Pulpits" by its gate. That week it carried the message *"No one in this world is useless who tries to lift the burden of it from another."* In the same way it hit my beloved Mentor then, it hit me like a hammer when he related this saga, and I have never forgotten it. *That* was exactly what he had witnessed. Someone so decrepit and feeble, you would have thought she could do nothing whatsoever for anyone, yet she had done everything in her poor power to help someone who was in fact in a far better condition than herself. He had seen a miracle without realising it, one which the notice had brought to his attention. Similarly I now realise why Death was, as it were, devouring those people as well as the little fox terrier in my experience. They were no longer serving! They had giving up on life, instead of trying to make it better for others, even if those whom they would be serving might be in a better condition than themselves. In other words they stopped fulfilling the "living demands" of life. I found it odd that a bus stop came into both my and my Mentor's experiences. In fact, after several "bus-stop experiences" over the years, I realise that bus-stops can be locales for the meeting of psychological conditions and archetypal patterns, from which a lot can be learned if we are conscious enough.

So in the simplest words, what I am really trying to say is that in order to truly "receive," you must first "give," the latter being a *Segulah*, i.e. a powerful magical activity, for achieving and maintaining פרנסה (*parnasah*), i.e. a good livelihood. In this regard, it is the principle of "giving" which is important, not the size of the gift, and this is why the sphere of *Chesed* (Loving-kindness) on the sefirotic Tree is so important. As noted elsewhere, this pertains to "*Tzedakah*," acts of loving-kindness, a word which is mistranslated "charity" in English, whilst it denotes "righteousness."[8] Of course, in Judaism the term "*Tzedakah*" refers to charitable deeds, regarding which I noted that "the most ideal form of *Tzedakah* is when the giver does not know who the receiver is, and the receiver does not know from whence the benefit derives."[9] Furthermore, I wrote that "true service is when we ourselves have the need to give, in as great a measure as the other person has the need to receive."[10]

Whilst money is neither the only nor the ultimate substance to be shared in the "*Art of Gifting*," it is an acknowledged vital component in successful living of humans amongst their own kind, whether we like to hear it or not. As noted elsewhere, "Money is really a form of energy exchange, but it is what has happened regarding human 'addiction' to money which has impacted our world in such a horrible manner."[11] Humans typically like to sideline this "addiction" by blaming money as the "root of all evil." I do not agree with the generally accepted statement that "money is the root of all evil." The original version of this statement in the Christian Bible reads "The *love* of money is the root of evil" (*1 Timothy 6:10*). In other words, it is the "addiction" called "greed," and not the money which is the problem. However, as I noted previously, "the entire concept of money has become so tainted over the centuries, that a lot of 'negative' energies, e.g. thoughts, feelings, etc., have become attached to it."[12] These impact "both the giver and the receiver, crippling us in some or other manner, hence it is said there are 'harsh judgements' associated with money."[13]

It is for this reason that we are taught that there should be a moderation of judgment, what Kabbalists termed "sweetening harsh judgments," which I noted previously refers "specifically to money and the role it plays in our lives."[14] In delineating the Kabbalistic "sweetening" principle, one commentator noted that "Mercy is called 'sweet,' and judgment is called 'bitter' or 'severe.' Mercy is sweetest when it is on its own, and judgment is most severe when it is alone. The real test of Mercy is its ability to sweeten a judgment. It does this by 'binding' or 'enveloping' the power of judgment within itself, and thereby transforming the very judgment into love. The *Zohar* (*3:176, 3:178a-b*) refers to this transformation when it instructs us to 'always include the left in the right'."[15] These concepts were greatly elucidated by Rabbi Nachman of Bratzlav, writing:

"Money is related to strict judgments. Thus it is written, 'and all the living substance that was at their *feet*' (*Deuteronomy 11:6*), on which the Rabbis commented: 'This refers to a person's money, which is what enables him to stand on his feet' (*Pesachim 119*). From this we learn that money is the 'feet.' Now it is written, 'Justice attends his *footsteps*' (*Isaiah 41:2*), and 'Justice is the holy kingship (*Malchut*)' (*Tikkuney Zohar, Introduction*), and *Malchut* is judgment. This indicates that money is related to judgment.

It is necessary to sweeten the severe judgments at their root, which lies at the level of *Binah*, 'Understanding,' as it is written, 'I am understanding, power is mine' (*Proverbs 8:14*). This is why the Tzaddik places his hands upon the money in order to sweeten the judgments. For there are three 'hands' in *Binah*: the 'great hand' (*Exodus 14:31*) and the 'strong hand' (*Deuteronomy 7:19* etc.), which together make up the 'high hand' (*Exodus 14:8*). When the money—i.e. the severe judgments—comes to the hands, which allude to the three hands of *Binah*, the judgments are sweetened at their source.

The severe judgments have their hold in this world of *Asiyah*. They must be sweetened by means of the three hands in each of the three higher worlds, *Atzilut*, *Beriyah* and *Yetzirah*. When one sweetens the severe judgment in the world of *Asiyah* through the three hands in the world of *Yetzirah*, the judgment is sweetened through the Name of Forty-two letters contained in the prayer '*Ana Becho'ach*': the numerical value of the Hebrew letters of the word יד (*Yad*—'hand') is 14 [י = 10 + ד = 4 = 14], and 14 x 3 = 42. In the world of *Bri'ah* the judgment is sweetened through the Names *EHYeH* and *YHV*, the numerical value of whose letters also adds up to 42. Higher still, in the world of *Atzilut*, the judgment is sweetened through the forty-two letters of the Name of *YHVH*, its expansion (*MaH*) and the expansion of the expansion—altogether 42 letters, three times *Yad* (14)."[16]

Rabbi Nachman's explication of "harsh judgments" and their "sweetening" may appear somewhat obscure and complex, but closer examination will soon afford greater clarity. The good Rabbi tells us that the money belonging to some person enables that individual to "stand on his feet." Considering what has been said about money, and the "harsh judgments" associated with it, you might think money to be aligned with *Gevurah* (Might) or *Din* (Judgement), whilst the hands of the kind, compassionate giver relate, as indicated, to *Binah* (Understanding). However, in the current instance we are informed that "money is the feet" and associated with *Malchut* (Kingship), the latter pertaining to the realm of physical manifestation. In fact, as I noted elsewhere regarding Rabbi Nachman's statements, the "'harsh realities' or the 'severe judgements' of cold harsh cash pertain to *Assiah*, this physical 'World of Action' we all live in."[17]

As far as practicalities are concerned, Rabbi Nachman maintained music to have "tremendous power to draw you to God,"[18] and that by singing, dancing and clapping your hands rhythmically you could "sweeten harsh judgements." However, he insisted that giving *Tzedakah* money to the poor is particularly meritorious, and, as I noted elsewhere as far as monetary donations are concerned, "the crippling forces ('severe judgments') attached to the money should be lightened ('sweetened') by the understanding benefactor."[19] Hence the statement regarding the *Tzaddik* placing his hands upon the money. Of course, it is not the amount of money you give, but the intention with which you give it that is important. In this regard, Rabbi Nachman maintained that "it is most important not to be stingy in the amount of money one gives in order that no severe judgments should remain hovering over one. It takes exceptional wisdom to know exactly how much a particular person should give to make sure that no harsh judgments remain."[20]

Basically we are informed that the forces of "harsh judgments" which cling to money are "rectified" by means of your own hands. However, Rabbi Nachman instructed us to "sweeten the judgments" by means of "three hands" in the "higher worlds" of *Yetzirah* (Formation), *Bri'ah* (Creation) and *Atzilut* (Emanation), the three "higher worlds" which my late Mentor related respectively to "Mind" (Formation), "Soul" (Creation) and "Spirit" (Emanation). We clearly understand that the first of the referenced "three hands" is in fact your own right hand, i.e. the "Great Hand" (*Gedulah*—Greatness) related to *Chesed* (Loving-kindness, and the second your left hand, i.e. the "Strong Hand," aligned with *Gevurah* (Might) on the sefirotic Tree. As noted elsewhere, the third hand titled the "High Hand," references "the 'Divine Power' which flows between your hands into the money intended as a donation."[21] As it is, your own hands are acknowledged to be highly specialised instruments by means of which you would not only give and take in life, but direct "Divine Forces" into the realm of physical manifestation. This is literally true, as we know from the many exercises in which the hands are employed to, as it were, "empower" individuals, objects, etc. We are instructed that the most holy Name of the Divine One is expressed in a unique manner in your hands, in fact, in every digit of your fingers, and this is said to pertain directly to the "*Mah*" extension of the Ineffable Name.

Kabbalah recognizes four "extensions" of the Ineffable Name, which, as noted elsewhere, pertain to the three possible spellings ("fillings") of the titles of the letters ה (*Heh*) and ו (*Vav*).[22] In this regard, the letter ה (*Heh*) can be spelled הא (*Heh-Alef*), הה (*Heh-Heh*) or הי (*Heh-Yod*), and ו (*Vav*) can be spelled ואו (*Vav-Alef-Vav*), ויו (*Vav-Yod-Vav*) or וו (*Vav-Vav*). The three possible spellings of the names of the said letters, are called:

    *Milui de-Alfin* (*Alef* filling);
    *Milui de-He'in* (*Heh* filling); and
    *Milui de-Yodin* (*Yod* filling).

Applying these details in the "expanded" spellings of the letters in the Ineffable Name (יהוה—*YHVH*), Kabbalists arrived at what are termed the "Forty-Five Letter Name of God," "Fifty-Two Letter Name of God," "Sixty-Three Letter Name of God," and the "Seventy-Two Letter Name of God," the latter being distinct from the "Name of Seventy-two Names." We are further informed, that each of these four "extensions" of the Ineffable Name align with one of the "Four Worlds" of Kabbalah, respectively the worlds of *Assiah, Yetzirah, Bri'ah* and *Atzilut*, as shown below:

> יוד הה וו הה (*Yod-vav-dalet Heh-heh Vav-vav Heh-heh*) comprises the "Fifty-Two Letter Name of God," and in *gematria* the combination בן (*Ben* or *Ban* [ב = 2 + ן = 50 = 52]), which is representative of the "Fifty-Two Letter Name of God," and aligned with the world of *Assiah* (Action);
>
> יוד הא ואו הא (*Yod-vav-dalet Heh-alef Vav-alef-vav Heh-alef*) comprises the "Forty-Five Letter Name of God," which corresponds in *gematria* to מה (*Mah* [מ = 40 + ה = 45]).
>
> יוד הי ואו הי (*Yod-vav-dalet Heh-yod Vav-alef-vav Heh-yod*) comprises the "Sixty-Three Letter Name of God," represented by the combination סג (*Sag* [ס = 60 + ג = 3 = 63])
>
> יוד הי ויו הי (*Yod-vav-dalet Heh-yod Vav-yod-vav Heh-yod*) comprises the "Seventy-Two Letter Name of God," which is related to the "Name of Seventy-Two Names." This *milui* of the Ineffable Name is appropriately represented by the combination עב (*Av* [ע = 70 + ב = 2 = 72]).

As noted earlier, Rabbi Nachman informed us that the "one sweetens the severe judgment in the world of *Asiyah* through the three hands in the world of *Yetzirah*."[23] In this regard, it would be the "power" of the מה (*Mah*) extension of the Ineffable Name, or "Forty-five Letter Name of God" aligned with *Olam ha-Yetzirah* (World of Formation), which is being expressed via the hands of the "understanding benefactor," as indicated in the following famous illustration:[24]

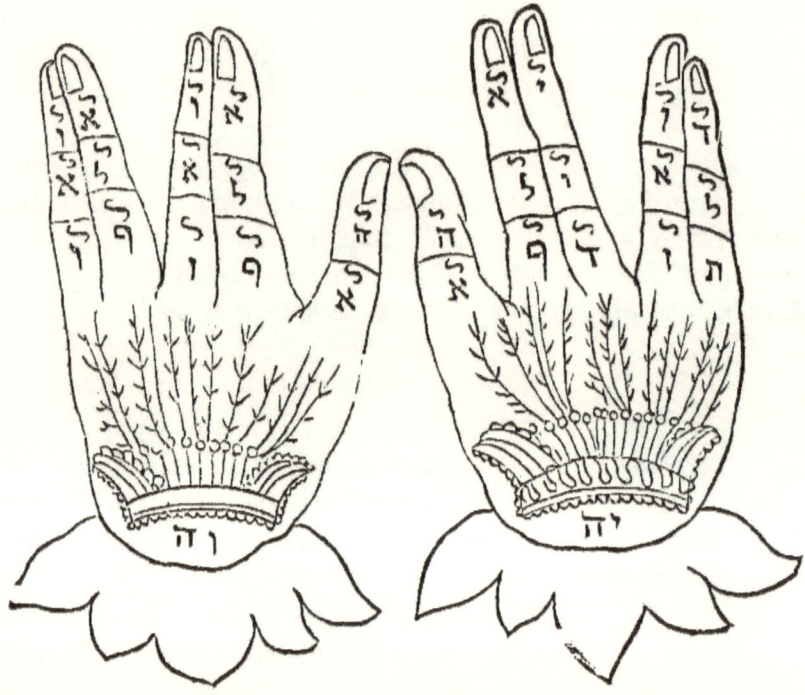

As indicated by the Hebrew letter pairs directly above the wrists of the two hands, it is clear that the right hand is associated with the letters י‎ה (YH) and the left with ה‎ו (VH), hence the two hands conjointly represent יהוה (YHVH). The ten fingers are aligned with the ten letters comprising the "*Mah* extension" of the Ineffable Name, i.e. יוד הא ואו הא (*Yod-vav-dalet Heh-alef Vav-alef-vav Heh-alef*), arranged in the following manner.

### Right Hand

י (*Yod*) spelled י (*Yod*—middle finger), ו (*Vav*—ring finger), ד (*Dalet*—little finger);

ה (*Heh*) spelled ה (*Heh*—thumb), א (*Alef*—index finger).

### Left Hand

ו (*Vav*) spelled ו (*Vav*—middle finger), א (*Alef*—ring finger), ו (*Vav*—little finger);

ה (*Heh*) spelled again ה (*Heh*—thumb), א (*Alef*—index finger).

However, we have only noted the said "extended spelling" of the Ineffable Name in terms, as it were, of the "tips" of the fingers, but there are further glyphs aligned with the remaining phalanges. This is where a particular peculiarity of the Hebrew alphabet is addressed, and what Rabbi Nachman meant with the statement that "in the world of *Atzilut*, the judgment is sweetened through the forty-two letters of the Name of *YHVH*, its expansion (*MaH*) and the expansion of the expansion—altogether 42 letters."[25]

As readers know well enough, every letter in Hebrew is a word comprised of letters, and those letters in turn are comprised of letters, etc. Hence a single Hebrew glyph can be infinitely meaningful to the one understanding and contemplating the component letters, which are, as it were, "hidden" inside that glyph. In this regard, consider the letter א. It is named אלף ("*Alef*"), a word comprising three letters which are equally words, i.e. אלף ("*Alef*"), ל ("*Lamed*"), and פ ("*Peh/Feh*"), and so forth *ad infinitum*. In other words, a single Hebrew glyph contains an enormous amount of information in its "expansions," as shown in this illustration of the "contents," so to speak, of the letter א (*Alef*) in terms of the standard spelling:

The French Kabbalist Carlos Suarès was particularly keen on examining the Hebrew alphabet in this manner.[26] Be that as it may, applying the same technique of further "expanding" the ten letters comprising the "*Mah* extension" of the Ineffable Name, we arrive at the following array of twenty-eight associated Hebrew glyphs:

Arranged over the twenty-eight phalanges of the ten fingers, we observe, in the shared illustration of the two hands, the letters comprising the first letter combination (יוד—*Yod*) arranged in the order: middle, ring and little finger, and the second letter combination (הא—*Heh*) arranged in the order: thumb and index finger of the right hand. In turn, the letters comprising the third letter combination (ואו—*Vav*) are arranged in the order: middle, ring and little finger, and the second letter combination (הא—*Heh*) is arranged in the order: thumb and index finger of the left hand.

Counting the 4 letters of יהוה (*YHVH*) pertaining to the two hands, the 10 letters spelling the "*Mah* extension" affiliated with the ten fingers, as well as the 28 glyphs comprising the further expansion of the said extension of the Ineffable Name in terms of the 28 phalanges of the fingers, Kabbalists arrived at the grand total of 42 "letters of the Name of *YHVH*" which Rabbi Nachman referenced in terms of "the judgment" being "sweetened" in the world of *Atzilut* (Emanation)."[27] As it is, the number forty-two is considered particularly important in terms of "sweetening the harsh judgments" on several levels of being. In this regard, we noted earlier that the *gematria* of the word יד (*Yad*—"hand") is 14 [י = 10 + ד = 4 = 14], and the five fingers of each hand comprises fourteen phalanges, i.e. 28 phalanges for both hands. However, emphasizing the special affinity between the numbers 14, 28 and 42, it was noted that whilst the numerical value of a single hand (יד—*Yad* ["hand"]) equals 14, the *gematria* of the "three hands" totals 3 x 14, i.e. 42. Furthermore, it was observed that the *gematria* of the word כח (*Ko'ach*—"might" or "Strength") equals 28 [כ = 20 + ח = 8 = 28]), and it is maintained that this is the primary spiritual force of the "Forty-two Letter Name of God" contained in the "*Ana Becho'ach*" prayer.[28]

Keeping these details in mind, you could now enact the following "magical" procedure of "*Sweetening the Harsh Judgments*" attached to money, which is particularly meaningful and effective. As noted earlier, we may "sweeten" the "severe judgment" in the "World of *Yetzirah*" by means of the "Name of Forty-two letters contained in the prayer '*Ana Becho'ach*'."[29] It is clear that it is the "Forty-two Letter Name of God," and not the "*Ana Becho'ach*" prayer which is being highlighted in this statement. However, whilst not included in the original practice which was shared with me nearly five decades ago, I personally like to commence and conclude the "*Sweetening the Harsh Judgments*" procedure with the *Ana Bechoach* Prayer. However, I do not include the standard ending at the recitation of this opening prayer, only doing so at the conclusion of the "Sweetening" procedure, which is as follows:

1. Utter complete *Ana Bechoach* Prayer, shared earlier in terms of the "Counting of the *Omer*."
2. [*Assiah*—"Action"] Recite aloud אני בינה לי גבורה (*Ani binah li Gevurah*—"I am Understanding, Power is Mine") [*Proverbs 8:14*].
3. Shape your fingers and hands into the wellknown "Double *Shin*" arrangement shape traditionally employed by High Priests, as indicated in the earlier shared hands illustration. In this manner each hand is indicating the initial ש (*Shin*) of the Divine Name שדי (*Shadai*), the Almighty One, whose power and protection are invoked by means of this action.
4. Place hands on the money, or hold hands over the money with palms facing downwards.
5. [*Yetzirah*] Whisper the "Forty-two letter Name" with great *Kavvanah* (focussed intention) concentration, whilst sensing the inherent power of the "Forty-two Letter Name of God" flow through your hands into the money. The "Forty-two Letter Name could be uttered either in seven six-letter or fourteen tri-letter combinations, these being:

### Six-letter Combinations

אבגיתצ קרעשטנ נגדיכש בתרצתג חקבטנע
יגלפזק שקוציח

Vocalised:
> Avgitatz Karastan Nagdichesh Batratztag Chakvetna Yaglefzok Shakutzit

### Tri-letter Combinations

אבג יתצ קרע שטנ נגד יכש בתר צתג
חקב טנע יגל פזק שקו ציח

Vocalised:
> AViGe YaToTzi KaRo' SaTaN' NaGiDa YeiCheiSha BiTaRo TzaTaG' CheKeVa TiN'I YaGaLi P'Z'Kei ShuKoVa TzoYaT'

6. [*Bri'ah*] Next turn your attention to the seven Hebrew glyphs comprising the Divine Names אהיה (*EH'YeH*) and יהו (*YHV*). These seven letters are said to align respectively with the seven sets of letters comprising the "Forty-two Letter Name of God." In this regard, while keeping your hands on or over the money, turn your attention to your heart which is said to be the seat of your Ru'ach (Awake Self) and the, as it were, "focus" of the "World of Soul" (*Bri'ah*-Creation) in your body. With a great "feeling appreciation," sense the seven letters of the Divine Names אהיה יהו (*Eh'yeh YHV*) in your heart. When ready, take a deep breath and during exhalation mentally express this Divine Name combination, sensing its power emanating from the palms of your hands into the money.

7. [*Atzilut*] Finally the practice of "sweetening the severe judgments" is concluded by aligning with the level of *Atzilut*, the "World of Emanation" which we noted earlier corresponds to "Spirit." In this instance, you would enunciate the מה (*Mah*) extension of the Ineffable Name over your hands. However, in this instance you start by visualising the four letters comprising the Ineffable Name, sensing them to be the size of mountains.

*The Oneness beyond All Being* / 405

This is followed by aligning the ten letters of the "*Mah*" extension of the Ineffable Name with the ten fingers in the following manner:

אה ואו הא יוד

**Right Hand**
י visualise and vocalise "Y*od*" over the middle finger;
ו visualise and vocalise "*Vav*" over the ring finger; and
ד visualise and vocalise "*Dalet*" over the little finger;

ה visualise and vocalise "*Heh*" over the thumb; and
א visualise and vocalise "*Alef*" over the index finger;

**Left Hand**
ו visualise and vocalise "*Vav*" over the middle finger;
א visualise and vocalise "*Alef*" over the ring finger; and
ו visualise and vocalise "*Vav*" over the little finger;

ה visualise and vocalise "*Heh*" over the thumb; and
א visualise and vocalise "*Alef*" over the index finger.

As noted elsewhere, "this act constitutes 'attachment' to the powers of the 'High Hand,' which must now be expressed through the fingers of your two hands. This is done by dividing the final twenty-eight letters into two groups of fourteen letters each, and in turn arranging these over the joints of the fingers."[30]

8. Whilst the plain utterance of the "*Mah*" extension of the Ineffable Name over the ten fingers is considered by some to be effective enough in "sweetening the severe judgments," it is in my estimation preferable to work the full procedure of focussing on the further expansion of the said extension of the Ineffable Name over the twenty-eight phalanges of the ten fingers. This is done in the following manner:

Focus on your right hand, the one named the "Great Hand" (*Gedulah*), and aligned with the first two letters of the Ineffable Name (יה). Visualise and sense the first fourteen letters literally flaming inside your fingers. Working from the upper phalanx to the bottom one of each finger, work the said technique in the following order:

a. the first three letters י-ו-ד (*Yod-Vav-Dalet*) correspond to the three phalanges of the right middle finger;
b. the next three letters ו-א-ו (*Vav-Alef-Vav*) correspond to the three phalanges of the right ring finger; and
c. the succeeding three letters ד-ל-ת (*Dalet-Lamed-Tav*) correspond to the three phalanges of the right little finger.

Collectively these three fingers and their associate letters comprise י (*Yod*) in the Ineffable Name. Repeat the action with the two sets of letters and fingers comprising the first ה (*Heh*) in the Ineffable Name:

a. the ה-א (*Heh-Alef*) align with the two phalanges of the right thumb; and finally
b. the א-ל-פ (*Alef-Lamed-Feh*) align with the three phalanges of the right index finger.

The sequence applied to your right hand, is repeated with the left hand, termed the "Strong Hand" (*Gevurah*), which in this instance is aligned with the concluding two letters of the Ineffable Name (וה). Visualise and sense the concluding fourteen letters of the "*Mah*" extension of the Ineffable Name, as it were, flaming inside the fingers of your left hand, doing so in the following sequence:

a. the first three letters of the remaining set ו-א-ו (*Vav-Alef-Vav*) correspond to the three phalanges of the left middle finger;
b. the next three letters א-ל-פ (*Alef-Lamed-Feh*) correspond to the three phalanges of the left ring finger; and

c. the succeeding three letters ו – א – ו (*Vav-Alef-Vav*) correspond to the three phalanges of the left little finger.

Again these three fingers on the left hand, as well as their associated letters, collectively comprise the ו (*Vav*) of the Ineffable Name. The remaining letters associated with the concluding ה (*Heh*) in the Ineffable Name, are aligned with the last two fingers of the left hand in the following manner:

a. the ה–א (*Heh-Alef*) align with the two phalanges of the left thumb; and
b. the final א–ל–פ (*Alef-Lamed-Feh*) align with the three phalanges of the left index finger.

Having visualised and sensed these letters virtually flaming inside the phalanges of your hands, conclude this portion of the procedure by inhaling and then exhaling the collective power of the invoked forces into the money on which your hands are resting.

9. As suggested, complete the procedure of "sweetening the harsh judgments," by reciting again the *Ana Bechoach* Prayer, this time concluding with the oft mentioned formula ברוך שם כבוד מלכותו לעולם ועד אמן (*Baruch Shem K'vod Malchuto l'Olam Va'ed Omein*— Blessed be the Name of His glorious Kingdom throughout eternity *Amen*).

The final step in this process is of course the "giving" itself. In this regard, the best form of benefaction is when "givers" do not know to whom they have given, and "receivers" do not know their benefactors. Whilst this is not always possible, the fundamental intention of the donors should always be no expectation whatsoever in terms of acknowledgment or recompense, not even a "thank you," from those who are benefitting from the one exercising *"The Art of Gifting."* It is almost as if the process of "gifting," necessitates you to separate your analytical mind from your hands. Regarding the hands employed in this special offering, it is worth noting that the ten fingers collectively represent the letter ' (*Yod*). The *gematria* of ' is 10, a number inclusive of all, and therefore called the "complete number." עשר (*Eser*), the Hebrew word for "ten," has the same spelling as *Osher* עשר—"wealth"). In this regard, I noted elsewhere that "it is understood that real abundance must be all-encompassing and without deficiency."[31] So, however small and insignificant the letter ' (*Yod*) may appear to be, it is truly great in meaning, and it is in this regard that I maintained that this glyph "could be considered the most primordial of all the Hebrew glyphs."[32] This tiny glyph "encompasses the beginning and the end of writing, and "its singularity is said to be designated by the word *Yachid* (יחיד—'single'), indicating the 'Singular Master,' the Divine One who is 'a complete and absolute unity'."[33]

## B. Self "Creation" vs "Uncreation"

Amongst the many remarkable lessons I learned from my late mentor, William G. Gray, is the one that you continuously affirm exactly who you are at every moment of your life, i.e. you say you are weak and you are weak; you say you are strong and you are strong; etc. He also maintained that you can lose faith in everything and be fine, but when you lose faith in yourself, you have lost everything. These factors are vital in understanding the process of *"Self Creation vs Self Uncreation,"* especially when it comes to dealing with what you might perceive to be the vicissitudes of life.

Most magical traditions offer techniques which are meant to deal with the numerous difficulties you may encounter in life, but few seem to focus on the great difficulty of the "person," i.e. of the very one trying to find a solution to a difficult situation. Amongst the many interesting ideas I have chanced upon in my encounters with *Practical Kabbalah*, is that you have to *BE* within yourself that which you want to establish in your world. This means that the "centre" (self) emanates or establishes the "circumference" ("external reality"), and this is the basic premise on which "*The Book of Self Creation*" is based.[34] This means that a "magical action" aimed at a specific outcome, could be doomed to failure whilst you are still contemplating an appropriate procedure relevant to the said desired result. In this regard, there are in my estimation fundamentally three factors which can hamper the outcome of a "magical action."

## 1. THE DESIRE FOR RESULTS

Having personally successfully worked a major amount of the magical techniques shared in this series of texts on Jewish Magic (*Practical Kabbalah*), I should emphasize that the *desire for results*, directly affects the outcome of any magical practice. As it is, the most successful "magical procedures" are worked by those who perform a magical procedure "for the heck of it," and then get it out of their minds as quickly as they possible can.

In this regard I have noted elsewhere, that "you must literally work because you enjoy it, practising for the sake of the 'art'......" and "perform a magical ritual because you want to do it, without caring whether it will work or not, or whether it will produce any effects or not." The emphasis is that you should not "seek any outcome, even if a working is done for a specific purpose," but to "simply work 'uninvolved,' which does not mean 'do not care' or not to put in effort. Just do not let spiritual, intellectual, egotistical, or emotional expectations cloud and destroy your efforts. Thus it is that at the end of the working, you should immediately wipe it from your mind."[35] In this regard, I wrote regarding the utterance of a "magical mantra" for a special purpose, that the magical action is complete when, "during the procedure, one begins to loose the desire for the end result, and when the words as well as their component letters are beginning to be but sounds without specific meanings, i.e, one is no longer, as it were, 'forcing' the words into the fixed meanings set by ones desire."[36] Thus I noted that the magical action "is halted when this stage is reached," following which you have to "forget the entire action so as to allow the *real* 'forces' behind the words to get on with the job."[37]

I recently witnessed a prime example of the effectiveness of "getting it out of your mind." A very dear friend and companion worked a Mercury "Planetary Magic" invocation for the purposes of boosting sales and finances. Shortly thereafter he was doing particularly well financially, and having particularly good interaction with a client. It suddenly occurred to him that he had completely forgotten that he had performed the said "Mercury procedure." He promptly posted me a "WhatsApp" message saying

"Invoked Mercury with a new client today, then forgot about it completely. Came away from the interaction thinking 'God I'm on form today! *Dohhh!!!*" To this I excitedly responded "Good man! Actually, the vital factor is that you 'forgot about it'! That is what makes the whole thing work. A desire for results actually kills it, hence, you simply work the technique and 'forget' about it! *Voila*.....simple and easy.....a prime example of immediate magic!"

Even in this instance the "magical outcome," like a very vulnerable infant, is in danger of being annihilated by the very one who engendered it. As noted, there are further factors which impede the successful outcome of magical activities.

## 2. THE DOUBT FACTOR

Having shared this incredible Tradition for several decades with a number of personal students, it has become fairly easy for me to distinguish who amongst them would become "successful magicians," and who would, as it were, "not make it." The practitioners who achieve the best results are those who do not question the validity of any of the techniques they are working, whilst those who constantly query "whether it will work" are mostly unsuccessful.

I recall having an unfortunate interaction with an individual who asked whether there was a technique for a specific purpose. On informing him that there was, he queried "Does it work?" to which I responded "No it doesn't!" He was outraged at my rejoinder, and queried how I could consider sharing with him a "magical technique" which was ineffective? I responded that the practice in question works well enough, and that it was actually *HE* himself who told me that it did not work. In other words, his query affirms his doubts, and therefore he could not work the magical practice successfully.

Plainly then, it is again a question of simply employing a magical technique relevant to your purpose, working the practice with great *Kavvanah* (focussed intention) without questioning the merits or demerits of the actual practice, and then "leaving well enough alone," as my late Mentor, William G. Gray, used to say.

## 3. REAFFIRMING THE *STATUS QUO*

Readers would probably have realised that successfully working any of the "Self Creation" techniques I have addressed in my works, does not pertain to ability alone. In fact, we are all "Self Creators," and are able to physically, mentally, emotionally and spiritually establish the reality we desire, but often what might have taken weeks, months, or even years to create, can be "uncreated" literally within minutes by, as it were, "resetting" and "re-empowering" the very situation we seek to transform. Again, every single, self aware individual on this world is a "master" at "Self Creation," with the majority being greater "masters" of instant "Self Uncreation"! The latter is probably the most difficult aspect of human nature for each practitioner of "Self Creation" to deal with.

For example, you might have been battling to disempower individuals from constantly targeting and abusing you. You might have taken the most powerful magical action to counteract this abusive behaviour, to the point where they should no longer affect you. Yet you reinstated that very abuse instantly with your *Kavvanah*, your focussed attitude, your mental, emotional and physical stance, when at the least sign of the abusive individuals making the slightest futile and totally impotent attempt to impact you negatively, you overreacted thereby handing power straight back to them by exclaiming "they are still doing me harm."

You may spend many months working an array of unique magical techniques in order to construct the most ideal scenario in terms of a desired outcome, yet could "uncreate" everything within literally two minutes flat by means of an emotional reaction to imagined scenarios which not only successfully annihilates all the work you may have done, but instantly affirms the very thing you do not want, but which you believe you are about to get. Of course, plain common sense informs each of us quite clearly that "it has not gone wrong until it has gone wrong," but common sense rarely prevails within the human psyche which often responds "I said the wrong thing, and now I have destroyed my chances," or "they want to destroy me, and they have succeeded in doing just that," etc., etc., etc. Every time you express something of that nature, especially when it is backed with emotions of anger, despair, etc., you are in fact creating and affirming the very situation you do not want. In other words, they have no power over you at all, and cannot harm you in any way beyond you handing power back to them by acknowledging that they have power over you.

Such behaviour can equally hamper the activities of anyone trying to help an individual to overcome personal difficulties. In this regard, I was once approached by an individual who was deeply concerned about his daughter being diagnosed with diabetes whilst she was pregnant with her first child. It was claimed that the said condition could negatively impact the pregnancy, and that she could even lose the child. I was naturally concerned and agreed to investigate the matter, the aim being to apply a magical healing technique which would support her throughout the remainder of her pregnancy, and ensure that both mother and child stay healthy. On investigating the matter closely, I ascertained that the lady in question did not suffer from actual diabetes at all, but was having "gestational diabetes," a common condition affecting literally thousands of pregnant women, and whilst it should be handled with care, it is not actually diabetes in the true sense of the word. I tried everything to allay the fears of the immediate family of the lady in question, but nothing worked. Their minds were made up that diabetes was the order of the day, and that her life and that of her unborn child were at stake.

Knowing the principles and possibilities of "Self Creation," I am perfectly aware of what this irrational belief could lead to, and hence resorted to one of the most important "magical" techniques, which is to convince the individual in question that I was employing the most "powerful magical practices" in order to "reverse" the disabling conditions. I also performed techniques pertaining to direct identification with the person in question, which were aimed at establishing a surrendered and peaceful state of mind. Instantly her health was back to normal, and the rest of the gestation and birthing process went exceptionally well. By accepting that she was aligned with someone whom they believed had some sort of hot line to that which is most powerful in manifestation, it was no longer necessary to fear debilitating self created scenarios. It is therefore vitally important to understand with absolute clarity that the one employing any technique, spiritual or otherwise, in order to overcome a difficult life situation, needs to maintain the correct stance at all times, which is fundamentally "You have no power. I give you power!" If you are able to maintain this attitude, the "centre" will control the "circumference" and you will be able to master any difficult situation.

Of course, there are situations which are far more complex and difficult to control. In this regard, I communicated a while back with an individual who mentioned that, in his own words, "he was a highly successful entrepreneur living a blessed life." He stated that suddenly, for no apparent reason, his health began to fail, he started to suffer great financial loss, and all relationships began to break up in an extreme manner. After some time he began to understand that this was not quite "natural," not that anything like that can ever be termed "natural" in any case. Be that as it may, he eventually ascertained that he was under direct psychic assault. It appears that the individual in question had been living with this situation for around ten years prior to approaching me, and during this time he consulted with a variety of spiritual advisers ranging from Shamans to those who promulgate the doctrines of a popular modern day Kabbalistic cult. He approached me in the desperate hope of employing *Practical Kabbalah*, in his own words, to "put on the figurative warrior garb and reclaim my life in a manner that feels aligned with my heritage, in alignment with *Hashem*" [my italics].

The said individual noted that he had some dealings with Kabbalah previously, having acquainted himself with the ten *sefirot*, scanned and attempted to "make some sense out of Zohar." However, he equally noted that the "solution can't be as simple as the *Ana B'choach* and the *Sh'ma* prayed with the right consciousness" [my italics]. As can be expected, there are a number of Hebrew Divine Names, including the "Forty-two Letter Name" on which the celebrated "*Ana B'choach*" prayer is based, which are specifically designed to deal with the problem of the person in question. There are equally a number of procedures which can be employed to work the "rectification," so to speak, e.g. *lachashim* (incantations), *kameot* (amulets), *segulot* (special magical procedures), etc. On selecting from amongst these, I suggested that he commence with a simple "*Hagah*," since Hebrew "mantric" procedures are one of the best ways of dealing speedily with the kind of problem to which the said individual was referring. Furthermore, any "Hebrew mantra" can be expanded upon and greatly empowered if needs be.

Having carefully considered the matter, I listed the remarkable and potent "magical qualities" of the earlier addressed אנקתם פסתם פספסים דיונסים (*Anaktam Pastam Paspasim Dionsim*) Divine Name construct. I suggested that the said individual employ the "Twenty-two Letter Name of God" as a *Hagah* (mantra), whispering or uttering it in the lowest voice he could muster inside his chest or solar plexus, the latter being the zone previously called the "liver." I further recommended that he he should perform this action continuously for around a week. Understanding that such a procedure could be problematic in terms of those with large, sensitive and quizzical ears in his immediate vicinity, I informed the said individual that the enunciation of the *Hagah* does not need to be aloud, but that it should be reiterated in his mind, heart, or solar plexus all day long.

I am perfectly aware that the individual in question could not keep focussing on his heart/chest/solar plexus the entire day, but he certainly could utter it in the back of his mind, and occasionally focus on sensing it, as it were, resonating inside his torso whenever the said Divine Name construct would come to mind. As delineated earlier, it would also be necessary to utter the *Hagah* as rhythmically as possible. I concluded this initial instruction by noting that, following the week of working the "Twenty-two Letter Name of God" in this manner, we could reassess, enlarge, or further empower the procedure. Having afforded the said individual the necessary time to work the initial "mantric magic," and having informed him that he should continue to recite the "Twenty-two Letter Name of God" as a *Hagah* until it became absolutely automatic to pronounce it virtually unconsciously at all times, I shared a more expanded version of the same "*Hagah*," i.e. the earlier addressed *Anaktam Pastam Paspasim Dionsim Yohach Kalach Tzamarchad Azbugah*, to be employed in conjunction with his personal name.

However, further interaction with the said individual thereafter, indicated that he was focussed virtually exclusively on the "evil" which had been done to him. He seemed to be fully occupied with this misfortune, stating that, in his own words, "I found PRECISELY what was done to me. I know who and I know how. It involves four specific demons and a host of angels and four sigils. There was a lengthy preparation/protection phase. I have every single detail including the sigils (which I haven't looked at) and the names of the spirits called upon." In his estimation, all the rabbis, psychics, and healers he approached were unable to help him. Furthermore, he noted that he found a number of "boastful magicians" online, who all appear young and arrogant, and thus he would not put his trust in any of them. Furthermore, despite the practices I already shared with him, he kept asking to be directed "as to how to reverse this curse aimed at my health, my home, my relationships, and my ability to see and think." Fundamentally doubting the efficacy of the recommended *Hagah*, he wanted to know if I had something stronger, and stated that he hoped I might, "at the very least," point him in the "right direction."

Naturally this raised a red flag for me, since I began to sense that he did not really believe the material I shared with him would "work the trick," so to speak. In fact, it became abundantly clear that he would simply "uncreate" whatever good he might receive from the many rectification techniques in *Practical Kabbalah* (Jewish Magic), which could have alleviated his plight directly. Thus I found it necessary to approach the said individual in the most direct, blunt manner possible, hoping that this would shock him out of what appeared to be a "self inflicted stupor," which was admittedly triggered by some or other unpleasant incident. I believe this "shock response" applies to all who are caught in the rut of self pity, self destruction, and the inability to recognise that they alone need to pull themselves up by their own bootstraps. In other words, no matter what anybody might do to benefit them, they will annihilate all that "goodness" by continuously wallowing in their own misery. Hence the necessity of the said "shock response," which I share, with some modification of the original statement, with all who suffer from this unfortunate affliction:

"You are facing your world with an image of total disaster. You are telling me that you know exactly who did whatever to you..... the *exact* number of demons employed.....that nobody understands.....that nobody can help you? I can give you a single

Divine Name, or even one considered to be of the least significance, which would dispel any measly evil, except for the one 'evil' called 'self' which is the most devious of them all. It tells you 'you are bewitched,' you 'know how'.....you 'know why'.....you 'know how to the exact four demons'! Nobody *can* help you, because you have become so totally obsessed with being bewitched, that you have indeed been bewitched by your own obsession. What do you want *me* to do about it? Where *does* it end? What do *you* want *me* to do? For heaven's sake, just kick them in the nuts and be done with it! That is a very clean, clear-cut, and most direct exorcism.

My late mentor of blessed memory told *me*, and I am telling *you* this straight from the horse's mouth, you can lose faith in everything and still be okay, but if you lose faith in your*SELF* you've lost *EVERYTHING!!* So my advice to you, which I am shouting from the rooftops is, 'pull yourself together,' no more no less. Come on, my magic is not pathetic when it comes to facing myself in the mirror of truth! That is your answer! Enough! Be done with it. 'They' of great insignificance started it, *you finish it* with that which is of great significance! *Omein netzach va-ed SELAH.*"

Having acknowledged that you indeed have the full capacity to be the creator of your own destiny, i.e. that you are the master of your own "Self Creation," you could meaningfully and successfully perform any of the practices which I have shared in these tomes on *Practical Kabbalah*. As far as spiritual protection is concerned, and as might be expected, there are many Divine Names and techniques employed in Jewish Magic to counteract "psychic assault." However, be it noted that the efficacy of these techniques are entirely dependent on the mindset of the practitioner, and therein lies the rub as I am sure you now understand well enough.

## C. At the End of Everything!

One of the most difficult issues for humans to deal with is the death of a loved one. Never mind how much one might want to explain it away with words like "a merciful release......," "he/she is in a better place," etc., the pain accompanying the loss of someone very dear to you is still extremely hard to bear. I once attended one of those psycho-spiritual courses in which one is faced with the question "What can I lose and still be me?" The fundamental intention of the presenter was to bring each participant to the realisation that you could lose everything, and that you would still be "you." However hard they tried, and whatever they did to convince me that I would still be the same after the loss of everything and everyone dear to me, my entire being would not budge an inch. I understand that I will still be around when I lose someone dear to me, but I will be so much less because they will no longer be here in the flesh.

I have encountered death many times in this lifetime, and with the demise of every human, or animal for that matter, whose physical presence was a shining star in my life, a portion of me also "died" with their passing. I have heard many an argument put forward by those who would persuade me of the folly of my behaviour in this regard, but none has thus far convinced me, nor has made me feel better about those who were dear to me, and whose departure left me with a profound sense of loss. In fact, to this day I yearn for the physical presence of those beings who made my life so meaningful. There is a uniqueness to each and everyone, whether of the human or animal kind, which resonates in specific ways in my soul, and I miss all of those who are no longer around. I am sure the same scenario applies to everyone who at some or other time has had to endure the inevitable demise of someone dear to him or her.

Regarding matters of life and death, I thought some readers might be interested in two very important Divine Name constructs respectively pertaining to "Birth" (incarnation) and "Death" (excarnation). These Divine Names comprise the conjunction of יהוה (*YHVH*) אדני (*Adonai*), i.e. יאהדונהי (vocalised in the current instance *Y'ahodovanaheiyo*), and איהדונויה (vocalised *Ay'dohonavayohei*). To understand the uniqueness of these Divine Name combinations, we need to consider that in *Kabbalah* the Ineffable Name is employed with specific reference to the sphere of *Tiferet* (Beauty) on the sefirotic Tree, whilst the Name *Adonai* pertains to the sphere of *Malchut* (Kingdom). We are often reminded of the particular fascination Kabbalists have with the relationship between *Tiferet* and *Malchut* in Jewish Mysticism. Respectively these two *sefirot* represent:

| *Tiferet* (Beauty [King]) | *Malchut* (Kingdom) |
|---|---|
| יהוה (*YHVH*) | אדני (*Adonai*) |
| Sun (Direct Light) | Moon (Reflected Light) |
| King | Queen |
| Upper | Lower |
| Male Principle | Female Principle |
| Lover | Beloved |
| Husband | Bride |

Engendering a "sacred marriage" between *Tiferet* (King) and *Malchut* (Queen-*Shechinah*), or the male and female aspects of the Divine One, is understood to be "the most important task that the mystic assumes in his quest."[38] In this regard, the sexual act itself is a physical expression of the "sacred union" of the Divine Male and Female Principles, i.e. when undertaken with the fully focussed intention of unifying the "Eternal One" (Divine Father) and the *Shechinah* (Divine Mother). We have been reminded that "*sexual intimacy* within the life of God is the paradigmatic expression of divine wholeness."[39] Furthermore, whilst we note the sexual act being employed with the intention of encouraging a "Sacred Marriage" between the masculine and feminine aspects of the Divine One, the visualisation and mental expression of יאהדונהי (*Y'ahodovanaheiyo*) is equally understood to facilitate the said "Sacred Marriage."

As noted above, two Divine Name constructs result from the conjunction of the Ineffable Name and *Adonai*, i.e. יאהדונהי and אידהנויה. The first combination, considered to be "Solar," aligns with "*B'rachot*" (Blessings), i.e. the channeling of "Direct Light" from *Tiferet* (Beauty) to *Malchut* (Kingdom), whilst the second combination, understood to be "Lunar," pertains to "*Kadishim*" (Sanctifications), i.e. the redirection of the Reflected Light back from *Malchut* (the "Lower Splendour") to *Tiferet* (the "Supernal Splendour"). This interplay between the mentioned *sefirot* refers to our relationship with the "Eternal Living Spirit." It is a kind of "inner sexuality" between the "Infinite One" and our "Selves," in which there is a continuous flow of "Divine Light" generated and projected by Divinity to us, which we then have to refocus and return for renewal in the "wholeness" of the "One-Beyond-All-Being," from whence it is re-projected to us, and so forth. Therefore contemplation of the said two Divine Name constructs is not only understood to facilitate the union of the Divine One and the *Shechinah*, but is said to facilitate the process of "opening the heart" in alignment with the "Spiritual Powers" inherent in the Divine Names. The fundamental motive is to literally infuse oneself with "Divine Force," in order to engender the unencumbered flow of "Divine Abundance" not only in ones life, but also outwards into the wider realm of physical manifestation.

We are reminded that the *gematria* (numerical value) of the יאהדונהי (*Y'ahodovanaheiyo* or *Yahadonahi*) Divine Name construct is equivalent to\ that of the word אמן (*Amen*), both being valued 91. Thus it is said *Amen* "reinforces" the sanctity of the "*Yahadonahi*," the latter being also known as the "Eight Letter Name of God." In terms of my earlier reference to the *Y'ahodovanaheiyo* and *Ay'dohonavayohei* Divine Name constructs being respectively aligned with *B'rachot* (Blessings) and *Kadishim* (Sanctifications), these being references to the actual applications of the associated Divine Name constructs in the Hebrew blessings and prayers for the deceased (*Kadish*), the reference is to the visualisation and mental expression of the יאהדונהי (*Y'ahodovanaheiyo*) combination when giving the *Omein* (*Amen*) response after a blessing, and doing the same with the אידהנויה (*Ay'dohonavayohei*) construct every time the *Omein* answer is given during the *Kadish* prayer. There are several reasons for doing this practice. As indicated earlier, in the case of the practice of mentally tracing and expressing the first Divine Name combination, the intention is to direct the flow of "Light" from the higher (*Tiferet*) to the lower (*Malchut*), which is the "sequence of the Sun," whilst in the instance of following the same procedure with the second Divine Name construct during *Kadish*, the intention is to reflect "Light" from the lower (*Malchut*) back to the higher (*Tiferet*), this being the "sequence of the Moon."

The basic difference between the two formats of the *YHVH/Adonai* Divine Name combination is the order of the letters. The "direct light" combination commences and ends with the letter

Yod (י), indicating the יחודא עלאה (*Yichuda Ila'ah*—"Higher Union") in which the whole of creation is united with the Eternal One beyond all manifestation. On the other hand, the "returning light" Divine Name construct begins with *Alef* (א), the "Life-death Principle of all that *Is* and all that *Is-not*," and ends with *Heh* (ה), the concluding letter of the Ineffable Name, in this instance indicating the return of the life-force into the higher "realms of spirit," this being יחודא תתאה (*Yichuda T'ta'ah*—"Lower Union").

You do not have to be Jewish or, for that matter, follow any traditional Jewish liturgy pertaining to uttering blessings and saying prayers for the deceased, in order to employ these remarkable Divine Name constructs effectively in terms of "Births" and "Deaths." You could simply visualise and whisper (or mentally utter) the יאהדונהי (*Y'ahodovanaheiyo*) Divine Name construct at the birth of a child, and conclude the action with the expression "*Omein (Amen) Baruch ha-Shem.*" In this manner, you facilitate the "Higher Union" and allow the "Solar" flow of "Direct Light" into the realm of manifestation and into the life of the newborn. On the other hand, in the case of the death of someone dear to you, you could just as easily visualise and whisper (or mentally utter) the אידהנויה (*Ay'dohonavayohei*) Divine Name combination, and thus facilitate the "Lower Union" whilst allowing the "Lunar" flow of "Reflected Light" to return with the soul of the dearly departed into the great Oneness within Universal Being, again concluding the action with the mentioned "*Omein (Amen) Baruch ha-Shem*," as I have done for my beloved friend Jonathan Helper, *alav ha-shalom v'zichrono livracha* (Peace be upon him and may his Memory be a Blessing)!

Finally, at the conclusion of this lengthy tome, I believe the most important realisation is that all life begins in "Consciousness" somewhere, and if "Consciousness" is continuous and contiguous, all death does is change us from one state to another. That may or may not be a "good" change as we understand the word, but, whatever the case may be, it is important that we comprehend that death is not a *separation* but rather an *incorporation*. In other words, however dreadful and painful the physical demise of those who are dear to you may be, and however much you may miss their physical, objective presence as you continue your earthlife, it is important to know that whilst deceased friends and companions are no longer separate and objective earth living entities, they do continue *inside* you in some degree for the rest of your earth life.

In my estimation the ultimate recognition of reality for the "magician," the one who is a "Self Creator," is that all things exist inside yourself—literally! God, the "Life-Spirit," or whatever you like to term the "Eternal Oneness of Being" beyond time, space and events, is conscious in and living through each and every one of us individually. We do the same on a much smaller scale, but fundamentally it is the selfsame process, since we are equally conscious individually through each other. Whilst we have been aware of our separate identities as humans for a very very long time, and have suffered many painful circumstances ensuing from this condition of "separateness," we are becoming more and more aware of the "Great Identity," realising ourselves as extensions of *IT*. In fact, it is all a question of "Know Thyself." I am you and you are me. We are each other. Mystics have been saying this for centuries, and it is only a matter of realising it—*MAKING IT REAL!*

**. ... ... ...Then no one would gather the strands woven from the songs of the clear spring and the heart of the world could not give the spring its present; the spring would dry up, and without the spring the heart of the world would cease to beat."**

It is a great and mysterious magic which joins the clear spring and the heart of the world. The heart cannot live without the spring, but without the heart the spring itself would dry up. Each day at dusk it receives a gift from the heart— one day, one single day for which it can continue to flow. When that day has passed, the spring begins to sing. Only the heart of the world hears that song, and it answers the spring with a song of its own. They sing strange, magic songs, songs without words, notes, or melody, joyous or sad. The songs of the clear spring and the heart of the world are woven of strands of light. These strands rise into the sky, reaching the seventh heaven, and high above the world they spread out like a net filled with glitter and sparkle.

Day after day God's greatest angel comes to fashion the net into a new day. When it is ready he gives it to the heart of the world, and the heart gives it to the clear spring. Then the spring can gush until the next evening's twilight. But the angel of God who shapes the new day from the shining net has to be created anew each time. His head, body, arms and legs come only from the good deeds of men; but evil deeds destroy him. If people help each other, and live in peace and the fear of God, they give the angel life. But if there are always on earth more of those who kill, or steal, or deceive, the angel will not appear. Then no one would gather the strands woven from the songs of the clear spring and the heart of the world could not give the spring its present; the spring would dry up, and without the spring the heart of the world would cease to beat.

— from *"The End of the World"*
(retold by Leo Pavlát in *Jewish Tales: The Eight Lights of the Hanukkiya*, Beehive Books, London 1986)

# REFERENCES & BIBLIOGRAPHY

## INTRODUCTION

1. **Swart, J.G.:** *The Book of Self Creation*, The Sangreal Sodality Press, Johannesburg 2009.
2. *Ibid.*
   **Swart, J.G.:** *The Book of Sacred Names*, The Sangreal Sodality Press, Johannesburg 2011.
   —*The Book of Seals & Amulets*, The Sangreal Sodality Press, Johannesburg 2014.
   —*The Book of Immediate Magic - Part 1*, The Sangreal Sodality Press, Johannesburg 2015.
3. *The Sixth and Seventh Books of Moses or, Moses' Magical Spirit-art, known as the Wonderful Arts of the Old Wise Hebrews, taken from the Mosaic books of the Cabala and the Talmud, for the good of mankind. Translated from the German, word for word, according to Old Writings, with Numerous Engravings*, The Arthur Westbrook Co., 1870.
   **Selig, G.A.:** *Secrets of the Psalms: A Fragment of the Practical Kabala, with Extracts from other Kabalistic writings, as translated by the author*, Dorene, Arlington 1929.
4. **Savedow, S.:** *Sepher Rezial Hemelach: The Book of the Angel Rezial*, Samuel Weiser Inc., York Beach 2000.
5. **Gaster, M.:** *The Sword of Moses*, Samuel Weiser Inc., New York 1973.
6. *Sepher ha-Razim: The Book of the Mysteries*, transl. M.A. Morgan, Society of Biblical Literature, 1983.
7. **Zacutto, M.:** *Shorshei ha-Shemot*, Hotza'at Nezer Shraga, Jerusalem 1999.
8. **Bohak, G.:** *A Fifteenth-Century Manuscript of Jewish Magic: MS New York Public Library, Heb. 190 (formerly Sassoon 56), Introduction, Annotated Edition with Facsimile*, Hotsa'at Keruv, Los Angeles 2014.

9. **Tirshom, J. ben E.:** *Shoshan Yesod Olam* in *Collectanea of Kabbalistic and Magical Texts*, Bibliothèque de Genève: Comites Latentes 145, Genève.
10. *Segulot, Hashva'ot v'Goralot*, Yemenite script, MIC. #8988, Jewish Theological Seminary.
*Mazalot v'Goralot*, Jerusalem - The National Library of Israel Ms. Heb. 28°3987.
*Liber Cabbalae Operativae* (1401–1500), Biblioteca Medicea Laurenziana, Firenze, IT-FI0100. Plut.44.22
**Tirshom, J. ben E.:** *Shoshan Yesod Olam, Op. cit.*
**Bar Meir, M.:** *Sefer Segulot*, Ms. hebr. oct. 131, Universitätsbibliothek JCS, Frankfurt am Main.
**Tzayach, J.:** *Even ha-Shoham*, Ms. 8° 416, Jerusalem.
—*Sheirit Josef*, Ms. 260. Vienna.
*Sefer Shimmush Tehillim*, Éliás Békéscsaba Klein, Budapest.
*Sefer Mishpatei ha-Olam* & *Sefer ha-Mivcharim*, Hotza'at Backal, Jerusalem.
*Sepher ha-Razim: The Book of the Mysteries, Op. cit.*
*Havdalah d'Rabbi Akiva*, Hotza'at Backal, Jerusalem 1996.
*Sefer Raziel ha-Malach*, Yarid ha-Sefarim, Jerusalem 2003.
*Refuah v'Chaim mi-Yerushalayim*, Hotza'at Backal, Jerusalem.
*Segulot ha-Avanim ha-Tovot*, Yarid ha-Sefarim, Jerusalem 2004.
**Balmes, A. Ben M. de:** *Mekanah Avraham*, Venice 1523.
Moshe ben Ya'akov of Kiev: *Sefer Shoshan Sodot*, Drukeray Y. A. Kriger, Koretz 1784.
**Halevi, B. ben Meir:** *Sefer Zechira ve-Einei Segulah*, Novly Dvor, 1798.
**Azulai, C.Y.D.:** *Sefer Avodat ha-Kodesh*, Jerusalem 1841.
—*Midbar Kedemot*, Mayan ha-Chochmah, Jerusalem 1957.
—*Shem ha-Gedolim*, Yerid ha-Sefarim, Jerusalem 2004.
**Badrashi, Y.:** *Yalkut Moshe*, Munkatch 1894.
Mi-Yerushalayim, R. ben A.: *Sefer Segulot*, Kahn & Fried, Munkatch 1906.
**Asher, Y.Y. ben:** *Toldot Yitzchak*, Bilgoraj 1909.
**Heschel, A.Y.:** *Shemirot uSegulot Niflot*, Warsaw 1913.
**Sifrin, Y.Y.Y.:** *Sha'ar Sefer Adam Yashar*, Lemberg.
**Vital, Chaim:** *K'tavim Chadashim l'Rabbi Chaim Vital*, Machon l'Hotza'at Sefarim v'Kitve-yad Ahavat shalom, Jerusalem 1988.
—*Sefer ha-Goralot*, Hotza'at Backal, Jerusalem.
**B'ruk, Y.S.:** *S'dei b'Samim*, Buchdruckerei "Grafia," Munkatsh.

**Chamui, A.:** *Devek Me'Ach*, Yarid ha-Sefarim, Jerusalem 2005.
—*He'Ach Nafshenu*, Yarid ha-Sefarim, Jerusalem 2007.
—*Nifla'im Ma'asecha*, Hotza'at Backal, Jerusalem 1972.
—*Bet El*, Eliyahu ben Amozeg va-chavero, Livorno 1878.
—*Yimlat Nafsho*, E.M. Devich ha-Kohen, Calcutta 1884.
—*Avi'ah Chidot*, S. Belforti va-chavero, Livorno 1879.
—*Avi'ah Chidot*, Hotza'at Backal, Jerusalem 1996.
—*Liderosh Elohim*, Mosdot "Mishpatim Yesharim," Bnei Barak 2011.
**Ochanah, R. ben C.:** *Sefer Mareh ha-Yeladim*, Yerid ha-Sefarim, Jerusalem 1990.
**Lifshitz, S.:** *Sefer Segulot Yisrael*, Kahn & Fried, Munkatch 1905; Mosdot Hifchadeti Shomrim, Jerusalem 1992.
**Reuven ben Avraham:** *Sefer ha-Segulot*, Mukatch 1906.
**Heller, S.:** *Sefer Refuot vi-Segulot*, Jerusalem 1907.
**Sharabi, S.; Duwayk, H.S.; & Legimi, E.Y.:** *Sefer Benayahu Ben Yehoyada*, Jerusalem 1911.
**Greenup, A.W.:** *Sefer ha-Levanah: The Book of the Moon*, London 1912.
**Ba'al Livushei Sarad:** *Refuot*, J. Schlensinger Buchhandlung, Vienna 1926.
**Mizrachi, E.A.:** *Refuah v'Chayim m'Yerushalayim*, Defus Yehudah vi-Yerushalayim, Jerusalem 1931.
**Rubenstein, Y.Y.:** *Zichron Yakov Yoshef*, Defus Yehudah vi-Yerushalayim, Jerusalem 1931.
**Roth, A.:** *Ahavat ha-Bore*, Jerusalem 1959.
**Kratchin, B.B.:** *Amtachat Binyamin*, Hotza'at Backal, Jerusalem 1966.
**Gaster, M.:** *The Sword of Moses*, Op. cit.
—*Studies and Texts in Folklore, Magic, Mediaeval Romance, Hebrew Apocrypha, and Samaritan Archaeology* (3 Volumes), Maggs Bros. Ltd., London 1925—1928.
**Sha'uli, M.C.:** *Marpeh ha-Bosem*, ha-Merkaz ha-Ruchani kehilati u-Vet Kneset "Sha'uli," Ashdod 1987.
**Keter, S. ben A.:** *Nechash ha-Nechoshet*, Baruch Keter, Jerusalem 1990.
**Lifshitz, S.:** *Sefer Segulot Yisrael*, Mosdot Hifchadeti Shomrim, Jerusalem 1992.
**Ba'al Shem, Elijah; Ba'al-Shem, Joel; ha-Kohen, N. ben Isaac; & Katz, N.:** *Mifalot Elokim*, Mechon Bnei Yishachar, Jerusalem 1994.
—*Sefer Toldot Adam*, Machon Bnei Yishaschar, Jerusalem 1994.

**Palagi, C.:** *Refuah v'Chayim*, Machon l'Hotza'at Sefarim v'Cheker Kitvei Rabotenu ha-Kadmonim, Jerusalem 1997.
**Zacutto, M.:** *Shorshei ha-Shemot, Op. cit.*
**Avraham Rimon of Granada:** *Brit Menuchah*, Machon Ramchal, Jerusalem 1998.
**Rosenberg, Y.:** *Refael ha-Malach*, Asher Klein, Jerusalem 2000.
**Tzubeiri, Y.:** *Emet v'Emunah*, Machon Shtilei Zeitim, Ramat Gan 2002.
**Shniori:** *Mikra'i Refu'i Kelali im Tatzlumim v'Iyurim Rabim Ner Mitzvah b'Torah Or*, New York 2003.
**Almagor, Y.M.:** *Sefer Otsrot Malachim: v'Kuntres Shimushe Sarim*, Hod ha-Sharon: Yisra'el Meir Almagor u-vanav 2005.
**Blau, L.:** *Das Altjüdische Zauberwesen*, K.J. Trübner, Strassburg 1898.
**Thompson, R.C.:** *Semitic Magic: Its Origins and Development*, Luzac & Co., London 1909.
**Witton Davies, T.:** *"Magic" Back and White, Charms and Counter Charms, Divination and Demonology among the Hindus, Hebrews, Arabs and Egyptians*, de Laurence, Scott & Co., Chicago 1910.
**Dahse, J.:** *Babylonian Oil Magic in the Talmud and in the Later Jewish Literature*, Jews' College, London 1913.
**Montgomery, J.A.:** *Aramaic Incantation Texts from Nippur*, University Museum, Philadelphia 1913.
**Ahrens, W.:** *Hebräische Amulette mit Magischen Zahlenquadraten*, Louis Lamm, Berlin 1916.
**Trachtenberg, J.:** *Jewish Magic and Superstition: A Study in Folk Religion*, Behrman's Jewish Book House Publishers, New York 1939.
**Schrire, T.:** *Hebrew Amulets*, Routledge & Kegan Paul, London 1966.
**Budge, E.A.:** *Amulets and Talismans*, University Books, New York 1968.
**Josephy, M.R. & Spertus, M.:** *Magic & Superstition in the Jewish Tradition: An Exhibition Organized by the Maurice Spertus*, Spertus College of Judaica Press, Chicago 1975.
**Rothenberg, J.; Lenowitz, H. & Doria, C.:** *A Big Jewish Book: Poems & Other Visions of the Jews from Tribal Times to Present*, Anchor Press, New York 1978.
**Shachar, I.:** *Jewish Tradition in Art: The Feuchtwanger Collection of Judaica*, transl. R. Grafman, The Israel Museum, Jerusalem 1981.

**Naveh, J. & Shaked, S.:** *Amulets and Magic Bowls: Aramaic Incantations of Late Antiquity*, The Magnes Press, Jerusalem 1985.
—*Magic Spells and Formulae: Aramaic Incantations of Late Antiquity*, The Magnes Press, Jerusalem 1993.
**Lustig, D.:** *Pela'ot Chachmeh ha-Kabbalah: v'He'avar ha-Kadum*, Hotza'at David ben Ze'ev, Tel Aviv 1987.
—*Wondrous Healings of the Wise Kabbalists and the Ancient Physicians*, D. Lustig, Tel Aviv 1989.
**Kaplan, A.:** *Meditation and Kabbalah*, Samuel Weiser Inc., York Beach 1988.
**Ruderman, D.B.:** *Kabbalah, Magic and Science: The Cultural Universe of a Sixteenth-Century Jewish Physician*, Harvard University Press, Cambridge 1988.
**Neusner, J.; Frerichs, E.S. & Flesher, P.V.M.:** *Religion, Science, and Magic: In Concert and in Conflict*, Oxford University Press, New York 1989.
**Schiffman, L.H. & Swartz, M.D.:** *Hebrew and Aramaic Incantation Texts from the Cairo Geniza: Selected Texts from Taylor-Schechter Box K1*, JSOT Press, Sheffield 1992.
**Idel, M.:** *The Magical and Neoplatonic Interpretations of the Kabbalah in the Renaissance* in Cooperman, B.D.: *Jewish Thought in the Sixteenth Century*, Harvard University Press, Cambridge 1983.
—*Golem: Jewish Magical and Mystical Traditions on the Artificial Anthropoid*, SUNY Press, Albany 1990.
—*Hasidism: Between Ecstasy and Magic*, SUNY Press, Albany 1995.
—*Kabbalah in Italy 1280-1510: A Survey*, Yale University Press, New Haven 2011.
**Nigal, G.:** *Magic, Mysticism, and Hasidism: The Supernatural in Jewish Thought*, Jason Aronson Inc., Northvale 1994.
Meyer, M.W. & Mirecki, P.A.: *Ancient Magic and Ritual Power*, E.J. Brill, Leiden 1995.
—*Magic and Ritual in the Ancient World*, E.J. Brill, Leiden 2001.
**Davis, E. & Frenkel, D.A.:** *Ha-Kami'a ha-Ivri: Mikra'i Refu'i Kelali im Tatzlumim v'Iyurim Rabim*, Machon l'Mada'e ha-Yahadut, Jerusalem 1995.
**Davis, E. & E.:** *Jewish Folk Art over the Ages: A Collector's Choice*, R. Mass, Jerusalem 1997.
**Huberman, I.:** *Living Symbols: Symbols in Jewish Art and Tradition*, Modan Publishers Ltd., Jerusalem 1996.

**Swartz. M.D:** *Scholastic Magic: Ritual and Revelation in Early Jewish Mysticism*, Princeton University Press, Princeton, 1996.
**Isaacs, R.J.:** *Divination, Magic, and Healing: The Book of Jewish Folklore*, Jason Aronson Inc., Northvale 1998.
—*Judaism, Medicine and Healing*, Jason Aronson Inc., Northvale 1998.
—*Ascending Jacob's Ladder: Jewish Views of Angels, Demons, and Evil Spirits*, Jason Aronson Inc., Northvale 1998.
**Lesses, R.M.:** *Ritual Practices to Gain Power: Angels, Incantations and Revelations in Early Jewish Mysticism*, Trinity Press International, Harrisburg 1998.
**Shwartz-Be'eri, O.:** *The Jews of Kurdistan: Daily Life, Customs, Arts and Crafts*, The Israel Museum, Jerusalem 2000.
**Kanarfogel, E.:** *Peering Through the Lattices: Mystical, Magical, and Pietistic Dimensions in the Tosafist Period*, Wayne State University Press, Detroit 2000.
**Janowitz, N.:** *Icons of Power: Ritual Practices in Late Antiquity*, The Pennsylvania State University Press, Pennsylvania 2002.
**Klein, M.:** *Not to Worry: Jewish Wisdom & Folklore*, The Jewish Publication Society, Philadelphia 2003.
**Winkler, G.:** *Magic of the Ordinary*, North Atlantic Books, Berkeley 2003.
**Noegel, S.B., Walker, J.T. & Wheeler, B.:** *Prayer, Magic and the Stars in the Ancient and Late Antique World*, The Pennsylvania State University Press, Pennsylvania 2003.
**Chajes, J.H.:** *Between worlds: Dybbuks, Exorcists, and Early Modern Judaism*, University of Pennsylvania Press, Philadelphia 2003.
**Green, A.:** *Judaic Artifacts: Unlocking the Secrets of Judaic Charms and Amulets*, Astrolog Publishing House, Hod Hasharon 2004.
**Etkes, I.:** *The Besht: Magician, Mystic and Leader*, Brandeis University Press, Lebanon 2005.
**Skemer, D.C.:** *Binding Words: Textual Amulets in the Middle Ages*, Pennsylvania State University Press, Pennsylvania 2006.
**Cooper, D.A.:** *Invoking Angels: For Blessings, Protection and Healing*, Sounds True Inc., Boulder 2006.
**Dennis, G.W.:** *The Encyclopedia of Jewish Myth, Magic and Mysticism*, Llewellyn Publications, Woodbury 2007.
**Bloom, M.:** *Jewish Mysticism and Magic: An Anthropological Perspective*, Routledge, New York & London 2007.

**Bohak, G.:** *Ancient Jewish Magic: A History*, Cambridge University Press, Cambridge 2008.
—*The Charaktêres in Ancient and Medieval Jewish Magic* in *Acta Classica Universitatis Scientiarum Debreceniensis*, Vol. 47, Univ Debreceniensis, Debrecen 2011
—*A Fifteenth-Century Manuscript of Jewish Magic, Op. cit.*
**Vukosavović, F.:** *Angels and Demons: Jewish Magic through the Ages*, Bible Lands Museum Jerusalem, Jerusalem 2010.

11. **Swart, J.G.:** *The Book of Sacred Names, Op. cit.*
12. **Vital, Chaim:** *Sefer Sha'arei Kedushah*, Aharon Barazani, Tel Aviv, 1995; Hotza'at Yeshivat ha-Shamash, Jerusalem 1997.
13. **Karo, J. ben E.:** *Shulchan Aruch*, Kehot Publishing Company, Brooklyn 1967.
14. **Zacutto, M.:** *Shorshei ha-Shemot, Op. cit.*

# CHAPTER 6

1. **Swart, J.G.:** *The Book of Self Creation*, Op. cit.
2. **Gikatilla, J.:** *Gates of Light: Sha'are Orah*, transl. Avi Weinstein, Alta Mira Press, Walnut Creek 1998.
3. *Ibid.*
4. **Riccius, P.:** *Portae Lucis: haec est porta Tetragrammaton, iusti intrabunt per eam*, Augsburg 1516.
5. **Pistorius, J.:** *Ars Cabalistica: hoc est recondita Theologiae et Philosophiae*, Vol. 1, Henricpetris, Basil 1587.
6. **Pfefferkorn, J.:** *The Jew's Mirror*, trans. R.I. Cape, Arizona Center for Medieval and Renaissance Studies, Tempe 2011.
   **Reuchlin, J.:** *Recommendation Whether to Confiscate, Destroy, and Burn All Jewish Books*, trans. P. Wortsman, Paulist Press, New York 2000.
   **Rummel, E.:** *The Case against Johann Reuchlin*, University of Toronto Press, Toronto 2002.
   **Price, D.H.:** *Johannes Reuchlin and the Campaign to Destroy Jewish Books*, Oxford University Press, Oxford 2011.
   **Shamir, A.:** *Christian Conceptions of Jewish Books: The Pfefferkorn Affair*, Museum Tusculanum Press, Copenhagen 2011.
7. **Kaplan, A.:** *Meditation and Kabbalah*, Op. cit.
8. **Gikatilla, J.:** *Gates of Light*, Op. cit.
9. **Kaplan, A.:** *Jewish Meditation: A Practical Guide*, Schocken Books Inc., New York 1985.
10. **Besserman, P.:** *The Shambhala Guide to Kabbalah and Jewish Mysticism*, Shambhala, Berkeley 1997.
    **Davis, A.:** *Meditation from the Heart of Judaism: Today's Teachers Share Their Practices, Techniques and Faith*, Jewish Lights Publishing, Woodstock 1997.
    **Fine, L.:** *Essential Papers on Kabbalah*, New York University Press, New York and London 1995.
    **Fisdel, S.A.:** *The Practice of Kabbalah: Meditation in Judaism*, Jason Aronson Inc., Northvale 1996.
    **Gray, W.G.:** *The Ladder of Lights*, Samuel Weiser Inc., York Beach, 1981.
    —*The Talking Tree*, Samuel Weiser Inc., New York 1977.
    —*The Tree of Evil*, Samuel Weiser Inc., York Beach, 1984.

—*Magical Ritual Methods*, Helios Book Service Ltd., Cheltenham 1969.
—*A Self Made by Magic*, Samuel Weiser Inc., New York 1976.
—*Qabalistic Concepts: Living the Tree*, (Previously *Concepts of Concepts*, Sangreal Sodality Series, Volume 3), Samuel Weiser Inc., York Beach 1997.
—*A Beginners Guide to Living Kabbalah*, The Sangreal Sodality Press, Parkmore 2009.
**Hoffman, E.:** *Opening the Inner Gates: New Paths in Kabbalah and Psychology*, Shambhala, Boston & London 1995.
**Kaplan, A.:** *Meditation and Kabbalah, Op. cit.*
—*Meditation and The Bible*, Samuel Weiser, York Beach 1978.
**Labowitz, S.:** *Miraculous Living: A Guided Journey in Kabbalah Through the Ten Gates of the Tree of Life*, Fireside, New York 1996.
**Rosenberg, A.:** *Jewish Liturgy as a Spiritual System: A Prayer-by-Prayer Explanation of the Nature and Meaning of Jewish Worship*, Jason Aronson Inc., Northvale 1997.
**Roth, J.:** *Jewish Meditation for Everyday Life: Awakening Your Heart, Connecting with God*, Jewish Lights Publishing, Woodstock 2009.
**Sherwin, B.L.:** *Kabbalah: An Introduction to Jewish Mysticism*, Rowman & Littlefield Publishers, Inc., Lanham 2006.
**Stewart, R.J.:** *The Miracle Tree: Demystifying the Qabalah*, New Page Books, Franklin Lakes 2003.

11. **Tzayach, Y.:** *Even ha-Shoham*, Ms. 8° 416, Jerusalem.
    **Kaplan, A.:** *Meditation and Kabbalah, Op. cit.*
12. **Swart, J.G.:** *The Book of Immediate Magic - Part 1, Op. cit.*
13. *Ibid.*
14. *Ibid.*
15. *Ibid.*
    **Anonymous:** *Ma'aseh ha-Tzafon* (*Tzafun*), privately owned manuscript.
16. *Ibid.*
17. *Ibid.*
18. **Regardie, I.:** *A Garden of Pomegranates*, Llewellyn Publications, 1970.
19. **Cordovero, M.:** *Pardes Rimmonim*, Yarid ha-Sefarim, Jerusalem 2000.
20. *Ibid.*
    **Robinson, I.:** *Moses Cordovero's Introduction to Kabbalah: An Annotated Translation of His Or Ne'erav*, The Michael Sharf Publication Trust of the Yeshiva University Press, New York 1994.

21. **Robinson, I.:** *Ibid.*
22. *Ibid.*
23. **Gikatilla, J.:** *Gates of Light: Sha'are Orah*, *Op. cit.*
24. *Ibid.*
25. *Ibid.*
26. **Robinson, I.:** *Moses Cordovero's Introduction to Kabbalah, Ibid.*
    **Cordovero, M.:** *Pardes Rimmonim*, *Op. cit.*
    **Chalfon, E.:** *Milon Ivri Kabbali*, Aharon Barzani u-Veno, Tel Aviv 1997.
27. **Fine, L.:** *Essential Papers on Kabbalah*, New York University Press, New York & London 1995.
    **Leet, L.:** *Renewing the Covenant: A Kabbalistic Guide to Jewish Spirituality*, Inner Traditions International, Rochester 1999.
    **Segal, E.:** *Reading Jewish Religious Texts*, Routledge, Oxon & New York 2012.
28. **Swart, J.G.:** *The Book of Immediate Magic - Part 1*, *Op. cit.*
29. **Gray, W.G.:** *The Rite of Light: A Mass of the Western Inner Mystery Tradition*, limited & numbered edition, Privately Printed, Cheltenham 1976 (Reprinted with explanations in *The Sangreal Sacrament*, Volume 2, Sangreal Sodality Series, Samuel Weiser Inc., York Beach, 1983).
30. **Gray, W.G.:** *A Beginners Guide to Living Kabbalah*, *Op. cit.*
31. *Ibid.*
32. *Ibid.*
33. *Ibid.*
34. **Tzayach, Y.:** *Sheirit Yosef*, Ms. 260, Vienna.
35. **Benyamini, S.:** *Pardes ha-Nisim Tehilim*, Shlomo Benyamini, Tel Aviv undated.
36. **Swart, J.G.:** *The Book of Immediate Magic - Part 1*, *Op. cit.*
37. **Anonymous:** *Ma'aseh ha-Tzafon (Tzafun)*, *Op. cit.*
38. **Swart, J.G.:** *The Book of Self Creation*, *Op. cit.*
39. **Swart, J.G.:** *The Book of Immediate Magic - Part 1*, *Op. cit.*
40. *Ibid.*
41. *Ibid.*
42. *Ibid.*
43. *Ibid.*
44. *Ibid.*
45. *Ibid.*
46. *Ibid.*
47. *Ibid.*
48. *Ibid.*
49. *Ibid.*

50. *Ibid.*
51. *Ibid.*
52. *Ibid.*
53. **Gikatilla, J.:** *Gates of Light: Sha'are Orah*, Op. cit.
    **Herrera, A.C. de:** *Gate of Heaven*, transl. K. Krabbenhoft, Brill Academic Publishers, Leiden 2002.
    **Robinson, I.:** *Moses Cordovero's Introduction to Kabbalah*, Op. cit.
    **Vidas, E. ben M. de & Benyosef, S.H.:** *The Beginning of Wisdom: Unabridged Translation of the Gate of Love from Rabbi Eliahu de Vidas' Reshit Chochmah*, KTAV Publishing House, Hoboken 2002.
    **Horowitz, S.S. ben A.:** *Sefer Shefa Tal*, Yarid ha-Sefarim, Jerusalem 2005.
    **Azulai, H.D.A.:** *Sefer Avodat ha-Kodesh: im kol ha-shiv'ah kochvei lechet*, Bet Hillel, Brooklyn 1982.
    **Reuchlin, J.:** *De Arte Cabalistica: On the Art of the Kabbalah*, transl. Martin & Sarah Goodman, Abaris Books Inc., New York 1983.
    **Kircher, A.:** *Oedipus Aegyptiacus*, Rome 1653.
    **Waite, A.E.:** *The Holy Kabbalah*, University Books Inc., New York 1960.
    **Westcott, W.W.:** *Sepher Yetzirah*, Occult Research Press, New York, 1887. Reprinted by Samuel Weiser, New York 1975.
    **Papus:** *The Qabalah*, Studies in Hermetic Tradition Vol. IV, Thorsons, Northamptonshire 1977.
    **Ginzburg, Y., Trugman, A.A., & Wisnefsky, M.Y.:** *The Alef-beit: Jewish Thought Revealed Through the Hebrew Letters*, Jason Aronson Inc., Northvale 1991.
    **Idel, M.:** *Ben: Sonship and Jewish Mysticism*, Continuum, London & New York 2007.
    **Ogren, B.:** *Renaissance and Rebirth: Reincarnation in Early Modern Italian Kabbalah*, Brill, Leiden & Boston 2009.
    **Ben Ya'ocov, Y.:** *Book of the Shining Path*, Page Publishing Inc., New York 2014.
    **Epstein, K.K. & Wineman, A.:** *Letters of Light: Passages from Ma'or va-Shemesh*, Pickwick Publications, Eugene 2015.
54. **Ginzburg, Y., Trugman, A.A., & Wisnefsky, M.Y.:** *Ibid.*
    **Finkel, A.Y.:** *The Essence of the Holy Days: Insights from the Jewish Sages*, Jason Aronson Inc., Northvale 1993.
    **Braun, M.A.:** *The Heschel Tradition: The Life and Teachings of Rabbi Abraham Joshua Heschel of Apt*, Jason Aronson Inc., Northvale 1997.

**Henoch, C.: Ramban:** Philosopher and Kabbalist: on the Basis of his Exegesis to the Mitzvoth, Jason Aronson Inc., Northvale 1998.

**Benyosef, S.H.:** *Living Kabbalah: A Guide to the Sabbath and Festivals in the Teachings of Rabbi Refael Moshe Luria*, Feldheim Publishers, Jerusalem 2006.

**Schachter-Shalomi, Z. & Miles-Yepez, N.:** *A Heart Afire: Stories and Teachings of the Early Hasidic Masters*, Jewish Publication Society, Philadelphia 2009.

55. **Gikatilla, J.:** *Gates of Light: Sha'are Orah, Op. cit.*
56. **Swart, J.G.:** *The Book of Immediate Magic - Part 1, Op. cit.*
57. **Gikatilla, J.:** *Gates of Light: Sha'are Orah, Op. cit.*
58. **Nulman, M.:** *The Encyclopedia of Jewish Prayer: The Ashkenazic and Sephardic Rites*, Jason Aronson Inc., Northvale 1993.

**Frankiel, T.:** *The Gift of Kabbalah: Discovering the Secrets of Heaven, Renewing your Life on Earth*, Jewish Lights Publishing, Woodstock 2001.

**Hoffman, L. & Brettler, M.:** *My People's Prayer Book: Kabbalat Shabbat (Welcoming Shabbat in the Synagogue)*, Jewish Lights Publishing, Woodstock 2005.

**Haber, Y.:** *Sefiros: Spiritual Refinement Through Counting the Omer*, TorahLab, Monsey & Jerusalem 2008.

**Windle, S. & Giesen, M. van der:** *Through the Gates: A Practice for Counting the Omer*, BookBaby, Cork 2012.

**Kedar, K.D.:** *Omer: A Counting*, Central Conference of American Rabbis, New York 2014.

59. **Gray, W.G.:** *A Self Made by Magic, Op. cit.*
60. **Swart, J.G.:** *The Book of Self Creation, Op. cit.*
61. **Gray, W.G.:** *A Self Made by Magic, Op. cit.*
62. **Swart, J.G.:** *The Book of Immediate Magic - Part 1, Op. cit.*
63. **Paprish, N. ben Y.M.:** *Sefer Mesilot Chochmah: bi-sh'loshim u-Shtayim N'tivot Chochmah*, Jerusalem 1914.
64. **Tzadok, A. ben:** *Sifre ha-Rav Ari'el bar Tzadok*, Yeshivat Benei N'vi'im, Chicago 2003.
65. **Swart, J.G.:** *The Book of Immediate Magic - Part 1, Op. cit.*
66. *Ibid.*
67. *Ibid.*
68. *Ibid.*
69. **Green, A.:** *Tormented Master: The Life and Spiritual Quest of Rabbi Nahman of Bratslav*, Jewish Lights Publishing, Woodstock 1992.

70. **Glotzer, L.R.:** *The Fundamentals of Jewish Mysticism: The Book of Creation and Its Commentaries*, Jason Aronson Inc., Northvale 1992.
    **Jacobson, S. & Ekman, G.R.:** *A Spiritual Guide to the Counting of the Omer: Forty-nine Steps to Personal Refinement according to the Jewish Tradition: the Forty-nine Days of Sefirah*, Vaad Hanochos Hatmimim, New York 1996.
    **Frankiel, T.:** *The Gift of Kabbalah, Op. cit.*
    **Strassfeld, M.:** *A Book of Life: Embracing Judaism as a Spiritual Practice*, Schocken Books, New York 2002.
    **Isaacs, R.H.:** *Siddur Kabbalat Shabbat*, Ktav Publishing House, Jersey City 2007.
    **Giller, P.:** *Shalom Shar'abi and the Kabbalists of Beit El*, Oxford University Press, Oxford & New York 2008.
    **Kantrowitz, M.:** *Counting the Omer: A Kabbalistic Meditation Guide*, Gaon Books, Santa Fe 2010.
    **Hermelin, S.:** *Journey Together: 49 Steps to Transforming a Family*, Urim Publications, Jerusalem & New York 2014.
71. **Hoffman, L. & Brettler, M.:** *My People's Prayer Book: Kabbalat Shabbat, Op. cit.*
72. *The Zohar*, Volume 5, transl. D.C. Matt (Pritzker edition), Stanford University Press, Stanford 2009.
73. **Kula, I. & Ochs, V.L.:** *The Book of Jewish Sacred Practices: CLAL's Guide to Everyday & Holiday Rituals & Blessings*, Jewish Lights Publishing, Woodstock 2001.
    **Gold, S.:** *The Magic of Hebrew Chant: Healing the Spirit, Transforming the Mind, Deepening Love*, Jewish Lights Publishing, Woodstock 2013.
74. **Spiegel, J.:** *Dancing with Angels: Jewish Kabbalah Meditation from Torah to Self-improvement to Prophecy*, online publication, http://www.cs.utah.edu/~spiegel/kabbalah/
75. **Shadur, J. & Shadur, Y.:** *Traditional Jewish Papercuts: An Inner World of Art and Symbol*, University Press of New England, Hanover 2002.
    **Swart, J.G.:** *The Book of Seals & Amulets, Op. cit.*
76. **Swart, J.G.:** *Ibid.*
77. **Cosman, M.P. & Jones, L.G.:** *Handbook To Life In The Medieval World*, Vol. 2, Facts on File Inc., New York 2008.
78. **Idelsohn, A.Z.:** *Jewish Liturgy and Its Development*, Shocken Books, New York 1967.
    **Kitov, E.:** *The Book of Our Heritage: The Jewish Year and Its Days of Significance*, Feldheim Publisher, Jerusalem 1997.

**Fine, L.:** *Judaism in Practice: From the Middle Ages through the Early Modern Period,* Shocken Books, Princeton University Press, Princeton 2001.
**Brettler, M.Z.:** *My People's Prayer Book: Traditional Prayers, Modern Commentaries,* edited by Hofmann, L.A., Volume 9, Jewish Light Publishing, Woodstock 2005.

79. **Swart, J.G.:** *The Book of Sacred Names, Op. cit.*
80. **Chefitz, M.:** *The Seventh Telling: The Kabbalah of Moshe Katan,* St. Martin's Press, New York 2001.
81. *Pirke Avot: Sayings of the Fathers,* Behrman House Inc., Springfield 1945.
    **Marcus, Y.:** *Pirkei Avot: Ethics of the Fathers with a New Commentary Anthologized from the Works of the Classic Commentators and the Chasidic Masters,* Kehot Publication Society, New York 2008.
82. **Cardin, N.B.:** *Visions of Holiness in the Everday,* United Synagogue of Conservative Judaism, Dept. Of Youth Activities, New York 1997.
    **Mintz, A. & Schiffman, L.H.:** *Jewish Spirituality and Divine Law,* Ktav Publishing House Inc., Jersey City 2005.
    **Koren, I.:** *The Mystery of the Earth: Mysticism and Hasidism in the Thought of Martin Buber,* United Synagogue of Conservative Judaism, Koninklijke Brill NV, Leiden 2010.
    **Green, A.:** The Heart of the Matter: *Studies in Jewish Mysticism and Theology,* The Jewish Publication Society, Philadelphia 2015.
83. **Siegel, R.; Strassfeld, M.; Strassfeld, S.; Copans, S. & Dudden, A.O.:** *The First Jewish Catalog: A Do-it-Yourself Kit,* The Jewish Publication Society, Philadelphia 1973.
    **Bláha, J.:** *Lessons from the Kabbalah and Jewish History,* Marek Konečný, Brno 2010.
84. **Swart, J.G.:** *The Book of Self Creation, Op. cit.*
85. *Ibid.*
86. **Wolfson, E.R.:** *Through a Speculum that Shines: Vision and Imagination in Medieval Jewish Mysticism,* Princeton University Press, Princeton 1994.
    —*Circle in the Square: Studies in the Use of Gender in Kabbalistic Symbolism,* State University of New York Press, Albany 1995.
    **Gafni, M.:** *The Mystery of Love,* Atria Books, New York 2003.
    **Green, A.:** *A Guide to the Zohar,* Stanford University Press, Stanford 2004.

**Idel, M.:** *Kabbalah and Eros,* Yale University Press, New Haven & London 2005.
**Hoffman, E. & Schachter-Shalomi, Z.M.:** *The Way of Splendor: Jewish Mysticism and Modern Psychology,* Rowman & Littlefield Publishers Inc., Lanham 2006.
**Rosler, I.B.:** *Eros Revisited: Love for the Indeterminate Other,* Lexington Books, 2007.

87. *The Zohar,* Volume 2, transl. D.C. Matt (Pritzker edition), Stanford University Press, Stanford 2004.
    —quoted in **Kaplan, A.:** *Meditation and Kabbalah, Op. cit.*
    **Leet, L.:** *Renewing the Covenant: A Kabbalistic Guide to Jewish Spirituality,* Inner Traditions International, Rochester 1999.
88. **Swart, J.G.:** *The Book of Self Creation, Op. cit.*
89. *The Zohar,* Volume 2, *Op. cit.*
    —quoted in **Kaplan, A.:** *Meditation and Kabbalah, Op. cit.*
    **Leet, L.:** *Renewing the Covenant, Op. cit.*
90. *Ibid.*
91. **Swart, J.G.:** *The Book of Self Creation, Op. cit.*
92. **Swart, J.G.:** *The Book of Sacred Names, Op. cit.*
93. *Ibid.*
    **Swart, J.G.:** *The Book of Seals & Amulets, Op. cit.*
    —*The Book of Immediate Magic - Part 1, Op. cit.*
94. *Siddur ha-Ari,* Yeshivat Sha'ar Ha-Shamayim, Mochon Sha'arei Ziv, Jerusalem 1983.
    **Koppel, Y.:** *Siddur m'ha-Arizal ha-Nikra b'Shem Kol Ya'akov,* Yaakov Koppel, Lemberg 1859.
    **Horowitz, I.:** *Siddur Sha'ar ha-Shamayim,* Ahavat Shalom, Jerusalem 1997.Brooklyn 1974.
    **Sharabi, S.:** *Siddur Nehar Shalom,* Yeshivat Nehar Shalom, Jerusalem 1997.
95. **Vital, Chaim:** *Sefer Sha'ar ha-Kavvanot,* Yeshivat ha-Mekubalim Maharchav, Jerusalem 2005.
    **Sharabi, S.; ha-Kohen, H.S. Dvek; Legimi, E.Y. & Luria, I. ben S.:** *Sefer Kavvanot Peratiyot: Kolel Kavvanot Nechutsot,* Defus ha-Achim Lifshits, Jerusalem 1911.
    **Sharabi, S.:** *Or Levanah,* s.n., Jerusalem 1974.
    **Katzin, Y.:** *Or ha-Levanah, Or ha-Chadash, Or ha-Chayim, Or ha-Chamah, Kavvanot ha-Sefirah, Pri Etz ha-Gan,* Jerusalem 1974.
    **Kaplan, A.:** *Meditation and Kabbalah, Op. cit.*
96. **Swart, J.G.:** *The Book of Sacred Names, Op. cit.*

97. **Baruch, S.Z. ben & Mangel, N.:** *Siddur Tehillat Hashem al pi Nusach ha-Ari Zal with English Translation, Annotated Edition*, Merkoz L'inyonei Chinuch Inc., Brooklyn 2003.
    **Cordovero, M.:** *Tefilah le-Moshe: Siddur ha-Ramak*, Volume 2, Herschenson & Schneidmesser, Prezysml 1892.
98. *Ibid.*
99. **Swart, J.G.:** *The Book of Seals & Amulets, Op. cit.*
100. **Swart, J.G.:** *The Book of Immediate Magic - Part 1, Op. cit.*
101. **Anonymous:** *Ma'aseh ha-Tzafon (Tzafun), Op. cit.*
102. **Jacobson, S. & Ekman, G.R.:** *A Spiritual Guide to the Counting of the Omer, Op. cit.*
103. *Ibid.*
    **Hermelin, S.:** *Journey Together, Op. cit.*
104. **Kaplan, A.:** *Innerspace: Introduction to Kabbalah, Meditation and Prophecy*, Moznaim Publishing Corporation, Jerusalem 1990.
105. *Ibid.*
106. **Gray, W.G.:** *A Beginners Guide to Living Kabbalah, Op. cit.*
107. **Swart, J.G.:** *The Book of Immediate Magic - Part 1, Op. cit.*
108. **Cooper, D.F.:** *Judaism 101: How to count the Omer contemplatively with Kabbalah*, https://davidfcooper.wordpress.com/2010/03/29/judaism-101-how-to-count-the-omer-contemplatively-with-kabbalah.
109. **Kaplan, A.:** *Innerspace, Op. cit.*
110. *Ibid.*
111. **Jacobson, S. & Ekman, G.R.:** *A Spiritual Guide to the Counting of the Omer, Op. cit.*
112. **Cooper, D.F.:** *Judaism 101: How to count the Omer contemplatively with Kabbalah, Op. cit.*
113. **Jacobson, S. & Ekman, G.R.:** *A Spiritual Guide to the Counting of the Omer, Op. cit.*
114. *Ibid.*
115. **Cooper, D.F.:** *Judaism 101: How to count the Omer contemplatively with Kabbalah, Op. cit.*
116. **Jacobson, S. & Ekman, G.R.:** *A Spiritual Guide to the Counting of the Omer, Op. cit.*
117. *Ibid.*
118. *Ibid.*
119. *Ibid.*
120. **Cooper, D.F.:** *Judaism 101: How to count the Omer contemplatively with Kabbalah, Op. cit.*
121. **Ginsburgh, Y.:** *Anatomy of the Soul*, Gal Einai, Jerusalem, New York & Los Angeles 2008.

122. *Ibid.*
123. *Ibid.*
124. **Jacobson, S. & Ekman, G.R.:** *A Spiritual Guide to the Counting of the Omer, Op. cit.*
125. *Ibid.*
126. **Hermelin, S.:** *Journey Together, Op. cit.*
127. *Ibid.*
128. *Ibid.*
129. **Jacobson, S. & Ekman, G.R.:** *A Spiritual Guide to the Counting of the Omer, Op. cit.*
130. **Cooper, D.F.:** *Judaism 101: How to count the Omer contemplatively with Kabbalah, Op. cit.*
131. **Shapiro, R.M.:** *Counting the Omer: A Personal Journal*, Simply Jewish Fellowship 2000.
132. **Jacobson, S. & Ekman, G.R.:** *A Spiritual Guide to the Counting of the Omer, Op. cit.*
133. *Ibid.*
134. **Cooper, D.F.:** *Judaism 101: How to count the Omer contemplatively with Kabbalah, Op. cit.*
135. **Jacobson, S. & Ekman, G.R.:** *A Spiritual Guide to the Counting of the Omer, Op. cit.*
136. **Swart, J.G.:** *The Book of Self Creation, Op. cit.*
137. *Ibid.*
138. **Hermelin, S.:** *Journey Together, Op. cit.*
139. **Jacobson, S. & Ekman, G.R.:** *A Spiritual Guide to the Counting of the Omer, Op. cit.*
140. **Hermelin, S.:** *Journey Together, Op. cit.*
141. **Jacobson, S. & Ekman, G.R.:** *A Spiritual Guide to the Counting of the Omer, Op. cit.*
142. **Cooper, D.F.:** *Judaism 101: How to count the Omer contemplatively with Kabbalah, Op. cit.*
143. **Jacobson, S. & Ekman, G.R.:** *A Spiritual Guide to the Counting of the Omer, Op. cit.*
144. *Ibid.*
145. **Hermelin, S.:** *Journey Together, Op. cit.*
146. *Ibid.*
147. *Ibid.*
148. *Ibid.*
149. **Jacobson, S. & Ekman, G.R.:** *A Spiritual Guide to the Counting of the Omer, Op. cit.*
150. **Cooper, D.F.:** *Judaism 101: How to count the Omer contemplatively with Kabbalah, Op. cit.*

151. **Jacobson, S. & Ekman, G.R.:** *A Spiritual Guide to the Counting of the Omer, Op. cit.*
152. *Ibid.*
153. **Gray, W.G:** *Qabalistic Concepts: Living the Tree*, (Previously *Concepts of Qabalah*, Sangreal Sodality Series, Volume 3), Samuel Weiser Inc., York Beach, 1997.
154. *Ibid.*
155. *Ibid.*
156. **Jacobson, S. & Ekman, G.R.:** *A Spiritual Guide to the Counting of the Omer, Op. cit.*
157. **Gray, W.G.:** *The Ladder of Lights, Op. cit.*
158. **Cooper, D.F.:** *Judaism 101: How to count the Omer contemplatively with Kabbalah, Op. cit.*
159. **Jacobson, S. & Ekman, G.R.:** *A Spiritual Guide to the Counting of the Omer, Op. cit.*
160. *Ibid.*
161. **Cooper, D.F.:** *Judaism 101: How to count the Omer contemplatively with Kabbalah, Op. cit.*
162. **Jacobson, S. & Ekman, G.R.:** *A Spiritual Guide to the Counting of the Omer, Op. cit.*
163. *Ibid.*
164. **Hermelin, S.:** *Journey Together, Op. cit.*
165. **Gray, W.G:** *Qabalistic Concepts, Op. cit.*
166. **Jacobson, S. & Ekman, G.R.:** *A Spiritual Guide to the Counting of the Omer, Op. cit.*
167. *Ibid.*
168. **Hermelin, S.:** *Journey Together, Op. cit.*
169. *Ibid.*
170. **Cooper, D.F.:** *Judaism 101: How to count the Omer contemplatively with Kabbalah, Op. cit.*
171. **Hermelin, S.:** *Journey Together, Op. cit.*
172. *Ibid.*
173. **Jacobson, S. & Ekman, G.R.:** *A Spiritual Guide to the Counting of the Omer, Op. cit.*
174. *Ibid.*
175. *Ibid.*
176. **Hermelin, S.:** *Journey Together, Op. cit.*
177. *Ibid.*
178. *Ibid.*
179. **Jacobson, S. & Ekman, G.R.:** *A Spiritual Guide to the Counting of the Omer, Op. cit.*
180. **Cooper, D.F.:** *Judaism 101: How to count the Omer contemplatively with Kabbalah, Op. cit.*

181. **Jacobson, S. & Ekman, G.R.:** *A Spiritual Guide to the Counting of the Omer, Op. cit.*
182. *Ibid.*
183. **Hermelin, S.:** *Journey Together, Op. cit.*
184. *Ibid.*
185. **Jacobson, S. & Ekman, G.R.:** *A Spiritual Guide to the Counting of the Omer, Op. cit.*
186. **Hermelin, S.:** *Journey Together, Op. cit.*
187. *Ibid.*
188. *Ibid.*
189. **Jacobson, S. & Ekman, G.R.:** *A Spiritual Guide to the Counting of the Omer, Op. cit.*
190. **Cooper, D.F.:** *Judaism 101: How to count the Omer contemplatively with Kabbalah, Op. cit.*
191. **Hermelin, S.:** *Journey Together, Op. cit.*
192. **Jacobson, S. & Ekman, G.R.:** *A Spiritual Guide to the Counting of the Omer, Op. cit.*
193. **Hermelin, S.:** *Journey Together, Op. cit.*
194. **Jacobson, S. & Ekman, G.R.:** *A Spiritual Guide to the Counting of the Omer, Op. cit.*
195. *Ibid.*
196. **Hermelin, S.:** *Journey Together, Op. cit.*
197. *Ibid.*
198. **Jacobson, S. & Ekman, G.R.:** *A Spiritual Guide to the Counting of the Omer, Op. cit.*
199. **Cooper, D.F.:** *Judaism 101: How to count the Omer contemplatively with Kabbalah, Op. cit.*
200. **Hermelin, S.:** *Journey Together, Op. cit.*
201. **Jacobson, S. & Ekman, G.R.:** *A Spiritual Guide to the Counting of the Omer, Op. cit.*
202. **Hermelin, S.:** *Journey Together, Op. cit.*
203. **Jacobson, S. & Ekman, G.R.:** *A Spiritual Guide to the Counting of the Omer, Op. cit.*
204. *Ibid.*
205. **Hermelin, S.:** *Journey Together, Op. cit.*
206. *Ibid.*
207. *Ibid.*
208. **Jacobson, S. & Ekman, G.R.:** *A Spiritual Guide to the Counting of the Omer, Op. cit.*
209. **Cooper, D.F.:** *Judaism 101: How to count the Omer contemplatively with Kabbalah, Op. cit.*
210. **Jacobson, S. & Ekman, G.R.:** *A Spiritual Guide to the Counting of the Omer, Op. cit.*

211. **Hermelin, S.:** *Journey Together, Op. cit.*
212. **Jacobson, S. & Ekman, G.R.:** *A Spiritual Guide to the Counting of the Omer, Op. cit.*
213. **Hermelin, S.:** *Journey Together, Op. cit.*
214. *Ibid.*
215. **Jacobson, S. & Ekman, G.R.:** *A Spiritual Guide to the Counting of the Omer, Op. cit.*
216. **Cooper, D.F.:** *Judaism 101: How to count the Omer contemplatively with Kabbalah, Op. cit.*
217. **Jacobson, S. & Ekman, G.R.:** *A Spiritual Guide to the Counting of the Omer, Op. cit.*
218. **Hermelin, S.:** *Journey Together, Op. cit.*
219. *Ibid.*
220. **Jacobson, S. & Ekman, G.R.:** *A Spiritual Guide to the Counting of the Omer, Op. cit.*
221. **Hermelin, S.:** *Journey Together, Op. cit.*
222. *Ibid.*
223. **Jacobson, S. & Ekman, G.R.:** *A Spiritual Guide to the Counting of the Omer, Op. cit.*
224. **Cooper, D.F.:** *Judaism 101: How to count the Omer contemplatively with Kabbalah, Op. cit.*
225. **Jacobson, S. & Ekman, G.R.:** *A Spiritual Guide to the Counting of the Omer, Op. cit.*
226. **Gikatilla, J.:** *Gates of Light, Op. cit.*
227. *Ibid.*
228. **Jacobson, S. & Ekman, G.R.:** *A Spiritual Guide to the Counting of the Omer, Op. cit.*
229. *Ibid.*
230. *Ibid.*
231. *Ibid.*
232. **Hermelin, S.:** *Journey Together, Op. cit.*
233. *Ibid.*
234. *Ibid.*
235. **Jacobson, S. & Ekman, G.R.:** *A Spiritual Guide to the Counting of the Omer, Op. cit.*
236. *Ibid.*
237. *Ibid.*
238. **Hermelin, S.:** *Journey Together, Op. cit.*
239. *Ibid.*
240. **Jacobson, S. & Ekman, G.R.:** *A Spiritual Guide to the Counting of the Omer, Op. cit.*
241. *Ibid.*
242. **Swart, J.G.:** *The Book of Self Creation, Op. cit.*

243. **Hermelin, S.:** *Journey Together, Op. cit.*
244. **Jacobson, S. & Ekman, G.R.:** *A Spiritual Guide to the Counting of the Omer, Op. cit.*
245. **Hermelin, S.:** *Journey Together, Op. cit.*
246. **Jacobson, S. & Ekman, G.R.:** *A Spiritual Guide to the Counting of the Omer, Op. cit.*
247. **Hermelin, S.:** *Journey Together, Op. cit.*
248. **Jacobson, S. & Ekman, G.R.:** *A Spiritual Guide to the Counting of the Omer, Op. cit.*
249. *Ibid.*
250. **Hermelin, S.:** *Journey Together, Op. cit.*
251. **Jacobson, S. & Ekman, G.R.:** *A Spiritual Guide to the Counting of the Omer, Op. cit.*
252. **Hermelin, S.:** *Journey Together, Op. cit.*
253. *Ibid.*
254. *Ibid.*
255. *Ibid.*
256. *Ibid.*
257. **Jacobson, S. & Ekman, G.R.:** *A Spiritual Guide to the Counting of the Omer, Op. cit.*
258. *Ibid.*
259. *Ibid.*
260. **Hermelin, S.:** *Journey Together, Op. cit.*
261. *Ibid.*
262. *Ibid.*
263. *Ibid.*
264. *Ibid.*
265. **Jacobson, S. & Ekman, G.R.:** *A Spiritual Guide to the Counting of the Omer, Op. cit.*
266. *Ibid.*
267. *Ibid.*
268. **Hermelin, S.:** *Journey Together, Op. cit.*
269. **Jacobson, S. & Ekman, G.R.:** *A Spiritual Guide to the Counting of the Omer, Op. cit.*
270. *Ibid.*
271. **Hermelin, S.:** *Journey Together, Op. cit.*
272. *Ibid.*
273. **Jacobson, S. & Ekman, G.R.:** *A Spiritual Guide to the Counting of the Omer, Op. cit.*
274. *Ibid.*
275. **Hermelin, S.:** *Journey Together, Op. cit.*
276. *Ibid.*
277. *Ibid.*

278. **Jacobson, S. & Ekman, G.R.:** *A Spiritual Guide to the Counting of the Omer, Op. cit.*
279. *Ibid.*
280. **Hermelin, S.:** *Journey Together, Op. cit.*
281. *Ibid.*
282. *Ibid.*
283. *Ibid.*
284. *Ibid.*
285. **Jacobson, S. & Ekman, G.R.:** *A Spiritual Guide to the Counting of the Omer, Op. cit.*
286. *Ibid.*
287. **Cooper, D.F.:** *Judaism 101: How to count the Omer contemplatively with Kabbalah, Op. cit.*
288. **Vital, H. ben Y. & Luria, I. ben S.:** *The Tree of Life: Chayyim Vital's Introduction to the Kabbalah of Isaac Luria: The Palace of Adam Kadmon*, transl. Menzi, D.W. & Z. Padeh, Jason Aronson Inc., Northvale 1999.
289. **Gray, W.G.:** *Qabalistic Concepts: Living the Tree, Op. cit.*
290. *Ibid.*
291. **Jacobson, S. & Ekman, G.R.:** *A Spiritual Guide to the Counting of the Omer, Op. cit.*
292. *Ibid.*
293. *Ibid.*
294. **Hermelin, S.:** *Journey Together, Op. cit.*
295. *Ibid.*
296. **Jacobson, S. & Ekman, G.R.:** *A Spiritual Guide to the Counting of the Omer, Op. cit.*
297. *Ibid.*
298. **Hermelin, S.:** *Journey Together, Op. cit.*
299. *Ibid.*
300. **Jacobson, S. & Ekman, G.R.:** *A Spiritual Guide to the Counting of the Omer, Op. cit.*
301. *Ibid.*
302. *Ibid.*
303. **Hermelin, S.:** *Journey Together, Op. cit.*
304. **Jacobson, S. & Ekman, G.R.:** *A Spiritual Guide to the Counting of the Omer, Op. cit.*
305. *Ibid.*
306. *Ibid.*
307. **Hermelin, S.:** *Journey Together, Op. cit.*
308. *Ibid.*
309. *Ibid.*
310. **Jacobson, S. & Ekman, G.R.:** *A Spiritual Guide to the Counting of the Omer, Op. cit.*

311. *Ibid.*
312. *Ibid.*
313. **Hermelin, S.:** *Journey Together, Op. cit.*
314. **Jacobson, S. & Ekman, G.R.:** *A Spiritual Guide to the Counting of the Omer, Op. cit.*
315. **Hermelin, S.:** *Journey Together, Op. cit.*
316. *Ibid.*
317. *Ibid.*
318. **Jacobson, S. & Ekman, G.R.:** *A Spiritual Guide to the Counting of the Omer, Op. cit.*
319. *Ibid.*
320. *Ibid.*
321. **Hermelin, S.:** *Journey Together, Op. cit.*
322. **Jacobson, S. & Ekman, G.R.:** *A Spiritual Guide to the Counting of the Omer, Op. cit.*
323. *Ibid.*
324. *Ibid.*
325. **Hermelin, S.:** *Journey Together, Op. cit.*
326. *Ibid.*
327. *Ibid.*
328. **Jacobson, S. & Ekman, G.R.:** *A Spiritual Guide to the Counting of the Omer, Op. cit.*
329. *Ibid.*
330. **Hermelin, S.:** *Journey Together, Op. cit.*
331. *Ibid.*
332. **Jacobson, S. & Ekman, G.R.:** *A Spiritual Guide to the Counting of the Omer, Op. cit.*
333. *Ibid.*
334. *Ibid.*
335. *Ibid.*
336. *Ibid.*
337. **Hermelin, S.:** *Journey Together, Op. cit.*
338. *Ibid.*
339. **Jacobson, S. & Ekman, G.R.:** *A Spiritual Guide to the Counting of the Omer, Op. cit.*
340. *Ibid.*
341. *Ibid.*
342. **Hermelin, S.:** *Journey Together, Op. cit.*
343. **Jacobson, S. & Ekman, G.R.:** *A Spiritual Guide to the Counting of the Omer, Op. cit.*
344. *Ibid.*
345. **Hermelin, S.:** *Journey Together, Op. cit.*
346. *Ibid.*

347. *Ibid.*
348. **Jacobson, S. & Ekman, G.R.:** *A Spiritual Guide to the Counting of the Omer, Op. cit.*
349. *Ibid.*
350. **Hermelin, S.:** *Journey Together, Op. cit.*
351. *Ibid.*
352. **Jacobson, S. & Ekman, G.R.:** *A Spiritual Guide to the Counting of the Omer, Op. cit.*
353. **Hermelin, S.:** *Journey Together, Op. cit.*
354. *Ibid.*
355. **Jacobson, S. & Ekman, G.R.:** *A Spiritual Guide to the Counting of the Omer, Op. cit.*
356. **Hermelin, S.:** *Journey Together, Op. cit.*
357. **Jacobson, S. & Ekman, G.R.:** *A Spiritual Guide to the Counting of the Omer, Op. cit.*
358. **Swart, J.G.:** *The Book of Self Creation, Op. cit.*
359. *Ibid.*
360. **Jacobson, S. & Ekman, G.R.:** *A Spiritual Guide to the Counting of the Omer, Op. cit.*
361. **Swart, J.G.:** *The Book of Seals & Amulets, Op. cit.*
362. **Jacobson, S. & Ekman, G.R.:** *A Spiritual Guide to the Counting of the Omer, Op. cit.*
363. *Ibid.*
364. *Ibid.*
365. *Ibid.*
366. **Hermelin, S.:** *Journey Together, Op. cit.*
367. **Jacobson, S. & Ekman, G.R.:** *A Spiritual Guide to the Counting of the Omer, Op. cit.*
368. **Hermelin, S.:** *Journey Together, Op. cit.*
369. **Jacobson, S. & Ekman, G.R.:** *A Spiritual Guide to the Counting of the Omer, Op. cit.*
370. *Ibid.*
371. *Ibid.*
372. *Ibid.*
373. **Hermelin, S.:** *Journey Together, Op. cit.*
374. *Ibid*
375. **Jacobson, S. & Ekman, G.R.:** *A Spiritual Guide to the Counting of the Omer, Op. cit.*
376. **Hermelin, S.:** *Journey Together, Op. cit.*
377. **Jacobson, S. & Ekman, G.R.:** *A Spiritual Guide to the Counting of the Omer, Op. cit.*
378. **Hermelin, S.:** *Journey Together, Op. cit.*

379. **Jacobson, S. & Ekman, G.R.:** *A Spiritual Guide to the Counting of the Omer, Op. cit.*
380. *Ibid.*
381. *Ibid.*
382. **Hermelin, S.:** *Journey Together, Op. cit.*
383. *Ibid*
384. *Ibid.*
385. *Ibid.*
386. *Ibid*
387. *Ibid.*
388. *Ibid.*
389. **Jacobson, S. & Ekman, G.R.:** *A Spiritual Guide to the Counting of the Omer, Op. cit.*
390. *Ibid.*
391. *Ibid.*
392. *Ibid.*
393. **Hermelin, S.:** *Journey Together, Op. cit.*
394. *Ibid*
395. *Ibid.*
396. *Ibid.*
397. *Ibid*
398. *Ibid.*
399. **Jacobson, S. & Ekman, G.R.:** *A Spiritual Guide to the Counting of the Omer, Op. cit.*
400. *Ibid.*
401. **Hermelin, S.:** *Journey Together, Op. cit.*
402. **Jacobson, S. & Ekman, G.R.:** *A Spiritual Guide to the Counting of the Omer, Op. cit.*
403. *Ibid.*
404. **Hermelin, S.:** *Journey Together, Op. cit.*
405. *Ibid*
406. **Jacobson, S. & Ekman, G.R.:** *A Spiritual Guide to the Counting of the Omer, Op. cit.*
407. **Hermelin, S.:** *Journey Together, Op. cit.*
408. **Jacobson, S. & Ekman, G.R.:** *A Spiritual Guide to the Counting of the Omer, Op. cit.*
409. **Hermelin, S.:** *Journey Together, Op. cit.*
410. *Ibid*
411. **Jacobson, S. & Ekman, G.R.:** *A Spiritual Guide to the Counting of the Omer, Op. cit.*
412. *Ibid.*1
413. **Hermelin, S.:** *Journey Together, Op. cit.*
414. *Ibid*

415. **Jacobson, S. & Ekman, G.R.:** *A Spiritual Guide to the Counting of the Omer, Op. cit.*
416. **Hermelin, S.:** *Journey Together, Op. cit.*
417. **Jacobson, S. & Ekman, G.R.:** *A Spiritual Guide to the Counting of the Omer, Op. cit.*
418. **Hermelin, S.:** *Journey Together, Op. cit.*
419. **Jacobson, S. & Ekman, G.R.:** *A Spiritual Guide to the Counting of the Omer, Op. cit.*
420. *Ibid*
421. *Ibid.*
422. **Jacobson, S. & Ekman, G.R.:** *A Spiritual Guide to the Counting of the Omer, Op. cit.*
423. *Ibid.*
424. *Ibid.*
425. **Hermelin, S.:** *Journey Together, Op. cit.*
426. **Jacobson, S. & Ekman, G.R.:** *A Spiritual Guide to the Counting of the Omer, Op. cit.*
427. *Ibid.*
428. *Ibid.*
429. **Hermelin, S.:** *Journey Together, Op. cit.*
430. *Ibid.*
431. **Jacobson, S. & Ekman, G.R.:** *A Spiritual Guide to the Counting of the Omer, Op. cit.*
432. *Ibid.*
433. **Hermelin, S.:** *Journey Together, Op. cit.*
434. **Jacobson, S. & Ekman, G.R.:** *A Spiritual Guide to the Counting of the Omer, Op. cit.*
435. *Ibid.*
436. *Ibid.*
437. **Swart, J.G.:** *The Book of Immediate Magic - Part 1, Op. cit.*
438. **Gibran, K.:** *Secrets of the Heart,* transl. Ferris, A.R., Signet Books, New York 1965.
439. **Gibran, K.:** *Tears and Laughter,* edited Wolf, M., Philosophical Library, New York 1949.
440. **Jacobson, S. & Ekman, G.R.:** *A Spiritual Guide to the Counting of the Omer, Op. cit.*
441. **Hermelin, S.:** *Journey Together, Op. cit.*
442. **Jacobson, S. & Ekman, G.R.:** *A Spiritual Guide to the Counting of the Omer, Op. cit.*
443. **Hermelin, S.:** *Journey Together, Op. cit.*
444. **Jacobson, S. & Ekman, G.R.:** *A Spiritual Guide to the Counting of the Omer, Op. cit.*
445. *Ibid.*
446. **Hermelin, S.:** *Journey Together, Op. cit*

447. *Ibid.*
448. *Ibid.*
449. **Jacobson, S. & Ekman, G.R.:** *A Spiritual Guide to the Counting of the Omer, Op. cit.*
450. *Ibid.*
451. *Ibid.*
452. **Hermelin, S.:** *Journey Together, Op. cit*
453. *Ibid.*
454. **Jacobson, S. & Ekman, G.R.:** *A Spiritual Guide to the Counting of the Omer, Op. cit.*
455. *Ibid.*
456. *Ibid.*
457. **Hermelin, S.:** *Journey Together, Op. cit*
458. *Ibid.*
459. *Ibid.*
460. *Ibid.*
461. **Jacobson, S. & Ekman, G.R.:** *A Spiritual Guide to the Counting of the Omer, Op. cit.*
462. *Ibid.*
463. **Hermelin, S.:** *Journey Together, Op. cit*
464. *Ibid.*
465. **Jacobson, S. & Ekman, G.R.:** *A Spiritual Guide to the Counting of the Omer, Op. cit.*
466. **Hermelin, S.:** *Journey Together, Op. cit*
467. **Jacobson, S. & Ekman, G.R.:** *A Spiritual Guide to the Counting of the Omer, Op. cit.*
468. **Hermelin, S.:** *Journey Together, Op. cit*
469. *Ibid.*
470. *Ibid.*
471. **Jacobson, S. & Ekman, G.R.:** *A Spiritual Guide to the Counting of the Omer, Op. cit.*
472. *Ibid.*
473. **Hermelin, S.:** *Journey Together, Op. cit*
474. *Ibid.*
475. *Ibid*
476. **Jacobson, S. & Ekman, G.R.:** *A Spiritual Guide to the Counting of the Omer, Op. cit.*
477. *Ibid.*
478. *Ibid.*
479. *Ibid.*
480. **Hermelin, S.:** *Journey Together, Op. cit*
481. *Ibid.*
482. **Jacobson, S. & Ekman, G.R.:** *A Spiritual Guide to the Counting of the Omer, Op. cit.*

483. *Ibid.*
484. **Hermelin, S.:** *Journey Together, Op. cit*
485. **Jacobson, S. & Ekman, G.R.:** *A Spiritual Guide to the Counting of the Omer, Op. cit.*
486. *Ibid.*
487. *Ibid.*
488. **Hermelin, S.:** *Journey Together, Op. cit*
489. *Ibid.*
490. *Ibid.*
491. *Ibid.*
492. **Jacobson, S. & Ekman, G.R.:** *A Spiritual Guide to the Counting of the Omer, Op. cit.*
493. *Ibid.*
494. *Ibid.*
495. *Ibid.*
496. **Hermelin, S.:** *Journey Together, Op. cit*
497. *Ibid.*
498. *Ibid.*
499. **Jacobson, S. & Ekman, G.R.:** *A Spiritual Guide to the Counting of the Omer, Op. cit.*
500. *Ibid.*
501. **Hermelin, S.:** *Journey Together, Op. cit*
502. *Ibid.*
503. **Jacobson, S. & Ekman, G.R.:** *A Spiritual Guide to the Counting of the Omer, Op. cit.*
504. *Ibid.*
505. **Gray, W.G.:** *Qabalistic Concepts: Living the Tree, Op. cit.*
506. *Ibid.*
507. *Ibid.*
508. *Ibid.*
509. *Ibid.*
510. *Ibid.*
511. *Ibid.*
512. **Jacobson, S. & Ekman, G.R.:** *A Spiritual Guide to the Counting of the Omer, Op. cit.*
513. *Ibid.*
514. *Ibid.*
515. *Ibid.*
516. **Hermelin, S.:** *Journey Together, Op. cit.*
517. *Ibid.*
518. *Ibid.*
519. **Jacobson, S. & Ekman, G.R.:** *A Spiritual Guide to the Counting of the Omer, Op. cit.*

520. *Ibid.*
521. **Hermelin, S.:** *Journey Together, Op. cit.*
522. *Ibid.*
523. *Ibid.*
524. **Jacobson, S. & Ekman, G.R.:** *A Spiritual Guide to the Counting of the Omer, Op. cit.*
525. *Ibid.*
526. **Hermelin, S.:** *Journey Together, Op. cit.*
527. *Ibid.*
528. **Jacobson, S. & Ekman, G.R.:** *A Spiritual Guide to the Counting of the Omer, Op. cit.*
529. *Ibid*
530. **Hermelin, S.:** *Journey Together, Op. cit.*
531. **Jacobson, S. & Ekman, G.R.:** *A Spiritual Guide to the Counting of the Omer, Op. cit.*
532. *Ibid.*
533. *Ibid.*
534. **Hermelin, S.:** *Journey Together, Op. cit.*
535. *Ibid.*
536. *Ibid.*
537. *Ibid.*
538. **Jacobson, S. & Ekman, G.R.:** *A Spiritual Guide to the Counting of the Omer, Op. cit.*
539. *Ibid.*
540. **Hermelin, S.:** *Journey Together, Op. cit*
541. **Jacobson, S. & Ekman, G.R.:** *A Spiritual Guide to the Counting of the Omer, Op. cit.*
542. **Hermelin, S.:** *Journey Together, Op. cit*
543. *Ibid.*
544. *Ibid.*
545. *Ibid.*
546. **Jacobson, S. & Ekman, G.R.:** *A Spiritual Guide to the Counting of the Omer, Op. cit.*
547. *Ibid.*
548. *Ibid.*
549. *Ibid.*
550. *Ibid.*
551. **Hermelin, S.:** *Journey Together, Op. cit*
552. *Ibid.*
553. *Ibid.*
554. **Jacobson, S. & Ekman, G.R.:** *A Spiritual Guide to the Counting of the Omer, Op. cit.*
555. *Ibid.*

556. **Hermelin, S.:** *Journey Together, Op. cit*
557. *Ibid.*
558. *Ibid.*
559. **Jacobson, S. & Ekman, G.R.:** *A Spiritual Guide to the Counting of the Omer, Op. cit.*
560. *Ibid.*
561. **Hermelin, S.:** *Journey Together, Op. cit*
562. *Ibid.*
563. *Ibid.*
564. **Jacobson, S. & Ekman, G.R.:** *A Spiritual Guide to the Counting of the Omer, Op. cit.*
565. *Ibid.*
566. *Ibid.*
567. *Ibid.*
568. *Ibid.*
569. *Ibid.*
570. **Hermelin, S.:** *Journey Together, Op. cit*
571. *Ibid.*
572. *Ibid.*
573. *Ibid.*
574. *Ibid.*
575. **Jacobson, S. & Ekman, G.R.:** *A Spiritual Guide to the Counting of the Omer, Op. cit.*
576. *Ibid.*
577. **Kedar, K.D.:** *Omer: A Counting*, CCAR Press, New York 2014.
578. *Ibid.*
579. *Ibid.*
580. **Ariel, D.S.:** *The Mystic Quest*, Schocken Books Inc., New York 1992.
581. *Ibid.*

# CHAPTER 7

1. **Swart, J.G.:** *The Book of Immediate Magic - Part 1*, Op. cit.
2. *Ibid.*
3. **Swart, J.G.:** *The Book of Seals & Amulets*, Op. cit.
4. **Swart, J.G.:** *The Book of Immediate Magic - Part 1*, Op. cit.
5. *Ibid.*
6. *Ibid.*
7. *Ibid.*
8. *Ibid.*
   **Swart, J.G.:** *The Book of Self Creation*, Op. cit.
9. *Ibid.*
10. **Eleazar ben Yehudah of Worms:** *Sefer ha-Chochmah*, MS Oxford-Bodleian 1568, relevant portions transl. in **Idel, M.:** *Kabbalah: New Perspectives*, Yale University Press, New Haven & London 1988.
    **Abulafia, A.:** *Imrei Shefer*, Aharon Barazani, Jerusalem 1999.
    — *Otzar Eden ha-Ganuz*, A. Gros, Jerusalem 2000.
    —*Sefer Chayei ha-Olam ha-Ba*, Aharon Barazani, Jerusalem 2001.
    —*Or ha-Sechel*, Aharon Barazani, Jerusalem 2001.
    —*Chayei Nefesh*, Aharon Barazani, Jerusalem 2001.
    —*Ner Elohim*, Aharon Barazani, Jerusalem 2002.
    —*Sefer ha-Tzeruf*, Aharon Barazani, Jerusalem 2003.
    —*The Path of Names*, transl. B. Finkel, J. Hirschman, D. Meltzer and G. Scholem, Trigram, Berkeley 1976.
    **Albotini, Y.:** *Sulam ha-Aliyah,*, Machon Sha'arei Ziv, Machon Sha'arei ziv, Jerusalem 1989.
    **Vital, Chaim:** *Pri Etz Chaim, Hotsa'at Eshel*, Tel Aviv 1961.
    —*Sefer Sha'ar Ru'ach ha-Kodesh*, Hotsa'at Kitve Rabeinu ha-Ari, Tel Aviv 1962; Mosdat Nehar Shalom, Jerusalem 1999.
    —*Sefer Sha'arei Kedushah*, Op. cit.
    —*K'tavim Chadashim l'Rabbi Chaim Vital*, Op. cit.
    —*Sha'ar ha-Kavvanot*, Yeshivat ha-shalom, Jerusalem 1997; Yeshivat ha-Mekubalim Maharchav, Jerusalem 2005.
    —*Sidur Tefilah mi-Kol ha-Shanah*, 3 Volumes, Zolkova.
    **Azulay, H.Y.D.:** *Shem ha-Gedolim*, Op. cit.
    —*Midbar Kedemot*, Op. cit.
    *Siddur ha-Ari*, Yeshivat Sha'ar Ha-Shamayim, Mochon Sha'arei Ziv, Jerusalem 1983.

**Horowitz, I.:** *Siddur Sha'ar ha-Shamayim, Op. cit.*
**Koppel, Y.:** *Siddur m'ha-Arizal ha-Nikra b'Shem Kol Ya'akov, Op. cit.*
**Sharabi, S.; ha-Kohen, H.S. Dvek; Legimi, E.Y. & Luria, I. ben S.:** *Sefer Kavvanot Peratiyot: Kolel Kavvanot Nechutsot*, Defus ha-Achim Lifshits, Jerusalem 1911.
**Sharabi, S.:** *Siddur Nehar Shalom, Op. cit.*
—*Or Levanah*, s.n., Jerusalem 1974.
**Katzin, Y.:** *Or ha-Levanah, Or ha-Chadash, Or ha-Chayim, Or ha-Chamah, Kavvanot ha-Sefirah, Pri Etz ha-Gan*, Jerusalem 1974.
**Weinstock, B.M.Y.:** *Siddur ha-Gaonim v'ha-Mekubalim*, 21 Volumes, Defus Shraga Weinfeld, Jerusalem 1970.
**Baruch, S.Z. ben & Mangel, N.:** *Siddur Tehillat Hashem al pi Nusach ha-Ari Zal, Op. cit.*
**Blumenthal, D.:** *Understanding Jewish Mysticism: The Philosophic Mystical Tradition and the Chassidic Tradition*, Volume II, KTAV Publishing House Inc., New York 1982.
**Kaplan, A.:** *Jewish Meditation: A Practical Guide, Op. cit.*
—*Meditation and Kabbalah, Op. cit.*
—*Meditation and The Bible, Op. cit.*
—*Innerspace, Op. cit.*
**Epstein, P.:** *Kabbalah: The Way of the Jewish Mystic*, Doubleday & Company, New York 1978.
**Besserman, P.:** *The Shambhala Guide to Kabbalah and Jewish Mysticism, Op. cit.*
**Idel, M.:** *Kabbalah: New Perspectives*, Yale University Press, New Haven & London 1988.
—*The Mystical Experience in Abraham Abulafia*, SUNY Press, Albany 1988.
—*Studies in Ecstatic Kabbalah*, SUNY Press, Albany 1988.
**Hoffman, E.:** *Opening the Inner Gates, Op. cit.*
**Fisdel, S.A.:** *The Practice of Kabbalah, Op. cit.*
**Verman, M.:** *The History and Varieties of Jewish Meditation*, Jason Aronson Inc., Northvale 1996.
**Davis, A.:** *Meditation from the Heart of Judaism, Op. cit.*
**Varetz, T.S.:** [with A. Sutton] *California Kabbalah: A Contemporary Initiation into Kabbalistic Meditation & Practice*, Zechariah Tzvi Shamayim V'aretz, eText 2001.
**Frankiel, T.:** *The Gift of Kabbalah, Op. cit.*
**Pinson, D.:** *Meditation and Judaism*, Rowman & Littlefield Publishers Inc., Lanham 2004.
—*Toward the Infinite: The Way of Kabbalistic Meditation*, Rowman & Littlefield Publishers, Inc., Lanham 2005.

**Cooper, D.:** *Ecstatic Kabbalah*, Sounds True Inc., Louisville 2005.
**Ribner, M.:** *Everyday Kabbalah: a Practical Guide to Jewish Meditation*, Healing and Personal Growth, Citadel, New York 2005.
**Sagiv, U.; Sopkin, B.; Sterne, D. & Schochet, J.I.:** *Love Like Fire and Water: A Guide to Jewish Meditation*, Jerusalem Connection, New York & Jerusalem, 2005.
**Roth, J.:** *Jewish Meditation for Everyday Life, Op. cit.*
**Gigi, D.:** *28 Jewelled Crown: A Comprehensive System of Jewish Meditation and Mysticism*, Maayan Hatum Publications, London 2009.
**Gefen, N.F.:** *Discovering Jewish Meditation: Instruction & Guidance for Learning an Ancient Spiritual Practice*, Jewish Lights Publishing, Woodstock 2011.
**Solomon, A.:** *Abraham Abulafia: Meditations on the Divine Name*, privately published: Lulu.com, 2011.
**Glick, Y.:** *Living the Life of Jewish Meditation: A Comprehensive Guide to Practice and Experience*, Jewish Lights Publishing, Woodstock 2014.
**Rubin, A.:** *Eye to the infinite: a Jewish Meditation Guidebook: How to Increase Divine Awareness*, Ayin el HoAyin Publications, 2016.

11. **Sadeh, P.:** *Jewish Folk Tales*, Collins, London 1990.
12. **Apta, Aharon of:** *Or ha-Ganuz* quoted in **Idel, M.:** *Hasidism, Op. cit.*
13. **Swart, J.G.:** *The Book of Self Creation, Op. cit.*
14. **Idel, M.:** *Hasidism, Op. cit.*
    **Cordovero, M.:** *Pardes Rimmonim, Op. cit.*
15. **Swart, J.G.:** *The Book of Self Creation, Op. cit.*
    —*The Book of Sacred Names, Op. cit.*
16. **Swart, J.G.:** *The Book of Immediate Magic - Part 1, Op. cit.*
17. **Swart, J.G.:** *The Book of Self Creation, Op. cit.*
18. **Feraro, S. & Lewis, J.R.:** *Contemporary Alternative Spiritualities in Israel*, Palgrave Macmillan, New York 2017.
19. **Varetz, T.S.:** [with A. Sutton] *California Kabbalah, Op. cit.*
20. *Ibid.*
21. *The Zohar*, Volume 8, transl. D.C. Matt (Pritzker edition), Stanford University Press, Stanford 2014.
22. **Scholem, G.:** *Major Trends in Jewish Mysticism*, Schocken Books Inc., Jerusalem 1941; New York 1946.
    —*On the Kabbalah and Its Symbolism*, Schocken Books Inc., New York 1965.
    —*Kabbalah*, Keter Publishing House, Jerusalem 1974.

**Jacobs, L.:** *Jewish Mystical Testimonies*, Schocken Books, New York 1977.
**Bar-Lev, Y.A.:** *Yedid Nefesh: Introduction to Kabbalah*, Privately Published, Petach-Tivka, 1988.
**Kaplan, A.:** *Innerspace: Introduction to Kabbalah, Meditation and Prophecy*, Moznaim Publishing Company, Jerusalem & New York 1991.
**Dan Cohn-Sherbok, D. & Cohn-Sherbok, L.:** *Jewish & Christian Mysticism: An Introduction*, The Continuum Publishing Company, New York 1994.
**Wolfson, E.R.:** *Circle in the Square: Studies in the Use of Gender in Kabbalistic Symbolism*, State University of New York Press, Albany 1995.
**Horowitz, I. & Krassen, M.:** *The Generations of Adam*, Paulist Press, New York 1996.
**Faierstein, M.M.:** *Jewish Mystical Autobiographies: Book of Visions and Book of Secrets*, Paulist Press, New York 1999.
**Drob, S.L.:** *Symbols of the Kabbalah: Philosophical and Psychological Perspectives*, Jason Aronson Inc., Northvale 2000.
—*Kabbalistic Metaphors: Jewish Mystical Themes in Ancient and Modern Thought*, Jason Aronson Inc., Northvale 2000.
**Klein, E.J.:** *Kabbalah of Creation: The Mysticism of Isaac Luria, Founder of Modern Kabbalah*, North Atlantic Books, Berkeley 2000.
**Cardoza, A.M.:** *Abraham Miguel Cardozo: Selected Writings*, transl. D.J. Halperin, Paulist Press, Mahwah 2001.
**Herrera, A.C. de & Krabbenhoft, K.:** *Abraham Cohen de Herrera Gate of Heaven*, Koninklijke Brill NV, Leiden 2002.
**Fine, L.:** *Physician of the Soul, Healer of the Cosmos: Isaac Luria and His Kabbalistic Fellowship*, Stanford University Press, Stanford 2003.
**Luzzatto, M. Chaim:** *138 Openings of Wisdom: Klach Pitchei ha-Chochmah*, transl. A.J. Greenbaum, Azamra Institute, Jerusalem 2005.
**Schneider, S.:** *Kabbalistic Writings on the Nature of Masculine & Feminine*, A Still Small Voice Publishing Group, Jerusalem 2007.
**Schneider, S.R.:** *Centers of Power: The Convergence of Psychoanalysis and Kabbalah*, Jason Aronson Inc., Lanham 2008.

23. **Ginsburgh, Y.:** *Kabbalah and Meditation for the Nations*, Gal Einai, Jerusalem, New York & Los Angeles 2006.

24. **Eisenberg. R.L:** *850 Intriguing Questions about Judaism: True, False, or In Between,* Rowman & Littlefield, Lanham, Boulder, New York & London 2015.
25. **Zacutto, M.:** *Shorshei ha-Shemot, Op. cit.*
26. **Eisenberg. R.L:** *850 Intriguing Questions about Judaism, Op. cit.*
27. *The Zohar,* Volume 1, transl. D.C. Matt (Pritzker edition), Stanford University Press, Stanford 2004.
28. *Ibid.*
29. **Swart, J.G.:** *The Book of Sacred Names, Op. cit.*
30. **Zacutto, M.:** *Shorshei ha-Shemot, Op. cit.*
31. *Ibid.*
32. **Swart, J.G.:** *The Book of Sacred Names, Op. cit.*
33. **Varetz, T.S.:** [with A. Sutton] *California Kabbalah, Op. cit.*
34. **Swart, J.G.:** *The Book of Self Creation, Op. cit*
35. *Ibid.*
36. *Ibid.*
37. *Ibid.*
38. **Varetz, T.S.:** [with A. Sutton] *California Kabbalah, Op. cit.*
39. *Ibid.*
40. *Ibid.*
41. *Ibid.*
    **Cordovero, M.:** *Pardes Rimmonim, Op. cit.*
42. **Varetz, T.S.:** [with A. Sutton] *California Kabbalah, Op. cit.*
43. *Ibid.*
44. **Abulafia, A.:** *Sefer Chayei ha-Olam ha-Ba, Op. cit.*
    **Kaplan, A.:** *Meditation and Kabbalah, Op. cit.*
45. **Swart, J.G.:** *The Book of Self Creation, Op. cit.*
    —*The Book of Immediate Magic - Part 1, Op. cit.*
46. *Ibid.*
47. *Ibid.*
48. *Ibid.*
49. **Swart, J.G.:** *The Book of Self Creation, Op. cit.*
50. **Swart, J.G.:** *The Book of Immediate Magic - Part 1, Op. cit.*
51. **Swart, J.G.:** *The Book of Self Creation, Op. cit.*
52. *Ibid.*
    **Swart, J.G.:** *The Book of Immediate Magic - Part 1, Op. cit.*
53. **Swart, J.G.:** *The Book of Sacred Names, Op. cit.*
    —*The Book of Immediate Magic - Part 1, Op. cit.*
54. *Ibid.*
    **Swart, J.G.:** *The Book of Self Creation, Op. cit.*
55. **Malachi, M.:** "*From the Depths of Silence*" in **Hoffman, E.:** *Opening the Inner Gates, Op. cit.*
56. **Swart, J.G.:** *The Book of Self Creation, Op. cit.*

57. *Ibid.*
58. **Swart, J.G.:** *The Book of Sacred Names, Op. cit.*
59. **Swart, J.G.:** *The Book of Immediate Magic - Part 1, Op. cit.*
60. **Swart, J.G.:** *The Book of Sacred Names, Op. cit.*
61. **Swart, J.G.:** *The Book of Immediate Magic - Part 1, Op. cit.*
62. *Ibid.*
    **Swart, J.G.:** *The Book of Sacred Names, Op. cit.*
63. **Swart, J.G.:** *The Book of Seals & Amulets, Op. cit.*
64. **Swart, J.G.:** *The Book of Sacred Names, Op. cit.*
65. *Ibid.*
66. *Ibid.*
67. **Swart, J.G.:** *The Book of Seals & Amulets, Op. cit.*
68. *Ibid.*
69. **Swart, J.G.:** *The Book of Immediate Magic - Part 1, Op. cit.*
70. *Ibid.*
71. **Swart, J.G.:** *The Book of Self Creation, Op. cit.*
72. **Swart, J.G.:** *The Book of Immediate Magic - Part 1, Op. cit.*
73. **Swart, J.G.:** *The Book of Self Creation, Op. cit.*
74. *Ibid.*
75. *Ibid.*
76. *Ibid.*
    **Swart, J.G.:** *The Book of Sacred Names, Op. cit*
    —*The Book of Seals & Amulets, Op. cit.*
    —*The Book of Immediate Magic - Part 1, Op. cit.*
77. **Swart, J.G.:** *The Book of Self Creation, Op. cit.*
78. *Ibid.*
79. *Ibid.*
80. **Swart, J.G.:** *The Book of Immediate Magic - Part 1, Op. cit.*
81. *Ibid.*
82. *Ibid.*
83. *Ibid.*
84. *Ibid.*
85. *Ibid.*
86. *Ibid.*
87. *Ibid.*
88. *Ibid.*
89. **Zacutto, M.:** *Shorshei ha-Shemot, Op. cit.*
90. **Swart, J.G.:** *The Book of Immediate Magic - Part 1, Op. cit.*
91. **Zacutto, M.:** *Shorshei ha-Shemot, Op. cit.*
92. **Swart, J.G.:** *The Book of Immediate Magic - Part 1, Op. cit.*
    —*The Book of Sacred Names, Op. cit*
    —*The Book of Seals & Amulets, Op. cit.*
93. *Ibid.*
94. *Ibid.*

95.     Ibid.
96.     Ibid.
97.     Ibid.
98.     **Swart, J.G.:** *The Book of Immediate Magic - Part 1*, Op. cit.
99.     Ibid.
        **Swart, J.G.:** *The Book of Sacred Names*, Op. cit
100.   Ibid.
101.   **Zacutto, M.:** *Shorshei ha-Shemot*, Op. cit.
        **Swart, J.G.:** *The Book of Sacred Names*, Op. cit
102.   Ibid.
103.   Ibid.
104.   Ibid.
105.   Ibid.
106.   Ibid.
107.   Ibid.
108.   **Benyamini, S.:** *Pardes ha-Nisim Tehilim*, Op. cit
109.   **Swart, J.G.:** *The Book of Self Creation*, Op. cit.
110.   **Thornton, F.B.:** *This is the Rosary*, Hawthorn Books, New York 1961.
        **Miller, J.D.:** *Beads and Prayers: The Rosary in History and Devotion*, Burns & Oates, London 2002.
        **Wiley, E. & Shannon, M.O.:** *A String and a Prayer: How to Make and Use Prayer Beads*, Red Wheel/Weiser, LLC, York Beach 2002.
        **Winston, K.:** *Bead One, Pray Too: A Guide to Making and Using Prayer Beads*, Church Publishing Incorporated, Harrisburg & New York 2008.
        **Dubin, L. & Togashi, K.:** *The Worldwide History of Beads: Ancient, Ethnic, Contemporary*, Thames & Hudson, London 2015.
111.   **Beer, R.:** *The Handbook of Tibetan Buddhist Symbols*, Serindia Publications, Inc., Chicago 2003.
        **Knapp, S.:** *The Heart of Hinduism: the Eastern Path to Freedom, Empowerment and Illumination: providing Knowledge of Reality distinguished from Illusion for the Welfare of All*, Rasbihari Lal & Sons, Vrindaban 2006.
        **Zerner A. & Farber, M.:** *Buddha Beads: Mala Mantras for Guidance, Wisdom, and Serenity*, Sterling Publishing Company Incorporated 2013.
        **Chapple, C.K.:** *Yoga in Jainism*, Routledge, Abingdon 2016.
112.   **Sabini, J.:** *Islam: A Primer*, AMIDEAST, Washington 2001.
        **Chebel, M. & Hamani, L.:** *Symbols of Islam*, Barnes & Noble, New York 2003.

**Netton, I.R.:** *Encyclopedia of Islamic Civilization and Religion*, Routledge, Abingdon 2008.
**Campo, J.E.:** *Encyclopedia of Islam*, Facts On File, Inc., New York 2009.

113. **Coles, J. & Budwig, R.:** *Beads: an Exploration of Bead Traditions around the World*, Simon & Schuster, East Roseville 1997.
**Koltuv, B.B.:** *Amulets, Talismans, and Magical Jewelry: A Way to the Unseen, Ever-Present*, Almighty God, Nicolas-Hays, Inc., Berwick 2005.
**Dubin, L.S.:** *The Worldwide History of Beads: Ancient, Ethnic, Contemporary*, Thames & Hudson, London 2010.
114. **Swart, J.G.:** *The Book of Sacred Names, Op. cit.*
115. *Ibid.*
116. *Ibid.*
117. *Ibid.*
118. **Swart, J.G.:** *The Book of Self Creation, Op. cit.*
119. *Ibid.*

# CHAPTER 8

1. **Campion, N.:** *An Introduction to the History of Astrology*, Institute for the Study of Cycles in World Affairs, London 1982.
   **Tester, S.J.:** *A History of Western Astrology*, The Boydell Press, Woodbridge 1987.
   **Barton, T.:** *Ancient Astrology*, Routledge, London 1994.
   **Hornung, E.:** *The Secret Lore of Egypt: Its Impact on the West*, Cornell University Press, Ithaca 2001.
   **Beck, R:** *A Brief History of Ancient Astrology*, Blackwell Publishing, Malden-Oxford-Carlton 2007.

2. **Mordell, P:** *Sefer Yetsirah*, P. Mordell, Philadelphia, 1914.
   **Stenring, K.:** *The Book of Formation*, KTAV, New York 1968.
   **Kalisch, I.:** *The Sepher Yetzirah: A Book of Creation*, L.H. Frank & Co., New York (Reprinted by the AMORC, San Jose, California, 1974).
   **Westcott, W.W.:** *Sepher Yetzirah*, Occult Research Press, New York, 1887. Reprinted by Samuel Weiser, New York 1975.
   **Suarès, C.:** *The Sepher Yetzirah: Including the Original Astrology according to the Qabala and its Zodiac*, Shambhala Publications Inc., Boulder 1976.
   **Friedman, I.:** *The Book of Creation: Sefer Yetzirah*, Samuel Weiser Inc., New York 1977.
   **Blumenthal, D.R.:** *Understanding Jewish Mysticism: The Merkabah Tradition and the Zoharic Tradition*, Volume 1, KTAV Publishing House Inc., New York 1978.
   **Kaplan, A.:** *Sefer Yetzirah: The Book of Creation In Theory and Practice*, Samuel Weiser Inc., York Beach 1990 (Revised edition with index 1997).
   **Hyman, A.P.:** *Sefer Yesira*, Mohr Siebeck, Tübingen 2004.
   *Mazalot v'Goralot, Op. cit.*
   **Musteri, S.:** *Chochmat ha-Mazalot bi-Tequfot u'Me'uberot v'ha-Kevi'ot: Kalendariv Hebraicum*, APVD Johann Froben, Basel 1527.
   *Mazalot*, Lublin 1557.
   *Sefer Mazalot shel Adam al Derech ha-Techunah*, Lublin 1557.
   *Seder 12 ha-Mazalot*, Hotsa'at Backal, Jerusalem 1973.
   **Ezra, A. ben M. Ibn; Levy, R. & Burgos, F.C.:** *The Beginning of Wisdom: An Astrological Treatise by Abraham ibn Ezra*, Oxford University Press, London 1939.

— **Epstein, M.B.; Hand, R. & Menachem, N. ben:** *The Book of Reasons* (*Sefer Ha'te'amim*), The Golden Hind Press, Berkeley Springs, 1994.
**Shlomo, S.:** *Abraham Ibn Ezra: The Book of Reasons: A Parallel Hebrew-English Critical Edition of the Two Versions of the Text*, Koninklijke Brill NV, Leiden 2007.
**Levy, R.:** *Astrological Works of Abraham ibn Ezra*, John Hopkins University Press, Baltimore 1927.
**Luzzatto, M. Chaim:** *Derech HaShem: The Way of God*, transl. A. Kaplan, Feldheim Publishers, Jerusalem & New York 1983.
**Ganz, D. bar S.:** *Nechmad v'Naim*, Jesnitz 1743.
**Trachtenberg, J.:** *Jewish Magic and Superstition*, *Op. cit.*
**Wertheimer, S.A.:** *Batei Midrashot: Esrim v'Chamishah Midrashei Chazal al pi kitvei yad mi-Genizat Yerushalayim u'Mitzrayim*, Vol. 1 & 2, Mosad ha-Rav Kook, Jerusalem 1952–1955.
*Encyclopedia Judaica*, Volume 3, The Macmillan Company, New York 1971.
**Glazerson, M.:** *Above the Zodiac: Astrology in Jewish Thought*, Jason Aronson Inc., Northvale 1997.
**Isaacs, R.J.:** *Divination, Magic, and Healing: The Book of Jewish Folklore*, Jason Aronson Inc., Northvale 1998.
**Erlanger, G.:** *Signs of the Times: The Zodiac in Jewish Tradition*, Feldman Publishing, Jerusalem 1999.
**Dobin, J.C.:** *Kabbalistic Astrology: The Sacred Tradition of the Hebrew Sages*, Inner Traditions International, Rochester 1999.
**Schwartz, D.:** *Studies on Astral Magic in Medieval Jewish Thought*, Brill, Leiden & Boston 2005.
**Bohak, G.; Harari, Y. & Shaked, S.:** *Continuity and Innovation in the Magical Tradition*, Koninklijke Brill NV, Leiden 2011.

3. **Swart, J.G.:** *The Book of Sacred Names*, *Op. cit.*
4. **Swart, J.G.:** *The Book of Self Creation*, *Op. cit.*
5. **Swart, J.G.:** *The Book of Immediate Magic - Part 1*, *Op. cit.*
6. *Siddur T'filah: Complete Prayer Book*, Shapiro, Vallentine & Co., London 1931.
7. **Swart, J.G.:** *The Book of Immediate Magic - Part 1*, *Op. cit.*
8. *Sefer ha-Kanah/Sefer ha-Pli'ah*, Koretz 1784.
9. **Swart, J.G.:** *The Book of Immediate Magic - Part 1*, *Op. cit.*
10. *Ibid.*
11. *Ibid.*
12. *Ibid.*
13. **Swart, J.G.:** *The Book of Sacred Names*, *Op. cit.*

14. *Ibid.*
    **Swart, J.G.:** *The Book of Seals & Amulets, Op. cit.*
15. **Leo, A.:** *Esoteric Astrology*, Destiny Books, Rochester 1983.
16. **Alouf, S.H.; Catton, S.; & Tawil, D.A.:** *Sidur Kol Yaakov ha-Shalem: ke minhag Aram Tsova* (Aleppo), Sephardic Heritage Foundation, New York 2001.
17. **Swart, J.G.:** *The Book of Sacred Names, Op. cit.*
18. **Swart, J.G.:** *The Book of Immediate Magic - Part 1, Op. cit.*
19. **Swart, J.G.:** *The Book of Sacred Names, Op. cit.*
20. *Ibid.*
21. **Mordell, P:** *Sefer Yetsirah, Op. cit.*
    **Stenring, K.:** *The Book of Formation, Op. cit.*
    **Kalisch, I.:** *The Sepher Yetzirah: A Book of Creation, Op. cit.*
    **Westcott, W.W.:** *Sepher Yetzirah, Op. cit.*
    **Suarès, C.:** *The Sepher Yetzirah, Op. cit.*
    **Friedman, I.:** *The Book of Creation: Sefer Yetzirah, Op. cit.*
    **Blumenthal, D.R.:** *Understanding Jewish Mysticism*, Volume 1, *Op. cit.*
    **Kaplan, A.:** *Sefer Yetzirah, Op. cit.*
    **Hyman, A.P.:** *Sefer Yesira, Op. cit.*
22. **Swart, J.G.:** *The Book of Seals & Amulets, Op. cit.*
23. *Sefer ha-Temunah*, attributed to Nehuniah ben HaKanah, Hotsa'at Nezer Sheraga, Jerusalem 1997.
    **Scholem, G.:** *Kabbalah, Op. cit.*
    —*Origins of the Kabbalah*, Princeton University Press, Princeton 1987.
    **Ginsburg, E.K.:** *The Sabbath in the Classical Kabbalah*, Suny Press, Albany 1989.
    **Hallamish, M.:** *An Introduction to the Kabbalah, Op. cit.*
    **Leet, L.:** *Renewing the Covenant: A Kabbalistic Guide to Jewish Spirituality*, Inner Traditions International, Rochester 1999.
    —*The Secret Doctrine of the Kabbalah: Discovering the Key to Hebraic Sacred Science*, Inner Traditions International, Rochester 1999.
    —*The Kabbalah of the Soul: The Transformative Psychology and Practices of Jewish Mysticism*, Inner Traditions International, Rochester 2003.
    —*The Universal Kabbalah, Op. cit.*
24. *Ibid.*
25. **Crowley, A.:** *777 Revised: vel prolegomena symbolica ad systemam sceptico-mysticae viae explicandae, fundamentum hieroglyphicum sanctissimorum scientiae summae*, Samuel Weiser Inc., New York 1970.

**Regardie, F.I. & Monnastre, C.:** *The Golden Dawn: A Complete Course in Practical Ceremonial Magic: the Original Account of the Teachings, Rites, and Ceremonies of the Hermetic Order of the Golden Dawn (Stella Matutina), as revealed by Israel Regardie*, 6th Edition, Revised and Enlarged, Llewellyn Publications, St. Paul 2003.
**Gray, W.G.:** *The Ladder of Lights, Op. cit.*
—*Magical Ritual Methods, Op. cit.*
—*Qabalistic Concepts: Living the Tree, Op. cit.*
**Parfitt, W.:** *The Elements of the Qabalah*, Element, New York 1991.
**Ashcroft-Nowicki, D.:** *The Ritual Magic Workbook: A Practical Course of Self-initiation*, Samuel Weiser Inc., York Beach 1998.
**Fortune, D. & Knight, G.:** *Principles of Hermetic Philosophy*, Thoth, Loughborough 1999.

26. **Halevi, Z. ben Shimon:** *A Kabbalistic Universe*, Samuel Weiser Inc., New York 1977.
27. **Idel, M.:** *Saturn's Jews: On the Witches' Sabbat and Sabbateanism*, Continuum International Publishing Group, New York 2011.
28. **Godwin, J.:** *Harmonies of Heaven and Earth: Mysticism in Music from Antiquity to the Avant Garde*, Inner Traditions International, Rochester 1987.
    —*The Harmony of the Spheres: A Sourcebook of the Pythagorean Tradition in Music*, Inner Traditions International, Rochester 1993.
29. **Kircher, A.:** *Oedipus Aegyptiacus, Op. cit.*
    **Papus:** *The Qabalah, Op. cit.*
    **Waite, A.E.:** *The Holy Kabbalah, Op. cit.*
30. **Kircher, A.:** *Ibid.*
31. **Kaplan, A.:** *Sefer Yetzirah, Op. cit.*
32. *Ibid.*
    **Buzaglo, S. ben M.:** *Kisei Melech*, Amsterdam 1769.
33. **Alemanno, Y.:** *Collectanaea*, Ms. Oxford, Bodeliana 2234.
    —*Untitled Manuscript*, Ms. Paris BN 849.
    **Roling, B.:** *Aristotelische Naturphilosophie und Christliche Kabbalah im Werk des Paulus Ritius*, Walter de Gruyter GmbH & Co. KG imprint, Max Niemeyer Verlag, Tübingen 2007.
34. **Idel, M.:** *Saturn's Jews, Op. cit.*
35. **Alemanno, Y.:** *Collectanaea, Op. cit.*
    —*Untitled Treatise, Op. cit.*

36. **Godwin, J.:** *The Harmony of the Spheres*, Op. cit.
    **Diemling, M. & Veltri, G.:** *The Jewish Body: Corporeality, Society, and Identity in the Renaissance and Early Modern Period*, Brill, Leiden & Boston 2009.
37. **Agrippa, H.C.:** *De Occulta Philosophia*, 3 Vols., Apud Godfridum & Marcellum, Beringos 1550.
    —*Three Books of Occult Philosophy*, transl. J. Freake [John French], Gregory Moule, London 1651.
38. **Leon-Jones, K.S. de:** *Giordano Bruno & the Kabbalah: Prophets, Magicians, and Rabbis*, Yale University Press, New Haven 1997.
39. **Schmidt-Biggemann, W.:** *Geschichte der Christlichen Kabbalah 1600—1660*, Part 2, Frommann-Holzboog Verlag e.K., Stuttgart-Bad Cannstatt 2013.
40. **Godwin, J.:** *The Harmony of the Spheres*, Op. cit.
41. **Vital, H. ben J,; Luria, I. ben S.; Menzi, D.W. & Padeh, Z.:** *The Tree of Life: Chayyim Vital's Introduction to the Kabbalah of Isaac Luria: the Palace of Adam Kadmon*, Jason Aronson Inc., Northvale 1999.
    **Yates, F.A.:** *Art of Memory: Selected Works of Francis Yates*, Vol. 3, Routledge, London & New York 2001.
    **Zinguer, I.; Melamed, A. & Shalev, Z.:** *Hebraic Aspects of the Renaissance: Sources and Encounters*, Koninklijke Brill NV, Leiden 2011.
42. **Swart, J.G.:** *The Book of Sacred Names*, Op. cit.
43. *Ibid.*
44. *Ibid.*
45. **Mordell, P:** *Sefer Yetsirah*, Op. cit.
    **Stenring, K.:** *The Book of Formation*, Op. cit.
    **Kalisch, I.:** *The Sepher Yetzirah: A Book of Creation*, Op. cit.
    **Westcott, W.W.:** *Sepher Yetzirah*, Op. cit.
    **Suarès, C.:** *The Sepher Yetzirah*, Op. cit.
    **Friedman, I.:** *The Book of Creation: Sefer Yetzirah*, Op. cit.
    **Blumenthal, D.R.:** *Understanding Jewish Mysticism*, Volume 1, Op. cit.
    **Kaplan, A.:** *Sefer Yetzirah*, Op. cit.
    **Hyman, A.P.:** *Sefer Yesira*, Op. cit.
46. **Suarès, C.:** *Ibid.*
    **Kaplan, A.:** *Ibid.*
    **Blumenthal, D.R.:** *Ibid.*
    **Posquieres, A. ben David [Raavad]:** *Sefer Yetzirah*, Mantua 1562; Horodna 1806.

**Vidzy, H. & Sulzbach, L.:** *Sefer Gan Yah: perush nechmad al Sefer Yetzirah*,ba-defus shel Leb Sulzbach u-venu le-ve Katzenelenbogen, Breslau 1831.

**ha-Bartzeloni, Y. bar B., Halberstam, S.J. & Kaufman, D.:** *Pirush Sefer Yetzirah*, Mekize Nirdamim, Berlin 1885.

**Ashkenazi, J. ben S.:** *Commentary on Sefer Yetzirah*, Epstein, Jerusalem 1961.

**Shabbetai Donnolo, Ra'avad, ha-Ramban (Nachmanides), Sa'adia ben Yosef, Eleazer m'Garmiza, Moses ben Jacob of Kiev, Moses ben Jacob Botarel, Eliyah ben Solomon m'Vilna (Gra), Yitzhak Eizik ben Yekutiel Zalman, Azriel ben Menachem, Shemuel ben Eliezer Aharon Lurya, David Castelli, Abraham ben David of Posquieres:** *Sefer Yetsirah: ha-Meyuchas le-Avraham avinu*, Levin-Epstein, Jerusalem 1964.

**Togarmi, B.:** *Commentary on Sefer Yetzirah*, published in **Scholem G.:** *Ha-Kabbalah shel Sefer ha-Temunah ve-shel Abraham Abulafia*, Akademon, Jerusalem 1969.

**Worms, E. ben Y. of; Dynow, Z.E.; Spira, H.L. & Spir, S.:** *Pirush ha-Rabbi Eleazer mi-Germiza al Sefer Yetzirah, Op. cit.*

**Weinstock, I.:** *An Anonymous Commentary on Sefer Yetzirah from the Foundation of Abraham Abulafia (attributed to Rabbi Abraham ibn Ezra)*, Mosad ha-Rav Kook, Jerusalem 1984.

*Sefer Yetzirah: ha-Meyuchas le-Avraham Avinu: v'alav kol ha-mefarshim ha-mekubalim* [Ten Commentaries], Yeshivat Kol Yehudah, Jerusalem 1990.

**Cordovero, M.:** *Sefer Yetsirah: ha-Meyuchas le-Avraham Avinu im Perush Or Yakar*, Chevrat Achuzat Yisra'el, Jerusalem 1988.

**Donnolo, S.:** *Sefer Chachmoni hu Perush al Sefer Yetzirah*, Hotsa'at Backal, Jerusalem 1994.

*Sefer Yetsirah: ha-Meyuchas le-Avraham Avinu: v'alav perush Raza d'Yetsirah*, Otiot, Jerusalem 2004.

**Uziyahu Sharbaf & Eizik ben Yekutiel Zalman:** *Sefer Yetsirah: ha-Meyuchas le-Avraham Avinu*, Amutat Shalhevet Techiyat ha-Aretz, Hebron 2008.

**ben Solomon, E. [ha-Gra] & Goldblat, H.T. ben Y.:** *Perush ha-Gra al Sefer Yetsirah: im be'ur yotser or*, Mishpachat Goldblat, Jerusalem 2012.

*Sefer Yetzirah im Perush Yotzer ha-Me'orot*, Hotzaat Sefarim Be'er Eliyahu, Israel 2014.

47. **Hyman, A.P.:** *Sefer Yesira, Op. cit.*
48. **Halevi, Y.:** *Sefer ha-Kuzari: Das Buch Kusari des Jehuda ha-Levi nach dem Hebräischen Texte des Jehuda Ibn Tibbon*, Friedrich Boigt's Buchhandlung, Leipzig 1869.

——*The Kuzari: An Argument for the Faith of Israel*, transl. H. Hirschfeld, Schocken Books, New York 1964.
49. **Tzayach, J.:** *Sheirit Josef*, Ms. 260. Vienna.
50. **MacKendrick, P. & Howe, H.M.:** *Classics in Translation - Volume I: Greek Literature*, University of Wisconsin Press, Madison 1980.
51. **Swart, J.G.:** *The Book of Seals & Amulets, Op. cit.*
52. **Gershon ben Solomon:** *The Gate of Heaven* (*Shaar ha-Shamayim*), transl. F.S. Bodenheimer, Kiryath Sepher, Jerusalem 1953.
53. *Ibid.*
    **Bachya ben Asher:** *Shulchan Arba*, Lemberg, 1858.
    **Tzayach, Y.:** *Even ha-Shoham*, Ms. 8° 416, Jerusalem.
    **Kaplan, A.:** *Meditation and Kabbalah, Op. cit.*
54. **Shamsian, A.:** *Chochmat ha-Partzuf Chochmat Kaf ha-Yad*, Avraham Shamsian, Safed.
    **Chamui, A.:** *Sefer Devek Me'Ach*, Yarid ha-Sefarim, Jerusalem 2005.
    *Chochmat ha-Yad v'ha-Sirtut*, Yarid ha-Sefarim, Jerusalem 2003.
    *Chochmat ha-Yad ha-Shalem* with commentary by Abraham Azulai, Hotza'at Backal, Jerusalem 1966.
    *Chochmat ha-Partzuf ha-Shalem*, Hotza'at Backal, Jerusalem 1966.
55. **Walker, L.:** *Changing with NLP: A Casebook of Neuro-linguistic Programming in Medical Practice*, Radcliffe Medical Press Ltd., Abingdon 2004.
    **Shah, N.:** *Introducing Neurolinguistic Programming (NLP): A Practical Guide*, Icon Books, London 2011.
    **Blyth, L. & Heron, H.:** *30 Days to NLP: An Introduction to Neuro Linguistic Programming*, Balboa Press, Bloomington 2016.
56. **Swart, J.G.:** *The Book of Immediate Magic - Part 1, Op. cit.*
57. *Ibid.*
58. *Ibid.*
59. *Ibid.*
60. *Ibid.*
61. *Ibid.*
62. *Ibid.*
63. *Ibid.*
64. *Ibid.*
65. *Ibid.*

66. *Pirush ha-Rabbi Eleazar m'Garniza al SeferYetzirah*, Verlag Moses Spiro, Przemysl 1883.
**Worms, E. ben Y. of; Dynow, Z.E.; Spira, H.L. & Spir, S.:** *Pirush ha-Rabbi Eleazer mi-Germiza al Sefer Yetzirah, Op. cit. Sefer Yetsirah: ha-Meyuchas le-Avraham Avinu: v'alav kol ha-mefarshim ha-mekubalim, Op. cit.*
67. **Tirshom, J. ben E.:** *Shoshan Yesod Olam, Op. cit.*
68. **Agrippa, H.C.:** *De Occulta Philosophia, Op. cit.*
—*Three Books of Occult Philosophy, Op. cit.*
**Barrett, F.:** *The Magus or Celestial Intelligencer, being a Complete System of Occult Philosophy in Three Books*, University Books Inc., New York 1967.
**Papus:** *Traité Élémentaire de Magie Pratique*, Chamuel, Paris 1893.
**Wallis Budge, E.A.:** *Amulets and Talismans, Op. cit.*
**Sepharial:** *The Book of Charms and Talismans*, W. Foulsham & Co., London 1923.
**Poinsot, M.C.:** *Encyclopédie des Sciences Occultes*, Les Éditions Georges-Anquetil, Paris 1925.
**Shah, S.I.:** *The Secret Lore of Magic: Books of the Sorcerers*, Frederick Muller Ltd., London 1957.
**Regardie, I.:** *How to Make and Use Talismans*, The Aquarian Press, Wellingborough 1972.
—*The Complete Golden Dawn System of Magic*, Falcon Press, Santa Monica 1987.
**MacLean, A.:** *A Treatise on Angel Magic*, Phanes Press, Grand Rapids 1990.
**Pennick, N.:** *Magical Alphabets*, Weiser Books, York Beach 1992.
**Fanger, C.:** *Conjuring Spirits: Texts and Traditions of Medieval Ritual Magic*, Sutton Publishing, Stroud 1998.
**Lehrich, C.I.:** *The Language of Demons and Angels: Cornelius Agrippa's Occult Philosophy*, Koninklijke Brill NV, Leiden 2003.
69. *Pirush ha-Rabbi Eleazar m'Garniza al SeferYetzirah, Op. cit.*
**Worms, E. ben Y. of; Dynow, Z.E.; Spira, H.L. & Spir, S.:** *Pirush ha-Rabbi Eleazer mi-Germiza al Sefer Yetzirah, Op. cit. Sefer Yetsirah: ha-Meyuchas le-Avraham Avinu: v'alav kol ha-mefarshim ha-mekubalim, Op. cit.*
70. **Swart, J.G.:** *The Book of Sacred Names, Op. cit.*
71. *Ibid.*

72. Posquieres, A. ben David [Raavad]: *Sefer Yetzirah, Op. cit.*
Shabbetai Donnolo, Ra'avad, ha-Ramban (Nachmanides), Sa'adia ben Yosef, Eleazer m'Garmiza, Moses ben Jacob of Kiev, Moses ben Jacob Botarel, Eliyah ben Solomon m'Vilna (Gra), Yitzhak Eizik ben Yekutiel Zalman, Azriel ben Menachem, Shemuel ben Eliezer Aharon Lurya, David Castelli, Abraham ben David of Posquieres: *Sefer Yetsirah: ha-Meyuchas le-Avraham avinu, Op. cit.*
*Sefer Yetsirah: ha-Meyuchas le-Avraham Avinu: v'alav kol ha-mefarshim ha-mekubalim, Op. cit.*
73. *Ibid.*
**Al-Biruni, A.M. Ibn A.:** *The Book of Instruction in the Elements of the Art of Astrology*, transl. Wright, R.R., Luzac & Co., London 1934.
**Warnock, C.:** *Mansions of the Moon: A Lunar Zodiac for Astrology and Magic*, Renaissance Astrology, Iowa City 2010.
74. **Greenup, A.W.:** *Sefer ha-Levanah: The Book of the Moon*, London 1912.
**Ibn Ezra, A.:** *The Book of the World (Sefer ha-Olam)*, edited by Fleisher, Y.L., Timishuara, Romania 1937.
—*The Book of Elections (Sefer ha-Mivcharim)*, edited by Fleisher, Y.L., Timishuara, Romania 1939.
**—& Sela, S.:** *Abraham Ibn Ezra, the Book of the World: A Parallel Hebrew-English Critical Edition of the Two Versions of the Text* (Abraham Ibn Ezra's Astrological Writings Vol. 2), Koninklijke Brill NV, Leiden 2010.
**—& Sela, S.:** *Abraham Ibn Ezra on Elections, Interrogations, and Medical Astrology: a Parallel Hebrew-English Critical Edition of the Book of Elections (3 Versions), the Book of Interrogations (3 Versions), and The Book of the Luminaries*, (Abraham Ibn Ezra's Astrological Writings Vol. 3), Koninklijke Brill NV, Leiden 2011.
**Langermann, Y.T.:** *The Jews and the Sciences in the Middle Ages*, Ashgate-Variorum, Aldershot-Brookfield, Singapore & Sydney 1999.
**Lancaster, I.:** *Deconstructing the Bible: Abraham Ibn Ezra's Introduction to the Torah*, RoutledgeCurzon, London 2003.
**Hehmeyer, I. & Schönig, H.:** *Herbal Medicine in Yemen: Traditional Knowledge and Practice, and Their Value for Today's World*, Koninklijke Brill NV, Leiden 2012.
75. *The Zohar*, Volume 3, transl. D.C. Matt (Pritzker edition), Stanford University Press, Stanford 2014.
76. *Ibid.*

77. *Tikunei ha-Zohar*, Jerusalem 1909.
    **Landau, R.:** *Tikunei ha-Zohar*, Lublin 1927.
    *Tikunei Zohar im m'forshim*, Jerusalem.
    *Sefer Tikunei Zohar*, Mechon Da'at Yosef, Jerusalem 1991.
78. **Gikatilla, J.:** *Gates of Light: Sha'are Orah*, Op. cit.
79. **Kaplan, A.:** *Sefer Yetzirah*, Op. cit.
    **Hyman, A.P.:** *Sefer Yesira*, Op. cit.
80. *Ibid.*
81. *Ibid.*
82. *Ibid.*
83. **Kaplan, A.:** *Sefer Yetzirah*, Op. cit.
84. **Swart, J.G.:** *The Book of Sacred Names*, Op. cit.
85. **Kaplan, A.:** *Sefer Yetzirah*, Op. cit.
86. **Posquieres, A. ben David [Raavad]:** *Sefer Yetzirah*, Op. cit.
    **Shabbetai Donnolo, Ra'avad, ha-Ramban (Nachmanides), Sa'adia ben Yosef, Eleazer m'Garmiza, Moses ben Jacob of Kiev, Moses ben Jacob Botarel, Eliyah ben Solomon m'Vilna (Gra), Yitzhak Eizik ben Yekutiel Zalman, Azriel ben Menachem, Shemuel ben Eliezer Aharon Lurya, David Castelli, Abraham ben David of Posquieres:** *Sefer Yetsirah: ha-Meyuchas le-Avraham avinu*, Op. cit.
    *Sefer Yetsirah: ha-Meyuchas le-Avraham Avinu: v'alav kol ha-mefarshim ha-mekubalim*, Op. cit.
    **Zacutto, M.:** *Shorshei ha-Shemot*, Op. cit.
    **Kaplan, A.:** *Sefer Yetzirah*, Op. cit.
87. *Ibid.*
88. *Ibid.*
89. *Ibid.*
90. **Winkler, G.:** *Magic of the Ordinary*, Op. cit.
91. **Kaplan, A.:** *Sefer Yetzirah*, Op. cit.
92. **Swart, J.G.:** *The Book of Immediate Magic - Part 1*, Op. cit.
93. **Swart, J.G.:** *The Book of Self Creation*, Op. cit.
94. *Ibid.*
95. *Ibid.*
96. *Ibid.*
97. *Ibid.*
98. **Trachtenberg, J.:** *Jewish Magic and Superstition*, Op. cit.
    **Bohak, G.:** *Ancient Jewish Magic*, Op. cit.
    **Ben-Amos, D.:** *On Demons*, published in **Dan, J.; Elior, R. & Schäfer, P.:** *Creation and Re-Creation in Jewish Thought: Festschrift in Honor of Joseph Dan on the occassion of His Seventieth Birthday*, Mohr Siebeck, Tübingen 2005.

**Dennis, G.W.:** *The Encyclopedia of Jewish Myth, Magic and Mysticism*, Op. cit.
**Isaacs, R.H.:** *Divination, Magic, and Healing*, Op. cit.
**Dynner, G.:** *Holy Dissent: Jewish and Christian Mystics in Eastern Europe*, Wayne State University Press, Detroit 2011.
**Patai, R. & Bar-Itzhak, H.:** *Encyclopedia of Jewish Folklore and Traditions*, Routledge, Abingdon & New York 2015.
**Harari, Y.:** *Jewish Magic before the Rise of Kabbalah*, Wayne State University Press, Detroit 2017.
**Saar, O.:** *Jewish Love Magic: From Late Antiquity to the Middle Ages*, Koninklijke Brill NV, Leiden 2017.

99. **Meyer, G.G.; Blum, K. & Cull, J.G.:** *Folk Medicine and Herbal Healing*, Thomas Publications, 1981.
**Lustig, D.:** *Pela'ot Chachmeh ha-Kabbalah: v'He'avar ha-Kadum*, Hotza'at David ben Ze'ev, Tel Aviv 1987.
—*Wondrous Healings of the Wise Kabbalists and the Ancient Physicians*, D. Lustig, Tel Aviv 1989.
**Patai, R.:** *The Jewish Alchemists: A History and Source Book*, Princeton University Press, Princeton 1994.
**Palevits, D. & Yaniv, Z.:** *Medicinal Plants of the Holy Land*, Modan Publishing House, Tel Aviv 2000.
**Lévy, I.J. & Lévy Zumwalt, R.:** *Ritual Medical Lore of Sephardic Women: Sweetening the Spirits, Healing the Sick*, University of Illinois Press, Urbana & Chicago 2002.

100. **Shtern, Y.P.:** *Practical Kabbalah and Natural Medicine in the Polish-Lituanian Commonwealth, 1690–1750*, published in **Dynner, G.:** *Holy Dissent*, Op. cit.

101. *Ibid.*

102. *Ibid.*

103. **Campbell Thompson, R.:** *Semitic Magic: Its Origins and Development*, Luzac 1908.
**Loeb, L.D. Outcaste (RLE Iran D):** *Jewish Life in Southern Iran*, Gordon and Breach Science Publishers, New York, London & Paris 1977.
**Meyer, G.G.; Blum, K. & Cull, J.G.:** *Folk Medicine and Herbal Healing*, Op. cit.
**Palevits, D. & Yaniv, Z.:** *Medicinal Plants of the Holy Land*, Op. cit.
**Lévy, I.J. & Lévy Zumwalt, R.:** *Ritual Medical Lore of Sephardic Women*, Op. cit.
**Lev, E. & Amar, Z.:** *Practical Materia Medica of the Medieval Eastern Mediterranean according to Cairo Geniza*, E.J. Brill, Leiden & Boston 2008.

104. **Zacutto, M.:** *Shorshei ha-Shemot, Op. cit.*
105. *Ibid.*
    **Swart, J.G.:** *The Book of Seals & Amulets, Op. cit.*
106. *Ibid.*
107. **Lev, E. & Amar, Z.:** *Practical Materia Medica of the Medieval Eastern Mediterranean according to Cairo Geniza, Op. cit.*
108. *Ibid.*
109. **Patai, R.:** *On Jewish Folklore*, Wayne State University Press, Detroit 1983.
110. *Ibid.*
111. **Lévy, I.J. & Lévy Zumwalt, R.:** *Ritual Medical Lore of Sephardic Women, Op. cit.*
112. *Ibid.*
113. **Culpeper, N.:** *The English Physician: Enlarged with Three Hundred, Sixty, and Nine Medicines*, George Sawbridge, Ludgate-Hill 1676.
    —*Culpeper's Complete Herbal, to which is now added upwards of One Hundred Additional Herbs, with a Display of their Medicinal and Occult Qualities*, Richard Evans, Spitalfields 1814.
    **Folkard, R.:** *PlantLore, Legends, and Lyrics: embracing the Myths, Traditions, Superstitions, and Folklore of the Plant Kingdom*, Sampson Low, Marston, Searle, and Rivington, London 1884.
    **Hulme, F.E.:** *Wild Fruits of the Country-Side*, Hutchinson & Co., London 1902.
    **von Nettesheim, H.C.A.:** *The Philosophy of Natural Magic: A Complete Work on Natural Magic, White Magic, Black magic*, DeLaurence Co., Chicago 1913.
    **Petulengro, L.:** Herbs, Health & Astrology, Keats Publishing Inc., New Canaan 1977.
    **Junius, M.M.:** *The Practical Handbook of Plant Alchemy: An Herbalist's Guide to Preparing Medicinal Essences, Tinctures, and Elixirs*, Healing Arts Press, Rochester 1985.
114. **Alfonso X:** *Lapidario del Rex Alfonso X: Codice Original*, A Cargo de J. Blasco, Madrid 1881.
    **Bahler, I. & Gatto, K.G.:** *The Lapidary of King Alfonso X the Learned*, University Press of the South, New Orleans 1997.
    **Agrippa, H.C.:** *The Philosophy of Natural Magic*, University Books, Secaucus 1974.
    **Jones, W.:** *History and Mystery of Precious Stones*, Richard Bentley and Son, London 1880.

**Kunz, G.F.:** *The Curious Lore of Precious Stones,* J.B. Lippencott Company, Philadelphia & London 1913.
**Kozminsky, I.:** *The Magic and Science of Jewels and Stones,* G.P. Putnam's Sons, New York & London 1922.
**Evans, J.:** *Magical Jewels of the Middle Ages and the Renaissance particularly in England,* Clarendon Press, Oxford 1922.
**Trachtenberg, J.:** *Jewish Magic and Superstition, Op. cit.*
**Fernie, W.T.:** *The Occult and Curative Powers of Precious Stones,* Rudolf Steiner Publications, New York 1973.
**Johari, H.:** *The Healing Power of Gemstones: In Tantra, Ayurveda, and Astrology,* Destiny Books, Rochester 1988.
**Dwivedi, B.:** *Be Your Own Astrologer: Ascendant Virgo: A Comprehensive Introduction,* Diamond Pocket Books (P) Ltd., New Delhi 2005.
**Schuh, C.P.:** *Mineralogy & Crystallography: On the History of These Sciences from Beginnings throughb 1919,* Electronic File, Tucson 2007.
**Shangari, H.:** *Gemstones: Magic or Science?,* Notion Press, Chetpet Chennai 2017.

115. **Alfonso X:** *Ibid.*
     **Bahler, I. & Gatto, K.G.:** *Ibid.*
116. **Trachtenberg, J.:** *Jewish Magic and Superstition, Op. cit.*
117. **Bohak, G.:** *Ancient Jewish Magic, Op. cit.*
118. **Trachtenberg, J.:** *Jewish Magic and Superstition, Op. cit.*
119. *Ibid.*
120. *Ibid.*
     **Etheridge, J.W.:** *The Targums of Onkelos and Jonathan ben Uzziel on the Pentateuch, with the Fragments of the Jerusalem Targum from the Chaldee: Genesis and Exodus,* Longman Green Longman & Roberts, London 1862.
     **Chlava, B. ben A. ben:** *Midrash Rabbeinu Bachya, Torah Commentary: Volume 3 - Shemot–Yitro,* transl. Munk E., Urim Publications, Jerusalem 1998.
     **Kozminsky, I.:** *The Magic and Science of Jewels and Stones, Op. cit.*
121. *Ibid.*
122. **Chlava, B. ben A. ben:** *Ibid.*
123. *Ibid.*
     **Trachtenberg, J.:** *Jewish Magic and Superstition, Op. cit.*
     **Etheridge, J.W.:** *The Targums of Onkelos and Jonathan ben Uzziel on the Pentateuch, Op. cit.*

**Kozminsky, I.:** *The Magic and Science of Jewels and Stones, Op. cit.*

124. **Shinan, A.:** *Midrash Shemot Rabbah: A Critical Edition based on a Jerusalem Manuscript with Variants, Commentary and Introduction,* Dvir, Tel Aviv 1984.
125. **Etheridge, J.W.:** *The Targums of Onkelos and Jonathan ben Uzziel on the Pentateuch, Op. cit.*
  **Trachtenberg, J.:** *Jewish Magic and Superstition, Op. cit.*
  **Chlava, B. ben A. ben:** *Midrash Rabbeinu Bachya, Op. cit.*
  **Kozminsky, I.:** *The Magic and Science of Jewels and Stones, Op. cit.*
126. *Ibid.*
127. *Ibid.*
128. **Trachtenberg, J.:** *Ibid.*
  **Chlava, B. ben A. ben:** *Ibid.*
129. **Chlava, B. ben A. ben:** *Ibid.*
130. *Ibid.*
  **Trachtenberg, J.:** *Jewish Magic and Superstition, Op. cit.*
  **Etheridge, J.W.:** *The Targums of Onkelos and Jonathan ben Uzziel on the Pentateuch, Op. cit.*
  **Kozminsky, I.:** *The Magic and Science of Jewels and Stones, Op. cit.*
131. *Ibid.*
132. *Ibid.*
133. **Etheridge, J.W.:** *Ibid.*
134. *Ibid.*
  **Trachtenberg, J.:** *Jewish Magic and Superstition, Op. cit.*
  **Chlava, B. ben A. ben:** *Midrash Rabbeinu Bachya, Op. cit.*
  **Kozminsky, I.:** *The Magic and Science of Jewels and Stones, Op. cit.*
135. *Ibid.*
136. *Ibid.*
137. **Shachar, I.:** *Jewish Tradition in Art, Op. cit.*
  **Davis, E. & Frenkel, D.A.:** *Ha-Kami'a ha-Ivri, Op. cit.*
138. **Alfonso X:** *Lapidario del Rex Alfonso X, Op. cit.*
  **Bahler, I. & Gatto, K.G.:** *The Lapidary of King Alfonso X the Learned, Op. cit.*
139. **Swart, J.G.:** *The Book of Self Creation, Op. cit.*
140. *Ibid.*
141. *Ibid.*
142. **Swart, J.G.:** *The Book of Immediate Magic - Part 1, Op. cit.*
143. *Ibid.*

144. *Ibid.*
145. **Swart, J.G.:** *The Book of Immediate Magic - Part 1, Op. cit.*
146. *Ibid.*
147. *Ibid.*
148. *Ibid.*
149. *Ibid.*
150. *Ibid.*
151. **Swart, J.G.:** *The Book of Seals & Amulets, Op. cit.*
152. **Swart, J.G.:** *The Book of Immediate Magic - Part 1, Op. cit.*
153. **Swart, J.G.:** *The Book of Seals & Amulets, Op. cit.*
154. **Swart, J.G.:** *The Book of Self Creation, Op. cit.*
155. **Swart, J.G.:** *The Book of Seals & Amulets, Op. cit.*
156. *Ibid.*
157. *Ibid.*
158. *Ibid.*
159. *Ibid.*
160. *Ibid.*
161. *Ibid.*
162. *Ibid.*
163. *Ibid.*
164. **Swart, J.G.:** *The Book of Sacred Names, Op. cit.*
165. **Swart, J.G.:** *The Book of Seals & Amulets, Op. cit.*
166. **Swart, J.G.:** *The Book of Immediate Magic - Part 1, Op. cit.*
167. *Ibid.*
168. *Ibid.*
    **Swart, J.G.:** *The Book of Self Creation, Op. cit.*
169. *Ibid.*
170. **Mathers, S.L. Macgregor:** *Key of Solomon the King: Clavicula Salomonis*, Routledge & Kegan Paul, London 1974.
171. **Gollancz, H.:** *Sepher Maphteah Shelomo* (*Book of the Key of Solomon*), Oxford University Press, London 1914.
172. **Mathers, S.L. Macgregor:** *Key of Solomon the King: Clavicula Salomonis, Op. cit.*
173. **Swart, J.G.:** *The Book of Self Creation, Op. cit.*
174. *Ibid.*
175. **Swart, J.G.:** *The Book of Immediate Magic - Part 1, Op. cit.*
176. **Swart, J.G.:** *The Book of Self Creation, Op. cit.*
177. **Swart, J.G.:** *The Book of Immediate Magic - Part 1, Op. cit.*
178. **Swart, J.G.:** *The Book of Self Creation, Op. cit.*
179. **Swart, J.G.:** *The Book of Immediate Magic - Part 1, Op. cit.*
180. **Swart, J.G.:** *The Book of Seals & Amulets, Op. cit.*
181. *Ibid.*

182. *Ibid.*
183. *Ibid.*
184. *Ibid.*

# CHAPTER 9

1. **Montagu, A.:** *Touching: The Human Significance of the Skin*, Harper and Row, New York 1986.
   **Paterson, M.:** *The Senses of Touch: Haptics, Affects and Technologies*, Bloomsbury Publications, London 2007
   **Hertenstein, M.J. & Weiss, S.J.:** *The Handbook of Touch: Neuroscience, Behavioral, and Health Perspectives*, Springer Publishing Company, New York 2011.
2. **Colwell, R. & Richardson, C.P.:** *The New Handbook of Research on Music Teaching and Learning: a Project of the Music Educators National Conference*, Oxford University Press, Oxford & New York 2002.
   **Mannes, E.:** *The Power of Music: Pioneering Discoveries in the New Science of Song*, Walker & Co., New York 2013.
   **Chamberlain, D.:** *Windows to the Womb: Revealing the Conscious Baby from Conception to Birth*, North Atlantic Books, Berkeley 2013.
   **Thompson, W.F.:** *Music in the Social and Behavioral Sciences: An Encyclopedia*, Sage Publications Inc., Los Angeles & Boston 2014.
3. **Gray, W.G.:** *Magical Ritual Methods*, Op. cit.
   —*Qabalistic Concepts: Living the Tree*, Op. cit.
4. **Rossel, S.; Borowitz, E.B. & Chanover, H.:** *When a Jew Prays*, Behrman House, New York 1973.
5. **Sillitoe, P.:** *An Introduction to the of Melanesia: Culture and Tradition*, Cambridge University Press, Cambridge 1998.
   **Glucklich, A.:** *Sacred Pain: Hurting the Body for the Sake of the Soul*, Oxford University Press, Oxford & New York 2001.
   **Van Gennep, A.:** *The Rites of Passage*, Routledge, London 2004.
   **Kilmartin, C. & Smiler, A.M.:** *The Masculine Self*, Sloan Publishing, Cornwall on Hudson 2015.
6. **Gardner, G.B.:** *Witchcraft Today*, Citadel Press, Secaucus 1954.
   —*The Meaning of Witchcraft*, Weiser Books, Boston 2004.
7. **Buckland, R.:** *Witchcraft from the Inside: Origins of the Fastest Growsing Religious Movement in America*, Llewellyn Publications, Minnesota 1995.
   **Cunningham, S.:** *The Truth About Witchcraft Today*, Llewellyn Publications, St. Paul 2001.

**Pearson, J.:** *Wicca and the Christian Heritage: Ritual, Sex and Magic*, Routledge, Abingdon 2007.

8. **Kapleau, P.:** *The Three Pillars of Zen: Teaching, Practice, and Enlightenment*, Beacon Press, Boston 1969.
**Uchiyama, K. Roshi:** *Opening the Hand of Thought: Foundations of Zen Buddhist Practice*, transl. T. Wright, J. Warner and S. Okumura, Wisdom Publications, New York 2005.

9. **Jennings, H.:** *Phallic Worship: A Description of the Mysteries of the Sex Worship of the Ancients with the History of the Masculine Cross: An Account of Primitive Symbolism, Hebrew Phallicism, Bacchic Festivals, Sexual Rites, and the Mysteries of the Ancient Faiths*, Privately Printed, London 1886.
—*Nature Worship: An Account of Phallic Faiths & Practices Ancient and Modern, including the Adoration of the Male and Female Powers in Various Nations and the Sacti Puja of Indian Gnosticism*, Privately Printed, London 1891.
—*Phallic Miscellanies: Facts and Phases of Ancient and Modern Sex Worship, as Illustrated Chiefly in the Religions of India: An Appendix of Additional and Explanatory Matter to the Volumes Phallism and Nature Worship*, Privately Printed, London 1891.
—*Phallicism: a Description of the Worship of Lingham-Yoni in Various Parts of the World, and in Different Ages: with an Account of Ancient & Modern Crosses, particularly of the Crux Ansata (or Handles Cross), and other Symbols connected with the Mysteries of Sex Worship*, Privately Printed, London 1892.
**Gamble, E.B.:** *The God Idea of the Ancients or Sex in Religion*, G.P. Putnam's Sons, New York & London 1897.
**Malinowski, B.:** *The Sexual Life of Savages in North-Western Melanesia*, Routledge & Kegan Paul Ltd., London 1929.
**Bloch, I.:** *Anthropological Studies in the Strange Sexual Practices in All Races of the World*, Falstaff Press, New York 1933.
**Scott, G.R.:** *Phallic Worship*, Panther, London 1970.
**Bullough, V.L. & Bullough, B.:** *Human Sexuality: An Encyclopedia*, Routledge, New York & London 2013.

10. **Martin, W. & Passantino, G.:** *The New Cults*, Regal Books, Ventura 1985.
**MacHovec, F.J.:** *Cults and Personality*, C.C. Thomas, Springfield 1989.
**Cowan, D.E. & Bromley, D.G.:** *Sects, Cults, and Alternative Religions: a World Survey and Sourcebook*, Blandford, London 1996.

**Berger, H.A.:** *Community of Witches: Contemporary Neo-Paganism and Witchcraft in the United States*, University of South California Press, Columbia 1999.
**Jenkins, P.:** *Mystics and Messiahs: Cults and New Religions in American History*, Oxford University Press, Oxford & New York 2000.
**Reis, E.:** *Spellbound: Woman and Witchcraft in America*, SR Books, Lanham 2004.
**Melton, J.G.:** *The Children of God: "The Family"*, Signature Books, Salt Lake City 2004.
**Ajemian, S.:** *The Children of God Cult, aka The Family*, Privately Published, Pasadena 2005.
**Kraemer, C.H.:** *Eros and Touch from a Pagan Perspective: Divided for Love's Sake*, Routledge, New York & London 2014.
**Cowan, D.E. & Bromley, D.G.:** *Cults and New Religions: a Brief History*, Blackwell Publishing, Malden 2016.

11. **Reich, W.:** *Selected Writings: An Introduction to Ogonomy*, Farrar, Straus & Giroux, New York 1960.
    **Mann, W.E.:** *Orgone, Reich and Eros. Wilhelm Reich's Theory of the Life Energy*, Simon and Schuster, New York 1973.
    **Boadella, D.:** *Wilhelm Reich: The Evolution of his Work*, Arkana, London 1985.
12. **Hartmann, F.:** *The Life and the Doctrines of Philippus Theophrastus, Bombast of Hohenheim known by the Name of Paracelcus*, John W. Lovell Company, New York 1891.
13. **Schiegl, H.:** *Healing Magnetism: The Transference of Vital Force*, Samuel Weiser, Maine 1987.
14. **Reichenbach, Baron K. von:** *Researches on Magnetism, Electricity, Heat, Light, Crystallization and Chemical Attraction in Relation to the Vital Force*, University Books, Secaucus 1974.
15. **Reich, W.:** *Reich Speaks of Freud: Wilhelm Reich Discusses His Work and His Relationship with Sigmund Freud*, Farrar, Straus & Giroux, New York 1967.
16. **Reich, W.:** *Selected Writings, Op. cit.*
17. **Wilson, R.A., Hyatt, C. & Holmes D.:** *Wilhelm Reich in Hell*, Falcon Press, Poenix 1987.
    **Regardie, F.I. & Monnastre, C.:** *The Golden Dawn, Op. cit.*
18. **Kleinfeld, V.A. & Dunn, C.W.:** *Federal Food, Druig, and Cosmetic Act: Judicial and Administrative Record 1953–1957*, Commerce Clearing House, New York 1958.
    **U.S. Department of Health, Education, and Welfare:** *United States Food and Drug Administration, Notices of Judgment Under the Federal Food, Drug, and Cosmetic Act: Given Pursuant to Section 705 of the Food, Drug, and Cosmetic Act 5381–5400: Drugs and Devices*, U.S. Government Print Office, Washington January 1959.

19. **Rutherford, A.:** *Outline of Pyramidology*, Institute of Pyramidology, Stanmore 1958.
    **Flanagan, G.P.:** *Pyramid Power*, De Vorss, Marina del Rey 1973.
    —*Beyond Pyramid Power*, DeVorss, Marina del Rey 1976.
    **Schull, B. & Petit, E.:** *The Psychic Power of Pyramids*, Coronet, London 1977.
    **Rixon, G.H.:** *Pyramid Power & Psychic Healing*, Pythagorean Press, Sydney 1980.
20. **Waite, A.E.:** *A New Encyclopedia of Freemasonry (ars magna latomorum) and of cognate instituted Mysteries; their Rites, Literature and History*, W. Rider & Son, Masonic History Company, London 1921.
    **Albert G Mackey, A.G.:** *A Lexicon of Freemasonry: containing Definitions of all its Communicable Terms, Notices of its Traditions and Antiquities, together with an Account of all the Rites and Mysteries of the Ancient World*, Richard Griffen & Company, London & Glasgow 1860.
    —with **Hughan, W.J. & Hawkins, E.L.:** *An Encyclopedia of Freemasonry and Its Kindred Sciences, Comprising the Whole Range of Arts, Sciences and Literature as Connected with the Institution*, Masonic History Company, Chicago 1924.
    **Regardie, I.:** *The Golden Dawn, Op. cit.*
    **Gilbert, R.A.:** *The Golden Dawn Companion: A Guide to the History, Structure, and Workings of the Hermetic Order of the Golden Dawn*, The Aquarian Press, Wellingborow 1986.
    **Zoja, L.:** *Drugs, Addiction and Initiation: The Modern Search for Ritual*, Sigo Press, Boston 1989.
    **McIntosh, C.:** *The Rosicrucians: The History, Mythology, and Rituals of an Esoteric Order*, Weiser Books, York Beach 1998.
    **Saunders, N., Saunders, A. & Pauli, M.:** *In Search of the Ultimate High: Spiritual Experiences through Psychoactives*, Rider, London, Sydney, Auckland & Johannesburg 2000.
21. **Gray, W.G.:** *My Autobiography*, Unpublished Manuscript, Sangreal Sodality William Gray Dossier: Temple Lux Occidentis in Extensio, Johannesburg, South Africa.
22. **Solomon, P.; Kubzansky, P.E.; Leiderman, P.H.; Mendelson, J.H., Trumbull, R.; & Wexler, D.:** *Sensory Deprivation: A Symposium Held at Harvard Medical School*, Harvard University Press, Cambridge 1960.
    **Zubek, J.P.:** *Sensory Deprivation: Fifteen Years of Research*, Appleton-Century-Crofts Educational Division/Meredith Corporation, New York 1969.

**Lilly, J.C.:** *The Deep Self: Profound Relaxation and the Tank Isolation Technique*, Simon and Schuster, New York 1977.

**— & Lilly, P.H.B.:** *The Quiet Center: Isolation and Spirit*, Ronin Publishing, Berkeley 2011.

**Spencer, L.:** *Flotation: A Guide for Sensory Deprivation, Relaxation, & Isolation Tanks*, Lulu.com 2015.

23. **Rosenfeld, E.:** *The Book of Highs: 250 Ways to alter Consciousness without Drugs*, Quadrangle, New York 1973.

**Cohen, D.:** *The Far Side of Consciousness*, Dodd, Mead & Company, New York 1974.

**Buckland, R.:** *Buckland's Complete Book of Witchcraft*, Llewellyn Publications, St. Paul 2002.

**Holzer, H.:** *Witches: True Encounters with Wicca, Wizards, Covens, Cults & Magick*, Black Dog & Leventhal, New York 2005.

**Willin, M.J.:** *Music, Witchcraft and the Paranormal*, Melrose Books, Cambridgeshire 2005.

24. **Blum, R.:** *Utopiates*, Atherton Press, New York 1964.

**Roberts, T.B.:** *Psychoactive Sacramentals: Essays on Entheogens and Religion*, Council on Spiritual Practices, San Francisco 2001.

*—Spiritual Growth with Entheogens: Psychoactive Sacramentals and Human Transformation*, Park Street Press, Rochester 2012.

**de Rios, M.D. & Oscar Janiger, O.:** *LSD, Spirituality, and the Creative Process: Based on the Groundbreaking Research of Oscar Janiger, M.D.*, Park Street Press, Rochester 2003.

**Kripal, J.J.:** *Esalen: America and the Religion of No Religion*, The University of Chicago Press, Chicago & London 2007.

**Ellens, J.H.:** *Seeking the Sacred with Psychoactive Substances: Chemical Paths to Spirituality and to God*, Praeger, Santa Barbara 2014.

**Richards. W.A.:** *Sacred Knowledge: Psychedelics and Religious Experiences*, Columbia University Press, New York 2016.

25. **Johnson, M.E.:** *The Rites of Christian Initiation: Their Evolution and Interpretation*, Liturgical Press, Collegeville 1999.

**Davies, D.:** *Death, Ritual, and Belief: The Rhetoric of Funerary Rites*, Continuum, London & New York 2002.

**Cross, A.R.:** *Recovering the Evangelical Sacrament: Baptisma Semper Reformandum*, Pickwick Publications, Eugene 2013.

26. **Eliade, M.:** *Rites and Symbols of Initiation: The Mysteries of Birth and Rebirth,* transl. Trask, W.R., Harper & Row, London & San Francisco 1958.
27. **Ginsburg, E.K.:** *The Sabbath in the Classical Kabbalah,* State University of New York Press, Albany 1989.
    **Wolfson, E.R.:** *Through a Speculum that Shines: Vision and Imagination in Medieval Jewish Mysticism,* Princeton University Press, Princeton 1994.
    —*Circle in the Square: Studies in the Use of Gender in Kabbalistic Symbolism,* State University of New York Press, Albany 1995.
    —*Language, Eros, Being: Kabbalistic Hermeneutics and Poetic Imagination,* Fordham University Press, New York 2005.
    **Ostow, M. & Arlow, J.A.:** *Ultimate Intimacy: The Psychodynamics of Jewish Mysticism,* Karnac Books, London 1995.
    **Fine, L.:** *Essential Papers on Kabbalah,* New York University Press, New York & London 1995.
    **Leet, L.:** *The Secret Doctrine of the Kabbalah: Discovering the Key to Hebraic Sacred Science,* Inner Traditions International, Rochester 1999.
    —*The Universal Kabbalah,* Inner Traditions International, Rochester 2004.
    **Drob, S.L.:** *Symbols of the Kabbalah, Op. cit.*
    **Livingstone, D.:** *The Dying God: The Hidden History of Western Civilization,* Writers Club Press, New York, Lincoln & Shanghai 2002.
    **Frankel, E.:** *Sacred Therapy: Jewish Spiritual Teachings on Emotional Healing and Inner Wholeness,* Shambhala, Boston 2005.
    **Scholem, G. & Ottmann, K.:** *Alchemy and kabbalah,* Spring Publications, Putnam 2006.
    **Campbell, J.:** *The Hero with a Thousand Faces,* New World Library, London & New York 2008.
    **Versluis, A.:** *The Secret History of Western Sexual Mysticism: Sacred Practices and Spiritual Marriage,* Destiny Books, Rochester 2008.
    **Mark, Z.:** *Mysticism and Madness: The Religious Thought of Rabbi Nachman of Bratslav,* Continuum, London & New York 2009.
    **Lundhaug, H.:** *Images of Rebirth: Cognitive Poetics and Transformational Soteriology in the Gospel of Philip and the Exegesis on the Soul,* Koninklijke Brill NV, Leiden 2010.

**Forshaw, P.J.:** *Lux in Tenebris: The Visual and the Symbolic in Western Esotericism*, Koninklijke Brill NV, Leiden 2016.
**Brodersen, E. & Glock, M.:** *Jungian Perspectives on Rebirth and Renewal: Phoenix Rising*, Routledge, London & New York 2017.

28. **Alister, I. & Hauke, C.:** *Contemporary Jungian Analysis: Post-Jungian Perspectives from the Society of Analytical Psychology*, Routledge, London & New York 1998.
**Campbell, J.:** *Pathways to Bliss: Mythology and Personal Transformation*, ReadHowYouWant, Sydney 2008.
**O'Connor, P.:** *Understanding Jung Understanding Yourself,* Routledge, London & New York 2015.

29. **Oliver, G.:** *The History of Initiation in Three Courses of Lectures: comprising a detailed Account of the Rites and Ceremonies, Doctrines and Discipline, of all the Secred and Mysterious Institutions of the Ancient World*, Printed for the Author and Published by Bro. Washbourn, London 1829.
**Eliade, M.:** *Rites and Symbols of Initiation, Op. cit.*
—*The Sacred and the Profane: The Nature of Religion*, transl. by Trask, W.R., Harcourt, Brace & World, New York 1959.
**Farb, P.:** *Man's Rise to Civilization as Shown by the Indians of North America*, Penguin Books, New York 1991.
**Cox, R.H., Betty Ervin-Cox, B. & Hoffman, L.:** *Spirituality and Psychological Health*, Colorado School of Professional Psychology Press, Colorado 2005.
**Smith, M.C.:** *Jung and Shamanism in Dialogue: Retrieving the Soul, Retrieving the Sacred*, Paulist Press, New York 2007.
**Corrigan, J.:** *The Oxford Handbook of Religion and Emotion*, Oxford University Press, Oxford & New York 2008.
**Tacey, D.:** *Gods and Diseases: Making Sense of Our Physical and Mental Wellbeing*, Routledge, New York 2013.

30. **Ferri, G.:** *The Psychology of Wilderness Survival*, Survival in the Bush, Hanover 1989.

31. **Hill, R.L.:** *Psychology and the Near-Death Experience: Searching for God*, White Crow Books, Hove 2015.

32. **Oliver, G.:** *The History of Initiation in Three Courses of Lectures, Op. cit.*
**Wundt, W.:** *Elements of Folk Psychology: Outlines of a Psychological History of the Development of Mankind* Vol. VII, Routledge, New York 2003.
**Hellholm, D., Vegge, T., Norderval, O. & Hellholm, C.:** *Ablution, Initiation, and Baptism: Late Antiquity, Early Judaism, and Early Christianity*, Walter de Gruyter GmbH & Co. KG, Berlin & Boston 2011.

33. **Elkins, D.P.:** *Rosh Hashanah Readings: Inspiration, Information, and Contemplation*, Jewish Lights Publishing, Woodstock 2006.
34. **Hatcher, B.A.:** *Hinduism in the Modern World*, Routledge, London & New York 2016.
35. **Rofé, H.:** *Reflections on Subud*, Humanity Publishing Company, 1958.
—*The Path of Subud*, Rider & Co., London 1959.
**Bennett, J.G.:** *Concerning Subud*, Hodder & Stoughton, London 1960.
**Geels, A.:** *Subud and the Javanese Mystical Tradition*, Curzon Press, Richmond 1997.
**Monbaron, S.:** *Subud the Coming New Age of Reality: The Most Complete Book on Subud*, Simar Enterprises, Sutherlin 1999.
36. **Monbaron, S.:** *Ibid.*
**Kiev, A. & Francis, J.L.:** *Subud and Mental Illness: Psychiatric Illness in a Religious Sect*, American Journal of Psychotherapy 18:I, New York 1964.
**Institute of Living:** *Digest of Neurology and Psychiatry: Volumes 32–33*, Institute Of Living, Hartford 1964.
**Raheem, A.:** *Soul Lightning: Awakening Soul Consciousness*, iUniverse, Lincoln 2005.
37. **Swart, J.G.:** *The Book of Self Creation, Op. cit.*
38. **Gray, W.G.:** *Inner Traditions of Magic*, Samuel Weiser Inc., New York 1978.
—*A Self Made by Magic, Op. cit.*
—*Qabalistic Concepts: Living the Tree, Op. cit.*
—*The Consecration of a Sangreal Temple*, unpublished Manuscript.
—*Sangreal Sodality Initiation Ceremonies: Initiation of the Cord*, unpublished manuscripts, Sangreal Sodality_William Gray Dossier: Temple Lux Occidentis in Extensio, Johannesburg, South Africa.
39. **Eleazar of Worms:** *Sefer ha-Shem*, MS British Museum 737.
40. **Dan, J.:** *Jewish Mysticism: The Middle Ages*, Jason Aronson Inc., Northvale & Jerusalem 1998.
41. **Scholem, G.:** *On the Kabbalah and Its Symbolism, Op. cit.*
42. **Eleazar of Worms:** *Sefer ha-Shem, Op. cit.*
**Wolfson, E.:** *Through a Speculum that Shines, Op. cit.*
43. **Wolfson, E.:** *Ibid.*
44. **Swart, J.G.:** *The Book of Self Creation, Op. cit.*

45. *Sefer ha-Malbush v'Tikkun me'il ha-Tzedakah* [*The Book of the Putting on and Fashioning of the Mantle of Righteousness*], MS British Museum, Margoliouth 752; MS Oxford Michael 473.
    **Wandrey, I.:** *Das Buch des Gewandes und Das Buch des Aufrechten: Dokumente eines Magischen Spätantiken Rituals*, Mohr Siebeck, Tübingen 2004.
    **Scholem, G.:** *On the Kabbalah and Its Symbolism, Op. cit.*
46. *Sêfer Ha-Malbûsh: The Book of the Garment*, transl. Feliciano, J.P., unpublished.
47. **Isaacs, R.H.:** *Rites of Passage: A Guide to the Jewish Life Cycle*, KTAV Publishing House, Inc., Hoboken 1992.
    **Artson, B.S.:** *On the Eighth Day in Every Generation: A Guide to the Brit Milah*, The Rabbinical Assembly, New York 1993.
    **Mark, E.W.:** *The Covenant of Circumcision: New Perspectives on an Ancient Jewish Rite*, Brandeis University Press published by University Press of New England, Hanover 2003.
    **Marcus, I.G.:** *The Jewish Life Cycle: Rites of Passage from Biblical to Modern Times*, University of Washington Press, Seattle & London 2004.
48. **Gollaher, D.:** *Circumcision: A History of the World's Most Controversial Surgery*, Al Saqi Bookshop, New York 2001.
    **Pedersen, L.E.:** *Dark Hearts: the Unconscious Forces that Shape Men's Lives*, iUniverse, Inc., Lincoln 2002.
49. **Berndt, R.M.:** *Australian Aboriginal Religion*, E.J. Brill, Leiden 1974.
    **Huxley, F.:** *The Way of the Sacred: Taboos, Rites & Symbols that fascinated Men through the Ages*, W.H. Allen & Co. Ltd., London 1980.
    **Elkin, A.P.:** *Aboriginal Men of High Degree: Initiation and Sorcery in the World's Oldest Tradition*, Inner Traditions, Rochester 1994.
    **Montagu, A.:** *Coming Into Being Among the Australian Aborigines*, Routledge, Abingdon 2004.
    **Favazza, A.R.:** *Bodies under Siege: Self-mutilation, Nonsuicidal Self-injury, and Body Modification in Culture and Psychiatry*, The John Hopkins University Press, Baltimore 2011.
    **Galvan, J.A.:** *They Do What? A Cultural Encyclopedia of Extraordinary and Exotic Customs from around the World*, ABC-CLIO, Santa Barbara 2014.
    **Charlesworth, M., Dussart, F. & Morphy, H.:** *Aboriginal Religions in Australia: An Anthology of Recent Writings*, Routledge, New York 2017.

Williams, V.: *Celebrating Life Customs around the World: From Baby Showers to Funerals: Volume 1 Birth and Childhood*, ABC-CLIO, LLC, Santa Barbara & Denver 2017.

50. **Needleman, J. & Baker, G.:** *Gurdjieff: Essays and Reflections on the Man and His Teachings*, The Continuum International Publishing Group Inc., New York 2004.
51. **Swart, J.G.:** *The Book of Self Creation, Op. cit.*
52. *Ibid.*
53. *The Fathers According to Rabbi Nathan*, transl. J. Goldin, Yale University Press, New Haven & London 1995.
54. **Swart, J.G.:** *The Book of Self Creation, Op. cit.*
55. *Ibid.*
56. *Ibid.*
57. *Ibid.*
58. **Gray, W.G:** *The Tree of Evil, Op. cit.*
59. **Swart, J.G.:** *The Book of Immediate Magic - Part 1, Op. cit.*
60. **Swart, J.G.:** *The Book of Self Creation, Op. cit.*
61. *Ibid.*
62. **Swart, J.G.:** *The Book of Immediate Magic - Part 1, Op. cit.*
63. **Swart, J.G.:** *The Book of Self Creation, Op. cit.*
64. *Ibid.*
65. **Pixley, O.C.B.:** *The Armour of Light, a Technique for Healing the Self and Others*, Favil Press, London 1957.
    — *The Armour of Light: A Technique of Healing the Self and Others*, Part 2, Helios Book Service Ltd., Cheltenham 1969.
    —*The Magnet: Advanced Technique: A Sequel to "The Armour of Light" a Technique of Healing the Self and Others*, Favil Press, London 1958.
    —*Olive Pixley's Spiritual Journey: Comprising Listening In, The Trail, Human Document*, Armour of Light Trust Council, Shere 1999.
    —*A Book of Talks: A Companion Reader to The Armour of Light Part II*, Armour of Light Trust Council, Shere 2002.
66. **Swart, J.G.:** *The Book of Self Creation, Op. cit.*
67. *Ibid.*
68. *Ibid.*
69. *Ibid.*
70. *Ibid.*
71. *Ibid.*
72. **Swart, J.G.:** *The Book of Immediate Magic - Part 1, Op. cit.*
73. *Ibid.*
    **Swart, J.G.:** *The Book of Self Creation, Op. cit.*
    —*The Book of Sacred Names, Op. cit.*
    —*The Book of Seals & Amulets, Op. cit.*

74. **Swart, J.G.:** *The Book of Self Creation, Ibid.*
75. *Ibid.*
76. *Ibid.*
77. *Ibid.*
78. *Ibid.*
    **Swart, J.G.:** *The Book of Immediate Magic - Part 1, Op. cit.*
79. *Ibid.*
80. *Ibid.*
81. **Swart, J.G.:** *The Book of Self Creation, Ibid.*
82. **Swart, J.G.:** *The Book of Immediate Magic - Part 1, Op. cit.*
83. **Swart, J.G.:** *The Book of Self Creation, Op. cit.*
84. *Ibid.*
85. *Ibid.*
86. *Ibid.*
87. **Swart, J.G.:** *The Book of Immediate Magic - Part 1, Op. cit.*
88. *Ibid.*
    **Swart, J.G.:** *The Book of Self Creation, Op. cit.*
89. *Ibid.*
90. *Ibid.*
91. Adapted from **Gray, W.G.:** *Shortened form of Initiation*, unpublished manuscript, Sangreal Sodality archives, Johannesburg.
92. *Ibid.*
93. *Ibid.*
94. *Ibid.*
95. *Ibid.*
96. *Ibid.*

# CHAPTER 10

1. **Swart, J.G.:** *The Book of Self Creation, Op. cit.*
2. **Swart, J.G.:** *The Book of Sacred Names, Op. cit.*
3. **Swart, J.G.:** *The Book of Immediate Magic - Part 1, Op. cit.*
4. **Kluger, Y.:** *A Psychological Interpretation of Ruth*, Daimon Verlag, Einsiedeln 1999.
5. **Hayden-Roy, P.A.:** *A Foretaste of Heaven: Friedrich Hölderlin in the Context of Württemberg Pietism*, Editions Rodopi V.B., Amsterdam 1994.
6. **Kluger, Y.:** *A Psychological Interpretation of Ruth, Op. cit.*
7. **Kramer, C.:** *Mashiach: Who? What? Why? How? Where? and When?*, Breslov Research Institute, Jerusalem 1994.
8. **Swart, J.G.:** *The Book of Self Creation, Op. cit.*
9. *Ibid.*
10. *Ibid.*
11. *Ibid.*
12. **Swart, J.G.:** *The Book of Sacred Names, Op. cit.*
13. *Ibid.*
14. *Ibid.*
15. **Varetz, T.S.:** [with A. Sutton] *California Kabbalah, Op. cit.*
16. **Nachman of Bratzlav:** *Likkutei Moharan*, Mechon Nachalat Tzvi, Jerusalem 2004.
    — with **Nathan Sternharz:** *Rabbi Nachman's Wisdom: Shevachay HaRan, Sichos HaRan*, transl. A. Kaplan, Breslov Research Institute, New York 1973.
17. **Swart, J.G.:** *The Book of Self Creation, Op. cit.*
18. **Nachman of Bratzlav:** *Likkutei Moharan, Op. cit.*
    —with **Nathan Sternharz:** *Rabbi Nachman's Wisdom, Op. cit.*
19. **Swart, J.G.:** *The Book of Self Creation, Op. cit.*
20. **Nachman of Bratzlav:** *Likkutei Moharan, Op. cit.*
    —with **Nathan Sternharz:** *Rabbi Nachman's Wisdom, Op. cit.*
21. **Swart, J.G.:** *The Book of Self Creation, Op. cit.*
22. **Swart, J.G.:** *The Book of Sacred Names, Op. cit.*
    —*The Book of Seals & Amulets, Op. cit.*
23. **Nachman of Bratzlav:** *Likkutei Moharan, Op. cit.*
    —with **Nathan Sternharz:** *Rabbi Nachman's Wisdom, Op. cit.*
24. **Horowitz, S.S. ben A.:** *Shefa Tal*, Hanau, 1612.
25. **Nachman of Bratzlav:** *Likkutei Moharan, Op. cit.*
    —with **Nathan Sternharz:** *Rabbi Nachman's Wisdom, Op. cit.*

26. **Suarès, C.:** *The Qabala Trilogy: The Cipher of Genesis, The Song of Songs, The Sepher Yetzirah*, Shambhala Publications Inc., Boulder 1985.
27. **Nachman of Bratzlav:** *Likkutei Moharan, Op. cit.*
—with **Nathan Sternharz:** *Rabbi Nachman's Wisdom, Op. cit.*
28. *Ibid.*
29. *Ibid.*
30. **Swart, J.G.:** *The Book of Sacred Names, Op. cit.*
31. *Ibid.*
32. *Ibid.*
33. *Ibid.*
34. **Swart, J.G.:** *The Book of Self Creation, Op. cit.*
35. *Ibid.*
36. **Swart, J.G.:** *The Book of Seals & Amulets, Op. cit.*
37. *Ibid.*
38. **Ariel, D.S.:** *The Mystic Quest, Op. cit.*
39. **Eilberg-Schwartz, H.:** *People of the Body: Jews and Judaism from an Embodied Perspective*, State University of New York Press, Albany 1992.

*also published by The Sangreal Sodality Press*

Shadow Tree Series
Volume 1

# THE BOOK OF SELF CREATION

Jacobus G. Swart

'*The Book of Self Creation*' is a study guide for all who seek God within and who prefer to steer the course of their lives in a personal manner. The doctrines and techniques addressed in this book will aid practitioners in the expansion of personal consciousness and spiritual evolution. Combining the principles and teachings of Kabbalah and Ceremonial Magic, the book offers step by step instructions on the conscious creation of physical life circumstances, such being always in harmony with the mind-set of the practitioner.

'The Book of Self Creation is a rich and resourceful workbook of practical kabbalah from the hands of a master kabbalist who is both compassionate and insightful.'
Caitlin Matthews, author of *Walkers Between the Worlds* and *Sophia, Goddess of Wisdom*.

The 'Shadow Tree Series' comprises a unique collection of Western Esoteric studies and practices which Jacobus Swart, spiritual successor to William G. Gray, has actuated and taught over a period of forty years. Regarding the author of this series, William Gray wrote 'It is well to bear in mind that Jacobus Swart is firstly and lastly a staunchly practicing member of the Western Inner Tradition and perforce writes from that specific angle alone. Moreover, he writes well, lucidly, and absolutely honestly.'

ISBN 978-0-620-42882-2                             *Paperback*

*also published by The Sangreal Sodality Press*

Shadow Tree Series
Volume 2

# THE BOOK OF SACRED NAMES

## Jacobus G. Swart

*'The Book of Sacred Names'* is a practical guide into the meditational and magical applications of ancient Hebrew Divine Names. Perpetuating the tenets of traditional Kabbalists who recognised the fundamental bond between 'Kabbalah' and 'Magic,' Jacobus Swart offers step by step instructions on the deliberate and conscious control of personal life circumstances, by means of the most cardinal components of Kabbalistic doctrines and techniques—Divine Names!

The material addressed in this tome derives from the extensive primary literature of '"*Practical Kabbalah*",' much of which is appearing in print for the first time in English translation.

The 'Shadow Tree Series' comprises a unique collection of Western Esoteric studies and practices which Jacobus Swart, spiritual successor to William G. Gray and co-founder of the Sangreal Sodality, has actuated and taught over a period of forty years. Having commenced his Kabbalah studies in Safed in the early 1970's, he later broadened his 'kabbalistic horizons' under the careful guidance of the famed English Kabbalist William G. Gray.

ISBN 978-0-620-50702-8                    *Paperback*

*also published by The Sangreal Sodality Press*

Shadow Tree Series
Volume 3

# THE BOOK OF SEALS & AMULETS

Jacobus G. Swart

Having introduced a 'nuts and bolts' insight into the inner workings of Ceremonial Magic and *"Practical Kabbalah"* in '*The Book of Self Creation*' and '*The Book of Sacred Names*,' Jacobus Swart unfolds further magical resources in *"The Book of Seals & Amulets."* This tome comprises a comprehensive investigation into the meaning and relevance of Celestial Alphabets, Magical Seals, Magic Squares, Divine and Angelic Names, etc., as well as their employment in Hebrew Amulets in order to benefit personal wellbeing in a most significant manner.

Continuing the standards set in the earlier volumes of this series, Jacobus Swart offers detailed instruction on the contents and construction of Hebrew Amulets. He again consulted the enormous array of relevant primary Hebrew literature, large sections of which are available to an English readership for the first time.

The 'Shadow Tree Series' comprises a unique collection of Western Esoteric studies and practices which Jacobus G. Swart, spiritual successor to William G. Gray and co-founder of the Sangreal Sodality, actuated and taught over a period of forty years. He commenced his Kabbalah odyssey in Safed in the early 1970's studying the doctrines of Lurianic Kabbalah. He also incorporated the teachings of his late mentor, the celebrated English Kabbalist William G. Gray, in his personal Kabbalistic worldview.

ISBN 978-0-620-59698-5                              *Paperback*

*also published by The Sangreal Sodality Press*

Shadow Tree Series
Volume 4

# THE BOOK OF IMMEDIATE MAGIC - PART 1

Jacobus G. Swart

*'The Book of Immediate Magic - Part One'* perpetuates the fundamental tenets of "Self Creation" in which it is maintained that the 'Centre' establishes the 'Circumference,' and that personal reality is emanated in harmony with personal 'Will.' Hence this tome comprises an enhancement and expansion of the magical doctrines of *Kabbalah Ma'asit* (*"Practical Kabbalah"*) addressed in the first three volumes of this "Shadow Tree Series" of Jewish Magical texts. Jacobus Swart claims that working "Immediate Magic" is neither impossible when we fully understand that consciousness is just one vast ocean, and that thoughts are the waves we make in it. It is all a matter of coordinating consciousness.

The 'Shadow Tree Series' comprises a unique collection of Western Esoteric studies and practices which Jacobus G. Swart, spiritual successor to William G. Gray and co-founder of the Sangreal Sodality, has actuated and taught over a period of forty years. He commenced his journey into the domain of Jewish Mysticism in the early 1970's investigating mainstream Kabbalah, later diversifying into the magical mysteries of Practical Kabbalah. He equally expanded his personal perspectives of the Western Magical Tradition under the careful tutelage of the celebrated English Kabbalist William G. Gray.

ISBN 978-0-620-69313-4                              *Paperback*

*also published by The Sangreal Sodality Press*

# THE LADDER OF LIGHTS
# (OR QABALAH RENOVATA)

## William G. Gray

The Tree of Life works in relation to consciousness somewhat like a computer. Data is fed in, stored in associative banks, and then fed out on demand. The difference between the Tree and a computer, however, is that a computer can only produce various combinations of the information that has been programmed into it. The Tree, operating through the intelligent consciousness of living beings, whether embodied in this world or not, acts as a sort of Universal Exchange throughout the entire chain of consciousness sharing its scheme, and the extent of this is infinite and incalculable.

The Tree of Life is a means and not an end. It is not in itself an object for worship or some idol for superstitious reverence. It is a means, a method, a map and a mechanism for assisting the attainment of the single objective common to all creeds, systems, mysteries and religions—namely, the mystical union of humanity and divinity. With this end in view, this book is an aid to whoever desires to climb the Tree of Life.

'.....the most original commentary on basic Kabbalistic knowledge that I have read for God knows how many years.'
Israel Regardie

'.....beautifully presented and set in excellent marching order.....For one new to the subject, this is a fine text and an exceptionally lucid introduction to a veiled and meditative lore which is still being enlarged from year to year.'
Max Freedom Long (*Huna Vistas*)

ISBN 978-0-620-40303-0                    *Paperback*

*also published by The Sangreal Sodality Press*

# AN OUTLOOK ON OUR INNER WESTERN WAY

## William G. Gray

'*An Outlook on Our Inner Western Way*' is a unique book. This is no dusty, quaint grimoire — it is a sane and simple method of true attainment for those who seek communion with their higher selves.

In this book, William Gray shows simply and lucidly, how to *live* the Western Inner Tradition. Tracing the cosmology of Western magic, he substantiates its vitality and urgency for our future.

William G. Gray is rated one of the most prolific — and controversial — occultists today. Blending keen insight, modern psychological models and an overall sense of practicality, his books have torn at the mouldy veils of so-called occult secrets, laying out a no-non sense foundation by which modern Western humanity may once again regain its precious magical soul.

ISBN 978-0-620-40306-1                *Paperback*

*also published by The Sangreal Sodality Press*

Sangreal Sodality Series
Volume 1

# WESTERN INNER WORKINGS

William G. Gray

The '*Sangreal Sodality Series*' is a home study course comprising the fundamental text books of the Sangreal Sodality, that revives the instrumentality inherent in our western Tradition. The series makes available to us, in our own cultural symbolism, a way to enlightenment that we can practice on a daily basis.

'*Western Inner Workings*' provides a practical framework for the western student's psycho-spiritual development. Each day includes a morning meditation, a mid-day invocation, evening exercises, and a sleep subject. Incorporating symbols that are 'close to home,' these rituals increase consciousness in comfortable increments.

ISBN 978-0-620-40304-7            *Paperback*

*also published by The Sangreal Sodality Press*

# A BEGINNERS GUIDE TO LIVING KABBALAH

## William G. Gray

This compendium comprises six Kabbalistic works by William G. Gray, some of which are appearing here in print for the first time. The texts included in this compilation are ranging from the simplest introduction to the Spheres and Paths of the Kabbalistic Tree of Life system, to related meditation techniques and associated ritual magical procedures, to an advanced system of what could be termed 'inter-dimensional spiritual communication.'

The title 'A Beginners Guide to Living Kabbalah' is perhaps somewhat misleading, as this compilation equally contains works of an advanced nature, and the ritual and meditation techniques addressed in this tome, pertain to both beginners as well as advanced practitioners of '"*Practical Kabbalah*".'

ISBN 978-0-620-42887-3          *Paperback*

*also published by The Sangreal Sodality Press*

# LESSONS LEARNED FROM OCCULT LETTERS

## William G. Gray

In this book William G. Gray, the renowned English Kabbalist and Ceremonial Magician, delineated some of the lessons he learned from the letters which passed between himself and Emil Napoleon Hauenstein, his Austrian mentor and friend, whom he affectionately called "E.N.H." Contrary to opinions expressed regarding Emil Napoleon Hauenstein's status as a "Magus," it should be noted that he was nothing of the kind. He classified himself a "mystic," and was a Martinist. Whilst he was an "Initiate" of the well-known French Occultist Papus (Gerard Encausse), he had a particularly poor opinion of ritual magic and never shared a single magical practice with William Gray.

On the other hand, E.N.H. addressed important psycho-spiritual occult principles and doctrines in his letters, and encouraged his young friend to acquire a greater understanding of what it means to be an "Occultist." William Gray gained a clear comprehension that "Goodness, Love, Truth, Kindness, and such Spiritual qualities in us that come direct from God must come *first*. Cleverness, intellectuality, and mental attributes can then be safely developed in the course of time." Since "Occultism is the study and practice of subjects and laws which are beyond the bounds and limitations of ordinary physical or even mental experience," Emil Napoleon Hauenstein directed his young protegé in unfolding a well-regulated "Self," who is in full control of all his personal faculties, whether these be physical, mental, emotional or spiritual. This is of particular importance in understanding, as William Gray noted, that "Occultism is *not* a pastime, it is a Power, a Purpose, a Progress, and a Path"—*a Way of Life!*

ISBN 978-0-620-79024-6               *Paperback*

www.ingramcontent.com/pod-product-compliance
Lightning Source LLC
Chambersburg PA
CBHW030102010526
44116CB00005B/69